USHER
iBT TOEFL
INTERMEDIATE TEST
LISTENING

어셔 iBT 토플 인터미디어트 테스트 리스닝

어셔 어학 연구소

USHER
iBT TOEFL INTERMEDIATE TEST
LISTENING
어셔 iBT 토플 인터미디어트 테스트 리스닝

초판 2쇄 발행 · 2023년 12월 1일
개정증보판 1쇄 발행 · 2025년 11월 1일

지은이 · 어셔 토플 연구소
펴낸곳 · (주) 어셔 어학 연구소
펴낸이 · 어셔 어학 연구소
주 소 · 서울시 서초구 잠원로 3길 40 태남빌딩 2층 어셔어학원
전 화 · 02) 595-5679
홈페이지 · www.usher.co.kr
ISBN · 979-11-85317-24-3

정 가 · 28,000원

저작권자 · ⓒ2019, 어셔 어학연구소

이 책 및 mp3 내용의 저작권은 저자에게 있습니다.
서면에 의한 저자와 출판사의 허락없이 내용의 일부 혹은 전부를 인용하거나, 발췌하는 것을 금합니다.

COPYRIGHT© 2019 by Usher Language Research Institute
All rights reserved including the rights of reproduction In whole or part in any form Printed in Korea

본 토플 교재는 iBT 토플 리스닝 영역에서 고득점을 얻길 원하는 학습자들을 위해 마무리 실전서로 출간된 책입니다.

■최신 iBT 토플 시험 경향 반영

과거 토플 형태인 PBT와 CBT를 거쳐 국내에서 2006년 9월 처음 시행된 iBT 형태의 토플 시험은 그동안 많은 변화를 보여왔습니다. 하지만 시중에는 여전히 iBT 토플 시험이 모습을 드러내기 전 시험 주관사인 ETS의 시험 방향 발표만을 듣고 만들거나 토플 시험 시행 후 어느정도 윤곽을 잡은 뒤 만들어낸 초기 형태의 문제지들을 세월이 지남에 따라 조금씩 개정하여 판매하는 경우가 많습니다. 그러나 안타깝게도 이 토플 책들은 최근 3년 사이에 크게 변화된 ETS의 출제 경향의 흐름을 읽지 못하고 그것을 반영하지 못한 부분이 많기에 최근 추세에 따른 문제지를 제작하게 되었습니다. 「USHER iBT TOEFL **INTERMEDIATE TEST LISTENING**」의 문제들은 최신 토플 시험 경향이 반영되어 여러분은 실제와 동일한 수준의 문제들을 그대로 경험하며 실전 감각을 익힐 수 있을 것입니다.

■토플 리스닝 고득점 취득을 위한 최상의 난이도

iBT 토플 리스닝 시험의 최근 변화 중 가장 큰 부분은 들려주는 시험 내용의 수준과 문제 난이도의 향상입니다. 과거 iBT 토플 시험은 내용이 단순한 형태이었으나, 최근의 토플 리스닝의 주제 및 내용들은 대학에서 다뤄지는 여러 학문 분야의 전문적인 내용들을 포함하고 있기 때문에 대충 듣고 내용을 추측해서 접근하면 틀리게끔 구성되어 있습니다. 또한 문제 역시 과거의 문제들은 짧은 강의 내용을 듣고 핵심 내용만 이해하면, 문제의 답이 쉽게 구별되었습니다. 그러나 최근의 iBT 토플 시험은 답 중에서 본문에 분명 정확하게 나왔던 내용이더라도 질문이 원하는 답이 아니면 정답으로 처리되지 않고 있으며, 보기의 한 단어나 일부분을 틀리게 하고 나머지 부분을 정답과 유사하게 만들어 수험자에게 혼란을 주는 경우가 늘어났습니다. 또한 표면적인 내용이 아닌 말 속에 숨어 있는 의도나 뉘앙스를 파악하는 추론 문제도 예전보다 많이 등장하고 있습니다. 본 토플 리스닝 교재에서는 이런 부분들을 포함하여 과거의 문제들과는 다른 차이점들을 성실히 반영하였습니다. 토플 시험에서 고득점을 원하는 학생들은 실제 시험과 가장 유사한 최상의 난이도를 가진 문제지를 원하는 경우가 많기에, 본 교재인 「USHER iBT TOEFL **INTERMEDIATE TEST LISTENING**」은 그 요구에 걸맞는 난이도로 제작되었습니다. '해설지'에서는 그러한 지문과 문제 하나하나에 대해 학습자가 정답과 오답의 이유를 논리적으로 이해할 수 있게 풀어냈습니다. 따라서 수험생들은 본 토플 교재를 통해 최상위 난 이도에 맞는 영어 실력 향상을 꾀할 수 있으며 이는 토플 고득점이라는 결과로 이어질 것입니다.

■독학용으로도 유용한 교재(토플학원에 다니지 못하는 학생을 위한 추천 교재)

토플학원에 다니지 않고 혼자서 토플 리스닝 시험을 준비하는 학생들이 가장 힘들어 하는 부분이, 해설지에서 문제의 답에 대한 설명을 보통 정답만 표시해 놓았거나, 별로 도움이 되지 않는 정답 이유만을 간략히 적고 끝나는 경우가 많다는 것입니다. 이에, 본 교재는 토플 어학원에 다니지 않고 혼자 토플 공부하는 학생들을 위해, 정답이 되는 부분에 대한 설명은 물론이고 오답이 되는 이유까지 구체적으로 설명해 두었습니다. 먼저 학습자가 스스로 문제를 분석한 뒤, 이 부분을 참고하여 공부하면 문제의 출제의도와 정답을 유추하는 능력을 향상시키는데 더욱 효과적일 것입니다. 또한, 모든 시험 문제들이 그렇듯이 ETS가 낸 토플 문제에도 반드시 오답 패턴이 있기에 이런 부분을 집중 분석하였고, 수험자들이 자신의 취약점을 파악하고 정리하여 같은 실수를 반복하지 않게 문제해결력을 키울 수 있도록 하였습니다.

■2019년 8월 바뀐 뉴토플에서 리스닝 파트는 1회 테스트를 구성하는 두개의 셋

(* 1개 세트는 conversation 1개, Lecture 2개이므로,

뉴토플 이전 테스트 1회는

세트 1 conversation 1개, Lecture 2

세트 2 conversation 1개, Lecture 2 로 구성되어있었으나

2019년 8월에 새롭게 바뀐 뉴토플에서는,
문제 길이, 문제 구성, 문제 난이도 모두 동일하게 유지한채

두번째 세트에서 Lecture 1개만 나오는 형태로 바뀜으로서, 즉,

테스트 1회는

세트 1 conversation 1개, Lecture 2

세트 2 conversation 1개 만으로 바뀌었을 뿐입니다.

하지만, 본 교재는, 학생들이 리스닝 시험에서 가장 힘들어 하는 부분중 하나가, 리딩 시험 3지문을 풀고(더미가 있으면 네 지문) 집중력이 떨어진 상태에서, 리스닝 시험을 볼때도, 집중력 유지가 필수이므로, 사라진 두번째 세트의 두번째 렉처를 본 교재에 부록으로 수록해 둠으로서, 시험장에서의 집중력 유지를 강화 하고자 합니다.

「USHER iBT TOEFL **INTERMEDIATE TEST LISTENING**」이 여러분의 꿈을 향한 과정 속에 함께하는 동반자가 될 수 있기를 바랍니다.

어셔 어학연구소

TABLE OF CONTENTS

USHER
USHER iBT TOEFL LISTENING
어셔 iBT 토플 리스닝

Introduction

	학생들이 자주하는 질문 Q&A	06
1	뉴 토플에 관하여	14
2	iBT TOEFL (iBT 토플) 시험 소개	15
3	iBT TOEFL Listening 소개	17
4	Listening Section 평가기준	21
5	본 iBT 토플 교재만의 특징	24
6	본 iBT 토플 교재의 구성	26
7	실력별 학습계획	30
8	Listening Strategies	
	1. 리스닝 학습 순서 및 방법	32
	2. 문제 분석 방법	38

문제 PART

TOEFL TEST 01
- Set 1 — 50
- Set 2 — 58

TOEFL TEST 02
- Set 1 — 68
- Set 2 — 76

TOEFL TEST 03
- Set 1 — 86
- Set 2 — 94

TOEFL TEST 04
- Set 1 — 104
- Set 2 — 112

TOEFL TEST 05
- Set 1 — 122
- Set 2 — 130

답지 — 139
Note Taking — 161
단어·구문 — 223
구문외우고·열번읽기 — 335

해설 PART

TOEFL TEST 01
- **Set 1-1 Conversation** — 398
  Accounting department
- **Set 1-2 Lecture 1** — 402
  Ice age
- **Set 1-3 Lecture 2** — 408
  Drama class
- **Set 2-1 Conversation** — 414
  Library employee
- **Set 2-2 Lecture 1** — 418
  Bioluminescence
- ***부록 Set 2-3 Lecture 2** — 424
  Muon detector

TOEFL TEST 02
- **Set 1-1 Conversation** — 432
  Math nights
- **Set 1-2 Lecture 1** — 436
  The accessibility of novels
- **Set 1-3 Lecture 2** — 442
  Predation risk effects
- **Set 2-1 Conversation** — 448
  Housing department
- **Set 2-2 Lecture 1** — 452
  Insight
- ***부록 Set 2-3 Lecture 2** — 458
  Shift from a nomadic lifestyle to sedentary settlements

TOEFL TEST 03
- **Set 1-1 Conversation** — 466
  Brain's Left and Right Hemisphere
- **Set 1-2 Lecture 1** — 470
  Younger Dryas
- **Set 1-3 Lecture 2** — 475
  Leonardo's philosophical thinking
- **Set 2-1 Conversation** — 480
  The championship games
- **Set 2-2 Lecture 1** — 484
  Earth's age
- ***부록 Set 2-3 Lecture 2** — 490
  Illegitimate theater

TOEFL TEST 04
- **Set 1-1 Conversation** — 498
  Final term papers
- **Set 1-2 Lecture 1** — 502
  Two galaxies
- **Set 1-3 Lecture 2** — 508
  Biomimetics
- **Set 2-1 Conversation** — 514
  19th century European art movements
- **Set 2-2 Lecture 1** — 518
  The advent of literacy and cheap books
- ***부록 Set 2-3 Lecture 2** — 524
  The Industrial Revolution

TOEFL TEST 05
- **Set 1-1 Conversation** — 532
  The reservation on a friday
- **Set 1-2 Lecture 1** — 536
  Early European art movements
- **Set 1-3 Lecture 2** — 542
  Antipredator adaptations
- **Set 2-1 Conversation** — 548
  Poetry reading
- **Set 2-2 Lecture 1** — 552
  Ethanol
- ***부록 Set 2-3 Lecture 2** — 558
  A solar nebula

■ 학생들이 자주하는 질문 Q&A

1. 왜 청취 부분 점수가 잘 안 나오는 걸까요? LC 공부는 어떻게 해야 하는지 감이 잘 안 잡혀요.

TOEFL Listening Section에서 고득점을 받지 못하는 이유는 다음 6가지 경우에 해당됩니다. 학습자의 영어 실력에 따라 한 가지가 부족할 수도 있고, 여러 가지 이유가 복합적으로 섞여 있을 수도 있습니다.

- A) 단어를 모르는 경우
- B) 영어 소리(발음)가 익숙치 않은 경우
- C) 문장이 잘 이해되지 않는 경우
- D) 논리적 사고력이 부족한 경우
- E) 문제스타일에 적응하지 못한 경우

이에 대한 청취 전략은 다음과 같습니다

(A) 단어를 모르는 경우

Spelling을 보았을 때는 아는 단어이지만 소리를 들었을 때 선뜻 의미가 생각나지 않는다면 리스닝에 있어서는 전혀 모르는 단어입니다. 이는 **머리 속에 단어의 글자와 의미만 있을 뿐 소리가 전혀 저장되어있지 않은 상태**이기 때문입니다. 많은 학생들이 딕테이션을 해보면 의외로 쉬운 단어들을 못 쓰곤 하는데, 그건 단어의 스펠링과 뜻은 머리속에 저장되어 있는데 발음 부분은 전혀 저장되어 있지 않거나 혹은 엉뚱한 소리로 저장되어 있어, native speaker의 발음을 들었을 때 빠르게 머리속 에 떠오르지 않기 때문이죠. 따라서 기존의 아는 단어라도 원어민 발음이 전혀 다른 경우가 많음으로 본인의 기억하고 있는 한국식 소리를 수정해야 들립니다. 방법은 전자사전이나 인터넷 사전에서 단어를 찾아 발음을 듣고 여러 번 따라 말해보는 것인데, 새로운 단어를 암기할 때에도 꼭 발음을 함께 기억하는 것이 중요합니다. 이렇게 정확하게 소리를 저장하고 발음하면 Speaking 시험에서도 효과를 볼 수 있습니다.

(B) 영어 소리(발음) 자체에 익숙치 않은 경우

리듬 언어인 영어는 이어져서 나는 소리가 많고, 강세 단어들은 소리가 높고 길고 강하게, 약세단어들은 뭉치거나 축약되어 낮고 약하고 빠르게 발음됩니다. 그래서 모든 음절을 또박또박 발음하는 한국어에 익숙한 학생들은, 이러한 영어 소리의 특징을 알지 못하기 때문에, 청취가 잘 안되어 힘들어 하는 경우가 많죠. 해결책은 **못들은 부분을 중점적으로 Shadowing하면서 발음을 여러 번 듣고 따라 하면서 외우는 것입니다. 이때 강세와 연음 부분에 특히 신경을 쓰면서 말해봅니다.** 따라하기 어려운 소리나 문장은 따로 노트에 정리하여 틈나는 대로 연습하는 것도 도움이 됩니다. 중요한 건 **원어민의 실제 발음, 억양, 말하는 속도**에 익숙해지는 것이므로 Shadowing을 할 때 이 부분들을 똑같이 흉내 내면서 연습하셔야 합니다.

(C) 문장이 잘 이해되지 않는 경우

단어는 하나씩 잘 들리지만, 문장이나 단락의 내용이 이해가 안되는 경우가 있습니다. 보통 학생들이 듣고 이해하지 못하는것을 걱정하는데, 기초적인 독해조차 안되기 때문에 내용을 들어도 무슨 말인지 파악하지 못하는 경우를 의외로 많이 봅니다. 만약 Reading Section에서 20점대 점수가 나온다면, 청취훈련을 통해 영어소리의 특징에 익숙해지면 소리가 잘 들리게 되어 리스닝 점수도 곧 상승합니다. 하지만 독해 점수가 낮은 학생들은 청취 훈련과 더불어 문장을 글로 봤을 때 빠르고 정확하게 이해하는 훈련도 병행해야 빠른 효과를 볼 수 있습니다.

Native Speaker가 말하는 내용을 단어로만 이해하고 구나 문장의 의미를 통으로 이해하지 못하는 경우, 첫째는 영어와 우리말이 어순이 다르기 때문에 원어민이 말하는 속도에 비해 한국인이 들으며 바로 이해하는 속도가 늦어지게 되어 발생합니다.

이를 극복하기 위해서는 **문장을 의미단위로 끊어서 들으며 순차해석하는 연습**을 꾸준히 해야 합니다. 문장을 개별적인 단어가 아닌 의미를 이루는 덩어리로 이해하면, 머리 속에서 처리속도가 빨라지기 때문에 원어민이 말하는 속도가 부담스럽지 않습니다. 예를 들어, '아버지가 방에 들어가서 가방을 들고 나오신다' 라는 문장을 본 한국인들은 초등학교 저학년이 아닌 이상 단어를 하나씩 파악하지는 않습니다. 그보다는 '아버지가 방에 들어가서, '가방을 들고 나오신다' 처럼 2개의 의미 덩어리로 이해하죠. 이 문장을 소리로 들어도 처리방식은 같을 것입니다. 그렇기 때문에 뉴스나 강의 같은 긴 문장이나 여러 가지 내용을 한국어로 오래 들어도 뇌가 피곤하지 않은 것입니다. 이를 영어에 대입하면, 한국 학생들이 어느 정도 자신이 있는 부분이 독해이기 때문에, 리스닝 스크립트를 가지고 직독직해가 빠르게 안 되는 사람은 귀를 뚫겠다고 소리를 아무리 많이 들어도 효과를 보기 힘듭니다. 그냥 단어들만 하나씩 알아들을 뿐이죠. 여러 개의 단어가 모여 다른 의미를 이루는 구어체 표현이나 문장들은 전혀 이해되지 않습니다. 따라서 Reading 부분의 지문을 해석할 때나 Listening의 스크립트를 해석할 때 낱개의 단어가 아닌 의미덩어리로 묶은 뒤 영어어순에 맞춰 이해해나가는 습관을 기르셔야 합니다. 이 때 영어어순에 따라 이해한다 함은 영어문장을 읽을 때 우리말로 완전한 문장을 만들거나 뒤에서부터 해석해오지 않고, 순차적으로 뜻만 생각하면서 빠르게 읽는 훈련을 하는 것입니다. 즉, 한 나라의 말을 다른 나라 말로 매끄럽게 옮기는 Translation(번역)이 아닌 읽는 문장의 내용이 무슨 뜻인지만 알면 되는 Comprehension(이해)을 연습하는 것이지요.

둘째, 특정 문장 구조가 안 들리는 경우인데, 이것은 그 문장의 구조가 익숙히 않기 때문입니다. 따라서 **해당 문장 구조 (예: 가정법, 사역동사, 등..)를 가진 예문을 3개 이상 찾아 말하면서 외우면**, 틀은 똑같고 단어만 바뀌어 나오므로 나중에 그 문장을 들었을 때 한번에 이해할 수 있게 됩니다. 단, 단순히 글로 암기하면 전혀 소용이 없고, 꼭 소리로 원어민의 속도와 똑같이 따라 발음해 보아야 합니다.

(D) 논리적 사고력이 부족한 경우

모든 소리가 잘 들리고 내용도 정확하게 이해했는데 문제를 풀면 계속 틀리는 경우는, 청취력의 문제라기보다는 대화나 강의의 Topic이 익숙치 않아 핵심내용을 빠르게 파악하지 못하거나, 글의 전개방식을 논리적으로 따라잡지 못해 발생합니다. 낯설거나 어렵게 느껴지는 주제를 담고 있는 내용들은 문제를 풀고 스크립트를 통해 내용을 확인한 뒤, 안 들리는 부분들을 골라 딕테이션과 섀도잉을 활용해 다시 한번 내용을 듣고 이해하는 습관을 기르셔야 합니다. 이때 그 분야에서 필수적으로 알아두어야 할 단어(word)나 어구(phrase)들을 꾸준히 외우는 작업 또한 병행하셔야 합니다.

또한 자신이 취약한 분야의 토픽(Topic)과 핵심어(Keyword)에 대한 배경지식을 꾸준히 습득하는 것이 필요합니다. 관련지식을 많이 알고 있을수록 들리는 내용도 많아지고 문제에 대한 감을 잡기가 쉽기 때문이죠. 이런 식으로 본인이 약하다고 생각되는 분야에 관련된 어휘, 문장, 배경지식을 많이 쌓아나가면, 내용에 대한 이해가 많아지면서 청취력에 큰 도움이 됩니다.

이와 더불어, Lecture의 경우 흐름이나 전개방식을 이해하는 것도 도움이 됩니다. 하나의 주제를 설명하는 방식은 논리적인 순서가 있기 때문에 이 흐름을 파악하게 되면, 들으면서 중요한 부분을 골라낼 수 있고 문제가 나오는 부분까지 예측하게 되는 것이죠. 이것은 Summary 훈련을 통하여 향상시킬 수 있는데, 강의의 내용파악 및 문제분석을 다 끝내고 완벽히 이해 한 상태에서, 본인이 종이에 요약을 하는 것입니다. 마치 중고등학생 시절에 중간·기말 고사를 앞두고 시험범위에 해당하는 내용을 핵심내용만 간추려 간략하게 정리하는 것처럼요. 이렇게 하면, 내용에 대한 이해가 확실해지면서, 보이지 않는 전체 골격을 파악하게 되고, 각 단락의 핵심이 뭔지 강의 전체에서 교수가 전달하고자 주제가 뭔지 금방 알게 됩니다. 결국 이것들이 문제를 통해 물어보는 사항들이므로, 청취를 하던서도 어떤 부분이 중요하고 문제가 어떻게 나올지 미리 예상할 수 있게 되는 것이지요. 또한 Summary는 문제를 처음 풀 때 기록했던 Note-taking과 비교해 보면, 본인이 내용을 들으면서 어떤 부분을 놓쳤는지 쉽게 알 수 있어 청취력 향상에도 도움이 많이 됩니다. Summary 샘플은 뒷장 P.37를 참조하세요.

■ 학생들이 자주하는 질문 Q&A

(E) 문제스타일에 적응하지 못한 경우

청취력도 훌륭하고 대화나 강의의 내용도 정확하게 이해했는데 예상외로 고득점이 안 나오거나 만점을 받지 못하는 경우가 있습니다. 주로 외국에서 공부하는 학생들이 이에 해당되는데요. 특히 학생들이 많이 틀리는 Main Idea, Inference(다시 들려주고 푸는 문제, Purpose/Intention, Imply, Opinion/Attitude) 문제 등은, 단순히 들었던 내용을 제대로 기억하는지 묻는 차원이 아닌 들은 내용을 바탕으로 문제의 출제 알맞는 정답을 고르는 것이기 때문에 논리적 사고력과 추론 능력이 필요합니다. 따라서, 이에 대한 처방은 본인이 **자주 틀리는 문제 유형과 출제의도를 정확히 분석한 후, 비슷한 문제를 반복하여 풀어봄으로써 정답을 골라내는 감을 기르는 것이 중요**합니다. **또한 LC 특유의 문제 풀이 유형을 충분히 숙지하고 있는지도 확인**해야 합니다. 모든 소리가 다 잘 들리고 내용도 정확하게 이해했는데 문제를 풀면 계속 틀리는 경우는, 청취력의 문제라기보다는 문제해결능력 부분을 향상시켜야 하는 경우가 대부분입니다. 이 때 **도움이 되는 것이 오답노트 정리**인데요. 틀린 문제를 계속 정리하다 보면, 문제를 낸 출제자의 의도, 문제에서 반복적으로 보이는 오답 패턴, 본인이 그 동안 잘 모르고 저질렀던 반복적인 실수 등이 파악되어 문제해결능력의 완성도를 높일 수 있는 길이 보일 것입니다. 본서에는 학습자들이 활용할 수 있도록 '오답정리표'를 각 테스트마다 제공하고 있습니다.

2. 효과적인 점수대별 학습 방법은 뭔가요?

시험점수 : 25점 이상~

이 점수대를 받는 학습자는 리스닝 실력이 '상' 단계로써, 청취력이 웬만큼 갖춰져 있다고 판단됩니다. Listening Section에서 고득점을 쟁취할 수 있는 비결은 두 가지 입니다. 첫째, 본인의 청취력 중 부족한 부분을 지속적으로 보충해 주셔야 합니다. 아무리 일반적인 영어청취가 뛰어나다 하더라도, 토플은 학문적인 내용들을 담고 있기 때문에, 본인이 취약한 분야나 토픽(Topic)이 있기 마련입니다. 따라서 대화와 강의의 음성파일을 듣고 내용 이해가 얼마나 정확하게 되고 있는지를 판단하고, 본인의 단어 실력이나 문장 표현에 대한 이해 등 어휘력이 어느 정도인지를 꼼꼼히 따져, 부족한 부분을 지속적으로 채워야 시험에 맞는 청취 실력으로 발전될 수 있습니다. 안들리는 부분은 스크립트(script)에 표시한 후, MP3파일을 이용하여 딕테이션(Dictation)과 새도잉(Shadowing)을 하면서 그 부분을 자신의 것으로 습득해 나가야 합니다. 또한 자신에게 낯선 토픽에 대한 배경지식을 인터넷을 통해 찾아보며 관련지식을 쌓아나가다 보면, 내용에 대한 이해가 많아지면서 청취력에 큰 도움이 됩니다. 둘째, 토플 LC 특유의 문제를 해결할 수 있는 문제풀이 능력을 향상시켜야 합니다. 오답노트 정리를 통하여 본인이 자주 틀리는 문제의 유형을 정확히 분석하고, 또한 비슷한 문제들을 계속 풀어봄으로써 토플 문제의 스타일에 익숙해지는 것이 중요합니다.

시험점수 : 20~25점대

리스닝 실력이 '중상' 단계로써 대화 및 강의의 전반적인 내용이 어느 정도 들리는 상태입니다. 이 단계는 정확한 청취력을 위해 연음, 속도, 의미덩어리 등 소리를 좀더 정확하게 잡아내는 연습을 꾸준히 해야 합니다. 그리고 각 문제 유형을 정확히 파악한 후 본인이 취약한 부분을 꼼꼼히 분석함과 동시에 논리적 이해력을 지속적으로 키워나갈 필요가 있습니다. 또한 강의를 들으며 세부사항을 명확하고 간략하게 효과적으로 Note-taking하는 훈련을 지속하여, 핵심 내용을 빠트리지 않고 잡아내는 연습도 필요합니다. Inference 및 Purpose 와 같이 단순히 들은 내용을 기억하여 푸는 문제가 아닌, 추론을 통하여 답을 골라야 하는 난이도가 꽤 있는 문제유형들을 자주 다뤄보는 것도 도움이 됩니다. 특히 본인이 틀린 문제는 반드시 그 이유를 확인하고 실수를 줄여나가는 것이 중요합니다.

| 토플 공부도우미 | www.usherin.usher.co.kr

시험점수 : 15~19점대

'중' 단계의 리스닝 실력을 지닌 이 점수대의 학생들은 청취를 할 때 기본적인 맥락(outline)은 이해하나, 세부사항의 구체적인 내용을 놓치거나 잘못 이해하는 경향이 있습니다. 이때는 집중적인 영어 청취 및 문장 따라 하기를 통해 내용을 좀더 명확하게 이해하는데 초점을 맞추는 청취력 향상에 주력하는 것이 좋습니다. 또한 리스닝의 각 문제 유형을 파악하여 ETS의 문제 스타일에 익숙해지는 것이 중요합니다. 문제를 분석할 때는 항상 스크립트에서 정답의 근거를 찾아 확인하는 습관을 가지고, 오답의 이유와 패턴을 파악하는 것도 많은 도움이 됩니다. 먼저 상대적으로 득점하기 쉬운 Conversation 먼저 공략하여 기본 점수를 획득하는 것이 좋으며, Lecture에서는 Main Idea 및 Detail 과 관련된 내용을 정확히 듣고 답을 골라내는 것과 Purpose & Attitude(화자의 의도 및 태도)를 파악하는 훈련을 꾸준히 해 나갈 필요가 있습니다.

시험점수 : ~14점대

토플 시험을 전혀 접해보지 못했거나 영어 리스닝 자체가 잘 안되는 학생은 가장 우선적으로 청취력을 키워야 합니다. 토플리스닝 시험은 말그대로 Listening Comprehension을 측정하는 시험으로, 영어를 알아듣는 부분과 내용을 논리적으로 이해하는 사고력 부분을 동시에 평가합니다. 따라서 기본적인 영어 청취가 안된다면 토플 리스닝 시험에 접근 자체가 불가능하게 됩니다. 이 점수대의 학생은 LC에 자주 나오는 단어와 표현들, 영어 문장들을 들으며 지속적으로 청취력 향상에 힘을 쓰면서, 기본적인 유형의 토플 시험을 풀어보는것이 도움이 됩니다. 그리고 상대적으로 점수를 확보하기 쉬운 Conversation을 먼저 공략하시기를 추천하며, 자세한 청취력 향상 방법은 이 책의 뒷장에 있는 P.35 '청취력 향상 훈련 방법'을 참고하시기 바랍니다.

3. 예전에 토플 시험을 본적이 있는데요. 요즘 시험은 Listening section이 훨씬 어려워진 것 같아요. 어떤 차이가 있는 건가요?

TOEFL(Test of English as a Foreign Language)이란 주로 영어권 국가에서 대학교 이상 수준의 학문을 공부하려는 외국인 학생의 영어실력을 평가하기 위하여 만들어진 시험입니다. 현재 TOEFL은 iBT(internet-Based Test) TOEFL이라 불리며, PBT(Paper-based Test)와 CBT(Computer-Based Test)를 거쳐 채택된 3세대 방식으로 읽기, 듣기, 말하기, 쓰기 등 다양한 분야의 영어실력을 평가하기 때문에 현재 세계적으로 가장 공신력있는 영어시험으로 자리 잡았죠. 현재 치뤄지고 있는 iBT Test는 처음 시행된 2006년 9월 이후에, 많은 변화를 거쳐왔고, LC도 다른 영역과 마찬가지로 많은 진화를 거듭하여 현재에 이르렀는데요. 우선 눈에 띄는 점은 들려주는 내용의 길이가 전반적으로 길어졌고, Native speaker의 말하는 속도도 점점 빨라지고 어투나 표현도 실제상황처럼 자연스러워졌다는 것입니다. 또한 Listening 영역은 크게 대화 (Conversaton)와 강의 (Lecture)로 구성되어 있는데, 이들의 주제가 예전에 비해 다양해지고 내용도 심화되고 있는 추세입니다. 문제도 예전과 달리 정답이 2개, 3개를 골라야 하는 문제도 자주 출제되고 있으며, 주제를 묻는 문제에 대한 정답을 고르는 문제가 어려워지고, 화자의 의도 및 태도를 묻는 등 추론형 문제 유형도 계속 증가하고 있습니다.

이처럼 청취력 위주의 영어 듣기 실력을 평가했던 과거의 시험 문제와 달리, 요즘은 내용을 정확하게 이해하는 고도의 청취력 뿐만 아니라, 내용 이면에 숨겨진 의도를 파악하는 분석력과 추론력, 흩어진 정보들을 모아 합성하는 통합적 사고력 등을 요구하는 문제들이 증가하고 있기 때문에 학생들이 예전에 비해 더 어렵다고 느끼고 있습니다.

■ 학생들이 자주하는 질문 **Q&A**

4. 효과적인 Note-taking 방법은 무엇인지 알려주세요.

리스닝을 하다 보면 짧지 않은 길이인 강의 내용을 모두 기억하기가 쉽지 않습니다. 이때는 청취를 하면서 도중에 중요하다고 판단되는 내용을 note-taking하면, 추후 문제를 풀 때 참고할 수 있으므로 도움이 됩니다. 그러나 대학교 수준의 전문적인 내용을 모국어가 아닌 외국어로 들으며 동시에 글을 쓴다는 것은 생각보다 쉽지 않은 일인데다, 완전히 청취에만 의존해서 듣게 되면 나중에 내용들이 혼란이 오기 때문에, 불안한 학생들은 어떻게 하면 노트테이킹을 잘 할 수 있는지 질문을 많이 합니다.

Note-taking은 말 그대로 '메모' 입니다. 한국어로 진행되는 강의를 교수님으로부터 들으며 메모를 한다고 생각해보세요. 여러분은 무엇을 적으려고 할까요? 당연히 중요하다고 판단되는 내용들을 간략하게 핵심단어 위주로 적을 것입니다. 손이 아무리 빨라도 말의 모든 내용을 다 적을 수 없기 때문에, 듣는 도중에 기억하기 힘든 용어(사람 이름, 지명, 전문 용어 등), 순서나 과정, 특징을 나타내는 단어 위주로 간략하게 적겠죠. 영어로 들으면서 하는 노트테이킹(Note-taking)도 이와 크게 다르지 않습니다. 핵심이 되는 내용을 본인이 알아보기 쉽게 간략하고 명료하게 적는 것이 효과적인 노트테이킹의 비결이죠. 이를 위해서는 평소에 자주 쓰이는 표현을 약자나 기호 등을 활용하여 받아쓰는 연습을 하는 것이 도움이 됩니다. 자세한 내용은 뒷장의 P.34 '효과적인 Note-taking방법' 을 참조하세요

5. 전 해외에서 유학하고 있는 학생인데요. 청취를 하면 내용은 이해가 잘 되는데, 문제를 풀면 많이 틀립니다. 뭐가 문제일까요?

첫째, 본인의 청취력 부분을 점검해 보셔야 합니다. 정말 내용이 완벽하게 이해가 되는 건지, 아니면 이해가 된다고 착각하는 것인지 스스로 의문해 보세요. 후자의 경우라면 정확한 이해가 아닌 거죠. 아니면 단어는 들리지만, 단어로 구성되는 문장이나, 그 문장들로 이뤄진 문단의 핵심내용이 이해가 안 되는 거죠. 들리는대로 다 이해하는데 문제가 풀리지 않는다는 건 상식적으로 말이 맞지 않는 부분이잖아요?^^ 대화내용에 대해서만 들릴 뿐, Lecture 부분에서 이해가 되지 않아 들리지 않을 수도 있고, 아니면 Lecture 내용이 문장 하나씩은 들리지만, 전체 내용이 가리키는 핵심 내용이 뭔지 정확히 잡아내지 못할 수도 있죠. 해외에서 있었다고 해서 모든 영어를 다 잘 듣지는 않습니다. 한국 사람들이 한국의 모든 말들을 다 이해하지 못하는 것과 마찬가지입니다. 한국어를 모국어로 쓰는 학생들 모두가 수능시험 언어영역에서 만점을 받지는 못하잖아요. 토플 Listening은 영어로 보는 언어영역 시험이라고 생각하시면 됩니다. 이런 수준의 시험에서는 단순히 청취력 뿐만이 아닌 분석력, 논리력, 통합 이해력, 순간 판단력도 필요합니다.

둘째, 해외에서 살다 온 학생들이 약한 부분이 바로 문법과 어휘입니다. 단어를 강제로 외웠거나 했던 경험도 없을 뿐더러, 초등학교 때부터 유학한 게 아니라면 문법을 따로 공부하지 않았을 겁니다. 그래서 수업을 듣고 문제를 풀어도 그저 느낌상으로만 이해를 해왔기 때문에 정확한 내용 파악이 안되며, Listening을 들어도 그저 기본적인 내용만 들리는 수준이기 때문에, Conversation 문제는 어느 정도 풀 수 있으나, 전문적인 강의 내용인 Lecture는 이해하기 힘들죠. 이 부분은 또한 논리적 사고력이 큰 역할을 담당하는데, 이것은 단순히 언어능력을 떠나서 내용의 구조나 흐름을 파악하고, 그 내용을 바탕으로 주제를 도출할 수 있는 분석력과 추리력이 요구되기 때문입니다. 또한 내용은 알아들었지만 문제를 제대로 풀지 못하는 건, 각각의 문장을 하나씩 이해해도, 강의 전체의 내용 흐름이나 구조 파악이 논리적으로 분석되지 않기 때문에, 주제라든가 예시를 드는 목적, 교수의 의도 등 전체적인 틀이 머리 속에서 잡히지 않는 경우가 많습니다. 또한 본인이 접하지 못했던 Topic에 대한 설명이 중점적으로 나오는 경우, 배경지식이 전혀 없거나 부족하기 때문에 내용을 정확하게 파악하는데 어려움을 겪게 됩니다. 따라서 중고등학교 때 배운 배경지식이 중요하고 또한 문제를 빠르고 정확하게 해석하는 것도 중요합니다. 이해를 해야 문제를 풀 수 있으니까요. 이와 같은 문제풀이 능력은, 토플이 아무래도 시험문제이다 보니 시험의 성격에 맞는 문제 이해력과 해결능력을 갖춰야 좋은 점수를 얻을 수 있도록 초점이 맞춰져 있기 때문이에요. 이를 위해서는 문제를 많이 풀어보고 자주 출제되는 유형을 알아가야 합니다. 하지만 단순히 문제만 많이 풀었다고 만족해서는 안됩니다. 왜 답의 근거가 그 부분인지, 내가 틀린

답은 왜 오답이 될 수 밖에 없는지를 이해하지 못하면 나중에 똑같은 문제를 다시 풀었을 때 계속 틀릴 수 밖에 없고, 결국 점수는 제자리 걸음을 하게 될테니까요.

6. 저는 단기간에 토플을 끝내야 하는데, 고득점을 빠르게 올릴 수 있는 방법은 없나요?

학생들마다 개인차이가 있기 때문에, 토플 리스닝을 끝내는데 얼마의 시간이 걸린다고 단정적으로 말씀드리기는 어렵습니다. 하지만 학습자가 중고등학교 때 쌓은 기본 영어 실력이 탄탄하다면 단기간에 고득점을 얻는 것이 가능합니다. 반면, 영어와 별로 친하지 않았거나 영어 소리와는 완전히 담을 쌓고 지냈다면, 청취력 자체를 기초부터 쌓으셔야 하기 때문에 단기간에 고득점을 받기가 어려울 수도 있습니다. 원하는 점수를 얻는데 걸리는 시간은 현재 본인의 실력, 공부에 투자하는 시간, 공부 방법 그리고 학생 본인의 의지 등에 따라 다릅니다. **각자의 실력에 맞는 공부방법은 위의 '2. 효과적인 점수대별 학습 방법은 뭔가요?' 를 참조하시기 바랍니다.**

또한, 목표기간이 짧다고 해서 기본적인 영어 청취력을 갖추지 않은 학생이 어려운 내용을 아무리 여러 번 듣고 문제를 풀어도 실력이 금방 향상되지는 않습니다. 기초부터 차곡차곡 밟아가는 것보다 오히려 더 많은 시간이 흐를지도 모르죠. 영어 수준은 본인이 취약한 부분을 꾸준히 메꾸는게 우선이라고 봅니다. 이것은 토플 성적만을 취득하기 위해서뿐만 아니라 제대로 된 영어 실력을 쌓는데도 도움이 됩니다. 특히, 토플 리스닝은 무조건 많이 듣는다고 해서 저절로 귀가 열리는게 아닙니다. 대학교 수준의 대화와 강의를 듣고 내용의 핵심을 파악해서 문제를 풀어야 하기 때문에, 총체적인 이해력과 내용의 포인트를 파악하는 분석력, 들은 정보를 바탕으로 문제가 요구하는 답을 골라내는 논리적 추론력 등, 단순한 청취 이외의 능력들도 함께 평가하고자 하는 시험입니다. **전반적인 토플 영어 청취실력 향상에 관한 방법은 앞장의 '1.왜 청취 부분 점수가 잘 안 나오는 걸까요? LC공부는 어떻게 해야 하는지 감이 잘 안 잡혀요.' 의 내용을 읽어보시기 바랍니다.**

7. 영어 공부를 한지 오래됐는데요. 리스닝을 따라갈 수 있을까요?

본인이 할 의지만 있다면 남들보다 시간이 조금 오래 걸릴지는 몰라도 다 따라오실 수 있습니다.^^ 다른 모든 section도 그렇지만, 단어는 리스닝의 첫 번째 기초이기 때문에, 뜻과 더불어 발음까지 정확하고 꼼꼼하게 외우면서 어휘의 양을 계속 누적시켜 나가야 합니다. 중고등 필수 영단어와 함께 토플단어를 외우면서 기초를 잡으시면 됩니다. 이때, 많은 학생들이 단순히 단어의 spelling과 뜻을 외우시는데, 영어는 한국어와 달리 글자와 소리가 일치하지 않는 부분이 많습니다. 따라서 각 단어의 소리를 하나씩 머리속에 입력하셔야 합니다. 이 작업은 그동안 영어공부를 글자 위주로 해온 한국 학생들이 가볍게 여기거나, 무시하는데 번거롭더라도 꼭 단어의 소리를 듣고 기억하셔야, 비단 리스닝 뿐만 아니라 speaking에도 큰 도움이됩니다.

또한 문법과 독해 공부도 꾸준히 하셔야 합니다. 리스닝의 기초는 어휘도 중요하지만, 문법도 큰 역할을 하니까요. 문법을 통해 문장구조 파악을 빨리 할 수 있어야 들리는 문장의 내용이 머리 속에서 빠르고 정확하게 이해되거든요. 한국 학생들이 어느 정도 공부해온 독해실력으로 리스닝 스크립트를 쭉 읽어나가는데, 처음에 문장을 한번 보고 문장의 구조나 의미가 들어오지 않는다면, 리스닝은 무리가 따릅니다. 이런 식으로 기본 영어 실력을 꾸준히 쌓아가면서, 청취 훈련을 하고 문제를 풀어나간다면, 좋은 결과를 얻으실 수 있을 겁니다.

■ 학생들이 자주하는 질문 Q&A

8. 청취력을 키우려면 무엇부터 공부해야 하나요?

당연히 어휘부터입니다. 특히 단어는 영어의 기초입니다. 토플 네 과목인 Reading, Listening, Writing, Speaking 전 영역에 있어서 기본적으로 꼭 알고 있어야 하는 필수적인 부분이며, 가장 많은 효과를 볼 수 있는 부분입니다. 특히 리스닝은 대학교 교양과목 수준의 내용을 듣고 이해하여 문제를 푸는 것이기 때문에, 전문적인 어휘가 많이 등장합니다. 따라서, 차곡차곡 어휘를 쌓아간다는 건 본인이 전쟁에 나가기에 앞서 총알을 챙기는 것과 같죠. 군인이 전쟁에 나가는데 총알이 없거나 턱없이 부족하다면 어떻게 될까요? 반면에 넉넉히 준비하고 있다면, 일단 전투에 임하는 자세가 달라지고 자신감이 샘솟는 것 뿐만 아니라 실제로 전투에서 이길 확률이 높아지겠죠.

주의하실 점은 단어 음원을 듣지 않은 상태에서 계속 외우기만 하면, 나중엔 쉬운 단어인데도 알아듣지 못하거나 엉뚱하게 다른 단어로 알아듣는 경우가 많다는 것입니다. 그러므로 스펠링과 함께 소리를 입력해주어야 하는데, 발음을 본인이 맘대로 창조하거나, 주변에서 한국인들끼리 통하는 소위 '된장' 발음은 지양하고, 정확한 소리를 기억해야 영어가 정확하게 들립니다. 또한 이런식으로 문장도 꾸준히 소리와 더불어 학습해 나간다면 얼마 안 있어 청취력이 빠르게 향상되는 걸 느끼실 수 있습니다

9. 저는 Reading Section에서는 점수가 20점 이상 꾸준히 나오는데, Listening Section은 10점대 초반으로 점수차가 많이 납니다. 뭐가 문제일까요?

기본적인 영어실력은 어느 정도 머리 속에 있는데, 청취를 해본 적이 없거나 영어소리에 익숙하지 않은 경우 이런 현상이 나타납니다. 실제 수업에서, 학생들에게 영어문장을 들려주고 딕테이션(Dictation)을 시킨 다음, 스크립트를 보고 체크해 보라고 하면, 학생 스스로도 놀라는 경우가 많습니다. 어렵거나 이상한 단어를 못 적은 것이 아니라, 다 아는 단어인데 소리로 만들었을 땐 안 들리거나 전혀 엉뚱한 단어로 들리기 때문에, 막상 적어보면 기본 어휘조차 잘 적지 못하는 것이지요. 또한 같은 문장을 글로 읽어보라고 하면, 쉽게 이해하고 해석합니다. 그러나 그 문장을 소리만 듣고 무슨 의미인지 얘기해 보라고 하면, 대답하지 못하는 경우를 많이 봅니다. 이것은 영어를 글자로만 공부했기 때문에 발생하는 문제인데요. 글자와 소리가 쉽게 매치되는 한국어와 달리, 영어는 특유의 강세와 리듬이 있으며, 철자를 보고 쉽게 발음이 판단이 안 되는 단어들도 많습니다. 그래서 한국인들이 느끼는 글자와 소리 사이의 괴리감이 발생하는 것이지요. 이것은 마치 한자를 보고 어떻게 발음 하냐고 물어보면 그 소리를 외우고 있지 않은 이상 선뜻 대답하지 못하는 것과 같습니다. 따라서 영어 소리 훈련을 통하여 머리 속에 저장된 글자 및 의미와 소리를 합치는 작업이 필요합니다. RC영역에서 성적이 어느 정도 나온다는 것은 어휘력, 문법, 문장력, 이해력 등 기본기가 갖춰있다는 뜻이기 때문에, 영어 소리의 특징에 익숙해지면 들은 내용이 머리 속에 이미 들어가있는 정보들과 빠르게 매치되면서 이해가 잘 되고, 이에 따라 문제를 정확하게 풀게 되어 점수가 오르는 것입니다.

해결 방법으로는, 어떤 단어나 표현을 외울 때 전자사전이나 인터넷 사전에서 우선 찾아서, 그 단어의 글자와 의미를 확인한 뒤 발음을 들어보세요. 또한, 여러 번 들어보고 3번 정도 똑같이 따라 말해보세요. 이렇게 함으로써 한 단어의 spelling, 뜻, 발음 이렇게 3가지를 동시에 머리속에 넣어 기억하는 겁니다. 영어 리스닝은 글자가 보이는 것이 아닌 소리만으로 뜻을 이해해야 하기 때문에, 소리 자체를 기억해야 나중에 들었을때 뜻과 함께 떠오르게 되어 청취를 하는데 효과적입니다. 또한 청취력이 어느정도 뒷받침되어진다 하더라도, 리딩과는 다른 리스닝 문제 특유의 유형을 파악하지 못하면 정답이 아닌 오답을 고르기 쉽기 때문에 점수가 잘 나오지 않을 수도 있습니다. 때문에 문제를 정확하게 분석하는 스킬을 기를 필요가 있습니다. 또한 Topic의 영향도 큰데, 자신이 취약한 주제가 나올 경우 친숙한 주제가 나올 때보다 난이도가 훨씬 어렵다고 느끼게 됩니다. 또한 내용을 들을때는 이해가 가지만 막상 문제를 풀 때 ETS가 출제하는 문제 유형이나 오답 방식에 익숙하지 않을 경우 정답이 아닌 오답을 고르게 됩니다. 이런 경우는 문제 해결력을 꾸준히 기르셔야 합니다.

10. 저는 학원을 다니지 않고 혼자 독학으로 토플 시험을 준비하고 있는데요. 어떻게 해야 효율적으로 공부 할 수 있나요?

학원에서 토플리스닝을 공부하는 경우에는 실제 문제 유형들을 접한 다음, 내용을 듣고 청취만을 바탕으로 본인이 알아들은 내용이 맞는지 파트너와 Discussion을 하고, 다시 선생님과의 내용 확인을 통해 단순히 내용만을 이해하는 것을 떠나 전반적인 강의의 구조와 내용전개 방식 등을 파악하는 훈련에 집중하게 됩니다. 또한 딕테이션 방법과 노트테이킹 요령, 각 문제별 유형과 대처법, 배경지식 쌓는 법 등 청취력을 향상시킬 수 있는 여러가지 팁들을 얻을 수 있죠.

반면에, 학생이 혼자서 토플 리스닝 시험을 준비하는 경우는 다음과 같은 순서로 공부하시면 효과를 보실 수 있습니다.

A) 실제시험과 비슷한 환경에서 긴장감있게 문제를 풀고 채점합니다. 그리고 나서 내용을 다시 들으면서 노트테이킹을 수정하세요. 이 때 처음에 놓쳤거나 잘못 들었던 내용을 정확히 잡으려고 노력합니다.
B) MP3를 전체적으로 다시 한 번 쭉 듣고나서, 안 들리는 부분을 한 문장씩 dictation합니다.
C) 스크립트 내용을 파악합니다. 이때 어휘나 표현, 문장을 정확히 해석하여 내용을 완벽하게 이해하기 위해, 이해가 안 가는 단어나 표현들은 사전이나 인터넷으로 확인합니다.
D) 문제를 분석합니다. 이때 틀린 문제 위주로 정답 근거를 스크립트에서 찾고, 본인이 선택한 오답의 이유를 분석해 봅니다.
E) 이제 완벽하게 이해한 강의의 내용을 summary해 봅니다. 핵심 내용 위주로 노트에 정리하면서 본인의 머리속에 배경지식으로 집어넣습니다.
F) Mp3를 다시 들으면서 내용을 다시 한번 정리하고, 딕테이션에서 수정한 부분이나 반복해서 들어도 잘 안들리는 문장은 소리를 그대로 따라하며 새도잉함으로써 귀를 열어줍니다.

☞ 자세한 학습 방법은 뒷장 P. 32 'Listening Strategies 1.리스닝 학습 순서 및 방법, 2. 문제 분석 방법' 을 참조하세요

11. 토플 리스닝 실력이 어느 정도 향상되었는지 한번 알아보고 싶은데, 어떻게 확인하죠?

본인이 공부를 잘 하고 있는지 혹은 내 실력이 어느정도 향상되었는지 알고 싶다면, 실제 시험을 보는 것도 좋지만 모의토플을 추천해 드리고 싶습니다. 모의 토플은 실제 토플 시험을 출제하는 ETS에서 주관하기 때문에 현재 시험과 가장 유사한 형태의 문제들을 체험해 볼 수 있는 좋은 기회입니다. Reading과 Listening 2과목만 따로 보는 것도 가능하기 때문에 실제 시험과 달리 부담이 덜하다는 장점이 있죠. 그리고 꼭 내 점수에 대한 평가를 위해서 뿐만아니라, 실제 시험을 앞두고 있다면 모의 시험을 통해 시험방식과 시험장 환경에 미리 적응하는 것도 나쁘지 않습니다. 실제 토플은 컴퓨터로 시험을 보는 것이어서 종이로 문제를 푸는 것과는 많이 다르거든요. 모의고사를 통해 모니터 화면에 익숙해 질 수 있는 기회를 가질 수 있고, 실제 시험 과정이 어떻게 진행되는지 경험할 수 있습니다. 또한 시험과 같은 환경에서 긴장감을 느끼며 문제를 풀기 때문에 실제 시험장에서 빨리 적응하는데 훈련이 됩니다. 더불어 모의 토플에 나오는 문제들은 과거 ETS가 출제한 문제들 이므로 실제 문제에 대한 감을 익힐 수도 있죠. 다만, 종이로 풀 때와 컴퓨터로 풀 때 점수 차이가 나는 학생들이 많기 때문에, 실제 iBT 시험과는 3~4점 정도 점수가 차이날 수도 있다는 가정하에 보셔야 합니다. 수능 전 모의고사를 여러 번 풀어 보듯이 실제 IBT문제를 접하기 전에 모의토플 시험을 신청하셔서 보시길 권해드립니다. 한 달에 1번씩 꾸준히 보고 본인만의 성적을 기록해 놓는 것도 좋은 방법입니다. 모의토플 응시는 www.toefltpo.com 또는 학원 (www.usherin.usher.co.kr)에 문의하시기 바랍니다.

 2019년 8월 1일 바뀌는 뉴 토플에 관하여
ETS가 공식 배포한 모의토플 테스트를 기준으로 안내

Writing

라이팅은 변동이 없는 유일한 파트입니다.

Reading

1. 문제가 지문당 14문제에서 10문제로 줄었습니다.
   (줄어든 문제 유형은 모두 가장 쉬운 문제 유형인, 단어와 fact문제입니다)
2. ·문제 풀이 시간은 지문당 20분에서 18분으로 줄었습니다.
   ·지문 길이는 기존과 같이 800자 내외 입니다. (변화 없습니다)

Listening

1. Set의 구성에 변화가 있습니다.
   예전 토플은 '1set= conversation+ lecture+lecture' 로만 구성 되었으나,
   뉴 토플은 첫번째 Set은 기존과 같이 conv+ lect + lect 이지만,
   두번째 Set은 conv + lect 로만 구성되어 lecture 한 지문이 사라졌습니다.
2. 이에 따라 문제 풀이 시간도 1개 set당 10분씩 배정 되었던것이,
   1st set : 10분(기존과 같음)
   2nd set : 7분으로 줄었습니다.
3. 청취시간(대화나, 강의 길이)은 기존과 같습니다
   ·conversation : 2분 30초 내외
   ·lecture 4분 30초내외

Speaking

· Task 1,5가 없어졌습니다.
   - 독립형 1,2번 문제중에서, 추상적이어서 상대적으로 학생들이 어려워하는 2번문제를 남겨두고, 1번 문제는 없어졌습니다.

2 iBT TOEFL (iBT 토플) 시험 소개
USHER iBT TOEFL **INTERMEDIATE TEST** LISTENING (어서 iBT 토플 인터미디어트 테스트 리스닝)

iBT TOEFL (iBT 토플)이란?

TOEFL(Test of English as a Foreign Language)이란 주로 영어권 국가의 대학교에 진학하는 외국인 학생의 영어실력을 평가하기 위하여 만들어진 시험입니다. 현재 TOEFL (토플)은 iBT(internet-Based Test) TOEFL이라 불리며, PBT(Paper-Based Test) 와 CBT(Computer-Based Test)를 거쳐 채택된 3세대 시험방식입니다. 읽기, 듣기, 말하기, 쓰기의 다양한 분야의 영어실력을 보기 때문에 현재 세계적으로 가장 공신력 있는 영어시험으로 자리잡았습니다.

iBT TOEFL (iBT 토플) 구성

시험순서	지문 개수	시간	세부사항	*더미 (Dummy)	만점
Reading (상대평가)	Passage 3개 (700단어 X 3개)	60~100분	Passage 당 18분 10문제	Passage 1개 더 출제 가능	30점
Listening (상대평가)	Conversation 2개	60~90분	Conversation 당 3분 5문제	Set 1개 (1Conversation + 2 Lecture) 더 출제 가능	30점
	Lecture 3개		Lecture 당 5분 6문제		
Speaking (절대평가)	Independent 1개 Intergrated 3개	15분 내외	-	없음	30점
Writing (절대평가)	Intergrated 1개 Independent 1개	55분 (25 + 30분)	-	없음	30점
총 약 4시간					총점 120점

*더미 (Dummy)란 원래 '꼭두각시, 연습용 인형'이란 뜻으로, TOEFL (토플)에서는 성적에 포함되지 않는 문제들을 일컫습니다. 원래의 출제 의도는 난이도 조절이었지만, iBT TOEFL (iBT 토플)에 와서 그 의미가 변하였으며, 외형상 실제 문제와 구분할 방법은 없습니다. (더 자세한 내용은 http://www.usherin.usher.co.kr 참조)

꼭 알아두세요!

접수	전화나 인터넷으로 최소 1주 전 등록	
비용	시험	- 미화 $ 210 (원화결제 가능)
	취소한 성적 복원	- 미화 $ 20
	성적 전송	- 미화 $ 20 (1개 기관당)
	일자 변경	- 미화 $ 60
	재채점	- 미화 $ 80 (1개 section당: 성적 불신시 speaking, writing만 가능)

2 iBT TOEFL (iBT 토플) 시험 소개

시험	한 달에 3회~5회 (토요일과 일요일에만 실시: http://ets.org/toefl에서 확인 가능)
시험장소	전국 27개 도시에 있는 Test Center 및 세계 각국의 ETS Test Center (안양, 아산, 부천, 부산, 천안, 청주, 춘천, 대구, 대전, 고성, 고양, 군포, 광주, 경기, 경주, 경산, 화성, 인천, 제주, 전주, 진주, 오산, 포천, 성남, 서울, 울산, 용인 등 27개 도시 - 토플 시험장에 대한 자세한 정보는 http://www.usherin.usher.co.kr 참조)
준비물	토플 web site에 등록되어 있는 신분증 지참
성적 발표일	토플 시험으로부터 최소 8일 ~ 최대 14일
성적 유효기간	2년
토플 시험 등록 취소	시험 등록 후 7일 까지 : 전액환불 시험 등록 후 8일 이후 : 금액의 50% 환불 시험보기 4일전 : 금액의 50% 환불 콜센터에 전화하거나 홈페이지에서 취소 (e-mail로는 불가능)

시험장에서!

1. 시험절차 시험장에 도착하면 여권 확인 후, 성적표에 나올 사진을 찍고 감독관의 안내에 따라 순서대로 시험을 시작한다.

2. 필기도구 연필과 종이는 감독관이 나누어주므로 따로 필요가 없고, 부족하면 얼마든지 더 달라고 할 수 있다. 다만, Section 시작 전에 종이에 필기할 경우, 부정행위로 간주될 수 있으므로 각별히 주의하자.

3. 헤드폰 음량 시험 도중 언제든지 조절할 수 있다.

4. 마이크 음량 시험 시작 직후와 Speaking Section 직전에 조절할 수 있다.

5. 휴식시간 Listening Section과 Speaking Section 사이에 10분의 휴식시간이 주어지고, 화장실에 가거나, 간식을 먹을 수 있다.
이 시간을 잘 활용해 Speaking에 대비하자!

6. 주의사항 각 응시자마다 시험 진행 시간이 다르기 때문에, 내가 Listening이나 Writing Section을 풀고 있을 때, 다른 사람의 목소리가 방해가 되는 경우가 많으니 염두해 두자.

3. iBT TOEFL Listening 소개
USHER iBT TOEFL **INTERMEDIATE TEST** LISTENING (어셔 iBT 토플 인터미디어트 테스트 리스닝)

iBT TOEFL Listening이란?

iBT TOEFL Listening 영역에서는 학생들이 미국 및 캐나다 등 영미권 국가에서 유학하는 동안, 학교 생활 및 강의의 내용을 이해하고 따라갈 수 있는 영어청취능력을 평가하고자 하는데 목적이 있습니다. 그러므로 리스닝 영역은 크게 2가지 종류의 테스트로 구성되어 있는데 바로 Conversation과 Lecture입니다. Conversation에서는 대학 캠퍼스에서 학생들이 겪을 수 있는 상황들(구내시설 이용, 교수와의 상담, 학생간의 토론)과 Lecture는 대학교 1, 2학년 학생들이 듣는 개론 수준의 교양과목 수업에 해당하는 다양한 강의들이 차지하고 있습니다. 특히 렉쳐는 다양한 Topics을 다루는 형태의 내용이 출제되지만 아주 전문적인 내용으로 구성되어 있지 않고, 국내 고등학교 수준까지의 학습 내용과 겹치기 때문에 너무 겁먹을 필요는 없습니다. 하지만 대화와 강의 내용을 단 한번만 듣고 문제를 풀어야 하기 때문에, 고도의 집중력과 정확한 청취력이 필요합니다. 또한 녹음 내용을 다 듣고 난 뒤에 문제가 화면에 나타나므로, 청취 내용을 이해하는 동시에 논리적으로 핵심을 정리하며 기억하거나 메모하는 능력이 요구됩니다. 또한 제한된 시간내에 문제와 4개의 답들을 빠르고 정확하게 파악하는 독해능력 또한 중요합니다.

iBT Listening 구성

2~3개 대화(Conversation) : 각 지문당 길이 - 3~4분 / 각각 5문항 출제

4~6개 강의(Lecture) : 한 지문당 길이 - 5~7분 / 각각 6문항 출제

→ 기본 2개 Set (1번째 Set : conversation 1개+lecture 2개,
2번째 Set : conversation 1개+lecture 1개) + 추가 1 Set(Dummy) 나올수도 안 나올수도 있음(리딩 더미에 따라)

☞ 시험문항수 : 34개 (1set(5+6+6)X2) + 추가 1 Set(Dummy)
☞ 시험시간 : 60분 + Dummy (추가 30분)
☞ 점수범위 : 0~30점

iBT Listening 내용

A. 대화 (Conversation)
캠퍼스에서 일어날 수 있는 상황(교무처, 기숙사, 도서관, 구내식당, 서점) + 교수연구실(강의내용 질문, 숙제 및 프로젝트 문의, 진로상담) + 학생간의 토론(강의내용 복습, 시험대비공부, 프로젝트 및 리서치 관련 대화)

B. 강의 (Lecture)
대학교 1, 2학년 교양과목에서 다루는 개론 수준의 학문분야로 다양한 Topics 포함(생물학, 환경학, 천문학, 지구과학, 인류학, 고고학, 역사, 예술, 문학, 마케팅, 경제, 경영 등)

3 iBT TOEFL Listening 소개

iBTListening 특징

Note-taking이 허용된다
대화와 강의 내용의 길이가 길어지고, 말의 속도(특히 conversation)가 빨라졌으며, 화자들의 어투가 자연스러워지고 실제 상황에서 쓰이는 표현들이 많이 등장하고 있다.
정답이 2개, 3개인 문제 형태가 출제된다.(Clik on 2 answers, Click on 3 answers)
들은 내용에 숨겨진 실질적인 의미나 화자의 의도, 다시 들려주는 부분을 듣고 화자의 의견이나 태도를 파악하는 문제유형이 증가하였다.
글의 구조 및 세부내용의 관계를 파악하는 순서 나열하기, 관련 내용 연결하기, OX맞추기 문제가 출제된다.

iBTListening 문제 유형 분석

난이도	기본문제유형	세부문제유형	문제유형 설명	지문당 문항수
상중하 (최근 어려워지는 추세임 - 약 20%차지)	Main Idea	Main Purpose Main Idea	방문목적 대화 및 강의 주제	1개
중하 (기본점수의 40% 이상 차지 - 청취력 확인)	Detail	Definition Example Characteristics Cause/Result Misunderstanding/Correction Requirement Suggestion Future action	용어가 가리키는 내용 찾기 본문 내용 사실여부 파악하기 문제점에 대한 화자의 제안	2 ~ 4개
중상 (변별력 목적 - 약 20 - 40% 차지)	Inference	Purpose Imply Opinion Headset	제공된 정보로 화자의 의도 및 태도 파악하기 다시 들려주는 부분 듣고 화자의 의도 파악하기	1 ~ 3개
중상 (변별력 목적- 약 20% 차지, 항상 출제되는 것은 아님)	Category	Organize Click on 2, 3 answers Matching Ordering	내용의 전개구조 파악하기 동일 범주에 해당하는 내용 찾기 주어진 정보를 알맞게 정렬하기 정보들의 관계를 연결하기	1 ~ 2개

iBT Listening 화면 구성

문제를 풀 때 화면 상단에 진행과정을 도와주는 툴바(Tool Bar)가 나타난다. 이것을 통해 헤드셋의 볼륨을 조절하고, 현재 풀고 있는 문제의 번호와, 다음 문제로 넘어가기, 해당 Set의 종료시간까지 얼마 남았는지 알 수 있다.

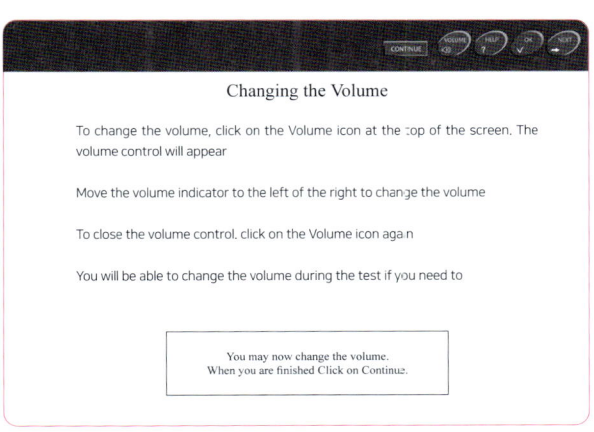

음량조절 화면

시험이 시작하기 전에 음량을 조절할 것인 묻는 화면으로 'VOLUME'을 클릭하면 음량을 조절할 수 있다.
시험을 보는 동안에도 음량 조절이 가능하다

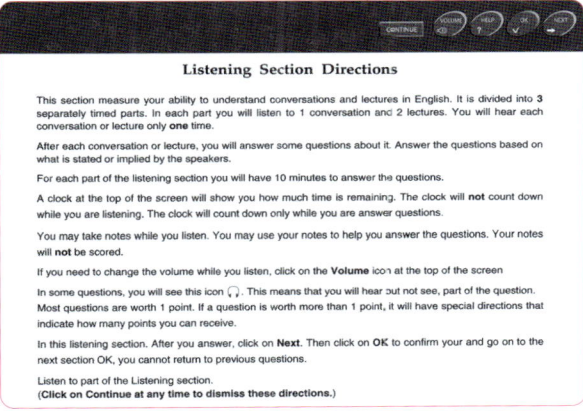

Listening Direction 화면

이 리스닝 시험 진행 방식에 대한 전반적인 설명이 나온다. 리스닝 파트에서는 17문제로 구성된 Part가 2~3번 나오며, 각 Part는 Conversation 1개와 Lecture 2개로 이루어져 있다는 설명이다.

대화 및 강의 내용을 들을 때 나오는 화면

대화가 나오는 동안 두 화자의 사진이 나오며 강의의 주제와 관련된 사진이 나오는 경우도 있다.
사진 아래의 바는 지문 분량의 진행정보를 알려준다.

3 iBT TOEFL Listening 소개

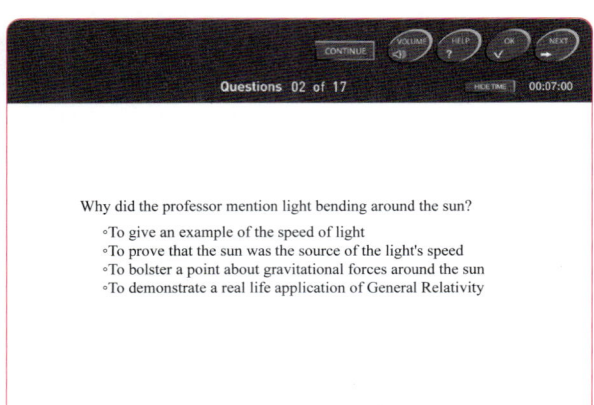

문제가 나오는 화면

문제가 나올 때 보이는 화면으로 문제를 들려주고 보기가 뜬다. 답을 클릭한 후 Next 버튼을 누르고 OK 버튼을 클릭하면 답이 확정되며 이전 화면으로 돌아갈 수 없으며, 답이 2개 이상인 문제는 반드시 모든 답을 클릭해야 다음 문제로 넘어갈 수 있다.

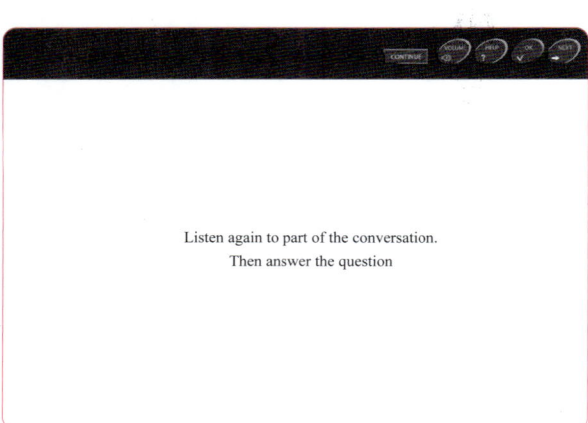

다시 들려주는 문제 유형의 Direction 화면

대화 및 강의의 일부를 다시 듣고 푸는 문제에서 주어지는 Direction화면이다. 이 화면이 나온 후 지문의 일부를 다시 들려준다.

4 Listening Section 평가기준 (ETS Scoring Criteria)
USHER iBT TOEFL INTERMEDIATE TEST LISTENING (어셔 iBT 토플 인터미디어트 테스트 리스닝)

리스닝 섹션의 문제를 통해 ETS가 평가하고자 하는 사항들을 설명한 것입니다. 학생들은 이 평가 기준을 통해 토플 리스닝 시험이 어떤 의도로 출제되는지 파악한 후, 이에 부합하는 어휘력, 청취력 및 논리적 사고력을 기르는데 힘쓴다면 고득점에 다가가기 훨씬 쉬울 것입니다.

High (22-30)

Test takers who receive a score at the HIGH level, as you did, typically understand conversations and lectures in English that present a wide range of listening demands. These demands can include **difficult vocabulary (uncommon terms, or colloquial or figurative language)**, complex grammatical structures, abstract or complex ideas and/or making sense of unexpected or seemingly contradictory information.

When listening to lectures and conversations like these, test takers at HIGH level typically can:

A. Understand **main idea** and **important details**, **whether they are stated or implied**;
B. **Distinguish more important ideas from less important ones**;
C. Understand how **information** is being **used** (for example, to provide **evidence** for a claim or describe **a step in a complex process**);
D. Recognize how pieces of information are **connected** (for example, in a **cause-and-effect relationship**);
E. Understand many different ways that speakers use language for **purpose other than to give information** (for example, to **emphasize a point**, express **agreement or disagreement**, or **convey intentions indirectly**); and
F. **Synthesize information, even when it is not presented in sequence**, and make **correct inferences** on the basis of that information.

Intermediate (15-21)

Test takers who receive a score at the INTERMEDIATE level, as you did, typically understand conversations and lectures in English that present a wide range of listening demands. These demands can include difficult vocabulary (uncommon terms, or colloquial or figurative language), complex grammatical structures and/or abstract or complex ideas. However, lectures and conversations that require the listener to make sense of unexpected or seemingly contradictory information may present some difficulty.

When listening to conversations and lectures like these, test takers at the INTERMEDIATE level typically can:

A. Understand explicitly stated main ideas and important details, especially if they are reinforced, but may have difficulty understanding main ideas that must be inferred or important details that are not reinforced.;
B. Understand how information is being used (for example, to provide support or describe a step in a complex process);
C. Recognize how pieces of information are connected (for example, in a cause-and-effect relationship);
D. Understand, though perhaps not consistently, ways that speakers use language for purposes other than to give information (for example, to emphasize a point, express agreement or disagreement, or convey intentions indirectly); and
E. Synthesize information from adjacent parts of a lecture or conversation and make correct inferences on the basis of that information, but may have difficulty synthesizing information from separate parts of a lecture or conversation.

4 Listening Section 평가기준 (ETS Criteria)

Low (0-14)

Test takers who receive a score at the **LOW** level, as you did, typically understand the main idea and some important details of conversations. However, test takers at the low level may have difficulty understanding lectures and conversations in English that involve abstract or complex ideas and recognizing the relationship between those ideas. Test takers at this level also may not understand sections of lectures and conversations that contain difficult vocabulary or complex grammatical structures.

Test takers at the **LOW** level typically can:

A. Understand main ideas when they are stated explicitly or marked as important, but may have difficulty understanding main ideas if they are not stated explicitly;

B. Understand important details when they are stated explicitly or marked as important, but may have difficulty understanding details if they are not repeated or clearly marked as important, or if they are conveyed over several exchanges among different speakers;

C. Understand ways that speakers use language to emphasize a point or to indicate agreement or disagreement, but generally only when the information is related to a central theme or is clearly marked as important; and

D. Make connections between the key ideas in a conversation, particularly if the ideas are related to a central theme or are repeated.

높음 (22-30)

높음(High) 수준의 점수를 받는 응시자는, 일반적으로 다양한 범위의 듣기 능력을 필요로 하는 영어 대화와 강의를 이해한다. 여기에서 요구되는 능력은 **어려운 어휘(자주 사용하지 않는 용어 또는 구어체 혹은 수사적 표현)**, 복잡한 문법구조, 추상적인 또는 복잡한 개념 그리고/또는 예상하지 못하거나 혹은 언뜻 보기에 모순적인 정보에 대한 이해를 포함한다.

이러한 강의와 대화를 들을 때, 높음 수준의 점수를 받는 응시자는 일반적으로 다음과 같은 것을 할 수 있다.

A. 제시되었든지 혹은 암시되었든지 간에 주제와 주요 세부사항을 이해할 수 있다.
B. 더 중요한 개념과 덜 중요한 개념을 구분할 수 있다.
C. 정보가 어떻게 사용되고 있는지(예: 주장에 대한 증거를 제공하기 위함인지 또는 복잡한 과정의 단계를 설명하기 위함인지)이해 할 수 있다.
D. 정보 조각들이 어떻게 연결되는지(예: 인과관계)이해 할 수 있다.
E. 정보를 제공하는 것 이외의 목적을 위해 화자가 언어를 사용하는 다른 방식들을 이해할 수 있다. (예: 핵심내용 강조하기, 동의나 반대 표현하기, 간접적으로 의도 전달하기) ; 그리고
F. 연속적으로 제시되어 있지 않더라도, 정보를 통합할 수 있고 그 정보에 기초해서 올바른 추론을 할 수 있다.

중간 (15-21)

중간(Intermediate) 수준의 점수를 받은 응시자는, 일반적으로 다양한 범위의 듣기 능력을 필요로 하는 영어 대화와 강의를 이해한다. 여기서 요구되는 능력은 어려운 어휘(자주 사용하지 않는 용어 또는 구어체 혹은 수사적 표현), 복잡한 문법 구조, 추상적이거나 또는 복잡한 개념들을 포함한다. 하지만, 강의와 대화에 있는 예상치 못하거나 혹은 언뜻 보기에 모순되게 제시 되는 정보를 청취자가 이해하는 것에 약간의 어려움을 느낀다.

이러한 강의와 대화를 들으면서, 중간 수준의 점수를 받는 응시자는 일반적으로 다음과 같은 것을 할 수 있다.

A. 명쾌하게 제시된 주제와 주요 세부사항을, 특히 이들이 강조되었을 때, 이해할 수 있다. 하지만 추론해야 하는 주제와 강조되지 않은 세부사항을 이해하는 데에는 어려움을 겪을 수 있다.
B. 정보가 어떻게 사용되고 있는지 이해할 수 있다. (예: 근거를 제공하거나 복잡한 절차의 단계를 묘사)
C. 정보 조각들이 어떻게 연결되어 있는지 파악할 수 있다. (예: 인과관계)
D. 지속적으로는 아닐지라도, 정보 제공 이외의 다른 목적을 위한 언어 사용 방법을 이해할 수 있다. (예: 강조하기, 동의나 반대 표현하기, 간접적으로 의도 전달하기) ; 그리고,
E. 강의나 대화에서 서로 인접해 있는 부분의 정보들을 합치고 그 정보에 기초해서 올바른 추론은 할 수 있지만, 떨어져 있는 정보를 합치는 것에는 어려움을 겪을 수 있다.

낮음 (0-14)

낮음(Low) 수준의 점수를 받는 응시자들은 일반적으로 대화의 주제와 몇몇 중요한 세부사항을 이해할 수 있다. 하지만 이 수준의 응시자는 추상적이거나 복잡한 개념을 포함한 영어 강의나 대화를 이해하거나, 그 생각들의 관계를 파악하는데 어려움을 겪을 수 있다. 이 수준의 응시자들은 또한 어려운 어휘나 복잡한 문법구조를 포함하는 강의와 대화의 부분들을 이해하지 못할 수 있다.

낮음 수준의 응시자들은 일반적으로 다음와 같은 것을 할 수 있다.

A. 명쾌하게 제시되거나 중요하다고 표시되어질 때 주제를 이해할 수 있지만, 만약 이들이 명쾌하게 제시되어 있지 않다면 주제를 이해하는데 어려움을 겪을 수 있다.
B. 명쾌하게 제시되거나 중요하다고 표시되어질 때 주요 세부사항을 이해할 수 있지만, 만약 그것이 반복되지 않거나 중요하다고 명확하게 표시되어 있지 않다면, 혹은 이들이 서로 다른 화자들을 통해 몇번의 대화를 거쳐 전달이 되면, 세부사항을 이해하는데 어려움을 겪을 수 있다.
C. 화자가 강조하기 위해 또는 동의나 반대를 나타내기 위해 언어를 사용하는 방식을 이해할 수 있지만, 일반적으로 정보가 중심 주제와 연결되어 있을 때나 중요하다고 명확하게 표시되어 있을 때에만 이해한다.
D. 특히 개념들이 중심 생각과 관련되어 있거나 반복되었을 때만, 대화에서 핵심 생각들 사이를 연결할 수 있다.

5 본 iBT 토플 교재만의 특징
USHER iBT TOEFL **INTERMEDIATE TEST** LISTENING (어셔 iBT 토플 인터미디어트 테스트 리스닝)

1 실제 iBT 토플 시험과 가장 유사한 실전서

최신 출제 경향 반영

최신 토플 시험 출제 경향을 완벽히 반영한 지문과 문제로 구성되었으며, 학생들이 어려워하는 주제인 물리학, 고고학, 인류학, 역사, 생물학, 건축학 등 지문 내용의 다양화와 상향된 난이도를 반영하여 본 교재를 통해 iBT 토플 리스닝 영역을 효과적으로 학습할 수 있다.

토플 고득점 달성을 위한 최상의 난이도

기존의 타교재와 비교해 최고 난이도의 지문과 문제로 구성된 본 교재를 학습함으로써 iBT 토플 리스닝 시험에 대한 감각을 확실하게 터득할 수 있어, 실제 시험에 철저히 대비할 수 있다.

2 효과적인 iBT 토플 리스닝 공부 방법 제시

체계적인 공부방법 설명

대부분의 기존 토플 교재들이 소홀히 하고 있는 부분인, 해석에만 초점을 맞춘 것이 아니라 학생들이 리스닝 시험에 접근하기 위해 효과적으로 공부하는 방법 자체를 설명하고 있다. 책의 서문에 나와 있는 리스닝 학습 순서 및 방법, 문제분석방법, 문제유형별 세부전략 등을 읽고 활용할 수 있다.

문제 유형별 전략 제시

각 문제의 유형별 세부 전략을 통해 고득점 달성에 필수인 가장 빠르고 효과적인 문제 접근 능력을 키워 논리적인 해결 능력을 향상시킬 수 있다.

| 토플 공부도우미 | www.usherin.usher.co.kr

3 토플 독학하는 수험생에게도 유용한 추천 학습서

수준별 학습 플랜 제시

학습자 개개인의 수준에 맞게 제시된 최적의 학습 플랜을 통해 체계적인 시간 관리와 효과적인 학습 방법을 익힐 수 있다. 스스로의 실력과 여건에 맞는 일정표를 작성하여 목표를 갖고 공부에 임하여 더 좋은 결과를 가질 수 있다.

정확한 해석 및 상세한 해설, 문제오답패턴 제시

정확한 지문 해석은 물론, 정답만을 짚어주는 기존의 해설서의 방식을 탈피하여, 정답의 근거 표시와 오답이 왜 틀렸는지에 대한 이유가 자세히 설명되어 있어 토플 리스닝을 독학으로 공부하는 학생들에게 큰 도움이 될 수 있다. 또한 모든 ETS 문제는 정답과 오답을 만드는데 패턴이 있는 만큼, 이런 패턴들을 모아 정리하였다.

셀프 체크 시스템

교재 서문의 'Listening Strategies 2. 문제분석방법과 각 테스트마다 있는 'Self-Check List 및 '오답정리표를 활용하여 정확한 문제 유형 파악과 본인이 반복적으로 실수하는 오답 패턴을 찾아 취약점을 집중적으로 공략할 수 있다.

본 iBT 토플 교재의 구성
USHER iBT TOEFL INTERMEDIATE TEST LISTENING (어셔 iBT 토플 인터미디어트 테스트 리스닝)

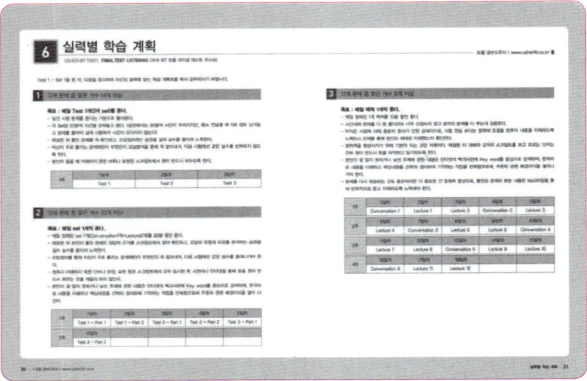

실력별 학습계획

각각 학생들의 실력 수준에 맞게 본 교재를 학습할 수 있는 학습플랜을 제시해 놓았습니다.

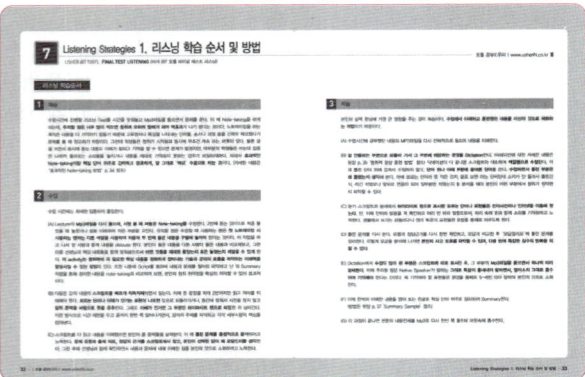

리스닝 학습순서 및 방법

학생들의 토플 리스닝 실력 향상을 위해 특별히 학습방법을 자세히 적어두었습니다. Listening Strategies 1. 리스닝 학습 순서 및 방법에서 '효과적인 Note-taking 방법', '청취력 향상훈련', 'Direction Sample', 'Summary Sample'등을 자세히 읽고 활용하시기 바랍니다. 또한 토플 리스닝 문제 유형과 오답 패턴 및 그에 따른 전략을 정리하였습니다. Listening Strategies 2. 문제분석방법, '문제유형별 세부전략', '문제유형과 Signals'을 참고하시기 바랍니다.

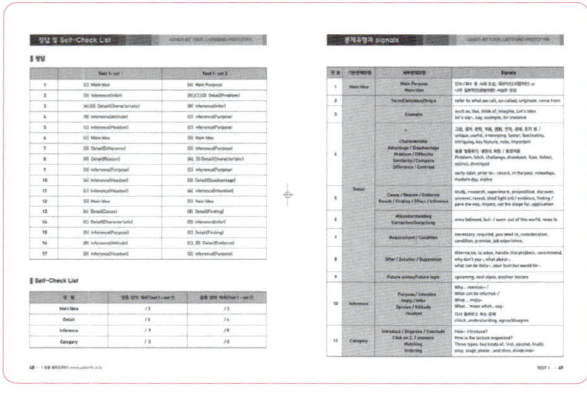

정답 및 Self-Check List

Test를 푼 후 정답을 맞출 때, 자신이 어떤 문제 유형을 틀렸는지 확인할 수 있도록 모든 문제의 정답 옆에 문제 유형을 표시하였습니다. 또한 자신의 문제 풀이 방식과 태도를 스스로 점검할 수 있도록 'Self-Check List'와 '오답정리표'를 제공하였습니다.

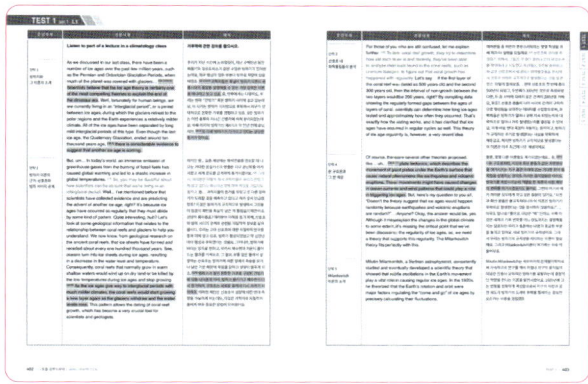

지문+해석, 해설

매회 테스트를 풀어본 후 심화학습을 할 수 있도록 해석과 자세한 해설, 정답의 근거를 제공하였습니다. 또한 토플을 혼자 공부하는 수험생들을 위해 본문에 정답의 단서가 되는 부분을 붉은색으로 표시하고, 각각 문제들의 유형 및 오답의 이유에 대한 상세한 설명을 넣어 공부의 편의성을 더하였습니다.

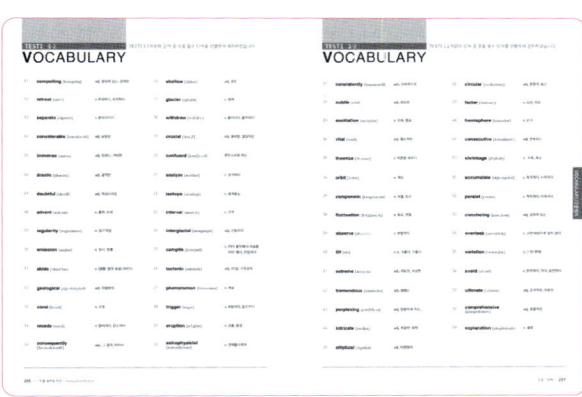

Vocabulary List

어휘 실력 향상을 위해 매 테스트에서 나온 어휘 중 필수 어휘만을 따로 선별하여 정리하였습니다. 이로 인해 번거롭게 사전을 찾을 필요없이 효율적으로 단어를 학습할 수 있습니다. 본문에 나온 토플 단어 정리를 해 두었습니다.

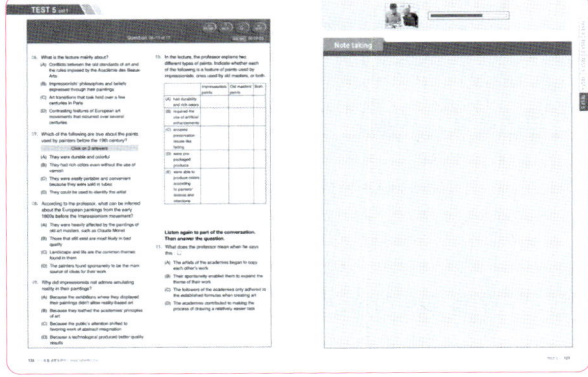

Test

실전 감각을 쌓을 수 있도록 총 3회분의 테스트를 수록하였고, 실제 시험 환경에 익숙해질 수 있도록 매 테스트를 실제 iBT 토플 시험과 동일한 형태의 화면으로 구성하였습니다. 시간을 맞춰 놓고 실전처럼 문제를 풀어주시기 바랍니다.

6 본 iBT 토플 교재의 구성

지문+해석, 해설 추가설명

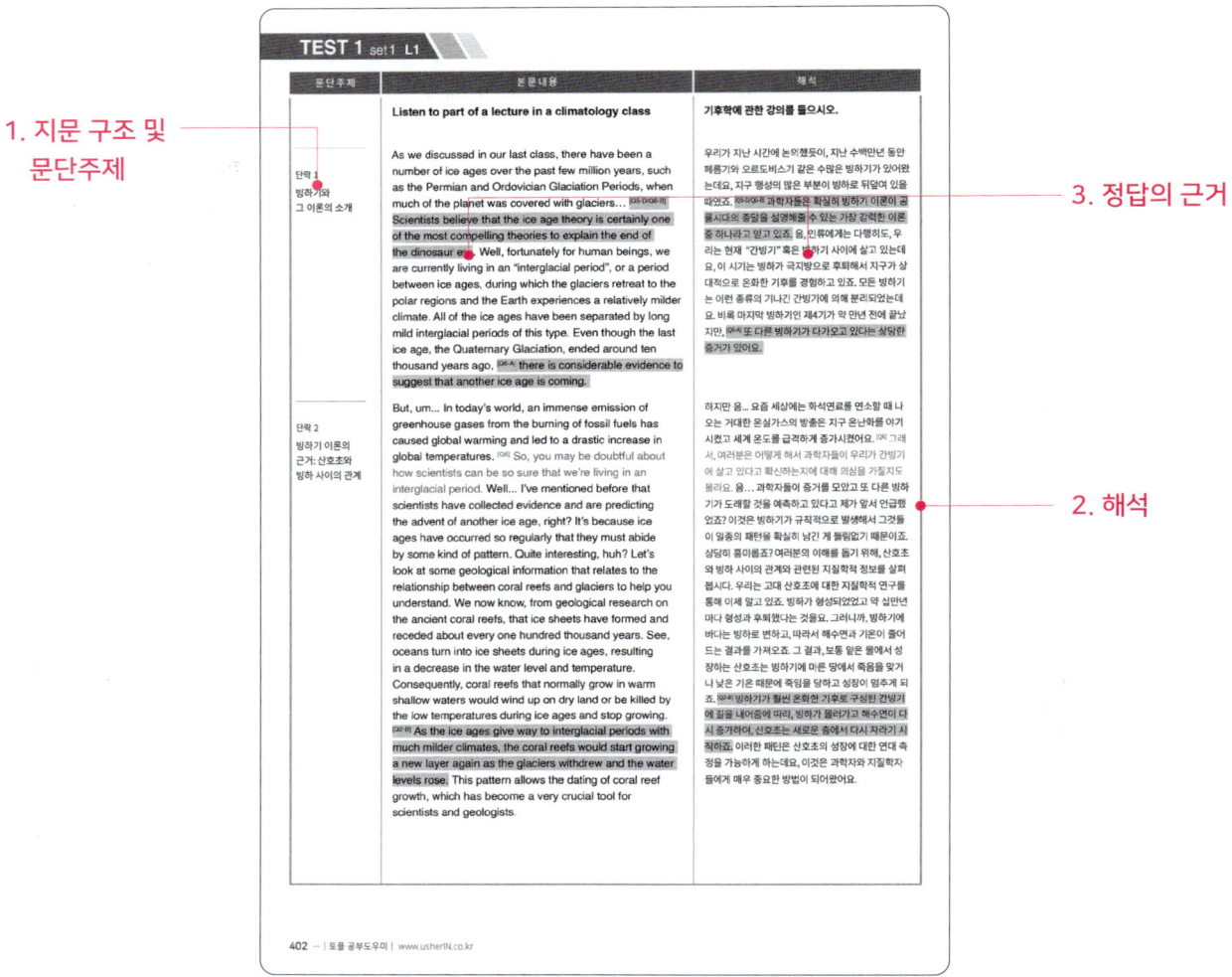

1. **지문구조 및 문단 주제**
   지문의 전체적인 흐름을 볼 수 있도록 지문의 핵심 내용을 요약하여 구조로 제시하였다.

2. **해석**
   지문 내용의 이해를 돕기 위해 정확한 해석을 제공하였다.

3. **정답의 근거**
   정답을 선택하는 데 단서가 되는 부분을 붉은 색으로 표시하여, 정답의 근거를 확실히 확인할 수 있도록 하였다.

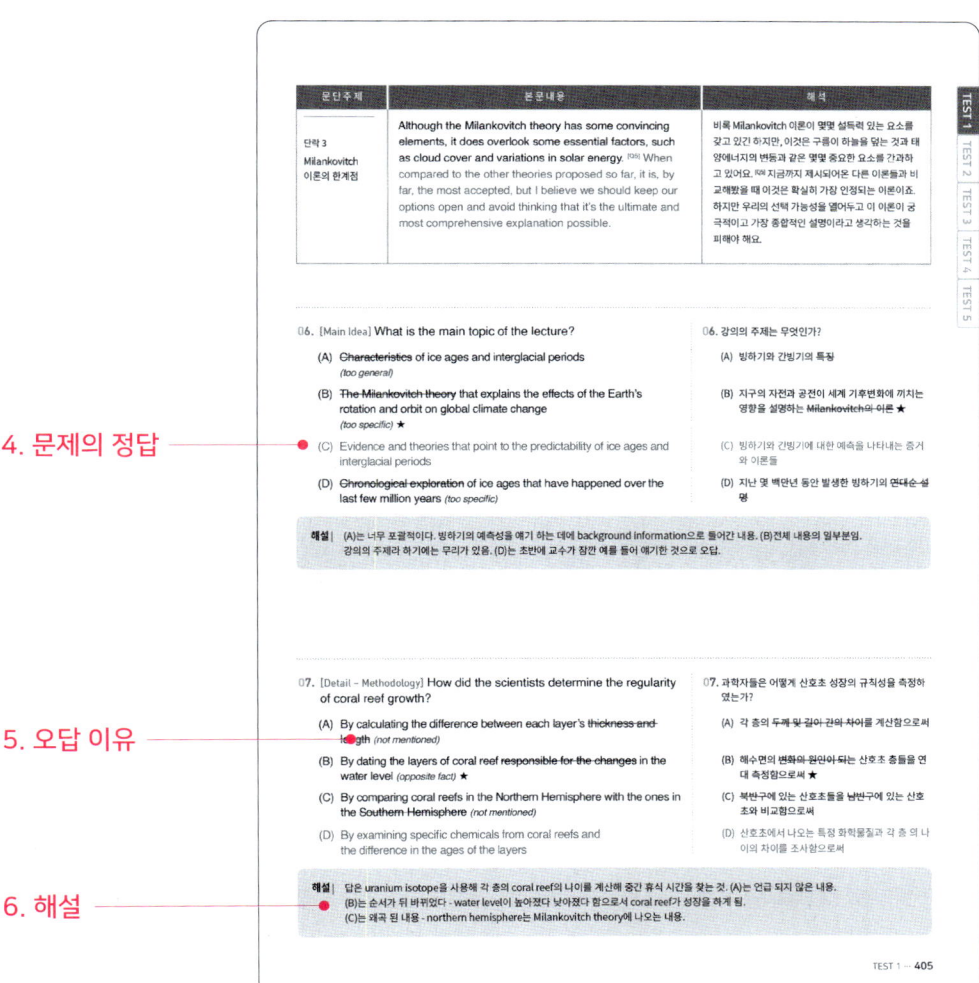

4. 문제의 정답
문제의 정답을 다른 색으로 표시하여 쉽게 알 수 있도록 했고, 찾기 쉽도록 옆의 해석 부분과 위치를 맞추었다.

5. 오답 이유
일반 문제들이 정답 근거만 제시하는 것에 반해, USHER iBT TOEFL INTERMEDIATE TEST LISTENING (어셔 iBT 토플 인터미디어트 테스트 리스닝)에서는, 오답의 이유도 밝혀 두어 혼자 공부하는 토플 독학생들에게 도움이 될 수 있도록 하였다.

6. 해설
각각의 문제 유형에 대한 표시, 정답이 되는 이유와 오답의 이유를 상세히 설명하여 혼자 공부하는 학생들에게 도움이 될 수 있도록 하였다.

7 실력별 학습 계획
USHER iBT TOEFL INTERMEDIATE TEST LISTENING (어셔 iBT 토플 인터미디어트 테스트 리스닝)

Test 1 - Set 1을 푼 뒤, 다음을 참고하여 자신의 실력에 맞는 학습 계획표를 짜서 공부하시기 바랍니다.

1 17개 문제 중 맞은 개수 14개 이상

목표 : 매일 Test 1개(2개 set)를 푼다.
- 실전 시험 문제를 푼다는 기분으로 풀어본다.
- 각 Set당 25분씩 시간을 맞춰놓고 푼다. (실전에서는 30분씩 시간이 주어지지만, 평소 연습할 때 5분 정도 남겨놓고 문제를 풀어야 실제 시험에서 시간이 모자라지 않는다)
- 채점한 뒤 틀린 문제를 꼭 확인하고, 오답정리하는 습관을 길러 실수를 줄이려 노력한다.
- 자신이 주로 틀리는 문제패턴이 무엇인지 오답분석을 통해 꼭 알아내서, 다음 시험에선 같은 실수를 반복하지 않도록 한다.
- 본인이 들을 때 이해하지 못한 어휘나 표현은 스크립트에서 찾아 반드시 외우도록 한다.

1주	1일차	2일차	3일차	4일차	5일차
	Test 1	Test 2	Test 3	Test 4	Teset 5

2 17개 문제 중 맞은 개수 10개 이상

목표 : 매일 set 1개씩 푼다.
- 매일 정해진 set 1개(Conversation1개+Lecture2개)를 30분 동안 푼다.
- 채점한 뒤 본인이 틀린 문제의 정답의 근거를 스크립트에서 찾아 확인하고, 오답의 유형과 이유를 분석하는 습관을 길러 실수를 줄이려 노력한다.
- 오답정리를 통해 자신이 주로 틀리는 문제패턴이 무엇인지 꼭 알아내어, 다음 시험에선 같은 실수를 줄여나가야 한다.
- 청취시 이해하지 못한 단어나 문장, 표현 등은 스크립트에서 모두 표시한 후 사전이나 인터넷을 통해 뜻을 찾아 반드시 외우는 것을 게을리 하지 않는다.
- 본인이 잘 알지 못하거나 낯선 주제에 관한 내용은 인터넷의 백과사전에 Key word를 중심으로 검색하여, 한국어로 내용을 이해하고 핵심내용을 간략히 정리하여 기억하는 작업을 반복함으로써 꾸준히 관련 배경지식을 쌓아 나간다.

1주	1일차	2일차	3일차	4일차	5일차
	Test 1 - Set 1	Test 1 - Set 2	Test 2 - Set 1	Test 2 - Set 2	Test 3 - Set 1
2주	**6일차**	**7일차**	**8일차**	**9일차**	**10일차**
	Test 3 - Set 2	Test 4 - Set 1	Test 4 - Set 2	Test 5 - Set 1	Test 5 - Set 2

3 17개 문제 중 맞은 개수 8개 이상

목표 : 매일 렉쳐 1개씩 푼다.

- 매일 정해진 1개 렉쳐를 10분 동안 푼다.
- 시간내에 문제를 다 못 풀더라도 너무 신경쓰지 말고 끝까지 문제를 다 푸는데 집중한다.
- 아직은 시험에 대해 충분히 준비가 안된 상태이므로, 시험 연습 보다는 청취에 초점을 맞추어 내용을 이해하도록 노력하고 문제를 통해 본인이 제대로 이해했는지 확인한다.
- 청취력을 향상시키기 위해 기본이 되는 것은 어휘이다. 채점한 뒤 대화와 강의의 스크립트를 보고 모르는 단어는 전부 찾아 반드시 뜻을 파악하고 암기하도록 한다.
- 본인이 잘 알지 못하거나 낯선 주제에 관한 내용은 인터넷의 백과사전에 Key word를 중심으로 검색하여, 한국어로 내용을 이해하고 핵심내용을 간략히 정리하여 기억하는 작업을 반복함으로써, 꾸준히 관련 배경지식을 쌓아나가야 한다.
- 문제를 다시 복습하는 것도 중요하지만 더 중요한 건 청취력 향상으로, 풀었던 문제의 본문 내용은 Mp3파일을 통해 반복적으로 듣고 이해하도록 노력해야 한다.

	1일차	2일차	3일차	4일차	5일차
1주	Conversation 1	Lecture 1	Lecture 2	Conversation 2	Lecture 3
	6일차	7일차	8일차	9일차	10일차
2주	Lecture 4	Conversation 3	Lecture 5	Lecture 6	Conversation 4
	11일차	12일차	13일차	14일차	15일차
3주	Lecture 7	Lecture 8	Conversation 5	Lecture 9	Lecture 10
	16일차	17일차	18일차	19일차	20일차
4주	Conversation 6	Lectuer 11	Lecture 12	Conversation 7	Lecture 13
	21일차	22일차	23일차	24일차	25일차
5주	Lecture 14	Conversation 8	Lecture 15	Lecture 16	Conversation 9
	26일차	27일차	28일차	29일차	30일차
6주	Lecture 17	Lecture 18	Conversation 10	Lecture 19	Lecture 20

8 Listening Strategies 1.리스닝 학습 순서 및 방법
USHER iBT TOEFL **INTERMEDIATE TEST LISTENING** (어셔 iBT 토플 인터미디어트 테스트 리스닝)

리스닝 학습순서

1 예습

수업시간에 진행할 리스닝 Test를 시간을 맞춰놓고 Mp3파일을 들으면서 문제를 푼다. 이 때 Note-taking을 하게 되는데, **주의할 점은 너무 많이 적으면 청취에 오히려 방해가 되어 역효과**가 나기 쉽다는 것이다. 노트테이킹을 하는 목적은 내용을 다 기억하기 힘들기 때문에 고유명사나 특징을 나타내는 단어들, 순서나 과정 등을 간략히 메모했다가 문제를 풀 때 참고하기 위함이다. 그런데 학생들은 청취가 시작됨과 동시에 무조건 계속 쓰는 버릇이 있다. 물론 글을 쓰면서 동시에 듣는 내용도 이해가 잘되고 기억을 할 수 있으면 문제가 없겠지만, 대부분의 학생들은 쓰는데 집중한 나머지 들려오는 소리들을 놓치거나 내용을 제대로 기억하지 못하는 경우가 비일비재하다. 따라서 **효과적인 Note-taking이란 핵심 단어 위주로 간략하고 명료하게, 말 그대로 '메모'수준으로 하는 것**이다. (자세한 내용은 p.34효과적인 Note-taking 방법 참조)

2 수업

수업 시간에는 최대한 집중하여 몰입한다.

(A) Lecture의 **Mp3파일을 다시 들으며, 시험 볼 때 써놓은 Note-taking을** 수정한다. 2번째 듣는 것이므로 처음 들었을 때 놓쳤거나 잘못 이해하여 적은 부분을 고친다. 유의할 점은 수정할 때 사용하는 펜은 **첫 노트테이킹 시 사용하는 펜과는 다른 색깔을 사용하여 처음과 두 번째 들은 내용을 구별해 놓아야 한다**는 것이다. 이 작업을 하고 나서 옆 사람과 함께 내용을 discuss 한다. 본인이 들은 내용을 다른 사람이 들은 내용과 비교해보고, 그런 다음 선생님과 핵심 내용들을 함께 맞춰봄으로써 **어떤 것들을 제대로 들었는지 혹은 놓쳤는지 깨달을 수 있게** 된다. **이 activity는 청취력에 꼭 필요한 핵심 내용을 정확하게 잡아내는 기술과 강의의 흐름을 파악하는 이해력을 향상시킬 수 있는 장점**이 있다. 또한 나중에 Script를 통하여 내용과 문제를 철저히 파악하고 난 뒤 Summary 작업을 통해 정리한 내용을 note-taking과 비교하여 보면, 본인의 청취 취약점을 확실히 파악할 수 있어 효과적이다.

(B) 다음은 강의 내용의 **스크립트를 빠르게 직독직해**하면서 읽는다. 이때 한 문장을 최대 2번까지만 읽고 의미를 이해해야 한다. **모르는 단어나 이해가 안가는 표현이 나오면** 앞으로 되돌아가거나, 중간에 멈춰서 사전을 찾지 말고 **앞뒤 문맥을 바탕으로 뜻을 유추**한다. 그래도 **이해가 안가면 그 부분만 하이라이트 펜으로 마킹**한 뒤 넘어간다. 이런 방식으로 시간 제한을 두고 끝까지 한번 쭉 읽어나가면서, 강의의 주제를 파악하고 각각 세부사항의 핵심을잡아낸다.

(C) 스크립트를 다 읽고 내용을 이해했으면 본인이 푼 문제들을 살펴본다. 이때 **틀린 문제를 중점적으로 분석**하려고 노력한다. **문제 유형과 출제 의도, 정답의 근거를 스크립트에서 찾고, 본인이 선택한 답이 왜 오답인지를 생각**한다. 그런 후에 선생님과 함께 확인하면서 내용과 문제에 대해 이해한 점을 본인의 것으로 소화하려고 노력한다.

3 복습

본인의 실력 향상에 가장 큰 영향을 주는 것이 복습이다. **수업에서 이해하고 훈련했던 내용을 자신의 것으로 체화하는 작업**이기 때문이다.

(A) 수업시간에 공부했던 내용의 MP3파일을 다시 전체적으로 들으며 내용을 이해한다.

(B) **잘 안들리는 부분으로 되돌아 가서 그 부분에 해당하는 문장을 Dictation**한다. (딕테이션에 대한 자세한 내용은 뒷장 p. 35 '청취력 향상 훈련 방법'참조) 딕테이션이 다 끝나면 스크립트와 대조하며 **색깔펜으로 수정**한다. 이 때 틀린 단어 위에 겹쳐서 수정하지 말고, **단어 위나 아래 부분에 올바른 단어를 쓴다. 수정하면서 틀린 부분은 왜 틀렸는지 생각**해 본다. 아예 모르는 단어라 못 적은 건지, 글로 보면 아는 단어인데 소리가 안들려서 틀린 건 지, 적긴 적었으나 앞뒤로 연음이 되어 일부분만 적었는지 등 분석을 해야 본인이 어떤 부분에서 취가 취약한지 파악할 수 있다.

(C) 듣기 스크립트와 문제에서 **하이라이트 펜으로 표시한 모르는 단어나 표현들은 전자사전이나 인터넷을 이용해 찾는다.** 단, 이때 단어의 발음을 꼭 확인하고 여러 번 따라 말함으로써, 머리 속에 뜻과 함께 소리를 기억하려고 노력한다. 생활에서 쓰이는 관용어구나 영어 특유의 표현들은 문장을 통째로 외우도록 한다.

(D) 틀린 문제를 다시 본다. 유형과 정답근거를 다시 한번 확인하고, 오답과 비교한 후 '청오답정리표'에 틀린 문제를 정리한다. 이렇게 오답을 분석해 나가면 **본인의 사고 오류를 파악할 수 있어, 다음 번에 똑같은 실수의 반복을 피할 수 있다.**

(E) Dictation에서 **수정이 많이 된 부분은 스크립트에 따로 표시한 후, 그 부분의 Mp3파일을 들으면서 하나씩 따라 말해본다.** 이때 주의할 점은 Native Speaker가 말하는 **그대로 똑같이 흉내내어 말하면서, 영어소리 그대로 흡수하여 기억해야** 한다는 것이다. 꼭 기억해야 할 표현들은 문장을 통째로 5, 6번 따라 말하며 본인의 것으로 소화한다.

(F) 이제 완벽히 이해한 내용을 영어 또는 한글로 핵심 단어 위주로 정리하여 Summary한다. (방법은 뒷장 p.37 'Summary Sample'참조)

(G) 이 과정이 끝나면 본문의 내용전체를 Mp3로 다시 한번 쭉 들으며 머릿속에 흡수한다.

8 Listening Strategies 1. 리스닝 학습 순서 및 방법

리스닝 학습방법

1 효과적인 Note-taking 방법

1. Note-taking의 목적 및 효과

A) 목적

대화(Conversation)는 내용이 짧고(3분정도) 물어보는 질문이 거의 패턴화 되어 있기 때문에 노트테이킹이 큰 역할을 하지는 않는다. 그러나 강의(Lecture)의 경우 길기 때문에(5~6분), 내용을 모두 기억하기란 쉽지 않으므로, 청취 **중에 중요하다고 판단되는 내용**을 메모하면 **문제를 풀 때 참고할 수 있어 유용**하다. 들으면서 동시에 기록하는 것은 쉽지 않기 때문에, **평소에 들으면서 주요내용을 파악하며 기억하기 어려운 부분을 빠르고 명료하게 받아쓰는 연습이 필요**하다.

B) 효과

효과적인 Note-taking은 **강의의 전체적인 흐름을 파악**하는 것과, **세부 정보를 기억하는데 도움**을 주며, 들려주는 **내용이 서로 어떤 연관성을 지니는가를 쉽게 파악**할 수 있도록 해준다.

▶ 유의점 : 대화 및 강의의 내용에 대한 이해를 하면서 Note-taking을 해야 효과적이며 청취를 통한 기본적인 이해가 없는 상태에서는 오히려 Listening에 방해가 될 수 있다.

▶ 방　향 : 모든 내용을 다 기록하려고 하기보다는, **핵심내용**만을 **논리적으로 간략하게 정리**해야 효과적이다.

2. Note-taking 요령

A) 세부사항을 간략하게 메모하기

세부사항을 기록할 때는 **Key Words를 이용하여 중심내용을 간략하게 정리**한다. 표기하기 쉽고 나중에 읽을 때 눈에 빨리 들어올 수 있도록, 평소에 글을 요약할 때 기호화 및 도식화하는 훈련을 하는 것이 도움이 된다. 또한 **각 세부 화제별로 내용을 묶어서 정리**할 수 있으면 좋다. 화제가 전화되거나 화자가 잠깐 중심 내용을 벗어난 얘기를 할 때는 Signal Words(Now, First of all, Another, Finally, etc)를 파악하면 변화를 알 수 있다.

B) 기호 및 약어

Note-taking시에는 들리는 말을 모두 받아쓰는 것이 아니라(시간소요, 뒤에 따라오는 내용 청취 방해), **기호 및 약어를 이용해서 간략하게 본인이 알아볼 수 있도록** 쓰는 것이 좋다.

【기호】	x : no, not	+ : and, plus, addition
	e.g. : example, instance	∵ : because, since
	→ : lead to, cause, go to	← : come from, originate from
	↑ : increase, rise, grow	↓ : decrease, decline, reduce
	/h : per hour	>, < : more / less than
【약어】	pl : people	etc : and so on, and so forth
	info : information	c : century
	tech : technology	Q : question
	vs : versus, compare	ea. : each
	S : step	T : types

3. Note - taking의 예

MT : Develop. of Piano.

    1) likes & dislikes of patron

      - Dev. of tech   inf.

    2)

Harp	Piano
String Quill pluck	Percu-Hammer Dynamic Convey emo.

    3) influence

      - mid class / mass pro   price ↓

      - lives of women ↑ : e.g. Clar Shu - pub recital

8 Listening Strategies 1. 리스닝 학습 순서 및 방법

Dictation Sample

문장의 의미상 꼭 필요한 핵심단어(강세단어)는 모두 적어야 합니다.

Listen to a conversation between a student and an employee in the university bookstore

S: Hi, bought this book beginning semester, but some things come up, like return

E: full refund, store policy have to return merchandise two weeks time purchased. but assigned textbooks, anything having to do with specific courses... wait, specific course?

S: Yeah, but actually...

E: for course books, deadline four weeks after beginning semester. So this fall semester, deadline October 1st.

S: Ouch, then missed ? But, why October 1st?

E: guess reasoning by October 1st, semester in full gear, everyone kind of knows what courses taking that semester.

딕테이션이 끝나면, **script와 비교하여, 색깔펜으로 틀린 단어를 수정**합니다.

B) 강의 내용의 **스크립트를 빠르게 직독직해** 합니다. 이때 한 문장을 최대 2번까지만 읽으면서 내용의 흐름을 따라 이해하고 해석해 나갑니다. 모르는 단어나 표현이 나와도 중간에 멈춰서 사전을 찾지 말고 그 부분만 하이라이트 펜으로 마킹한 뒤, 앞뒤 문맥을 바탕으로 뜻을 유추하면서 끝까지 한번 쭉 읽어나갑니다. 글의 마지막까지 다 읽었으면 이제 표시해 두었던 단어나 표현을 사전에서 찾아 확인합니다.

C) 이제 섀도잉을 하시되 Dictation 단계에서 많이 틀린 곳을 script에 하이라이트 펜으로 표시한 후, 그 부분만 한 문장씩 끊어서 따라 말해보세요. 긴 문장은 의미단위로 나누어 여러 번 따라 말해본 후에, 잘되면 붙여서 그 문장 전체를 한번에 따라 말합니다. 잘 안되는 문장(발음이 꼬이거나, 길어서 한번에 말하지 못하는 문장등...)은 좀 더 많이 따라해서 소리가 익숙해지도록 합니다. 특히 통째로 외워야 하는 어휘나 생활표현(colloquial expression) 등은 소리와 뜻이 머리 속에 합쳐서 기억될 수 있도록 **문장자체를 소리로 암기**해주셔야 합니다. 5번 정도 이상 Native speaker의 발음과 스피드를 똑같이 흉내내면서 연습하면 발음뿐만 아니라 그 문장 자체가 머리 속에 남게 되며 이렇게 익힌 표현들은 speaking 및 Writing 시험에서도 큰 효과를 발휘하게 됩니다.

D) **script를 보지말고 mp3를 다시 들으며 전체 내용을 머리 속에 정리**합니다. 이미 해석한 내용이므로 소리 파일을 중간에 멈추지 말고 native speaker의 속도를 그대로 따라가면서 내용을 이해하려고 노력합니다.

이런 식으로 대화 및 강의를 훈련하다 보면, 일정한 양이 쌓이면서 영어 소리에 대한 귀가 점차 열리게 됩니다. 더불어 본인의 발음까지 교정되기 때문에, Listeing 뿐만 아니라 speaking 시험에도 상당한 도움을 받을 수 있습니다. 명심할 것은 **"내가 말할 수 있는건 다~~ 들린다"**는 사실입니다. 리스닝은 입과 귀를 동시에 사용해서 뚫는 것이 가장 빠르고 효과적인 방법입니다.

2 Summary

▶ Summary를 하는 목적은?
1) 강의내용을 구조(structure) 및 흐름(flow)을 파악, 문제 예측 가능
2) 핵심내용만을 기억하여 추후 배경지식으로 활용
3) 리스닝과 동시에 진행되는 Note-taking의 기본골격 연습

Summary Sample

예1) 영어요약 - Conversation
1. **Purpose** : To find out about volunteering for archeology project
2. **Issue**
   A) **Need to have any experience with these kinds of projects?**
      → Not really. Most students have little or no experience with research
   B) **Specific contents on the project**
      1. Studying history of campus
      2. The site where they'll be studying :
         - The main lecture hall ; once farmhouse and barn
         - Excavating the site to see artifacts things
         - No travelling involved
3. **Suggestion:**
   A) **What the project offers for the student**
      - Any extra credit in class?   can arrange something
      - Professor thinks extra credit is always good incentive for students
   B) **Training schedule?**
      - Professor will schedule a training class when it's convenient for everyone

예2) 한글 요약 - Lecture
MI: 가장 오래된 동굴 미술 - 프랑스의 Chauvet cave
1. Chauvet 동굴의 연대 측정
   - 3만년 이상
   - 오래되었으나 원시적 X, 걸작품 O
   - Chauvet 동굴 연대측정에 대한 의심 : Altamira and Lasco 동굴보다 훨씬 오래됨
                                        근거) 다른 실험실의 결과 확인 X
2. 동굴 그림들의 배경
   1) 구석기 : 날씨가 현저히 다른 때보다 추웠음, 동굴에서 주거 - 동굴 벽에 그림 그렸음
   2) Chauvet : 사람이 살았던 흔적 없음
            - 인간 거주 흔적 없으나, 보러는 왔었음 - 증거) 숯의 흔적
            - 무엇이 그들로 하여금 그림 그리게 했나? : 알 수 없음
3. Chauvet 동굴벽화가 말해주는 것
   1) 구석기 : 초식동물
   2) Chauvet 초기벽화 : 크고 위험한 동물, But 인간은 그리지 않음 - 왜 특정 동물인가? : 알 수 없음

8 Listening Strategies 2. 문제 분석 방법
USHER iBT TOEFL INTERMEDIATE TEST LISTENING (어셔 iBT 토플 인터미디어트 테스트 리스닝)

실전에서 문제를 풀때, 본인이 정답이라고 생각되는 보기가 빨리 눈에 띄었다 하더라도 침착하게 남은 보기 모두를 끝까지 확인하는 습관을 길러야 합니다. 최근 토플리스닝 문제의 경향은 정답과 흡사한 오답이 등장하는 경우가 예전에 비해 현저히 증가하여, 수험자들에게 혼란을 주는 경우가 많다는 것입니다. 따라서 문제와 답을 하나씩 끝까지 확인하여 실수의 가능성을 최소화함으로써, 내용을 정확하게 듣고도 문제의 의도에 맞는 정답을 고르지 못하거나, 출제자가 의도적으로 만들어 놓은 함정에 빠져 아까운 점수를 잃는 경우를 없애야 합니다. 이를 위해, 평소에 훈련할 때 정답의 근거 파악과 본인이 틀린 문제는 왜 틀렸는지를 꼼꼼히 분석하는 습관을 기르는 것이 도움이 됩니다.

정답과 오답을 분석하는 방법은 다음과 같습니다.

1. 문제에서 정답을 확인한 뒤 script에서 답의 근거가 해당되는 위치를 찾아 표시합니다.
2. 각각 오답의 유형을 분석한 뒤 표시합니다. (아래 Example1 참조)
3. 틀린문제와 답은 오답정리표에 따로 기록하여 다시 한번 정리한 뒤, 추후 복습용으로 활용합니다.
   (▶ 오답정리표는 각 테스트에 위치)

오답 유형

Type 1	선택하려는 답이 지문에서 **언급이 안된 경우** (not mentioned)
Type 2	선택하려는 답이 지문의 사실과 **반대되거나 잘못된 정보**를 주는 경우 (opposite / wrong fact)
Type 3	선택하려는 답이 **지문에서 정확히 언급이 되었지만 문제에서 요구하는 답이 아닌 경우** (fact, but not related to the question)
Type 4	선택하려는 답이 그럴싸하게 정답인 듯 보이지만 **한 단어 또는 일부 때문에 오답이 되는 경우** (one word or partial error)

Example 1 : 정답 및 오답 표시

6. What does the professor mainly discuss?

   (A) Some characteristics that are common in several languages : 정답
   (B) A way to represent languages that are genetically related : Type1
   (C) Which languages probably evolved from Proto-Indo-European : Type3
   (D) Linguists' opinions about why languages change over time : Type1

문제 유형별 세부 전략

1 방문 목적 및 강의 주제

대화(conversation)나 강의(Lecture)의 중심내용을 찾는 문제 유형으로, Conversation은 찾아온 목적이나 대화의 중심내용, Lecture는 강의의 주제를 주로 물어본다.

【 질문형태 】
- Why does the student talk to the employee?
- Why does the student go to see his professor?
- Why does the professor ask to see the student?
- What is the conversation mainly about?
- What do the speakers mainly discuss?
- What is the lecture mainly about?
- What is the purpose of the lecture?

【 전 략 】

A) 처음에 나오는 Direction 및 내용의 도입부를 집중해서 듣는다.
앞부분을 놓치지 않는다. 대화 및 강의는 앞부분에서 중심내용이 무엇인지 파악할 수 있는 경우가 많으므로 앞부분에 특별한 주의를 기울여 전체적인 내용이 무엇일지 예측하면서 들어야 한다. 대화 및 강의 내용이 나오기 전에 들려주는 Direction에서 앞으로 설명될 분야가 언급되기 때문이다. 이를 통해 학생의 대화상대가 직원인지 혹은 교수인지를 알 수 있고, 강의의 경우 해당 강의의 과목을 미리 파악할 수 있어 내용을 따라가는데 도움이 된다. 또한 대화나 강의의 앞부분에 특별한 주의를 기울여 들으면, 주로 도입부에서 중심내용이 무엇인지 파악할 수 있는 실마리나 힌트를 얻게 경우가 많으므로, 앞부분의 내용과 함께 전체적인 내용이 무엇일 것인지 예측하면서 들어야 한다.
- **Conversation** : 주로 화자들이 인사를 나눈 다음에 찾아온 목적이나 대화의 중심내용이 언급됨. 최근에는 도입부 분에서 다른 얘기를 하다가, 중간 부분에서 찾아온 이유나 중심내용을 시작하는 경우도 증가하고 있음.
- **Lecture** : 지난 수업에서 다루었던 내용을 간략히 언급한 후에, 주로 강의의 주제나 방향에 대해 언급됨. 도입부분에서 주제가 뚜렷이 언급되지 않고 강의의 내용 전체를 끝까지 듣고 유추해야 하는 경우도 증가하고 있음.

B) 중심내용을 언급하는 표시어(signal words)에 집중하며 듣는다.
중심내용을 언급할 때 자주 쓰이는 표현이 있는데, 이 표시어 앞뒤로 중심내용이 등장하는 경우가 많으므로 집중해서 들어야 한다.
- **Conversation** : I'm here because ~, That's why I came by. I want to(I'd like to) talk to you about ~.
  I was wondering If ~
- **Lecture** : Today, we will be discussing ~, Let's look at~, We'll be continuing ~ , Today, we're going to look at ~

▶ 주의 : 도입부에서 주제가 확실히 언급되지 않는 경우가 간혹 있는데, 이때는 지문 전체를 듣고 전반적인 내용을 파악한 후 문제에서 적합한 답을 찾아야 함.

8 Listening Strategies 2. 문제 분석 방법

2 세부사항

대화나 강의를 통해 알 수 있는 세부사항을 파악하는 문제로, 주로 화자가 언급한 내용 중 주제와 관련된 중요한 세부사항을 묻는 경우가 대부분이다.

【 질문형태 】

What does the man / professor say about~ ?
According to the conversation/professor, how does~?
What are some reasons that~?
What are two features/characteristics/ factors of~ ?
What are the two examples the man gives facors of~?
According to the conversation / lecture, what can be inferred from~ ?

【 전   략 】

A) **주제와 관련**하여 주요 세부 사항을 주의깊게 듣는다.

화자는 중심내용과 밀접하게 관련된 세부사항을 언급하므로 이를 주의깊게 파악하여 들으며 기억하거나 메모한다.
- **Conversation** : 문제점, 예시, 제안, 충고, 필요요건, 반응 등
- **Lecture** : 이유, 특징, 부연설명, 방법, 결과, 질문, 질문에 대답하는 내용, 강조하고자 하는 내용 등

B) 새로이 소개되는 **용어**를 주의깊게 듣는다.

강의에서 화자가 새로이 소개하는 용어가 있다면 그에 대한 정의 및 부가 설명이 뒤이어 오는 경우가 많고, 이 용어는 강의내용 상 반드시 이해해야 할 개념인 경우가 대부분이므로, 문제로 이어질 가능성이 크다. 따라서 용어는 나오는대로 기억하거나 메모할 필요가 있다.

C) **예시**를 사용하여 설명할 때 주의깊게 듣는다

주제와 관련하여 예시를 사용해 내용을 설명하는 경우는 토플 리스닝 렉쳐에서 많이 사용하는 방법이다. 따라서 예시를 나타내는 표시어가 들리면 긴장하여 듣고, 특히 주제와 관련하여 어떤 부분을 설명하는지 연결하여 들을 필요가 있다.

D) **화제가 전환되는 부분**을 파악하며 듣는다

화자가 중간에 화제를 전환하거나 중심내용에서 잠깐 벗어나 다른 얘기를 할 때, 이를 파악하며 듣는 것은 전체적인 내용의 흐름과 화자의 목적, 세부 내용과 중심내용의 관계 등을 이해하는 데 필요하다.

E) **표시어(signal words)**를 통해 내용들간의 관계를 파악하며 듣는다.

용어, 예시, 특징, 비교/대조, 요건, 제안, 인과관계, 분류, 순차적인 관계 등을 나타내는 표시어를 주의깊게 들으면 내용들을 더 쉽게 파악할 수 있다.
- 용어 : It's called"'-, What we call"'-, so-called"'-, It's referred as"'-

- 예시 : For example, For instance, Let's say, say, take, such as, like, think of, imagine
- 특징 : It's interestingA., unique, fascinating, intriguing, important, useful, note, unusual, odd, weird, strange
- 비교/대조 : early, later, compare, contrast, analogy, evolve, develop, in the past, decades ago,
            in ancient times, today, nowadays, modern day
- 요건 : required, necessary, consider, condition, premise, experience, you need to~.
- 제안 : to solve/handle this problem, recommend, Why don't you~.?, What about~?, What can be done~.,
        Your best bet would beA.
- 인과관계/증거/결과/발견/영향 : study, research, experiment, project, find, discover, uncover, reveal, evidence,
                              impact, pave the way, application
- 순서/분류 : step, stage, phase, and then, divide intoA., three types, two kinds of, first, second, finally

3 내용의 사실 이해 문제

지문에서 들은 정보를 바탕으로 추론할 수 있는 사실을 묻는 문제이다. Purpose는 화자가 특정 내용을 언급한 목적이 무엇인지 문제로 지문에서 직접적으로 드러나지 않고, 간접적으로 알 수 있는 정보에 대해 묻는다. 세부사항에 해당하는 내용을 물어보기도 하고 지문의 특정 부분 내용을 다시 들려준 후 문제를 푸는 형태로 출제되기도 한다. 겉으로 드러나는 말 뒤에 숨어있는 내용이 암시하는 바와 이 말을 하는 화자의 의도를 묻는 문제이기 때문에, 화자가 특정한 언급을 한 의도가 무엇인지 파악하고 화자의 의견이나 이 유형은 세부사항에 해당하는 내용을 물어보기도 하고 지문의 특정 부분을 다시 들려 준 후 문제로 푸는 형태로 출제되기도 한다.

【 질문형태 】

Why does the professor mention/ discuss / talk about~ ?
What does the professor imply about ~?
What can be inferred about ~?
What is the professor's opinion/attitude/stance towards~?
How does the professor feel about~?
Why does the student say this :
What does the man/ woman mean when he/she says this :
What does the professor imply when he/she says this :
What will the man/ woman probably do next?

8 Listening Strategies 2. 문제 분석 방법

【전　략】

A) 문제가 나올수 있는 부분을 예측하며 듣는다.
　　화자가 자신의 의도를 직접적으로 말하지 않고 간접적인 방식으로 돌려 말할 때, 자신의 의견이나 평가 또는 강조나 동의를 구할 때, 놓치지 않고 화자의 의도나 태도를 생각하며 듣는다.

B) 화자의 어조를 통해 태도를 파악하며 듣는다.
　　화자의 어조가 긍정적, 부정적, 비판적, 불확실인지 등을 판단하여, 화자의 의견이나 강의 대상에 대한 평가와 화자의 숨어있는 태도를 정확히 파악하며 듣는다.

C) 화자가 언급한 말의 이면적인 뜻을 생각하며 듣는다.
　　화자가 직접적으로 말하지는 않았으나 화자가 한말을 통해 간접적으로 알 수 있는 사실을 추론하며 듣는다. 제시된 사실을 단순히 그대로 받아들이지 말고 화자가 말하고자 하는 바가 무엇인지를 생각하며 듣는다.

D) 맥락을 파악하며 듣는다.
　　다시 들려주는 부분의 맥락을 통해 화자가 한말의 의도를 파악한다. 예전과 달리 최근에는 다시 들려주는 부분이 줄어들었기 때문에, 처음에 내용을 들을 때 흐름을 정확히 파악하며 들어야 문제가 물어보는 위치를 기억할 수 있다.

4 내용의 암시 및 화자의 의도 파악

화자가 어떤 방식으로 내용을 전개하여 정보를 전달하는지 묻는 문제이다. 지문에 언급된 여러가지 정보들 간의 연관성을 이해하는지를 묻는 문제유형으로, 정보들이 어떻게 조직되어 있는지를 확인하거나 흩어져 있는 정보들이 어떻게 서로 연결되는지 파악, 범주별로 알맞은 정보를 연결하거나 사건 및 절차를 순차적으로 나열하는 문제 등이 출제된다.

【질문형태】
　　How does the professor introduce/ conclude ~?
　　How is the lecture/discussion organized?
　　How does the professor emphasize his point about~?
　　What are the features/characteristics/ factors of~ ? Click on 2/3 answers
　　In the lecture/conversation, ~. Indicate whether each of the following is a ~.

	Included	Not Included
Statement A		
Statement B		
Statement C		

Match each of the following to types of ~.

	Type A	Type B	Type C
Example 1			
Example 2			

The professor explains the steps in the process of ~. Put these steps in order.

Step 1	
Step 2	

【 전　　략 】

A) 나올 수 있는 가능성있는 문제를 예측하며 듣는다.

　　화자의 정보전달 방식을 파악하는 필요하다. 지문의 큰 구조를 이해하면서 화자가 어떤 방식으로 정보를 전달하는지 유의하면서 듣는다. 화자가 정보를 전달하는 전개 방식에는 두 가지 사항의 비교 혹은 대조, 시간 흐름에 따른 나열, 구체적인 예 제시, 장단점 기술 등이 있으며, 이러한 형태의 문제는 대화보다 강의에서 등장하는 경우가 많다.

B) 하나 이상의 범주에 포함되는 정보들이 나열될 때, 주의깊게 듣거나 메모한다.

　　하나의 범주에 대한 정보들 (ex: conversation - 특정과목을 수강등록하기 위한 조건들/Lecture-성층화산의 특징들), 두 개 이상의 범주에 관한 정보들 (ex: 비교/대조, 장점/단점)이나 정답을 2개 이상 고르는 문제 (Click on 2 answers, Click on 3 answers), 관련된 정보들을 연결하는 문제, 그리고 몇가지 정보들이 특정한 순서 및 전개 방식으로 전달될 때 (ex: 절차, 과정, 사건), Ordering 문제를 예상하며 듣는다.

C) 자주 쓰이는 표시어(signal words)를 주의 깊게 듣는다.

　- 특징/요건 : requirement, condition, necessary, include, reasons, features
　- Matching : types, features, characteristics, points
　- Ordering : steps, stages, phase, divide into

8 Listening Strategies 2. 문제 분석 방법

5 문제 유형과 Signals

번호	기본문제유형	세부문제유형	Signals
1	Main Idea	Main Purpose Main Idea	국부적인(지엽적인) or 너무 일반적인(광범위한) 사실은 오답, 시제 및 단수 / 복수 주의
2	Details	Term/Definition/Irigin	refer to, what we call, so-called, originate, come from
3		Example	such as, like, think of, imagine, Let's take, let's say~, say, example, for instance
4		Characteristic Advantage / Disadvantage Problem / Difficulty Similarity / Compare Difference / Contrast	그림, 음악, 문학, 무용, 영화, 연극, 공예, 조각 등 unique, useful, interesting, faster, fascinating, intriguing, key feature, note, important 동물 멸종위기, 생명의 위협 / 환경적응 Problem, hitch, challenge, drawback, flaw, defect, extinct, destroyed early-later, prior to~, recent, in the past, nowadays, modern day, evolve
5		Cause / Reason / Evidence Result / Finding / Effect / Influence	study, research, experiment, project(find, discover, uncover, reveal, shed light on) / evidence, finding / pave the way, impact, set the stage for, application
6		Misunderstanding Correction/Surprising	once believed, but~ / seem out of this world, news to
7		Requirement / Condition	necessary, required, you need to, consideration, condition, premise, job experience,
8		Offer / Solution / Suggestion	Alternative, to solve, handle this problem, recommend, why don't you~, what about~, what can be done~, your best bet would be~,
9		Future action/Future topic	upcoming, next class, another lecture
10	Inference	Purpose / Intention Imply / Infer Opinion / Attitude Headset	Why... mention~ / What can be inferred~/ What... imply~ What... mean when...say~ 다시 들려주고 푸는 문제 check ,understanding, agree/disagree
11	Category	Introduce / Organize / Conclude Matching Ordering	How~ introduce? How is the lecture organized? Three types, two kinds of, first, second, finally step, stage, phase , and then, divide into~

6 Listening Lecture 기출 Topic

아래는 과거 토플 리스닝 시험 Lecture에서 출제되었던 토픽(Topics)들을 모아놓은 것입니다. 쭉 살펴보고 본인이 익숙하지 않은 것들은 인터넷을 통해 검색해서 내용의 개요를 알아두면 도움이 될 것입니다. 리스닝에 나오는 토픽들은 또한 리딩과 라이팅에도 주제가 겹쳐 나오는 경우가 종종 있기 때문에, 배경지식으로 알아두면 여러모로 쓸모가 있습니다.

Social Science (사회과학)

Anthropology : calendar, Aztec, Maya, Egypt, Inuit People, Neolithic age, Inca, Artic pottery, Natufians, Fertile Crescent, etc.

Archaeology : GPR(Ground Penetrating Radar), Passage Grave, Stone Henge, Troy, hieroglyph, Anasazi, radiocarbon dating, etc.

Psychology / Child Development : memory, blind spot, imagination, hypersomnia, stress, Placebo effect, child attachment, Piaget, Montessori, Separation Anxiety disorder, reciprocal helping & altruistic helping, insight, social-evaluations, etc.

History / U.S. history : Gold Rush, eyeglasses, printing press, railroad, Tourism, U.S. President, Navajo, Clovis people, Iroquois People, Prehistoric Nevada, feudalism, Civil War, etc.

Linguistics : Grice's maxim, human language vs. animal communication, tree model, universal grammar, Webster, etc.

Business / Economics : AHP, famine, Sherman Act, boom & bust, function & project, Segmentation, etc.

Sociology : AMA, guilds, Labor Union, Zif's law, bureaucracy, etc.

Mass Communication : Newspaper, magazine, radio, etc.

Philosophy : Socrates, paradigm shift, Plato, etc.

Art (예술)

Painting : Cubism, Dadaism, Impressionism, Naturalism, fresco painting, Jackson Pollack, Picasso, etching, Paul Cezanne, Vincent Van Gogh, Johannes Jan Vermeer, Frida Kahlo, Andrew Warhol, Chauvet cave painting, Hudson River School, etc.

Literature : Book of Kells, detective novel, memoir vs. autobiography, Sherwood Anderson, Postmodernism, parchment & palimpsest, Mary Shelley's Frankenstein, etc.

Film / Theater : films in 1920s~30s, Nickelodeon, sound editing, well-made play, Method Acting, classical acting vs naturalism, structure of Greek theare, etc.

Music history : drum, opera, piano vs harpsichord, saxophone, records sale & radio in early 1900s, etc.

Architecture : roof style, Central Park, straw bale house, architect Frank, pedestrian mall, etc.

Crafts & Sculpture : stained glass, Navajo textile, Roman sculpture(polychrome), etc.

Photography : pin-hole camera, Camera obscura(Johannes Vermeer), etc.

8 Listening Strategies 2. 문제 분석 방법

Social Science (사회과학)

Biology

- **Botany** : maple syrup, pollination, rare tree, Mangrove, Venus flytrap, symbiosis(coral reefs), etc.

- **Zoology & Insectology** : bat, bird, snake, Polar bear, Humming bird, wolf, animal communication (dolphin, honey bee), habitat and the adaptation (bird migration, habitat selection, camouflage, hibernation, etc), cicada, dragonfly, spider's web, termite, etc.

- **Marine biology** : dolphin, whale, pearl, Spartina, squid, salmon, chemosynthesis, etc.

- **Taxonomy** : classification, binomial nomenclature, etc.

Environmental Science & Ecology : Eutrophication, phosphorous cycle, oil making, drying up lakes, greenhouse effect, glacier, alternative energy(ethanol), renewable energy, predation risk effects carbon capture(post combustion & pre combustion), etc.

Paleontology : Archaeopteryx, Amber, living fossil, dinosaur(cold blooded vs warm blooded), etc.

Physiology : lens of eyes, joints, sleep cycle, neuron, brain, etc.

Social Science (사회과학)

Astronomy : asteroid, comet, geocentric model, planet formation, star formation, stellar parallax, Supernova, Milky Way, Variables, Mercury, life on Mars, Venus, Saturn, Pluto, Protostar, albedo, Kuiper belt, Sagittarius galaxy, etc.

Geology : limestone cave, continental drift theory, rocks, Zircon, hoodoo, sand dune, seismic waves, volcanoes, Tundra, K-T boundary, etc.

Chemistry : charcoal, carbon & diamond, decaffeination, ice molecular structure, Leidenfrost Effect, Periodic Table, graphene, etc.

Physics : rainfall, standing waves, properties of light/sound (speed of light, resonance), Electromagnetic radiation (e.g. gamma ray), etc.

Earth Science : climate change, length of a day, ocean's salinity, Plate Tectonics, Flotsam Science, carbon sequestration, etc.

Engineering : airfoil, Bicycle Canada Bridge, Eiffel Tower, Hoover Dam, Shape Memory Alloy, semiconductor switch, etc.

Meteorology : hail, rain, snow, lightening, etc.

USHER
iBT TOEFL
INTERMEDIATE TEST
LISTENING | 문제집

어셔 iBT 토플 인터미디어트 테스트 리스닝 문제집

어셔 어학 연구소

www.usherin.usher.co.kr

USHER
iBT TOEFL
INTERMEDIATE LISTENING
TEST 1

TEST 1 set 1

Listening Section Directions

This section measures your ability to understand conversations and lectures in English. It is divided into 3 separately timed parts. In each part you will listen to 1 conversation and 2 lectures. You will hear each conversation or lecture only **one** time.

After each conversation or lecture, you will answer some questions about it. Answer the questions based on what is stated or implied by the speakers.

For each part of the listening section you will have 10 minutes to answer the questions.

A clock at the top of the screen will show you how much time you have remaining. The clock will **not** count down while you are listening. The clock will count down only while you are answer questions.

You may take notes while you listen. You may use your notes to help you answer the questions. Your notes will **not** be scored.

If you need to change the volume while you listen, click on the **Volume** icon at the top of the screen.

In some questions, you will see this icon . This means that you will hear, but not see. part of the question. Most questions are worth 1 point. If a question is worth more than 1 point, it will have special directions that indicate how many points you can receive.

In this listening section. After you answer each question, click on **Next**. Then click on **OK** to confirm your answer and go on to the next section, you cannot return to previous questions.

Listen to part of the Listening section.

(Click on Continue at any time to dismiss these directions.)

리스닝 섹션은 PART 1, PART 2로 나누어져 있습니다.
PART 1에서는 세 지문을 듣게 됩니다. 10분 동안 질문에 답하세요.
지문을 듣는 동안 시간이 줄어들지 않습니다.

Note taking

TEST 1 set 1 C

Question 1~5 of 17

01. Why does the student visit the accounting department?

(A) He needs help with a term paper that he's having a difficult time with.

(B) He would like to talk to the professor about his major's job prospects.

(C) He needs the professor's advice as to which career to pursue after earning his degree.

(D) He wants to discuss and explore options other than his current major.

02. Why is the student considering switching his major?

(A) Because it's hard for him to keep up with the amount of mathematical work.

(B) Because his first choice has too many mandatory examinations.

(C) Because he is struggling in terms of his academic performance in his current major.

(D) Because there are only a limited number of job options after graduation for his current major

03. According to the professor, what is the biggest drawback of the new major the student is considering?

(A) The society is leaning more towards generalists as opposed to specialists.

(B) It could encumber the student with too many examinations.

(C) It's relatively tougher to pursue a career after earning a degree in the field.

(D) It entails an abundant amount of mathematical work.

04. What is the student most likely to do after his consultation with the professor?

(A) He will follow the school's procedures and fill out the papers needed to switch majors.

(B) He will delay his decision and collect more information about his options.

(C) He will take a break this semester and narrow his interests and options.

(D) He will spend the rest of his time at his college with his current major.

Listen again to part of the conversation. Then answer the question.

05. What does the professor imply when she says:

(A) That the student is one of the top students in her class.

(B) That she doesn't feel the need to help the student with his problem.

(C) That she doesn't understand why the student is having a hard time with his term paper.

(D) That it's difficult to understand why the student feels uncertain about his major.

Note taking

TEST 1 set 1 L1

Question 06~11 of 17

06. What is the main topic of the lecture?

(A) Characteristics of ice ages and interglacial periods

(B) The Milankovitch theory that explains the effects of the Earth's rotation and orbit on global climate change

(C) Evidence and theories that point to the predictability of ice ages and interglacial periods

(D) Chronological exploration of ice ages that have happened over the last few million years

07. How did the scientists determine the regularity of coral reef growth?

(A) By calculating the difference between each layer's thickness and length

(B) By dating the layers of coral reef responsible for the changes in the water level

(C) By comparing coral reefs in the Northern Hemisphere with the ones in the Southern Hemisphere

(D) By examining specific chemicals from coral reefs and the difference in the ages of the layers

08. Which of the following is true about the Earth's tilt?

(A) The sun's gravity exerts a great influence on the Earth's tilt.

(B) It does not have any significant impact on the global climate.

(C) More tilt results in extreme summers and mild winters.

(D) Small changes in the Earth's tilt could lead to substantial changes in the global climate.

09. What are the causes of ice ages according to Milutin Milankovitch?

Click on 2 andswers

(A) The relative position of the Earth's axis

(B) Changes in ocean currents and wind patterns

(C) Continental drift and volcanic eruptions

(D) The elliptical orbit of the Earth

10. What is the professor's attitude towards the Milankovitch theory?

(A) He takes a detached position and also opens up the possibility of other theories.

(B) He criticizes the theory and debases the validity of it.

(C) He acknowledges the absolute creditability of the theory.

(D) He believes the theory is the most historically accurate one.

11. What does the professor imply when she says:

(A) That there is not enough evidence to support his claim of the advent of another ice age.

(B) That he is also doubtful of the hypothesis scientists have established.

(C) That it is very difficult to predict when another ice age will take place.

(D) That it's hard for students to believe that another ice age will come.

Note taking

TEST 1 set 1 L2

Question 12~17 of 17

12. What is the lecture mainly about?

    (A) The location and organization of theaters in ancient Greece
    (B) The establishment of the theater world in the 5th century B.C.E.
    (C) Exploration of the aspects of Greek theaters in comparison to modern ones
    (D) Distinct roles that the Greeks' chorus and actors played in contrast to those of today

13. How does the professor distinguish the chorus of the Greeks from today's chorus?

    (A) The Greek chorus sang and danced on stage
    (B) The Greek chorus' roles weren't as significant as today's
    (C) Today, theaters are built indoors, while ancient theaters were built outdoors in nature.
    (D) The Greek choruses often took a more active role in the play.

14. What was the purpose of the skēnē in early theaters?

    (A) It helped the audience in the back rows hear the play more easily.
    (B) It served to portray every single scene of the play through multiple background images.
    (C) Although it was just a wooden platform, it played a considerable role.
    (D) It was a background image that made the play look more elaborate.

15. What does the professor imply when she interprets the meaning of the term, "theatron"?

    (A) That the literal interpretation of the Greek term doesn't match with its practical function.
    (B) That the interpretation of the term is controversial among scholars.
    (C) That it's ironic that the shape of theatron was a semi-circle instead of a square.
    (D) That it's very likely that everyone in the audience was able to watch the play.

16. Why was the bowl shape of the theatron so important?

    (A) It widened the viewing range of the audience.
    (B) The shape enabled more viewers, thus making the play more profitable.
    (C) It effectively funneled the sound upward and delivered it to the audience.
    (D) It was well incorporated with nature, and, thus, made the theater grand and prestigious.

Listen again to part of the lecture. Then answer the question.

17. Why does the professor say this:

    (A) She doesn't want the student to interrupt her lesson.
    (B) Her next discussion would automatically answer the student's question.
    (C) She needs time to collect her thoughts before she answers the student's question.
    (D) She is not certain about the credibility of her answer, so she thinks more research needs to be done.

**You have reached the end of this part of the test.
Click on Continue to go on.**

Note taking

TEST 1 set 2

Listening Section Directions

This section measures your ability to understand conversations and lectures in English. It is divided into 3 separately timed parts. In each part you will listen to 1 conversation and 2 lectures. You will hear each conversation or lecture only **one** time.

After each conversation or lecture, you will answer some questions about it. Answer the questions based on what is stated or implied by the speakers.

For each part of the listening section you will have 10 minutes to answer the questions.

A clock at the top of the screen will show you how much time you have remaining. The clock will **not** count down while you are listening. The clock will count down only while you are answer questions.

You may take notes while you listen. You may use your notes to help you answer the questions. Your notes will **not** be scored.

If you need to change the volume while you listen, click on the **Volume** icon at the top of the screen.

In some questions, you will see this icon 🎧. This means that you will hear, but not see. part of the question. Most questions are worth 1 point. If a question is worth more than 1 point, it will have special directions that indicate how many points you can receive.

In this listening section. After you answer each question, click on **Next**. Then click on **OK** to confirm your answer and go on to the next section, you cannot return to previous questions.

Listen to part of the Listening section.

(Click on Continue at any time to dismiss these directions.)

리스닝 섹션은 PART 1, PART 2로 나누어져 있습니다.
PART 1에서는 세 지문을 듣게 됩니다. 10분 동안 질문에 답하세요.
지문을 듣는 동안 시간이 줄어들지 않습니다.

Note taking

TEST 1 set 2 C

Question 1~5 of 17

01. Why does the student go to see the librarian?

(A) To ask directions to a different university that has the book that he needs

(B) To ask whether the library can fix some damaged pages of a book

(C) To get help finding a different book that contains more information that he needs

(D) To get help finding information that he needs for his assignment

02. What can be inferred about the library?

(A) It often encounters cases similar to that of the student.

(B) It only has a single copy of each book.

(C) It has had problems regarding the delivery of materials from other places.

(D) It does not own many books regarding the Great Depression.

03. What will the student probably do next?

(A) Try to decipher what he can from the damaged pages.

(B) Leave his contact information and head out of the library.

(C) Search for a book that may have the information that he needs.

(D) Talk to the librarian's colleague over the phone.

04. Which of the following is true about the book in the other library?

(A) It has not been checked out yet.

(B) It will definitely get to the student by tomorrow.

(C) It belongs to a library in New York that is probably closed.

(D) It belongs to a library that the librarian's friend owns.

Listen again to part of the conversation. Then answer the question.

05. Why does the student say this:

(A) To suggest that he is used to the library's poor management of the books

(B) To show that it's unbelievable to him that only the pages of use to him are damaged

(C) To show his anger towards the likely outcome of his assignment

(D) To ask the librarian how he could decipher the reference pages

Note taking

06. What is the lecture mainly about?

(A) The characteristics of the deep-zone layer of the ocean and its organisms.

(B) Two strategies, active and passive defense, that organisms use when dealing with predators.

(C) The use of an evolutionary trait by organisms in the deepest layer of the ocean.

(D) The defensive strategies of sea animals and a general exploration of each strategy.

07. Which of the following is NOT true about bioluminescence?

(A) Its primary source of power is generated by both bacteria and chemicals.

(B) Its application in the medical field is plausible.

(C) It enables fish to generate light within themselves, without any external help.

(D) In most cases, it's blue, but it can sometimes be other colors, such as red.

08. According to the professor, why are crystal jellyfish influential to our society?

(A) Because they generate blue light and blue light is a great resource when exploring the deep-zone of the ocean.

(B) Because their bioluminescent chemical is used in cancer detection.

(C) Because the chemical responsible for its bioluminescence can be used as a light source.

(D) Because its bioluminescence works as a gathering signal for squid, and it helps fishermen catch squid more efficiently.

09. How did scientists prove that bioluminescence attracts predators' predators?

(A) They observed that flashes of light mimicking a jellyfish's flashes attracted squid.

(B) They put squid and jellyfish together and witnessed that the jellyfish flashed more when squid were around.

(C) They spotted the heaviest accumulations of squid around jellyfish habitats.

(D) They noticed that while the jellyfish's predators tried to feed on their prey, they were attacked.

10. How is passive defense strategy different from active defense strategy?

(A) A passive defense strategy is the direct use of flashing lights at predators.

(B) A passive defense strategy is used prior to any engagement between predator and prey.

(C) A passive defense strategy enables the jellyfish to change its skin color.

(D) A passive defense strategy enables organisms to seem daunting to the predator.

11. Why does the professor mention the principle of camouflage?

(A) To explain that bioluminescence and camouflage are two examples of the same phenomenon.

(B) To claim that bioluminescence is also inherent in terrestrial animals, such as frogs.

(C) To indicate that bioluminescent organisms are capable of changing their skin color as well as the color of their flashes.

(D) To imply that the use of bioluminescence is similar to that of camouflage.

Note taking

TEST 1 set2 L2

Question 12~17 of 17

12. What is the purpose of the lecture?

(A) Explaining the advancements made in the development of the muon detector

(B) Explaining the differences between the ancient muon detector and the modern muon detector

(C) Explaining a type of technology that archaeologists have utilized when excavating historic sites

(D) Explaining how excavation sites, such as the Egyptian pyramids, have been explored by archaeologists

13. What is the professor's opinion about the misconceptions that cartoons give students regarding archaeology?

(A) He approves of the idea that archaeology doesn't entail any high-tech tools.

(B) He opposes the student's opinion that archaeologists don't have any sophisticated skills.

(C) He believes that cartoons have led many people to believe that most archaeological exploration is accomplished through guessing and luck.

(D) He is critical of the portrayal of archaeology in cartoons and thinks it is only meant to demean the profession.

14. How are archaeologists able to determine the structure of excavation sites?

(A) They use a particle detector to measure muons, thus allowing them to produce a visual image of the internal structure.

(B) They extract isotopes from the chemicals found in the excavation sites and use them to draw structures.

(C) They scan the structures using energy they reclaim from cosmic rays.

(D) They use a form of technology that is a combination of the x-ray machine and the muon scanner.

15. Which of the following are the deficiencies of early muon detectors?

Click on 2 answers

(A) The direction from which the scanning process could be performed was very limited.

(B) It took too much time to produce a visual image of the structure.

(C) It was very unstable in terms of image quality.

(D) It wasn't practically portable.

16. Why is the modern muon detector still considered to be imperfect?

(A) It takes a great deal of time to produce an image.

(B) It works only if it is placed beneath the object to be scanned.

(C) It does not function well under certain circumstances, such as on hot volcanic sites.

(D) Although it's light and easily portable, it fails to include every small detail.

Listen again to part of the lecture. Then answer the question

17. What does the professor imply when he says this :

(A) That the student understands the reason that muon detectors are the only practical solution in some cases

(B) That the muon detector is applicable to various fields.

(C) That the muon detector is often used to map out the interiors of volcanoes.

(D) That the muon detector is only practical when examining volcanoes.

You have reached the end of this part of the test.
Click on **Continue** to go on.

Note taking

모범 답안·지문·해석 P.427

www.usherin.usher.co.kr

USHER

iBT TOEFL
INTERMEDIATE LISTENING
TEST 2

Listening Section Directions

This section measures your ability to understand conversations and lectures in English. It is divided into 3 separately timed parts. In each part you will listen to 1 conversation and 2 lectures. You will hear each conversation or lecture only **one** time.

After each conversation or lecture, you will answer some questions about it. Answer the questions based on what is stated or implied by the speakers.

For each part of the listening section you will have 10 minutes to answer the questions.

A clock at the top of the screen will show you how much time you have remaining. The clock will **not** count down while you are listening. The clock will count down only while you are answer questions.

You may take notes while you listen. You may use your notes to help you answer the questions. Your notes will **not** be scored.

If you need to change the volume while you listen, click on the **Volume** icon at the top of the screen.

In some questions, you will see this icon 🎧. This means that you will hear, but not see. part of the question. Most questions are worth 1 point. If a question is worth more than 1 point, it will have special directions that indicate how many points you can receive.

In this listening section. After you answer each question, click on **Next**. Then click on **OK** to confirm your answer and go on to the next section, you cannot return to previous questions.

Listen to part of the Listening section.

(Click on Continue at any time to dismiss these directions.)

리스닝 섹션은 PART 1, PART 2로 나누어져 있습니다.
PART 1에서는 세 지문을 듣게 됩니다. 10분 동안 질문에 답하세요.
지문을 듣는 동안 시간이 줄어들지 않습니다.

Note taking

TEST 2 set 1 C

Question 1~5 of 17

01. Why does the professor want to speak to the student?

(A) To ask him to help plan the math nights that the department is arranging
(B) To suggest that he teach a group of 7th graders at the math nights
(C) To ask him to write the questions for a math night with problems related to calculating probability
(D) To inquire about his interest in a job at the math nights that the university is hosting

02. According to the professor, what is the university department trying to accomplish through the math nights?

Click on 2 answers

(A) Guiding kids in considering their futures using mathematics
(B) Helping parents and their kids understand important math concepts
(C) Building intimate relationships between parents and their kids
(D) Improving the level of mathematics in 7th grade

03. Why is the student reluctant to take the offer that the professor suggests at first?

(A) Because he already has a job, which is a burden for him
(B) Because he believes the job won't provide good teaching experience
(C) Because he doesn't think he's capable of explaining 7th grade math concepts to kids and parents
(D) Because the classes he is taking are already too much to handle

04. Why does the professor need to get the student's answer as soon as possible?

(A) Because she needs to get approval from the schools at which the university is hosting the math nights.
(B) Because she needs to let the administrator know in 15 hours
(C) Because the administrator has to approve the employment of workers by next week
(D) Because she is going on vacation next week and won't be reachable

Listen again to part of the conversation. Then answer the question.

05. Why does the professor imply when she says this?

(A) To distinguish the training course from other regular classes the student has taken
(B) To let the student know about the potential non-monetary compensation that the job provides
(C) To tell the student that the training course is a way of giving back to the community
(D) To inform the student that she will be receiving homework assignments in the training course, just like any other class

Note taking

06. What is the main topic of the lecture?

(A) The reasons that purchasing books was so difficult in the 19th century

(B) The differences between the composition of American and British novels

(C) The prestigious English authors of the 19th century and their works

(D) The methods that English readers used to gain access to novels in the 19th century.

07. Why does the professor mention Arthur Conan Doyle?

(A) To illustrate the type of novels that were praised and bought by C.E. Mudie.

(B) To provide an example of a great novelist from 19th century Britain.

(C) To support his claim that novels were more expensive in England than in America

(D) To give an example of a hindrance that discouraged readers from buying books

08. According to the professor, how were lending libraries different from today's libraries?

(A) Lending libraries were located in cities, but never in rural areas

(B) Lending libraries profited by requiring an annual fee from all borrowers.

(C) At lending libraries, people needed to pay a certain amount every time they borrowed books.

(D) Lending libraries had large quantities of newspapers and magazines.

09. Which of these characteristics is true about the serial publication form?

(A) The serial publication form was more preferred by readers than lending libraries

(B) All of a novel's contents were updated and presented to people on a daily basis.

(C) Contents were released in a newspaper or magazine rather than being published as a novel.

(D) All writers who used the serial publication form ended each episode with a suspenseful ending to attract more readers.

10. Why were most of the authors who used the serial publication form criticized by the public?

(A) Because they would employ unwelcome methods at the end of their stories to attract more readers

(B) Because they unnecessarily prolonged their novels to earn more profits

(C) Because they were against the practice of lending libraries

(D) Because the pure purpose of newspapers and magazines was tainted

Listen again to part of the lecture. Then answer the question.

11. What does the professor mean when he says this:

(A) That C.E. Mudie was also the head of a book publishing company

(B) That library owners during the 19th century were more influential than present-day librarians

(C) That the influence of C.E. Mudie's preferences greatly affected publishers' decisions.

(D) That C.E. Mudie's conceited attitude was ridiculed by the public.

Note taking

12. What is the lecture mainly about?

(A) The process of restoring biodiversity to an infertile region.
(B) The influence of the interactions between predators and prey on an environment.
(C) The success of Yellowstone National Park to protect the wildlife in it.
(D) Interactions of predators and prey and their relative effects on each other.

13. According to the professor, what is true about animals' predatory nature?

Click on 2 andswers

(A) It causes them to cease to employ their survival mechanisms in the presence of their predators.
(B) It maintains balance in the ecosystems' biodiversity.
(C) It works as a driving force for the growth or decline of a population.
(D) It can ultimately cause a species' extermination or extinction.

14. Which of the following could cause an increase in the predation risk effects of a species?

(A) Competition for food sources between various species.
(B) An animal's failure to fully exploit its survival skills and methods.
(C) A rapid explosion in a species' population.
(D) The appearance of a previously nonexistent population of predators.

15. According to the professor, why did Yellowstone National Park fail to accomplish its mission to protect the wild life in the park?

(A) Because it ignored the importance of imposing any rules on free hunting.
(B) Because carnivores, except bears, were not protected at the time.
(C) Because it failed to foresee the level of elk hunting and indirectly caused an increase in the wolf population.
(D) Because it provided regulatory protection only for the herbivores.

16. Which of the following was an effect or result of the disappearance of wolves from the park?

(A) An increase in the growth rate of aspen seedlings.
(B) Increased hunting of carnivores as their replacements.
(C) The loss of habitats for birds.
(D) A decrease in the population of the wolves' predators.

17. How did the researchers solve the problem created by the disappearance of the wolves from the national park?

(A) They recreated an environment where predators and prey co-existed.
(B) They artificially precluded the elk from feeding on the seedlings of aspens.
(C) They imposed restrictions on the free-hunting of herbivores.
(D) They segregated the prey's habitats from those of the predators.

You have reached the end of this part of the test.
Click on **Continue** to go on.

Note taking

Listening Section Directions

This section measures your ability to understand conversations and lectures in English. It is divided into 3 separately timed parts. In each part you will listen to 1 conversation and 2 lectures. You will hear each conversation or lecture only **one** time.

After each conversation or lecture, you will answer some questions about it. Answer the questions based on what is stated or implied by the speakers.

For each part of the listening section you will have 10 minutes to answer the questions.

A clock at the top of the screen will show you how much time you have remaining. The clock will **not** count down while you are listening. The clock will count down only while you are answer questions.

You may take notes while you listen. You may use your notes to help you answer the questions. Your notes will **not** be scored.

If you need to change the volume while you listen, click on the **Volume** icon at the top of the screen.

In some questions, you will see this icon 🎧. This means that you will hear, but not see. part of the question. Most questions are worth 1 point. If a question is worth more than 1 point, it will have special directions that indicate how many points you can receive.

In this listening section. After you answer each question, click on **Next**. Then click on **OK** to confirm your answer and go on to the next section, you cannot return to previous questions.

Listen to part of the Listening section.
(Click on Continue at any time to dismiss these directions.)

리스닝 섹션은 PART 1, PART 2로 나누어져 있습니다.
PART 1에서는 세 지문을 듣게 됩니다. 10분 동안 질문에 답하세요.
지문을 듣는 동안 시간이 줄어들지 않습니다.

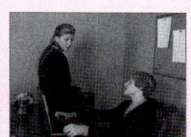

Note taking

Question 1~5 of 17

01. Why did the man go to see the administrator in the housing department?

(A) To donate the stuff he left behind when he left last semester

(B) To organize his plan to build a link between a charity organization and his university

(C) To inquire about a job advertisement he saw in the school paper

(D) To retrieve the stuff that he couldn't take with him last semester

02. What did the man think happened to the stuff he left behind?

(A) That someone who lived in his dorm after he left took it and used it

(B) That it was donated to a charity organization for a good cause

(C) That it was simply thrown away

(D) That the housing department took it and held it for future inquiries by its owner

03. What can be inferred about the charity organization that the student contacted?

(A) That it directly sends the donated things, such as clothes and dishes, to children in Africa.

(B) That the university needs to collect the donated things and drop them off at the organization

(C) That it wants to have a meeting with the university's administration to discuss it first

(D) That it will pick up the students' donated items every semester as long as the university administration permits them to

04. What does the administrator suggest is the fastest way to advertise the new donation program?

(A) Advertising it in the school's paper

(B) Putting advertisements on the bulletin board in the student center

(C) Having the school's TV station announce it every morning

(D) Putting flyers and notices on the walls of the campus buildings.

Listen again to part of the conversation. Then answer the question.

05. What does the administrator mean when she says this:

(A) All of the students went to the beach as a school trip.

(B) The student is supposed to be in Africa helping kids in school.

(C) The student had told the administrator about spending his summer break at the beach.

(D) She wonders why he is on campus before students are required to be there.

Note taking

TEST 2 set2 L1

Question 06~11 of 17

06. What is the lecture mainly about?

(A) Gamma waves and their role in facilitating brain activity and enhancing the brain's capacity

(B) Isaac Newton's work and his approach to problem solving

(C) The professor's advice on the final term paper that he has assigned to his students

(D) General exploration and explanation of insight with supporting details

07. Why does the professor mention Isaac Newton at the beginning?

(A) To remind his students of the famous apple story

(B) To present an account that illustrates the concept of insight

(C) To encourage his students to take an "Isaac Newton" approach to solving problems

(D) To open up a discussion about well-known physicians of the 1600's

08. Which of the following is a characteristic of the preparatory stage?

(A) The visual cortex is enhanced, thereby facilitating problem solving that requires the brain to visualize.

(B) Sensory areas, other than the visual and auditory cortexes, shut down.

(C) The parts of the brain devoted to speech and language production are activated.

(D) The lobes that sense external stimuli temporarily stop functioning.

09. What can be inferred about gamma waves from the passage?

(A) There needs to be more research on the cause of their production.

(B) They are the core of the sensory system, including the visual and auditory cortexes.

(C) They are formed right after the speech-language-production part of the brain becomes active.

(D) They are only helpful in the communication between nearby cells.

10. What is the primary function of the gamma rhythms?

(A) They help in the transition from a tense, stressed brain to a relaxed brain.

(B) They block signals from the sensory areas of the brain during the search phase.

(C) They form the connecting networks between distant cells.

(D) They enable the activation of the speech-language-production part of the brain.

Listen again to part of the lecture. Then answer the question

11. Why does the professor say this :

(A) To claim that most of Newton's discoveries were rather accidental

(B) To make the point that Newton's leisure time actually helped him with his discovery

(C) To show admiration to the amount of work Newton put into his unexpected discovery

(D) To help his students visualize the design of the experiment that Newton executed with an apple.

Note taking

12. What is the main topic of the lecture?

    (A) The means that Natufians employed to survive in a harsh environment
    (B) A part of the world where a lifestyle shift occurred centuries ago
    (C) Distinct characteristics of the Natufians' lifestyle in the eastern Mediterranean region
    (D) A change in lifestyles that happened thousands of years ago and its evidence

13. Which of the following initiated the shift to permanent settlements?

    (A) The end of a cold era that resulted in a dramatic change in the world's climate
    (B) The glaciers that remained stable in the Mediterranean region after the ice age
    (C) An increase in rainfall as a result of the end of the last ice age
    (D) The advent of tools that eased agricultural practices

14. How did the Natufians make their houses strong and stable?

    (A) The Natufians only used heavy stones to build the walls of their houses.
    (B) The Natufians built houses that dug deep into the ground.
    (C) The Natufians arranged their houses in a semicircular shape that bound them to one another.
    (D) The Natufians built the lower parts of their houses with stones and dug them into the ground.

15. Which of the following are NOT true about the Natufians' agriculture?

    Click on 2 andswers

    (A) The Natufians planted and harvested grains on a seasonal basis.
    (B) Large quantities of mortars were used to grind seeds and grains.
    (C) Grains such as wheat were cherished, whereas grains such as oats were ignored.
    (D) The Natufians took advantage of the vast areas of fertile soil and continually relied on the abundant wild plants as a food source.

16. Why did the professor mention migratory birds and young gazelles?

    (A) To give examples of the Natufians' domesticated animals
    (B) To inform her students that migratory animals took up a large portion of the Natufians' diet
    (C) To explain that the Natufians used the animals' feathers and leather to withstand the harsh conditions.
    (D) To present another available food source to support the claim of permanent residence

Listen again to part of the lecture. Then answer the question.

17. What does the professor imply when she says:

    (A) Sedentary settlements have apparent differences from cultures with nomadic lifestyles
    (B) What she stated as pre-conditions of the shift in lifestyle aren't enough to prove a permanent settlement
    (C) Her students must have learned about the physical evidence found in the region previously
    (D) She wants to give the students a chance to answer because they've asked her a similar question before

Note taking

www.usherin.usher.co.kr

USHER

iBT TOEFL
INTERMEDIATE LISTENING
TEST 3

TEST 3 set 1

Listening Section Directions

This section measures your ability to understand conversations and lectures in English. It is divided into 3 separately timed parts. In each part you will listen to 1 conversation and 2 lectures. You will hear each conversation or lecture only **one** time.

After each conversation or lecture, you will answer some questions about it. Answer the questions based on what is stated or implied by the speakers.

For each part of the listening section you will have 10 minutes to answer the questions.

A clock at the top of the screen will show you how much time you have remaining. The clock will **not** count down while you are listening. The clock will count down only while you are answer questions.

You may take notes while you listen. You may use your notes to help you answer the questions. Your notes will **not** be scored.

If you need to change the volume while you listen, click on the **Volume** icon at the top of the screen.

In some questions, you will see this icon 🎧. This means that you will hear, but not see. part of the question. Most questions are worth 1 point. If a question is worth more than 1 point, it will have special directions that indicate how many points you can receive.

In this listening section. After you answer each question, click on **Next**. Then click on **OK** to confirm your answer and go on to the next section, you cannot return to previous questions.

Listen to part of the Listening section.
(Click on Continue at any time to dismiss these directions.)

리스닝 섹션은 PART 1, PART 2로 나누어져 있습니다.
PART 1에서는 세 지문을 듣게 됩니다. 10분 동안 질문에 답하세요.
지문을 듣는 동안 시간이 줄어들지 않습니다.

Note taking

TEST 3 set 1 C

Question 1~5 of 17

01. Why does the student visit the professor?

(A) To ask the professor for advice on his brain research

(B) To ask for help with designing an experiment to study the brain

(C) To get a better understanding of a recent lecture

(D) To get an idea of what neuropsychologists do in their field

02. According to the professor, why did Roger Walcott Sperry decide to split the patient's brain in half?

(A) To treat his patient for severe convulsions

(B) To collect more data about the two hemispheres of the brain

(C) To analyze the function of the corpus callosum of the brain

(D) To make sure his patient's mental abnormalities do not relapse

03. What was the student's misconception about the left and right hemispheres in relation to visual fields?

(A) That the right hemisphere dictates the perception of objects in the left visual field

(B) That once the brain was split, the visual fields would never be balanced again

(C) That the left hemisphere is connected with the left visual field

(D) That the right hemisphere corresponds to spatial abilities

04. How is the left hemisphere different from the right hemisphere?

(A) The left hemisphere is specialized in imagination and creative thinking

(B) The left hemisphere primarily involves the task of analysis and logical reasoning

(C) The left hemisphere specializes in auditory tasks

(D) The left hemisphere plays a role in processing rhetorical tasks

Listen again to part of the conversation. Then answer the question.

05. Why does the professor say this :

(A) To elucidate one of the side effects that the patient suffered after the surgery

(B) To see if the student recognizes the elements used in the experiment

(C) To illustrate that the left and right hemispheres of the brain aren't different in terms of their functions and tasks

(D) To show his doubt that the student is paying enough attention to him

Note taking

TEST 3 set 1 L1

06. What is the lecture mainly about?

(A) Exploration of the events that took place during the Younger Dryas period with scientific research

(B) The last ice age that caused the demise of the Clovis civilization and extinction of species in North America

(C) The characteristics of nanodiamonds and the black mat in which they are found

(D) In-depth theories of the Younger Dryas period with supporting details

07. According to the professor, what gave rise to the initiation of the Younger Dryas?

(A) The extinction of the species including mammoths in North America

(B) The disrupted ocean currents and global wind patterns caused by deglaciation

(C) The change in ocean currents in the Atlantic Ocean caused by an influx of lake water

(D) The end of the ice age that took place about 12,900 years ago

08. How were Kennett and his team able to support their claim that comets struck the Earth?

(A) By using an electron microscope and finding minerals that are synchronous with the Younger Dryas

(B) By dating mammals' bones that have remained in the black mat throughout centuries

(C) By examining the crater that's been assumed to be created by the asteroid 12,900 years ago

(D) By running computer simulations and calculating the possibility of the occurrence of asteroids during the Younger Dryas

09. Which of the following is true about the critics' perspective about Kennett and his team's finding of nanodiamonds?

(A) That although the theory is not sufficient enough as of now, there is hope that there will be additional evidence in near future

(B) That their work is incomplete in a sense that other places than the impact-sites haven't been examined

(C) That their hypothesis is purely based on coincidental events rather than periodic phenomena

(D) That their finding doesn't support their claim that asteroids struck the Earth

10. What is the professor's overall attitude towards the "Clovis comet hypothesis"?

(A) He takes a negative standpoint of the theory by giving an argument in line with the critics

(B) He seems to be emotionally detached and doesn't disclose any subjective perspective on the hypothesis

(C) He takes a fairly neutral stance by illustrating that it's quite possible that additional evidence will be found in the future

(D) He explains that the hypothesis is just another ephemeral theory like the one that involves the demise of dinosaurs

11. Why does the professor mention the extinction of dinosaurs at the end?

(A) To deliver a message that evidence to support Kennett's theory could also be used to prove the dinosaur theory

(B) To make a comparison with Kennett's theory in that it fails to entail proven evidence

(C) To further support his claim that new discoveries that could validate Kennett's theory are just yet to be found

(D) To point out that the demise of dinosaurs was also caused by impacts

Note taking

12. What is the purpose of the lecture?

  (A) To discuss Leonardo da Vinci's philosophical thinking embedded in his work
  (B) To explain the fundamental roots of creating computer programs
  (C) To illustrate the distinctive characteristics of technological design developers
  (D) To show that human needs and wants are considered in various fields in today's society

13. What part of Leonardo da Vinci's work does the professor stress as a critical aspect of his work?

  (A) His inventive and spontaneous thinking process
  (B) His well-rounded insight as a philosopher, an artist, and a polymath
  (C) His enlightened perspectives in the various fields he studied
  (D) His designs that were meant to satisfy people's problems

14. Why does the professor stop from further explaining old computing?

  (A) Because he believes old computing is relatively less significant than new computing
  (B) Because he wishes to discuss old computing next time
  (C) Because he supposes that new computing is the main point of his lecture, not old computing
  (D) Because he thinks old computing is not related to new computing in any way

15. According to the professor, how do developers in the field of technology design, new computing, get their ideas?

  (A) They study works by Leonardo da Vinci and apply his rules to their work
  (B) They get advice from increasingly popular websites with a massive database
  (C) They refer to the public's demands and its purposes of using computers
  (D) They develop their work based on futuristic and revolutionary thinking

16. In the lecture, the professor explains two branches of technological design. Indicate whether each of the following is a feature of old computing, new computing, both, or neither.

	old-computing	new-computing	both	neither
(A) Concerns the effectiveness and usability of computers				
(B) Develops technologies involved in improving computer speed				
(C) Contributes to simplifying computer components that could otherwise be perplexing				
(D) Involves the application of philosophy for the ultimate benefit of the society				

17. What do Leonardo da Vinci's work and new computing have in common?

  (A) They are both conservative; they preserve and consist of the old principles and ideas
  (B) Both are easily exploitable and accessible by the public
  (C) Both comprise profound scientific research and experiments
  (D) They contain advances in both philosophical and mechanical aspects

Note taking

TEST 3 set 2

Listening Section Directions

This section measures your ability to understand conversations and lectures in English. It is divided into 3 separately timed parts. In each part you will listen to 1 conversation and 2 lectures. You will hear each conversation or lecture only **one** time.

After each conversation or lecture, you will answer some questions about it. Answer the questions based on what is stated or implied by the speakers.

For each part of the listening section you will have 10 minutes to answer the questions.

A clock at the top of the screen will show you how much time you have remaining. The clock will **not** count down while you are listening. The clock will count down only while you are answer questions.

You may take notes while you listen. You may use your notes to help you answer the questions. Your notes will **not** be scored.

If you need to change the volume while you listen, click on the **Volume** icon at the top of the screen.

In some questions, you will see this icon. This means that you will hear, but not see. part of the question. Most questions are worth 1 point. If a question is worth more than 1 point, it will have special directions that indicate how many points you can receive.

In this listening section. After you answer each question, click on **Next**. Then click on **OK** to confirm your answer and go on to the next section, you cannot return to previous questions.

Listen to part of the Listening section.
(Click on Continue at any time to dismiss these directions.)

리스닝 섹션은 PART 1, PART 2로 나누어져 있습니다.
PART 1에서는 세 지문을 듣게 됩니다. 10분 동안 질문에 답하세요.
지문을 듣는 동안 시간이 줄어들지 않습니다.

Note taking

TEST 3 set2 C

Question 1~5 of 17

01. What does the coach want to talk about with the student?

   (A) An upcoming interview for an internship at the university that the coach is promoting
   (B) The student's contributions to the team as the new captain
   (C) The reason the student is undecided about attending the championship
   (D) The transportation methods by which the team can get to the championship games

02. According to the student, why is the interview for the internship position a problem?

   (A) He prioritizes the internship position over the soccer captain position
   (B) The transportation system doesn't take the student to the interview place directly
   (C) It's not practical for an applicant to reschedule an interview
   (D) The interview time overlaps with the championship games

03. What was the student's misconception about the championship game?

   (A) That the champion is decided through a single game
   (B) That it's very burdensome to get to the championship place using public transportation
   (C) That the championship comprises several games over few days
   (D) That it actually takes place one day after the arrival at the game venue

04. What is the student most likely to do about the 'internship or championship' dilemma?

   (A) He will try to explain his situation to the agency and delay his interview
   (B) He will have to abandon the championship game for the internship position
   (C) He will attempt to attend both of the events
   (D) He is going to give up on the interview because he wishes to participate in all of the games

Listen again to part of the conversation. Then answer the question.

05. What does the student imply when he says this :

   (A) That the interview for the internship is more important than the championship
   (B) That he has taken both into contemplation, and it's difficult for him to give up on the internship interview
   (C) That once he misses this internship interview, he will never get another chance
   (D) That he doesn't want to let the championship game hinder his path

Note taking

TEST 3 set2 L1

Question 06~11 of 17

06. What is the main topic of the lecture?

(A) Contrasting theories and opinions regarding the age of the earth
(B) Scientific studies of heat diffusion
(C) Lord Kelvin's successful research that has helped today's scientists determine the earth's age
(D) Research of the mechanisms behind the early formation of the earth

07. How did Lord Kelvin establish the fundamentals of this theory?

(A) He theorized that earth's heat loss occurred through heat convection
(B) He established that the layers beneath earth's crust became solid through a cooling process
(C) He posited the laws of thermodynamics to explain earth's cooling process
(D) He demonstrated the direction in which heat contained in a solid body flowed

08. Why does the professor mention the boiling kettle?

(A) To help his students understand that the earth was very hot when it formed
(B) To illustrate that the liquid interior of the earth worked as a heat source for the entire earth
(C) To explain the mechanism of heat diffusion to his students
(D) To explain how the melting point of rocks is calculated

09. According to the critics of Lord Kelvin's theory, which of the following was false about his calculations?

(A) He failed to take all variables of heat production into account
(B) He underestimated the amount of heat produced by radioactivity
(C) He falsely assumed that asteroids and comets actually struck the earth
(D) His calculations included no evidence of the earth's heat loss

10. What basic assumption was Perry's theory based upon that differed from Kelvin's?

(A) That the earth's heat loss followed a circular path rather than diffusion
(B) That the interior of the earth was in a liquid, or semi-liquid, state
(C) That the cooling process took place while the earth was being solidified
(D) That the trapped heat diffused inward not outward

Listen again to part of the lecture.
Then answer the question.

11. What does the professor mean when he says this :

(A) Perry's challenge to Kelvin encouraged a major shift in the social structure in the contemporary society
(B) Perry's argument resembles a society in which the less powerful citizens rebel against the authority
(C) Kelvin abused his assistants and employees including Perry
(D) Perry's action was thought to be impetuous and rebellious by the society at the time

Note taking

Question 12~17 of 17

12. What is the main topic of the lecture?

    (A) One of the major cultural changes in American theater history with supporting details
    (B) General discussions of various aspects of vaudeville theaters after the civil war
    (C) Biography of Benjamin Franklin Keith and details of his figure as a successful businessman
    (D) Social changes in lifestyle that directly affected the popularity of popular theater

13. Which of the following were the primary forces that bolstered the establishment of a new form of theater art?

    Click on 2 answers

    (A) Increasing urban populations at the end of the 19th century
    (B) Adaptation of foreign cultures brought in by immense immigration movements
    (C) Growth in the employment and income rates
    (D) Economic depression in rural areas caused by mass movements to the cities

14. Why does the professor compare vaudeville theaters to convenience stores?

    (A) To posit that bigger-marketed industries soon surpassed vaudeville theaters
    (B) To accentuate the thought that vaudeville theaters were as common as convenience stores
    (C) To elucidate that Vaudevillian performances were low-quality
    (D) To explain that a myriad of entertainments was accessible in vaudeville theaters, collectively

15. How did Benjamin Franklin Keith make his vaudeville theater exceptional?

    (A) He increased the operating hours of his theater and embellished them with ornaments
    (B) He built his theater inside a luxurious hotel to make it seem more grandiose
    (C) He decorated the performers' costumes with extravagant details
    (D) He allowed the admission of women and children into his theater when most theaters didn't

16. What is the difference between the traditional theaters of the American Civil War era and the one established by Benjamin Franklin Keith?

    (A) Freedom of speech was greatly suppressed in Keith's theater under the government's control
    (B) Serious literary shows were predominant during the civil war due to the government's censorship law
    (C) The use of vulgarity and inappropriate behavior were greatly discouraged in Keith's theater
    (D) The traditional theaters had a strong theme of illegitimate theater

Listen again to part of the lecture. Then answer the question.

17. What does the professor imply when she says this :

    (A) That Keith's theater mainly consisted of romantic and humorous elements
    (B) That the women and children's influence was greater than that of men during the time
    (C) That Keith advocated the equality of his audience and was able to make more profits than the discriminatory theaters
    (D) That Keith's theaters consisted of elements that attracted more female and young customers than male customers

**You have reached the end of this part of the test.
Click on Continue to go on.**

Note taking

www.usherin.usher.co.kr

USHER

iBT TOEFL
INTERMEDIATE LISTENING
TEST 4

TEST 4 set 1

Listening Section Directions

This section measures your ability to understand conversations and lectures in English. It is divided into 3 separately timed parts. In each part you will listen to 1 conversation and 2 lectures. You will hear each conversation or lecture only **one** time.

After each conversation or lecture, you will answer some questions about it. Answer the questions based on what is stated or implied by the speakers.

For each part of the listening section you will have 10 minutes to answer the questions.

A clock at the top of the screen will show you how much time you have remaining. The clock will **not** count down while you are listening. The clock will count down only while you are answer questions.

You may take notes while you listen. You may use your notes to help you answer the questions. Your notes will **not** be scored.

If you need to change the volume while you listen, click on the **Volume** icon at the top of the screen.

In some questions, you will see this icon 🎧. This means that you will hear, but not see. part of the question. Most questions are worth 1 point. If a question is worth more than 1 point, it will have special directions that indicate how many points you can receive.

In this listening section. After you answer each question, click on **Next**. Then click on **OK** to confirm your answer and go on to the next section, you cannot return to previous questions.

Listen to part of the Listening section.
(Click on Continue at any time to dismiss these directions.)

리스닝 섹션은 PART 1, PART 2로 나누어져 있습니다.
PART 1에서는 세 지문을 듣게 됩니다. 10분 동안 질문에 답하세요.
지문을 듣는 동안 시간이 줄어들지 않습니다.

Note taking

TEST 4 set 1 C

Question 1~5 of 17

01. What is the conversation mainly about?

(A) The student's last term paper for the semester in her Biology class

(B) Honeybees' usage of their dances and the magnetic field as their survival mechanism

(C) Student's request that the professor extends the deadline for the Biology paper that is due soon

(D) The professor's advice on the student's difficulty of grasping the concept of honeybees' navigation methods

02. What is the main idea addressed in the student's paper?

(A) How honeybees accomplish communication using earth's magnetic field

(B) Comparison between plants' biological clocks and honeybees' internal clocks

(C) Insects' survival and foraging methods

(D) Communication and navigation methods utilized by honeybees

03. According to the student, what affects honeybees' decision to use either the round dance or the waggle dance?

(A) Their position in the highly complex social structure

(B) The strength of the earth's magnetic field they sense

(C) The location of their food sources with respect to that of their hives

(D) Their individual and distinctive duties

04. How are honeybees able to navigate?

(A) By sensing earth's magnetic field with iron in their bodies

(B) By responding to and orienting themselves to external stimuli, such as wind

(C) By using their internal, biological clock to detect the amount of sunlight

(D) By detecting traces of iron in earth's magnetic field

05. What is the student most likely to do after the conversation with the professor?

(A) She will finish her other assignments before revising her Biology paper

(B) She will revise her paper using her original sources

(C) She will come back to the professor for help again

(D) She will find another suitable source of information

Note taking

06. What is the lecture mainly about?

(A) Comparison between the distinct properties and characteristics of two galaxies

(B) Discoveries regarding the relationship between two galaxies that differ in size

(C) The effect of gravitational forces on the formation and coordination of galaxies

(D) The origin of our solar system, which has been misunderstood for a long time

07. Why does the professor mention 'two identical stacks of paper'?

(A) To give his students a better understanding of how galaxies are initially formed

(B) To help his students grasp the idea that stars of several galaxies are always jumbled up

(C) To help his students understand the universally accepted method of distinguishing galaxies using the colors blue and red

(D) To simplify the concept of the technology that was developed to distinguish galaxies from one another

08. What property of galaxies helped the research team make a distinction between two different chemical compositions?

(A) The gravitational pull that exists between galaxies

(B) The galaxies' emission of light photons created by their heat energy

(C) Bigger galaxies' tendency to fuse with relatively smaller galaxies

(D) The unique chemical patterns found at the center of each galaxy

09. According to the professor, why is a special type of device needed to measure chemical patterns of galaxies?

(A) Because the light that galaxies radiate is not within the visible-light spectrum

(B) Because galaxies become so dark that they are not visible through a regular telescope

(C) Because galaxies release light composed of blinding chemicals

(D) Because the distance between galaxies and Earth makes it impossible for ordinary telescopes to detect them

10. What do scientists imply about the future of the Milky Way and Sagittarius galaxies?

(A) That the entirety of the Milky Way will be absorbed by Sagittarius

(B) That fusion of the galaxies will eventually cause both to be completely destroyed

(C) That the gravitational force between the Moon and Earth will eventually interrupt the one between two galaxies

(D) That the incessant attractive force will ultimately lead to total disappearance of the Sagittarius

Listen again to part of the lecture. Then answer the question.

11. What does the professor imply when he says this :

(A) That the gravitational pull from the Earth inhibited physical contact between galaxies

(B) That the astronomers from the past didn't believe that it was possible for galaxies to affect each other

(C) That the gravitational force that once existed no longer exists

(D) That the previous generations were conservative and never made attempts to override existing theories

Note taking

TEST 4 set 1 L2

Question 12~17 of 17

12. What is the lecture mainly about?

(A) Methods of color production employed by diverse species with feathers and scales
(B) Pros and cons of biomimicry used in many industries and potential threats
(C) The application of natural processes in modern commercial endeavors
(D) Contributing factor to the development of structural coloration in the modern society

13. According to the professor, why aren't plants able to absorb the green wavelength?

(A) Because the green wavelengths are used during photosynthesis so the chloroplasts absorb them
(B) Because the chlorophyll in the leaves reflects the green wavelengths of light from the sun's rays
(C) Because the leaves of plants have strong affinity for all colors but green
(D) Because the wavelength of green the sun disseminates is not substantial enough for plants to detect

14. How do Morpho butterflies appear as blue when no pigment is existent in their bodies?

(A) Their scales are too pale to absorb the blue wavelengths in ultraviolet light
(B) The unique chemical called schemochromes makes them reflect the blue wavelength
(C) The multiple surfaces of their scales reflect the blue light from the ultraviolet spectrum
(D) Their wing movements and the angle at which the sunlight hits them makes them appear to be blue

15. What property of the scales of Morpho butterflies makes the wings water-resistant?

(A) The air-filled gaps in between their scales
(B) The adhesive forces between each layer of their scale
(C) The rough, multi-layered structure of their scale caused by the chemical called schemochromes
(D) Their individual cells' hemophilic membrane that prevents the entrance of water

16. In the lecture, the professor explains two different ways in which colors are created in nature. Indicate whether each of the following is a feature of pigmentation, structural coloration, or none.

	Pigmentation	Structural Coloration	None
(A) Requires thin layers of films or scales and light			
(B) Heavily involves original thinking			
(C) Also known as schemochrome			
(D) Less exploited by business people when designing products			

Listen again to part of the lecture. Then answer the question.

17. What does the professor mean when she says this :

(A) That the ketchup would slide off the shirt without staining it
(B) That all everyday commodities like the shirt could be modified the same way
(C) That using pigments on the shirt isn't necessary anymore because the shirts are already structurally colored
(D) That applying the discipline of structural coloration to shirts is as effective as the layers of the butterflies' wings

You have reached the end of this part of the test.
Click on **Continue** to go on.

Note taking

TEST 4 set 2

Listening Section Directions

This section measures your ability to understand conversations and lectures in English. It is divided into 3 separately timed parts. In each part you will listen to 1 conversation and 2 lectures. You will hear each conversation or lecture only **one** time.

After each conversation or lecture, you will answer some questions about it. Answer the questions based on what is stated or implied by the speakers.

For each part of the listening section you will have 10 minutes to answer the questions.

A clock at the top of the screen will show you how much time you have remaining. The clock will **not** count down while you are listening. The clock will count down only while you are answer questions.

You may take notes while you listen. You may use your notes to help you answer the questions. Your notes will **not** be scored.

If you need to change the volume while you listen, click on the **Volume** icon at the top of the screen.

In some questions, you will see this icon 🎧. This means that you will hear, but not see. part of the question. Most questions are worth 1 point. If a question is worth more than 1 point, it will have special directions that indicate how many points you can receive.

In this listening section. After you answer each question, click on **Next**. Then click on **OK** to confirm your answer and go on to the next section, you cannot return to previous questions.

Listen to part of the Listening section.

(Click on Continue at any time to dismiss these directions.)

리스닝 섹션은 PART 1, PART 2로 나누어져 있습니다.
PART 1에서는 세 지문을 듣게 됩니다. 10분 동안 질문에 답하세요.
지문을 듣는 동안 시간이 줄어들지 않습니다.

Note taking

Question 1~5 of 17

01. Why does the student visit the professor?

(A) To organize her thoughts and get advice on an upcoming assignment

(B) To discuss the Barbizon paintings that she will observe in the art museum around the corner

(C) To consult with the professor on the problems she's having with her group members

(D) To inquire about the lifestyle of French painters in the in the mid-19th century

02. According to the student, what property of the Fontainebleau Forest did the painters of the Barbizon school cherish?

(A) Its distinct landscape features that other forests did not have

(B) The existence of its untouched nature

(C) The fusion of modern civilization and preserved relics from ancient times

(D) Its location just outside of the village in Paris where the painters lived

03. How did the Barbizon way of landscape painting differ from that of an earlier period?

(A) The former's artists used imagination as a key component

(B) The latter presented an honest, truthful depiction of nature

(C) The former didn't require any part of paintings to be fabricated

(D) The former's artists mostly worked in forests undisturbed by modern civilization

04. Why does the professor mention Théodore Rousseau?

(A) To explain that he was one of the most prestigious artists of the time

(B) To give the student an exemplary person whom she could possibly use for her assignment

(C) To support his claim that the student's paper is well-organized and comprehensive

(D) To claim that Théodore Rousseau was responsible for founding the Barbizon school

Listen again to part of the conversation. Then answer the question.

05. What does the professor imply when he says this :

(A) That the student didn't pay enough attention to the presentation guidelines

(B) That the student may be trying to present too much information

(C) That he made a change in the requirements of the assignment and shortened the presentation's duration

(D) That in his opinion, all presentations should be concise and informative within 5 minutes

Note taking

TEST 4 set2 L1

Question 06~11 of 17

06. What is the main purpose of the lecture?

(A) To discuss the causes and effects of the development of accessible literature in the early modern period

(B) To explain remarkable works by French scholars, such as Michel de Montaigne

(C) To compare and contrast the revolution that took hold in the 19th century with the early modern period

(D) To address the transition from the manuscript culture to print culture

07. Why does the professor mention what happened in England in the 19th century at the beginning of the lecture?

(A) To explain that the printing revolution continued all the way through the 19th century

(B) To explain how classics were divided into triple-deckers of three volumes

(C) To imply that the last class' discussion shares a similarity with today's lecture

(D) To introduce the idea that revolutions have taken place throughout Europe since the printing era began

08. Which of the following are the characteristics of cheap books made during the early modern period?

Click on 2 answers

(A) They contained light stories that most people enjoyed reading

(B) Unlike those of the medieval period, they avoided philosophical topics like medieval knights and religious stories

(C) They required sophisticated logical reasoning skills

(D) They were easily accessible and sometimes sold by street vendors

09. What does the professor imply about the oral tradition?

(A) That it was a reliable source of preserving ideas and stories for future generations

(B) That its role didn't vanish or succumb to printing machines

(C) That it died out when the printing era began taking over

(D) That its importance surpassed that of the printing machines

10. According to the professor, what was the contemporary public's opinion of Montaigne's essays?

(A) They were thought of as innovative and experimental

(B) They were viewed adversely because of their argumentative tendency

(C) They were most popular and sensational with politicians of his time

(D) The authorities ironically favored them, for they identified their shortcomings

Listen again to part of the lecture. Then answer the question.

11. What does the professor imply when she asks this :

(A) That the focus of attention should be on the people of the period not the technology

(B) That she believes other technologies facilitated the revolution's longevity

(C) That the biggest contribution to the early modern period was the scholars' work

(D) That she's in line with those who argue that the printing technology was the essence of the revolution

Note taking

TEST 4 set2 L2

Question 12~17 of 17

12. What is the lecture mainly about?

    (A) The continuing history and development of bicycles
    (B) Comparison between advances in automobile technology before and after the Industrial Revolution
    (C) The causes and effects of the Industrial Revolution in the 18th century
    (D) Technological development in transportation over several decades

13. What does the professor identify as the earliest steam-powered vehicles' problem?

    (A) They were so heavy that their engines could not power their bodies
    (B) They could not be utilized on rough roads because of their massive density
    (C) They were slower than other transportation methods
    (D) They were prone to sudden breakdowns and stalling

14. Why were Baron Karl Drais' horseless carriages criticized by the public?

    (A) Because the draft animals used were abused by their owners
    (B) Because they failed to accommodate more people than previous inventions
    (C) Because their use was limited to certain landscapes
    (D) Because they employed 'draft people,' which was viewed as immoral

15. How does the professor react to the student's doubt that the Laufmaschine was the first bicycle?

    (A) She takes the same stance and does not understand why researchers call it the first bicycle
    (B) She opposes the student's point and explains why it was the first bicycle
    (C) She partially shares the opinion of the student
    (D) She believes that the Laufmaschine deserves credit as the first bicycle along with other two types, the Penny-farthing and the boneshaker

16. Why did the public's opinions about the Laufmaschine vary in France and Germany?

    (A) Because the French had different taste in bicycles than the German people
    (B) Because the idea of utilizing human-powered transportation wasn't popular in France at the time
    (C) Because it received a fair amount of acclaim and recognition when it was demonstrated in Germany
    (D) Because geographical conditions in the regions where the machine was introduced were very different

Listen again to part of the lecture. Then answer the question.

17. What does the professor imply when she says this :

    (A) That she believes everyone in her class has done research before the lecture
    (B) That the students can figure out the problem using common sense
    (C) That she has as little knowledge of the concept as the students
    (D) That she has previously explained the concept to the class

**You have reached the end of this part of the test.
Click on Continue to go on.**

Note taking

모범 답안·지문·해석 P.527

www.usherin.usher.co.kr

USHER

iBT TOEFL
INTERMEDIATE LISTENING
TEST 5

TEST 5 set 1

Listening Section Directions

This section measures your ability to understand conversations and lectures in English. It is divided into 3 separately timed parts. In each part you will listen to 1 conversation and 2 lectures. You will hear each conversation or lecture only **one** time.

After each conversation or lecture, you will answer some questions about it. Answer the questions based on what is stated or implied by the speakers.

For each part of the listening section you will have 10 minutes to answer the questions.

A clock at the top of the screen will show you how much time you have remaining. The clock will **not** count down while you are listening. The clock will count down only while you are answer questions.

You may take notes while you listen. You may use your notes to help you answer the questions. Your notes will **not** be scored.

If you need to change the volume while you listen, click on the **Volume** icon at the top of the screen.

In some questions, you will see this icon 🎧. This means that you will hear, but not see. part of the question. Most questions are worth 1 point. If a question is worth more than 1 point, it will have special directions that indicate how many points you can receive.

In this listening section. After you answer each question, click on **Next**. Then click on **OK** to confirm your answer and go on to the next section, you cannot return to previous questions.

Listen to part of the Listening section.
(Click on Continue at any time to dismiss these directions.)

리스닝 섹션은 PART 1, PART 2로 나누어져 있습니다.
PART 1에서는 세 지문을 듣게 됩니다. 10분 동안 질문에 답하세요.
지문을 듣는 동안 시간이 줄어들지 않습니다.

Note taking

TEST 5 set 1 C

Question 1~5 of 17

01. Why does the student visit the employee at the community center?

(A) Because his soccer coach has asked him to hand in a reservation form
(B) Because he is supposed to have a job interview
(C) Because he needs to book a space for an upcoming club activity
(D) Because he needs to meet the deadline for the club registration date

02. What can be inferred about the student from the conversation?

(A) That it's natural for him to know almost everything about his town
(B) That he is late because traffic jams occur frequently on Main Street
(C) That he is not familiar with the town because he has just moved there
(D) That he knows for certain that the traffic jam was caused by a vehicle accident

03. Why has the student's coach asked him to make an arrangement specifically with the employee?

(A) Because he wants to exploit the special treatment she gives him in regard to the reservation fee
(B) Because he knows pretty much everything about the town
(C) Because his team has not received funds from the sports department
(D) Because he wants to invite the employee to the soccer practice next Friday

04. What is the student most likely to do right after the conversation?

(A) He will give out the guest passes to his team members
(B) He and his coach will sign the registration forms and return them
(C) He will ask for guest passes for the number of people in his team
(D) He will visit the team members individually to get their signatures on the registration form

Listen again to part of the conversation. Then answer the question.

05. What does the student mean when he says this :

(A) That he's surprised that the job interview finished 20 minutes ago
(B) That he had not expected the misunderstanding that occurred
(C) That he's having a hard time trying to understand how the employee could make such a silly mistake
(D) That he happens to know the other guy with whom the employee has mixed him up

Note taking

TEST 5 set 1 L1

Question 06~11 of 17

06. What is the lecture mainly about?
 (A) Conflicts between the old standards of art and the rules imposed by the Académie des Beaux-Arts
 (B) Impressionists' philosophies and beliefs expressed through their paintings
 (C) Art transitions that took hold over a few centuries in Paris
 (D) Contrasting features of European art movements that occurred over several centuries

07. Which of the following are true about the paints used by painters before the 19th century?
 Click on 2 answers
 (A) They were durable and colorful
 (B) They had rich colors even without the use of varnish
 (C) They were easily portable and convenient because they were sold in tubes
 (D) They could be used to identify the artist

08. According to the professor, what can be inferred about the European paintings from the early 1800s before the Impressionism movement?
 (A) They were heavily affected by the paintings of old art masters, such as Claude Monet
 (B) Those that still exist are most likely in bad quality
 (C) Landscape and life are the common themes found in them
 (D) The painters found spontaneity to be the main source of ideas for their work

09. Why did impressionists not admire emulating reality in their paintings?
 (A) Because the exhibitions where they displayed their paintings didn't allow reality-based art
 (B) Because they loathed the academies' principles of art
 (C) Because the public's attention shifted to favoring work of abstract imagination
 (D) Because a technological produced better quality results

10. In the lecture, the professor explains two different types of paints. Indicate whether each of the following is a feature of paints used by impressionists, ones used by old masters, or both.

	Impressionists' paints	Old masters' paints	Both
(A) had durability and rich colors			
(B) required the use of artificial enhancements			
(C) aroused preservation issues like fading			
(D) were pre-packaged products			
(E) were able to produce colors according to painters' desires and intentions			

Listen again to part of the lecture. Then answer the question.

11. What does the professor mean when he says this :
 (A) The artists of the academies began to copy each other's work
 (B) Their spontaneity enabled them to expand the theme of their work
 (C) The followers of the academies only adhered to the established formulas when creating art
 (D) The academies contributed to making the process of drawing a relatively easier task

Note taking

Question 12~17 of 17

12. What is the main topic of the lecture?

(A) The interaction between predators and prey and its effects on both

(B) The definition of autotomy as an animal's reaction to threat

(C) An antipredator adaptation of a reptile species and its effects

(D) A variety of evolutionary traits that predators have developed to increase their chances of capturing prey

13. How is autotomy in geckos different from that in lizards?

(A) Geckos drop their tails when under threat, but only at night

(B) Lizards release their fragile skin to slip away from predatory attacks

(C) The former employ autotomy when they're in direct contact with their predators

(D) The former have multiple fracture planes, whereas the latter have only one

14. What does the professor imply about the studies that explain the voluntary detachment of tails?

(A) That they fall short of proving that tails have their own nervous systems

(B) That they've yet to effectively validate the phenomenon with sufficient evidence

(C) That improvements need to be made regarding the understanding of differences between geckos and lizards

(D) That they're complete and the discovery of body structures like fracture planes is the evidence viewed as immoral

15. Which of the following is true about the regenerated tails of lizards?

(A) Regeneration begins about four to twelve weeks after the detachment

(B) They are different from the original tails in terms of their physical compositions

(C) They are smaller and weaker than the original tails

(D) Lizards aren't able to autotomize regenerated tails again

16. Why do lizards lose a great amount of energy after tail autotomization?

(A) Because lizards' energy storage mechanisms are located in the section of the tail that isn't detached

(B) Because regenerating tails requires a massive amount of energy

(C) Because lizards need to compensate for their restricted movement

(D) Because lizards suffer from degradation of their social status and expend extra energy earning it back

17. How do lizards adapt to living without their tails and overcome the disadvantages it causes?

(A) They develop additional traits, such as crypsis and mimesis

(B) They change their behavior patterns and the time of their activity

(C) They exert more energy to speed their tail regeneration

(D) They forage in social groups rather than hunting individually

You have reached the end of this part of the test.
Click on **Continue** to go on.

Note taking

TEST 5 set 2

Listening Section Directions

This section measures your ability to understand conversations and lectures in English. It is divided into 3 separately timed parts. In each part you will listen to 1 conversation and 2 lectures. You will hear each conversation or lecture only **one** time.

After each conversation or lecture, you will answer some questions about it. Answer the questions based on what is stated or implied by the speakers.

For each part of the listening section you will have 10 minutes to answer the questions.

A clock at the top of the screen will show you how much time you have remaining. The clock will **not** count down while you are listening. The clock will count down only while you are answer questions.

You may take notes while you listen. You may use your notes to help you answer the questions. Your notes will **not** be scored.

If you need to change the volume while you listen, click on the **Volume** icon at the top of the screen.

In some questions, you will see this icon 🎧. This means that you will hear, but not see. part of the question. Most questions are worth 1 point. If a question is worth more than 1 point, it will have special directions that indicate how many points you can receive.

In this listening section. After you answer each question, click on **Next**. Then click on **OK** to confirm your answer and go on to the next section, you cannot return to previous questions.

Listen to part of the Listening section.
(Click on Continue at any time to dismiss these directions.)

리스닝 섹션은 PART 1, PART 2로 나누어져 있습니다.
PART 1에서는 세 지문을 듣게 됩니다. 10분 동안 질문에 답하세요.
지문을 듣는 동안 시간이 줄어들지 않습니다.

Note taking

TEST 5 set 2 C

Question 1~5 of 17

01. Why does the student visit the professor?

(A) To get help with distinguishing conventional poetry readings from poetry slams
(B) To discuss the poetry reading event that recently took place on campus
(C) To organize her thoughts on her paper
(D) To examine the significance of Allen Ginsberg as a prominent leader of the Beat Generation

02. What can be inferred about the student?

(A) That she was momentarily handicapped due to an injury
(B) That she is distressed about the poetry reading she missed recently
(C) That she did not spend much time planning her paper
(D) That she dislikes conventional poetry reading

03. According to the professor, what was the focal point of the Beat Generation?

(A) Connecting with the audience and involving them in the creation process
(B) A contentious attitude toward traditional beliefs and values
(C) Implicit acceptance by main-stream society
(D) Violent riots and rebellion against the government

04. Why does the professor mention Allen Ginsberg?

(A) To explain that his practice of reading poetry in poetry slams inspired lots of young writers
(B) To illustrate his philosophies as a poet to introduce the Beat Generation
(C) To show the difference between the styles of conventional poetry readings and poetry slams
(D) To demonstrate that conventional poetry reading and poetry slams can be classified into a spectrum

Listen again to part of the conversation. Then answer the question.

05. What does the professor imply when he says this :

(A) That he wishes to avoid giving away too much information to the student
(B) That he is not familiar with the details of the topic
(C) That the details are too complicated for him to explain on the spot
(D) That he thinks that the student is apathetic about her research topic

Note taking

TEST 5 set2 L1

Question 06~11 of 17

06. What is the main topic of the lecture?

(A) Social responsibilities and the production of ethanol as a fuel source

(B) The efficiency of ethanol in contrast to that of gasoline

(C) The pros and cons of an alternative to gasoline as a fuel

(D) The deficiency of gasoline alternatives with supporting details

07. What can be inferred about ethanol fuel from the lecture?

(A) Most countries are using it, contributing to a dramatic increase in its production

(B) Its use has been accepted by many despite its relatively short history

(C) The quality of the energy it produces is substandard and inferior to gasoline

(D) It's too costly for countries without ethanol fermentation technology to produce

08. According to the professor, how does the use of ethanol fuel contribute to the welfare of society?

(A) Since it requires extra transportation, it creates jobs for distributors

(B) Because growing and harvesting crops just happens, it doesn't require much labor

(C) It inhibits the use of environmentally harmful chemicals, such as fertilizers and oil

(D) It works as a catalyst for businesses in countries with abundant amount of agricultural resources

09. Which of the following are environmental impacts of ethanol fuel?

Click on 2 answers

(A) It takes about 1.5 gallons of ethanol to produce the same amount of CO_2 as 1 gallon of gasoline

(B) Creating ethanol from corn is energy-intensive in that it requires the production of toxic chemicals

(C) It completely eradicates the emission of carbon dioxide

(D) Fermenting corn kernels and purifying ethanol entails the use of fossil fuels

10. Why can't ethanol be transported via pipelines like oil?

(A) Because its high flammability makes it unsuitable for such a transportation method

(B) Because it starts a chemical reaction and causes rusting in response to its contact with steel

(C) Because it loses its usefulness as a fuel when tainted by water

(D) Because it's economically impossible to build a pipeline network just for ethanol

Listen again to part of the lecture. Then answer the question.

11. What does the professor imply when he says this :

(A) That most people don't realize that the alcohol they drink is a corn product that can be used as a fuel

(B) That corn, unlike all other crops, is used in the production of alcohol

(C) That not all corn products are edible

(D) That it makes more sense if the students understand how alcoholic beverages are produced

Note taking

TEST 5 set2 L2

Question 12~17 of 17

12. What is the lecture mainly about?

   (A) Proven theories regarding the formation of Earth and its ability to maintain liquid water
   (B) Geological differences between planets such as Earth, Mars, and the Moon
   (C) The climate conditions of planets in regard to their ability to maintain liquid water
   (D) The influence of water and greenhouse gases on the planets of our solar system

13. According to the professor, what role did greenhouse gases play in the early formation of Earth?

   (A) They prevented water from vaporizing into space
   (B) They produced heat and maintained constant warmer temperatures
   (C) They worked as a barrier and minimized the impact of meteors on Earth
   (D) They kept heat from escaping the atmosphere

14. What can be inferred about the volcanic activity theory suggested in the lecture?

   (A) It is outdated and its proponents have now shifted to the lunar cataclysm theory
   (B) It doesn't take into account the greenhouse gases that prevented heat from escaping into space
   (C) It falls short of validating all origins of liquid water on Earth
   (D) It fails to take the transformation of liquid water into account and explain it thoroughly

15. Why does the professor mention the Apollo missions?

   (A) To praise NASA's accomplishments, which brought significant changes to the history of mankind
   (B) To support his claim that the tests on meteorites proved that asteroids struck Earth around 4 billion years ago
   (C) To argue that meteors hit Earth around the time they struck other planets when Earth was forming
   (D) To prove his point that asteroids are usually incinerated in Earth's atmosphere before they reach the surface

16. Which of the following is true about Mars?

   (A) It lacks a key feature of Earth that shields it from solar winds
   (B) Its water was vaporized due to the lack of a strong magnetic field
   (C) It was not subjected to the same bombardment as Earth, hence the different resemblance of oceans and greenhouse gases
   (D) It doesn't sustain water because of low its gravitational force

Listen again to part of the lecture. Then answer the question.

17. What does the professor mean when she says this :

   (A) When meteors continuously struck Earth, it began to be negatively affected by them
   (B) The effect of the meteors' hitting Earth was quite insubstantial
   (C) Little strokes of meteor yield inconsequential amounts of by-products
   (D) When accumulated in large quantities, the small impact of the meteors caused a great change

You have reached the end of this part of the test.
Click on **Continue** to go on.

Note taking

www.usherin.usher.co.kr

USHER

iBT TOEFL
INTERMEDIATE LISTENING
답지

정답 및 Self-check list
문제유형과 signals
오답 정리표

정답 및 Self-Check List

정답

	TEST 1 - set 1	TEST 1 - set 2
1	(D) Detail	(D) Main Idea
2	(A) Detail	(C) Inference
3	(C) Detail	(C) Inference
4	(B) Inference	(C) Detail
5	(D) Inference	(B) Inference
6	(C) Main Idea	(C) Main Idea
7	(D) Detail	(A) Detail
8	(D) Detail	(B) Detail
9	(A), (D) Detail	(A) Detail
10	(A) Inference	(B) Detail
11	(D) Inference	(D) Inference
12	(C) Main Idea	(C) Main Idea
13	(D) Detail	(C) Inference
14	(D) Detail	(A) Detail
15	(A) Inference	(A), (D) Detail
16	(C) Detail	(A) Detail
17	(B) Inference	(A) Inference

Self-Check List

유 형	맞춘답의 개수(Test 1 - set 1)	맞춘답의 개수(Test 1 - set 2)
Main Idea	/ 2	/ 3
Detail	/ 9	/ 8
Inference	/ 6	/ 6
전 체	/ 17	/ 17

문제유형과 signals

번호	기본문제유형	세부문제유형	Signals
1	Main Idea	Main Purpose Main Idea	국부적(지엽적인) or 너무 일반적인(광범위한) 사실은 오답, 시제 및 단수 / 복수 주의
2	Detail	Term/Definition/Origin	refer to, what we call, so-called, originate, come from
3	Detail	Example	such as, like, think of, imagine, Let's take, let's say~, say, example, for instance
4	Detail	Characteristic Advantage / Disadvantage Problem / Difficulty Similarity / Compare Difference / Contrast	그림, 음악, 문학, 무용, 영화, 연극, 공예, 조각 등 / unique, useful, interesting, faster, fascinating, intriguing, key feature, note, important 동물 멸종위기, 생명의 위협 / 환경적응 Problem, hitch, challenge, drawback, flaw, defect, extinct, destroyed early-later, prior to~, recent, in the past, nowadays, modern day, evolve
5	Detail	Cause / Reason / Evidence Result / Finding / Effect / Influence	study, research, experiment, project(find, discover, uncover, reveal, shed light on) / evidence, finding / pave the way, impact, set the stage for, application
6	Detail	Misunderstanding Correction/Surprising	once believed, but~ / seem out of this world, news to
7	Detail	Requirement / Condition	necessary, required, you need to, consideration, condition, premise, job experience,
8	Detail	Offer / Solution / Suggestion	Alternative, to solve, handle this problem, recommend, why don't you~, what about~, what can be done~, your best bet would be~,
9	Detail	Future action/Future topic	upcoming, next class, another lecture
10	Inference	Purpose / Intention Imply / Infer Opinion / Attitude Headset	Why... mention~ / What can be inferred~/ What... imply~ What... mean when...say~ 다시 들려주고 푸는 문제 check ,understanding, agree/disagree
11	Category	Introduce / Organize / Conclude Matching Ordering	How~ introduce? How is the lecture organized? Three types, two kinds of, first, second, finally step, stage, phase , and then, divide into~

오답정리표 : Test 1

정답

번 호	문제 유형	틀린 답번호	오답유형	출제의도파악 (문제 및 정답 요약)
sample	Purpose	Test1-15	T1	교수가 Wood Thrush를 언급한 이유는 → 동물의 Displacement activities가 주변 환경으로부터 어떤 영향을 받는지에 대한 예
1	Main Purpose Main Idea Introduce Organize Conclusion			
2	Term Definition Origin			
3	Example			
4	Characteristic Advantage Disadvantage Problem Difficulty Similarity Compare Difference Contrast			

#				
5	Cause, Reason, Evidence Result, Finding, Effect, Influence			
6	Misunderstanding Correction Surprising			
7	Requirement Condition			
8	Offer Solution Suggestion			
9	Future action Future topic			
10	Purpose Intention Imply Infer Opinion Attitude Headset			
11	Introduce Organize Conclude Matching Ordering			

정답 및 Self-Check List

USHER iBT TOEFL INTERMEDIATE TEST LISTENING

정답

	TEST 2 - set 1	TEST 2 - set 2
1	(D) Main Idea	(B) Main Idea
2	(A), (B) Detail	(C) Detail
3	(B) Detail	(D) Inference
4	(C) Detail	(A) Detail
5	(A) Inference	(D) Inference
6	(D) Main Idea	(D) Main Idea
7	(D) Detail	(B) Inference
8	(B) Detail	(D) Detail
9	(C) Detail	(A) Inference
10	(A) Detail	(C) Detail
11	(C) Inference	(B) Inference
12	(B) Main Idea	(D) Main Idea
13	(B), (C) Detail	(A) Detail
14	(D) Detail	(D) Detail
15	(D) Detail	(A), (C) Detail
16	(C) Detail	(D) Inference
17	(A) Detail	(B) Inference

Self-Check List

유 형	맞춘답의 개수(TEST 2 - set 1)	맞춘답의 개수(TEST 2 - set 2)
Main Idea	/ 3	/ 3
Detail	/ 12	/ 7
Inference	/ 2	/ 7
전 체	/ 17	/ 17

문제유형과 signals

번호	기본문제유형	세부문제유형	Signals
1	Main Idea	Main Purpose Main Idea	국부적(지엽적인) or 너무 일반적인(광범위한) 사실은 오답, 시제 및 단수 / 복수 주의
2	Detail	Term/Definition/Origin	refer to, what we call, so-called, originate, come from
3		Example	such as, like, think of, imagine, Let's take, let's say~, say, example, for instance
4		Characteristic Advantage / Disadvantage Problem / Difficulty Similarity / Compare Difference / Contrast	그림, 음악, 문학, 무용, 영화, 연극, 공예, 조각 등 / unique, useful, interesting, faster, fascinating, intriguing, key feature, note, important 동물 멸종위기, 생명의 위협 / 환경적응 Problem, hitch, challenge, drawback, flaw, defect, extinct, destroyed early-later, prior to~, recent, in the past, nowadays, modern day, evolve
5		Cause / Reason / Evidence Result / Finding / Effect / Influence	study, research, experiment, project(find, discover, uncover, reveal, shed light on) / evidence, finding / pave the way, impact, set the stage for, application
6		Misunderstanding Correction/Surprising	once believed, but~ / seem out of this world, news to
7		Requirement / Condition	necessary, required, you need to, consideration, condition, premise, job experience,
8		Offer / Solution / Suggestion	Alternative, to solve, handle this problem, recommend, why don't you~, what about~, what can be done~, your best bet would be~,
9		Future action/Future topic	upcoming, next class, another lecture
10	Inference	Purpose / Intention Imply / Infer Opinion / Attitude Headset	Why... mention~ / What can be inferred~/ What... imply~ What... mean when...say~ 다시 들려주고 푸는 문제 check ,understanding, agree/disagree
11	Category	Introduce / Organize / Conclude Matching Ordering	How~ introduce? How is the lecture organized? Three types, two kinds of, first, second, finally step, stage, phase , and then, divide into~

오답정리표 : TEST 2

정답

번호	문제 유형	틀린 답번호	오답유형	출제의도파악 (문제 및 정답 요약)
sample	Purpose	TEST2-15	T1	교수가 Wood Thrush를 언급한 이유는 → 동물의 Displacement activities가 주변 환경으로부터 어떤 영향을 받는지에 대한 예
1	Main Purpose Main Idea Introduce Organize Conclusion			
2	Term Definition Origin			
3	Example			
4	Characteristic Advantage Disadvantage Problem Difficulty Similarity Compare Difference Contrast			

5	Cause, Reason, Evidence Result, Finding, Effect, Influence			
6	Misunderstanding Correction Surprising			
7	Requirement Condition			
8	Offer Solution Suggestion			
9	Future action Future topic			
10	Purpose Intention Imply Infer Opinion Attitude Headset			
11	Introduce Organize Conclude Matching Ordering			

정답 및 Self-Check List

USHER iBT TOEFL INTERMEDIATE TEST LISTENING

정답

	TEST 3 - set 1	TEST 3 - set 2
1	(C) Main Idea	(C) Main Idea
2	(A) Detail	(D) Detail
3	(C) Detail	(A) Detail
4	(B), (D) Detail	(C) Detail
5	(A) Inference	(B) Inference
6	(D) Main Idea	(A) Main Idea
7	(C) Detail	(D) Detail
8	(A) Detail	(C) Detail
9	(B), (D) Detail	(A) Detail
10	(C) Inference	(B) Detail
11	(C) Inference	(B) Inference
12	(B) Main Idea	(A) Main Idea
13	(D) Detail	(A), (C) Detail
14	(C) Inference	(D) Inference
15	(C) Detail	(A) Detail
16	Old Computing-(B) / New Computing-(A) / Both-(D) / Neither-(C) Detail	(C) Detail
17	(D) Detail	(C) Inference

Self-Check List

유 형	맞춘답의 개수 (TEST 3 - set 1)	맞춘답의 개수 (TEST 3 - set 2)
Main Idea	/ 3	/ 3
Detail	/ 10	/ 10
Inference	/ 4	/ 4
전 체	/ 17	/ 17

문제유형과 signals

번 호	기본문제유형	세부문제유형	Signals
1	Main Idea	Main Purpose Main Idea	국부적(지엽적인) or 너무 일반적인(광범위한) 사실은 오답, 시제 및 단수 / 복수 주의
2	Detail	Term/Definition/Origin	refer to, what we call, so-called, originate, come from
3		Example	such as, like, think of, imagine, Let's take, let's say~, say, example, for instance
4		Characteristic Advantage / Disadvantage Problem / Difficulty Similarity / Compare Difference / Contrast	그림, 음악, 문학, 무용, 영화, 연극, 공예, 조각 등 / unique, useful, interesting, faster, fascinating, intriguing, key feature, note, important 동물 멸종위기, 생명의 위협 / 환경적응 Problem, hitch, challenge, drawback, flaw, defect, extinct, destroyed early-later, prior to~, recent, in the past, nowadays, modern day, evolve
5		Cause / Reason / Evidence Result / Finding / Effect / Influence	study, research, experiment, project(find, discover, uncover, reveal, shed light on) / evidence, finding / pave the way, impact, set the stage for, application
6		Misunderstanding Correction/Surprising	once believed, but~ / seem out of this world, news to
7		Requirement / Condition	necessary, required, you need to, consideration, condition, premise, job experience,
8		Offer / Solution / Suggestion	Alternative, to solve, handle this problem, recommend, why don't you~, what about~, what can be done~, your best bet would be~,
9		Future action/Future topic	upcoming, next class, another lecture
10	Inference	Purpose / Intention Imply / Infer Opinion / Attitude Headset	Why... mention~ / What can be inferred~/ What... imply~ What... mean when...say~ 다시 들려주고 푸는 문제 check ,understanding, agree/disagree
11	Category	Introduce / Organize / Conclude Matching Ordering	How~ introduce? How is the lecture organized? Three types, two kinds of, first, second, finally step, stage, phase , and then, divide into~

오답정리표 : TEST 3

정답

번 호	문제 유형	틀린 답번호	오답유형	출제의도파악 (문제 및 정답 요약)
sample	Purpose	TEST3-15	T1	교수가 Wood Thrush를 언급한 이유는 → 동물의 Displacement activities가 주변 환경으로부터 어떤 영향을 받는지에 대한 예
1	Main Purpose Main Idea Introduce Organize Conclusion			
2	Term Definition Origin			
3	Example			
4	Characteristic Advantage Disadvantage Problem Difficulty Similarity Compare Difference Contrast			

5	Cause, Reason, Evidence Result, Finding, Effect, Influence			
6	Misunderstanding Correction Surprising			
7	Requirement Condition			
8	Offer Solution Suggestion			
9	Future action Future topic			
10	Purpose Intention Imply Infer Opinion Attitude Headset			
11	Introduce Organize Conclude Matching Ordering			

정답 및 Self-Check List

USHER iBT TOEFL INTERMEDIATE TEST LISTENING

정답

	TEST 4 - set 1	TEST 4 - set 2
1	(A) Main Idea	(A) Main Purpose
2	(D) Main Idea	(B) Detail
3	(C) Detail	(C) Detail
4	(A) Detail	(B) Inference
5	(D) Inference	(B) Inference
6	(B) Main Idea	(A) Main Purpose
7	(D) Detail	(C) Inference
8	(B) Detail	(A), (D) Detail
9	(A) Detail	(B) Inference
10	(D) Inference	(B) Detail
11	(B) Inference	(A) Inference
12	(C) Main Idea	(D) Main Idea
13	(B) Detail	(B) Detail
14	(C) Detail	(D) Detail
15	(A) Detail	(B) Detail
16	Pigmentation-(D) / Structural Coloration-(A),(C) / Neither-(B) Detail	(D) Detail
17	(A) Inference	(D) Inference

Self-Check List

유형	맞춘답의 개수(TEST 4 - set 1)	맞춘답의 개수(TEST 4 - set 2)
Main Idea	/ 4	/ 3
Detail	/ 9	/ 8
Inference	/ 4	/ 6
전 체	/ 17	/ 17

문제유형과 signals

번호	기본문제유형	세부문제유형	Signals
1	Main Idea	Main Purpose Main Idea	국부적(지엽적인) or 너무 일반적인(광범위한) 사실은 오답, 시제 및 단수 / 복수 주의
2	Detail	Term/Definition/Origin	refer to, what we call, so-called, originate, come from
3		Example	such as, like, think of, imagine, Let's take, let's say~, say, example, for instance
4		Characteristic Advantage / Disadvantage Problem / Difficulty Similarity / Compare Difference / Contrast	그림, 음악, 문학, 무용, 영화, 연극, 공예, 조각 등 / unique, useful, interesting, faster, fascinating, intriguing, key feature, note, important 동물 멸종위기, 생명의 위협 / 환경적응 Problem, hitch, challenge, drawback, flaw, defect, extinct, destroyed early-later, prior to~, recent, in the past, nowadays, modern day, evolve
5		Cause / Reason / Evidence Result / Finding / Effect / Influence	study, research, experiment, project(find, discover, uncover, reveal, shed light on) / evidence, finding / pave the way, impact, set the stage for, application
6		Misunderstanding Correction/Surprising	once believed, but~ / seem out of this world, news to
7		Requirement / Condition	necessary, required, you need to, consideration, condition, premise, job experience,
8		Offer / Solution / Suggestion	Alternative, to solve, handle this problem, recommend, why don't you~, what about~, what can be done~, your best bet would be~,
9		Future action/Future topic	upcoming, next class, another lecture
10	Inference	Purpose / Intention Imply / Infer Opinion / Attitude Headset	Why... mention~ / What can be inferred~/ What... imply~ What... mean when...say~ 다시 들려주고 푸는 문제 check ,understanding, agree/disagree
11	Category	Introduce / Organize / Conclude Matching Ordering	How~ introduce? How is the lecture organized? Three types, two kinds of, first, second, finally step, stage, phase , and then, divide into~

오답정리표 : TEST 4

USHER iBT TOEFL INTERMEDIATE TEST LISTENING

정답

번호	문제유형	틀린 답번호	오답유형	출제의도파악 (문제 및 정답 요약)
sample	Purpose	TEST4-15	T1	교수가 Wood Thrush를 언급한 이유는 → 동물의 Displacement activities가 주변 환경으로부터 어떤 영향을 받는지에 대한 예
1	Main Purpose Main Idea Introduce Organize Conclusion			
2	Term Definition Origin			
3	Example			
4	Characteristic Advantage Disadvantage Problem Difficulty Similarity Compare Difference Contrast			

#				
5	Cause, Reason, Evidence Result, Finding, Effect, Influence			
6	Misunderstanding Correction Surprising			
7	Requirement Condition			
8	Offer Solution Suggestion			
9	Future action Future topic			
10	Purpose Intention Imply Infer Opinion Attitude Headset			
11	Introduce Organize Conclude Matching Ordering			

정답 및 Self-Check List

USHER iBT TOEFL INTERMEDIATE TEST LISTENING

정답

	TEST 5 - set 1	TEST 5 - set 2
1	(C) Main Purpose	(C) Main Purpose
2	(A) Inference	(A) Inference
3	(A) Detail	(B) Detail
4	(B) Inference	(C) Detail
5	(B) Inference	(A) Inference
6	(D) Main Idea	(C) Main Idea
7	(A), (D) Detail	(B) Inference
8	(B) Inference	(D) Detail
9	(D) Detail	(B), (D) Detail
10	Impressionists' paints-(A),(D) / Old masters' paints-(B),(C) / Both-(E) Detail	(C) Detail
11	(C) Inference	(A) Inference
12	(C) Main Idea	(C) Main Idea
13	(C) Detail	(D) Detail
14	(B) Inference	(C) Inference
15	(B) Detail	(B) Detail
16	(C) Detail	(A) Detail
17	(B) Detail	(D) Inference

Self-Check List

유 형	맞춘답의 개수(TEST 5 - set 1)	맞춘답의 개수(TEST 5 - set 2)
Main Idea	/ 3	/ 3
Detail	/ 8	/ 8
Inference	/ 6	/ 6
전 체	/ 17	/ 17

문제유형과 signals

번호	기본문제유형	세부문제유형	Signals
1	Main Idea	Main Purpose Main Idea	국부적(지엽적인) or 너무 일반적인(광범위한) 사실은 오답, 시제 및 단수 / 복수 주의
2	Detail	Term/Definition/Origin	refer to, what we call, so-called, originate, come from
3	Detail	Example	such as, like, think of, imagine, Let's take, let's say~, say, example, for instance
4	Detail	Characteristic Advantage / Disadvantage Problem / Difficulty Similarity / Compare Difference / Contrast	그림, 음악, 문학, 무용, 영화, 연극, 공예, 조각 등 / unique, useful, interesting, faster, fascinating, intriguing, key feature, note, important 동물 멸종위기, 생명의 위협 / 환경적응 Problem, hitch, challenge, drawback, flaw, defect, extinct, destroyed early-later, prior to~, recent, in the past, nowadays, modern day, evolve
5	Detail	Cause / Reason / Evidence Result / Finding / Effect / Influence	study, research, experiment, project(find, discover, uncover, reveal, shed light on) / evidence, finding / pave the way, impact, set the stage for, application
6	Detail	Misunderstanding Correction/Surprising	once believed, but~ / seem out of this world, news to
7	Detail	Requirement / Condition	necessary, required, you need to, consideration, condition, premise, job experience,
8	Detail	Offer / Solution / Suggestion	Alternative, to solve, handle this problem, recommend, why don't you~, what about~, what can be done~, your best bet would be~,
9	Detail	Future action/Future topic	upcoming, next class, another lecture
10	Inference	Purpose / Intention Imply / Infer Opinion / Attitude Headset	Why... mention~ / What can be inferred~/ What... imply~ What... mean when...say~ 다시 들려주고 푸는 문제 check ,understanding, agree/disagree
11	Category	Introduce / Organize / Conclude Matching Ordering	How~ introduce? How is the lecture organized? Three types, two kinds of, first, second, finally step, stage, phase , and then, divide into~

오답정리표 : TEST 5

정답

번 호	문제 유형	틀린 답번호	오답유형	출제의도파악 (문제 및 정답 요약)
sample	Purpose	TEST5-15	T1	교수가 Wood Thrush를 언급한 이유는 → 동물의 Displacement activities가 주변 환경으로부터 어떤 영향을 받는지에 대한 예
1	Main Purpose Main Idea Introduce Organize Conclusion			
2	Term Definition Origin			
3	Example			
4	Characteristic Advantage Disadvantage Problem Difficulty Similarity Compare Difference Contrast			

#				
5	Cause, Reason, Evidence Result, Finding, Effect, Influence			
6	Misunderstanding Correction Surprising			
7	Requirement Condition			
8	Offer Solution Suggestion			
9	Future action Future topic			
10	Purpose Intention Imply Infer Opinion Attitude Headset			
11	Introduce Organize Conclude Matching Ordering			

www.usherin.usher.co.kr

USHER
iBT TOEFL
INTERMEDIATE LISTENING
Note Taking

Note taking TEST 1 Set1-C (#1)

U. accounting dept.
 paper on net profits of Google: impressive
recently feel strong need to switch majors Q1
enter college하기 전, research → accounting이 나한테 맞겠다!
                    but doubting decision
                     business management로 바꿀까 고민중

grades. participation X bad Q5
academic performance가 이유 X
amount of math required. takes more time than b.m. Q2
Job prospects? → 아직 안봄
accounting : 有 variety of options.
exp. in finance. Global marketing. Etc. → (accounting graduates)
                          likely to get hired
        ex) financial analyst/auditor/financial manager …
Q3 B.M: broad & general. X a specialist. ∴ D↓
                    easier to secure jobs

B.M : X ⊕ move.
 job prospects 말고도 many other aspects: examinations, $, etc.
switching major: X easy.
take time & do more research 하고 결정 Q4

TEST 1 Set1-C (#2)

University accounting department.
 paper on net profits of Google: impressive
recently feel strong need to switch majors Q1
enter college하기 전, research 했을 때 → accounting이 나한테 맞겠다고 판단.
　　　　　　　　　　　　　　but doubting decision
　　　　　　　　　　　　　　　business management로 바꿀까 고민중

grades. participation 안 나쁜데? Q5
academic performance가 이유가 아님
amount of math required(많음) takes more time than business management Q2
Job prospects? → 아직 안봄
accounting: variety of options in career paths 있음
회사들이 experience in finance. global marketing 등 경험 있는 사람 구직 할때
　　　　　　→ accounting graduates likely to get hired
　　　　　　ex) financial analyst/auditor/financial manager …
Q3 Business Management: broad & general. X a specialist. ∴ D ↓
　　　　　　　　　　　easier to secure jobs

Business Management로 전공 바꾸는 건 not a positive move.
 job prospects 말고도 many other aspects 고려해야 해 : examinations, $, etc.
switching major : not easy.
→ take time & do more research 하고 결정할게요 Q4

Note taking TEST 1 Set1-L1 (#1)

Ice ages (past few m yrs) (ex. Permian. Ordo ~) 多 glaciers
　theory
　　　compelling exp for end of 공룡 era
　humans: interglacial period ← ice ages 사이 (glaciers → polar regions)
　　　　　　　　　　　　　　　　(+) mild climate

last ice age (Quaternary ~ (?)): 10,000 yrs ago에 끝남.
有evidence that another ice age is coming
greenhouse gases … Global warming/temp ↑

Q6　int. glac. Period 인지 어떻게 알아?
　ice ages occur regularly. <u>Pattern</u> 있을꺼야
　　coral reefs and glaciers
　　… ice sheets formed/receded every 10,000 yrs

ocean → ice sheers → water level & temp ↓ → coral reefs : dry land → killed/stop growing
ice age → int. period : coral sheets 새로자람

　　　∴ dating of coral reef growth 가능. <u>crucial tool</u>
Q2　<u>determine how old each layer is.</u>
　　<u>analyze chem (ex. uranium isotopes)</u>

　　　∴ coral growth regular
　　　1st layer: 500　　2nd: 300
　　　　　　interval = 200

　　　∴ figure out ice age: how long & how often
　　　　but 이 theory very recent idea

　　other theories: plate tectonics … (earthquakes & volcanic eruptions)
　　　　　　　　　　movements → Δ ocean currents (+) wind patterns … ice age.
　　Q: theory = "ice age random"　∴ ↓ random
　　A: yes. Missing critical point (regularity*)
　　M theory: subtle oscillations → regular ice ages.
　　　1920s: Earth's rotation & orbit = major factors by calculating fluctuations

Q4　① Δ angle of E's tilt = 3°/41,000 yrs
　　More tilt = extreme summer/winter
　　Less　　milder

Q3　<u>Small fluctuations …　effects. How?</u>
　→　perplexing & intricate systems
　小 변화도　大 Δ로

Q4　② E's orbit around sun = elliptical
　　E & S 가장 가까울 때 : (present) Jan　　milder summers in
　　11,000 yrs ago: July. Extreme summers/winters
　　→ climate change
　　　(+) impact on formation & ebbing of ice sheets
　　　　　cooler summers → snow accumulate　　ice age
　　　　　warmer summer → ice sheets shrinkage　　int g period

　　(M theory:) convincing but overlooks cloud cover & v in solar E
Q5　└→ <u>by far the most accepted. but keep options open.</u>

TEST 1 Set1-L1 (#2)

Ice ages (in the past few few million years) (ex. Permian. Ordovician Glaciation Periods)
   ↳ Earth covered with glaciers
Ice age theory = compelling explanation for end of 공룡 era
현재 humans: interglacial period = period between ice ages   glaciers → polar regions
                                                                  (+) mild climate

last ice age (Quaternary Glaciation): 10,000 years ago에 끝남.
有evidence that another ice age is coming
greenhouse gases … Global warming/temperature ↑

Q6 interglacial Period 인지 어떻게 알아?
ice ages occur regularly. Pattern 있을꺼야
 coral reefs and glaciers
… ice sheets formed/receded every 10,000 years

ocean → ice sheers → water level & temperature ↓ → coral reefs : dry land → killed/stop growing
ice age → interglacial period : coral sheets 새로자람

   ∴ dating of coral reef growth 가능. crucial tool
Q2 determine how old each layer is.
    analyze chemicals (ex. uranium isotopes)
    ∴ coral growth regular
    1st layer: 500   2nd: 300
              interval = 200

   ∴ figure out ice age: how long & how often
     but 이 theory는 very recent idea

other theories: plate tectonics … earthquakes & volcanic eruptions
                  movements → change ocean currents & wind patterns … ice age.
Q: theory = "ice age random" 이라고 주장하지 않나요? ∵ earthquakes & volcanic eruptions random
   A: yes. Missing critical point (regularity*)
Milankovitch theory: subtle oscillations → regular ice ages.
    1920s : found that Earth's rotation & orbit are major factors by calculating fluctuations
Q4 ① change in angle of earth's tilt = 3°/41,000 years
     More tilt = extreme summer/winter
     Less tilt = milder summer/winter
Q3 Small fluctuations … 大effects. How?
  → ∵ earth는 perplexing & intricate systems
   작은 fluctuations도 큰 변화로 이어질 수 있음
Q4 ② Earth's orbit around sun = elliptical
    Earth and sun 가장 가까울 때 ┌ present : January milder summers in northern hemisphere
                              └ 11,000 years ago July ∴ extreme summers and winters
   → climate change
     (+) impact on formation & ebbing of ice sheets
     Northern Hemisphere: cooler summers → snow accumulate ∴ ice age
                         warmer summer → ice sheets shrinkage ∴ interglacial period
Milankovitch theory: convincing but overlooks cloud cover & variation in solar energy
   Q5 ↳ by far the most accepted. but keep options open for other theories.

Note taking TEST 1 Set 1-L2 (#1)

drama class
how structure & stage relate
   beg. of theater development
    1st theater : 5c BCE by Greeks
      outdoors. top of a hill. natural scenery ★
       오늘 theater의 basic element ≐ ancient times
      Q1 today : sim & diff. certain things unchanged / modified / abandoned

where choruses performed : orchestra (dancing place)
      ancient times : dance & sing on stage (+) commentary
                           (what char were doing / thinking)
     ↳ primary role : interaction w/ audience
       importance ↓ over time
     ↳ involvement so ★. 有 distinct personality. (Aristotle)
                   Q2 有 active role in drama

Politis : action scenes abridged
   bull killed Politis : pronounced dead by messenger
   intense fighting scene 생략. ??
  Q6 곧 answer 할게
Stage / skene (Greek) - ① structure only
                 - ② structure (+) stage (우리 수업 정의)
   ↳ evolved
     wooden platform → ornate & decorative
  est. of theater … Q3 background scenery

ex) front wall of building = temple or palace
   problem : X tech to Δ background for every scene
   1 decorated skene로 entire play 쭉
     ↳ ∴ impractical to portray every single scene
       (+) events condensed into words
        X visual images
      ∴ Politis 죽는 장면 → messenger
    other examples 보여줄게 next lesion

seating area : theatron
   ironic : theatron = "seeing place"
   多 rows, 14,000 spectators
   위에 있는 人 : X watch. Only hear
   theatron ≒ bowl. Seats spreading outwards / upwards.
        sometimes ▽
  Q5 bowl shape : effective. Capture sound.
             efficiently delivered ↑
some ppl put emphasis on today's theater (+) overlook ancient
   If 옛날 theater X → then 오늘 theater X

drama class

last class : how structure & stage relate

beginning of theater development

   1st theater : 5c BCE by Greeks

     outdoors. top of a hill. natural scenery incorporated into setting.

   오늘 theater의 basic element = ancient times

   Q1 today : similarity & differences. certain things that remained unchanged/modified/abandoned

     where choruses performed : orchestra (= "dancing place")

       ancient times : dance & sing on stage & commentary

             (what characters were doing/thinking)

        ↳ primary role: interaction with audience

          importance ↓ over time

        ↳ involvement so significant. " 有 distinct personality" - Aristotle

               Q2 有 active role in drama

Politis : action scenes abridged

     bull killed Politis: pronounced dead by messenger

  intense fighting scene 생략. 어떻게 된거에요?

Q6 → 곧 answer 할게

   Stage / skene (Greek) - ① structure only

                 - ② structure (+) stage (우리 수업 정의)

      ↳ evolved

         wooden platform → ornate & decorative

  establishment of theater ⋯ Q3 background scenery

ex) front wall of building = temple or palace

  problem : no technology to change background for every scene

    1 decorated skene로 entire play 동안 쭉 쓰임

      ↳ ∴ impractical to portray every single scene

        (+) events have to be condensed into words

          X visual images

      ∴ Politis 죽는 장면 → messenger

      other examples 다음시간에 보여줄게

seating area : theatron

Q4 ironic ∵ theatron = "seeing place"

   多 rows. 14,000 spectators

   위에 있는 사람 : 보지 않고 Only hear

   theatron ≒ bowl. Seats spreading outwards / upwards.

         sometimes semicircular

Q5 bowl shape: effective. capture sound.

         efficiently delivered it upwards

  some people put emphasis on today's theater & overlook ancient

   옛날 theater 없었으면 오늘 theater도 없음

Note taking TEST 1 Set2-C (#1)

USHER

paper on wall street crash (1929) Great Depression

책: "Time of Great Struggle"

→ ref pgs : damaged. Q5 can't decipher

another copy X. 그게 only copy.

ref pgs 없으면 can't finish assignment

online? other sources?

내일까지!

order 하면 take too long

track 해서 다른 library에 있나 볼께

Q4 ① New York

얼마나 걸려요?

내일 but X know 어떤 delays can happen

Q2 experienced similar issues

다른 방법으로 받을 순 X?

usually X personal favors but former colleague가 거기서 근무. will ask.

fax → 사서 → 학생

시차 eastern time. Q4 지금 very late there.

그럼 언제?

library 지금 X open. but 有 home #

거기에도 없으면 노답

Q3 여기서 다른 책들 찾아봐.

문자 남겨주세요. 번호 여기에 남겨

paper on wall street crash (1929) Great Depression

Q1 책: "Time of Great Struggle"

→ reference pages : damaged. Q5 can't decipher

another copy 없음. 그게 only copy.

ref pages 없으면 can't finish assignment

online에서 자료 찾아봤어? other sources?

과제 내일까지! order 하면 take too long

track 해서 다른 library에 있나 볼게

Q4 1권 in a library in New York

얼마나 걸려요?

내일까지 올걸. but don't know 어떤 delays can happen

Q2 → 전에 experienced similar issues

다른 방법으로 받을 순 없나요?

usually personal favors 안들어주는데 former colleague가 거기서 근무. will ask.

fax → 사서 → 학생

(시차) eastern time. Q4 지금 very late there.

그럼 언제?

library 지금 closed. but former colleague home number 있음

거기에도 없으면 노답

Q3 여기서 다른 책들 찾아봐.

문자 남겨주세요. 번호 여기에 남겨

Note taking TEST 1 Set2-L1 (#1)

1st 2 layers of ocean & marine life

  today: last layer. deep-zone layer

    - dangerous

    - ↓ level of oxygen.

    - ↑ water pressure

    - X light

      = X vision

  produce chem light - bioluminescence

  Q2 → bacteria? X

      produce own light.

      대부분: light = blue. but other colors도 有

      no visual sense 아니에요? X, 有. limited. only detect blue light

      dragon fish: red light (大 advantage)

Q1 (+) of bio- (usefulness - protection)

  active & passive defense strategy

  Ex) crystal jellyfish - influential in med field.

        Q3 chem resp for light generation

          → locate cancerous tumor

  detect threat → flash light at pred

  active defense (2 theories)

  ① to seem daunting, scare off

  ② exposes pred to its own pred

  Q4 experiment : artificially recreated flashes of jellyfish.

      → squid followed flashes

passive defense strategy

  Q5 - used to avoid encountering predators

  Q6 (- camouflage : conceal from pred. Δ color

      - bio~ works similarly

    sea anemones: use conspicuous colors. deliver warning message.

TEST 1 Set2-L1 (#2)

first 2 layers of ocean & marine life

today: last layer. deep-zone layer

- dangerous
- low level of oxygen.
- high water pressure
- no light
    = no vision

produce chemical light - bioluminescence

Q2 → bacteria? X

박테리아가 아니라 produce own light.

대부분: light = blue. but other colors도 있음

no visual sense 아니에요? no, 있음 but limited. only detect blue light

dragon fish: red light (huge advantage)

Q1 benefits of bioluminescence (usefulness - protection)

active & passive defense strategy

ex) crystal jellyfish - influential in medical field.

Q3 chemical responsible for light generation

→ locate cancerous tumor

detect threat → flash light at predator

active defense (2 theories)

① to seem daunting, scare off predators

② exposes predator to its own predator

Q4 experiment: artificially recreated flashes of jellyfish.

→ squid followed flashes

passive defense strategy

Q5 - used to avoid encountering predators

Q6 - camouflage: conceal from predators. change color
   - bioluminescence works similarly

sea anemones: use conspicuous colors. deliver warning message.

Note taking TEST 1 Set2-L2 (#1)

cartoons - archaeological elements
   misconceptions - image of archaeologists?
        Q2 → 여기저기 dig. X require sophisticated skill.
          → 맞아 but 사실은 그렇지 X
            a lot more professional. Includes high-tech tools
   institutions devoted   effort - dev tech
     - particle detector - muon detector
     다른 inventions but today's focus: muon detector
Q1 muon detector - uses muons (result from cosmic rays)
        cosmic rays collide w/ E's atmosphere → subatomic particles로 break = muons
muons - highly stimulated & energized   Q3 ∴ can pass through 고체
               → create visual image
               ≒ photograph
ex) excavation of ancient temple/Egyptian pyramid
   pass through dense materials 할 때 muons lose E
   impediment 많이 penetrate → E 많이 lose

chamber → temple walls
    chamber : lighter than temple walls
         → reflect more muons

past: 有 risk of damaging artifacts. ∴ X sophisticated tools
  muon detector 有 ⋯ X damage while excavating
since invention → 多 modifications
earliest form: used when looking for burial chambers. Egyptian pyramids. Giza (1967)
   2 major (-)
    Q4 1) only functional beneath the object
      X work at the side
    2) big & heavy
Today : X perfect
   Q5 issues. ½ yr to produce an image
   Japanese scientists working on interiors of volcanoes.
     X 다른 방법. best tool we have for now. Q6

TEST 1 Set2-L2 (#2)

cartoons - archaeological elements
  misconceptions - image of archaeologists?
            Q2 → 여기저기 dig. doesn't require sophisticated skill.
              → 맞아 but 사실은 그렇지 않아
                a lot more professional. Includes high-tech tools
institutions devoted tremendous efforts - develop technology
  - particle detector - muon detector
      有 다른 inventions 있지만 but today's focus: muon detector
Q1 muon detector - uses muons (result from cosmic rays)
        cosmic rays collide with Earth's atmosphere
         → subatomic particles로 break
           이게 바로 muons
muons - highly stimulated & energized
      Q3 ∴ can pass through 고체 → create visual image
                ≒ photograph
  ex) excavation of ancient temple/Egyptian pyramid
    pass through dense materials 할 때 muons lose Energy
    impediment 많이 penetrate → Energy 많이 lose

chamber → temple walls
      chamber: lighter than temple walls
              → reflect more muons

  past : always at risk of damaging artifacts. ∴ no sophisticated tools
  with muon detector ⋯ avoid damage while excavating
  since invention → 많은 modifications 거침

earliest form: used when looking for burial chambers.
        Egyptian pyramids. Giza (1967)
  2 major drawbacks :   1) only functional beneath the objet
                Q4   doesn't work at the side
                     2) big & heavy
Today : still imperfect
    Q5 有 issues 있음. ½ year 걸림 to produce an image
    Japanese scientists working on interiors of volcanoes. Q6
    다른 방법 없음. best tool we have for now.

Note taking TEST 2 Set1-C (#1)

수학 prof. & S.

Q1 나 찾음? 응 job offer. new program. math nights.
　　　　　　　　　　　　　　└→ schools host math-related
　　　　　　　　　　　　　　　　games. parents & kids.
　　　　　　　　　　　　　　　　Loved it when young

enjoyed? helped improve math skills?
　→ was horrible & loathed math before attending
　　ironic ∵ math major
　　Δ the way I looked at math
　　parents supportive of math major decision

바로 그거야. Q2 help figure out future. teaching math concepts.

intriguing. math puzzles만? X concerned about $

Q3 gaining math teaching 경험 ★. puzzles X 도움
　→ X worry. explain math concepts → kids & parents.
　　level of math taught in school ↑

Q5 7th grade math level 수준정도
　　└→ X underestimate. high level - graphing. prob.

부모: 아이들 가르치기 힘듦

but 나 바쁨

15h/semester

X bad.

언제까지 결정?

ASAP. Q4 ∵ complete list of workers 다음주까지 → administrator (sign & approve)

Priority. 종 inquired about job.

TEST 2 Set1-C (#2)

수학 professor & student 대화

Q1 저 찾았어요? 응. job offer. new program. Launch : math nights.
　　　　　　　　　　　　　　　　　　　　↳ schools host math-related
　　　　　　　　　　　　　　　　　　　　　　games.
　　　　　　　　　　　　　　　　　　　　　parents & kids 같이 참여
　　　　　　　　　　　　　　　　　　　　　　Loved it when young

　enjoyed it? helped improve math skills?
　　　→ was horrible at math & loathed math before attending
　　　　ironic : since currently a math major
　　　　changed the way I looked at math
　　　　parents supportive of decision to major in math

바로 그거야 : Q. to help kids figure out future & teach math concepts.
　　　intriguing. math puzzles만 풀어요? not concerned about money
　　　Q3 want to gain math teaching experience
　　　　　solving kids' puzzles doesn't help
　　　→ don't worry. explain math concepts to kids & parents.
　　　　　level of math taught in school : higher
　　　Q5 7th grade math level 정도의 수준
　　　　↳ underestimate하면 안돼. high level – graphing. probability
　　　　부모 : 아이들 가르치기 힘듦

but 나 바쁨
　15h/semester만 하면 돼
　not bad 하네요
　언제까지 결정해야돼요?
　　As soon as possible. Q4 ∵ have to complete list of workers
　　　　　　　　　　　by next week
　　　　　　　　　　　　→ administrator (sign & approve)
　　Priority. many people inquired about the job.

Note taking   TEST 2   Set1-L1 (#1)

USHER

popular English authors of 19c (ex. Charles Dickens)

Q1 accessibility of novels

    classics at the time : v expensive

    $ required to buy 1 book = a laborer's avg. weekly wage

    high cost ∴ triple deckers
- single book published in 3 volumes
  - Q2 ex) Arthur Conan Doyle. Sherlock Holmes
- discouraged Brit readers from purchasing novels
- publishers : "X good place to launch business"

        ex) Moby Dick : $1.50 (America)

                    $7.80 (England)

Q3 lending library: annual fee. Some: "ridiculous" but good deal

    Mudie's : largest national company

        有 branches in major cities
- 책 대량 구매.
- brilliant ∴ benefits & smart enough to take advantage of triple deckers

        (3V ∴ x3 profit)
- huge purchases ∴ great influence over publishers' novel selections
- conservative. Publishers avoid novels w/ possibly offensive content

Q6 - 大 power of selection. Influential

Serial Publication Form
- novels divided into chapters

Q4 each published weekly / monthly in magazine / newspaper

    (chronological order)
- caused authors to write longer novels

    ∵ got paid by # of episodes
- Charles Dickens came up w/ new version of S.P.F

    simplified → illustrations/ad (+) chapters

Q5 - criticism : cliffhangers. suspenseful endings로 대부분 끝남

    but Charles Dickens : X cliffhangers. cinematic effects.

        more settled endings.

        ∴ praised by public. attracted readers.

popular English authors of 19th century (ex. Charles Dickens)

Q1 accessibility of novels

  classics at the time : very expensive

  money required to buy one book = a laborer's average weekly wages

  high cost due to triple deckers
    ↳ single book published in 3 volumes
     Q2 ex) Arthur Conan Doyle, Sherlock Holmes
    ↳ discouraged British readers from purchasing novels
    ↳ publishers : "England is not a good place to launch business"
     ex) Moby Dick : $1.50 (America)
          $7.80 (England)

Q3 lending library : annual fee. Some thought it was ridiculous but was still a good deal

  Mudie's: largest national company
    had branches in major cities
   ↳ 책 대량 구매
   ↳ brilliant ∵ benefits & smart enough to take advantage of triple deckers
       (3 volumes ∴ 3 times as much profit)
   ↳ huge purchases ∴ great influence over publishers' novel selections
   ↳ conservative. publishers avoid novels with possibly offensive content
 Q6 ↳ huge power of selection. Influential

Serial Publication Form
 ↳ novels divided into chapters
 Q4 each published weekly / monthly in magazine / newspaper
   (chronological order)
 ↳ caused authors to write longer novels
   ∵ got paid by the number of episodes
 ↳ Charles Dickens came up with new version of Serial Publication Form
   Simplified it to only illustrations / advertisements (+) chapters
Q5 ↳ criticism : cliffhangers. suspenseful endings로 대부분 끝남
   but Charles Dickens : X cliffhangers. cinematic effects.
     more settled endings.
     ∴ praised by public. attracted readers.

Note taking TEST 2 Set1-L2 (#1)

Q1 interaction of pred & prey (+) effects. survival methods.
    apex predators (tigers & lions) 빼고 有 natural predators
  Today: ecosystem
      └▹ where wild organisms interact
      └▹ ≒ communities
      └▹ sig role in ecology
  effects of predation
Q2 animals' predatory nature → populations
                      → shaping biodiversity
  food chain : herbivore (vegan) → plants
              carnivore (meat-eating)
       ★ for healthy balance btw populations
     Δ animal behavior ≒ Δ ecosystem
      ex) X natural predators → cease to employ survival mechanism
                      x pressure
Q3 suddenly introduced : immed. terminated.
            X prep to use defense mechanism.
            → eaten
            <u>or</u> force themselves to modify original behaviors/adapt new ones
     "predation risk effects"
     → 有 example?
     → Yellowstone National Park (1872)
        protect landscape & wildlife
     Q4 → protection limited (ex. carnivores X protected)
    → Continually hunted
      (wolves. coyotes. etc.)
  (1962) wolves: wiped out
      ∴ elk (prey) range of activity ↑
       →herbivores
     ∴ range of food ↑
  aspen seedlings: main food source
    → devoured
    ∴ never → 🌳
Q5 🌳↓ … birds : (-) affected
      ↳ lost habitats. biodiversity ↓
  researchers: "mission failing"
Q6 ∴ reintroduced wolves (1995)
  wolves absent → balance re-established.
    elk → more nimble & attentive. Activity range ↓
      biodiversity restored.

TEST 2 Set1-L2(#2)

Q1 interaction of predator & prey (+) effects. survival methods.
apex predators (tigers & lions) 빼고 natural predators 있음.
Today: ecosystem
　　└▸ where wild organisms interact
　　　└▸ analogous to communities
　　　└▸ significant role in ecology
effects of predation
animals' predatory nature ⎡ affects populations   ⎫ Q2
　　　　　　　　　　　　　⎣ shapes biodiversity   ⎭
food chain :
　⎡ carnivore (meat-eating)
　⎢ ↓
　⎢ herbivore (vegan)
　⎢ ↓
　⎣ plants
　└▸ important for healthy balance between populations
　　changes in animal behavior ≒ changes in ecosystem
　　　ex) no natural predators → cease to employ survival mechanism
　　　　　　　　　　　　　because no pressure
　　　↳ suddenly introduced : immediately terminated.
　　　　　　　　　　unprepared to use defense mechanism.
Q3　　　　　　　　　→ eaten
　　　　　　　　or force themselves to modify original behaviors/adapt new ones
　　　　　　　　"predation risk effects"
　　　　　　　　→ 有 example?
　　　　　　　　→ Yellowstone National Park (1872)
　　　　　　　　　protect landscape & wildlife
　　　　　　　　　　→ protection limited (ex. carnivores X protected)
　　　　　　　　　　→ Continually hunted (wolves, coyotes, etc.)
　　　　　　　　　(1962) wolves : wiped out
　　　　　　　　　　∴ elk (prey) range of activity ↑
　　　　　　　　　└▸ herbivores
　　　　　　　　　　∴ range of food ↑
　　　　　　　　　aspen seedlings : main food source
　　　　　　　　　└▸ devoured
　　　　　　　　　　∴ never mature into trees
Q5 trees ↓ … birds : negatively affected
　　　　└▸ lost habitats, biodiversity ↓
　　researchers : "mission failing"
　　Q6 ∴ reintroduced wolves (1995)
　　wolves absent → balance re-established.
　　　elk → more nimble & attentive, activity range ↓
　　　　biodiversity restored.

Note taking TEST 2 Set2-C (#1)

USHER

왜왔어? beach X? Q5

    last semester : donating stuff X take home.

             left abruptly. 문 앞에 box

  summer courses 들은 사람 used. Thank You letter.

     Q2 → 다 버려진줄. Q1 donation formalize before summer break.

        다른 학생들도 same problem.

             too heavy for plane. 물건들 throw away/leave in dorm.

           (useful - 옷, 책, dishes)

Q3 charity organizations 연락.

    그 중 하나: pickups every semester

    sell → profits → children. Africa

    talk to admin? yes.

    meeting. sat. w/ managers.

    X complicated procedure

    spread word - flyers & notices?

  Q4 fastest way = ad in U newspaper

    name & #. will contact ASAP

왜왔어? beach에 안갔구? Q5

　last semester: donating stuff that I couldn't take home.
　　　　　　left abruptly. 문 앞에 box에 두고 감.
　　summer courses 들은 사람이 씀. Left Thank You letter.
　Q2 → 다 버려진줄. Q1 donation formalize before summer break 하러옴
　다름 학생들도 face same problem.
　　　　too heavy for plane한 물건들 throw away/leave in dorm.
　　　　　(useful한 things – 옷, 책, dishes)
　Q3 charity organizations 연락.
　　　그 중 하나: pickups every semester
　　　sell → profits → children in Africa
　　　talk to administration? yes.
　　　meeting this Saturday with managers.
　　　not a complicated procedure
　　　spread word – flyers & notices?
　　　Q4 ↳ fastest way = advertisement in university newspaper
　　　　　name & number 남겨두고가. will contact as soon as possible

Note taking TEST 2 Set2-L1 (psychology) (#1)

final term paper.
approach problems : spend hours (solution) → step back (break)
　　　　　　　　　　　　　　　　　　　　↳ computer. dog
　　　　　　　　　　　　　→ sudden light bulb = "insight"
Isaac Newton - ★ mathematician & physicist (1600s)
　　🍎 story : moon's orbit figure out → 산책

　🌳　Ⓕ (gravity) = moon's orbit 원인

Q6 X practical effort. simply 🍎목격. "insight" Q2
　experiments : - word puzzles. 2 unusual patterns (brain activity)
　　　① frontal lobe
　　　　- forehead
　　　　- decision-making
　　　　- activated. Preparatory phase
　　　　　other sensory areas shut down
　　　　　　Q3 시각 & 청각 cortexes slowed
　　　　　　　→ 잠시 shut down.
　　　　　　　∵ could distract
　　　② search phase
　　　control speech & lang f(x)
　　　just before brain part activated.
　　　　　　: rhythm / waves
　　Q4 X consensus on why generated.
　　　→ most accepted : caused by formation
　　　　　　　　　　　　of new links btw cells
　　　≒ telephone network
　　　try to solve problem → fail → 포기 → brain relax
　　　　　　　　→ γ wave 생성
　　Q5 → build network btw remote cells
　　　　↑ network … faster solution

TEST 2 Set2-L1 (psychology) (#2)

final term paper.
approach problems : spend hours (to find solution) → step back (break)
　　　　　　　　　　　　　　　　　　　　　　↳ computer. dog
　　　　　　　　　　　　　　→ sudden light bulb ≒ "insight"
Isaac Newton - prestigious mathematician & physicist (1600s)
　　apple story : trying to figure out moon's orbit → 산책

　　　　Force (gravity) = moon's orbit 원인

Q6 no practical effort. simply apple 목격. ("insight") Q2
　　experiments - word puzzles. 2 unusual patterns (brain activity)
　　　　① frontal lobe
　　　　　　- forehead에 위치
　　　　　　- decision-making
　　　　　　- activated. Preparatory phase
　　　　　　　　other sensory areas shut down
　　　　　　　　　　Q3 시각 & 청각 cortexes slowed
　　　　　　　　　　　　→ 잠시 shut down.
　　　　　　　　　　　　∵ could distract
　　　　② search phase
　　　　　　control speech & language functions
　　　　　　just before brain part activated.
　　　　　　　　: gamma rhythm / waves
　　Q4 no consensus on why generated.
　　　　→ most accepted: caused by formation of new links between cells
　　　　　　≒ telephone network
　　　　　　　try to solve problem → fail → 포기
　　　　　　　→ brain relax
　　Q5　↳ gamma wave 생성 → build network between remote cells
　　　　　More network … faster solution

Note taking TEST 2 Set2-L2 (archaeology) (#1)

social Δs. ancient ppl.
today : 1 major social Δ
    most sig Δ : nomadic lifestyle → sedentary
    cause : Δs in climate conditions
Q2 glaciers → polar regions. drastic climate Δ
        ∴ 정착 & cultivate
    focus : E. Mediterranean (Lebanon)
      → infertile. X suitable for habitation.
      18,000 yrs ago : grasslands & woods.
          大 convenience
      5,000 yrs ago : climate Δ. rainfall ↑ ⋯ precipitation ↑
          ⊖ richer / fertile soil & ecosystem
Q6 physical evidence : houses
    architectural remains ⋯ confirm existence. settlement
   Natufians
    → housing settlements: uniform. identical. rigid structure. semicircle

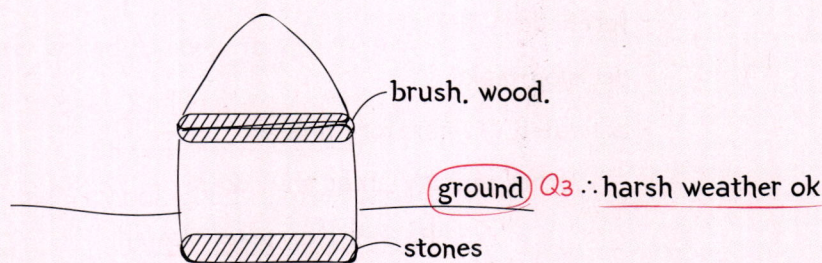

floors : holes ⋯ posts & beams (roof support)
→ intricate ∴ sedentary lifestyle

tools – harvest
   region : Q4-D 大 rich soil. 多 cereal grains
      Q4-B ∴ harvest wheat. oats ← stone mortars
      Q4-A tools : harvest (o). planting (x)
        unintentional planting ⋯ continual reliance
          → wind.
          ∴ X actual planting.
   Q5 hunting (food source)
      bones (migratory birds. Gazelles)
      winter ←   → spring/summer

      ∴ N – permanent settlement (E. Med region)

TEST 2 Set2 -L2 (archaeology) (#2)

social changes. ancient people.
today : 1 major social change
　　　most significant change : nomadic lifestyle → sedentary
　　　cause : changes in climate conditions
　　Q2 glaciers → polar regions. drastic climate change
　　　　　∴ 정착 & cultivate
　　　　focus : Eastern Mediterranean (today's Lebanon)
　　　　　↳ infertile. not suitable for habitation.
　　　　　18,000 years ago : grasslands & woods.
　　　　　　　　　huge convenience
　　　　　5,000 years ago : climate change. rainfall ↑ … precipitation ↑
　　　　　　　　= richer/fertile soil & ecosystem
Q6 physical evidence : houses
　　　architectural remains … confirm existence, settlement
　　　Natufians
　　　　↳ housing settlements : uniform. Identical. rigid structure. semicircle

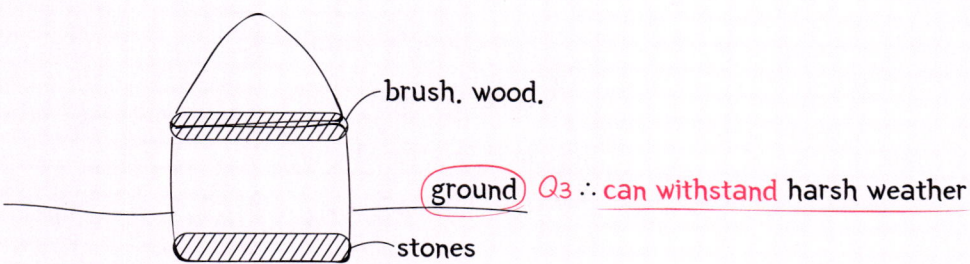

floors : holes … posts & beams (roof support)
→ intricate ∴ sedentary lifestyle

tools - harvest
　　region : Q4-D huge areas of rich soil. abundant cereal grains
　　　　Q4-B ∴ harvest wheat. oats ← stone mortars
　　　　Q4-A tools : harvest (o). planting (x)
　　　　　　unintentional planting … continual reliance
　　　　　　　↳ wind.
　　　　　　　∴ didn't do actual planting.
　　　Q5 hunting (food source)
　　　　bones (migratory birds. Gazelles)
　　　　　winter ←　　　　　→ spring/summer

　　∴ Natufians - permanent settlement (Eastern Mediterranean region)

Note taking — TEST 3 Set1-C (#1)

brain research

Q1 좌/우 diff f(x). (daydreaming)

→ commissural fibers. "corpus callosum"

signals

split? yes.   ex) Sperry 1960s. Noble Prize (Psych/Med) - 1981

Q2 epilepsy (seizures) → split brain

X other options

surgery: successful.

side effects: insuff speech prod.

why? Communication btw hemispheres X?

eye sight normal

(X recog left visual field.

(O recog right   "

Q3 (left hem. malfunctioning?

   (→ X. left hem - right v.f.

             R - L

each hem - specialize in certain tasks

ex) Q4 L : analytical. verbal

R : spatial, music, creativity

communication X

symptom 평생? → X.   ability to learn.

brain research

Q1 좌/우뇌 serve different functions 설명 듣고 started (daydreaming)

→ commissural fibers. "corpus callosum"
    signals 주고 받음

split 가능? yes.   ex) Roger Walcott Sperry 1960s.
                  Noble Prize (Psychology / Medicine) - 1981
        Q2 cure for epilepsy (seizures) → split brain
           no other options
           surgery: successful.
           but patient had side effects : insufficient speech production
       why? Communication between hemispheres cut-off 때문?
           eye sight normal
           (X recognize left visual field.
             O recognize right visual field.
      left hemisphere malfunctioning?
Q3 (→ 아님. left hemisphere - right visual field
          right hemisphere - left visual field

each hemisphere - specialize in certain tasks
  ex) Q4 left : analytical. verbal
      right : spatial, music, creativity
      communication disabled
      symptom 평생 안고 살았어요? → no, brain has ability to learn.

historical global climate Δ

12,900 yrs ago : Younger Dryas

Q2 ┌→ driving force
   │   lake. ―freshwater→ Atlantic Ocean
   └   Canada

   Oceanic currents disrupted.
   warmer temp.
   (+) calamity … extinction. mammals. Clovis ppl

Q1 Kennett : YD impact. Clovis comet

   comet fragments → N. America
   ① disrupt ocean currents (lake water)
   ② 35 genera extinct (comets…fire…animals + Clovis X)

   evidence?
   - soil (carbon): 16 sites
                                    → color
   Q3 ┌ nanodiamonds from (black mat)
      └ electron microscopes (electrostatic. electromagnetic lenses)
   → critical evidence ∵ F of asteroid impacts create

   (-) "impact signs missing ∵ 그 전에 fragmented"
        but impossible to X w/o trace
            ∴ asteroid occurrence prove X
   (-) X evidence of population ↓ / wildfires
            ∴ Clovis ppl & species X → invalid.

Q4 nanodiamonds?
   → common. found in non-impact sites

Q5 fundamentally wrong?
   → X. theories일뿐
   valid evidence X found yet ★

Q6 공룡 extinction : criticism   but evidence found.
   needs time.

TEST 3 Set1-L1 (#2)

historical global climate **change**

12,900 **years** ago: Younger Dryas

Q2 ├─ → driving force
   │   lake. ─freshwater─▷ Atlantic Ocean
   └─ Canada

   Oceanic currents disrupted.
   warmer temp**erature**.
   (+) calamity … extinction **of** mammals. Clovis **people**

Q1 Kennett: YD impact. Clovis comet

   comet fragments → **North** America
   ① disrupt ocean currents (lake water)
   ② 35 genera extinct (comets … fire … **demise of** animals + Clovis)
   evidence?
       - soil (**rich in** carbon): 16 sites → **distinctive** color
   Q3 ┌ nanodiamonds from (black mat)
      └ electron microscopes (electrostatic. electromagnetic lenses)
      → critical evidence ∵ **Force** of asteroid impacts create

(−) "impact signs missing ∵ **hit the ground**하기 전에 fragmented"
     but impossible to **vanish without** trace
         ∴ asteroid occurrence prove 하지 않음
(−) **no** evidence of population **decline** / wildfires
         ∴ Clovis **people** & species **extinction** → invalid.

nanodiamonds?
   → **more** common **than we think** ┐
      found in non-impact sites   ┘ Q4

Q5 fundamentally wrong?
      → X. theories일뿐
      valid evidence **not** found **yet** ★

Q6 ex) 공룡 extinction: criticism 많았으나 evidence 결국 found.
        needs time.

Note taking TEST 3 Set1-L2 (#1)

USHER

designing computers ┌ exterior – simpler (sophistication)
　　　　　　　　　 └ interior
personal computer – diff color, shapes, sizes.
　　　　　　　　 – lighting mods, body fillers …
　　　　　　　　　 → trend

Q1 Tech design & How developers design / invent
　　　– philosophical aspects – Leonardo da Vinci
　　　　　　　　　　↳ talented 르네상스 artist.
　　　　　　　　　　　polymath, music …
　　　　　　　　　　　anatomy – blend of 철학, 과학, art.
　　　　　　Q2 ★ understanding of human needs & problems → design
　　　　　　Q6 philosophical & technological aspects

– tech design ┌ old
　　　　　　　└ new　computing : computing power/speed ↑, tech
　　　　　　　　　　　　　　　　: focus = satisfying ppl's needs & desires
　　　　　　　　　　　　　　　　　what ppl can do w/ computers
　　　　　　　　　　Q4 users' demand/desire
　　　　　　　　　　　　→ programs
　　　　　　　　　　　　- efficient
　　　　　　　　　　　　- useful
　　　　　　Q5 ┤ - manageable
　　　　　　　　　　　　- executable
　　　　　　　　　　　　→ user-friendly ★
　　　　　　　　　　　　　usability (+) usefulness
　　　　　　　　　　　　　expertise X
　　ex) term paper, research, info.
　　　　websites → X organized, frustrating
　　　　① info million clicks away
　　　　② unnecessary info.
　　　　　→ fail
　　Human – centered computing ★

TEST 3 Set1-L2 (#2)

designing computers ┌ exterior - simpler (in terms of sophistication)
　　　　　　　　　　└ interior
personal computer - different color, shapes, sizes.
　　　　　　　　 - lighting mods, body fillers …
　　　　　　　　→ growing trend

Q1 Tech design & How developers design / invent
　　- philosophical aspects - Leonardo da Vinci
　　　　　　　　　　↳ talented Renaissance artist.
　　　　　　　　　　　polymath, music, etc.
　　　　　　　　　　　anatomy - blend of philosophy, science, art.
　　　　　　　Q2 ★ understanding of human needs & problems → design
　　　　　　　　Q6 philosophical & technological aspects
　　- technological design ┌ old computing : computing power/speed ↑, technical specifications
　　　　　　　　　　　　　└ new computing : focus = satisfying people's needs & desires
　　　　　　　　　　　　　　　　what people can do with their computers
　　　　　　　　　　　Q4 users' demand/desire
　　　　　　　　　　　　　→ programs
　　　　　　　Q5 ┌ - efficient
　　　　　　　　 │ - useful
　　　　　　　　 │ - manageable
　　　　　　　　 └ - executable
　　　　　　　　　　　→ user-friendly ★
　　　　　　　　　　　usability (+) usefulness
　　　　　　　　　　　expertise ✗
　　　　　　　ex) term paper, research, information
　　　　　　　　　websites → unorganized, frustrating
　　　　　　　　　① information million clicks away
　　　　　　　　　② unnecessary information
　　　　　　　　　　→ fail
　　　　　　Human - centered computing ★

Note taking TEST 3 Set2-C (#1)

great game last night

State Championships

    improvement. team captain ··· team cooperation ↑

Q1 X participate in championship games

Q2 interview 날짜 = 떠나는 날짜 (겹침)

  internship interview. U ad agency

  reschedule? → X good impression as candidate

              popular & competitive position

Wed afternoon에 떠남

games : Thurs morning start

public transportation? → athletics dept would cover cost

bus schedule. 3am. other methods : transfer

X enough rest. **Q3** championship - 3 games. 1 each day.

                            → forgot

  miss first game해도 will be big help

  explain situation to agency → **Q5** X sense of inability. irresponsibility.

                                        internship chance rare

Q4 public transportation 더 알아볼게요 → 2nd game

TEST 3 Set2-C (#2)

great game last night

State Championships

　huge improvement. team captain 많은 이후 team cooperation improved

Q1 unable to participate in championship games

Q2 interview 날짜 = 떠나는 날짜 (겹침)

　internship interview. University advertising agency

　reschedule 할 수는 없어? → won't give good impression as candidate
　　　　　　　　　　　　　　　popular & competitive position

Wednesday afternoon에 떠남

games : Thursday morning start

public transportation? → athletics department would cover cost

bus schedule. 3am. other methods : transfer 많이 해야 됨

그렇게 되면 can't get enough rest.　Q3 championship - 3 games. 1 each day.
　　　　　　　　　　　　　　　　　　　→ forgot

　miss first game해도 will be big help

　explain situation to agency → Q5 don't want to give a sense of inability. irresponsibility.
　　　　　　　　　　　　　　　　internship chance rare

Q4 public transportation 더 알아볼게요 → 2nd game

Note taking TEST 3 Set2-L1 (#1)

Earth : 4.54b yrs old
　radiometric / radioactive dating ⋯ cosmic materials ages ≒ E's age
　　　　　　　　　　　　　　　　　　　　Q1 disputed

Lord Kelvin's theory
　- laws of thermodynamics —apply→ understanding of E
　- theory assumption : E molten state → solid body
　　　　　　　　　　　　　　= rock's melting point
　　　　　　　　　　　　　(600 ~ 1200°C)
　　　　　　　　　heat to outer space "thermal diffusion"
　　　　　　　ex) boil water (coffee)
　Q3　→ craving X → kettle freezer → temp ↓
　　　　　→ temp. gradient
　　　　　surface layer cool 1st
　　　law of heat transfer high temp —heat→ low temp
　Q2　∴ calculation : diff btw original & current temp.
　　　　→ E ≤ 100m yrs old

(-) sedimentation & erosion : take millions of yrs ∴ X make sense
　　errors in K's calculations
　　early 1900s : radioactivity & heat release from radioactive decay
　　→ discovered
Q4 (=) additional heat source - absent
　　but insignificant. ∴ X greatly affected
- assistant : John Perry (patron of employer)
　Q6 ↳ coup d'etat
　　　↳ discredit calculations (1895)
　　　↳ assumption (solid E) = wrong
　　　↳ Q5
　　　　　　crust
　　　　　liquid
　　　　semi-liquid ┘ thermal diffusion X happen. convection
　　　↳ hot material circulation
　　　　　heat → circular pathway. X outward diffusion
　　　　　　∴ cooling : slower
　　　↳ P's calculation (3b yrs) ≒ 4.54 b
　　　　　(+) lack of tech
　　　↳ X recog from contemp ∴ diff framework
　　　↳ continental drift proven ⋯ recog

TEST 3 Set2-L1 (#2)

Earth : 4.54 billion years old
   radiometric / radioactive dating … cosmic materials ages ≒ Earth's age
                                             Q1 disputed

Lord Kelvin's theory
  - laws of thermodynamics —apply to→ understanding of Earth
  - theory assumption : Earth molten state → solid body
                       = rock's melting point
                         (600 ~ 1200°C)
                          radiate heat to outer space "thermal diffusion"
                       ⎛ ex) boil water for coffee
                    Q3 ⎜   → craving went away → put kettle in freezer
                       ⎜   → temperature drop
                       ⎝   temperature gradient
                         surface layer cool first
                     ⎛ law of heat transfer high temperature —heat→ low temperature
                 Q2 ⎨ ∴ calculation : difference between original & current temperature
                     ⎝ → Earth's age no more than 100 million years old

(-) sedimentation & erosion : take millions of years
      ∴ Kelvin's calculation doesn't make sense
  errors in Kelvin's calculations
  early 1900s : radioactivity & heat release from radioactive decay
              → discovered
          Q4 (=) additional heat source - absent
          but considered insignificant. ∴ calculation not greatly affected
  - assistant : John Perry (patron of employer)
    Q6 → coup d'etat
      → discredit calculations (1895)
      → assumption (solid E) = wrong
      → Q5
             (crust / liquid / semi-liquid) ⎤ thermal diffusion doesn't happen. instead, convection
      → hot material circulation
         heat → circular pathway. ✗ outward diffusion
           ∴ cooling : slower
      → Perry's calculation (3 billion years) ≒ 4.54 billion years
         (+) lack of technology
      → didn't receive recognition from contemporaries ∵ whole different framework
      → continental drift proven 되고 recognized

Note taking — TEST 3 Set2-L2 (#1)

USHER

last class : legitimate theater = form of theatrical art
→ spoken words
X singing / dancing / music

GB's Licensing Act (1737) … restraints on media
limited permission to perform serious literary shows
(ex Romeo & Juliet)
theaters under govt control
aka illegitimate theater

Q1 Theatrical dev (US)
cultural Δ as N & S conflict ↓ after Civil War

Q2 Jobs ↑, rural ppl → cities (1870~1920)
(+) Int'l immigration … city population ↑
∴ urban productivity & incomes ↑

Q2 덜 힘든 jobs + more $ … leisure activities / 여행
(+) new era of theatrical arts
= "popular theater"
≒ illegitimate theater (serious plays rare)
→ V~ (main form)
 └→ origin : obscure
- described satirical songs (France)
- "voice of the city"
- "songs of the town"

Popular theater : 10 unrelated acts (wide spectrum)
= access to every type
Q3 ex) convenience store. "quality" X but range
taste 상관없이 다 =

Benjamin Franklin Keith
Gaiety Museum (Boston, 1883)
Bijou Theater
① continuous performances - doors open 24/7
role of ent = amuse ppl whenever
performers repeat acts
operate 12hrs daily
urban income ↑ : exploit through continuous perf.
① fill theater w/ ↑ ppl
② innovations
② extravagant decorations

success - policy of cleanliness & order (stern businessman)
rules ┌ **Q5** X profanity / offensive lang.
       │ **Q6** ∴ appeal to women & children
       └ audience X allowed to interrupt perf.
civil war era : low-brow behavior
→ educated appropriate theater behaviors

next class : entrepreneurs that followed

TEST 3 Set2-L2 (#2)

last class : legitimate theater = form of theatrical art
　　　　　　　　　　　　　→ spoken words
　　　　　　　　　　　　　X singing / dancing / music
　　　　Great Britain's Licensing Act (1737) ··· restraints on media
　　　　　　　　　　　limited permission to perform serious literary shows
　　　　　　　　　　　(ex. Romeo and Juliet)
　　　　　　　　　　　theaters under governmental control
　　　　　　　　　　　= "illegitimate theater"

Q1 Theatrical development in the United States
　　　huge culture changes as the North and South conflict waned after Civil War
Q2 Jobs increased. rural people → cities (1870~1920)
　　　　(+) International immigration ··· city population increased
　　　　∴ urban productivity & incomes increased
Q2 덜 힘든 jobs + more money ··· leisure activities / 여행
　　　　　　　　(+) new era of theatrical arts
　　　　　　　　= "popular theater"
　　　　　　　　≒ illegitimate theater (serious plays rare)
　　　　　　　　　→ Vaudeville (main form)
　　　　　　　　　　　↳ origin : obscure
　　　　　　　　　　　- described satirical songs (France)
　　　　　　　　　　　- "voice of the city"
　　　　　　　　　　　- "songs of the town"

Popular theater : 10 unrelated acts (wide spectrum)
　　　　　had access to every type
　　　Q3 ex) convenience store. "quality" products 없지만 wide range
　　　　　taste 상관없이 다 있었음

Benjamin Franklin Keith
　　Gaiety Museum (Boston. 1883)
　　Bijou Theater
　　　① continuous performances - doors always open
　　　　　　　　　　　　role of entertainment = to amuse people whenever
　　　② innovations　　　had performers repeat acts
　　　　　　　　　　　operate 12 hours daily
　　　　　　　　　　　urban income increase를 exploit through continuous performances
　　　　　　　　　　　　　① fill theater with more people
　　　　　　　　　　　　　② extravagant decorations

　success - policy of cleanliness & order (stern businessman)
　　　　rules ┌ Q5 forbade profanity/offensive language
　　　　　　　│ Q6 ∴ appeal to women & children
　　　　　　　└ audience not allowed to interrupt performances
　　　　　　　　civil war era : low-brow behavior
　　　　　　　　　→ educated appropriate theater behaviors

next class : entrepreneurs that followed

Note taking TEST 4 Set1-C (#1)

semester almost over. relaxing?
　　　→ X. Q1 final term papers due. overwhelmed.
　　　　　deadline extend 해줘서 thank you.
first draft X effort?
　　　→ X. ton of research. 봤어요?
yes.　few Qs. main theme?
　　　→ Q2 honeybees. communicating (+) magnetic field 활용법
　　　　　　　　　　　　　　　　　　　？
　　　　　　　　　　　　　　　　　navigate

　　　그니까 ① communicate ② navigate?
　　　　　→ yes
　　　　paper : vague
　　　2 types of dances to deliver messages.
　Q3 ┌ ① round dance : food source nearby
　　　└ ② waggle dance : food source far away from hive
　　　　→ food-location signals
　Q4 iron-rich granules in cells
　　　　→ sense magnetic field
　　　　≒ internal compass
　　　advice : paper lacks clear connection
　　　　　(btw communication & navigation)
　　　source - X academic.
　　　　　　misused concepts.
　　　　　　subjective.
　Q5 find another source.
　　　　　(+) clarify

semester almost over. relaxing?

→ no. Q1 final term papers due. overwhelmed.

deadline extend 해줘서 thank you.

first draft에 didn't put in effort?

→ no. did a ton of research. 읽어봤어요?

yes. have a few Questions. main theme?

→ Q2 honeybees. way of communicating (+) magnetic field 활용법

magnetic field 사용해서 communicate?

→ X. navigate

그러니까 ① communicate ② navigate?

→ yes

paper : vague

2 types of dances to deliver messages.

Q3 ｛ ① round dance : food source nearby
② waggle dance : food source far away from the hive

→ food-location signals

Q4 iron-rich granules in cells

→ sense magnetic field

≒ internal compass

advice : paper lacks clear connection

between communication & navigation

source - not academic.

a lot of misused concepts.

subjective.

Q5 find another source.

(+) clarify

Note taking TEST 4 Set1-L1 (#1)

어제 : solar system + contents
오늘 : Q1 2 galaxies - Milky Way. Sagittarius.
　　larger galaxies absorb stars from smaller galaxies.
　MW > S (×10,000)
　　↳ stars 빨려 들어감
Q6 gravitationally bound (x) fusing together (o)
　　　　　　　　　→ Evidence
　prev. researchers prove 못한 이유
Q2 ⎰ ex) shred 2 (=) paper
　　⎱ pure white → sort 불가능
　　 1 blue/1 red → sort 가능.
　galaxy study 하기 시작 : 구성. properties …
　　→ Q3 thermal E. (heat from infrared radiation / light)
　　　ex) detecting devices. bulky goggles
　　　　　　→ night vision … detect thermal radiation
　　　　　　temp determines radiation's color (blue ~ red)
　　　body-scanning process. measure temp
　Q4 (-) 눈으로 구분 못함.
　　infrared light = X within visible spectrum.
　　　　→ device required : infrared telescope.
　　　　　　≒ regular telescope
　　　　　　diff : location. infrared radiation ↓E
　　　　　　　　→ 다음시간. remind me ∵ ★
　composition of stars
　　→ peripheral space : diff.　unusual chem patterns
　　　　　　　　(X sync w/ MW)
　　　　　　　secondary source of chem comp
　　　　　　　　= Sagittarius Galaxy
　　→ how much absorbed 알아냄
　　　attractive F = gravitational F
　　　　↳　　≒ F btw Earth & Moon (but much stronger)
　　　↳ caused MW to absorb S
　　　　∴ S : elongated
　　　Q5 if continues : S 완전히 destroyed
　　　　→ galaxies are bound (x)
　　　　　ever-evolving (o)
　　　next time : contradictory point about solar system

어제 : solar system + contents
오늘 : Q1 2 galaxies - Milky Way. Sagittarius.
    larger galaxies absorb stars from smaller galaxies.
    Milky Way > Sagittarius (10,000 times bigger)
    ↑ stars 빨려 들어감
Q6 gravitationally bound (x) fusing together (o)
                → Evidence 있음
previous researchers prove 못한 이유
Q2 (ex) shred 2 identical stacks of paper
      pure white → sort 불가능
      1 blue/1 red → sort 가능.
galaxy study 하기 시작 : 구성. properties …
  → Q3 thermal energy. (heat from infrared radiation / light)
    ex) detecting devices. bulky goggles
          → night vision … detect thermal radiation
        temperature determines radiation's color (range : blue to red)
    body-scanning process. measure temperature
Q4 (-) 눈으로 구분 못함.
    infrared light = not within visible spectrum.
      → device required : infrared telescope.
          ≒ regular telescope
        difference : location. infrared radiation has lower energy
          → 다음시간에 remind me ∵ important
    composition of stars
      → peripheral space : different. contained unusual chemical patterns
        (didn't sync with the Milky Way)
        secondary source of chemical composition found
          = Sagittarius Galaxy
  → determined how much was absorbed
    attractive force = gravitational force
              ≒ force between Earth & Moon (but much stronger)
      ↳ caused the Milky Way to absorb Sagittarius
      ∴ Sagittarius : elongated
    Q5 if continues : Sagittarius 완전히 destroyed
      → galaxies are bound (x)
        ever-evolving (o)
    next time : contradictory point about solar system

Note taking TEST 4 Set1-L2 (#1)

Biomimetics : Q1 imitating natural components → commercial products
　　새 / 나비 : unique structures (features, scales)
　　　ex) Morpho 나비 : green / blue scales on wings
　　　　　　　→ pigmentation, structural coloration
　　　　　colors of plants : green (Q2 ∵ chlorophyll, green pigment in chloroplasts)
　　　　　　　　　↳ green wavelength reflected, X absorbed.
　　　　　　　　　　→ evidence X.
　　　　　　　　　assumption : green = det. to photosynthesis

Structural Coloration (schemochrome)
　　-Morpho 나비 ①Robert / Isaac 　②Thomas
　　　　　　　　　　　　　　　　↳ structural color : ┌ thin layers of films / scales
　　　　wings : rows of scales (+) gaps　　　　　　　　└ light

Q3 light hits → interact → absorb / reflect
　　blue reflected ∴ visible
- business ppl design 할 때 exploit
　　→ can eliminate toxic elements
- energy - efficient, X env. damaging　∵ X additional E consumption required
　　　　　　　　　　　　　　　(+) waterproof

Q4 wings : gaps filled w/ gas, water-barrier
　　　adhesive F : ┌ attraction btw droplets
　　　　　　　　　└ E water stick to solid
　　　　　　　∴ water → flatten out on smooth surfaces
　　　　　　　but Morpho 나비's wings : bumpy / rough (+) air in gaps
　　　　　　　　　　　　　　∴ X flatten out & slide off
　　　　　　　　　　　　　　(+) 먼지 같이 roll off
　　　　　　　ex) shirt manufacturers
　　　　　　　　　→ (=) principles
　　　　　Q6 (hamburger in S/C shirt
　　　　　　　　if) ketchup on shirt → same result

Q5 great promise for future
　　((-) (1) replicating aspects of natural mechanism
　　　　(2) understanding of phenomena
　　　　(3) ensure replication X work as impediment to thinking process
　　　　　→ original thinking barely involved
　　　　　　∵ observe → exploit

　　　　　　noteworthy benefits

TEST 4 Set1-L2 (#2)

Biomimetics : Q1 imitating natural components → commercial products
    새 / 나비 : unique structures (features, scales)
      ex) Morpho 나비 : green / blue scales on wings
            → pigmentation, structural coloration
               colors of plants : green (Q2 ∵ chlorophyll, green pigment in chloroplasts)
                      ↳ green wavelength reflected, unabsorbed.
                          → evidence 아직 없음.
                      assumption : green = detrimental to photosynthesis

Structural Coloration (schemochrome)
    -Morpho 나비 ①Robert Hooke / Isaac Newton ②Thomas Young
                                          ↳ structural color : ⎡ thin layers of films / scales
     wings : rows of scales (+) gaps   ⎣ light

Q3 light hits scales → interact with it → absorb / reflect certain wavelengths
    blue reflected ∴ visible
 - business people design 할 때 exploit
      → can eliminate toxic elements
 - energy - efficient, not environmentally damaging ∵ no additional energy consumption required
                                                      (+) waterproof

Q4 wings : gaps filled with gas, water-barrier
        adhesive force : ⎡ attraction between droplets
                       ⎣ energy that causes water to stick to solid
          ∴ water → flatten out on smooth surfaces
             but Morpho 나비's wings : bumpy / rough (+) air in gaps
                           ∴ doesn't flatten out & slide off
                            (+) 먼지 같이 roll off
              ex) shirt manufacturers
                 → incorporates same principles
             Q6 hamburger in structural coloration shirt
                if) spill ketchup on shirt → same result

Q5 great promise for future
    (-) (1) replicating aspects of natural mechanism
       (2) understanding of phenomena
       (3) ensure that replication doesn't work as impediment to thinking process
          → original thinking barely involved
             ∵ simply observe → exploit

    presents noteworthy benefits

Note taking TEST 4 Set2-C (#1)

Q1 group presentation on 19c European art movement

topic : Barbizon school. French painters (1830~1880)

⤷ name : village outside Paris ∴ primary workplace : F~ forest

Q2 ⤷ preserved nature
genuine rep. of nature

⤷ painting : shared understanding of landscape
faithful painters. 보이는거 capture. X figurative elements

⤷ vs. traditional French landscape painting ⎤
(imaginative elements)   ⎬ Q3
→ diff btw two 포함시켜   ⎦

⤷ preliminary sketches in forest → studio에서 finish

⤷ intentionally left details looking 미완성
→ concise & informative. 5 min. X hour. Q5
→ missing central figure (paragon)

Q4 ex. Rousseau (most noteworthy)
research on life & paintings

⤷ 주변 art museum에 Barbizon paintings.
gonna stop by

Q1 group presentation on 19th century European art movement

topic : Barbizon school. French painters (1830~1880)

↳ name : village outside of Paris ∴ primary workplace : Fontainebleau forest

Q2 { preserved nature / genuine representation / of nature

↳ painting : shared understanding of landscape

faithful painters. 보이는거 capture. avoided figurative elements

↳ vs. traditional French landscape painting

(included imaginative elements) ⎫
→ difference between the two 포함시켜 ⎭ Q3

↳ preliminary sketches in forest → studio에서 finish

↳ intentionally left details looking unfinished

→ concise & informative 하게 해. 5 minutes. not an hour. Q5

→ missing central figure (paragon)

Q4 ex. Théodore Rousseau (one of the most noteworthy artists)

research on his life & paintings

↳ 주변에 위치한 art museum에 Barbizon paintings 전시

gonna stop by

Note taking TEST 4 Set2-L1 (#1)

last class : access to books 19c English public
      (classics → triple-deckers)
    books $$ ∴ accessible / cheaper methods : lending libraries. magazines / newspapers

Q2 (≒) 현상 (15c ~ 17c)
Q1 Early Modern Period (Middle Ages 이후)
  - advent of literacy (+) cheap books readily available to general public.
      → small pamphlets
      → chivalry. religious stories (saints vs. demons)
    Q3 ⎧ → light & entertaining
        ⎩ → X philosophical. everyday ppl 즐김
      → simple. cheaply-made ≠ Middle Ages (철학. art. science)
    Q3 → common. hawkers & peddlers

  - stimulus / input
    Elizabeth Eisenstein
    1970s : "printing cheap books … 2 sig. long-term effects"
      ① printing tech. new standards
        이전에는 stories passed down orally
        Q4 → X 완전 eradicated   ∵ convenient
      ② permanent preservation
        employed by critics (evidence. diff perspectives)
        ex) Montaigne (prestigious writer)
        Q5 controversial essays (det. to tradition)
        father of modern skepticism
        had access to info from books
        → borrowed ideas / concepts
        POV well conveyed
        1580 에쎄 : politics. religion. human nature.

  - Driving force of revolution : Printing machines or ppl?
    French Rev & Industrial Rev
      ↳ 10 yrs   ↳ 50~70 yrs : long time for a rev ⎤
    Printing Rev : ~300 yrs. X enough of a driving F ⎦ Q6

TEST 4 Set2-L1 (#2)

last class : access to books by the 19th century English public
　　　(classics → triple-deckers)
　　　books : very expensive　∴ more accessible / cheaper methods
　　　　　　　　　　　　　: lending libraries, magazines / newspapers

Q2 Similar Phenomenon (15th ~ 17th century)
Q1 Early Modern Period (Middle Ages 이후)
　　- advent of literacy (+) cheap books readily available to general public.
　　　　→ small pamphlets
　　　　→ chivalry, religious stories (saints vs. demons)
　　　Q3 ┌ → light & entertaining
　　　　 └ → X philosophical, everyday people이 즐김
　　　　→ simple, cheaply-made ≠ Middle Ages (철학, art, science)
　　　Q3 → common, even sold by hawkers & peddlers
　- stimulus / input
　　　Elizabeth Eisenstein
　　　1970s : "printing cheap books resulted in 2 significant long-term effects"
　　　　① printing tech, new standards for books
　　　　　이전에는 stories passed down orally
　　　　　Q4 → X 완전 eradicated　∴ convenient
　　　　② permanent preservation
　　　　　employed by critics (evidence, differing perspectives 참고)
　　　　　ex) Montaigne (prestigious writer)
　　　　　Q5 controversial essays (detrimental to tradition)
　　　　　　father of modern skepticism
　　　　　　had access to information from books
　　　　　　→ borrowed ideas / concepts
　　　　　　Points of view : well conveyed
　　　　　　1580 Essais : politics, religion, human nature.

　　- Driving force of revolution : Printing machines or people?
　　　　French Revolution & Industrial Revolution
　　　　　↳ 10 years　　　 ↳ 50~70 years : long time for a revolution
　　　　Printing Revolution : about 300 years, not enough of a driving force　Q6

Note taking TEST 4 Set2-L2 (#1)

Industrial Revolution (1760 ~ 1820/1840)
  ↳ most prominent period ∵ developmental boom. advances (medication. 교통. food)
  ↳ England → Europe → US

Q1 Transportation
  - steam - powered vehicles : mid-18c
  Q2 (-) too heavy (3,600kg)
     → X practical for 교통 unless on 완전 flat surfaces
  locomotives
  new resources (early 20c) → internal combustion powered vehicles
  Q6 human-powered transportation (more popular)
     ┌ bicycles
     ├ skateboards
     ├ velomobiles
     └ cabin cycles
  1800s - limited choices
     ① horseless carriages (4 wheels)
        diff models
        4 riders
        (+) convenience on rough roads
     Q3 (-) too heavy. humans → draft animals → mechanical E
        owners criticized for abuse   ∴ use ↓
     ② Drais : Dandy horse / Laufmachine (?)
                  = running machine
                  = fast / foot
              ≈ bicycle w/o pedals
        ┌ penny-farthing (1870)
     Q4 ├ boneshaker (1860s)
        └ Laufmachine (1818) - earlier
        ┌ 독일에서 first demonstrated
        └ France - Ignored
     Q5 geographical diff
        ┌ G ┌ 14km in less than 1h
        │   └ smooth level surfaces
        └ F - slope/mud. injuries downhill
           X benefits
         ∴ Drais Δ marketing strategy
            recreation > transportation
            parks : rent out
            sig : inspired other inventors

TEST 4 Set2-L2 (#2)

Industrial Revolution (1760~1820 / 1840)
  ↳ most prominent period ∵ developmental boom. advances in medication. transportation. food…
  ↳ England → Europe → United States

Q1 Transportation
  - steam-powered vehicles : mid-18th century
  Q2 (-) too heavy (3,600kg)
       → X practical for transportation unless on 완전 flat surfaces
     locomotives
     new resources (early 20th century) → internal combustion powered vehicles
  Q6 human-powered transportation (more popular than steam engines)
       ┌ bicycles
       ├ skateboards
       ├ velomobiles
       └ cabin cycles
     1800s - limited choices
       ① horseless carriages (4 wheels)
           different models available
           accommodated 4 riders
           (+) convenience on rough roads
         Q3 (-) too heavy. humans → draft animals → mechanical energy
              owners criticized for abuse ∴ use waned
       ② Baron Karl Drais: Dandy horse / Laufmaschine
              = running machine
              = fast / foot
              ≒ bicycle without pedals
         ┌ penny-farthing (1870)
       Q4│ boneshaker (1860s)
         └ Laufmaschine (1818) - several decades earlier
           ┌ 독일에서 first demonstrated
           └ France - Ignored
       Q5 geographical differences
           ┌ Germany ┌ covered 14km in less than 1 hour
           │   └ traveled smooth level surfaces
           │ France - went up slopes / through mud
                     could cause injuries downhill
                     hardly any benefits over walking
                    ∴ Drais changed marketing strategy
                        recreation > transportation
                        rented them out in parks
                        significance : inspired other inventors

Note taking TEST 5 Set1-C (#2)

USHER

traffic jam, car accident

major accident on other side

community center

   Q2 인생 대부분 여기서 ∴ know everything

   website

Q1 reservation for soccer practice (next Fri)

   Mr. James
      ∧
    Mike

Q5 job interview w/ Bryan James 20 min ago

     → mixed up

   reservation : next Fri

   manager asked to come to you

   ↳ name : Coach Stillman
             Steven

   met in high school, good relationship (30 yrs)

   normally - pay to make reservation on Fri (X cheap ∴ v. popular)

   Q3 but discount? → X, free.

Q4 Reservation forms → you & Steven sign → receive guest passes

     → pass 꼭 가져오기. Security guards X let in w/o

traffic jam. car accident

major accident on the other side

community center

   Q. 인생 대부분 여기서 살음 ∴ know everything about this town

      website 가르쳐줄게

  Q1 → here to make a reservation for soccer practice (next Friday)

      Mr. James
         ∧
       Mike

Q5 job interview with Bryan James 20 minutes ago

      → mixed up

    reservation : next Friday

    manager asked to come to you

     ↳ name : Coach Steven Stillman

    met in high school. good relationship for 30 years

    normally - need to pay to make reservation on a Friday

        (isn't cheap because very popular)

  Q3 but discount? → no. free.

  Q4 Reservation forms → you & Steven sign → receive guest passes

     → pass 꼭 가져오기. Security guards won't let in without

Note taking TEST 5 Set1-L1 (#1)

early European art movements
Q1 15 ~ 19c → contemp art
painting styles / 철학 / perspectives 다양 → but share one 특징
       mixed / developed own paints
     Q2 exp → colorful & durable paints (+) preserve
         ↓3c
     transition (l1700s ~ e1800s)
     l1700s → exp ⋯ stability
     tech innovations
     glue in canvases
     → diff for paint to stick
     glue dry 하면서 paint crack / fade
     모르고 transitioned
    Q3 ∴ e1800s : disaster. longevity

Experimentation & Innovation
previously : artists trained under master painters
    → interactive. intensive
e1800s : art standards transformed
"Academy ~"
= group of art academies. 프랑스 주변
  ↳ rules / guidelines impose. artists 이거에 adhere
  ↳ artists educated at academies
 ∴ their pref = new standard
  ex) valued religious / historical themes
   caused to conceal individual feelings
   realistic. conservative colors
    ∴ individuality & creativity → diff to discern
  Q6 → spared responsibility of originality

Another art movement
Impression, Sunrise 모네 (Impressionist movement)
      (+) Sisley. Pissarro. etc.
 ↳ ∴ "Impressionism" → Independence. rebellion
    X apply academies' regulations
      ∴ unnatural
  own exhibitions ⋯ awareness ↑

    → imagination & subjectivity ★
     X reality
  Q4 → photography ↑ 해질때
    more accurate / realistic 불가능. futile.
     ∴ imagination
  → pre-packaged paints
  Q5 ⎧ - durability
    - rich colors
    - artificial enhancements
Next class : 5 Impressionist works. techniques. color usage

TEST 5 Set1-L1 (#2)

early European art movements
   15th ~ 19th century → contemporary art
painting styles / 철학 / perspectives 다양 → but share one 특징
                         mixed / developed own paints
                   Q2 experimentation → colorful & durable paints (+) preserve
                              ↓3 centuries
                    transition (late 1700s~early 1800s)
                    late 1700s → experimentation ⋯ stability
                    technological innovations
                    glue in canvases
                  → difficult for paint to stick
                    glue dry 하면서 paint crack / fade
                    모르고 transitioned
             Q3 ∴ early 1800s : disaster. (longevity-wise)

Experimentation & Innovation
previously : artists trained under master painters
              → interactive. intensive
early 1800s : art standards transformed
"Académie des Beaux-Arts"
= group of art academies. 프랑스 주변
    rules / guidelines impose함. artists 이거에 adhere
    artists educated at academies
    their preference = new standard
    ex) valued religious / historical themes
        caused to conceal individual feelings
        realistic. conservative colors
        ∴ individuality & creativity → difficult to discern
      Q6 → spared responsibility of originality
Another art movement
Impression, Sunrise. Claude Monet (Impressionist movement)
              (+) Sisley. Pissarro. etc.
   ∴"Impressionism" → Independence. rebellion
               X apply academies' regulations
                   ∴ unnatural
    own exhibitions ⋯ awareness ↑
              → imagination & subjectivity ★
                 X reality
     Q4 → photography popular 해질때 develop
            more accurate / realistic 불가능. futile.
               ∴ imagination으로 승부
      → pre-packaged paints
          - durability
          - rich colors
          - artificial enhancements

Note taking TEST 5 Set1-L2 (#1)

prey animals' tech : antipredator adaptations
  ↳ camouflaging methods (crypsis, mimesis)
      → Δ skin / scale colors & patterns
      ex) dark frogs → red / yellow (signal of danger / toxicity)

Autotomy
  ↳ detach part of body → distract
  ↳ usually invertebrates
  ↳ vertebrates (salamanders, lizards ⋯)
        ↳ drop limbs

Lizards
  ↳ drop tails] Q1
  ↳ X need physical contact for A to occur
        Q2 ↔ gecko (skin release)
  ↳ 1st stage of A = voluntary decision to 위협적 stimuli
Q3 ↳ Qs about neural / physical basis. Research needed
  ↳ internal trigger, fracture plane
          ↳ help A tails
             contract muscles btw vertebrae
             잘린 꼬리 temp. wiggle
             How? → next time
  ↳ escape → tail healing process
Q4 (healed tails ≠ originals
       cartilage ↙   ↘ vertebrae
         재생 = 4~12 w
  ↳ become less effective pred
        sig E loss ↔ fat reserves (E storage) X lost (tail base)
  ↳ lack of tail
      Q5 - X move freely. ∴ expend more E
         - ↓ attractiveness to opposite-sex
         - female : fewer eggs, weaker offspring
         - male : ↓ social status
    → X 완전 vulnerable, ever-evolving. Q6 ex) Δ activity time

TEST 5 Set1-L2 (#2)

prey animals' technique : antipredator adaptations
  └→ camouflaging methods (crypsis, mimesis)
        → change skin / scale colors & patterns
        ex) dark frogs → red / yellow (signal of danger / toxicity)

Autotomy
  └→ detach part of body → distract
  └→ usually invertebrates
  └→ vertebrates (salamanders, lizards …)
        └→ drop limbs

Lizards
  └→ drop tails] Q1
  └→ don't need physical contact for autotomy to occur
        Q2 ↔ geckos' skin release (needs physical contact)
  └→ initial stage of autotomy = voluntary decision to 위협적 stimuli
Q3 └→ Questions about neural/physical basis. Research needed
  └→ internal trigger, fracture plane
        └→ help autotomize tails
           contract muscles between vertebrae
           잘린 꼬리 temporarily wiggle
           How? → next time
  └→ escape → tail healing process
     Q4 (healed tails ≠ originals
          cartilage ↙   ↘ vertebrae
          재생 = 4~12 weeks
  └→ become less effective predator
        significant energy loss ↔ fat reserves (energy storage) aren't lost (tail base)
  └→ lack of tail
     Q5 - can't move freely. ∴ expend more energy
        - reduced attractiveness to opposite-sex
        - female : lay fewer eggs, weaker offspring
        - male : lowered social status
  → not completely vulnerable, ever-evolving. Q6 ex) change activity time

Note taking TEST 5 Set2-C (#1)

Q2 injury
   poetry reading. 최근 attend
Q1 term paper idea 고민. but can't broaden perspective
   reading - conventional. mood : quiet / calm. audience 조용히 listened
   other way of sharing? - poetry slam (Beat Generation)
            1948 Jack K~ (pioneer)
         Q3 express attitude (politics & rejection of values)

Poetry slam ─┬─ competitive
             ├─ poets compete. judged by audience (3~5)
             ├─ Q4 ex. Allen Ginsberg (★ leader of Beat G)
             ├─ energetic. loud. role of audience ★
             │   ↳ primary f(x) : poem 듣기 (conventional readings)
             │   involvement discouraged
             │   silence expected
             │   ↳ poetry slam : audience responds (yelling/cheering)
             └─ needed to arouse emotions (connection w/ audience)
                  ∴ topics controversial
                Q5 research는 너가 해

TEST 5 Set2-C (#2)

Q2 injury

   poetry reading. 최근 attend

Q1 term paper idea 고민. but can't broaden perspective

   reading - conventional. mood : quiet / calm. audience 조용히 listened

   other way of sharing? - poetry slam (Beat Generation)

                 1948 Jack Kerouac (pioneer)

             Q3 express attitude towards politics & rejection of values

Poetry slam ─ competitive
            ├ poets compete. judged by 3~5 audience members
            ├ Q4 ex. Allen Ginsberg (prominent leader of Beat Generation)
            ├ energetic. loud. role of audience : significant

Conventional Readings	Poetry Slam
primary function of audience : poem듣기 nvolvement discouraged silence expected	Audience responds by yelling / cheering

            └ needed to arouse emotions (to build connection with audience)
                 ∴ topics controversial

Q5 research는 너가 해

Note taking — TEST 5 Set2-L1 (#1)

alternative to petroleum - based fuel (ex. gasoline)
　　↳ most suitable & efficient

Q6 ethanol - alcohol in 술
　　↳ corn product
　　ferment corn (sugar) —chem rxn→ ethanol & CO_2
　　　　　　　　↓
　　　　concentrated form
　　　　　　　　↓
　　　　　　　fuel

supplies E. internal combustion engines
used in Brazil. US. alt.

Q2 2000 ~ 2007 ethanol prod : 17b → 52b L

(+) ─ renewable (gasoline X renewable. limited
　　　　　ethanol - X fossil fuel. crops = → ok)
　　─ econ impact. crops : labor. econ security (farmers). Q3 trade
　　─ env. friendly. ∵ less CO_2

(-) ─ quality. less E. more input
　　　　　1.5 gallons ethanol (=) 1 gallon gasoline
　　─ Q4 fertilizers needed. det. to env.
　　　　↳ Q4 prod : use fossil fuel
　　　　　　(=) ethanol fermentation & distillation
　　　　　　∴ X 완전 env. friendly
　　─ transporting & distributing Ethanol　E input
　　　　　Q5 X pipelines. tainted (H_2O)
　　─ future harm. kernel 부분 사용 = part we eat
　　─ future : prod Ethanol > feeding ppl
　　─ highly flammable. X ideal alt

HW : other sources. alt to corn in ethanol prod & analyze (+)

TEST 5 Set2 -L1 (#2)

alternative to petroleum - based fuel (ex. gasoline)
  └→ thought to be the most suitable & efficient

Q6 ethanol - alcohol in 술
  └→ corn product
    ferment corn (produce sugar) —chemical reaction→ ethanol & CO_2
                                                    ↓
                                              concentrated form
                                                    ↓
                                                  fuel

supplies energy to internal combustion engines
used in Brazil. US. as alternative to gasoline

Q2 2000 ~ 2007 ethanol production : 17 billion → 52 billion L

(+) ┬ renewable (gasoline non-renewable. supply : limited
    │   ethanol - not a fossil fuel. crops 있으면 ok)
    ├ economic impact. crops : require labor. economic security for farmers. Q3 trade
    └ environmentally friendly. ∴ less CO_2

(-) ┬ quality. less energy produced. more input needed
    │   1.5 gallons of ethanol (=) 1 gallon of gasoline
    ├ Q4 fertilizers needed. detrimental to environment
    │   └→ Q4 production : uses fossil fuel
    │   same with ethanol fermentation & distillation
    │   ∴ X 완전 environmentally friendly
    ├ transporting & distributing Ethanol : requires huge energy input
    │   Q5 can't use pipelines. easily tainted by water
    ├ future harm. kernel 부분 사용 = the part we eat
    ├ future : production of Ethanol prioritized over feeding people
    └ highly flammable. X ideal alternative

HW : other sources. alternative to corn in ethanol production & analyze benefits

Note taking TEST 5 Set2-L2 (#1)

cloud of dust / gas → solar system (core accretion model)
    (solar nebula)
collapse of cloud 일부 → conc. of cosmic material at center → Sun
      → terrestrial planets (build-up of remaining materials)

Earth
   dense elements → bottom ··· core
   lighter   "   → crust

Q1 Life - sustaining ability
liquid water = ★ for life. distinguishing facet of Earth
   ↳ rare on other planets (freezes / vaporizes)
     water's origin on Earth - theory
     ① water remain ∵ accumulation of greenhouse gases (volcanic activity)
                  Q2 ↳ trap heat. prevent from escaping atmosphere
                        ↳ maintained Earth's temp.
                            ∴ water : liquid

     Q3 volcanic activity 말고도 other factors : meteorites

        meteorites → edge of A →   frictional F ↗ disintegrate
                                       ↘ reach Earth
        Intense electricity ··· same conditions
                    (heat fragments → 1,000°C)
                → 2 by-products : CO_2 & water vapor
                  ∴ warmer temp & water
               Q6 하나로는 부족 but "little strokes fell great oaks"

   ② Lunar cataclysm
      asteroid & celestial bodies collide (3.8 ~ 4.1b yrs ago)
    Q4 (evidence : impact melt rocks collected. Apollo missions
           → 4b yrs
         ∴ asteroids struck early planets
      theoretical meteors burned up in E's A → by-products
      meteoric H_2O → oceans
      GG heat 가둬서 correct temp

Diff btw E & Mars
Meteors → same consequence
but Q5 E : = strong magnetic field at core (protects it from solar winds & charged particles)
   Mars : X   "   subject to solar winds (blow away GG)
                ∴ temp ↓. water freezes

cloud of dust / gas → solar system (core accretion model)
   (solar nebula)
collapse of cloud 일부 → concentration of cosmic material at the center → Sun
      → advent of terrestrial planets (build-up of remaining materials)

Earth
dense elements → bottom ··· core
lighter elements → crust

Q1 Life - sustaining ability
liquid water = essential for life. the most distinguishing facet of Earth
   rare on other planets (freezes / vaporizes)
   water's origin on Earth - theory
      ① water remained due to accumulation of greenhouse gases (produced by volcanic activity)
         Q2 ┌→ trap heat. prevent it from escaping the atmosphere
            └→ maintained Earth's temperature
                  ∴ water remained liquid
         Q3 volcanic activity 말고도 other factors : meteorites

            meteorites → edge of atmosphere → huge frictional force ╱ disintegrate
                                                                    ╲ reach Earth
            Intense electricity로 same conditions 재현
                  (heat fragments to 1,000°C)
                  → 2 by-products : CO2 & water vapor
                     warmer temperature & water
                  Q6 하나로는 부족 but "little strokes fell great oaks"

      ② Lunar cataclysm
         millions of asteroid & celestial bodies collide (3.8 ~ 4.1 billion years ago)
         evidence : impact melt rocks collected during the Apollo missions
         Q4 ┌ → dated to 4 billion years ago
            └   ∴ many asteroids struck early planets
               theoretical meteors burned up in Earth's atmosphere → produced by-products
               meteoric water → oceans
               greenhouse gases는 heat 가둬서 correct temperature 만듬

   Differences between Earth & Mars
   Meteors → same consequence
   but Q5 Earth : has strong magnetic field at core (protects it from solar winds
                              & charged particles)
         Mars : doesn't have strong magnetic field. subject to solar winds
                     (blow away greenhouse gases)
                  ∴ temperature falls. water freezes

www.usherin.usher.co.kr

USHER

iBT TOEFL
INTERMEDIATE LISTENING
단어 · 구문

TEST1 1-1
VOCABULARY

TEST1 1-1지문의 단어 중 토플 필수 단어를 선별하여 정리하였습니다.

01	**net profit** [nét práfit]	n. 순이익
02	**phenomenal** [finámənl]	adj. 경이로운
03	**impressed** [ɪm|prest]	adj. 인상 깊게 생각하는
04	**assure** [əʃúər]	v. 장담하다, 확언하다
05	**ensure** [ɪnʃúər]	v. 보장하다
06	**route** [raʊt]	n. (어떤 일을 달성하는) 길[방법/경로]
07	**accounting** [ə|kaʊntɪŋ]	n. 회계 (업무)
08	**doubt** [daʊt]	v. 확신하지 못하다, 의문[의혹]을 갖다
09	**participation** [pɑːr|tɪsɪ|peɪʃn]	n. 참여도
10	**performance** [pər|fɔːrməns]	n. (과제 등의) 수행[실행]
11	**acquire** [əkwáiər]	v. 습득하다
12	**overwhelming** [òuvərhwélmɪŋ]	adj. 부담스러운
13	**variety** [və|raɪəti]	n. 여러 가지, 갖가지
14	**career** [kə|rɪr]	n. 직업
15	**analyst** [ænəlɪst]	n. 분석가
16	**auditor** [ɔ́ːditər]	n. 회계 감사관
17	**specialist** [spéʃəlist]	n. 전문가
18	**former** [|fɔːrmə(r)]	adj. 과거[이전]의
19	**burdensome** [|bɜːrdnsəm]	adj. 부담스러운, 힘든
20	**rash** [ræʃ]	adj. 경솔한
21	**prospect** [práspekt]	n. 가망, 가능성
22	**aspect** [|æspekt]	n. 측면
23	**examination** [ɪg|zæmɪ|neɪʃn]	n. 시험
24	**impetuous** [impétʃuəs]	adj. 성급한, 충동적인

구문정리

본문 중 중요 구문 정리한 내용입니다. 우선 암기하고 많이 읽으시기 바랍니다.

TEST1 1-1 | Accounting department

Set1 Conversation에 등장하는 단어들 중 필요한 단어들을 선별하였습니다.

#	구문	의미
01	accounting department	회계부서; 회계 학과
02	paper on	~에 대한 paper
03	net profits	순이익
04	keep up the good work	잘 해내다
05	assure O that	O에게 that절을 확신시키다
06	do a great job	일을 잘 했다
07	ask for	~을 묻다, 찾다
08	feel the need	필요를 느끼다
09	need to do	~할 필요
10	switch majors	전공을 바꾸다
11	look into	~을 살피다
12	prior to	~에 앞서, 먼저
13	do research	연구를 하다
14	now that	~이기 때문에
15	doubt decision	결정을 의심하다
16	think about	~에 대해 생각하다
17	switch A to B	A를 B로 변경하다
18	look like	~처럼 보이다
19	do badly	잘 못하다
20	at this point	현 시점에서
21	try my best	최선을 다하다
22	academic performance	학업 성취
23	consider ~ing	ing하는것을 고려하다
24	require O to do	O가 to do 하는것을 요구하다
25	acquire degree	학점을 획득하다
26	in the field	~ 분야에서
27	take time to do	to do 하는데 ~한시간이 걸리다
28	earn a degree	학위를 얻다
29	at times	때로는 (=sometimes)
30	look at	~을 보다
31	job prospects	취업 전망
32	forget to do	to do 할것을 잊어버리다
33	degree in	~분야의 학위
34	a variety of	다양한
35	career paths	진로
36	with experience in	~점에서 경험을 가진
37	be likely to do	to do 할 가능성이 있다
38	get hired	취업 되다
39	what about	~하는 게 어때
40	demand for	~에 대한 수요
41	people with a degree in	~의 학위를 가진 사람
42	have easy time ing	~함에 있어 쉬운 시간을 보내다
43	secure jobs	직업을 구하다 (s)
44	that's not the case with	그것은 ~의 경우에 해당하지 않는다
45	hard to do	~하기 힘들다
46	get a job	일자리를 얻다 (g)
47	long term	장기적
48	I'm not so sure if	~인지 아닌지 확신할 수 없다
49	get your point	네말을 알겠다
50	make decision	결정하다
51	other than	~외에
52	need to do	~할 필요가 있다
53	deal with	처리하다, 다루다
54	make money	돈을 벌다
55	and so on	기타 등등
56	of course not	물론 아니다
57	take step	조치를 취하다
58	take time	시간을 가지다
59	do research	연구 하다
60	thank you for	~에 대해 감사하다

TEST1 1-2
VOCABULARY

TEST1 1-2지문의 단어 중 토플 필수 단어를 선별하여 정리하였습니다.

USHER

01	**compelling** [kəmˈpelɪŋ]	adj. 설득력 있는, 강력한
02	**retreat** [rɪˈtriːt]	v. 후퇴하다, 퇴각하다
03	**separate** [ˈsépərèit]	v. 분리시키다
04	**considerable** [kənsídərəbl]	adj. 상당한
05	**immense** [iméns]	adj. 엄청난, 거대한
06	**drastic** [ˈdræstɪk]	adj. 급격한
07	**doubtful** [ˈdaʊtfl]	adj. 의심스러운
08	**advent** [ǽdvent]	n. 출현, 도래
09	**regularity** [ˌregjuˈlærəti]	n. 정기적임
10	**emission** [imíʃən]	n. 방사, 방출
11	**abide** [əbáid bai]	v. (법률·합의 등을) 따르다
12	**geological** [dʒìːəládʒikəl]	adj. 지질학의
13	**coral** [kɔ́ːrəl]	n. 산호
14	**recede** [risíːd]	v. 멀어지다, 감소하다
15	**consequently** [ˈkɑːnsəkwentli]	adv. 그 결과, 따라서
16	**shallow** [ˈʃæloʊ]	adj. 얕은
17	**glacier** [ˈgleɪʃər]	n. 빙하
18	**withdraw** [wɪðˈdrɔː]	v. 물러나다, 철수하다
19	**crucial** [ˈkruːʃl]	adj. 중대한, 결정적인
20	**confused** [kənˈfjuːzd]	혼란스러워 하는
21	**analyze** [ǽnəlàiz]	n. 분석하다
22	**isotope** [áisətòup]	n. 동위원소
23	**interval** [íntərvəl]	n. 간격
24	**interglacial** [ìntərgléiʃəl]	adj. 간빙기의
25	**compile** [kəmˈpaɪl]	v. (여러 출처에서 자료를 따와) 엮다, 편집하다
26	**tectonic** [tektánik]	adj. (지질) 구조상의
27	**phenomenon** [finámənàn]	n. 현상
28	**trigger** [trígər]	v. 유발하다, 일으키다
29	**eruption** [irʌpʃən]	n. 분출, 발생
30	**astrophysicist** [æstroufízəsist]	n. 천체물리학자

TEST1 1-2
VOCABULARY

TEST1 1-2지문의 단어 중 토플 필수 단어를 선별하여 정리하였습니다.

31	**consistently** [kənsístəntli]	adv. 지속적으로
32	**subtle** [sʌtl]	adj. 미묘한
33	**oscillation** [àsəléiʃən]	n. 진동, 동요
34	**vital** [ˈvaɪtl]	adj. 필수적인
35	**theorize** [ˈθiːəraɪz]	v. 이론을 세우다
36	**orbit** [ɔ́ːrbit]	n. 궤도
37	**component** [kəmpóunənt]	n. 부품, 요소
38	**fluctuation** [flʌktʃuéiʃən]	n. 동요, 변동
39	**observe** [əbˈzɜːrv]	v. 관찰하다
40	**tilt** [tilt]	v. n. 기울다, 기울기
41	**extreme** [ɪkˈstriːm]	adj. 극도의, 극심한
42	**tremendous** [triméndəs]	adj. 엄청난
43	**perplexing** [pərpléksiŋ]	adj. 당황하게 하는,
44	**intricate** [íntrikət]	adj. 복잡한, 얽힌
45	**elliptical** [ilíptikəl]	adj. 타원형의
46	**circular** [ˈsɜːrkjələ(r)]	adj. 원형의, 둥근
47	**factor** [ˈfæktə(r)]	n. 요인, 인자
48	**hemisphere** [hémisfiər]	n. 반구
49	**consecutive** [kənsékjutiv]	adj. 연속되는
50	**shrinkage** [ʃríŋkidʒ]	n. 수축, 축소
51	**accumulate** [əkjúːmjulèit]	v. 축적하다, 누적하다
52	**persist** [pərsíst]	v. 계속하다, 지속하다
53	**convincing** [kənvínsiŋ]	adj. 설득력 있는
54	**overlook** [ˌoʊvərˈlʊk]	v. 고려 대상으로 삼지 않다
55	**variation** [vɛəriéiʃən]	n. (~의) 변형
56	**avoid** [əˈvɔɪd]	v. 방지하다, 막다, 모면하다
57	**ultimate** [ˈʌltɪmət]	adj. 궁극적인, 최후의
58	**comprehensive** [kàmprihénsiv]	adj. 종합적인
59	**explanation** [ˌekspləˈneɪʃn]	n. 설명

구문정리

본문 중 중요 구문 정리한 내용입니다. 우선 암기하고 많이 읽으시기 바랍니다.

TEST1 1-2 | Ice age
Set1 Lecture1에 등장하는 단어들 중 필요한 단어들을 선별하였습니다.

01	a number of	수많은
02	over the years	수년간
03	such as	~와 같은
04	cover A with B	A로 B를 덮다
05	fortunately for	다행스럽게도
06	human beings	인간, 인류
07	live in a period	~한 시대에 살다
08	retreat to	~로 퇴각하다
09	separate A by B	A를 B에 의해 분리하다
10	fossil fuel	화석 연료
11	lead to	~를 야기하다
12	increase in	~라는 점에서 증가
13	be doubtful about	~에 대해 의심하다
14	be sure that	~를 확신하다
15	so ~ that	너무 ~해서 ~하다
16	abide by	지키다, 따르다
17	look at	~을 살피다
18	relate to	~에 대해 언급하다 ; ~와 연관되다
19	relationship between A and B	A와 B사이의 관계
20	help O do	O가 do 하도록 돕다
21	research on	~에 대한 연구
22	every~ years	매 ~해마다
23	turn into	~이 되다 (t)
24	result in	결국 ~이 되다 (r)
25	decrease in	~라는 점에서의 감소
26	stop ~ing	ing 하는것을 그만하다
27	give way to	~로 바뀌다, 대체되다
28	start ~ing	ing하는것을 시작하다
29	let me explain	설명해줄게
30	be able to do	to do할 수 있다
31	figure out	알아내다, 이해하다
32	with regularity	규칙적으로
33	let's say	예를 들면
34	in cycles	주기적으로
35	of course	물론
36	might have caused	야기할수도 있다.

구문정리

TEST1 1-2 | Ice age

본문 중 중요 구문 정리한 내용입니다. 우선 암기하고 많이 읽으시기 바랍니다.
Set1 Lecture1에 등장하는 단어들 중 필요한 단어들을 선별하였습니다.

37	play a role in	~라는 점에서 역할을 하다
38	change in	~라는 점에서의 변화
39	to some extent	어느 정도까지
40	critical point	중요기점, 임계점
41	fit with	~와 맞다
42	changes in the angle of	~의 각 변화
43	with respect to	~에 대하여
44	effect on	~에 대한 영향
45	It is because	이유는 ~이다.
46	compose A of B	A를 B로 구성되다
47	stay on	계속하다
48	contribute to	~에 기여하다
49	guess from	~로 추측하다
50	at times	때때로 (sometimes)
51	closer to	~ 근처에
52	at present	현재
53	approach to	~로의 접근
54	in the northern hemisphere	북반구에서
55	on the contrary	그와는 반대로
56	conclude from	~로부터 결론을 내리다
57	have a impact on	~에 영향을 주다
58	for instance	예를 들어
59	allow O to do	O가 to do 하는 것을 허락하다
60	throughout the year	일 년 내내
61	on the other hand	반대로
62	bring about	야기하다
63	right now	지금 당장
64	variation in	~라는 점에서의 변화
65	compare A to B	A를 B와 비교하다
66	so far	지금까지
67	by far	훨씬, 단연코
68	keep O O.C	O를 O.C로 유지하다
69	avoid ~ing	ing 하는것을 피하다

TEST1 1-3
VOCABULARY

TEST1 1-3지문의 단어 중 토플 필수 단어를 선별하여 정리하였습니다.

01	**structure** [ˈstrʌktʃə(r)]	n. 구조
02	**perform** [pərˈfɔːrm]	v. 공연[연주/연기] 하다
03	**development** [dɪˈveləpmənt]	n. 발달, 성장
04	**modern** [ˈmɑːdərn]	adj. 현재의 근대의
05	**architect** [ˈɑːrkɪtekt]	n. 건축가
06	**ensure** [ɪnˈʃʊər]	v. 보장하다
07	**scenery** [ˈsíːnəri]	n. 경치, 풍경, 무대
08	**incorporate** [ɪnkɔ́ːrpərèitid]	v. 통합하다
09	**element** [ˈelɪmənt]	n. 요소, 성분
10	**similarity** [ˌsɪməˈlærəti]	n. 유사점
11	**difference** [ˈdɪfrəns]	n. 차이
12	**modify** [ˈmɑːdɪfaɪ]	v. 수정[변경]하다, 바꾸다
13	**abandon** [əˈbændən]	v. 버리다
14	**discussion** [dɪˈskʌʃn]	n. 논의, 상의
15	**chorus** [kɔ́ːrəs]	n. 현상
16	**discrepancy** [dɪskrépənsi]	n. 불일치, 차이
17	**provide** [prəˈvaɪd]	v. 제공하다
18	**commentary** [ˈkɑːmənteri]	n. 해설
19	**theme** [θiːm]	n. 주제, 테마
20	**occasional** [əkéiʒənəl]	adj. 가끔의, 때때로
21	**direct** [dɪˈrekt]	adj. 직접적인
22	**involvement** [ɪnˈvɑːlvmənt]	n. 관여, 개입
23	**primary** [ˈpraɪmeri]	adj. 주된, 주요한, 기본적인
24	**interact** [ˈɪntərækt]	v. 소통하다, 교류하다
25	**diminish** [dɪmíːnɪʃ]	v. 감소하다, 낮아지다, 줄어들다
26	**distinct** [dɪˈstɪŋkt]	adj. 뚜렷한, 분명한
27	**philosopher** [fəˈlɑːsəfə(r)]	n. 철학자
28	**reenactment** [riːænˈæktmənt]	n. 재연, 재현
29	**witness** [ˈwɪtnəs]	v. 목격하다
30	**abridge** [əbrídʒ]	v. 요약하다, 단축하다, 줄이다

TEST1 1-3
VOCABULARY

TEST1 1-3지문의 단어 중 토플 필수 단어를 선별하여 정리하였습니다.

31	**chariot** [tʃǽriət]	n. (고대의 전투나 경주용) 마차[전차]
32	**officially** [əfíʃəli]	adv. 공식적으로
33	**intense** [inténs]	adj. 강렬한, 강한, 심한
34	**relay** [ríːleɪ]	v. (정보, 뉴스 등을) 전달하다
35	**unfamiliar** [ˌʌnfəˈmɪliə(r)]	adj. 익숙지 않은, 낯선
36	**interpretation** [intə̀ːrprətéiʃən]	n. 해석, 설명
37	**scholar** [ˈskɑːlə(r)]	n. 학자
38	**strictly** [ˈstrɪktli]	adv. 엄격히, 엄하게
39	**merely** [ˈmɪrli]	adv. 한낱, 그저, 단지
40	**modification** [màdəfikéiʃən]	n. 수정, 변경, 조절
41	**ornate** [ɔːrnéit]	adj. 화려하게 장식한, 화려한
42	**decorative** [ˈdekəreɪtɪv]	adj. 장식이 된
43	**establishment** [ɪˈstæblɪʃmənt]	n. 설립, 수립, 확립
44	**technology** [tekˈnɑːlədʒi]	n. (과학) 기술
45	**impractical** [ɪmˈpræktɪkl]	adj. 비현실적인
46	**portray** [pɔːrtréi]	v. 묘사하다, 그리다, 표현하다
47	**condense** [kəndéns]	v. 압축하다, 응축하다
48	**accommodate** [əkάmədèit]	v. 수용하다, 맞추다
49	**spectator** [ˈspekteɪtər]	n. 관중
50	**construct** [kɑːnstrʌkt]	v. 건설하다
51	**resemble** [rɪˈzembl]	v. 닮다, 비슷[유사]하다
52	**enable** [ɪˈneɪbl]	v. (무엇을) 가능하게 하다
53	**regardless** [rɪˈgɑːrdləs]	adv. 개의치 [상관하지] 않고
54	**devote** [divóut]	v. …에 쏟다
55	**pleasure** [ˈpleʒə(r)]	n. 기쁨, 즐거움
56	**emphasis** [émfəsis]	n. 강조, 중점, 중시
57	**overlook** [óuvər lùk]	v. 간과하다

구문정리 — TEST1 1-3

본문 중 중요 구문 정리한 내용입니다. 우선 암기하고 많이 읽으시기 바랍니다.

Drama class
Set1 Lecture2에 등장하는 단어들 중 필요한 단어들을 선별하였습니다.

01	up to now	이때까지, 지금까지
02	look at	~을 보다
03	perform play	공연하다
04	be related to	~와 관계되어 있다
05	each other	서로서로
06	be aware that	~을 알다, 인지하다
07	in modern sense	현대적인 의미에서
08	be supposed to do	to do 하기로 되어있다, 해야 한다
09	on the top of	~의 꼭대기에
10	in this way	이러한 방법으로
11	incorporate A into B	A를 B에 통합시키다
12	on the other hand	반면에
13	the same as	~와 마찬가지로
14	look into	조사하다
15	go along	진행되다
16	begin A with B	A를 B와 함께 시작하다
17	perform roles	배역들을 연기하다
18	in ancient time	고대에
19	as far as	~하는 한
20	in order to do	to do 하기 위해
21	need to do	to do 할 필요가 있다
22	on top of	~ 외에 (in addition to); ~ 위에
23	on the stage	무대에서
24	commentary on	~에 대한 논평
25	a variety of	다수의
26	interact with	~와 상호작용을 하다
27	react to	~에 반응하다
28	different from	~와 다른
29	over time	시간이 지나면서
30	so that	너무 ~해서 그 결과 ~ 하다
31	consider O to do	O가 to do 한다고 생각하다
32	have a role in	~라는 점에서 역할을 맡다
33	send off	보내다
34	announce A to B	A에게 B를 알리다
35	spring from	돌출하다
36	walk off	떠나다
37	in front of	~의 앞에
38	would have been	(추측) ~이었을 것이다

TEST1 1-3 | Drama class

본문 중 중요 구문 정리한 내용입니다. 우선 암기하고 많이 읽으시기 바랍니다.
Set1 Lecture2에 등장하는 단어들 중 필요한 단어들을 선별하였습니다.

39	put A into words	A를 말로 나타내다
40	relay A to B	A를 B에게 전달하다
41	be about to do	막 ~하려는 참이다
42	move on to	~로 이동하다
43	answer the question	질문에 답하다
44	hang on a minute	잠깐만 기다려라
45	take a look at	~을 보다
46	refer to A as B	A를 B라고 언급하다
47	sound unfamiliar	생소하게 들리다
48	use O to do	O를 to do 하기위해 사용하다
49	both A and B	A B둘다
50	the latter	후자
51	prior to	~에 앞서
52	with no significance	중요하지않은
53	go through	겪다
54	act as	~로서 역할하다
55	according to	~에 따르면
56	have to do	to do 할 필요가 있다
57	for O to do	의미상 주어
58	condense A into B	A 를 B로 압축 시키다
59	instead of	~대신에
60	that's why	그게 이유다
61	take place	일어나다
62	in fact	사실
63	show A B	A에게 B를 보여주다
64	in the lesson	수업에서
65	call A B	A를 B라고 부르다
66	such~ that~	~ 해서(원인) ~(결과) 하다
67	result in	그결과 ~이 되다
68	cut in half	반으로 가르다
69	so that	그래서(결과)
70	regardless of	~에 상관없이
71	devote A to B	A를 B에 바치다
72	introduce A to B	A를 B에게 소개하다
73	put emphasis on	~을 강조하다
74	keep that in mind	그것을 명심하다

TEST1 2-1
VOCABULARY

TEST1 2-1지문의 단어 중 토플 필수 단어를 선별하여 정리하였습니다.

01	**Wall Street** [wɔːl striːt]	n. 월가, 미국 금융 시장
02	**Great Depression** [greit dipréʃən]	n. 대공황
03	**resource** [ríːsɔːrs]	n. 자료
04	**reference** [ˈrefrəns]	참고[인용] 문헌
05	**damaged** [dǽmidʒd]	손해를 입은, 하자가 생긴
06	**wrinkled** [ˈrɪŋkld]	adj. 주름이 있는
07	**decipher** [disáifər]	v. 판독하다, 해독하다
08	**odds** [adz]	n. 가능성, 확률
09	**assignment** [əsáinmənt]	n. 과제
10	**track** [træk]	v. 추적하다
11	**delay** [dɪˈleɪ]	n. 지연, 지체
12	**shipment** [ʃípmənt]	n. 배송, 발송
13	**personal** [ˈpɜːrsənl]	adj. 개인적인
14	**favor** [féivər]	n. 부탁
15	**patron** [péitrən]	n. 단골, 고객
16	**colleague** [kɑ́liːg]	n. 동료

TEST1 2-1 | Library employee

본문 중 중요 구문 정리한 내용입니다. 우선 암기하고 많이 읽으시기 바랍니다.

Set2 Conversation에 등장하는 단어들 중 필요한 단어들을 선별하였습니다.

01	work on	~에 공들이다
02	paper on	~에 대한 문서
03	look for	찾다
04	come across	우연히 만나다
05	give A B	A에게 B를 주다
06	let O do	O가 do 하게 하다
07	check if	인지 아닌지 확인하자
08	it seems like	~처럼 보이다
09	try ing	ing 해보다
10	be sure	확신하다
11	the thing is	사실, 근데
12	need to do	to do 할 필요가 있다
13	research for	~에 대한 연구
14	by (time)	~까지
15	take too long	너무 오래 걸리다
16	see if	인지 아닌지 보자
17	as long as	~하는 한
18	browse for	(인터넷) 검색하다
19	want to do	to do 하기를 원하다
20	take time to do	to do하는데 시간이 걸리다
21	way to do	to do 하는 방법
22	do favor	호의를 베풀다
23	during working hours	근무시간 동안에
24	ask if	~인지 아닌지 물어보다
25	be of	~에 속하다
26	in situation	상황에
27	give A to B	A를 B에게 주다
28	be able to do	to do 할 수 있다
29	time difference	시차
30	Eastern time	동부시간
31	think about	생각하다
32	get in touch with	~와 접촉하다
33	ring O	O에게 전화하다
34	checke out	대출하다(책)
35	you never know	누가 알아? [아무도 모르는 거라고] (특히 미래에 좋은 일이 있을지도 모른다는 뜻을 나타낼 때 씀)
36	sound like	~처럼 들리다
37	for now	당분간
38	leave A B	A에게 B를 남겨주다
39	work out	해결하다
40	make sure	확실히 하다
41	wait for	~를 기다리다
42	be going to do	to do 하기로 되어있다
43	thanks for	~에 대해 감사하다
44	as soon as possible	가능한 빨리

TEST1 2-2
VOCABULARY

TEST1 2-2지문의 단어 중 토플 필수 단어를 선별하여 정리하였습니다.

01	**layer** [	ler]	n. 층 [단계]
02	**marine** [məri:n]	adj. 바다의 해양의
03	**contain** [kən	teɪn]	v. ~이 들어있다
04	**discuss** [dɪ	skʌs]	v. 상의[의논/논의]하다
05	**distinguishable** [dɪstíŋgwiʃəbl]	adj. 구별할 수 있는, 두드러진
06	**challenging** [ʧǽlindʒiŋ]	adj. 도전적인, 어려운
07	**survive** [sər	vaɪv]	v. 살아남다, 생존하다
08	**pressure** [	preʃə(r)]	n. 압력
09	**devoid of** [dɪvɔ́id ʌv]	adj. 결여된, 없는
10	**condition** [kən	dɪʃn]	n. 상태
11	**equivalent** [ikwívələnt]	adj. 동등한, 등가의
12	**vision** [	vɪʒn]	n. 시력
13	**bioluminescence** [báioulù:mənésəns]	n. 생체 발광
14	**thrive** [θraɪv]	v. 번성하다, 성장하다
15	**uninhabitable** [|ʌnɪn|hæbɪtəbl]	adj. 주거하기에 부적합한
16	**adapt** [ə	dæpt]	v. (상황에) 적응하다
17	**interesting** [	ɪntrəstɪŋ]	adj. 재미있는, 흥미로운
18	**harsh** [hɑ:rʃ]	adj. 가혹한, 냉혹한
19	**trait** [treɪt]	n. 특성
20	**present** [	preznt]	adj. 있는, 존재하는
21	**glow** [gloʊ]	v. 빛나다
22	**generate** [	dʒenəreɪt]	v. 발생시키다, 만들어 내다
23	**illumination** [ɪ|lu:mɪ|neɪʃn]	n. 빛
24	**inherit** [ɪn	herɪt]	v. 상속받다, 물려받다
25	**occasionally** [ə	keɪʒnəli]	adv. 가끔
26	**functional** [	fʌŋkʃənl]	adj. 실용적인, 기능적인
27	**environment** [ɪn	vaɪrənmənt]	n. (주변의) 환경
28	**extent** [ɪk	stent]	n. 정도, 규모
29	**detect** [ditékt]	v. 감지하다, 탐지하다
30	**fortunate** [	fɔ:rtʃənət]	adj. 운 좋은, 다행한
31	**capable** [	keɪpəbl]	adj. (능력, 특질상) ~을 할 수 있는
32	**standard** [	stændərd]	n. 기준
33	**tremendous** [trə	mendəs]	adj. 엄청난
34	**advantage** [əd	væntɪdʒ]	n. 이점, 장점
35	**usefulness** [	ju:sfəlnəs]	n. 유용성
36	**aid** [eɪd]	v. 돕다
37	**reproductive** [|ri:prə|dʌktɪv]	adj. 생식[번식]의
38	**communication** [kə|mju:nɪ|keɪʃn]	n. 의사소통

TEST1 2-2
VOCABULARY

TEST1 2-2지문의 단어 중 토플 필수 단어를 선별하여 정리하였습니다.

39	**strategy**	[ˈstrætədʒi]	n. 전략
40	**employ**	[ɪmplɔ́i]	v. 사용하다, 이용하다
41	**defense**	[diféns]	n. 방어
42	**active**	[ˈæktɪv]	adj. 능동의
43	**passive**	[ˈpæsɪv]	adj. 수동적인
44	**zone**	[zoʊn]	n. 지역
45	**utilize**	[ˈjuːtəlaɪz]	v. 활용하다
46	**influential**	[ˌɪnfluˈenʃl]	adj. 영향력이 있는, 영향력이 큰
47	**organism**	[ˈɔːrɡənɪzəm]	n. 유기체
48	**responsible**	[rɪˈspɑːnsəbl]	adj. 책임지고 있는
49	**locate**	[ˈloʊkeɪt]	v. ~의 정확한 위치를 찾아내다
50	**cancerous**	[kǽnsərəs]	adj. 암의
51	**tumor**	[tjúːmər]	n. 종양
52	**initially**	[ɪˈnɪʃəli]	adv. 처음에
53	**threat**	[θret]	n. 위협
54	**flash**	[flæʃ]	v. 비치다, 비추다
55	**consensus**	[kənsénsəs]	n. 합의, 의견 일치
56	**daunting**	[dɔ́ːntɪŋ]	adj. 벅찬, 주눅이 들게 하는
57	**illustrate**	[ˈɪləstreɪt]	v. (실례, 도해 등을 이용하여) 분명히 보여주다
58	**thief**	[θiːf]	n. 도둑, 절도범
59	**steal**	[stiːl]	v. 훔치다, 도둑질하다
60	**jewelry**	[dʒúːəlri]	n. 보석류, 장신구
61	**posit**	[ˈpɑːzɪt]	v. 사실로 상정하다
62	**expose**	[ɪkˈspoʊz]	v. 드러내다
63	**hypothesize**	[haɪˈpɑːθəsaɪz]	v. 가설을 세우다
64	**artificially**	[ɑ̀ːrtəfíʃəli]	adv. 인위적으로
65	**recreate**	[ˌriːkriˈeɪt]	v. 재현하다
66	**signal**	[ˈsɪɡnəl]	n. 신호
67	**attract**	[əˈtrækt]	v. 끌어들이다
68	**encounter**	[ɪnˈkaʊntə(r)]	v. 맞닥뜨리다, 접하다
69	**camouflage**	[kǽməflὰːʒ]	v. 위장하다
70	**conceal**	[kənˈsiːl]	v. 감추다, 숨기다
71	**deliberately**	[dɪˈlɪbərətli]	adv. 고의로, 의도적으로
72	**mechanism**	[ˈmekənɪzəm]	n. 방법, 매커니즘
73	**conspicuous**	[kənspíkjuəs]	adj. 눈에 띄는, 두드러지는
74	**toxic**	[tάksik]	adj. 유독한

구문정리

TEST1 2-2 | Bioluminescence

본문 중 중요 구문 정리한 내용입니다. 우선 암기하고 많이 읽으시기 바랍니다.
Set2 Lecture1에 등장하는 단어들 중 필요한 단어들을 선별하였습니다.

01	look at	~을 살피다
02	move on to	~로 이동하다
03	name A B	A를 B라고 부르다
04	so far	지금까지
05	for O to do	의미상주어
06	devoid of	~이 없는
07	would like to do	to do 하고싶다
08	lack of	~의 부족
09	come to mind	생각이 나다
10	kind of	약간, 어느 정도
11	equivalent to	~와 같은
12	may have done	~했을지도 모른다(m)
13	enable O to do	O가 ~할 수 있게 하다
14	a type of	유형의, 일종의
15	call A B	A를 B라고 부르다
16	different from	~와 다른(f)
17	In fact	사실
18	inherit A from B	A를 B로부터 물려받다
19	from generation to generation	대대로
20	use O to do	O를 ~하기 위해 사용하다
21	In most cases	대부분의 경우에
22	in the sense	~한 의미로
23	be of help	도움되다
24	no at all	전혀 아니다.
25	need to do	to do 할 필요가 있다
26	to some extent	어느정도는
27	come as	=be (이다.)
28	ability to do	~할 수 있는 능력
29	make sense	의미가 통하다
30	limit A to B	A를 B에 제한하다
31	be capable of ~ing	~ing 할 수 있다
32	enable O to do	O가 to do 하는것을 가능케 하다
33	in the darkness	어둠속에
34	apply A to B	A를 B에 적용하다
35	of course	물론
36	advantage over	~이상의 장점
37	move on	계속하다
38	look into	~을 조사하다
39	when it comes to	~에 관한 한
40	deal with	~을 다루다
41	serve a purpose	도움되다
42	such as	~와 같은

구문정리

TEST1 2-2 | Bioluminescence

본문 중 중요 구문 정리한 내용입니다. 우선 암기하고 많이 읽으시기 바랍니다.
Set2 Lecture1에 등장하는 단어들 중 필요한 단어들을 선별하였습니다.

#	구문	뜻
43	aid in	~라는 점에서 돕다
44	want to do	to do하기를 원하다
45	take a guess	추측을 해보다
46	protect A aginst B	A를 B로부터 보호하다
47	teach A B	A에게 B를 가르치다
48	apply to	~에 적용하다
49	both A and B	A와 B 둘 다
50	for a purpose	어떤 목적으로
51	consider A (to be) B	A를 B로 여기다
52	in the field	분야에서
53	responsible for	~에 책임이 있는
54	flash light at	~에 불을 밝히다
55	in two different senses	두가지 다른 의미에서
56	What I mean is	내말은 ~ 이다
57	as to	~에 관하여
58	play a role in	~라는점에서 역할을 하다
59	scare off	~에게 겁을 주다
60	in a sense	어떤 의미에서
61	Let's say	예를 들면
62	in the middle of	~의 도중에
63	steal A from B	A를 B로부터 훔치다
64	try to do	to do 하는 것을 시도하다
65	run away	달아나다
66	expose A to B	A를 B에 노출시키다
67	feed on	~을 먹다
68	focus on	~에 초점을 맞추다
69	whether or not	~인지 아닌지
70	guess what	맞춰봐, 알겠니?
71	different than	~와는 다른 (t)
72	in that	~라는 점에서
73	avoid ~ing	ing 하는 것을 피하다
74	discussion on	~에 대한 논의
75	conceal A from B	A를 B로부터 숨기다
76	for instance	예를 들면
77	either A or B	A 또는 B
78	make O O.C	O를 O.C한 상태로 만들다
79	make O do	O가 do 하게 만들다
80	deliver a message to	~에게 메시지를 전달하다
81	as if	마치 ~인 것 처럼
82	consider A as B	A를 B로 여기다

TEST1 2-3
VOCABULARY

TEST1 2-3지문의 단어 중 토플 필수 단어를 선별하여 정리하였습니다.

01	**cartoon**	[kɑːrˈtuːn]	n. 만화 영화
02	**childhood**	[ˈtʃaɪldhʊd]	n. 어린 시절
03	**portray**	[pɔːrˈtreɪ]	v. 묘사하다
04	**archaeological**	[ˌɑːrkiəˈlɑdʒikəl]	adj. 고고학의
05	**element**	[ˈelɪmənt]	n. 요소
06	**misconception**	[ˌmìskənsépʃən]	n. 오해, 잘못된 생각
07	**archaeology**	[ˌɑːrkiˈɑːlədʒi]	n. 고고학
08	**discover**	[dɪˈskʌvə(r)]	v. 발견하다
09	**significant**	[sɪgˈnɪfɪkənt]	adj. 중요한
10	**valuable**	[ˈvæljuəbl]	adj. 소중한, 귀중한
11	**judgmental**	[dʒʌdʒˈméntl]	adj. 판단의, 판단을 내린
12	**require**	[rɪˈkwaɪə(r)]	v. 필요로 하다, 요구하다
13	**sophisticated**	[səˈfístəkèitid]	adj. 정교한, 복잡한
14	**institution**	[ˌɪnstɪˈtuːʃn]	n. 기관
15	**devote**	[dɪˈvóut]	v. 쏟다, 기울이다
16	**tremendous**	[trɪˈméndəs]	adj. 엄청난, 거대한
17	**enrich**	[ɪnˈrɪtʃ]	v. 질을 높이다, 풍요롭게 하다
18	**detector**	[dɪˈtektə(r)]	n. 탐지기
19	**invention**	[ɪnˈvenʃn]	n. 발명품
20	**develop**	[dɪˈveləp]	v. 발달하다
21	**cosmic**	[ˈkɑːzmɪk]	adj. 우주의
22	**subatomic**	[ˌsʌbəˈtɑːmɪk]	adj. 원자보다 작은
23	**collide**	[kəˈlaɪd]	v. 충돌하다, 부딪치다
24	**atmosphere**	[ˈætməsfɪr]	n. (지구의) 대기
25	**consequently**	[ˈkɑːnsəkwentli]	adv. 그 결과, 따라서
26	**particle**	[ˈpɑːrtɪkl]	n. 입자
27	**property**	[ˈprɑːpərti]	n. 속성, 특성
28	**exploit**	[ɪkˈsplóit]	v. 활용하다, 이용하다
29	**basically**	[ˈbeɪsɪkli]	adv. 근본적으로
30	**stimulate**	[ˈstɪmjuleɪt]	v. 자극하다
31	**energize**	[ˈenərdʒaɪz]	v. 동력을 공급하다
32	**penetrate**	[ˈpenɪtreɪt]	v. 관통하다
33	**advantage**	[ædˈvæntidʒ]	n. 이점, 장점
34	**excavate**	[ˈékskəvèit]	v. 파다, …을 발굴하다
35	**artifact**	[ˈɑːrtəfækt]	n. 인공물, 공예품
36	**tomb**	[tuːm]	n. 무덤

TEST1 2-3
VOCABULARY

TEST1 2-3지문의 단어 중 토플 필수 단어를 선별하여 정리하였습니다.

37	**straightforward** [|streɪt|fɔ:rwərd]	adj. 간단한, 복잡하지 않은
38	**complicated** [kámpləkèitid]	adj. 복잡한, 어려운
39	**post** [poust]	n. 기둥
40	**impediment** [impédəmənt]	n. 장애, 방해
41	**hindrance** [híndrəns]	n. 장애, 방해
42	**density** [dénsəti]	n. 밀도
43	**decipher** [disáifər]	v. 판독하다, 해독하다
44	**blocked** [blakt]	adj. 막힌
45	**deflected** [difléktid]	adj. 아래로 굽은
46	**dense** [dens]	adj. 밀집한
47	**visualize** [|vɪʒuəlaɪz]	v. 시각화하다
48	**vividly** [vívidli]	adv. 생생하게, 선명하게
49	**represent** [|reprɪ|zent]	v. 나타내다, 상징하다
50	**strike** [straɪk]	v. 부딪치다
51	**eventually** [ɪ|ventʃuəli]	adv. 결국
52	**reflect** [rɪ|flekt]	v. 반사하다
53	**damage** [|dæmɪdʒ]	v. 훼손하다
54	**ensure** [ɪn|ʃʊr]	v. 보장하다
55	**safety** [|seɪfti]	n. 안전
56	**avoid** [ə|vɔɪd]	v. 방지하다, 막다, 모면하다
57	**despite** [dɪ|spaɪt]	pre. …에도 불구하고
58	**practical** [|præktɪkl]	adj. 현실적인
59	**strenuous** [strénjuəs]	adj. 힘이 많이 드는, 몹시 힘든, 격렬한
60	**modification** [|mɑ:dɪfɪ|keɪʃn]	n. 수정
61	**enhance** [ɪn|hæns]	v. 향상하다, 증진
62	**flaw** [flɔ:]	n. 결점, 결함
63	**functional** [fʌŋkʃənl]	adj. 작동하는
64	**internal** [ɪntə́:rnl]	adj. 내부의
65	**burdensome** [bə́:rdnsəm]	adj. 부담이 되는, 짐스러운
66	**improve** [imprú:v]	v. 개선하다, 증진시키다
67	**advance** [ædvǽns]	n. 발전, 발달
68	**alternative** [ɔ:ltə́:rnətiv]	n. 대안
69	**explore** [ɪk|splɔ:(r)]	v. 답사하다, 탐구하다
70	**deficiency** [dɪ|fɪʃnsi]	n. 부족, 결함
71	**overcome** [ouˈvərkə,m]	v. 극복하다, 이겨내다

구문정리

TEST1 2-3 | Muon detector

본문 중 중요 구문 정리한 내용입니다. 우선 암기하고 많이 읽으시기 바랍니다.
Set2 Lecture2에 등장하는 단어들 중 필요한 단어들을 선별하였습니다.

01	almost all	대부분
02	might have done	~했을지도 모른다
03	give A B	A에게 B를 주다
04	ask A B	A에게 B를 묻다
05	get A from B	A를 B로 부터 얻다
06	hope to do	to do 하기를 바라다
07	something significant	중요한 무언가
08	try to do	to do 하기를 시도하다
09	seem to do	to do 하는 것처럼 보인다
10	That is how	방법은 ~이다
11	in a sense	어떤 의미에서는
12	carry out	수행하다
13	involve A in B	A를 B에 관여하게하다
14	in contrast to	~에 반하여
15	such as	예를 들어; ~와 같은
16	devote A to B	A를 B에 바치다
17	in fact	사실
18	one of the 복수명사	복수명사 중 하나
19	to be more specific	더 구체적으로 말하면
20	mean to do	to do 할 작정이다
21	as well	또한
22	would like to do	to do 하고싶다
23	focus on	~에 주력하다, 초점을 맞추다
24	in the next class	다음 수업 시간에
25	get back to	~으로 돌아가다
26	call A B	A를 B라고 부르다
27	result from	~로 부터 기인하다
28	travel through	~를 지나 여행하다
29	at the speed of	~의 속도로
30	close to	가까운
31	collide with	~와 충돌하다
32	break down into	~로 부수다
33	know A as B	A를 B라고 알다
34	wonder about	~에 대해 궁금해하다
35	be of help	힘이 되다, 도움되다
36	in the field of	~의 분야에서
37	after all	결국에는, 어쨌든
38	be able to do	to do 할 수 있다
39	take advantage of	~를 이용하다
40	use O to do	O를 to do하는데 사용하다
41	similar to	~와 유사한
42	want to do	to do 하는 것을 원하다
43	need to do	to do하는 것을 필요로하다
44	figure out	이해하다, 알아내다

구문정리

TEST1 2-3 | Muon detector

본문 중 중요 구문 정리한 내용입니다. 우선 암기하고 많이 읽으시기 바랍니다.

Set2 Lecture2에 등장하는 단어들 중 필요한 단어들을 선별하였습니다.

45	bury inside	~안에 묻다		65	avoid ~ing	~ing 하기를 피하다
46	fill A with B	A를 B로 채우다		66	enough to be	~이기에 충분한
47	go through	겪다		67	a lot of	많은
48	in this case	이 경우에는		68	look for	~를 찾다
49	the 비교급, the 비교급	~할수록 더 ~하다		69	at that time	그 당시에
50	on the other hand	반면에		70	place A on B	A를 B에 두다
51	pose hinderance to	~에게 방해를 야기하다		71	it is difficult for O to do	O가 to do하는것은 어렵다
52	the number of	~의 숫자		72	there is	~이 있다
53	depend on	~에 의존하다, 의지하다		73	work out	해답을 내다
54	have a hard time ~ing	~ing 함에 있어 어려움을 겪다		74	take O to do	O를 ~하기 위해 쓰다, 취하다
55	make sense	의미가 통하다, 이해하다		75	half a year	반년(6개월)
56	turn A into B	A를 B로 바꾸다		76	in some ways	어떤 점에서는, 어떻게 해서든
57	as I mentioned previously	이전에 언급했듯이		77	not at all	전혀
58	help O do	O가 ~하는 것을 돕다		78	for six months	6개월 동안
59	in the middle of	~의 중앙에		79	assure O that	O에게 that절을 보장하다
60	between A and B	A와 B사이에		80	this way	이방법으로
61	pass through	~를 거쳐가다		81	map out	상세히 나타내다
62	in other words	다시 말해서		82	go inside	안으로 들어가다
63	in the past	과거에		83	at the moment	바로 지금 (now)
64	at risk of	~의 위험에 처한				

TEST2 1-1
VOCABULARY

TEST2 1-1 지문의 단어 중 토플 필수 단어를 선별하여 정리하였습니다.

1	**offer** [ɔ́:fər]	v. 제안하다, 권하다
2	**department** [dɪ|pɑ́:rtmənt]	n. 부서
3	**launch** [lɔ:ntʃ]	v. 개최하다, 추진하다
4	**community** [kə|mjú:nəti]	n. 지역 사회
5	**participate** [pɑ:r|tɪsɪpeɪt]	v. 참가하다, 참여하다
6	**experience** [ɪk|spɪriəns]	n. 경험
7	**improve** [ɪmprú:v]	v. 향상시키다, 개선하다
8	**loath** [loʊθ]	adj. 혐오하다, 몹시 질색하다
9	**attend** [ə|tend]	v. 참석하다
10	**ironic** [airánik]	adj. 아이러니한, 모순적인
11	**major** [méidʒər]	n. 전공
12	**supportive** [sə|pɔ́:rtɪv]	adj. 힘을 주는
13	**contribute to** [kən|trɪbju:t]	v. 기여하다, 이바지하다
14	**develop** [dɪ|veləp]	v. 성장하다
15	**profound** [prə|faʊnd]	adj. 깊은, 심오한
16	**fundamental** [|fʌndə|mentl]	adj. 근본적인, 본질적인
17	**concept** [|kɑ́:nsept]	n. 개념
18	**intriguing** [ɪn|trí:gɪŋ]	adj. 아주 흥미로운, 흥미를 자아내는
19	**relatively** [|relətɪvli]	adv. 상대적으로, 비교적
20	**decade** [dékeid]	n. 십년
21	**underestimate** [ə|ndəre|stəmei,t]	v. 과소평가하다
22	**current** [kə́:rənt]	adj. 현재의, 지금의
23	**generally** [dʒénərəli]	adv. 일반적으로, 대개
24	**entail** [ɪntéil]	v. ~을 수반하다
25	**stuff** [stʌf]	n. 물질, 물건, 것(것들)
26	**calculate** [kǽlkjulèit]	v. 계산하다, 산출하다
27	**probability** [prɑ̀bəbíləti]	n. 확률
28	**barely** [béərli]	adv. 거의 ~아니게, 간신히
29	**involve** [ɪnvɑ́lv]	v. 포함하다, 수반하다
30	**complete** [kəmplí:t]	v. 완료하다, 끝마치다
31	**administrator** [ədmínistrèitər]	n. 행정관, 관계자
32	**approve** [əprú:v]	v. 승인하다
33	**priority** [praiɔ́:rəti]	n. 우선, 중요, 먼저
34	**inquire** [inkwáiər]	v. 문의하다

구문정리

TEST2 1-1 | Math nights

본문 중 중요 구문 정리한 내용입니다. 우선 암기하고 많이 읽으시기 바랍니다.

Set1 Conversation에 등장하는 단어들 중 필요한 단어들을 선별하였습니다.

01	look for	~을 찾다
02	want to do	to do 하기를 원하다
03	offer A B	A에게 B를 제공하다
04	relate A to B	A와 B를 관련시키다
05	hear of	~에 대해 듣다(소문등으로)
06	talk about	~에 대해 이야기하다
07	participate in	~에 참가하다
08	love ~ing	~ing 하는것을 좋아하다
09	have experience with	경험을 가지다
10	help O do	O가 ~하는 것을 돕다
11	improve skill	솜씨를 닦다
12	to be honest with you	솔직히 말하자면
13	not only A but (also) B	A뿐만 아니라 B또한
14	now that	~ 이므로, ~ 이기 때문에
15	look at	~을 보다
16	supportive of	~을 지원하는
17	decision to do	to do 하려는 결정
18	choose to do	to do 하는것을 선택하다
19	major in	~을 전공하다
20	try to do	to do 하는것을 시도하다
21	contribute to	~에 기여하다
22	figure out	~을 알아내다, 이해하다
23	teach A B	A에게 B를 가르치다
24	intriguing to	~에게 흥미롭다
25	do a puzzle	퍼즐하다
26	be concerned with	~에 관심이 있다 ; ~와 관계 있다
27	I'd like to do	to do하고 싶다
28	focus on	~에 초점 맞추다
29	have to do	to do 해야한다
30	worry about	~에 대해 걱정하다
31	explain A to B	A를 B에게 설명하다
32	as well	~또한
33	you see	있잖아 (무엇을 설명할 때)
34	get adj	점점 adj 해지다
35	over decades	수십년동안
36	have a time ~ing	~하는데 시간을 가지다
37	nothing higher than	~ 이상은 아닌
38	sound hard	어렵게 들린다
39	for O to do	의미상 주어
40	relate to	~을 이해하다
41	the thing is	실은(중요한 사실·이유·해명을 언급하려고 할 때 씀)
42	keep up with	따라잡다, 뒤쳐지지 않다
43	a lot of	많은
44	add A to B	A를 B에 더하다
45	give A B	A에게 B를 주다
46	per semester	학기당
47	difficult of~	~하기 어렵다
48	the 비교급, the 비교급	~할수록, ~하다
49	let us know	우리에게 알려줘
50	need to do	~할 필요가 있다
51	take long	오래 걸리다
52	give you a call	너에게 전화하다
53	by the end of the week	주말까지
54	thank A for B	A에게 B때문에 감사하다

TEST2 1-2
VOCABULARY

TEST2 1-2 지문의 단어 중 토플 필수 단어를 선별하여 정리하였습니다.

01	**research** [rɪ	sɜːrtʃ]	v. 연구하다, 조사하다
02	**popular** [	pɑːpjələ(r)]	adj. 인기 있는
03	**discussion** [dɪ	skʌʃn]	n. 논의, 상의
04	**accessibility** [æksèsəbíləti]	n. 접근성
05	**purchase** [	pɜːrtʃəs]	v. 구입하다, 구매하다
06	**extremely** [ɪk	striːmli]	adv. 극도로, 극히
07	**laborer** [léibərər]	n. 노동자
08	**wage** [weɪdʒ]	n. 임금, 급료
09	**costly** [	kɔːstli]	adj. 값비싼
10	**publish** [pʌblɪʃ]	v. 출판하다
11	**separate** [	seprət]	adj. 분리된
12	**discourage** [dɪs	kɜːrɪdʒ]	v. 낙담시키다, 단념시키다
13	**ingrained** [ɪngréind]	adj. 뿌리깊은, 깊이 배어든
14	**launch** [lɔːntʃ]	v. 시작하다
15	**profitable** [prɑ́fitəbl]	adj. 수익성이 좋은, 이익이 되는
16	**unfortunate** [ənfɔ́ːrtʃənət]	adj. 불행한, 유감스러운
17	**burdensome** [bə́ːrdnsəm]	adj. 귀찮은, 짐스러운, 부담이 되는
18	**expense** [ikspéns]	n. 비용, 지출, 희생
19	**medium** [míːdiəm]	n. 방법, 방식
20	**invent** [invént]	v. 발명하다, 개발하다, 고안하다
21	**lend** [lend]	v. 빌려주다
22	**annual** [ǽnjuəl]	adj. 연간의, 매년의
23	**borrow** [bɑ́rou]	v. 빌리다
24	**ridiculous** [ridíkjuləs]	adj. 말도 안 되는, 터무니없는
25	**consider** [kənsídər]	v. 고려하다
26	**satisfy** [sǽtisfài]	v. 만족시키다, 충족시키다
27	**quantity** [kwɑ́ntəti]	n. 양, 수량
28	**beneficial** [bènəfíʃəl]	adj. 이로운, 유익한

TEST2 1-2
VOCABULARY

TEST2 1-2 지문의 단어 중 토플 필수 단어를 선별하여 정리하였습니다.

29	**brilliant**	[bríljənt]	adj. 훌륭한, 뛰어난, 멋진
30	**influence**	[ínfluəns]	n. 영향
31	**conservative**	[kənsə́:rvətiv]	adj. 보수적인
32	**avoid**	[əvɔ́id]	v. 피하다
33	**content**	[kάntent]	n. 콘텐츠, 내용
34	**offensive**	[əfénsiv]	adj. 모욕적인, 불쾌한
35	**divide**	[diváid]	v. 나누다, 분할하다
36	**chronological**	[krɑˌnəlɑˈdʒikəl]	adj. 연대순의
37	**burden**	[bə́:rdn]	n. 부담감, 부담, 짐
38	**ameliorate**	[əmí:ljərèit]	v. 개선하다
39	**lengthy**	[léŋkθi]	adj. 오랜, 긴
40	**intend**	[inténd]	v. 의도하다
41	**digress**	[daigrés]	v. [주제에서] 벗어나다
42	**serialization**	[sìəriəlizéiʃən]	n. 연재
43	**simplify**	[símpləfài]	v. 단순화하다, 간소화하다
44	**illustration**	[ìləstréiʃən]	n. 삽화
45	**advertisement**	[ædvərtáizmənt]	n. 광고
46	**criticism**	[krítəsìzm]	n. 비판, 비난
47	**periodically**	[pìəriάdikəli]	adv. 정기적으로, 주기적으로
48	**proponent**	[prəpóunənt]	n. 지지자
49	**installment**	[instɔ́:lmənt]	n. 연재물
50	**ensure**	[inʃúər]	v. ~하기 위해, 보장하다, 확보하다
51	**consistent**	[kənsístənt]	adj. 일관된, 지속적인
52	**suspenseful**	[səspénsfəl]	adj. 긴장감 넘치는
53	**cinematic**	[sìnəmǽtik]	adj. 영화의
54	**approach**	[əpróutʃ]	n. 접근, 접근법
55	**dramatization**	[dræmətizéiʃən]	n. 각색, 희곡화

구문정리

본문 중 중요 구문 정리한 내용입니다. 우선 암기하고 많이 읽으시기 바랍니다.

TEST2 1-2 | The accessibility of novels

Set1 Lecture1에 등장하는 단어들 중 필요한 단어들을 선별하였습니다.

01	ask O to do	O가 to do하는것을 요구하다 (a)
02	such as	~와 같은
03	I would like to do	to do 하고 싶다
04	at the time	그당시에
05	used to do	~하곤 했다
06	gain access to	~에 접근하다
07	talk about	~에 대해 이야기하다
08	refer to A as B	A를 B라고 언급하다
09	the amount of	~양
10	require O to do	O가 to do 하는것을 요구하다 (r)
11	equal to	~와 같은
12	weekly wage	주급
13	do research	조사하다
14	due to	~때문에
15	call A B	A를 B라 부르다
16	in three volumes	세권으로
17	for instance	예를 들어(i)
18	let's say	예를 들어 (s)
19	a series of	일련의
20	be aware of	~을 알다
21	have to do	to do 해야한다
22	not just A , but also B	A뿐만 아니라 B도(j)
23	discourage A from B	A를 B하지 못하게 막다
24	so ~ that	너무 ~해서 ~이다
25	unfortunate for	~에게 불행한
26	sell A for B	A를 B의 값을 받고팔다
27	look at	살피다
28	so-called	소위, 이른바
29	pay fee	요금을 지불하다
30	run business	사업을 운영하다
31	thousands of	수천의
32	at once	즉시, 당장
33	satisfy the need	필요를 충족시키다
34	in large quantities	대량으로
35	worry about	~에 대해 걱정하다
36	sell A to B	A를 B에게 팔다
37	beneficial for	~에게 이로운
38	possible for O to do	O가 to do 하는것을 가능한

구문정리

TEST2 1-2 | The accessibility of novels

본문 중 중요 구문 정리한 내용입니다. 우선 암기하고 많이 읽으시기 바랍니다.
Set1 Lecture1에 등장하는 단어들 중 필요한 단어들을 선별하였습니다.

#	구문	의미
39	not only A but also B	A뿐만 아니라 B또한(o)
40	enough to do	to do 할만큼 충분히
41	take advantage of	~을 이용하다
42	think about	~에 대해 생각하다
43	make profit	이익을 내다
44	three times as much	3배 많은
45	fulfill plan	계획 달성하다
46	exerted an influence over	~에 영향력을 행사하다
47	put A into B	A를 B에 넣다
48	turn A into B	A를 B로 바꾸다
49	move on to	~로 나아가다, 계속 진행하다
50	hear of	(소문으로) 듣다
51	divide A into B	A를 B로 나누다
52	in chronological order	시간순으로
53	come as	=be (~이다)
54	way to do	to do 하는 방법
55	cause O to do	O가 to do 하는것을 야기하다
56	get done	~ 되다
57	try to do	~하는것을 시도하다
58	make up	채우다; 만들다
59	make O O.C	O를 O.C로 만들다
60	come up with	생각해 내다
61	instead of	~대신에
62	fill up	가득 채우다
63	other than	~을 제외하고
64	along with	~에 따라, ~와 함께
65	contribution to	~에 기여
66	criticism form the public	대중으로부터의 비판
67	need O to do	O가 to do 하는것을 필요로 하다
68	rush out	~을 급히 만들어 내다
69	keep O ~ing	O를 ing한 상태로 유지하다
70	end with	~으로 끝나다
71	walk down the street	거리를 거닐다
72	walk off	떠나 버리다
73	into the distance	먼곳으로
74	A is praised by B	A가 B에 의해 칭찬받다
75	be opposed to	~에 반대하다

TEST2 1-3
VOCABULARY

TEST2 1-3지문의 단어 중 토플 필수 단어를 선별하여 정리하였습니다.

01	**interaction** [iˌntərækˈʃən]	n. 상호작용,
02	**predator** [prédətər]	n. 포식자
03	**prey** [prei]	v. 잡아먹다, n. 먹이
04	**relative** [rélətiv]	adj. 비교상의, 상대적인
05	**survival** [sərváivəl]	n. 생존 adj. 살아남기 위한
06	**method** [méθəd]	n. 방법, 방식, 수단
07	**apex** [éipeks]	n. 정점
08	**ecosystem** [ékousístəm]	n. 생태계
09	**analogous** [ənǽləgəs]	adj. 유사한, 비슷한
10	**occupy** [άkjupài]	v. 차지하다
11	**integrative** [íntəgrèitiv]	adj. 통합하는, 완전하게 하는
12	**ecology** [ikάlədʒi]	n. 생태 환경
13	**biodiversity** [báiou divə́:rsəti]	n. 생물의 다양성
14	**herbivore** [ə́:rbəvɔ̀:r]	n. 초식동물
15	**carnivore** [kά:rnəvɔ̀:r]	n. 육식동물
16	**vegan** [víːgən]	n. 채식주의자
17	**commensurate** [kəménsərət]	adj. 상응하는, 비례하는, 동등한
18	**phenomenon** [finάmənὰn]	n. 현상
19	**cease** [siːs]	v. 중단하다
20	**alert** [ələ́ːrt]	adj. 기민한
21	**appearance** [əpíərəns]	n. 출연
22	**carefree** [keˈrfriˌ]	adj. 걱정없는, 태평한
23	**existence** [igzístəns]	n. 존재
24	**immediately** [imíːdiətli]	adv. 즉시, 바로
25	**terminate** [tə́ːrmənèit]	v. 끝내다
26	**defense** [diféns]	n. 방어
27	**impact** [ímpækt]	n. 영향
28	**modify** [mάdəfài]	v. 변경하다
29	**adapt** [ədǽpt]	v. (상황에) 적응하다
30	**predation** [pridéiʃən]	n. 포식, 포식관계

TEST2 1-3
VOCABULARY

TEST2 1-3지문의 단어 중 토플 필수 단어를 선별하여 정리하였습니다.

31	**visualize** [víʒuəlàiz]	v. 시각화하다, 마음에 떠올리다	44	**roam** [roum]	v. 돌아다니다
32	**primary** [ˈpraɪmeri]	adj. 주된, 주요한	45	**devour** [diváuər]	v. 먹어치우다, 잡아먹다
33	**inhabit** [inhǽbit]	v. 거주하다, 서식하다	46	**mature** [mətjúər]	v. 어른이 되다, 성숙해지다
34	**region** [ˈriːdʒən]	n. 지역	47	**accomplish** [əkɑːmplɪʃ]	v. 완수하다, 성취하다
35	**exception** [ɪkˈsepʃn]	n. 예외	48	**initially** [iníʃəli]	adv. 처음에, 당초에
36	**continually** [kəntínjuəli]	adv. 계속해서, 끊임없이, 줄곧	49	**complex** [kəmpléks]	adj. 복잡한
37	**peculiar** [pɪˈkjuːliə(r)]	adj. 이상한, 특이한	50	**absent** [ǽbsənt]	adj. 부재의, 없는, 결여된
38	**forcibly** [fɔ́ːrsəbli]	adv. 강제적으로	51	**minimize** [mínəmàiz]	v. 최소화하다
39	**regulation** [règjuléiʃən]	n. 규제, 규정, 법규	52	**nimble** [nímbl]	adj. 민첩한, 재빠른
40	**impose** [impóuz]	v. 부과하다, 적용하다, 제한하다	53	**attentive** [əténtiv]	adj. 주의깊은, 세심한
41	**disappearance** [dìsəpíːərəns]	n. 사라짐, 소멸, 실종	54	**range** [reɪndʒ]	n. 다양성, 범위
42	**thrive** [θraiv]	v. 번창하다, 성장하다	55	**restrict** [ristríkt]	v. 제한하다, 금지하다
43	**dramatically** [drəmǽtikəli]	adv. 극적으로, 급격하게	56	**hinder** [híndər]	v. 방해하다, 저해하다

구문정리 TEST2 1-3

Predation risk effects

본문 중 중요 구문 정리한 내용입니다. 우선 암기하고 많이 읽으시기 바랍니다.
Set1 Lecture2에 등장하는 단어들 중 필요한 단어들을 선별하였습니다.

01	start from	~에서 시작하다
02	leave off	중단하다
03	talk about	~에 대해 말하다
04	effect on	~에 대한 영향
05	each other	서로서로
06	employ O to do	O를 to do 하기 위해 사용하다
07	except for	~을 제외하고
08	apex predator	최상위 포식자
09	such as	~와 같은
10	enough to do	~하기에 충분한
11	be going to do	~할 예정이다
12	bring A into B	A를 B로 가져오다
13	refer to	지칭하다, 언급하다
14	interact with	~와 상호작용하다
15	one another	서로서로
16	In a sense	어떤 의미에서
17	analogous to	~와 비슷한
18	play a role in	~라는 점에서 역할을 하다
19	look at	보다
20	both A and B	A와 B 둘 다
21	branch of	부분의
22	as opposed to	~와는 대조적으로
23	in terms of	~라는 점에서
24	be aware of	~을 알다
25	prey on	~을 잡아먹다
26	be a key to ing	~ing함에 있어 중요하다
27	change in	~라는 점에서의 변화
28	commensurate with	~에 비례한
29	for instance	예를 들어(i)
30	live in	~에 살다
31	cease to do	to do 하는 것을 멈추다
32	look around	둘러보다
33	no longer	더 이상 ~이 아닌
34	live with	~와 동거하다; 감수하다
35	try to do	to do 하기를 시도하다
36	introduce A to B	A를 B에 소개하다
37	be prepared to do	to do 할 준비가 되어있다
38	defense mechanisms	방어기제
39	for a long time	장기간
40	it is likely that	that절 일것 같다
41	as soon as	하자마자
42	think of	~을 생각하다
43	force O to do	O가 to do하도록 강요하다
44	due to	~때문에
45	call A B	A를 B라고 부르다
46	exert influence on	~에 대해 영향력을 발휘하다

TEST2 1-3 | Predation risk effects

Set1 Lecture2에 등장하는 단어들 중 필요한 단어들을 선별하였습니다.

#	구문	뜻
47	have hard time -ing	~ing 하는데 어려움을 겪다
48	of course	물론
49	be sure	확신하다
50	go on a trip	여행가다
51	that of	앞 명사 반복(단수)
52	chance to do	to do 할 기회
53	not only A but also B	A뿐만 아니라 B도
54	in the beginning	맨처음에
55	limit A to B	A를 B로 제한하다
56	for example	예를 들어 (e)
57	at the time	그 당시에
58	with the exception of	~을 제외하고
59	over the course of	~동안
60	as a result of	~의 결과로서
61	not surprisingly	당연히
62	wipe out	완전히 없애버리다
63	prey upon	~을 잡아먹다
64	in this case	이 경우에 있어서
65	In addition to	~에 더하여
66	as well	또한
67	want to do	~하기를 원하다
68	take a guess	추측하다
69	feed on	~을 먹다
70	starting ing	ing 하는것을 시작하다
71	without fear	안심하고
72	along with	~와 함께
73	you got it	그렇고 말고, 바로 그거야
74	mature into	~로 성숙하다
75	decrease in	~에서의 감소
76	the number of	숫자
77	rely upon	~에 의존하다
78	as a means of	수단으로서
79	be at risk of -ing	~ing 할 위기에 처해있다
80	solve the problem	문제를 해결하다
81	start with	~와 함께 시작하다
82	wish to do	to do 하기를 소망하다
83	increase in	~에서의 증가
84	now that	~이기 때문에
85	absent from	~에 없는, 결석한
86	food chain	먹이사슬
87	need to do	~해야 할 필요가 있다
88	restrict A to B	A를 B로 한정하다
89	from a distance	멀리서
90	impose A on B	A를 B에 부과하다
91	allow O to do	O가 to do 하는 것을 허락하다
92	return to	복귀하다

TEST2 2-1
VOCABULARY

TEST2 2-1지문의 단어 중 토플 필수 단어를 선별하여 정리하였습니다.

01	**suppose** [səpóuz]	v. 추측하다, 가정하다
02	**stuff** [stʌf]	n. 물건, 물질, 것(것들)
03	**generous** [dʒénərəs]	adj. 관대한, 후한, 너그러운
04	**gesture** [dʒéstʃər]	n. 몸짓
05	**abruptly** [əbrʌ́ptli]	adv. 갑자기, 돌연히
06	**expect** [ikspékt]	v. 예상하다, 기대하다
07	**formalize** [fɔ́ːrməlàiz]	v. ~을 형식화하다, 정식화하다
08	**summer break** [sʌ́mər breik]	n. 여름방학
09	**donation** [dounéiʃən]	n. 기부, 기증
10	**experience** [ikspíəriəns]	n. 경험, 경력
11	**dorm** [dɔːrm]	n. 기숙사
12	**useful** [júːsfl]	adj. 유용한, 쓸모 있는
13	**contact** [kɑ́ntækt]	v. 연락하다, 접촉하다
14	**charity** [tʃǽrəti]	n. 자선단체
15	**organization** [ɔ̀ːrɡənəzéiʃn]	n. 단체, 기구
16	**schedule** [skédʒuːl]	v. 일정을 잡다
17	**store** [stɔːr]	v. 저장하다, 보관하다
18	**profit** [práfit]	n. 이익, 수익, 이윤
19	**administration** [ədmìnistréiʃən]	n. 관리[행정]
20	**complicated** [kámpləkèitid]	adj. 복잡한
21	**procedure** [prəsíːdʒər]	n. 절차, 과정
22	**specific** [spəsífik]	adj. 구체적인, 특정한
23	**request** [rikwést]	n. 요청
24	**process** [prɑ́ːses]	n. 과정, 절차
25	**spread** [spred]	v. 퍼뜨리다, 확산시키다
26	**flyer** [fláiər]	n. 광고 전단
27	**notice** [nóutis]	n. 공고문, 안내문
28	**bulletin board** [búlitən bɔːrd]	n. 게시판
29	**advertisement** [ædvərtáizmənt]	n. 광고
30	**permission** [pərmíʃn]	n. 허락, 허가

구문정리

TEST2 2-1 | Housing department

본문 중 중요 구문 정리한 내용입니다. 우선 암기하고 많이 읽으시기 바랍니다.

Set2 Conversation에 등장하는 단어들 중 필요한 단어들을 선별하였습니다.

01	long time no see	오랜만이야
02	what bring you here?	왜 왔니?
03	be supposed to do	~하기로 되어있다
04	spend time	시간을 보내다
05	talk about	~에 대해 얘기하다
06	take home with me	집에 가져가다
07	of course	물론
08	so~ that~	너무 ~해서 ~ 하다
09	in front of	~의 앞쪽에
10	take a course	수업을 받다
11	for O to do	의미상 주어
12	here it is	여기 있습니다
13	make O do	O가 do하게 만들다
14	have been done	당해오다 (동사형태 4번)
15	throw out	~를 내쫓다
16	want to do	~하기를 원하다
17	summer break	여름방학
18	a lot of	많은
19	leave A in B	A를 B에 두다
20	too ~ to	너무 ~해서 ~할 수 없다
21	carry with	~에 휴대하다
22	you know	알지
23	come from	~에서 나용
24	charity organization	3자선 단체
25	be willing to do	기꺼이 ~하다
26	every semester	매학기
27	use O to do	O를 ~하기 위해 사용하다
28	need to do	O가 to do 하는 것을 필요로 하다
29	let's see	어디 한 번 보자
30	agree with 상대 on 주제	~랑 ~주제에 대해 동의하다
31	think so	동감하다
32	follow procedure	절차를 따르다
33	have to do	to do 해야한다
34	go through	~을 살펴보다
35	spread the word	말을 퍼뜨리다, 소문내다
36	put A on B	A를 B위에 두다
37	bulletin board	게시판
38	sound like	~처럼 들리다
39	put A in the newspaper	A를 신문에 게재하다
40	almost all	거의 전부
41	that way	그와 같이
42	seem like	~처럼 보이다
43	work out	해결하다
44	as soon as	~하자마자
45	get permission	허가를 얻다

TEST2 2-2 VOCABULARY

TEST2 2-2지문의 단어 중 토플 필수 단어를 선별하여 정리하였습니다.

01	**struggle** [strʌgl]	v. 어려움을 겪다
02	**confront** [kən|frʌnt]	v. 직면하다, 마주하다
03	**adversity** [ædvə́:rsəti]	n. 고난, 역경
04	**daily** [déili]	adj. 매일의, 일상적인
05	**frustrated** [frʌstreitid]	adj. 실망한, 낙담한
06	**approach** [əpróuʧ]	v. 접근하다
07	**tenaciously** [tənéiʃəsli]	adv. 끈기 있게
08	**unreachable** [ʌnrí:ʧəbl]	adj. 도달할 수 없는
09	**socialize** [sóuʃəlàiz]	v. 어울리다, 교제하다
10	**grasp** [græsp]	v. 파악하다, 이해하다
11	**phenomenon** [finámənàn]	n. 현상
12	**insight** [ínsàit]	n. 통찰
13	**renowned** [rináund]	adj. 유명한, 저명한
14	**presitgious** [prestídʒəs]	adj. 명망 있는, 고귀한
15	**mathematician** [mæθəmətíʃən]	n. 수학자
16	**impact** [ímpækt]	v. ~에 영향을 주다
17	**aspect** [ǽspekt]	n. 측면
18	**orbit** [ɔ́:rbit]	n. 궤도
19	**reach** [ri:ʧ]	v. 도달하다, 이르다
20	**withdraw** [wiðdrɔ́: wiθ-]	v. 철수하다, 인출하다
21	**stroll** [stroul]	n. 산책
22	**conclude** [kənklú:d]	v. 결론짓다
23	**gravity** [grǽvəti]	n. 중력
24	**practical** [prǽktikəl]	adj. 실질적인
25	**establish** [istǽbliʃ]	v. 설립하다, 세우다
26	**fundamental** [fʌndəméntl]	adj. 기본적인, 근본적인, 중요한
27	**governing** [gʌvərniŋ]	adj. 지배적인
28	**neuroscientist** [njùərousáiəntist]	n. 신경과학자
29	**analyze** [ǽnəlàiz]	v. 분석하다
30	**subject** [sʌbdʒikt]	n. 피험자

TEST2 2-2
VOCABULARY

TEST2 2-2지문의 단어 중 토플 필수 단어를 선별하여 정리하였습니다.

31	**participate** [pa:rtísəpèit]	v. 참여하다
32	**monitor** [mánətər]	v. 감시하다, 관찰하다
33	**unusual** [ənjuːʒuˌəl]	adj. 특이한, 독특한
34	**forehead** [fɔ́:rid, fɔ́:rhèd]	n. 이마
35	**frontal lobe** [frʌntl loub]	n. 전두엽
36	**initiate** [iníʃièit]	v. 시작하다, 개시하다
37	**logic** [ládʒik]	n. 논리
38	**prepatory** [pripǽrətɔ̀:ri]	adj. 예비의, 준비의
39	**sensory** [sénsəri]	adj. 감각의
40	**detect** [ditékt]	v. 탐지하다
41	**external** [ikstə́:rnl]	adj. 외부의
42	**visual** [víʒuəl]	adj. 시각의
43	**auditory** [ɔ́:ditɔ̀:ri]	adj. 청각의
44	**cortex** [kɔ́:rteks]	n. 대뇌 피질
45	**occipital** [aksípitəl]	adj. 후두의
46	**temporal** [témpərəl]	adj. 관자놀이의, 측두의
47	**vital** [váitl]	adj. 중요한, 필수적인
48	**dominate** [dámənèit]	v. ~을 지배하다, 압도하다
49	**momentarily** [mòuməntérəli]	adv. 잠시
50	**blocked** [blakt]	adj. 막힌
51	**distract** [distrǽkt]	v. 방해하다, 산만하게 하다
52	**devoted** [divóutid]	adj. 헌신적인
53	**activated** [ǽktəvèitid]	adj. 활성화된
54	**significant** [signífikənt]	adj. 중요한, 의미 있는
55	**phase** [feiz]	n. 단계
56	**consensus** [kənsénsəs]	n. 합의
57	**intriguing** [intríːgiŋ]	adj. 흥미를 유발하는
58	**miserably** [mízərəbli]	adv. 비참하게, 초라하게
59	**dormant** [dɔ́:rmənt]	adj. 휴면의, 활동하지 않는
60	**obtain** [əbtéin]	v. 얻다, 획득하다
61	**remote** [rimóut]	adj. 먼, 가깝지 않은

구문정리

본문 중 중요 구문 정리한 내용입니다. 우선 암기하고 많이 읽으시기 바랍니다.

TEST2 2-2 | Insight
Set2 Lecture1에 등장하는 단어들 중 필요한 단어들을 선별하였습니다.

#	구문	뜻
01	almost all	대부분(most)
02	struggle with	~으로 고심하다
03	term paper	학기말 리포트
04	last week	지난주
05	confront adversity	역경에 직면하다
06	on a daily basis	매일매일
07	right now	지금 당장
08	in a similar way	유사한 방법으로
09	spend time ing	ing하면서 시간을 보내다
10	try to do	to do 하기를 시도하다
11	come up with	~을 생각해내다
12	step back	한 걸음 물러나다 ; (~에서) 한 걸음 물러나 생각하다
13	take a break	휴식을 취하다
14	socialize with	~와 교제하다
15	walk the dog	개를 산책 시키다
16	keep A off	멀리하다 피하다
17	go on	(불·전기 등이) 들어오다
18	out of reach	손이 닿지 않는
19	be sure	확신하다
20	put aside	무시하다
21	struggle with	~로 고심하다, 싸우다
22	look at	보다
23	pop up	튀어오르다
24	think of	~을 생각하다, 떠올리다
25	hundreds of years ago	수 백년 전에
26	be aware of	~을 알다
27	get done	수동으로 해석할것
28	figure out	~을 이해하다, 파악하다
29	keep A in B	A를 B에 유지시키다
30	reach a point	~의 수준에 도달하다
31	have to do	~해야만 한다
32	withdraw from	~에서 철수하다
33	decide to do	to do 하기를 결정하다
34	take a stroll	산책하다
35	and such	등등
36	fall to the ground	땅으로 떨어지다
37	be able to do	to do 할 수 있다
38	cause O to do	O가 to do 하는 것을 야기하다
39	keep O from ~ing	O가 -ing 하는 것을 막다
40	fly out of	~로부터 날아가다 ('=from)
41	put A into B	A를 B에 넣다
42	fall to	~로 떨어지다
43	help O do	O가 do 하는 것을 돕다
44	apply A to B	A를 B에 적용하다
45	wonder about	~에 대해 궁금해하다
46	at this point	현시점에서
47	a great deal of	많은
48	carry out the experiment	실험을 수행하다

구문정리 TEST2 2-2

Insight

본문 중 중요 구문 정리한 내용입니다. 우선 암기하고 많이 읽으시기 바랍니다.

Set2 Lecture1에 등장하는 단어들 중 필요한 단어들을 선별하였습니다.

#	구문	뜻
49	take place	발생하다
50	participate in	~에 참가하다
51	task A with B	A에게 B의 일을 맡기다, 주다
52	a set of	일련의
53	try -ing	~ing 하는 것을 시도하다
54	take an action	행동을 취하다
55	base A on B	A를 B에 기초하다
56	come into play	작동하기 시작하다
57	shut down	멈추다, 폐쇄하다
58	such as	~와 같은
59	of course	물론
60	play a role	역할을 하다
61	enable O to do	O가 ~하는 것을 가능하게 하다
62	it seems that	~처럼 보이다
63	switch off	끄다
64	love to do	to do 하고 싶다
65	enough to do	~하기에 충분한
66	stay on	계속 하다 [계속 남아 있다]
67	distract A from -ing	A가 ing 하는 것을 방해하다, 분산시키다
68	focus on	~에 집중하다
69	task at hand	당면한 문제
70	so-called	소위
71	come as	=be ~이다
72	devote to	~에 헌신하다
73	know A as B	A를 B로 알다
74	far from	~에서 멀리
75	one another	서로서로
76	connect A to B	A를 B로 연결하다
77	no matter where	어디든지간에
78	as long as	~하는 한
79	sort of	일종의
80	work the same way	같은 방식으로 작동하다
81	solve a problem	문제를 해결하다
82	fail at	~점에서 실패하다(a)
83	give up	포기하다
84	according to	~에 따르면
85	be supposed to do	to do 하기로 되어 있다
86	help O do	O가 ~하는 것을 돕다
87	fail to do	to do하는데 실패하다 (t)
88	the more, the faster	더 많으면, 더 빠르다
89	find a solution	해답을 찾다
90	be stuck	꼼짝 못하다; 막히다
91	at some point	어느 순간에는
92	go out	외출하다
93	enjoy the view	경치를 즐기다
94	in front of	~의 앞에

TEST2 2-3
VOCABULARY

TEST2 2-3지문의 단어 중 토플 필수 단어를 선별하여 정리하였습니다.

01	**social** [sóuʃəl]	adj. 사회적인, 사회의
02	**ancient** [éinʃənt]	adj. 고대의, 옛날의
03	**narrow** [nǽrou]	v. ~을 좁히다, ~의 (범위를) 한정하다
04	**major** [méidʒər]	adj. 주요한
05	**occur** [əkə́:r]	v. 발생하다, 일어나다
06	**century** [sénʧəri]	n. 세기, 100년
07	**significant** [signífikənt]	adj. 중요한, 상당한
08	**nomadic** [noumǽdik]	adj. 유목의, 유목민의
09	**sedentary** [sédntèri]	adj. 정착의
10	**settlement** [sétlmənt]	n. 정착
11	**initiate** [iníʃièit]	v. 시작하다
12	**climate** [kláimit]	n. 기후
13	**ultimately** [ʌ́ltəmətli]	adv. 결국
14	**trigger** [trígər]	v. 일으키다
15	**shift** [ʃift]	n. 변화, 전환
16	**glacier** [gléiʃər]	n. 빙하
17	**polar region** [póulər rí:dʒən]	n. 극지방
18	**drastic** [drǽstik]	adj. 급격한
19	**globe** [gloub]	n. 세계, 지구
20	**enable** [inéibl]	v. 가능하게 하다, 할 수 있게 하다
21	**cultivate** [kʌ́ltəvèit]	v. 재배하다
22	**crop** [krap]	n. 농작물, 수확, 곡물
23	**wander** [wándər]	v. 돌아다니다, 배회하다
24	**similar** [símələr]	adj. 비슷한, 유사한
25	**exemplary** [igzémpləri]	adj. 전형적인, 모범적인
26	**coastal plain** [kóustəl plein]	n. 해안 평야, 연안 평지
27	**Eastern Mediterranean** [í:stərn mèdətəréiniən]	n. 동부 지중해
28	**infertile** [infə́:rtəl]	adj. 메마른, 불모의
29	**suitable** [sú:təbl]	adj. 적합한, 적절한, 알맞은, 적당한
30	**habitation** [hæ̀bitéiʃən]	n. 거주
31	**grassland** [grǽˌslæ̀nd]	n. 초원, 목초지
32	**convenience** [kənví:njəns]	n. 편의, 편리
33	**survival** [sərváivəl]	n. 생존
34	**undoubtedly** [ʌ̀ndáutidli]	adv. 의심할 여지 없이, 분명히
35	**attractive** [ətrǽktiv]	adj. 매력적인
36	**advent** [ǽdvent]	n. 출현, 도래

TEST2 2-3
VOCABULARY

TEST2 2-3지문의 단어 중 토플 필수 단어를 선별하여 정리하였습니다.

37	**precipitation** [prisìpətéiʃən]	n. 강우, 강수량
38	**fertile** [fə́:rtl]	adj. 비옥한
39	**verify** [vérəfài]	v. 검증하다, 증명하다
40	**statistical data** [stətístikəl déitə]	n. 통계자료
41	**architectural** [à:rkətéktʃərəl]	adj. 건축술의, 건축의
42	**remains** [riméinz]	n. 잔여물, 잔해
43	**vital** [váitl]	adj. 중요한, 필수적인, 주요한
44	**existence** [igzístəns]	n. 존재
45	**uniform** [júːnəfɔ̀:rm]	adj. 일정한, 균일한
46	**identical** [aidéntikəl]	adj. 동일한, 똑같은
47	**rigid** [rídʒid]	adj. 강직한, 단단한
48	**semicircle** [sémisə̀:rkl]	n. 반원, 반원형
49	**partially** [pá:rʃəli]	adv. 부분적으로, 일부, 어느 정도
50	**construct** [kənstrʌ́kt]	v. 건설하다
51	**withstand** [wiðstǽnd]	v. 견디다, 이겨내다
52	**occasional** [əkéiʒənəl]	adj. 가끔의, 때때로
53	**harsh** [ha:rʃ]	adj. 가혹한
54	**excavate** [ékskəvèit]	v. ~을 발굴하다
55	**indicate** [índikèit]	v. 나타내다, 가리키다
56	**post** [póust]	n. 기둥, 말뚝
57	**beam** [bi:m]	n. 대들보
58	**intricate** [íntrikət]	adj. 복잡한
59	**seasonal** [síːzənl]	adj. 계절적인, 주기적인
60	**valuable** [vǽljuəbl]	adj. 가치있는, 귀중한
61	**harvest** [há:rvist]	v. [농작물을] 수확하다, 거둬들이다
62	**mortar** [mɔ́:rtər]	n. 절구, 막자사발
63	**inhabit** [inhǽbit]	v. 거주하다, 서식하다
64	**vast** [væst]	adj. 광대한, 방대한
65	**abundant** [əbʌ́ndənt]	adj. 풍부한, 많은
66	**assumption** [əsʌ́mpʃən]	n. 가정, 추측
67	**chance** [tʃæns]	n. 확률, 가능성
68	**slim** [slim]	adj. 희박한, 적은
69	**unintentional** [ʌninténʃənl]	adj. 본의 아닌, 의도치 않은
70	**reliance** [riláiəns]	n. 의존
71	**sprout** [spraut]	v. 싹트다
72	**migratory** [máigrətɔ̀:]	adj. 이주하는, 이동성의
73	**permanent** [pə́:rmənənt]	adj. 영구적인

구문정리

TEST2 2-3 | Shift from a nomadic lifestyle to sedentary settlements

본문 중 중요 구문 정리한 내용입니다. 우선 암기하고 많이 읽으시기 바랍니다.
Set2 Lecture2에 등장하는 단어들 중 필요한 단어들을 선별하였습니다.

#	구문	뜻
01	go through	겪다
02	a bit	조금
03	look at	~를 살피다, 보다
04	in history	역사상
05	shift from A to B	A에서 B로 이동
06	change in	~라는 점에서의 변화
07	recede to	~로 물러나다; 쇠퇴하다
08	across the globe	전세계에 걸쳐
09	enable O to do	O가 to do 하는 것을 가능하게 하다
10	cultivate crops	작물을 재배하다
11	instead of	~대신에
12	from place to place	이곳저곳, 이리저리
13	there is	~이 있다
14	a number of	많은
15	at about the same time	거의 비슷한 시간대에
16	focus on	~에 주력하다, 초점을 맞추다
17	as you may know	너가 알다시피
18	suitable for	~에 알맞은
19	at this time	이때에
20	be likely to do	to do 할 가능성이 높다
21	a great deal of	다량의
22	depend on	~에 의존하다
23	the amount of	~의 양
24	attractive to	~에게 매력적인
25	on top of	~뿐만 아니라 (in addition to)
26	the advent of	~의 출현
27	result in	~를 낳다(결과)
28	equal to	~와 같은, 동등한
29	be able to do	~할 수 있다
30	support a claim	주장을 지지하다
31	must have done	~했음에 틀림없다
32	have been done	당해오다
33	play a role in	역할을 하다
34	help O do	O가 do하는 것을 돕다
35	know A as B	A를 B로 알다
36	Take A into account	A를 고려하다
37	identical to	~와 같은, 동일한
38	arrange in a semicircle	반원형으로 정렬하다, 배치하다
39	upper parts of	~의 윗 부분
40	be made of	~로 구성되다

구문정리

TEST2 2-3 | Shift from a nomadic lifestyle to sedentary settlements

본문 중 중요 구문 정리한 내용입니다. 우선 암기하고 많이 읽으시기 바랍니다.
Set2 Lecture2에 등장하는 단어들 중 필요한 단어들을 선별하였습니다.

41	line A with B	A를 B로 덧대다, 둘러싸다	61	along with	~와 함께
42	enough to do	to do 하기 충분한	62	used to do	to do하곤 하다
43	come up with	생각해내다	63	large quantities of	다량의
44	a way to do	to do 하는 방법	64	as I previously stated	이전에 언급했듯이
45	and whatnot	~따위, 등등	65	take advantage of	이용하다
46	use O to do	O를 ~하는데 사용하다	66	remember ~ing	ing 하는것을 기억하다
47	not at all	전혀, 털 끝 만큼도	67	that of	앞에 반복된 명사 피하기(단수)
48	move to	~로 거처를 옮기다, 이사하다	68	have yet to do	아직 ~ 하지 않았다
49	You have a point, but	당신 말도 일리는 있지만.	69	might have done	~일지도 모른다
50	something important	중요한 무언가	70	during this time	이 시기 동안
51	want to do	to do 하기를 원하다	71	according to	~에 따르면
52	take a guess	추측하다	72	reliance on	~할 수 있었을 것이다
53	give away	주다	73	could have done	~에 대한 의존
54	seem to be	~인 것 처럼 보이다	74	speaking of	~을 증명하다
55	in many ways	여러모로	75	flow to	~로 흐르다
56	put so much effort into	~에 많은 노력을 들이다	76	show up	나타나다
57	leave behind	두고가다, 뒤에 남기다	77	try to do	to do 하려고 노력하다
58	on a seasonal basis	계절마다	78	take place	발생하다
59	That's my point	내말이 그말이야	79	year around	1년 내내
60	be going to do	~할 예정이다	80	point to	나타내다, 시사하다

TEST3 1-1
VOCABULARY

TEST3 1-1 지문의 단어 중 토플 필수 단어를 선별하여 정리하였습니다.

01	**daydream** [bríljənt]	n. 백일몽
02	**corpus callosum** [ǀkɔ́:rpəs kəlóusəm]	n. 뇌량
03	**fiber** [fáibər]	n. 섬유
04	**seizure** [sí:ʒər]	n. 발작, 경련
05	**epilepsy** [épəlèpsi]	n. 뇌전증, 간질
06	**neurological** [njùərəládʒikəl]	adj. 신경학상의
07	**hemisphere** [hémisfiər]	n. 반구
08	**uniformly** [jú:nəfɔ́:rmli]	adv. 한결같이
09	**specialize** [spéʃəlàiz]	v. 전문화하다, 특수화하다
10	**spatial** [spéiʃəl]	adj. 공간의
11	**analytical** [ænəlítik, -ikəl]	adj. 분석적인, 분석의
12	**verbal** [və́:rbəl]	adj. 말의, 구두의
13	**cease** [si:s]	v. 중단하다
14	**irrational** [irǽʃənl]	adj. 비이성적인, 비합리적인, 불합리한
15	**insufficient** [ìnsəfíʃənt]	adj. 불충분한, 부족한
16	**visual field** [víʒuəl][fi:ld]	n. 시야
17	**clarify** [klǽrəfài]	v. 명백히하다
18	**stimulus** [stímjuləs]	n. 자극
19	**function** [fʌ́ŋkʃən]	n. 기능
20	**correspond to** [kɔ̀:rəspánd]	v. 해당하다, 일치하다, 부합하다
21	**regardless** [rigá:rdlis]	adv. 상관없이, 관계없이
22	**recognize** [rékəgnàiz]	v. 인식하다, 인지하다, 알아보다
23	**neuropsychology** [njùərəsaikálədʒi]	n. 신경 심리학
24	**psychology** [saikálədʒi]	n. 심리
25	**malfunction** [mælfəˈŋkʃən]	n. 오동작, 고장, 기능 불량
26	**dangerous** [déindʒərəs]	adj. 위험한
27	**perceive** [pərsí:v]	v. 인지하다
28	**successful** [səksésfəl]	adj. 성공한
29	**vice versa** [váisə və́:rsə]	adv. 반대로, 거꾸로
30	**bear** [bɛər]	v. 부담하다, 참다
31	**brain** [brein]	n. 뇌

TEST3 1-1 | Brain's Left and Right Hemisphere

본문 중 중요 구문 정리한 내용입니다. 우선 암기하고 많이 읽으시기 바랍니다.
Set1 Conversation에 등장하는 단어들 중 필요한 단어들을 선별하였습니다.

#	구문	뜻
1	serve function	역할, 기능을 하다 (s)
2	kind of	약간, 어느 정도
3	go back	되돌아가다
4	key point	요점
5	consist of	~로 구성되다
6	call A B	A를 B라 부르다
7	it is possible to do	to do 하는 것이 가능하다
8	give A B	A에게 B를 주다
9	carry out	연구를 수행하다, 이행하다 (f)
10	earn prize	상을 타다
11	look for	~을 찾다, 바라다
12	characterize by	~로 특징짓다
13	come up with	생각해내다
14	cut A in half	A를 절반으로 자르다
15	That sounds dangerous to me	그건 내게 위험하게 들린다
16	perceive A as B	A를 B로 인지하다
17	There were no other options	다른 선택들이 없었다.
18	go well	일이 잘 되어 가다
19	except that	~을 제외하면
20	side effects	부작용
21	such as	~와 같은
22	have defect	결함을 가지고 있다
23	cut off	차단하다; 잘라내다
24	perform function	기능하다 (f)
25	put A in B	A를 B에 넣다
26	what if	~라면 어떻게 될까?
27	regardless of	~와 상관없이
28	correspond to	~에 일치하다
29	carry out tasks	일들을 수행하다
30	in-depth	깊히, 상세히
31	be able to do	to do 할 수 있다
32	come to the conclusion	~라는 결론에 도달하다
33	specialize in	~을 전문으로 하다
34	for instance	예를 들면
35	associate A with B	A를 B와 연관짓다
36	in the first place	첫째로
37	have to do	to do 해야만 한다
38	bear with	~을 견디다
39	for the rest of one's life	남은 평생동안
40	must have done	~했었음에 틀림 없다
41	ability to do	to do 하는 능력
42	over time	시간이 흐르면서
43	vice versa	반대로도, 역으로도 또한

TEST3 1-2
VOCABULARY

TEST3 1-2 지문의 단어 중 토플 필수 단어를 선별하여 정리하였습니다.

01	global [glóubəl]	adj. 세계적인
02	climate [kláimit]	n. 기후
03	historical [histó:rikəl]	adj. 역사의
04	discussion [diskʌ́ʃən]	n. 논의
05	continue [kəntínju:]	v. 계속하다
06	occur [əkə́:r]	v. 발생하다
07	previously [prí:viəsli]	adv. 이전에
08	warming [wɔ́:rmiŋ]	n. 온난화, 따뜻해짐
09	correct [kərékt]	adj. 정확한, 올바른, 옳은
10	earth [ə:rθ]	n. 지구
11	background [bǽkgrauˌnd]	n. 배경
12	knowledge [nálidʒ]	n. 지식
13	generally [dʒénərəli]	adv. 일반적으로, 대개, 보통
14	point to [pɔint] [tú]	n. 가리키다
15	driving force [dráiviŋ fɔ:rs]	n. 원동력, 추진력
16	influx [ínflʌks]	n. 유입
17	Atlantic Ocean [ætlǽntik óuʃən]	n. 대서양
18	oceanic [òuʃiǽnik]	adj. 대양의
19	current [kə́:rənt]	n. 해류

20	calamity [kəlǽməti]	n. 재난
21	concurrently [kənkə́:rəntli]	adv. 동시에, 겸임하여
22	cause [kɔ:z]	v. 초래하다, 일으키다
23	camel [kǽməl]	n. 낙타
24	mammoth [mǽməθ]	n. 맘모스
25	species [spí:ʃi:z]	n. 종
26	area [ɛ́əriə]	n. 지역
27	extinction [ikstíŋkʃən]	n. 소멸
28	so-called [sou-kɔ:ld]	adj. 소위, 이른바
29	trace [treis]	n. 흔적
30	attempt [ətémpt]	v. 시도하다
31	explain [ikspléin]	v. 설명하다
32	archaeologist [à:rkiáləjist]	n. 고고학자
33	impact [ímpækt]	n. 영향
34	hypothesis [haipáθəsis]	n. 가설, 가정, 추측
35	bundle [bʌ́ndl]	n. 묶음
36	comet [kámit]	n. 혜성
37	fragment [frǽgmənt]	n. 파편
38	strike [straik]	v. 타격, 치다

TEST3 1-2
VOCABULARY

TEST3 1-2 지문의 단어 중 토플 필수 단어를 선별하여 정리하였습니다.

39	**continent** [kάntənənt]	n. 대륙
40	**genus** [dʒíːnəs]	n. (생물 분류상의) 속
41	**extinct** [ikstíŋkt]	adj. 멸종한
42	**sudden** [sʌdn]	adj. 갑작스러운
43	**flow** [flou]	n. 흐름, 유동, 유입
44	**alter** [ɔ́ːltər]	v. 바꾸다
45	**demise** [dimáiz]	n. 사망, 죽음, 서거
46	**depend** [dipénd]	v. 의존하다
47	**sustenance** [sʌstənəns]	n. 생계
48	**convincing** [kənvínsiŋ]	adj. 설득력 있는
49	**interpret** [intə́ːrprit]	v. 해석하다, 이해하다
50	**soil** [sɔil]	n. 흙
51	**rich** [ritʃ]	adj. 풍부한
52	**carbon** [kάːrbən]	n. 탄소
53	**extract** [ikstrǽkt]	v. 추출하다
54	**examine** [igzǽmin]	v. 조사하다, 살펴보다, 관찰하다
55	**biological** [bàiəlάdʒikəl]	adj. 생물학의
56	**inorganic** [ìnɔːrgǽnik]	adj. 무생물의
57	**specimen** [spésəmən]	n. 표본
58	**cell** [sel]	n. 세포
59	**comprise** [kəmpráiz]	v. …을 구성하다
60	**electrostatic** [ilèktrəstǽtik]	adj. 정전기학의,
61	**electromagnetic** [ɪ|lektroʊmæg|netɪk]	adj. 전자기의, 전자석의 정전기의
62	**revisit** [rivízit]	v. (어떤 아이디어, 주제를) 다시 논의하다
63	**distinctive** [distíŋktiv]	adj. 독특한, 특유의
64	**asteroid** [ǽstərɔ̀id]	n. 소행성
65	**support** [səpɔ́ːrt]	v. 뒷받침하다
66	**crater** [kréitər]	n. 분화구
67	**arise** [əráiz]	v. 발생하다, 일어나다
68	**decline** [dikláin]	n. 감소, 하락
69	**remain** [riméin]	v. 남다
70	**disputable** [dispjúːtəbl]	adj. 논의의 여지가 있는
71	**wildfire** [waiˈldfaiˌər]	n. 도깨비불
72	**irrefutable** [ìrifjúːtəbl, iréfjətəbl]	adj. 반박할 수 없는
73	**hardly** [hάːrdli]	adv. 거의…아니다, 거의…할 것 같지 않다
74	**fundamentally** [fʌndəméntəli]	adv. 근본적으로
75	**rebuttal** [ribʌtl]	n. 반박

구문정리

TEST3 1-2 | Younger Dryas

본문 중 중요 구문 정리한 내용입니다. 우선 암기하고 많이 읽으시기 바랍니다.
Set1 Lecture1에 등장하는 단어들 중 필요한 단어들을 선별하였습니다.

01	one of the periods	기간 중 하나
02	for about a thousand years	약 천년 동안
03	correct me if I'm wrong	내가 틀리다면, 바로잡아 주세요
04	from what I've read	읽은 바에 의하면
05	For those without this background knowledge	배경 지식 없는 사람들을 위해서
06	let me explain	내가 설명 해줄게
07	driving force	추진력, 원동력
08	point to	가리키다, 암시하다
09	influx of A to B	A의 B로의 유입
10	The world's second largest	세계에서 두번째로 큰
11	bring A to B	A를 B로 가져오다
12	in the area	지역에서
13	such as	예를 들어, ~와 같은
14	so-called	소위, 이른바
15	disappear without a trace	흔적 없이 사라지다
16	attempt to do	to do 하려고 시도하다
17	come up with	생각해 내다
18	call A B	A를 B라고 부르다
19	a bundle of	한 꾸러미의
20	have an effect	효과를 갖다
21	genera of	~의 속 (동,식물의 종)
22	go extinct	멸종하다
23	according to	~에 따르면
24	suggest that	~을 제안하다, 제시하다
25	set A on fire	A에 불을 지르다
26	demise of	~의 종말, 멸종, 서거
27	depend on	~에 의존하다
28	That sounds convincing	그럴듯 하게 들린다, 설득력 있게 들린다
29	rich in	~이 풍부한
30	be able to do	to do 할 수 있다

구문정리

TEST3 1-2 — Younger Dryas

본문 중 중요 구문 정리한 내용입니다. 우선 암기하고 많이 읽으시기 바랍니다.
Set1 Lecture1에 등장하는 단어들 중 필요한 단어들을 선별하였습니다.

#	구문	뜻
31	come in handy	쓸모가 있다, 도움이 되다
32	obtain A from B	A를 B로부터 얻다
33	discovery of	~의 발견
34	consider A (to be) B	A를 B라고 고려하다
35	support claim	주장을 지지하다
36	point out	(주의를 기울이도록) 언급하다, 지적하다
37	fall short	부족해지다
38	in some way	어떤 점에서는
39	at least	적어도, 최소한
40	it is impossible for O to do	O가 to do 하는 것이 불가능하다
41	without a trace	흔적없이, 묘연히
42	There is no evidence of	~의 증거가 없다
43	disappearance of	~의 실종, 소멸
44	be said to do	~라고 한다
45	have been done	당해오다 (동사형태 4번)
46	That seems convincing to me	그것은 나에게 설득력 있게 들린다
47	it is irrefutable that	that절은 반박할 수 없다
48	look for	~을 찾다, 구하다
49	thousand years ago	수 천년 전에
50	consider that	~을 고려하면
51	occurrence of	~의 출현
52	not at all	전혀
53	a lot of	많은
54	prove A (to be) B	A가 B라는 것을 증명하다
55	that's the case here	여기서도 그렇다
56	as well	또한, 마찬가지로
57	base A on B	A를 B에 기반을 두다
58	in the case of	~한 경우에는, ~에 관하여는, ~에 관하여 말하면
59	a series of	일련의
60	time to do	to do 할 시간

TEST3 1-3
VOCABULARY

TEST3 1-3지문의 단어 중 토플 필수 단어를 선별하여 정리하였습니다.

01	**major** [méidʒər]	adj. 주요한, 중대한
02	**category** [kǽtəgɔ̀:ri]	n. 범주
03	**relatively** [rélətivli]	adv. 비교적으로
04	**interior** [intíəriər]	n. 실내
05	**sophistication** [səfìstəkéiʃən]	n. 교양, 세련
06	**introduction** [ìntrədʌ́kʃən]	n. 도입, 전래
07	**chassis** [tʃǽsi]	n. 차대, 새시
08	**method** [méθəd]	n. 방법, 방식
09	**technological** [tèknəládʒikəl]	adj. 기술적인
10	**invent** [invént]	v. 발명하다
11	**software** [sɔ́ːftwèr]	n. 소프트웨어, 프로그램
12	**philosophical** [fìləsáfik, -ikəl]	adj. 철학의
13	**illustrate** [íləstrèit]	v. 설명하다, 분명히 보여주다
14	**diverse** [divə́:rs]	adj. 다양한
15	**inventive** [invéntiv]	adj. 창의성이 풍부한
16	**profound** [prəfáund]	adj. 심오한
17	**polymath** [pálimæθ]	n. 박식가
18	**contribution** [kàntrəbjúːʃən]	n. 기여
19	**engineering** [èndʒiníəriŋ]	n. 공학, 기술
20	**architecture** [á:rkitèktʃər]	n. 건축
21	**anatomy** [ənǽtəmi]	n. 해부학
22	**demonstrate** [démənstrèit]	v. 나타내다, 설명하다
23	**blend** [blend]	n. 혼합
24	**focal point** [fóukəl pɔint]	n. 초점

TEST3 1-3
VOCABULARY

TEST3 1-3지문의 단어 중 토플 필수 단어를 선별하여 정리하였습니다.

25	**primary** [práimeri]	adj. 주요한, 주된
26	**crux** [krʌks]	n. 핵심
27	**sense** [sens]	n. 의미
28	**compute** [kəmpjúːt]	v. 컴퓨터로 계산하다
29	**vital** [váitl]	adj. 중요한, 필수의
30	**benefit** [bénəfit]	v. 도움이 되다
31	**irrelevant** [iréləvənt]	adj. 관계가 없는
32	**prevalent** [prévələnt]	adj. 널리 퍼진
33	**elucidate** [ilúːsədèit]	v. 밝히다
34	**satisfy** [sǽtisfài]	v. 만족시키다
35	**capacity** [kəpǽsəti]	n. 용량
36	**myriad** [míriəd]	n. 무수함, 무수히 많음

37	**socialize** [sóuʃəlàiz]	v. 사회화하다
38	**disseminate** [disémənèit]	v. 퍼뜨리다, 유포하다
39	**usability** [jùːzəbíləti]	n. 편리성, 사용하기 쉬움
40	**usefulness** [júːsfəlnis]	n. 유용성
41	**demand** [dimǽnd]	v. 요구하다
42	**manageable** [mǽnidʒəbl]	adj. 처리하기 쉬운
43	**executable** [éksəkjùːtəbl]	adj. 실행할 수 있는
44	**user-friendly** [júːzər-fréndli]	adj. 사용하기 쉬운
45	**substantial** [səbstǽnʃəl]	adj. 상당한, 실질적인
46	**expertise** [èkspərtíːz]	n. 전문적 기술
47	**frustrated** [frʌstreitid]	adj. 답답한
48	**jumble** [dʒʌmbl]	v. 뒤섞다

구문정리 TEST3 1-3

본문 중 중요 구문 정리한 내용입니다. 우선 암기하고 많이 읽으시기 바랍니다.

Leonardo's philosophical thinking
Set1 Lecture2에 등장하는 단어들 중 필요한 단어들을 선별하였습니다.

01	let's review	~을 돌아보자, 살펴보자
02	when it comes to	~에 관하여
03	in terms of	~라는 면에서
04	think about	~에 대해 생각하다
05	look like	~인 것 처럼 보이다
06	come in shapes and sizes	~한 모양들과 색들로 나온다
07	have done	해오다 (동사형태 3번)
08	take place	일어나다
09	a number of	다수의
10	distinguish A from B	A를 B와 구별하다
11	and so on	등등
12	want to do	to do 하기를 원하다
13	focus on	초점을 맞추다
14	the other side	반대쪽
15	apply A to B	A를 B에 적용하다
16	more than	~이상
17	involve A in B	A를 B에 포함시키다
18	in the process	~과정에서
19	refer to	~을 언급하다
20	as you know	알다시피
21	not to mention	말 할 것도 없이
22	make a great contribution	크게 이바지하다
23	a blend of	~의 혼합
24	both A and B	A와 B 둘 다
25	focal point	초점
26	the crux of	~의 중심
27	In this sense	이런 의미에서
28	devote A to B	A를 B에 헌신하다
29	cast doubt on	~을 의심하다
30	get a wrong idea	오해하다
31	play a role in	~에서 역할을 하다
32	go deep into	깊이 파고들다
33	irrelevant to	~와 관계 없는
34	way of thinking	사고방식
35	prevalent in	~에 널리 퍼져 있는
36	in contrast to	~와 대조적으로
37	approach to	~에의 접근
38	satisfy a need	수요를 충족시키다

구문정리

TEST3 1-3 | Leonardo's philosophical thinking

본문 중 중요 구문 정리한 내용입니다. 우선 암기하고 많이 읽으시기 바랍니다.

Set1 Lecture2에 등장하는 단어들 중 필요한 단어들을 선별하였습니다.

39	focus on	~에 집중하다
40	instead of	~ 대신에
41	disseminate A to B	A를 B로 퍼뜨리다, 전파하다
42	try to do	to do 하려고 노력하다
43	on behalf of	~을 대신하여
44	the public	대중
45	it is important for developers to know	개발자들이 아는것은 중요하다
46	what kind of	어떤 종류의
47	need to do	to do 할 필요가 있다
48	make sure	확실하게 하다
49	not only A but also B	A 뿐만 아니라 B도
50	user-friendly	사용하기 쉬운
51	along with	~와 함께
52	make sense	의미가 통하다
53	hard to do	to do 하기 어려운
54	put A in a situation	A 를 ~한 상황에 두다
55	work on	~에 애쓰다
56	term paper	학기말 과제(리포트)
57	go on a website	웹사이트에 가다 (= go to)
58	of course	물론
59	what if	만약 ~라면
60	in a way	~한 방법으로
61	make O done	O가 done 되어지게 만들다
62	look for	찾다
63	clicks away	클릭만큼 먼, 클릭만큼 떨어진
64	jumble A with B	A와 B를 뒤섞다
65	a bunch of	다수의
66	fail to do	to do 하는 것에 실패하다
67	meet the demand	수요를 충족 시키다
68	come into play	작용하기 시작하다
69	solve a problem	문제를 해결하다
70	as a matter of fact	사실은
71	such as	예를 들어, ~같은
72	tend to do	to do 하는 경향이 있다
73	in that	~라는 점에서
74	communicate with	~와 연락하다
75	get on	올라타다

TEST3 2-1
VOCABULARY

TEST3 2-1지문의 단어 중 토플 필수 단어를 선별하여 정리하였습니다.

01	**championship** [tʃǽmpiənʃip]	n. 챔피언쉽, 선수권
02	**improvement** [imprúːvmənt]	n. 개선
03	**cooperation** [kouɑ̀pəréiʃən]	n. 협동조합, 협력
04	**beginning** [bigíniŋ]	n. 시작
05	**advance** [ædvǽns]	n. 발전
06	**significanctly** [signífikəntli]	adv. 상당히, 현저히
07	**sidetrack** [saiˈdtræˌk]	v. 탈선시키다
08	**participate** [paːrtísəpèit]	v. 참여하다
09	**consult** [kənsʌ́lt]	v. 상담하다
10	**advertising** [ǽdvərtàiziŋ]	n. 광고
11	**agency** [éidʒənsi]	n. 대행사, 기관
12	**alternative** [ɔːltǽːrnətiv]	n. 대안
13	**reschedule** [rìːskédʒuːl]	v. 재조정하다, 예정을 다시 세우다
14	**popular** [pɑ́pjulər]	adj. 인기 있는, 유명한
15	**competetive** [kəmpétətiv]	adj. 경쟁의, 경쟁적인
16	**consider** [kənsídər]	v. 고려하다
17	**public Transportation** [pʌ́blik trænspərtéiʃən]	n. 대중교통
18	**department** [dipɑ́ːrtmənt]	n. 학과, 부서
19	**athletics** [æθlétiks]	n. 체육
20	**cover** [kʌ́vər]	v. 부담하다
21	**schedule** [skédʒuːl]	n. 일정
22	**miss** [mis]	v. 놓치다
23	**situation** [sitʃuéiʃən]	n. 상황
24	**sense** [sens]	n. 의미
25	**inability** [inəbíləti]	n. 할 수 없음, 무능력
26	**irresponsibility** [ìrispɑ̀nsəbíləti]	n. 무책임
27	**devote** [divóut]	v. 헌신하다
28	**passionate** [pǽʃənət]	adj. 열정적인
29	**decision** [disíʒən]	n. 결정
30	**suggest** [səgdʒést]	v. 제안하다
31	**look into** [luk intu]	v. …을 들여다보다, 살펴보다

구문정리

TEST3 2-1 | The championship games

본문 중 중요 구문 정리한 내용입니다. 우선 암기하고 많이 읽으시기 바랍니다.
Set2 Conversation에 등장하는 단어들 중 필요한 단어들을 선별하였습니다.

01	got a minute?	시간 있니?
02	of course	물론
03	would have done	~했을지도 모른다 (추측)
04	make it to	~에 도착하다
05	at the beginning of	~의 초반에서, 처음에
06	have done	해오다(동사형태 3번)
07	by the way	그런데(대화에서 화제를 바꿀 때)
08	call A in	A를 부르다, 전화하다
09	get sidetracked	옆길로 새다
10	be able to do	to do 할 수 있다
11	participate in	참여하다
12	should have done	~했어야 했을지 모른다 (추측)
13	consult with	~와 협의하다
14	in the first place	우선
15	on the day	그날에
16	step up	나아가다, ~를 증가시키다, 강화하다
17	alternative way	대안, 다른 방법
18	or something	~따위, 등등
19	think about	~에 대해 생각하다
20	give A B	A에게 B를 주다
21	ask to do	to do 하는 것을 요청하다
22	let's see	어디 한번 보자
23	on Wednesday	수요일에
24	consider ~ing	~ing 하는 것을 고려하다, 숙고하다
25	public transportation	대중 교통
26	cover the cost	경비를 대다
27	look into	~를 조사하다
28	available time	이용 가능 시간, 가용시간
29	in the morning	아침에, 새벽에
30	a million times	수 백만번
31	consist of	~로 구성되다
32	each day	매일, 날마다
33	even if	~에도 불구하고 (=even though)
34	a big help to	~에 큰 도움
35	want to do	to do 하는 것을 원하다
36	why not	~하는 게 어때
37	try to do	to do 하는 것을 시도하다
38	like I said	내가 말한 바와 같이
39	hate to do	to do 하기를 싫어하다
40	devote A to B	A를 B에 바치다
41	reach a point	수준에 도달하다, 지점에 도달하다
42	come around	돌아오다
43	as well	또한
44	support a decision	결정을 지지하다
45	make a decision	결정을 내리다
46	let A down	A를 내려가게 하다, 기대를 저버리다, 실망시키다
47	wish A B	A에게 B를 빌어주다

TEST3 2-2 VOCABULARY

TEST3 2-2지문의 단어 중 토플 필수 단어를 선별하여 정리하였습니다.

01	**geologist** [dʒiálədʒist]	n. 지질학자
02	**radiometric** [rèidioumétrik]	adj. 방사 측정의
03	**radioactive** [rei͵diouæˈktiv]	adj. 방사성
04	**cosmic** [kázmik]	adj. 우주의
05	**material** [mətíəriəl]	n. 성분, 물질
06	**meteorite** [míːtiəràit]	n. 운석
07	**debris** [dəbríː]	n. 파편
08	**asteroid** [ǽstərɔ̀id]	n. 소행성
09	**comet** [kámit]	n. 혜성
10	**terrestrial** [təréstriəl]	adj. 지구의, 육지의
11	**analogous** [ənǽləgəs]	adj. 유사한, 비슷한
12	**theory** [θíːəri]	n. 이론
13	**dispute** [dispjúːt]	n. 분쟁, 논쟁
14	**regard** [rigáːrd]	v. 관련되다, 간주하다, 여기다, 보다
15	**explore** [ikspló:r]	v. 살펴보다, 탐구하다
16	**thermodynamics** [θə̀ːrmoudainǽmiks]	n. 열역학
17	**contribution** [kàntrəbjúːʃən]	n. 기여
18	**development** [divéləpmənt]	n. 개발, 발전, 발달
19	**physics** [fíziks]	n. 물리학
20	**rudimentary** [rùːdəméntəri]	adj. 초보의
21	**molten** [móultən]	adj. 용해된, 녹은
22	**state** [steit]	n. 상태
23	**frigid** [frídʒid]	adj. 몹시 추운, 냉담한
24	**phenomenon** [finámənàn]	n. 현상
25	**posit** [pázit]	v. 사실로 상정하다
26	**thermal** [θə́ːrməl]	adj. 열의
27	**diffusion** [difjúːʒən]	n. 유포, 발산, 보급
28	**concept** [kánsept]	n. 개념
29	**craving** [kréiviŋ]	n. 갈망
30	**kettle** [kétl]	n. 주전자

TEST3 2-2
VOCABULARY

TEST3 2-2지문의 단어 중 토플 필수 단어를 선별하여 정리하였습니다.

31	**process** [práses]	n. 과정
32	**gradient** [gréidiənt]	n. 변화도
33	**outermost** [auˈtərmouˌst]	adj. 가장 바깥쪽의
34	**layer** [léiər]	n. 층
35	**property** [prápərti]	n. 특성
36	**estimate** [éstəmèit]	v. 추정하다, 계산하다
37	**speculate** [spékjulèit]	v. 추측하다, 내다보다
38	**acknowledgment** [æknálidʒmənt]	n. 인정
39	**acclaim** [əkléim]	n. 호평
40	**induce** [indjúːs]	v. …하게 하다, 유발하다
41	**initially** [iníʃəli]	adv. 처음에
42	**uproar** [ʌpróːr]	n. 소동
43	**sedimentation** [sèdəməntéiʃən]	n. 퇴적, 침전
44	**erosion** [iróuʒən]	n. 침식
45	**error** [érər]	n. 오차, 오류
46	**insignificant** [insignífikənt]	adj. 미미한
47	**discredit** [diskrédit]	v. …을 신용하지 않다, 불신하다
48	**crust** [krʌst]	n. 지각
49	**scrutiny** [skrúːtəni]	n. 정밀 조사
50	**convection** [kənvékʃən]	n. 대류
51	**circulation** [sɔ̀ːrkjuléiʃən]	n. 순환
52	**pathway** [pæˈθweiˌ]	n. 진로
53	**rate** [reit]	n. 속도
54	**lack** [læk]	n. 부족, 결핍
55	**construct** [kənstrʌkt]	v. 구성하다, 세우다
56	**recognition** [rèkəgníʃən]	n. 인정
57	**continental drift** [kàntənéntl drift]	n. 대륙이동
58	**deserve** [dizɔ́ːrv]	v. …을 받을 만하다

구문정리 TEST3 2-2

본문 중 중요 구문 정리한 내용입니다. 우선 암기하고 많이 읽으시기 바랍니다.

Earth's age
Set2 Lecture1에 등장하는 단어들 중 필요한 단어들을 선별하였습니다.

01	analogous to	~와 비슷한
02	prior to	~에 앞서
03	let's look at	~을 살펴보자
04	be sure	~을 확신하다
05	hear of	~에 대해 듣다
06	a contribution to	~에 대한 기여
07	be able to do	to do 할 수 있다
08	apply A to B	A를 B에 적용하다
09	base A on B	A를 B에 근거하다
10	in a state	~의 상태로
11	It is said that	~이라고 한다
12	melting point	녹는 점
13	radiate A into B	A를 B로 내뿜다
14	term A B	A를 B라고 칭하다
15	more or less	거의, 대략
16	for those of you not familiar with	~와 익숙하지 않은 사람들을 위해
17	let O do	O가 do 하게 하다
18	give A B	A에게 B를 주다
19	let's say	예를 들어
20	go away	떠나다
21	put A into B	A를 B에 넣다
22	want to do	to do 하기를 원하다
23	what happen	무슨 일이 일어나는지
24	much more	훨씬 더
25	from A to B	A부터 B까지
26	difference between A and B	A와 B 사이의 차이
27	just below	바로 아래에
28	according to	~에 의하면
29	at temperature	온도에
30	flow to	~로 흐르다

구문정리

TEST3 2-2 | Earth's age

본문 중 중요 구문 정리한 내용입니다. 우선 암기하고 많이 읽으시기 바랍니다.

Set2 Lecture1에 등장하는 단어들 중 필요한 단어들을 선별하였습니다.

31	use O to do	O를 to do 하기 위해 사용하다	46	have been done	당해오다 (동사형태 4번)
32	by ~ing	~ 함으로써	47	prove O (to be) O.C	O가 O.C라는 것을 증명하다
33	no more than	단지, ~일 뿐 (=only)	48	name A B	A를 B라고 이름 붙이다
34	receive acclaim from	~로 부터 환호를 받다	49	it is like	이것은 ~ 같다
35	It is because	이유가 ~이기 때문이다	50	in fact	사실
36	hundreds of millions of	수 억의	51	instead of	~의 대신에
37	make sense	이치에 맞다	52	not only A but also B	A 뿐만 아니라 B 도
38	less than	~보다 적은	53	large amounts of	많은 양의
39	as time passed	시간 지남에 따라	54	at a rate	~의 속도로
40	look for	찾다	55	close to	~에 가까운
41	just as	꼭 ~ 처럼	56	lack of	~의 부족
42	release from	~로 부터 풀어주다	57	receive recognition from ~	~로부터 인정을 받다
43	be absent from	~에 결석하다, 없다	58	construct A on B	A를 B위에 건설하다
44	the amount of	~의 양	59	begin ~ing	~ing 하는 것을 시작하다
45	consider O (to be) O.C	O를 O.C로 간주하다			

TEST3 2-3 VOCABULARY

TEST3 2-3지문의 단어 중 토플 필수 단어를 선별하여 정리하였습니다.

01	**legitimate** [lɪˈdʒɪtɪmət]	adj. 합법적인, 적법한
02	**theatrical** [θiˈætrɪkl]	adj. 연극의, 공연의
03	**component** [kəmˈpoʊnənt]	n. 요소, 구성요소
04	**restraint** [rɪˈstreɪnt]	n. 규제
05	**permit** [pərˈmɪt]	v. 허락하다, 허용하다
06	**serious** [ˈsɪəriəs]	adj. 진지한, 생각을 요하는
07	**literary** [ˈlɪtəreri]	adj. 문학의
08	**censorship** [ˈsensərʃɪp]	n. 검열
09	**bar** [bɑː(r)]	v. 막다, 금지하다
10	**illegitimate** [ɪləˈdʒɪtəmət]	adj. 불법의
11	**gradually** [ˈɡrædʒuəli]	adv. 점점, 서서히
12	**wane** [weɪn]	v. 약해지다, 시들해지다
13	**rural** [ˈrʊrəl]	adj. 시골의, 지방의
14	**flock** [flɑːk]	v. 떼지어 가다
15	**population** [ˌpɑːpjuˈleɪʃn]	n. 인구
16	**consequence** [ˈkɑːnsəkwens]	n. 결과
17	**urban** [ˈɜːrbən]	adj. 도시의, 도회지의
18	**productivity** [ˌprɑːdʌkˈtɪvəti]	n. 생산성
19	**skyrocket** [ˈskaɪrɑːkɪt]	v. 급등하다, 치솟다
20	**strenuous** [ˈstrenjuəs]	adj. 힘이 많이 드는, 몹시 힘든, 격렬한
21	**demographic** [ˌdèːməɡræfik]	adj. 인구통계학의, 인구학의
22	**catalyst** [ˈkætəlɪst]	n. 촉매
23	**era** [ˈɪrə; ˈerə]	n. 시대
24	**flourish** [ˈflɜːrɪʃ]	v. 번성하다, 번창하다
25	**origin** [ˈɔːrɪdʒɪn]	n. 기원, 근원
26	**obscure** [əbˈskjʊr]	adj. 잘 알려져있지 않은, 모호한
27	**satirical** [səˈtɪrɪkl]	adj. 풍자적인
28	**theorize** [ˈθiːəraɪz]	v. 이론을 제시하다, 이론을 세우다
29	**unrelated** [ˌʌnrɪˈleɪtɪd]	adj. 관련없는, 관계없는
30	**acrobatics** [ˌækrəˈbætɪks]	n. 곡예

TEST3 2-3
VOCABULARY

TEST3 2-3지문의 단어 중 토플 필수 단어를 선별하여 정리하였습니다.

31	**comedy** [ˈkɑːmədi]	n. 코미디, 희극
32	**property** [ˈprɑːpərti]	n. 속성, 특성
33	**distracting** [dɪstræktɪŋ]	adj. 집중 안되게 하는, 산만하게 하는
34	**visualize** [ˈvɪʒuəlaɪz]	v. 마음속에 그려보다, 상상하다
35	**convenience store** [kənˈviːniəns stɔː(r)]	n. 편의점
36	**quality** [ˈkwɑːləti]	adj. 양질의, 고급의
37	**commodity** [kəˈmɑːdəti]	n. 상품, 물품
38	**exceptional** [ɪkˈsepʃənl]	adj. 특출한, 특별한
39	**entrepreneurial** [ˌɒntrəprəˈnɜː(r)iəl]	adj. 사업가의, 기업가의
40	**establishment** [ɪˈstæblɪʃmənt]	n. 설립
41	**continuous** [kənˈtɪnjuəs]	adj. 계속되는
42	**endeavor** [indévər, en-]	n. 노력, 시도
43	**triumph** [ˈtraɪʌmf]	n. 큰 업적, 대성공, 승리
44	**outstanding** [aʊtˈstændɪŋ]	adj. 뛰어난, 걸출한
45	**amuse** [əˈmjuːz]	v. 즐겁게 하다, 재미있게 하다
46	**throughout** [θruːˈaʊt]	p. ~동안 죽, 내내
47	**operate** [ˈɑːpəreɪt]	v. 운영하다, 영업하다
48	**partake** [pɑːrˈteɪk]	v. 참가하다
49	**leisure** [ˈliːʒər]	n. 여가
50	**exploit** [ɪkˈsplɔɪt]	v. 이용하다
51	**captivate** [ˈkæptɪveɪt]	v. 마음을 사로잡다, 매혹하다
52	**extravagant** [ɪkˈstrævəgənt]	adj. 낭비하는, 낭비벽이 있는
53	**lavish** [ˈlævɪʃ]	adj. 호화로운
54	**luxurious** [lʌɡˈʒʊriəs]	adj. 호화로운
55	**tempting** [ˈtemptɪŋ]	adj. 솔깃한, 구미가 당기는
56	**elucidate** [iˈluːsɪdeɪt]	v. 설명하다
57	**entrepreneur** [ˌɑːntrəprəˈnɜː(r)]	n. 사업가, 기업가
58	**fixed** [fɪkst]	adj. 고정된, 확고한
59	**cleanliness** [ˈklenlinəs]	n. 청결, 깨끗함
60	**stern** [stɜːrn]	adj. 엄중한, 근엄한

TEST3 2-3
VOCABULARY

TEST3 2-3지문의 단어 중 토플 필수 단어를 선별하여 정리하였습니다.

61	**abide** [əˈbaɪd]	v. 참다, 따르다
62	**forbade** [fə(r)ˈbæd]	forbid(막다, 금지하다)의 과거
63	**profanity** [prəˈfænəti]	n. 신성모독, 불경
64	**offensive** [əˈfensɪv]	adj. 모욕적인, 불쾌한
65	**restriction** [rɪˈstrɪkʃn]	n. 제한, 규제
66	**low-brow** [ˈloʊbraʊ]	adj. 교양없는, 저속한
67	**stamp** [stæmp]	v. 발을 구르다
68	**strive to** [straɪv]	v. 분투하다
69	**biography** [baɪˈɑːgrəfi]	n. 전기
70	**figure** [ˈfɪɡjər]	n. 인물, 인물의 모습
71	**popularity** [ˌpɑːpjuˈlærəti]	n. 인기
72	**bolster** [ˈboʊlstə(r)]	v. 강화하다
73	**adaptation** [ˌædæpˈteɪʃn]	n. 적응
74	**immense** [ɪˈmens]	adj. 엄청난, 어마어마한

75	**mass** [mæs]	adj. 대량의, 대규모의
76	**posit** [ˈpɑːzɪt]	v. 상정하다
77	**surpass** [sərˈpæs]	v. 능가하다, 뛰어넘다
78	**accentuate** [əkˈsentʃueɪt]	v. 강조하다
79	**myriad** [ˈmɪriəd]	n. 무수함, 무수히 많음
80	**collectively** [kəˈlektɪvli]	adv. 집합적으로, 총괄하여
81	**embellish** [ɪmˈbelɪʃ]	v. 장식하다, 꾸미다
82	**ornament** [ˈɔːnəmənt]	n. 장식품
83	**grandiose** [ˈɡrændioʊs]	adj. 거창한
84	**suppress** [səˈpres]	v. 억누르다, 참다
85	**predominant** [prɪˈdɑːmɪnənt]	adj. 두드러진, 뚜렷한
86	**vulgarity** [vʌlˈɡærəti]	n. 상스러움, 음란물
87	**advocate** [ˈædvəkeɪt]	v. 지지하다, 옹호하다
88	**discriminatory** [dɪˈskrɪmɪnətɔːri]	adj. 차별적인

구문정리

TEST3 2-3 | Illegitimate theater

본문 중 중요 구문 정리한 내용입니다. 우선 암기하고 많이 읽으시기 바랍니다.
Set2 Lecture2에 등장하는 단어들 중 필요한 단어들을 선별하였습니다.

01	rely on	~에 의지하다
02	due to	~때문에
03	put restraints on	~에 제한을 가하다, 억제하다
04	permit O to do	O가 to do 하는 것을 허가하다
05	get an idea	아이디어를 얻다
06	bar A from ing	A가 ~ ing 하는것을 금지하다
07	under control	통제되는
08	refer to A as B	A를 B라고 언급하다
09	look at	~을 살펴보다
10	conflict between A and B	A와 B 사이의 갈등
11	become available to	~에 사용 가능하게 되다
12	a number of	다수의
13	flock to	~로 모여들다
14	as a consequence	~의 결과로서
15	as well	마찬가지로
16	turn attention to	~로 주의를 돌리다
17	work as	~로서 일하다, 작용하다
18	in that	~라는 점에서
19	at the time	그 당시, 당시에
20	His dress is that of a gentle man, but his manners are those of a clown.	앞 명사 반복
21	sound familiar	친근하게 들리다
22	get hung up on	~에 매달리다, 집착하다
23	have nothing to do with	~와 아무 관련이 없다
24	consist of	~로 구성되다
25	a series of	일련의
26	a wide spectrum of	광범위한
27	such as	~와 같은
28	and so on	기타 등등
29	fail to do	to do 하는 것을 실패하다
30	have access to	~에 접근할 수 있다.

구문정리

TEST3 2-3 | Illegitimate theater

본문 중 중요 구문 정리한 내용입니다. 우선 암기하고 많이 읽으시기 바랍니다.
Set2 Lecture2에 등장하는 단어들 중 필요한 단어들을 선별하였습니다.

#	구문	의미
31	help O do	O가 do 하는 것을 돕다
32	in the same sense	그 같은 의미로
33	taste in	~라는 점에서의 취향
34	begin with	~으로 시작하다
35	allow O to do	O가 to do 하는 것을 가능케 하다
36	all day	하루종일 (a)
37	throughout the day	온종일 (t)
38	design O to do	O를 to do 하기 위해 설계하다
39	leisure activity	여가활동
40	intend to do	to do 할 작정이다, 의도이다
41	in two ways	두 가지 방법으로
42	fill A with B	A를 B로 채우다
43	decorate A with B	A를 B로 장식하다
44	walk into	~로 걸어들어가다
45	for a purpose	~한 목적으로
46	come to	(결국) ~이 되다.
47	abide by	따르다, 지키다, 준수하다
48	prevent A from B	A를 B로부터 보호하다
49	offensive language	거친 말투
50	appeal to	~에 호소하다
51	place A on B	A를 B에 놓다
52	in any way	이렇든 저렇든, 어떻게든
53	strive to do	to do 하기를 시도하다
54	run out of time	시간이 다되다
55	continue discussion on	~에 대한 토론을 계속하다
56	be sure to do	to do를 꼭 하다, to do 하는 것을 확실히 하다
57	do search on	~에 대한 조사, 연구를 하다

TEST4 1-1
VOCABULARY

TEST4 1-1지문의 단어 중 토플 필수 단어를 선별하여 정리하였습니다.

01	**semester** [sɪˈmestə(r)]	n. 학기
02	**relaxing** [rɪˈlæksɪŋ]	adj. 편한
03	**leisure** [ˈliːʒər]	n. 여가
04	**overwhelm** [ˌoʊvərˈwelm]	v. 압도하다, 격한 감정이 휩싸다
05	**extend** [ɪkˈstend]	v. 연장하다
06	**deadline** [ˈdedlaɪn]	n. 기한, 마감시간
07	**generous** [ˈdʒenərəs]	adj. 후한, 관대한
08	**draft** [dræft]	n. 초안
09	**from scratch** [frʌm skrætʃ]	아무 것도 없이
10	**summarize** [ˈsʌməraɪz]	v. 요약하다
11	**honeybee** [ˈhʌnibiː]	n. 꿀벌
12	**magnetic field** [mægˈnetɪk fiːld]	n. 자기장
13	**facilitate** [fəˈsɪlɪteɪt]	v. ~하게 하다, 가능하게 하다
14	**course** [kɔːrs]	n. 항로, 길
15	**navigate** [ˈnævɪgeɪt]	v. 길을 찾다, 방향을 읽다
16	**vague** [veɪg]	adj. 모호한
17	**grasp** [græsp]	v. 이해하다, 파악하다
18	**separatey** [ˈseprətli]	adv. 따로따로, 별도로
19	**article** [ˈɑːrtɪkl]	n. 글, 기사
20	**nearby** [ˈnɪrbaɪ]	adj. 인근의, 가까운 곳의
21	**waggle dance** [ˈwægl dæns]	n. 벌의 8자 춤
22	**perplexing** [pərˈpleksɪŋ]	adj. 복잡한
23	**hive** [haɪv]	n. 벌집
24	**iron-rich** [ˈaɪərn rɪtʃ]	adj. 철이 풍부한
25	**granule** [ˈgrænjuːl]	n. 작은 알갱이, 과립
26	**cell** [sel]	n. 세포
27	**sense** [sens]	v. 감지하다, 느끼다
28	**compass** [ˈkʌmpəs]	n. 나침반

TEST4 1-1
VOCABULARY

TEST4 1-1지문의 단어 중 토플 필수 단어를 선별하여 정리하였습니다.

29	**biological** [ˌbaɪəˈlɑːdʒɪkl]	adj. 생물의, 생물체의
30	**refer** [rɪˈfɜːr]	v. 참조하다, 참고하다
31	**citation** [saɪˈteɪʃn]	n. 인용
32	**source** [sɔːrs]	n. 원천, 근원, 출처
33	**subjective** [səbˈdʒektɪv]	adj. 주관적인
34	**comprehensive** [ˌkɑːmprɪˈhensɪv]	adj. 포괄적인, 종합적인
35	**clarify** [ˈklærəfaɪ]	v. 명확하게 하다, 분명히 말하다
36	**forage** [ˈfɔːrɪdʒ; ˈfɑː-]	v. 동물이 먹이를 찾다
37	**address** [əˈdres]	v. 말하다, (어떤 주제를) 다루다
38	**utilize** [ˈjuːtəlaɪz]	v. 활용하다, 이용하다
39	**comparison** [kəmˈpærɪsn]	n. 비교
40	**internal** [ɪnˈtɜːrnl]	adj. 내부의
41	**insect** [ˈɪnsekt]	n. 곤충
42	**accomplish** [əˈkɑːmplɪʃ]	v. 완수하다, 해내다, 간소화하다
43	**complex** [kəmˈpleks]	adj. 복잡한
44	**structure** [ˈstrʌktʃə(r)]	n. 구조
45	**receive** [rɪˈsiːv]	v. 받다
46	**individual** [ˌɪndɪˈvɪdʒuəl]	adj. 각각의, 개개의
47	**distinctive** [dɪˈstɪŋktɪv]	adj. 독특한, 구별된
48	**external** [ɪkˈstɜːrnl]	adj. 외부의, 바깥의
49	**stimuli** [stímjulài]	n. stimulus(자극)의 복수
50	**detect** [dɪˈtekt]	v. 알아내다, 감지하다
51	**possess** [pəˈzes]	v. 소유하다
52	**revise** [rɪˈvaɪz]	v. 수정하다
53	**original** [əˈrɪdʒənl]	adj. 원래의, 본래의
54	**suitable** [ˈsuːtəbl]	adj. 적합한, 적절한, 알맞은

구문정리

TEST4 1-1 | Final term papers

본문 중 중요 구문 정리한 내용입니다. 우선 암기하고 많이 읽으시기 바랍니다.

Set1 Conversation에 등장하는 단어들 중 필요한 단어들을 선별하였습니다.

#	구문	뜻	#	구문	뜻
01	do you have a minute?	잠시 시간 좀 내주시겠어요?	16	have a chance to do	to do 할 기회를 가지다
02	how have you been?	어떻게 지냈니? 잘 지냈니?	17	over the weekend	주말에
03	The semester is almost over	학기가 거의 끝났다	18	that's why	그게 이유다
04	must be	~임에 틀림 없다(추측)	19	come by	잠시 들르다
05	leasure time	여가시간	20	way of ~ing	~ing 하는 방법
06	be due	~할 예정이다	21	communicate with	~와 의사소통하다
07	be overwhelmed	주체를 못하다, 압도되다	22	one another	서로서로
08	extend the deadline	기한을 연장하다	23	in the process	과정에서
09	of course	물론	24	use O to do	O를 to do 하기 위해 사용하다
10	put effort into	공을 들이다	25	help O to do	O가 to do 하는 것을 돕다
11	the first draft	초안, 초고	26	start to do	to do 하는 것을 시작하다
12	start from scratch	처음부터 시작하다, 제로에서 다시 시작하다	27	a bit	약간
13	do research	조사하다	28	magnetic field	자기장
14	a ton of	많은	29	in that sense	그러한 점에서
15	I was wondering if	~인지 아닌지 궁금하다	30	difficult to do	to do 하는 것은 어렵다

구문정리

TEST4 1-1 | Final term papers

본문 중 중요 구문 정리한 내용입니다. 우선 암기하고 많이 읽으시기 바랍니다.

Set1 Conversation에 등장하는 단어들 중 필요한 단어들을 선별하였습니다.

31	employ O to do	O를 to do 하기 위해 사용하다		46	seem to do	to do 하는 것처럼 보이다
32	deliver a message	메시지를 전달하다		47	lack a connection	연결성이 부족하다
33	perform dance	춤추다		48	refer to	언급하다
34	what's called	~라고 불리는 것		49	Is there something wrong with	~에 무슨 문제 있나요?
35	tell others that	다른 이들에게 that절을 말하다(=tell A B)		50	a lot of	많은
36	far away	멀리 떨어진		51	fail to do	to do 하는 것을 실패하다
37	a sort of	일종의		52	the other side of	~의 반대편
38	work as	~로서 일하다		53	I suggest you find	나는 네가 찾기를 권한다 (should생략)
39	fit into	~에 꼭 들어맞다		54	relation to	~와의 관계
40	right after	그 직후		55	sound like	~처럼 들리다
41	even if	비록 ~라 할지라도		56	thank A for B	A에게 B에 대해 감사하다
42	lose one's way	길을 잃다		57	need to do	to do 할 필요가 있다
43	due to	~때문에		58	meet the deadline	마감을 맞추다 (= make the deadline)
44	get back	돌아오다		59	stop by	잠시 들리다
45	on course	진로에 따라서, 예정 방향으로				

TEST4 1-2
VOCABULARY

TEST4 1-2지문의 단어 중 토플 필수 단어를 선별하여 정리하였습니다.

01	**Sagittarius** [ˈsædʒɪˌteriəs]	n. 궁수자리
02	**solar** [ˈsoʊlə(r)]	adj. 태양의
03	**content** [ˈkɑːntent]	n. 속에 든 것, 내용물
04	**galaxy** [ˈɡæləksi]	n. 은하계, 은하
05	**remnant** [ˈremnənt]	n. 나머지, 남은 부분
06	**absorb** [əbˈsɔːrb; əbˈzɔːrb]	v. 흡수하다, 빨아들이다
07	**astonishing** [əˈstɑːnɪʃɪŋ]	adj. 정말 놀라운, 믿기 힘든
08	**gravitational** [ˌɡrævɪˈteɪʃənl]	adj. 중력의
09	**seldom** [ˈseldəm]	adv. 좀처럼 ~ 않는, 거의 ~ 않는
10	**bound** [baʊnd]	adj. 얽매인, 묶인
11	**fuse** [fjúːz]	v. 융합시키다
12	**validate** [ˈvælɪdeɪt]	v. 입증하다, 타당화하다
13	**absurd** [əbˈsɜːrd]	adj. 우스꽝스러운, 터무니없는
14	**controversial** [ˌkɑːntrəˈvɜːrʃl]	adj. 논란이 많은, 논쟁적인
15	**arise** [əˈraɪz]	v. 생기다, 발생하다
16	**previous** [ˈpriːviəs]	adj. 이전의, 기존의
17	**cosmologist** [kɑzˈmɑːlədʒɪst]	n. 우주론자
18	**shred** [ʃred]	v. 갈가리 자르다, 찢다
16	**stack** [stæk]	n. 무더기, 더미
20	**pure** [pjʊr]	adj. 다른 것이 섞이지 않은
21	**supernatural** [ˌsuːpərˈnætʃrəl]	adj. 초자연적인
22	**scenario** [səˈnærioʊ]	n. 시나리오, 이야기
23	**distinguish** [dɪˈstɪŋɡwɪʃ]	v. 구별하다
24	**determine** [dɪˈtɜːrmɪn]	v. 알아내다, 밝히다
25	**property** [ˈprɑːpərti]	n. 속성
26	**thermal** [ˈθɜːrml]	adj. 열의
27	**radiate** [ˈreɪdieɪt]	v. 내뿜다, 발하다
28	**infrared radiation** [ˌɪnfrəˈred ˌreɪdiˈeɪʃn]	n. 적외선
29	**give off** [ɡɪv ɔːf, ɑf]	v. 내뿜다, 발하다
30	**warzone** [ˈwɔːr zoʊn]	n. 교전지역
31	**scrutinize** [ˈskruːtənaɪz]	v. 세심히 살피다, 면밀히 조사하다
32	**discern** [dɪˈsɜːrn]	v. 차이점을 식별하다

USHER iBT TOEFL INTERMEDIATE TEST LISTENING

단어 · 구문

TEST4 1-2
VOCABULARY

TEST4 1-2지문의 단어 중 토플 필수 단어를 선별하여 정리하였습니다.

33	**crucial** [ˈkruːʃl]	adj. 중대한, 중요한
34	**astronomer** [əˈstrɑːnəmə(r)]	n. 천문학자
35	**composition** [ˌkɑːmpəˈzɪʃn]	n. 구성 요소들, 구성
36	**peripheral** [pəˈrɪfərəl]	adj. 주변적인, 지엽적인
37	**sync** [sɪŋk]	v. 맞추다
38	**attempt** [əˈtempt]	n. 시도
39	**telescope** [ˈtelɪskoʊp]	n. 망원경
40	**dissimilar** [dɪˈsɪmɪlə(r)]	adj. 같지 않은, 다른
41	**attractive** [əˈtræktɪv]	adj. 당기는, 이끄는
42	**stretch** [stretʃ]	v. 잡아당기다, 늘이다
43	**elongated** [ɪˈlɔːŋɡeɪtɪd]	adj. (비정상적으로) 가늘고 긴
44	**elliptical** [ɪˈlɪptɪkl]	adj. 타원형의
45	**incorporate** [ɪnˈkɔːrpəreɪt]	v. 포함하다, 합치다
46	**evolve** [ɪˈvɑːlv]	v. 발달시키다
47	**dwarf** [dwɔːrf]	n. 왜소함
48	**identical** [aɪˈdentɪkl]	adj. 동일한, 똑같은
49	**grasp** [ɡræsp]	v. 이해하다
50	**jumble** [ˈdʒʌmbl]	v. 뒤섞다
51	**simplify** [ˈsɪmplɪfaɪ]	v. 간소화하다, 단순화하다
52	**relatively** [ˈrelətɪvli]	adv. 상대적으로, 비교적
53	**emission** [iˈmɪʃn]	n. 배출
54	**photon** [ˈfoʊtɑːn]	n. 광자
55	**fuse** [fjuːz]	v. 섞다, 융합하다
56	**entirety** [ɪnˈtaɪərəti]	n. 전체, 전부
57	**inhibit** [ɪnˈhɪbɪt]	v. 저해하다, 방해하다
58	**incessant** [ɪnˈsesnt]	adj. 끊임없는, 쉴새없는
59	**physical** [ˈfɪzɪkl]	adj. 물리적인, 신체의
60	**contact** [ˈkɑːntækt]	n. 접촉
61	**conservative** [kənˈsɜːrvətɪv]	adj. 보수적인
62	**override** [ˌoʊvərˈraɪd]	v. 기각하다, 무시하다
63	**existing** [ɪɡˈzɪstɪŋ]	adj. 기존의

구문정리

TEST4 1-2 | Two galaxies

본문 중 중요 구문 정리한 내용입니다. 우선 암기하고 많이 읽으시기 바랍니다.

Set1 Lecture1에 등장하는 단어들 중 필요한 단어들을 선별하였습니다.

01	talk about	~에 더해 이야기 하다
02	consist of	~로 구성되다
03	name A B	A를 B라 이름 짓다
04	have done	해오다 (동사형태 3번)
05	tend to do	to do 하는 경향이 있다
06	absorb A from B	A를 B로부터 흡수하다
07	relate to	~와 관련되다
08	you see	있잖아 (무엇을 설명할 때)
09	be 1000 times bigger	~보다 1000배 크다
10	be being done	당해오는 중이다 (동사형태 7번)
11	pull A into B	A를 B에 넣다
12	be absorbed by	~에 의해 흡수되다
13	think O to do	O가 to do하다고 생각하다
14	fuse together	합쳐져서 하나가 되다
15	validate the point	그 포인트를 입증하다
16	due to	~때문에
17	lack of	~의 부족
18	view A as B	A를 B로 간주하다
19	to begin	먼저, 우선
20	go over	~을 검토하다
21	help O do	O가 do 하는 것을 돕다
22	let's say	예를 들면
23	be able to do	to do 할 수 있다
24	supernatural power	초자연적인 힘
25	what if	만약 ~라면
26	easy to do	to do 하기 쉬운
27	extent to	~정도까지
28	begin by	~으로 시작하다 (= with, at, on)
29	make A of B	A를 B로 만들다
30	give off	(냄새, 열, 빛 등을) 내다, 발하다
31	This might sound familiar to you	너에게 익숙하게 들릴수도 있다
32	for those not familiar with ~	~와 익숙하지 않은 사람들을 위해서
33	think about	~에 대해 생각하다
34	detecting device	탐지장치
35	employ A in B	A를 B에서 사용하다
36	at night	밤에

구문정리

TEST4 1-2 | Two galaxies

본문 중 중요 구문 정리한 내용입니다. 우선 암기하고 많이 읽으시기 바랍니다.
Set1 Lecture1에 등장하는 단어들 중 필요한 단어들을 선별하였습니다.

#	구문	뜻
37	enable O to do	O가 to do 하는 것을 가능하게 하다
38	regardless of	~와 관계없이
39	range from A to B	A부터 B까지 이르다, 걸쳐있다
40	at the airport	공항에서
41	go through	~을 살펴보다
42	distinguish A from B	A를 B로부터 구분하다
43	apply A to B	A를 B에 적용시키다
44	ability to do	to do 할 수 있는 능력
45	look at	~을 살피다
46	discern one from another	하나를 다른것으로부터 구별하다
47	Infrared light	적외선
48	a part of	~의 한 부분
49	require O to do	O가 to do 하는 것을 요구하다
50	a sort of	일종의
51	differ from	~와 다르다
52	take O to do	O를 to do 하는데 필요로 하다
53	let's get back	본론으로 다시 돌아가보자
54	be sure to do	to do 하는 것을 확실히 하다
55	begin ~ing	~ing 하는 것을 시작하다
56	seem to do	to do 하는 것처럼 보이다
57	sync with	~와 맞다, 동기화되다
58	attempt to do	to do 하려는 시도
59	identify A as B	A를 B로 확인하다
60	attractive force	인력, 당기는 힘
61	dissimilar from	~와 다른
62	except that	~이라는 것을 제외하면
63	in the latter case	후자의 경우에
64	cause O to do	O가 to do 하는 것을 야기하다
65	for so long	오랫동안
66	stretch out	뻗다
67	transform A into B	A를 B로 변형시키다
68	incorporate A into B	A를 B에 포함시키다
69	no longer	더 이상 ~않는
70	next time	다음에 ~할때에
71	contradictory point	모순되는 포인트
72	belong to	~에 속하다

TEST4 1-3
VOCABULARY

TEST4 1-3지문의 단어 중 토플 필수 단어를 선별하여 정리하였습니다.

01	**basically** [	beɪsɪkli]	adv. 원래는, 실은
02	**imitate** [	ɪmɪteɪt]	v. ~를 흉내내다, 모방하다
03	**for the purpose of ~**	~의 목적으로, ~을 위해
04	**commercial** [kə	mɜːrʃl]	adj. 상업의, 영리적인
05	**mesmerize** [	mezməraɪz]	v. 최면을 걸듯 마음을 사로잡다, 완전 넋을 빼놓다
06	**pigmentation** [|pɪgmen|teɪʃn]	n. 색소 형성, 염색
07	**coloration** [|kʌlə|reɪʃn]	n. 착색, 채색, 배색
08	**the former and the latter**	전자와 후자
09	**be familiar with ~**	~에 친숙하다, 익숙하다
10	**common** [	kɑːmən]	adj. 보통의, 흔히 있는
11	**perception** [pər	sepʃn]	n. 인식
12	**due to ~**	~ 때문에
13	**chlorophyll** [	klɔːrəfɪl]	n. 엽록소
14	**chloroplast** [	klɔːrəplæst]	n. 엽록체
15	**wavelength** [	weɪvleŋθ]	n. 파장
16	**absorb** [əb|sɔːrb;əb|zɔːrb]	v. ~를 흡수하다
17	**a wide range of ~**	광범위한
18	**fail to V**	V하는 것을 실패하다
19	**detrimental** [|detrɪ|mentl]	adj. 손해를 입히는, 해로운, 반(反)하는
20	**photosynthesis** [|foʊtoʊ|sɪnθəsɪs]	n. 광합성
21	**require** [rɪ	kwaɪə(r)]	v. ~를 요구하다, 필요로하다
22	**be composed of ~**	~로 구성되다
23	**row** [roʊ]	n. 줄, 열
24	**scale** [skeɪl]	n. (물고기, 뱀 따위의) 비늘
25	**pigment** [	pɪgmənt]	n. (조직, 세포 중의) 색소
26	**exactly** [ɪg	zæktli]	adv. 바로, 꼭
27	**exploit** [ɪk	splɔɪt]	v. ~을 이용하다, 착취하다
28	**dye** [daɪ]	n. 물감
29	**chemical** [	kemɪkl]	n. 화학 제품
30	**fabric** [	fæbrɪk]	n. 옷감, 직물
31	**fiber** [fáibər]	n. 섬유
32	**manufacturer** [|mænju|fæktʃərə(r)]	n. 제조업자, 제작자
33	**eliminate** [ɪ	lɪmɪneɪt]	v. 제거하다, 삭제하다
34	**formula** [	fɔːrmjələ]	n. 기본 원칙, 해결책
35	**additionally** [ə'dɪʃənəli]	adv. 게다가, 더구나
36	**energy-efficient**	adj. 에너지가 적게 드는, 효율이 좋은
37	**water-proof**	adj. 방수의, 내수성의
38	**so that**	그 결과, 그러므로, 그 때문에
39	**be filled with~**	~로 채워져있다
40	**droplet** [	drɑːplət]	n. 물방울
41	**several** [	sevrəl]	adj. 몇몇의
42	**adhesive** [əd|hiːsɪv;əd|hiːzɪv]	adj. 들러붙는, 부착력이 있는, 점착성의
43	**attraction** [ə	trækʃn]	n. 인력
44	**flatten out**	평평하게 되다(하다)

TEST4 1-3
VOCABULARY

TEST4 1-3지문의 단어 중 토플 필수 단어를 선별하여 정리하였습니다.

45	bumpy [ˈbʌmpi]	adj. 울퉁불퉁한		67	noteworthy [ˈnoʊtwɜːrði]	adj. 주목할 만한
46	come into contact with~	~와 닿다, 접촉하다		68	employ [ɪmˈplɔɪ]	v. ~을 쓰다, 이용하다
47	preserve [prɪˈzɜːrv]	v. ~을 보존하다		69	pros and cons	장단점, 찬반 양론, 이해 득실
48	slide off ~	~에서 미끄러 떨어지다, 미끄러지다		70	potential [pəˈtenʃl]	adj. 잠재적인
49	roll off	굴러 떨어지다		71	threat [θret]	n. 위협
50	affinity [əˈfɪnəti]	n. 친화성, 유사성		72	process [ˈprɑːses;ˈproʊses]	n. 작용
51	solid [ˈsɑːlɪd]	adj. 고체의		73	application [ˌæplɪˈkeɪʃn]	n. 적용
52	matter [ˈmætə(r)]	n. 물질		74	contributing factor	기여 요인
53	phenomena [fəˈnɑːmɪnə]	n. 현상		75	the sun's rays	직사광선
54	prevalent [ˈprevələnt]	adj. 널리 퍼진, 만연한, 일반적인		76	substantial [səbˈstænʃl]	adj. 충분한, 상당한
55	incorporate [ɪnˈkɔːrpəreɪt]	v. ~을 집어넣다, 포함하다, 함유하다		77	detect [dɪˈtekt]	v. ~을 감지하다
56	greasy [ˈɡriːsi;ˈɡriːzi]	adj. 기름진		78	hemophiliac [ˌhiːməˈfɪliæk]	adj. 혈우병에 걸린
57	accidentally [ˌæksɪˈdentəli]	adv. 우연히		79	membrane [ˈmembreɪn]	n. 막
58	spill [spɪl]	v. ~을 엎지르다		80	neutral [ˈnuːtrəl]	adj. 중립적인
59	layered [ˈleɪərd]	adj. 층을 이루고 있는		81	stance [stæns]	n. 태도
60	integration [ˌɪntɪˈɡreɪʃn]	n. 통합, 결합		82	consideration [kənˌsɪdəˈreɪʃn]	n. 고려 사항
61	have a negative impact on ~	~에 부정적인 영향을 미치다		83	biased [ˈbáiəst]	adj. 편향된, 선입견이 있는
62	imperative [ɪmˈperətɪv]	adj. 필수적인, 중요한		84	abuse [əˈbjuːz]	v. ~을 남용하다, 학대하다
63	ensure [ɪnˈʃʊr]	v. ~을 확실하게 하다, 보증하다		85	social awareness	사회적 인식
64	impediment [ɪmˈpedɪmənt]	n. 방해, 방해물		86	in order to V	V하기 위해서
65	barely [ˈberli]	adv. 거의 ~ 않다		87	discipline [ˈdɪsəplɪn]	n. 단련법, 훈련, 규율
66	be involved in ~	~에 참여하다				

구문정리

TEST4 1-3 | Biomimetics

본문 중 중요 구문 정리한 내용입니다. 우선 암기하고 많이 읽으시기 바랍니다.

Set1 Lecture2에 등장하는 단어들 중 필요한 단어들을 선별하였습니다.

01	call A B	A를 B라 칭하다
02	for the purpose of	~의 목적으로
03	give A B	A에게 B를 주다
04	make O O.C	O를 O.C 상태로 만들다
05	integrate A into B	A를 B에 통합시키다
06	be sure	~을 확신하다
07	such as	~와 같은
08	for instance	예를 들어
09	in a way	방법으로
10	the former	전자
11	the latter	후자
12	familiar with	~와 친숙한
13	look at	~을 살펴보다
14	due to	~때문에
15	find A in B	A를 B에서 발견하다
16	be absorbed by	~에 의해 흡수 되다
17	that's why	그게 바로 ~ 한 이유이다
18	a wide range of	광범위한
19	fail to do	to do 하기를 실패하다
20	detrimental to	~에 해로운
21	through the process	과정을 통해서
22	produce A from B	A를 B로부터 만들다
23	know A as B	A를 B로 알다
24	compose A of B	A를 B로 구성하다
25	interact with	~와 상호작용하다
26	just as	마치 ~ 처럼
27	I don't know if	~인지 아닌지 나는 모른다
28	you see	있잖아
29	eliminate A from B	A를 B로 부터 제거하다
30	require O to do	O가 to do 하는 것을 요구하다

구문정리 TEST4 1-3

본문 중 중요 구문 정리한 내용입니다. 우선 암기하고 많이 읽으시기 바랍니다.

Biomimetics
Set1 Lecture2에 등장하는 단어들 중 필요한 단어들을 선별하였습니다.

#	구문	뜻
31	apply A to B	A를 B에 적용시키다
32	forget to do	to do 하는 것을 잊어버리다
33	so that	그래서 그결과
34	fill A with B	A를 B로 채우다
35	work as	~로서 일하다
36	drop A on B	A를 B에 떨어뜨리다
37	pull together	함께 일하다, 협력하다
38	The boy grew up to be a fine youth	to 부정사 부사적 용법 > 결과
39	cause O to do	O가 to do 하는 것을 야기하다
40	stick to	~에 들러붙다, 고수하다, 지키다
41	flatten out	평평해지다
42	in a way	이러한 방법으로
43	in a term	~용어로서
44	come into contact with	~와 접촉하다
45	allow O to do	O가 to do 하는 것을 허락하다
46	attach A to B	A를 B에 붙이다
47	roll off	굴러 떨어지다
48	be prevalent in	~에 만연하다
49	interesting to	~에게 흥미로운
50	spill A on B	A를 B에 쏟다
51	of course	물론
52	have an impact on	~에 영향을 끼치다
53	let O do	O가 do 하게 하다
54	refer to	~을 언급하다
55	need to do	to do 할 필요가 있다
56	impediment to	~에 대한 장애
57	involve A in B	A를 B에 포함하다

TEST4 2-1
VOCABULARY

TEST4 2-1지문의 단어 중 토플 필수 단어를 선별하여 정리하였습니다.

01	**movement** [ˈmuːvmənt]	n. 운동, 동향
02	**sort** [sɔːrt]	v. ~을 분류하다, 구분하다
03	**school** [skuːl]	n. 학파
04	**catch one's attention**	~의 이목을 끌다
05	**source** [sɔːrs]	n. 근원, 원인
06	**locate** [ˈloʊkeɪt]	v. 정착하다, ~에 잡다
07	**primary** [ˈpraɪmeri]	a. 주요한, 최초의
08	**nearby** [ˌnɪrˈbaɪ]	a. 바로 가까이의
09	**attract** [əˈtrækt]	v. (주위, 흥미 따위)~를 끌다
10	**preserve** [prɪˈzɜːrv]	v. ~을 보존하다, 간수하다
11	**unaffected** [ˌʌnəˈfektɪd]	a. ~에 영향을 받지 않은
12	**modern civilization**	현대 문명
13	**genuine** [ˈdʒenjuɪn]	a. 진짜의
14	**when it comes to**	~에 관한, ~에 대하여
15	**strive to V** [straɪv]	v. ~하려고 애쓰다, 노력하다
16	**adhere to ~** [ədˈhɪr]	v. 엄수하다, 고수하다, 충실하다
17	**figurative** [ˈfɪɡərətɪv]	a. 형상 묘사의, 비유적인
18	**landscape painting**	n. 풍경화
19	**imaginative** [ɪˈmædʒɪnətɪv]	a. 상상의, 상상력이 만들어낸
20	**inspire** [ɪnˈspaɪər]	v. (감정, 사상 따위를) 일어나게 하다
21	**presentation** [ˌpriːzenˈteɪʃn]	n. 발표, 설명
22	**preliminary** [prɪˈlɪmɪneri]	n. 임시의, 예비의
23	**intentionally** [ɪnˈtenʃənəli]	n. 의도적으로, 고의로
24	**leave O O.C**	O를 O.C하게 하다, 두다
25	**concise** [kənˈsaɪs]	a. 간결한
26	**informative** [ɪnˈfɔːrmətɪv]	a. 유익한
27	**proceed** [proʊˈsiːd]	v. 나아가다, 행해지다
28	**comprehensive** [ˌkɑːmprɪˈhensɪv]	a. 포괄적인, 종합적인, 많은 것을 포함하는, 광범위한

TEST4 2-1
VOCABULARY

TEST4 2-1지문의 단어 중 토플 필수 단어를 선별하여 정리하였습니다.

29	**paragon** [ˈpærəgɑːn]	n. 매우 우수한 사람, 모범, 전형
30	**figure out**	v. 알아내다
31	**prominent** [ˈprɑːmɪnənt]	a. 탁월한, 저명한
32	**noteworthy** [ˈnoʊtwɜːrði]	a. 주목할 만한
33	**by the way**	그런데, 말이 난 김에
34	**exhibit** [ɪɡˈzɪbɪt]	v. ~을 전시하다
35	**look forward to ~**	~를 기대하다
36	**organize** [ˈɔːrɡənaɪz]	v. ~을 모아 정리하다, ~을 준비하다
37	**go over**	v. 반복하다
38	**inquire** [ɪnˈkwaɪər]	v. 묻다
39	**property** [ˈprɑːpərti]	n. 속성
40	**cherish** [ˈtʃerɪʃ]	v. ~을 소중히 하다, 중히 여기다
41	**distinct** [dɪˈstɪŋkt]	a. 확실한, 뚜렷한, 분명한
42	**untouched** [ʌnˈtʌtʃt]	a. 손상되지 않은, 손을 대지 않은, 처음 상태로 있는
43	**existence** [ɪɡˈzɪstəns]	n. 존재, 실존, 현존
44	**fusion** [ˈfjuːʒn]	n. 융합, 통합
45	**relic** [ˈrelɪk]	n. 유물, 유품
46	**depiction** [dɪˈpɪkʃn]	n. 묘사, 서술
47	**fabricate** [ˈfæbrɪkeɪt]	n. 제조하다, 제작하다, ~을 만들어내다
48	**undisturbed** [ˌʌndɪˈstɜːrbd]	a. 방해받지 않은, 평온한
49	**prestigious** [preˈstɪdʒəs]	a. 유명한, 명성이 있는
50	**exemplary** [ɪɡˈzempləri]	a. 모범적인, 전형적인, 좋은 예가 되는
51	**well-organized**	a. 잘 정리된
52	**be responsible for ~**	~의 원인이 되다
53	**pay attention to ~**	~에 주목하다, 유의하다
54	**requirement** [rɪˈkwaɪərmənt]	n. 필요 조건, 요건, 요구되는 것
55	**shorten** [ˈʃɔːrtn]	v. 짧게 하다, 축소하다, 줄이다
56	**duration** [duˈreɪʃn]	n. 지속 시간, 기간

구문정리

TEST4 2-1 | 19th century European art movements

본문 중 중요 구문 정리한 내용입니다. 우선 암기하고 많이 읽으시기 바랍니다.
Set2 Conversation에 등장하는 단어들 중 필요한 단어들을 선별하였습니다.

01	do you have a minute	시간 있으세요?
02	what can I do for you?	무엇을 도와드릴까요?
03	have done	해오다(동사형태 3번)
04	catch attention	주목을 끌다
05	from A to B	A부터 B까지
06	why don't you	~하는게 어때?
07	tell A B	A에게 B를 말하다
08	learn from	~로부터 배우다
09	start with	~와 시작하다
10	from what I have read	읽은 바에 의하면
11	come from	~로부터 오다
12	when it comes to	~에 관한 한
13	by that I mean	그래서 내 말은
14	strive to do	to do 하려 매진하다, 몰두하다
15	adhere to	~을 고수하다
16	I am not sure if	~인지 아닌지 확실하지 않다
17	different from	~와 다른
18	add A to B	A를 B에 추가하다
19	be able to do	to do 할 수 있다
20	need to do	to do 할 필요가 있다
21	research on	~에 대한 연구
22	try to do	to do 하려고 시도하다
23	make O O.C	O를 O.C로 만들다
24	let's see	어디 보자
25	do research	조사, 연구를 하다
26	figure out	~을 알아내다, 이해하다
27	one of the 복수명사	복수명사 중의 하나
28	include A in B	A를 B에 포함시키다
29	by the way	그런데 (대화에서 화제를 바꿀때)
30	be going to do	to do 할 것이다
31	stop by	잠시 들르다
32	be all set	준비가 되어 있다
33	no problem at all	전혀 문제가 안된다
34	look forward to	~을 기대하다

TEST4 2-2 VOCABULARY

TEST4 2-2지문의 단어 중 토플 필수 단어를 선별하여 정리하였습니다.

01	**access** [	ækses]	n. 접근권, 접촉 기회
02	**public** [	pʌblɪk]	n. 대중, 일반인
03	**specifically** [spə	sɪfɪkli]	adv. 구체적으로, 명확하게
04	**classics** [	klæsɪks]	n. 고전
05	**divide** [dɪ	vaɪd]	v. 나누다
06	**triple-decker** [trɪpl-dékər]	n. 3부작
07	**volume** [	vɑ:lju:m;-jəm]	n. 권
08	**come up with** [kʌm ʌp wɪð;wɪθ]	v. 제시하다, 떠올리다
09	**accessible** [ək	sesəbl]	adj. 접근가능한
10	**phenomenon** [fə	nɑ:mɪnən]	n. 현상
11	**century** [	sentʃəri]	n. 세기, 100년
12	**investigate** [ɪn	vestɪgeɪt]	v. 조사하다
13	**era** [|ɪrə;|erə]	n. 시대
14	**literature** [lítərətʃər]	n. 문학
15	**controversial** [|kɑ:ntrə|vɜ:rʃl]	adj. 논쟁의 여지가 있는
16	**refer** [rifə:r]	v. 부르다, 말하다
17	**early** [	ɜ:rli]	adj. 초기의
18	**modern** [	mɑ:dərn]	adj. 현대의
19	**succeeding** [səksí:dɪŋ]	adj. 계속되는, 다음의
20	**advent** [	ædvent]	n. 도래
21	**literacy** [	lɪtərəsi]	n. 글을 읽고 쓸 줄 아는 능력, 문해력
22	**readily** [	redɪli]	adv. 쉽게
23	**available** [ə	veɪləbl]	adv. 구할 수 있는, 이용할 수 있는
24	**general** [	dʒenrəl]	adj. 일반적인
25	**especially** [ɪ	speʃəli]	adv. 특히
26	**pamphlet** [	pæmflət]	n. 팜플렛
27	**chivalry** [ʃívəlri]	n. 기사도
28	**medieval** [mì:dí:vəl, mè-]	adj. 중세의
29	**knight** [naɪt]	n. 기사
30	**adventure** [əd	ventʃə(r)]	n. 모험
31	**explore** [ɪk	splɔ:(r)]	v. 탐험하다
32	**religious** [rɪ	lɪdʒəs]	adj. 종교적인
33	**saint** [seɪnt]	n. 성인
34	**demon** [	di:mən]	n. 악령, 악마
35	**cover** [	kʌvə(r)]	v. (어떤 내용을) 다루다
36	**entertaining** [|entər|təɪnɪŋ]	adj. 재미있는, 즐거움을 주는

TEST4 2-2
VOCABULARY

TEST4 2-2지문의 단어 중 토플 필수 단어를 선별하여 정리하였습니다.

37	philosophical	[ˌfɪləˈsɑːfɪkl]	adj. 철학적인
38	component	[kəmˈpoʊnənt]	n. 요소, 부분
39	everyday	[ˈevrideɪ]	adj. 일상적인, 일반적인
40	embellish	[ɪmˈbelɪʃ]	v. 장식하다
41	manuscript	[ˈmænjuskrɪpt]	n. 필사본
42	hawker	[ˈhɔːkə(r)]	n. 행상인
43	peddler	[ˈpedlə(r)]	n. 행상인
44	stimulus	[ˈstɪmjələs]	n. 자극제
45	input	[ˈɪnpʊt]	n. 투입
46	radical	[ˈrædɪkl]	adj. 근본적인, 철저한
47	initiate	[ɪˈnɪʃieɪt]	v. 개시되게 하다, 시작하게 하다
48	dramatic	[drəˈmætɪk]	adj. 극적인
49	civilization	[ˌsɪvələˈzeɪʃn]	n. 문명
50	scholar	[ˈskɑːlə(r)]	n. 학자
51	transition	[trænˈzɪʃn; trænˈsɪʃn]	n. 이행, 전환
52	unrecognized	[ʌnˈrekəɡnaɪzd]	adj. 인식되지 못한, 인정받지 못하는
53	significant	[sɪɡˈnɪfɪkənt]	adj. 중요한, 의미있는
54	standard	[ˈstændərd]	n. 표준, 기준
55	make way for	[meɪk weɪ fə®]	v. ~에 길을 내어주다
56	profitable	[ˈprɑːfɪtəbl]	adj. 수익성이 있는, 이윤이 남는
57	prior	[ˈpraɪə(r)]	adj. 사전의, 이전의
58	oral	[ˈɔːrəl]	adj. 구두의, 입을 통한
59	hypothesis	[haɪˈpɑːθəsɪs]	n. 가설
60	eradicate	[ɪˈrædɪkeɪt]	v. 뿌리뽑다, 없애버리다
61	express	[ɪkˈspres]	v. 나타내다, 표현하다
62	convenient	[kənˈviːniənt]	adj. 편리한
63	enable	[ɪˈneɪbl]	v. ~을 할 수 있게 하다
64	permanent	[ˈpɜːrmənənt]	adj. 영구적인, 영원한
65	preservation	[ˌprezərˈveɪʃn]	n. 보존
66	material	[məˈtɪriəl]	n. 자료
67	authority	[əˈθɔːrəti; əˈθɑːr-]	n. 권위, 권한
68	perspective	[pərˈspektɪv]	n. 관점, 시각
69	elucidate	[iˈluːsɪdeɪt]	v. 더 자세히 설명하다
70	prestigious	[preˈstɪdʒəs]	adj. 명망있는, 일류의
71	notable	[ˈnoʊtəbl]	adj. 중요한, 주목할 만한
72	detrimental	[ˌdetrɪˈmentl]	adj. 해로운

TEST4 2-2
VOCABULARY

TEST4 2-2지문의 단어 중 토플 필수 단어를 선별하여 정리하였습니다.

#	단어	발음	뜻
73	**skepticism**	[sképtəsìzm]	n. 회의론, 회의주의
74	**biography**	[baɪɑ́:grəfi]	n. 전기
75	**scrutinize**	[ˈskru:tənaɪz]	v. 세세히 조사하다
76	**convey**	[kənˈveɪ]	v. 생각, 감정을 전달하다
77	**noteworthy**	[ˈnoʊtwɜ:rði]	adj. 주목할 만한
78	**driving force**	[ˈdraɪvɪŋ fɔ:rs]	n. 원동력
79	**actualize**	[ˈæktʃuəlaɪz]	v. 현실로 만들다, 실현하다
80	**last**	[læst, lɑ́:st]	v. 계속하다, 지속하다
81	**unfortunate**	[ʌnˈfɔ:rtʃənət]	adj. 불운한, 불행한
82	**credit**	[krédit]	n. 칭찬, 인정
83	**remarkable**	[rɪˈmɑ:rkəbl]	adj. 놀랄만한, 주목할만한
84	**compare**	[kəmˈper]	v. 비교하다
85	**contrast**	[kənˈtræst]	v. 대조하다
86	**briefly**	[ˈbri:fli]	adv. 잠시, 간단히
87	**mechanically**	[məkǽnikəli]	adv. 기계로
88	**sophisticated**	[səˈfɪstɪkeɪtɪd]	adj. 복잡한, 정교한
89	**logical**	[ˈlɑ:dʒɪkl]	adj. 논리적인, 타당한
90	**reasoning**	[ˈri:zənɪŋ]	n. 추론
91	**vendor**	[ˈvendə(r)]	n. 행상인, 노점상
92	**reliable**	[rɪˈlaɪəbl]	adj. 믿을 수 있는, 신뢰할만한
93	**vanish**	[ˈvænɪʃ]	v. 사라지다
94	**succumb**	[səˈkʌm]	v. 굴복하다, 무릎을 꿇다
95	**surpass**	[sərˈpæs]	v. 능가하다, 뛰어넘다
96	**contemporary**	[kənˈtempəreri]	adj. 동시대의, 현대의
97	**innovative**	[ˈɪnəveɪtɪv]	adj. 혁신적인
98	**experimental**	[ɪkˌsperɪˈmentl]	adj. 실험적인
99	**adversely**	[ˈædvɜ:rs]	adv. 역으로, 부정적으로
100	**argumentative**	[ˌɑ:rgjuˈmentətɪv]	adj. 따지기 좋아하는, 시비를 거는
101	**ironically**	[aɪrɑ́nikəli]	adv. 역설적으로, 반어적으로
102	**shortcoming**	[ˈʃɔ:rtkʌmɪŋ]	n. 단점, 결점
103	**longevity**	[lɑ:nˈdʒevəti; lɔ:n-]	n. 장수, 오래 감
104	**crux**	[krʌks]	n. 가장 중요한 부분

TEST4 2-2

The advent of literacy and cheap books

Set2 Lecture1에 등장하는 단어들 중 필요한 단어들을 선별하였습니다.

01	look at	~을 보다
02	access to	~에의 접근
03	divide A into B	A를 B로 나누다
04	due to	~때문에
05	come up with	생각해내다
06	way to do	to do 하는 방법
07	make O O.C	O를 O.C로 만들다
08	exist from A to B	A에서 B까지 존재하다
09	all the way	내내, 시종일관
10	move on to	~로 이동하다
11	be going to do	to do 할 예정이다
12	refer to A as B	A를 B로 언급하다
13	modern period	근대
14	mark A by B	A를 B로 표시하다
15	available to	이용 가능한
16	cover a subject	주제를 다루다
17	go on	시작하다; 계속하다
18	between A and B	A와 B 사이
19	don't get the worng idea	오해하다
20	enjoy ~ing	~ing 하는 것을 즐기다
21	nothing like	전혀 ~ 같지 않은
22	a range of	다양한
23	from A to B	A에서 B까지
24	so ~ that ~	너무 ~해서 그 결과 ~ 하다
25	in this case	이 경우에 있어서
26	change in	~에서의 변화
27	transition from A to B	A에서 B로의 전환
28	His dress is that of a gentleman, but his manners are those of a clown.	반복되는 명사 반복 피하기
29	responsible for	~에 원인이 있는
30	result in	그 결과 ~ 하다
31	long-term effect	장기 효과
32	in detail	상세하게

구문정리

TEST4 2-2 | The advent of literacy and cheap books

본문 중 중요 구문 정리한 내용입니다. 우선 암기하고 많이 읽으시기 바랍니다.
Set2 Lecture1에 등장하는 단어들 중 필요한 단어들을 선별하였습니다.

33	worry about	~을 두려워하다
34	bring about	초래하다
35	a set of	한 벌의
36	make way for	~을 위해 길을 열어주다
37	that way	그런 상태로, 그런 방법으로
38	prior to the advent of	~의 출현 이전에
39	pass down	전해지다
40	there would be	~이 있었을 것이다
41	continue to do	to do 하기를 계속하다
42	at the time	그 당시에
43	refer to	언급하다
44	one of the 복수명사	복수명사 중 하나
45	consider A as B	A를 B로 간주하다
46	detrimental to	~에 유해한
47	go into	들어가다
48	where were we?	우리가 어디까지 얘기했었죠?
49	as I mentioned earlier	앞서 언급했듯이
50	point of view	관점
51	for instance	예를 들어
52	call A B	A를 B라 부르다
53	a view on	~에 관한 의견
54	enough of	~의 충분한 양
55	driving force	원동력
56	make it possible for people to develop	사람들이 개발 하는것을 가능하게 하다
57	take into consideration	고려하다
58	the account of	~의 이야기
59	enough to do	to do 하기에 충분한
60	keep O O.C	O를 O.C로 유지하다
61	get the credit	공적을 인정 받다

TEST4 2-3
VOCABULARY

TEST4 2-3지문의 단어 중 토플 필수 단어를 선별하여 정리하였습니다.

01	**discussion** [dɪˈskʌʃn]	n. 논의, 검토, 고찰
02	**mention** [ˈmenʃn]	v. 언급하다, ~에 대해 말하다
03	**prominent** [ˈprɑːmɪnənt]	a. 두드러진, 뚜렷한, 중요한
04	**developmental** [dɪˌveləpˈmentl]	a. 발전의
05	**in every aspect of**	모든 면에서, 모든 견지에서
06	**due to**	~ 때문에
07	**powered** [ˈpaʊərd]	a. 동력을 장치한, 힘이 있는
08	**burdensome** [ˈbɜːrdnsəm]	a. 짐이 되는, 부담이 되는
09	**manufacturing** [ˌmænjuˈfæktʃərɪŋ]	a. 제조의, 제조하는, 제작하는
10	**practical** [ˈpræktɪkl]	a. 실지의, 실용적인, 실리적인
11	**flat** [flæt]	a. 평평한, 기복이 없는, 수평의
12	**petroleum** [pəˈtroʊliəm]	n. 석유
13	**combustion** [kəmˈbʌstʃən]	n. 연소, 격동
14	**mark** [mɑːrk]	v. ~을 두드러지게 하다, 설계하다
15	**be aware of**	~를 인식하다
16	**well-known** [ˌwel ˈnoʊn]	a. 잘 알려진
17	**when it comes to**	~에 관한 한, ~라면
18	**patent** [ˈpætnt]	v. ~의 특허를 얻다, ~을 독자 개발해 자기것으로 삼다
19	**accommodate** [əˈkɑːmədeɪt]	v. ~을 수용하다, ~을 태우다
20	**up to**	~까지, ~만큼
21	**despite** [dɪˈspaɪt]	prep. ~에도 불구하고
22	**operation** [ˌɑːpəˈreɪʃn]	n. 조작, 운전
23	**bothersome** [ˈbɑːðərsəm]	a. 귀찮은, 번거로운, 성가신
24	**draft animal**	짐수레 끄는 동물, 역축(役畜)
25	**horrendous** [həˈrendəs]	a. 끔찍스러운, 소름끼치는
26	**criticize** [ˈkrɪtɪsaɪz]	v. ~을 비판하다

TEST4 2-3
VOCABULARY

TEST4 2-3지문의 단어 중 토플 필수 단어를 선별하여 정리하였습니다.

27	**debase** [dɪˈbeɪs]	a. ~의 인격을 떨어뜨리다, 끌어내리다
28	**abuse** [əˈbjuːs]	v. ~을 학대하다, 혹사하여 해를 끼치다
29	**wane** [weɪn]	v. 줄다, 작아지다, 적어지다
30	**come up with**	v. ~이 생각나다, 떠오르다
31	**somewhat** [ˈsʌmwʌt]	ad. 어느 정도, 얼마간, 다소
32	**resemble** [rɪˈzembl]	v. ~을 닮다, ~와 공통점이 있다
33	**translate** [trænsˈleɪt]	v. ~을 번역하다, 옮기다
34	**come from**	~에서 오다, ~출신이다
35	**extension** [ɪkˈstenʃn]	n. 확장, 연장선
36	**straddle** [ˈstrædl]	v. 양다리를 벌리고 앉다, 양다리를 걸치다
37	**humongous** [hjuːˈmʌŋgəs]	a. 거대한, 엄청나게 큰
38	**refer to**	~에 대해 언급하다, 관계가 있다
39	**whichever** [wɪtʃˈevər]	pron. 어느 것이든, 어느 쪽이든
40	**be on the same page**	(~에 대해) 이해 하고 있는 내용이 같다
41	**chronologically** [ˌkrɑːnəˈlɑːdʒɪkli]	ad. 연대순으로
42	**introduce** [ˌɪntrəˈduːs]	v. ~를 널리 알리다, ~를 창안하다, 시작하다
43	**several** [ˈsevrəl]	a. 몇몇의, 여러가지의
44	**decade** [ˈdekeɪd]	n. 10년간
45	**fair** [fer]	a. 상당한
46	**amount** [əˈmaʊnt]	n. 양
47	**acclaim** [əˈkleɪm]	n. 환호, 찬사, 호평
48	**recognition** [ˌrekəgˈnɪʃn]	n. 인정, 포상
49	**largely** [ˈlɑːrdʒli]	n. 대부분, 주로
50	**ignore** [ɪgˈnɔːr]	v. ~를 무시하다, 모르는 체하다
51	**geographical** [ˌdʒiːəˈgræfɪkl]	a. 지리학의, 지리상의, 지리적인
52	**reaction** [riˈækʃn]	a. 반응, 대응

VOCABULARY

TEST4 2-3 — TEST4 2-3지문의 단어 중 토플 필수 단어를 선별하여 정리하였습니다.

53	**demonstrate** [ˈdemənstreɪt]	a. ~을 실물로 선전하다
54	**cover** [ˈkʌvər]	v. ~을 가다, 답파하다
55	**level** [ˈlevl]	a. 평탄한, 높낮이가 없는
56	**surface** [ˈsɜːrfɪs]	a. 지표면, 외면
57	**forestland** [fɔ́ːristlæ̀nd]	n. 삼림지
58	**injury** [ˈɪndʒəri]	n. 부상, 상해
59	**strategy** [ˈstrætədʒi]	n. 전략
60	**recreation** [ˌriːkriˈeɪʃn]	n. 여가
61	**rent out**	~을 빌려주다, 임대하다
62	**ingenious** [ɪnˈdʒiːniəs]	a. 영리한, 독창적인
63	**inspire** [ɪnˈspaɪər]	v. ~에 영감을 주다
64	**descend** [dɪˈsend]	v. 유래되다
65	**stall** [stɔːl]	v. 오도가도(꼼짝) 못하게 만들다, ~를 세우다
66	**be prone to do**	~하기 쉽다
67	**landscape** [ˈlændskeɪp]	n. 지표, 지형
68	**immoral** [ɪˈmɑːrəl]	a. 부도덕한, 도의에 어긋나는
69	**stance** [stæns]	n. 태도, 자세
70	**oppose** [əˈpoʊz]	v. ~에 반대하다
71	**partially** [ˈpɑːrʃəli]	ad. 부분적으로
72	**deserve credit as**	~이라고 평가받을 자격이 있다
73	**along with**	~와 함께, ~에 더하여
74	**utilize** [ˈjuːtəlaɪz]	v. ~을 이용하다, 활용하다
75	**by now**	지금쯤은 이미
76	**figure out**	v. ~을 이해하다
77	**common sense** [ˌkɑːmən ˈsens]	n. 상식, 상식적 판단력

구문정리

본문 중 중요 구문 정리한 내용입니다. 우선 암기하고 많이 읽으시기 바랍니다.

TEST4 2-3 | The Industrial Revolution

Set2 Lecture2에 등장하는 단어들 중 필요한 단어들을 선별하였습니다.

01	take place	일어나다, 발생하다
02	as I mentioned	내가 말했듯이
03	boom in	~의 급증
04	every aspect of	~의 모든 측면
05	due to	~때문에
06	advance in	~점에서의 진보, 발전
07	and so on	기타 등등
08	spread across	~전역에 퍼지다
09	would like to do	to do 하고 싶다
10	focus on	~에 주력하다, 초점을 맞추다
11	come about	발생하다
12	practical for	~에 실용적인
13	turn to	~에 의지하다
14	such as	예를 들어, ~와 같은
15	lead to	~로 이어지다, 초래하다
16	mark the end of	종료하다, ~의 끝을 나타내다
17	by now	지금쯤은, 이제
18	be aware of	~을 알다
19	along with	~와 함께
20	when it comes to	~에 관한 한
21	start with	~와 함께 출발하다
22	call A B	A를 B라고 부르다
23	up to	~까지
24	accept A as B	A를 B로 받아들이다
25	work as	~으로 일하다
26	criticize A for B	A를 B의 이유로 비판하다
27	come up with	생각해내다
28	refer to A as B	A를 B라고 언급하다, 부르다
29	translate to	~로 번역하다
30	come from	~로부터 나오다
31	as if	마치 ~인 것 처럼
32	think of	~를 생각하다, 떠올리다

308 ··· | 토플 공부도우미 | www.usherin.usher.co.kr

구문정리

TEST4 2-3 | The Industrial Revolution

본문 중 중요 구문 정리한 내용입니다. 우선 암기하고 많이 읽으시기 바랍니다.
Set2 Lecture2에 등장하는 단어들 중 필요한 단어들을 선별하였습니다.

33	refer to	~을 언급하다
34	introduce A as B	A를 B로 소개하다
35	be on the same page	이해하고 있는 내용이 같다, 동의하다
36	chronologically speaking	연대기적으로(시간순으로) 말해서,
37	several decades earlier than	~보다 몇십년 전 이전에
38	starting point	출발점
39	receive acclaim	환호를 받다
40	an amount of	상당한
41	in an hour	한시간 내에
42	less than	~보다 적은
43	take twice as long	두배 길게 걸리다
44	need to do	to do 할 필요가 있다
45	look at	~를 보다
46	in contrast	그에 반해서
47	use O to do	O를 to do 하기 위해 사용하다
48	go up	올라가다
49	lose control	통제를 잃다, 제어할 수 없게 되다
50	for these reasons	이러한 이유들 때문에
51	be interested in	~에 흥미, 관심이 있다
52	succumb to	~에 굴복하다
53	strive to do	to do 하려고 분투하다, 노력하다
54	keep O O.C	O를 O.C로 유지하다
55	marketing strategy	마케팅 전략
56	use for	~를 위한 사용
57	rather than	~보다는, 대신에
58	bring A to B	A를 B로 가져오다
59	rent out	~를 임대하다
60	want O to do	O가 to do 하기를 원하다
61	as ~ as	~만큼 ~한
62	inspire O to do	O가 to do 하기를 고무하다, 격려하다
63	descend from	~에서 전해내려오다, 기원되다

TEST5 1-1
VOCABULARY

TEST5 1-1 지문의 단어 중 토플 필수 단어를 선별하여 정리하였습니다.

01	**traffic jam** [|træfɪk dʒæm]	n. 교통체증
02	**major** [|meɪdʒə(r)]	adj. 큰, 중대한
03	**accident** [|æksɪdənt]	n. 사고
04	**highway** [|haɪweɪ]	n. 고속도로
05	**injure** [|ɪndʒə(r)]	v. 부상을 입히다
06	**community center** [kə|mjuːnəti séntər]	n. 문화센터, 구민회관
07	**majority** [mə|dʒɔːrəti; -|dʒɑːr-]	n. 다수
08	**complicated** [|kɑːmplɪkeɪtɪd]	adj. 복잡한
09	**suppose** [sə|poʊz]	v. ~라고 여겨지다
10	**out of the blue**	갑자기, 난데없이
11	**apology** [ə|pɑːlədʒi]	n. 사과
12	**confuse** [kən|fjuːz]	v. (사람을) 혼란시키다
13	**reservation** [|rezər|veɪʃn]	n. 예약
14	**be on the same page**	~에 대해 이해하고 있는 내용이 같다
15	**recommend** [|rekə|mend]	v. 추천하다
16	**wonder** [|wʌndə(r)]	v. 놀라다, 궁금하다
17	**deviate** [|diːvieɪt]	v. 벗어나다
18	**extremely** [ɪk|striːmli]	adv. 극도로, 매우
19	**willing** [|wɪlɪŋ]	adj. 기꺼이 하는, 적극적인
20	**generous** [|dʒenərəs]	adj. 너그러운, 관대한
21	**security** [sə|kjʊrəti]	n. 보안, 경비
22	**guard** [gɑːrd]	n. 경비요원, 경비원
23	**track somebody /something down**	~을 찾아내다
24	**hand in** [hænd ɪn]	v. 제출하다
25	**upcoming** [|ʌpkʌmɪŋ]	adj. 다가오는, 곧 있을
26	**registration** [|redʒɪ|streɪʃn]	n. 등록, 신고
27	**vehicle** [|viːhɪkl]	n. 차량, 탈것
28	**arrangement** [ə|reɪndʒmənt]	n. 준비, 주선, 약속
29	**exploit** [ɪk|splɔɪt]	v. 이용하다
30	**mix somebody/something up with somebody/something**	v. ~를 ~와 혼동하다

TEST5 1-1

The reservation on a friday

Set1 Conversation에 등장하는 단어들 중 필요한 단어들을 선별하였습니다.

01	I'm here for a meeting with	~와 만나러 왔습니다.
02	must be	~임에 틀림 없다
03	look for	~을 찾다
04	Were you waiting long?	오래 기다리셨나요?
05	traffic jam	교통체증
06	must have been	~이었음에 틀림 없다
07	car accident	차사고
08	leading road to	~로 가는 주요 도로
09	what's happening	도대체 어떻게 된거야
10	on the other side of	~의 반대편에는
11	familiar with	~와 친숙한
12	spend time	시간을 보내다
13	the majority of	다수의
14	come in	들어오다
15	take a seat	자리에 앉다
16	need to do	to do 할 필요가 있다
17	make O OC	O를 O.C로 만들다
18	make a reservation	예약하다
19	expect O to do	O가 to do 하기를 기대하다
20	give A B	A에게 B를 주다
21	be supposed to do	to do 하기로 되어 있다
22	job interview	면접
23	mix A up with B	A와 B를 혼동하다
24	for a second	잠시 동안

TEST5 1-1

The reservation on a friday
Set1 Conversation에 등장하는 단어들 중 필요한 단어들을 선별하였습니다.

#	표현	뜻
25	want to do	to do 하는 것을 원하다
26	ask O to do	O에게 to do 하기를 부탁하다
27	be on the same page	(~에 대해) 이해하는 내용이 같다
28	no wonder	~은 놀랄 일이 아니다
29	I am following	이해하고 있는 중이다
30	go way back	오랫동안 알고 지내다
31	have a relationship	관계를 맺다
32	a little bit	조금
33	pay to	~에 지불하다
34	be willing to do	기꺼이 to do 하다
35	I did not see that coming.	그건 예상하지 못했다
36	make sure	~임을 확인하다
37	both A and B	A와 B 둘 다
38	be done	당하다 (동사형태 2번)
39	guest pass	손님용 입장권
40	bring in	도입하다
41	Are we clear?	우리 분명해 졌지요?
42	loud and clear	아주 이해하기 쉽게 (무전: 감도 매우 양호함)
43	tell o to do	o가 to do 하라고 말하다, 시키다
44	let in	~을 들어오게 하다
45	say hello to	~에게 안부를 전하다
46	of course	물론
47	track down	~을 찾아내다

TEST5 1-2
VOCABULARY

TEST5 1-2지문의 단어 중 토플 필수 단어를 선별하여 정리하였습니다.

01	movement [ˈmuːvmənt]	n. (사람들이 조직적으로 벌이는) 운동
02	contemporary [kənˈtempəreri]	adj. 동시대의, 현대의
03	myriad [ˈmɪriəd]	n. 무수함, 무수히 많음
04	philosophy [fəˈlɑːsəfi]	n. 철학
05	perspective [pərˈspektɪv]	n. 관점, 시각
06	embed [ɪmˈbed]	v. 넣다, 박아넣다
07	sophisticated [səˈfɪstɪkeɪtɪd]	adj. 정교한, 복잡한
08	delicate [ˈdelɪkət]	adj. 섬세한
09	pop [pɑːp]	v. 잠깐 가다, 들르다
10	experimentation [ɪkˌsperɪmenˈteɪʃn]	n. 실험
11	durable [ˈdʊrəbl]	adj. 내구성이 있는, 오래가는
12	preserve [prɪˈzɜːrv]	v. 보존하다
13	ornate [ɔːrˈneɪt]	adj. 현란한
14	stability [stəˈbɪləti]	n. 안정, 안정성
15	canvas [ˈkænvəs]	n. 캔버스, 화폭
16	obsolete [ˌɑːbsəˈliːt]	adj. 쓸모가 없는, 구식의
17	crack [kræk]	v. 갈라지다, 금이 가다
18	fade [feɪd]	v. 바래다, 희미해지다
19	regrettably [rɪˈgretəbli]	adv. 유감스럽게, 애석하게
20	strenuous [ˈstrenjuəs]	adj. 힘이 많이 드는, 몹시 힘든
21	disaster [dɪˈzæstə(r)]	n. 재난, 재앙
22	longevity [lɑːnˈdʒevəti; lɔːn-]	n. 장수, 오래 지속됨
23	interactive [ˌɪntərˈæktɪv]	adj. 상호적인, 상호작용을 하는
24	intensive [ɪnˈtensɪv]	adj. 집중적인
25	rebuild [ˌriːˈbɪld]	v. 다시 세우다, 재건하다
26	adhere [ədˈhɪr]	v. 고수하다, 지키다
27	conceal [kənˈsiːl]	v. 감추다, 숨기다
28	earnest [ˈɜːrnɪst]	adj. 진중한
29	conservative [kənˈsɜːrvətɪv]	adj. 보수적인
30	discern [dɪˈsɜːrn]	v. 알아차리다, 포착하다

TEST5 1-2
VOCABULARY

TEST5 1-2지문의 단어 중 토플 필수 단어를 선별하여 정리하였습니다.

31	**spare** [sper]	v. 내어주다
32	**originality** [ərɪdʒəˈnæləti]	n. 독창성, 창의성
33	**figure** [ˈfɪɡjər]	n. 인물
34	**pursuit** [pərˈsuːt]	n. 추구, 쫓음
35	**rebellion** [rɪˈbeljən]	n. 반란, 모반
36	**abstain** [əbˈsteɪn]	v. 피하다, 삼가다
37	**awareness** [əˈwernəs]	n. 인식, 관심
38	**distinguish** [dɪˈstɪŋɡwɪʃ]	v. 구별하다
39	**subjectivity** [sʌbdʒekˈtívəti]	n. 주관성
40	**emulate** [ˈemjuleɪt]	v. 모방하다, 따라가다
41	**portable** [ˈpɔːrtəbl]	adj. 휴대가 쉬운, 휴대용의
42	**attempt** [əˈtempt]	v. 시도하다, 애써 해보다
43	**representation** [ˌreprɪzenˈteɪʃn]	n. 표현, 묘사, 표상
44	**futile** [ˈfjuːtl]	adj. 헛된, 소용없는
45	**landscape** [ˈlændskeɪp]	n. 풍경, 풍경화
46	**tidbit** [ˈtídbɪt]	n. 재밌는 이야기, 별미
47	**pre-package** [priːˈpækɪdʒ]	v. 판매하기 전에 포장하다
48	**durability** [djùərəbíləti]	n. 내구성
49	**readily** [ˈredɪli]	adv. 손쉽게, 순조롭게
50	**available** [əˈveɪləbl]	adj. 구할 수 있는, 이용할 수 있는
51	**varnish** [ˈvɑːrnɪʃ]	n. 광택제 / v. 광택제를 바르다
52	**master** [ˈmæstə(r)]	n. 대가, 거장
53	**artificial** [ˌɑːrtɪˈfɪʃl]	adj. 인공의
54	**enhancement** [ɪnˈhænsmənt, en-]	n. 향상, 상승
55	**impose** [ɪmˈpoʊz]	v. 부과하다, 도입하다
56	**spontaneity** [ˌspɑːntəˈneɪəti]	n. 자발적임, 자연스러움, 즉흥성
57	**admire** [ədˈmaɪə(r)]	v. 중요하게 생각하다
58	**loathe** [loʊð]	v. 싫어하다, 혐오하다
59	**abstract** [ˈæbstrækt]	adj. 추상적인
60	**supplement** [ˈsʌplɪmənt]	n. 보충, 추가
61	**costly** [ˈkɔːstli]	adj. 비싼
62	**formula** [ˈfɔːrmjələ]	n. 공식

구문정리

TEST5 1-2 | **Early European art movements**
Set1 Lecture1에 등장하는 단어들 중 필요한 단어들을 선별하였습니다.

본문 중 중요 구문 정리한 내용입니다. 우선 암기하고 많이 읽으시기 바랍니다.

01	go over	점검하다, 검토하다	17	make sense	의미가 통하다, 이해가 되다
02	key point	요점	18	want O to do	O가 to do 하기를 원하다
03	move on to	~로 (새로운 일, 주제로) 옮기다, 넘어가다	19	go to waste	쓸모없게 되다
04	a myriad of	무수한	20	between A and B	A와 B 사이에
05	embed A in B	A를 B에 끼워넣다	21	have an understanding of	~에 대해 이해하다
06	pay attention to	~에 주의를 기울이다	22	on one's own	혼자, 스스로
07	come up with	생각해내다	23	by the end of	~의 끝 무렵에
08	back then	그 당시에, 과거 그때에	24	lead to	~로 이어지다, 초래하다
09	pop into	~을 잠깐 방문하다	25	become obsolete	구식이 되다, 노후화 되다
10	ask for	~을 청하다, 구하다	26	due to	~때문에
11	need to do	to do 할 필요가 있다	27	make it difficult for O to do	O가 to do 하는 것을 어렵게 만들다
12	go through	겪다	28	cause O to do	O가 to do 하는 것을 야기하다
13	a lot of	많은	29	would have done	~했을 것이다
14	not only A but also B	A 뿐만 아니라 B도	30	in terms of	~의 면에서, ~에 관하여
15	set A apart from B	A를 B로부터 구별하다	31	in a setting	환경에서
16	want to do	to do 하기를 원하다	32	hear of	~에 대해 듣다

구문정리

TEST5 1-2 — Early European art movements

본문 중 중요 구문 정리한 내용입니다. 우선 암기하고 많이 읽으시기 바랍니다.
Set1 Lecture1에 등장하는 단어들 중 필요한 단어들을 선별하였습니다.

#	구문	뜻
33	a group of	한 무리의
34	begin to do	to do 하는 것을 시작하다
35	adhere to	고수하다
36	impose A on B	A를 B에 부과하다
37	such as	예를 들어, ~와 같은(s)
38	for instance	예를 들어 (i)
39	in a way that	~한 방법으로
40	make O do	O가 do 하게 만들다
41	difficult to do	to do 하기 어려운
42	in opposition to	~에 반대하여
43	show A B	A에게 B를 보여주다
44	regard A as B	A를 B라고 여기다, 간주하다
45	one of the leading figures	중요 인물(거물) 중 하나
46	along with	~와 함께
47	contribute to	~에 기여하다
48	give A B	A에게 B를 주다
49	abstain from	~을 삼가다, 그만두다
50	apply A to B	A를 B에게 적용하다
51	hold an exhibition	전시회를 열다, 개최하다
52	differ from	~와 다르다
53	distinguish A from B	A를 B로부터 구별하다
54	attempt to do	to do 하는 것을 시도하다
55	take off	급격히 인기를 얻다; 이륙하다
56	gain popularity	인기를 얻다
57	instead of	~대신에
58	add A to B	A를 B에 추가하다, 첨가하다
59	because of	~때문에
60	in contrast to	~에 대조하여
61	protect O from ~ing	O가 ~ing 하는 것으로부터 막다
62	for long periods	오랜 기간 동안
63	in addition to	~뿐만 아니라
64	for the same reason	같은 이유로
65	look at	~를 보다, 살피다

TEST5 1-3
VOCABULARY

TEST5 1-3지문의 단어 중 토플 필수 단어를 선별하여 정리하였습니다.

01	**predation** [prɪ	deɪʃn]	n. 포식
02	**adaptation** [|ædæp|teɪʃn]	n. 적응
03	**evolutionary** [|i:və|lu:ʃəneri]	adj. 진화의
04	**camouflage** [	kæməflɑ:ʒ]	v. 위장하다
05	**crypsis** [ˈkrɪp-səs]	n. 은폐
06	**mimesis** [mɪ|mi:sɪs;maɪ|mi:sɪs]	n. 모방
07	**scale** [skeɪl]	n. 비늘
08	**instantaneous** [|ɪnstən|teɪniəs]	adj. 즉각적인
09	**vivid** [	vɪvɪd]	adj. 생생한, 선명한
10	**toxicity** [tɑ:k	sɪsəti]	n. 유독성
11	**behavioral** [bihéivjərəl]	adj. 행동의, 행동에 관한
12	**mechanism** [	mekənɪzəm]	n. 방법, 메커니즘
13	**off-topic** [ɔ:f	tɑ:pɪk]	adj. 주제에서 벗어난
14	**autotomy** [ɔ:tátəmi]	n. 자기 절단, 자절
15	**detach** [dɪ	tætʃ]	v. 떼다, 분리하다
16	**momentarily** [|moʊmən|terəli]	adv. 잠깐, 잠깐동안
17	**distract** [dɪ	strækt]	v. 주의를 딴 데로 돌리다
18	**thereby** [|ðer|baɪ]	adv. 그렇게 함으로써, 그래서
19	**escape** [ɪ	skeɪp]	v. 달아나다, 탈출하다
20	**invertebrate** [ɪn	vɜ:rtɪbrət]	n. 무척추동물
21	**squid** [skwɪd]	n. 오징어
22	**vertebrate** [	vɜ:rtɪbrət]	n. 척추동물
23	**salamander** [	sæləmændə(r)]	n. 도롱뇽
24	**lizard** [	lɪzərd]	n. 도마뱀
25	**gecko** [	gekoʊ]	n. 도마뱀붙이
26	**limb** [lɪm]	n. 팔다리, 사지
27	**release** [rɪ	li:s]	v. 내버리다, 방출하다 n. 내버림, 풀어 줌
28	**activate** [	æktɪveɪt]	v. 작동시키다, 활성화시키다
29	**physical** [	fɪzɪkl]	adj. 신체의, 물리적인
30	**contact** [	kɑ:ntækt]	n. 접촉, 닿음
31	**distinction** [dɪ	stɪŋkʃn]	n. 뚜렷한 차이, 대조
32	**voluntary** [	vɑ:lənteri]	adj. 자발적인, 자진한

TEST5 1-3
VOCABULARY

TEST5 1-3지문의 단어 중 토플 필수 단어를 선별하여 정리하였습니다.

33	reflex	[ˈriːfleks]	n. 반사, 반사 반응
34	stimuli	[stímjulài]	n. stimulus(자극)의 복수
35	voluntarily	[ˈvɑːlənterəli]	adv. 자발적으로, 자진해서
36	neural	[ˈnʊrəl]	adj. 신경의
37	internal	[ɪnˈtɜːrnl]	adj. 내부의
38	trigger	[ˈtrɪɡə(r)]	n. 촉발 요인, 자극제
39	incite	[ɪnˈsaɪt]	v. 조장하다, 일으키다
40	structure	[ˈstrʌktʃə(r)]	n. 구조
41	facilitate	[fəˈsɪlɪteɪt]	v. 가능하게 하다, 용이하게 하다
42	fracture plane	[ˈfræktʃə(r) pleɪn]	파단면
43	whereas	[ˈwerˈæz]	c. 반면에
44	vertebrae	[ˈvɜːrtɪbrə]	n. 척추뼈, 등골
45	autotomize	[ɔːˈtɑːtəmàɪz]	v. 자절하다, 자기절단하다
46	contract	[kənˈtrækt]	v. 수축하다, 수축시키다
47	sever	[ˈsevə(r)]	v. 자르다, 잘라내다, 절단하다
48	temporarily		adv. 일시적으로
49	wiggle	[ˈwɪɡl]	v. 씰룩씰룩 움직이다
50	freaky	[ˈfriːki]	adj. 이상한, 기이한
51	nervous	[ˈnɜːrvəs]	adj. 신경의
52	stimulate	[ˈstɪmjuleɪt]	v. 자극하다, 불러일으키다
53	initially	[ɪˈnɪʃəli]	adv. 처음에
54	doubtful	[ˈdaʊtfl]	adj. 확신이 없는, 미심쩍은
55	detachment	[dɪˈtætʃmənt]	n. 분리
56	track	[træk]	n. 선로, 진로
57	regenerate	[rɪˈdʒenəreɪt]	v. 재생시키다, 재생되다
58	identical	[aɪˈdentɪkl]	adj. 동일한, 똑같은
59	comprise	[kəmˈpraɪz]	v. …으로 구성되다, 이뤄지다
60	cartilage	[ˈkɑːrtɪlɪdʒ]	n. 연골, 물렁뼈
61	significant	[sɪɡˈnɪfɪkənt]	adj. 중요한, 상당한
62	reserve	[rɪˈzɜːrv]	n. 비축, 비축물
63	storage	[ˈstɔːrɪdʒ]	n. 저장
64	base	[beɪs]	n. 맨 아래 부분

TEST5 1-3
VOCABULARY

TEST5 1-3지문의 단어 중 토플 필수 단어를 선별하여 정리하였습니다.

65	revolve around		~을 중심으로 돌아가다
66	forage	[ˈfɔːrɪdʒ; ˈfɑː-]	v. 먹이를 찾다
67	expend	[ɪkˈspend]	v. (에너지, 돈, 시간을) 쏟다, 들이다
68	negate	[nɪˈɡeɪt]	v. 무효화하다, 효력이 없게 만들다
69	reduction	[rɪˈdʌkʃn]	n. 축소
70	lay	[léi]	v. 알을 낳다
71	offspring	[ˈɔːfsprɪŋ; ˈɑːf-]	n. 자식, 새끼
72	lower	[ˈloʊə(r)]	v. ~을 내리다, 낮추다
73	status	[ˈsteɪtəs, ˈstætəs]	n. 사회적 지위
74	redundant	[rɪˈdʌndənt]	adj. 불필요한, 쓸모없는
75	completely	[kəmˈpliːtli]	adv. 완전히, 전적으로
76	vulnerable	[ˈvʌlnərəbl]	adj. (~에) 취약한, 연약한
77	ever-evolving		계속 진화하는
78	diurnal	[daɪˈɜːrnl]	adj. 낮의, 주행성의
79	nocturnal	[nɑːkˈtɜːrnl]	adj. 밤의, 야행성의
80	vice versa	[váisə-vɔ́ːrsə, váis-, váisi-]	adv. 거꾸로, 반대로, 역도 같음
81	species	[ˈspiːʃiːz]	n. 종
82	alteration	[ˌɔːltəˈreɪʃn]	n. 변화, 개조
83	reptile	[ˈreptaɪl, ˈreptl]	n. 파충류
84	multiple	[ˈmʌltɪpl]	adj. 많은, 다수의
85	sufficient	[səˈfɪʃnt]	adj. 충분한
86	phenomenon	[fəˈnɑːmɪnən]	n. 현상
87	composition	[ˌkɑːmpəˈzɪʃn]	n. 구성요소들, 구성
88	in terms of		~의 면에서, ~에 관해서
89	massive	[ˈmæsɪv]	adj. 거대한
90	compensate	[ˈkɑːmpenseɪt]	v. 보상하다
91	degradation	[ˌdeɡrəˈdeɪʃn]	n. 악화, 저하
92	earn	[ɜːrn]	v. ~을 확보하다, 얻다
93	exert	[ɪɡˈzɜːrt]	v. 가하다, 행사하다

구문정리

TEST5 1-3 | Antipredator adaptations

본문 중 중요 구문 정리한 내용입니다. 우선 암기하고 많이 읽으시기 바랍니다.
Set1 Lecture2에 등장하는 단어들 중 필요한 단어들을 선별하였습니다.

01	key point	요점
02	employ O to do	O를 to do 하는데 사용하다
03	avoid predation	포식을 피하다
04	call A B	A를 B라 부르다
05	over centuries	몇 세기 동안
06	a wide range of	광범위한
07	such as	~와 같은
08	allow O to do	O가 to do 하는 것을 허용하다
09	for instance	예를 들어
10	change into	~으로 바꾸다
11	poison to	~에 대한 독성
12	warn O off	O에게 경고하다
13	in the same way	같은 방법으로
14	use O to do	O를 to do 하는데 이용하다
15	hear of	~에 대해 듣다
16	buy A B	A에게 B를 사주다, 얻어주다
17	find A in B	A를 B에서 찾다
18	look at	~을 살펴보다
19	concentrate on	~에 집중하다
20	ability to do	to do 할 수 있는 능력
21	need to do	to do 할 필요가 있다
22	for autotomy to occur	자가 절단이 일어나기 위해서
23	different from	~와는 다른
24	in contact with	~와 접촉하는
25	draw a distinction	구별하다
26	it seems that	~처럼 보이다
27	reflex to ~	~에 대한 반사작용
28	There are still questions about~	~에 관하여 여전히 질문들이 있다
29	basis for~	~에 대한 근거
30	serve one purpose	한가지 목적에 맞다, 도움이 되다
31	help O do	O가 do 하는 것을 돕다
32	between A and B	A와 B 사이
33	as if	마치 ~처럼
34	it is possible that	that절 할 가능성이 있다

TEST5 1-3 | Antipredator adaptations

본문 중 중요 구문 정리한 내용입니다. 우선 암기하고 많이 읽으시기 바랍니다.
Set1 Lecture2에 등장하는 단어들 중 필요한 단어들을 선별하였습니다.

#	구문	뜻
35	try to do	to do 하려고 시도하다
36	on track	궤도에 올라, 바르게
37	healing process	치유과정
38	identical to	~와 동일한
39	rather than	~라기 보다는
40	serve function	기능하다
41	more or less	거의
42	take time	시간이 걸리다
43	depend on	~에 의존하다, 신뢰하다
44	you see	있잖아
45	an amount of	상당한 양의
46	not so much	~정도는 아닌
47	at the base of	~의 바닥에, 기슭에
48	the lack of	~의 부족
49	daily life	일상생활
50	feed on	~을 잡아먹다
51	use A for B	A를 B를 위해 사용하다
52	expend energy ~ing	~ing 하는데 에너지를 쓰다
53	reduction in	~라는 점에서의 감소
54	attractiveness to	~에 대한 매력
55	in addition	게다가
56	lay egg	알을 낳다
57	result in	~을 야기하다
58	suffer from	~로 고통 받다
59	social status	사회적 지위
60	go into	~에 들어가다, 검토하다
61	leave O O.C	O를 O.C의 상태로 남기다
62	according to	~에 의하면
63	spend time ~ing	~ing 하는데 시간을 보내다
64	look out for	~을 조심하다, 주의하다
65	vice versa	역(반대) 또한 같음
66	depending on	~에 따라

TEST5 2-1
VOCABULARY

TEST5 2-1지문의 단어 중 토플 필수 단어를 선별하여 정리하였습니다.

01	**horrible** [ˈhɔːrəbl;ˈhɑːr-]	a. 끔찍한
02	**injury** [ˈɪndʒəri]	n. 부상
03	**suffer** [ˈsʌfə(r)]	v. 시달리다, 고통받다
04	**reading** [ˈriːdɪŋ]	n. 낭독
05	**come up with ~**	~을 생각해내다
06	**contemplation** [ˌkɑːntəmˈpleɪʃn]	n. 숙고
07	**broaden** [ˈbrɔːdn]	v. ~를 넓히다
08	**perspective** [pərˈspektɪv]	n. 관점, 시각
09	**conventional** [kənˈvenʃənl]	a. 상투적인, 통례적인
10	**overall** [ˌoʊvərˈɔːl]	a. 전부의, 전반적인
11	**quiet** [ˈkwaɪət]	a. 조용한
12	**share** [ʃer]	v. ~를 이야기하다, 분배하다, 나누다
13	**pioneer** [ˌpaɪəˈnɪr]	n. 개척자, 선구자, 주창자
14	**coin** [kɔɪn]	v. (신어, 거짓말 따위)를 만들어내다
15	**proponent** [prəˈpoʊnənt]	n. 지지자, 옹호자
16	**anti-conformist**	n. (전통, 관습 따위에) 반대하는 사람, 순응하지 않는 사람
17	**rejection** [rɪdʒékʃən]	n. 거부
18	**contemporary** [kənˈtempəreri]	n. 현대의, 동시대의
19	**fascinating** [ˈfæsɪneɪtɪŋ]	a. 매혹적인, 황홀케 하는
20	**competitive** [kəmˈpetətɪv]	a. 경쟁의, 경쟁적인
21	**engage in ~**	~에 참가하다, ~를 시작하다
22	**judge** [dʒʌdʒ]	v. ~를 판단하다
23	**clear up**	v. ~를 마무리하다, 해결하다; (의문, 오해 따위)를 풀다
24	**prominent** [ˈprɑːmɪnənt]	a. 두드러진, 주목을 끄는

VOCABULARY

TEST5 2-1

TEST5 2-1지문의 단어 중 토플 필수 단어를 선별하여 정리하였습니다.

25	**noteworthy** [noʊtwɜːrði]	a. 주목할 만한, 눈부신, 현저한
26	**known for**	~로 알려진, 유명한
27	**engaging** [ɪnˈgeɪdʒɪŋ]	a. 매력적인, 애교 있는
28	**emphasize** [ˈemfəsaɪz]	v. ~를 강조하다, 중시하다
29	**highly** [ˈhaɪli]	ad. 매우, 꽤
30	**discouraged** [dɪsˈkʌrɪdʒd]	a. 낙심한, 낙담한
31	**yell** [jel]	v. 고함치다, 외치다
32	**just as**	꼭 ~처럼
33	**controversial** [ˌkɑːntrəˈvɜːrʃl]	a. 논쟁의 여지가 있는, 물의를 일으키는
34	**assignment** [əˈsaɪnmənt]	n. 숙제, 과제
35	**distinguish** [dɪˈstɪŋgwɪʃ]	v. ~을 구별하다, 분간하다
36	**momentarily** [ˌmoʊmənˈterəli]	ad. 잠시, 잠깐
37	**handicapped** [ˈhændikæpt]	a. 신체적(정신적) 장애가 있는
38	**seldom** [ˈseldəm]	ad. 좀처럼 ~ 않는, ~의 경우가 거의 없는
39	**prefer to ~**	~를 선호하다
40	**contentious** [kənˈtenʃəs]	a. 논쟁을 불러일으키는, 논쟁을 좋아하는
41	**implicit** [ɪmˈplɪsɪt]	a. 절대적인, 맹목적인, 무조건의
42	**acceptance** [əkˈseptəns]	n. 수용, 용인, 인정
43	**main-stream society**	주류 사회
44	**riot** [ˈraɪət]	n. 폭동, 반란
45	**rebellion** [rɪˈbeljən]	n. 반란, 폭동, 저항
46	**inspire** [ɪnˈspaɪə(r)]	v. ~를 일어나게 하다, ~를 불어넣다
47	**give away**	v. ~를 거저 주다, 증여하다
48	**be familiar with ~**	~와 친숙하다, 익숙하다
49	**run out of**	~을 다 써버리다, 없어지다
50	**shortly** [ˈʃɔːrtli]	ad. 곧, 바로

구문정리

TEST5 2-1 | Poetry reading

본문 중 중요 구문 정리한 내용입니다. 우선 암기하고 많이 읽으시기 바랍니다.
Set2 Conversation에 등장하는 단어들 중 필요한 단어들을 선별하였습니다.

01	come on in	들어와요
02	I'm glad to see you	만나서 반가워요
03	on your feet	완전히 회복한
04	what brings you here?	무슨 일로 오셨나요?
05	try to do	to do 하는 것을 시도하다
06	come up with	~을 생각해내다
07	term paper	학기말 리포트
08	seem to do	to do 할 모양이다
09	tell A B	A에게 B를 말하다
10	what kind of	어떤 종류의
11	need to do	to do 할 필요가 있다
12	come from	~에서 나오다
13	of course	물론
14	listened to	~을 듣다
15	You know what I mean?	무슨 말인지 알지?
16	sound like	~처럼 들리다
17	wonder if	~인지 아닌지를 궁금해하다
18	go back	돌아가다
19	different from	~와 다른
20	a number of	다수의
21	engage in	~에 관여하다
22	I'm not following	이해하지 못하는 중이다
23	look at A as B	A를 B로서 보다
24	clear A up	A를 설명하다, 해결하다
25	one of the leaders	리더들 중 하나
26	known for	~로 알려진
27	at the end of	~의 끝에
28	as well	또한
29	respond to	~에 대응하다, 반응하다
30	by ~ing	~ing 함으로써
31	would have done	~했을지도 모른다
32	arouse emotions	정서를 환기시키다
33	in order to do	to do 하기 위해서
34	a connection with	~와의 관계, 연고
35	be going to do	to do 할 것이다
36	do research	연구하다, 조사하다
37	get the details	자세히 알아보다
38	as to	~에 관하여
39	look forward to ~ing	~ing 하는 것을 기대하다
40	good luck with	~가 잘 되길 바래

TEST5 2-2
VOCABULARY

TEST5 2-2지문의 단어 중 토플 필수 단어를 선별하여 정리하였습니다.

01	**discuss** [dɪˈskʌs]	v. ~을 논의하다, 토론하다
02	**alternative to~** [ɔːlˈtɜːrnətɪv]	~의 대안
03	**petroleum** [pəˈtroʊliəm]	n. 석유
04	**internal** [ɪnˈtɜːrnl]	a. 내부의
05	**combustion** [kəmˈbʌstʃən]	n. 연소
06	**locomotive** [ˌloʊkəˈmoʊtɪv]	n. 기관차
07	**you name it**	(같은 종류의 것을 몇 가지 열거한 다음에) 그 밖에 무엇이든지
08	**rely on ~**	~을 의지하다, 믿다
09	**suitable** [ˈsuːtəbl]	a. 적절한
10	**discover** [dɪˈskʌvər]	v. ~을 발견하다, 알아내다
11	**alcoholic** [ˌælkəˈhɔːlɪk]	a. 알코올성의, 알코올이 든
12	**ideal** [aɪˈdiːəl]	a. 이상적인
13	**fit** [fɪt]	n. 적합성, 적합도
14	**make sense**	이치에 맞다
15	**think of A as B**	A를 B로 생각하다
16	**pre-made**	a. 미리 만들어진, 기성의
17	**edible** [ˈedəbl]	a. 식용이 되는, 먹을 수 있는
18	**grain** [ɡreɪn]	n. 곡물
19	**ferment** [fərˈment]	v. ~을 발효시키다
20	**go through**	겪다
21	**a series of ~**	일련의
22	**ultimately** [ˈʌltɪmətli]	ad. 궁극적으로, 마침내
23	**by-product** [ˈbaɪ prɑːdʌkt]	n. 부산물, 부생성물, 부작용, 부차적 결과
24	**be distilled into ~**	증류하여 ~로 만들어지다
25	**concentrate** [ˈkɑːnsntreɪt]	v. ~을 농축하다, 응집하다
26	**purify** [ˈpjʊrɪfaɪ]	v. ~에서 불순물을 제거하다, 정화하다
27	**be used as ~**	~로 사용되다
28	**additive** [ˈædətɪv]	n. 첨가제, 부가물, 첨가물
29	**in a number of ~**	많은
30	**fairly** [ˈferli]	ad. 꽤

TEST5 2-2
VOCABULARY

TEST5 2-2지문의 단어 중 토플 필수 단어를 선별하여 정리하였습니다.

31	first of all	무엇보다도
32	unlike [ˌʌnˈlaɪk]	prep. ~와는 다른, ~같지 않은
33	be aware that ~	~를 인식하다
34	extracted from ~	~에서 추출된
35	run out	v. (물자, 돈 따위가) 떨어지다, 끊기다
36	fossil fuel [ˈfɑːsl fjuːəl]	화석 연료
37	available [əˈveɪləbl]	a. 유효한, 이용할 수 있는
38	speaking of ~	~에 관하여 말하다, 평하다; ~이라는 말을 쓰다
39	security [səˈkjʊrəti]	n. 안정
40	furthermore [ˌfɜːrðərˈmɔːr]	ad. 그 위에, 게다가, 더욱이, 더군다나
41	bring prosperity to ~	~가 번영하게 되다, 번창하게 되다
42	emit [iˈmɪt]	v. ~을 방출하다
43	point out	지적하다
44	basically [ˈbeɪsɪkli]	ad. 기초적으로, 본래, 본질적으로
45	equivalent to ~	~와 동등한, 같은
46	sow [soʊ]	v. ~을 뿌리다, 파종하다
47	supplement [ˈsʌplɪmənt]	n. 보충물, 추가물
48	fertilizer [ˈfɜːrtəlaɪzər]	n. 비료
49	deterimental to ~	~에 해로운
50	harm [hɑːrm]	v. ~에게 해를 끼치다, ~을 상하게 하다
51	be drenched in ~	~에 담가지다, 흠뻑 젖다
52	off the track	(목표, 주제에서) 벗어나서; (열차가) 탈선하여
53	entail [ɪnˈteɪl]	v. ~을 일으키다, 수반하다
54	fermentation [ˌfɜːrmenˈteɪʃn]	n. 발효, 발효작용
55	distillation [ˌdɪstɪˈleɪʃn]	n. 증류, 증류작용
56	on top of that	무엇보다도
57	tremendous [trəˈmendəs]	a. 엄청난, 터무니없는, 거대한
58	input [ˈɪnpʊt]	n. 투입
59	pipeline [ˈpaɪplaɪn]	n. 수송관
60	tainted [ˈteɪntɪd]	a. 더러워진, 썩은, 부패한

TEST5 2-2
VOCABULARY

TEST5 2-2지문의 단어 중 토플 필수 단어를 선별하여 정리하였습니다.

61	**mention** [ˈmenʃn]	v. ~을 이야기하다; 언급하다
62	**practically** [ˈpræktɪkli]	ad. 실제로는, 사실상은
63	**leak** [liːk]	v. ~을 새게하다, 누출시키다
64	**hold** [hoʊld]	v. ~을 지니다, 품다, 믿다
65	**by that**	그것에 의하여; 그 결과, 그 때문에
66	**kernel** [ˈkɜːrnl]	n. (콩 껍질 속의) 열매
67	**priority over ~**	~보다 중요함, 우선 사항
68	**flammable** [ˈflæməbl]	a. 가연성의, 불타기 쉬운
69	**wrap up**	v. ~을 요약하다, 매듭짓다
70	**assignment** [əˈsaɪnmənt]	n. 과제
71	**sugar cane** [ʃʊɡər ˈkeɪn]	n. 사탕 수수
72	**pros and cons**	n. 장단점
73	**deficiency** [dɪˈfɪʃnsi]	n. 결핍, 부족, 결함
74	**costly** [ˈkɔːstli]	a. 값비싼, 비용이 많이 드는
75	**substandard** [ˌsʌbˈstændərd]	a. 표준 이하의
76	**inferior to ~**	a. ~보다 떨어지는, 열등한
77	**distributor** [dɪˈstrɪbjətər]	n. 도매업자, 배급업자
78	**induce** [ɪnˈduːs]	v. ~을 일으키다, 야기시키다, 유발하다
79	**transition** [trænˈzɪʃn]	n. 변천, 변화, 이동
80	**settlement** [ˈsetlmənt]	n. 부락, 정착지
81	**chemical** [ˈkemɪkl]	n. 화학 물질
82	**catalyst** [ˈkætəlɪst]	n. 촉매제
83	**business** [ˈbɪznəs]	n. 무역, 상업
84	**abundant** [əˈbʌndənt]	a. 풍부한
85	**energy-intensive**	a. 에너지 집약적인, 에너지가 많이 필요한
86	**eradicate** [ɪˈrædɪkeɪt]	v. ~을 근절하다, 박멸하다, 절멸시키다
87	**flammability** [ˌflæməˈbɪləti]	n. 연소성, 인화성
88	**chemical reaction**	화학 반응
89	**rust** [rʌst]	v. 녹슬다, 부식하다
90	**in response to ~**	~에 응하여, 답하여
91	**usefulness** [ˈjuːsfəlnəs]	n. 유용함, 쓸모 있음;

구문정리 TEST5 2-2 | Ethanol

본문 중 중요 구문 정리한 내용입니다. 우선 암기하고 많이 읽으시기 바랍니다.
Set2 Lecture1에 등장하는 단어들 중 필요한 단어들을 선별하였습니다.

01	a lot of	많은
02	effort goes into ~ing	~ing 하는데 노력을 들이다
03	alternative to	~에 대한 대안
04	such as	~와 같은
05	used in	~에 사용되는
06	you name it	전부; 무엇이든지 말해 봐요
07	rely on	~에 의지하다
08	believe A to be B	A를 B라고 믿다
09	know A as B	A를 B로 알다
10	for those of you not familiar with it	이것과 익숙하지 않은 사람들을 위해서
11	familiar with	~와 친숙한
12	find A in B	A를 B에서 찾다
13	sound like	~처럼 들리다
14	fit for	~에 적합한
15	make sense	이치에 맞다
16	think of A as B	A를 B로 간주하다
17	use A as B	A를 B로 사용하다
18	in the United States	미국에서
19	begin with	~으로 시작하다
20	go through	겪다
21	a series of	일련의
22	chemical reaction	화학반응
23	distill A into B	A를 B로 증류하다
24	different from	~와 다른
25	in that	~라는 점에서
26	supply A to B	A를 B에 공급하다
27	internal combustion engines	내연 기관
28	a number of	많은
29	increase from A to B	A에서 B까지 증가하다
30	considering that	~을 고려하면
31	of course	물론
32	first of all	우선
33	be sure	~을 확신하다
34	be aware that	that절을 알다
35	extract A from B	A를 B에서 추출하다
36	run out	다 쓰다

구문정리

TEST5 2-2 | Ethanol

본문 중 중요 구문 정리한 내용입니다. 우선 암기하고 많이 읽으시기 바랍니다.
Set2 Lecture1에 등장하는 단어들 중 필요한 단어들을 선별하였습니다.

37	in contrast	그와 반대로, 대조적으로
38	as long as	~하는 한
39	speaking of	~에 관해서 말하면
40	have an impact	영향을 가지다, 주다
41	you see	있잖아
42	bring A to B	A를 B로 가져오다
43	depend on	~에 의존하다
44	environmentally friendly	친환경적인
45	negative aspects	부정적인 측면
46	point out	지적하다
47	quality difference	질 차이
48	difference between	~사이의 차이점
49	in other words	다시 말해서
50	require O to do	O가 to do 하기를 요구하다
51	equivalent to	~와 동등한, 맞먹는
52	in terms of	~라는 점에서
53	energy efficiency	에너지 효율
54	familiar with	~와 익숙한
55	detrimental to	~에 유해한
56	drenched in	~로 흠뻑 젖은
57	You are off the track	너는 주제에서 벗어나 있다
58	entail the use of	~의 사용을 수반하다
59	as ~ as ~	~만큼 ~한
60	on top of	~뿐만 아니라 (in addition to)
61	mix A with B	A와 B를 섞다
62	Am I missing something?	내가 뭔가를 놓치고 있는 건가요?
63	forget to do	to do 하는 것을 잊어버리다
64	it is impossible to do	to do 하기 불가능하다
65	take O to do	O를 to do 하는데 팔요로 하다
66	across the country	전국에 걸쳐서
67	part of	~부분의
68	seem like	~처럼 보이다
69	in the future	미래에
70	priority over	~보다 우선(권)
71	wrap up	매듭짓다
72	give A B	A에게 B를 주다

TEST5 2-3
VOCABULARY

TEST5 2-3지문의 단어 중 토플 필수 단어를 선별하여 정리하였습니다.

01	**solar system** [ˈsoʊlər sɪstəm]	n. 태양계
02	**dust** [dʌst]	n. 먼지
03	**nebula** [ˈnebjələ]	n. 성운
04	**accretion** [əˈkriːʃn]	n. 부착물
05	**collapse** [kəˈlæps]	n. 붕괴
06	**concentration** [ˌkɑːnsnˈtreɪʃn]	n. 응축
07	**cosmic** [ˈkɑːzmɪk]	a. 우주의
08	**ultimately** [ˈʌltɪmətli]	ad. 궁극적으로
09	**advent** [ˈædvent]	n. 도래, 출현
10	**terrestrial planet**	지구형 행성
11	**take place**	v. 일어나다, 발생하다
12	**shortly after**	금세, 곧
13	**formation** [fɔːrˈmeɪʃn]	n. 형성
14	**dense** [dens]	a. 빽빽한, 밀집한
15	**sink** [sɪŋk]	v. 가라앉다, 빠지다
16	**form** [fɔːrm]	v. 형성되다, 형성시키다
17	**crust** [krʌst]	n. 지각
18	**regarding** [rɪˈgɑːrdɪŋ]	prep. ~에 관하여, 대하여
19	**uninhabitable** [ˌʌnɪnˈhæbɪtəbl]	a. 사람이 살 수 없는, 주거하기에 부적합한
20	**liquid** [ˈlɪkwɪd]	n. 액체; a. 액체 형태의, 액상의
21	**be essential for**	~에 필수적인
22	**presence** [ˈprezns]	n. 존재, 있음
23	**distinguish** [dɪˈstɪŋgwɪʃ]	v. 구별하다
24	**facet** [ˈfæsɪt]	n. 측면, 양상
25	**rarely** [ˈrerli]	ad. 드물게, 좀처럼 ~않고
26	**freeze** [friːz]	v. 얼다, 얼리다
27	**vaporize** [ˈveɪpəraɪz]	v. 증발하다, 기화하다
28	**abundant** [əˈbʌndənt]	a. 풍부한
29	**elucidate** [iˈluːsɪdeɪt]	v. 설명하다
30	**accumulation** [əkjùːmjuléiʃən]	n. 축적, 누적, 축재
31	**volcanic** [vɑːlˈkænɪk]	a. 화산의, 화산 작용에 의해 만들어진
32	**greenhouse gas** [ˌgriːnhaʊs ˈgæs]	온실 가스
33	**trap** [træp]	v. 가두다, 끌어모으다
34	**prevent A from B**	A를 B로부터 막다, 예방하다

TEST5 2-3
VOCABULARY

TEST5 2-3지문의 단어 중 토플 필수 단어를 선별하여 정리하였습니다.

35	**play a role in**	~에서 역할을 하다
36	**consequently** [|kɑ:nsəkwentli]	ad. 그 결과, 따라서
37	**geologist** [dʒi|ɑ:lədʒɪst]	n. 지질학자
38	**fragment** [|frægmənt]	n. 조각, 파편
39	**meteorite** [|mi:tiəraɪt]	n. 운석
40	**retain** [rɪ|teɪn]	v. 유지하다, 보유하다
41	**contend** [kən|tend]	v. 주장하다
42	**bring A to B**	A를 B로 가져오다, 데려오다
43	**reach** [ri:tʃ]	v. ~에 이르다, 도달하다
44	**edge** [edʒ]	n. 끝, 가장자리, 모서리
45	**encounter** [ɪn|kaʊntə(r)]	v. 맞닥뜨리다, 부딪히다
46	**frictional force**	마찰력
47	**disintegrate** [dɪs|ɪntɪgreɪt]	v. 해체되다, 분해되다, 산산조각 나다
48	**mid-air** [ˌmɪd ˈer]	a. 허공의
49	**catalyst** [|kætəlɪst]	n. 촉매제
50	**intense** [ɪn|tens]	a. 강렬한
51	**by-product** [ˈbaɪ prɑ:dʌkt]	n. 부산물, 부생성물
52	**carbon dioxide**	n. 이산화탄소
53	**water vapor**	n. 수증기
54	**contribute** [kən|trɪbju:t]	v. 기여하다, 공헌하다
55	**meteor** [|mi:tiə®]	n. 유성, 운석
56	**yield** [ji:ld]	v. ~를 산출하다, ~을 가져오다
57	**proverb** [|prɑ:vɜ:rb]	n. 속담
58	**stroke** [stroʊk]	n. 치기, 때리기
59	**oak** [oʊk]	n. 오크 나무
60	**date** [deɪt]	v. ~의 연대(시기)를 산정하다, 추정하다
61	**cataclysm** [|kætəklɪzəm]	n. 지각의 격변, 대변동
62	**hypothetical** [haɪpə|θetɪkl]	a. 가설의
63	**take A into account**	A를 고려하다
64	**asteroid** [|æstəroɪd]	n. 소행성
65	**collide** [kə|laɪd]	v. 충돌하다
66	**Mercury** [|mɜ:rkjəri]	n. 수성
67	**Mars** [mɑ:rz]	n. 화성
68	**collect** [kəˈlekt]	v. 모으다, 집합시키다

VOCABULARY

TEST5 2-3

TEST5 2-3지문의 단어 중 토플 필수 단어를 선별하여 정리하였습니다.

69	**manned** [mænd]	유인의		85	**bombardment** [bɑmbá:rdmənt]	n. 포격, 폭격
70	**spaceflight** [speɪsflàit]	n. 우주 비행, 우주 여행		86	**likely** [ˈlaɪkli]	a. ~할 것 같은, ~할 것으로 예상되는
71	**originally** [əˈrɪdʒənəli]	ad. 원래, 본래		87	**result in**	그 결과 ~가 되다
72	**strike** [straɪk]	v. 치다, 부딪히다		88	**consequence** [ˈkɑnsəkwens]	n. 결과; 연속
73	**experiment** [ɪkˈspɛrɪmənt]	n. 실험		89	**magnetic field** [mægˌnetɪk ˈfi:ld]	n. 자기장
74	**carry out**	수행하다, 이행하다		90	**core** [kɔ:(r)]	n. 핵심, 중요한, 핵, 근원
75	**theoretical** [ˌθi:əˈretɪkl]	a. 이론의, 이론적인		91	**protect A from B**	A를 B로부터 보호하다
76	**meteor** [ˈmi:tiə®]	n. 유성, 별똥별		92	**charged particle**	하전 입자(전하를 띄고 있는 입자)
77	**mention** [ˈmenʃn]	v. 말하다, 거론하다		93	**electron** [ɪˈlektrɑ:n]	n. 전자
78	**subsequently** [ˈsʌbsɪkwəntli]	ad. 그뒤, 나중에		94	**proton** [ˈproʊtɑ:n]	n. 양성자
79	**meteoric** [ˌmi:tiˈɔ:rɪk]	a. 유성의; 일약 ~한		95	**upper** [ˈʌpə(r)]	a. 위쪽의, 상부의
80	**accumulate** [əˈkju:mjəleɪt]	v. 모으다, 축적하다		96	**go into**	~을 검토하다, ~을 연구하다
81	**remain** [rɪˈmeɪn]	v. 계속 ~이다, 남다		97	**complex** [kəmˈpleks]	a. 복잡한
82	**resemble** [rɪˈzembl]	v. 닮다, 비슷하다		98	**stay on**	남아 있다, 눌러 앉다, 유임하다
83	**in terms of ~**	~의 측면에서, ~에 관하여		99	**blow away**	불어 날리다
84	**be subjected to**	~을 받다, 당하다		100	**exist** [ɪgˈzɪst]	v. 존재하다, 실재하다, a. 현존하다

구문정리

TEST5 2-3 | A solar nebula

본문 중 중요 구문 정리한 내용입니다. 우선 암기하고 많이 읽으시기 바랍니다.
Set2 Lecture2에 등장하는 단어들 중 필요한 단어들을 선별하였습니다.

01	start as	~로서 시작하다
02	know A as B	A를 B로 알다
03	according to	~에 따르면
04	at its center	중심에서
05	take place	일어나다, 발생하다
06	shortly after	직후에, 곧
07	begin to do	to do 하는 것을 시작하다
08	build up	쌓아 올리다, 창조하다
09	to the bottom	바닥까지
10	look at	~를 자세히 살피다, 보다
11	tend to do	to do 하는 경향이 있다
12	be able to do	to do 할 수 있다
13	try to do	to do 하려고 시도하다
14	be essential for	~에 필수적이다
15	in small quantities	소량으로
16	either A or B	A 또는 B
17	depend on	~에 의존하다
18	go over	훑어보다, ~를 조사하다, 점검하다
19	one of the theories	이론들 중 하나
20	it is believed that	that절이라고 믿어지다
21	due to	~때문에
22	volcanic activity	화산활동
23	around the time of	~무렵에
24	be familiar with	~에 익숙하다, 친숙하다
25	greenhouse gas	온실가스
26	prevent O from ~ing	O가 ~ing 하는 것을 막다
27	play a role in	역할을 하다
28	cause O to do	O가 to do 하는 것을 야기하다, 초래하다
29	in fact	사실
30	may have done	했을지도 모른다 (추측 m)
31	bring A to B	A를 B로 가져오다
32	contribute to	~에 기여하다

구문정리

본문 중 중요 구문 정리한 내용입니다. 우선 암기하고 많이 읽으시기 바랍니다.

TEST5 2-3 | A solar nebula

Set2 Lecture2에 등장하는 단어들 중 필요한 단어들을 선별하였습니다.

#	구문	뜻
33	in order for O to do	O가 to do 하기 위해서
34	need to do	to do 할 필요가 있다
35	reach the edge of	~의 가장자리에 닿다
36	frictional force	마찰력
37	manage to do	가까스로 to do 하다
38	use O to do	O를 to do 하기 위해 사용하다
39	burn up	전소되다, 타오르다
40	introduce A to B	A를 B에게 소개하다, 도입하다
41	of course	물론
42	by-product	부산물
43	as the old proverb states	옛 속담이 말하듯
44	little strokes fell great oaks	열번찍어 안넘어 가는 나무 없다
45	date from	~부터 시작되다
46	have you heard of~?	~에 대해 들어봤나요?
47	take into account	~을 고려하다
48	collide with	~와 충돌하다
49	come from	~에서 나오다
50	be dated to	~까지 연대 추정되다
51	a number of	많은
52	carry out	수행하다, 완수하다
53	in terms of	~라는 면에서
54	subject A to B	A를 B에 노출시키다
55	difference between A and B	A와 B 사이의 차이점
56	result in	~을 야기하다 (결과)
57	magnetic field	자기장
58	protect A from B	A를 B로부터 보호하다
59	such as	예를 들어, ~와 같은
60	release A from B	A를 B로부터 방출하다
61	go into detail	상세히 들어가다, 설명하다
62	stay on topic	주제에 집중하다, 머무르다
63	blow away	불어날리다
64	(Do) you see where I'm going with this?	내가 무엇을 말하려는지 알겠어요?

USHER

iBT TOEFL
INTERMEDIATE LISTENING
구문 외우고·열번 읽기

Accounting department

Listen to a conversation between a student and a professor in a university 01) **accounting department**

P: Hi, Sam. I saw your 02) **paper on** the 03) **net profits** of Google this year. Your work was phenomenal… I was very impressed.

S: Oh, I'm very glad to hear that. Thank you so much.

P: No problem! I hope you 04) **keep up the good work**. So, what brought you here today? If it's about the paper, I've just 05) **assured you that** you've 06) **done a great job** on it.

S: Well…that's not what I'm here about… I'm actually here to 07) **ask for** your help with… umm… What's been concerning me recently is that I 08) **feel the** strong 09) **need to** 10) **switch majors**.

P: Okay… What are you 11) **looking into** right now?

S: Well, 12) **prior to** entering college, I 13) **did** some **research** to ensure that I would choose the right route for myself, and I thought that accounting would be a suitable major. 14) **Now that** I'm here, however, I have been 15) **doubting** my **decision**… I'm 16) **thinking about** 17) **switching to** Business Management.

P: Let's see… Your grades… Your participation in class… It doesn't' 18) **look like** you're 19) **doing badly** 20) **at this point**.

S: You're right. I've always 21) **tried my best**, but my 22) **academic performance** isn't the reason I'm 23) **considering switching** majors. I guess it's the amount of math 24) **required to** 25) **acquire a degree** 26) **in the field**. And, I think it 27) **takes a lot more time to** 28) **earn a degree** in accounting than it does in business management.

P: That's true. It can be quite overwhelming 29) **at times**. Have you 30) **looked at** the 31) **job prospects** of both?

S: Oh yeah! I totally 32) **forgot to check that out**.

P: You see, graduates who have 33) **degrees in** the accounting field have 34) **a variety of** options when choosing their 35) **career paths**. When a company is seeking 36) **a person with experience in finance**, global marketing, or other business-related fields, accounting graduates 37) **are** very **likely to** 38) **get hired**. For instance, you could be a financial analyst, an auditor, a financial manager, and so on.

S: Mmm… I see. 39) **What about** business management?

P: Well, my belief is that the problem with business management is that since the major itself is very broad and general, you won't really be a specialist in any field like an accounting major would be. Therefore, the 40) **demand for** 41) **people with a degree in** business management in the industry is relatively lower. So, as I mentioned before, accounting graduates 42) **have a** relatively **easy time** 43) **securing jobs**, but 44) **that's** usually **not the case with** business management graduates.

S: Are you implying that 45) **it's hard to** 46) **get a job** with a degree in business management?

P: Umm… From what I've seen through my former graduate students, I would say so. I understand that you're having a hard time with your first choice and the burdensome amount of work involved, but, looking at the 47) **long term**, 48) **I'm not so sure if** business management would be a positive move for you.

S: I 49) **get your point**… I guess I shouldn't 50) **make** a rash **decision**, huh?

P: Exactly. 51) **Other than** the job prospects, there are also many other aspects to consider, like the examinations you will 52) **need to** 53) **deal with**, how much 54) **money** you can **make**, 55) **and so on**.

S: Right… Okay, I guess I shouldn't be swayed by my impetuous emotions…

P: 56) **Of course not**… Switching majors is certainly not an easy 57) **step to take**, you know?

S: Yes… Well, I'll 58) **take my time** and 59) **do** some more **research** before I make a decision about whether or not to change my major. 60) **Thank you for** your advice, professor. I really appreciate it.

P: No problem, Sam. I'm available anytime you need me. Good luck!

TEST 1 SET 1-1

Accounting department

Listen to a conversation between a student and a professor in a university accounting department

P: Hi, Sam. I saw your paper on the net profits of Google this year. Your work was phenomenal… I was very impressed.

S: Oh, I'm very glad to hear that. Thank you so much.

P: No problem! I hope you keep up the good work. So, what brought you here today? If it's about the paper, I've just assured you that you've done a great job on it.

S: Well…that's not what I'm here about… I'm actually here to ask for your help with… umm… What's been concerning me recently is that I feel the strong need to switch majors.

P: Okay… What are you looking into right now?

S: Well, prior to entering college, I did some research to ensure that I would choose the right route for myself, and I thought that accounting would be a suitable major. Now that I'm here, however, I have been doubting my decision… I'm thinking about switching to Business Management.

P: Let's see… Your grades… Your participation in class… It doesn't' look like you're doing badly at this point.

S: You're right. I've always tried my best, but my academic performance isn't the reason I'm considering switching majors. I guess it's the amount of math required to acquire a degree in the field. And, I think it takes a lot more time to earn a degree in accounting than it does in business management.

P: That's true. It can be quite overwhelming at times. Have you looked at the job prospects of both?

S: Oh yeah! I totally forgot to check that out.

P: You see, graduates who have degrees in the accounting field have a variety of options when choosing their career paths. When a company is seeking a person with experience in finance, global marketing, or other business-related fields, accounting graduates are very likely to get hired. For instance, you could be a financial analyst, an auditor, a financial manager, and so on.

S: Mmm… I see. What about business management?

P: Well, my belief is that the problem with business management is that since the major itself is very broad and general, you won't really be a specialist in any field like an accounting major would be. Therefore, the demand for people with a degree in business management in the industry is relatively lower. So, as I mentioned before, accounting graduates have a relatively easy time securing jobs, but that's usually not the case with business management graduates.

S: Are you implying that it's hard to get a job with a degree in business management?

P: Umm… From what I've seen through my former graduate students, I would say so. I understand that you're having a hard time with your first choice and the burdensome amount of work involved, but, looking at the long term, I'm not so sure if business management would be a positive move for you.

S: I get your point… I guess I shouldn't make a rash decision, huh?

P: Exactly. Other than the job prospects, there are also many other aspects to consider, like the examinations you will need to deal with, how much money you can make, and so on.

S: Right… Okay, I guess I shouldn't be swayed by my impetuous emotions…

P: Of course not… Switching majors is certainly not an easy step to take, you know?

S: Yes… Well, I'll take my time and do some more research before I make a decision about whether or not to change my major. Thank you for your advice, professor. I really appreciate it.

P: No problem, Sam. I'm available anytime you need me. Good luck!

Ice age

Listen to part of a lecture in a climatology class

P: As we discussed in our last class, there have been 01) **a number of** ice ages 02) **over the** past few million **years**, 03) **such as** the Permian and Ordovician Glaciation Periods, when much of the planet 04) **was covered with** glaciers… Scientists believe that the ice age theory is certainly one of the most compelling theories to explain the end of the dinosaur era. Well, 05) **fortunately for** 06) **human beings**, we are currently 07) **living in an** "interglacial **period**", or a period between ice ages, during which the glaciers 08) **retreat to** the polar regions and the Earth experiences a relatively milder climate. All of the ice ages have 09) **been separated by** long mild interglacial periods of this type. Even though the last ice age, the Quaternary Glaciation, ended around ten thousand years ago, there is considerable evidence to suggest that another ice age is coming.

But, um… In today's world, an immense emission of greenhouse gases from the burning of 10) **fossil fuels** has caused global warming and 11) **led to** a drastic 12) **increase in** global temperatures. So, you may 13) **be doubtful about** how scientists can 14) **be so sure that** we're living in an interglacial period. Well… I've mentioned before that scientists have collected evidence and are predicting the advent of another ice age, right? It's because ice ages have occurred 15) **so regularly that** they must 16) **abide by** some kind of pattern. Quite interesting, huh? Let's 17) **look at** some geological information that 18) **relates to** the 19) **relationship between** coral reefs **and** glaciers to 20) **help you understand**. We now know, from geological 21) **research on** the ancient coral reefs, that ice sheets have formed and receded about 22) **every** one hundred thousand **years**. See, oceans 23) **turn into** ice sheets during ice ages, 24) **resulting in** a 25) **decrease in** the water level and temperature. Consequently, coral reefs that normally grow in warm shallow waters would wind up on dry land or be killed by the low temperatures during ice ages and 26) **stop growing**. As the ice ages 27) **give way to** interglacial periods with much milder climates, the coral reefs would 28) **start growing** a new layer again as the glaciers withdrew and the water levels rose. This pattern allows the dating of coral reef growth, which has become a very crucial tool for scientists and geologists.

For those of you who are still confused, 29) **let me explain** further. To date coral reef growth, they try to determine how old each layer is and recently, they've 30) **been able to analyze** chemicals found in the coral reefs, such as uranium isotopes, to 31) **figure out** that coral growth has happened 32) **with regularity**. 33) **Let's say**… If the first layer of the coral reef was dated as 500 years old and the second 300 years old, then the interval of non-growth between the two layers would be 200 years, right? By compiling data showing the regularly formed gaps between the ages of layers of coral, scientists can determine how long ice ages lasted and approximately how often they occurred. That's exactly how the dating works, and it has clarified that ice ages have occurred 34) **in** regular **cycles as well**. This theory of ice age regularity is, however, a very recent idea.

35) **Of course**, there are several other theories proposed, like… uh… plate tectonics, which describes the movement of giant plates under the Earth's surface that cause natural phenomena like earthquakes and volcanic eruptions. Those movements 36) **might have caused** changes in ocean currents and wind patterns that could 37) **play a role in triggering** ice ages. But, here's my question to you all, "Doesn't the theory suggest that ice ages would happen randomly because earthquakes and volcanic eruptions are random?"… Anyone? Okay, the answer would be, yes. Although it may explain the 38) **changes in** the global climate 39) **to some extent**, it's missing the 40) **critical point** that we've been discussing: the regularity of ice ages, so, we need a theory that supports this regularity. The Milankovitch theory 41) **fits** perfectly **with** this.

Milutin Milankovitch, a Serbian astrophysicist, consistently studied and eventually developed a scientific theory that showed that subtle oscillations in the Earth's movement play a vital role in causing regular ice ages. In the 1920s, he theorized that the Earth's rotation and orbit were major factors regulating the "come and go" of ice ages by precisely calculating their fluctuations.

First, by observing the 42) **changes in the angle** of the Earth's tilt 43) **with respect to** its axis, Milankovitch was able to conclude that the tilt changes about three degrees every forty-one thousand years. Furthermore, he was able to conclude that more tilt leads to more extreme summers and winters, and less tilt results in the opposite, milder summers and winters. You might be wondering how small fluctuations in the Earth's tilt could lead to such tremendous 44) **effects on** the climate. Um… 45) **It's because** the Earth 46) **is composed of** such perplexing and intricate systems that even very minimal fluctuations can result in huge changes. Well… It's not important to discuss these systems in this lecture, so let's 47) **stay on** topic.

Now, there was another 48) **contributing** factor **to** the global climate change that Milankovitch proposed. He also claimed that the Earth's orbit around the sun is elliptical, rather than perfectly circular. As you may have already 49) **guessed from** what I've just said, 50) **at times**, the Earth is 51) **closer to** the sun than it is at other times. 52) **At present**, the Earth's closest 53) **approach to** the sun occurs in January, resulting in milder summers 54) **in the northern hemisphere**. 55) **On the contrary**, however, eleven thousand years ago, the closest approach of the Earth to the sun happened in July, making summers and winters much more extreme.

Okay… So now we know the two contributing factors he proposed: the changes in the Earth's tilt and Earth's uneven orbital pattern around the sun. What can we 56) **conclude from** this? Well… We know they cause climate changes, sometimes cooler summers or warmer summers. These two phenomena could also 57) **have** a huge **impact on** the formation and ebbing of ice sheets. 58) **For instance**, in the northern hemisphere where most of the Earth's landmass is found, consecutive cooler summers would 59) **allow** snow **to accumulate** and persist 60) **throughout the year**. What do you think that will lead to? Of course, an ice age! 61) **On the other hand**, consecutive warmer summers would cause the shrinkage of ice sheets, which would 62) **bring about** an interglacial period, like the one we're living in 63) **right now**.

Although the Milankovitch theory has some convincing elements, it does overlook some essential factors, such as cloud cover and 64) **variations in** solar energy. When 65) **compared to** the other theories proposed 66) **so far**, it is, 67) **by far**, the most accepted, but I believe we should 68) **keep our options open** and 69) **avoid thinking** that it's the ultimate and most comprehensive explanation possible.

Ice age

Listen to part of a lecture in a climatology class

P: As we discussed in our last class, there have been a number of ice ages over the past few million years, such as the Permian and Ordovician Glaciation Periods, when much of the planet was covered with glaciers… Scientists believe that the ice age theory is certainly one of the most compelling theories to explain the end of the dinosaur era. Well, fortunately for human beings, we are currently living in an "interglacial period", or a period between ice ages, during which the glaciers retreat to the polar regions and the Earth experiences a relatively milder climate. All of the ice ages have been separated by long mild interglacial periods of this type. Even though the last ice age, the Quaternary Glaciation, ended around ten thousand years ago, there is considerable evidence to suggest that another ice age is coming.

But, um… In today's world, an immense emission of greenhouse gases from the burning of fossil fuels has caused global warming and led to a drastic increase in global temperatures. So, you may be doubtful about how scientists can be so sure that we're living in an interglacial period. Well… I've mentioned before that scientists have collected evidence and are predicting the advent of another ice age, right? It's because ice ages have occurred so regularly that they must abide by some kind of pattern. Quite interesting, huh? Let's look at some geological information that relates to the relationship between coral reefs and glaciers to help you understand. We now know, from geological research on the ancient coral reefs, that ice sheets have formed and receded about every one hundred thousand years. See, oceans turn into ice sheets during ice ages, resulting in a decrease in the water level and temperature. Consequently, coral reefs that normally grow in warm shallow waters would wind up on dry land or be killed by the low temperatures during ice ages and stop growing. As the ice ages give way to interglacial periods with much milder climates, the coral reefs would start growing a new layer again as the glaciers withdrew and the water levels rose. This pattern allows the dating of coral reef growth, which has become a very crucial tool for scientists and geologists.

For those of you who are still confused, let me explain further. To date coral reef growth, they try to determine how old each layer is and recently, they've been able to analyze chemicals found in the coral reefs, such as uranium isotopes, to figure out that coral growth has happened with regularity. Let's say… If the first layer of the coral reef was dated as 500 years old and the second 300 years old, then the interval of non-growth between the two layers would be 200 years, right? By compiling data showing the regularly formed gaps between the ages of layers of coral, scientists can determine how long ice ages lasted and approximately how often they occurred. That's exactly how the dating works, and it has clarified that ice ages have occurred in regular cycles as well. This theory of ice age regularity is, however, a very recent idea.

Of course, there are several other theories proposed, like… uh… plate tectonics, which describes the movement of giant plates under the Earth's surface that cause natural phenomena like earthquakes and volcanic eruptions. Those movements might have caused changes in ocean currents and wind patterns that could play a role in triggering ice ages. But, here's my question to you all, "Doesn't the theory suggest that ice ages would happen randomly because earthquakes and volcanic eruptions are random?"… Anyone? Okay, the answer would be, yes. Although it may explain the changes in the global climate to some extent, it's missing the critical point that we've been discussing: the regularity of ice ages, so, we need a theory that supports this regularity. The Milankovitch theory fits perfectly with this.

Milutin Milankovitch, a Serbian astrophysicist, consistently studied and eventually developed a scientific theory that showed that subtle oscillations in the Earth's movement play a vital role in causing regular ice ages. In the 1920s, he theorized that the Earth's rotation and orbit were major factors regulating the "come and go" of ice ages by precisely calculating their fluctuations.

First, by observing the changes in the angle of the Earth's tilt with respect to its axis, Milankovitch was able to conclude that the tilt changes about three degrees every forty-one thousand years. Furthermore, he was able to conclude that more tilt leads to more extreme summers and winters, and less tilt results in the opposite, milder summers and winters. You might be wondering how small fluctuations in the Earth's tilt could lead to such tremendous effects on the climate. Um… It's because the Earth is composed of such perplexing and intricate systems that even very minimal fluctuations can result in huge changes. Well… It's not important to discuss these systems in this lecture, so let's stay on topic.

Now, there was another contributing factor to the global climate change that Milankovitch proposed. He also claimed that the Earth's orbit around the sun is elliptical, rather than perfectly circular. As you may have already guessed from what I've just said, at times, the Earth is closer to the sun than it is at other times. At present, the Earth's closest approach to the sun occurs in January, resulting in milder summers in the northern hemisphere. On the contrary, however, eleven thousand years ago, the closest approach of the Earth to the sun happened in July, making summers and winters much more extreme.

Okay… So now we know the two contributing factors he proposed: the changes in the Earth's tilt and Earth's uneven orbital pattern around the sun. What can we conclude from this? Well… We know they cause climate changes, sometimes cooler summers or warmer summers. These two phenomena could also have a huge impact on the formation and ebbing of ice sheets. For instance, in the northern hemisphere where most of the Earth's landmass is found, consecutive cooler summers would allow snow to accumulate and persist throughout the year. What do you think that will lead to? Of course, an ice age! On the other hand, consecutive warmer summers would cause the shrinkage of ice sheets, which would bring about an interglacial period, like the one we're living in right now.

Although the Milankovitch theory has some convincing elements, it does overlook some essential factors, such as cloud cover and variations in solar energy. When compared to the other theories proposed so far, it is, by far, the most accepted, but I believe we should keep our options open and avoid thinking that it's the ultimate and most comprehensive explanation possible.

Drama class

Listen to part of a lecture in an introduction to drama class

P: 01) **Up to now** we've been 02) **looking at** how the structure of a play and the stage where the 03) **play is performed** 04) **are related to** 05) **each other**. Let's look back to the very beginning of theater development. You guys 06) **are aware that** the first theaters were built by the Greeks in the 5th century B.C.E. right? Well, although 07) **in our modern sense**, theaters 08) **are supposed to be** indoors, back then, they were built outdoors in nature, usually 09) **on the top of** a hill. By locating them 10) **in this way**, the Greek architects ensured that the natural scenery 11) **was** well **incorporated into** the theaters' settings. 12) **On the other hand**, the basic elements of today's theater are essentially 13) **the same as** in ancient times… So, today we will be 14) **looking** more deeply **into** their similarities and differences, and as we 15) **go along**, you'll notice how certain things in the theater world remain unchanged and others were modified or abandoned.

Let's 16) **begin** our discussion **with** the space where the choruses 17) **performed** their **roles** 18) **in ancient times**. Just like today's theater, the performing area for the chorus was called the orchestra, which meant "the dancing place" in ancient Greek. 19) **As far as** I'm concerned, the similarities they share end about there. 20) **In order to understand** the discrepancy, you 21) **need to notice** that the chorus in ancient times had an extra role 22) **on top of** that of today's choruses. Yes, they certainly did dance and sing 23) **on the stage** like they do today, but they also provided 24) **commentary on** 25) **a variety of** aspects of the play, including its theme, what the characters were thinking, and what they were doing. Their occasional direct involvement in the plays clearly showed that one of their primary roles was to 26) **interact with** the audience and 27) **react to** the drama **with** them. This is quite 28) **different from** today's choruses, isn't it? One could argue that the importance of the chorus has diminished greatly 29) **over time**. Anyway… Does anyone know any other differences between today's choruses and ancient ones?

S: Well, I've heard that the choruses' involvement was 30) **so** significant **that** they 31) **were considered to have** a distinct personality like any other character on stage.

P: Yes. That's exactly what Aristotle, the Greek philosopher, explained about the choruses' role… That they also 32) **had** an active **role in** the drama! Yes, John?

S: Um… I saw Politis last summer, you know, the reenactment of the ancient one, and I witnessed something very strange during the play… It seemed like some of the action scenes were abridged. You see, when Politis 33) **was sent off**, a messenger appeared on stage and 34) **announced to** the audience **that** while Politis was riding in his chariot, a giant monster, a bull, if I remember correctly, 35) **sprang** forth **from** the ocean and killed Politis. Then, as the messenger 36) **walked off**, Politis was carried back on stage, and he was officially pronounced dead 37) **in front of** the audience. I mean, the intense fighting scene, which 38) **would have been** great to watch, was 39) **put into words** and 40) **relayed to** us by a messenger. I don't understand… What happened to the scene? Is this how the theaters presented their scenes in ancient times?

P: Great point! I 41) **was just about to** 42) **move on to** a topic that will 43) **answer your question**, so 44) **hang on a minute**.

Okay. Now that we've looked at the chorus, let's 45) **take a look at** where the actors performed. The modern term for where the actors perform is called the stage, as you all know. The Greeks, however, 46) **referred to** it **as** the skēnē. I'm sure it 47) **sounds unfamiliar to** all of you, as even scholars have two totally different interpretations of the word. Some scholars 48) **use** the term strictly **to refer to** the structure behind the stage, whereas others use it in reference to 49) **both** the structure **and** the stage itself. In this class, we'll be using the term with 50) **the latter** purpose. Anyway, the skēnē evolved throughout the centuries. 51) **Prior to** the advent of theaters, it was merely a wooden platform 52) **with no significance**, but it 53) **went through** a lot of modifications and became much more ornate and decorative over time. With the establishment of theaters, it 54) **acted as** background scenery. For instance, the front wall of the building was decorated, sometimes as a temple or as a palace, 55) **according to** the setting of the story. Well… The problem with this was that they didn't have the technology to change the background for every scene like we do today.. Instead, they had only one decorated skēnē, and that 56) **had to last** throughout the entire play. Therefore, as you mentioned, John, it was impractical 57) **for them to portray** every single scene of the play, and sometimes some of the events had to be 58) **condensed into** words 59) **instead of** visual images. 60) **That's why** the entire fight scene in Politis had to be reported by the messenger… The setting in which the fight 61) **took place** was not the same as the one in which the rest of the play happened. 62) **In fact**, I'll 63) **show you** some other great **examples** of plays like the one that John mentioned 64) **in the** next **lesson**.

Anyway, the last aspect of the Greek theaters we will be discussing today is the seating area for the audience, which they called the theatron. Well, it's just an idea, but I think it's quite ironic that they 65) **called it** the **theatron**, which meant the 'seeing place,' when some theaters had numerous rows and accommodated about 14,000 spectators per play… I'm sure some of the people in the upper part of the place couldn't even watch the show and had to hear it instead… Anyway, the theatron was constructed in 66) **such** a way **that** it resembled a bowl, with rows of seats spreading outwards and upwards… Sometimes, they were 68) **cut in half**, 67) **resulting in** a semi-circular shape. The bowl shape was very effective because it enabled the capturing of the sound and efficiently delivered it upwards, 69) **so that** everyone, 70) **regardless of** his/her seat location, could hear the performers.

Okay. That should cover today's discussion. Well, you see, I've 71) **devoted** a long time **to studying** the fields of drama and theater, and I get a sense of great joy and pleasure whenever I 72) **introduce** new students like you **to** my approach… Some people might 73) **put** great **emphasis** on today's theaters and overlook the very first theaters used by the Greeks, but the way I look at it is that modern theater wouldn't exist without the basic elements of the ancient theaters, so try to 74) **keep that in mind**.

Drama class

Listen to part of a lecture in an introduction to drama class

P: Up to now we've been looking at how the structure of a play and the stage where the play is performed are related to each other. Let's look back to the very beginning of theater development. You guys are aware that the first theaters were built by the Greeks in the 5th century B.C.E. right? Well, although in our modern sense, theaters are supposed to be indoors, back then, they were built outdoors in nature, usually on the top of a hill. By locating them in this way, the Greek architects ensured that the natural scenery was well incorporated into the theaters' settings. On the other hand, the basic elements of today's theater are essentially the same as in ancient times… So, today we will be looking more deeply into their similarities and differences, and as we go along, you'll notice how certain things in the theater world remain unchanged and others were modified or abandoned.

Let's begin our discussion with the space where the choruses performed their roles in ancient times. Just like today's theater, the performing area for the chorus was called the orchestra, which meant "the dancing place" in ancient Greek. As far as I'm concerned, the similarities they share end about there. In order to understand the discrepancy, you need to notice that the chorus in ancient times had an extra role on top of that of today's choruses. Yes, they certainly did dance and sing on the stage like they do today, but they also provided commentary on a variety of aspects of the play, including its theme, what the characters were thinking, and what they were doing. Their occasional direct involvement in the plays clearly showed that one of their primary roles was to interact with the audience and react to the drama with them. This is quite different from today's choruses, isn't it? One could argue that the importance of the chorus has diminished greatly over time. Anyway… Does anyone know any other differences between today's choruses and ancient ones?

S: Well, I've heard that the choruses' involvement was so significant that they were considered to have a distinct personality like any other character on stage.

P: Yes. That's exactly what Aristotle, the Greek philosopher, explained about the choruses' role… That they also had an active role in the drama! Yes, John?

S: Um… I saw Politis last summer, you know, the reenactment of the ancient one, and I witnessed something very strange during the play… It seemed like some of the action scenes were abridged. You see, when Politis was sent off, a messenger appeared on stage and announced to the audience that while Politis was riding in his chariot, a giant monster, a bull, if I remember correctly, sprang forth from the ocean and killed Politis. Then, as the messenger walked off, Politis was carried back on stage, and he was officially pronounced dead in front of the audience. I mean, the intense fighting scene, which would have been great to watch, was put into words and relayed to us by a messenger. I don't understand… What happened to the scene? Is this how the theaters presented their scenes in ancient times?

P: Great point! I was just about to move on to a topic that will answer your question, so hang on a minute.

Okay. Now that we've looked at the chorus, let's take a look at where the actors performed. The modern term for where the actors perform is called the stage, as you all know. The Greeks, however, referred to it as the skēnē. I'm sure it sounds unfamiliar to all of you, as even scholars have two totally different interpretations of the word. Some scholars use the term strictly to refer to the structure behind the stage, whereas others use it in reference to both the structure and the stage itself. In this class, we'll be using the term with the latter purpose. Anyway, the skēnē evolved throughout the centuries. Prior to the advent of theaters, it was merely a wooden platform with no significance, but it went through a lot of modifications and became much more ornate and decorative over time. With the establishment of theaters, it acted as background scenery. For instance, the front wall of the building was decorated, sometimes as a temple or as a palace, according to the setting of the story. Well… The problem with this was that they didn't have the technology to change the background for every scene like we do today.. Instead, they had only one decorated skēnē, and that had to last throughout the entire play. Therefore, as you mentioned, John, it was impractical for them to portray every single scene of the play, and sometimes some of the events had to be condensed into words instead of visual images. That's why the entire fight scene in Politis had to be reported by the messenger… The setting in which the fight took place was not the same as the one in which the rest of the play happened. In fact, I'll show you some other great examples of plays like the one that John mentioned in the next lesson.

Anyway, the last aspect of the Greek theaters we will be discussing today is the seating area for the audience, which they called the theatron. Well, it's just an idea, but I think it's quite ironic that they called it the theatron, which meant the 'seeing place,' when some theaters had numerous rows and accommodated about 14,000 spectators per play… I'm sure some of the people in the upper part of the place couldn't even watch the show and had to hear it instead… Anyway, the theatron was constructed in such a way that it resembled a bowl, with rows of seats spreading outwards and upwards… Sometimes, they were cut in half, resulting in a semi-circular shape. The bowl shape was very effective because it enabled the capturing of the sound and efficiently delivered it upwards, so that everyone, regardless of his/her seat location, could hear the performers.

Okay. That should cover today's discussion. Well, you see, I've devoted a long time to studying the fields of drama and theater, and I get a sense of great joy and pleasure whenever I introduce new students like you to my approach… Some people might put great emphasis on today's theaters and overlook the very first theaters used by the Greeks, but the way I look at it is that modern theater wouldn't exist without the basic elements of the ancient theaters, so try to keep that in mind.

TEST 1 SET 2-1

Library employee

Listen to a conversation between a student and a library employee

S: Hi, could you help me with something? I really need your help.

L: Of course, how may I help you?

S: Well, I am 01) **working on** 02)**a paper on** the Wall Street Crash of 1929, you know the Great Depression, and while I was 03)**looking for** resources, I 04)**came across** this book, "Time of Great Struggle." But, its reference pages are all damaged and wrinkled, and I can't really decipher anything. What are the odds?

L: 05)**Give me one second**; 06) **let me** 07) **check if** we have another copy for you.

S: Sure.

L: Well… 08) **It seems like** the book you're holding is the only copy we have in the library…

S: Oh no… I can't finish my assignment without the reference pages…

L: Have you 09) **tried ordering** a copy of the book online? 10) **I'm sure** you could try other sources

S: 11) **The thing is,** I 12) **need to finish** my 13) **research for** the assignment 14) **by tomorrow**, so ordering a new copy will 15) **take too long**…

L: Hmm… let me try tracking the book and 16) **see if** any other libraries have it.

S: Sure, 17) **as long as** I can get the book.

L: I'm 18) **browsing for** the book… and… actually, there's one university in New York! Do you 19) **want to try** that?

S: Great! **How long** will it 20) **take** for it **to get** here?

L: Well, I think it could get here by tomorrow if we ordered it right now, but you never know what kind of delays can happen during shipment. We've experienced some of these issues before.

S: Oh no… Is there any other 21) **way to get** the book **from** the university?

L: Well, I usually do not 22) **do** personal **favors** for patrons 23) **during working hours**, but…a former colleague of mine works at that university. Maybe I can 24) **ask if** he can help.

S: That'd be great. But how do you think he could 25) **be of any help** 26) **in** my current **situation**?

L: Well, he could fax over the pages that you need, and then I could 27) **give them to you**.

S: Perfect! How soon do you think you'll 28) **be able to contact** him?

L: Well, you're forgetting the 29) **time difference**. They're on 30) **Eastern Time**, so…. it's very late there now

S: I hadn't 31) **thought about** that. Okay, so…what time will you be able to 32) **get in touch with** him?

L: Actually, I'm sure the library is not open right now, but I have his home number. I'll 33) **ring him** right now and see what he can do, but... If the book 34) **is** already **checked out**, I don't know what else I could do for you... Perhaps you could stay here and **try finding** other books on the Great Depression. 35) **You never know**.

S: Okay, that 36) **sounds like** all I can do 37) **for now**. Could you 38) **leave me a message** if that 39) **works out** or not? I really **want to** 40) **make sure** I'm not 41) **waiting for** something that 42) **'s not going to happen**.

L: Sure, just leave your phone number here.

S: 43) **Thanks for** your help.

L: I will **let you know** 44) **as soon as possible**.

Library employee

Listen to a conversation between a student and a library employee

S: Hi, could you help me with something? I really need your help.

L: Of course, how may I help you?

S: Well, I am working on a paper on the Wall Street Crash of 1929, you know the Great Depression, and while I was looking for resources, I came across this book, "Time of Great Struggle." But, its reference pages are all damaged and wrinkled, and I can't really decipher anything. What are the odds?

L: Give me one second; let me check if we have another copy for you.

S: Sure.

L: Well… It seems like the book you're holding is the only copy we have in the library…

S: Oh no… I can't finish my assignment without the reference pages…

L: Have you tried ordering a copy of the book online? I'm sure you could try other sources

S: The thing is, I need to finish my research for the assignment by tomorrow, so ordering a new copy will take too long…

L: Hmm… let me try tracking the book and see if any other libraries have it.

S: Sure, as long as I can get the book.

L: I'm browsing for the book... and… actually, there's one university in New York! Do you want to try that?

S: Great! How long will it take for it to get here?

L: Well, I think it could get here by tomorrow if we ordered it right now, but you never know what kind of delays can happen during shipment. We've experienced some of these issues before.

S: Oh no… Is there any other way to get the book from the university?

L: Well, I usually do not do personal favors for patrons during working hours, but…a former colleague of mine works at that university. Maybe I can ask if he can help.

S: That'd be great. But how do you think he could be of any help in my current situation?

L: Well, he could fax over the pages that you need, and then I could give them to you.

S: Perfect! How soon do you think you'll be able to contact him?

L: Well, you're forgetting the time difference. They're on Eastern Time, so…. it's very late there now

S: I hadn't thought about that. Okay, so…what time will you be able to get in touch with him?

L: Actually, I'm sure the library is not open right now, but I have his home number. I'll ring him right now and see what he can do, but... If the book is already checked out, I don't know what else I could do for you... Perhaps you could stay here and try finding other books on the Great Depression. You never know.

S: Okay, that sounds like all I can do for now. Could you leave me a message if that works out or not? I really want to make sure I'm not waiting for something that's not going to happen.

L: Sure, just leave your phone number here.

S: Thanks for your help.

L: I will let you know as soon as possible.

Bioluminescence

Listen to part of a lecture in a marine biology class

P: Last class we [01] **looked at** the first two layers of the ocean and the marine life they contain. Well, today, we'll be [02] **moving on to** the last, darkest layer of the ocean, [03] **named** the deep-zone layer. Unlike the other two we've discussed [04] **so far**, the deep-zone has some distinguishable characteristics. Yes, Isabella?

S: From what I've read, professor, the zone is quite a dangerous and challenging place [05] **for marine life to survive**… it doesn't have as high of an oxygen level as the other two, the water pressure is high, and oh, it's also completely [06] **devoid of** any light.

P: You're right. And, I [07] **would like to discuss** the last condition: [08] **lack of** light. Well, what first [09] **comes to mind** when you hear that there is no light in the zone?

S: Well, I'm a little confused… I mean… I know that there are organisms living down there, but no light is [10] **kind of** [11] **equivalent to** no vision, right? So, how is it possible that there are organisms that thrive there without a problem?

P: Good question! Although the environment is seemingly uninhabitable, the marine life that lives there has adapted quite interesting ways to survive the harsh conditions. As you [12] **may have already guessed**, the organisms that live in the zone have developed a trait that [13] **enables them to produce** [14] **a type of** chemical light, [15] **called** "bioluminescence."

S: Um, correct me if I'm wrong, but isn't it the bacteria that are present in the water or within the organisms that glow, not the fish themselves?

P: Well, you're not completely wrong. There are fish like that, but that's a whole [16] **different** category **from** bioluminescence. [17] **In fact**, most fish with bioluminescence, which is, again, a chemical trait, not a type of bacteria, generate illumination within themselves to produce their own light. Okay now, we all know marine life down there has a chemical [18] **inherited** [19] **from generation to generation** that they [20] **use to produce** light … [21] **In most cases**, the light is blue... but other colors are also seen occasionally.

S: Professor, I understand that the color blue is the most functional color in the water [22] **in the sense** that it travels the farthest in such an environment, but how [23] **is** that **of** any **help**, considering that… I mean… I thought the organisms in the deep-zone couldn't see anything because they had [24] **no visual senses at all**. For bioluminescence to be functional, it [25] **needs to be** seen, right?

P: Well, [26] **to some extent**, you're right. But, it may [27] **come as** a surprise to you that the fish in the zone actually do have the [28] **ability to see**… but their visual senses are very limited. They only detect blue light, which is very fortunate since blue is the color of light that bioluminescence produces in most cases. It [29] **makes sense** now, doesn't it? Although their vision [30] **is limited to** one specific color, blue, they [31] **are capable of generating** it themselves, thus [32] **enabling them to see** [33] **in the darkness**. Uh… there is one special type of fish, named the dragon fish, **to** which the blue light standard does not [34] **apply**. They generate and see red light instead, and [35] **of course**, this ability presents a tremendous [36] **advantage over** others. Well… Dragon fish are not the topic of today's discussion, so let's [37] **move on**.

P: We were talking about the benefits of bioluminescence. The main one we'll be [38] **looking into** is the usefulness of bioluminescence [39] **when it comes to** [40] **dealing with** predators and their threats. Just for your information, though, it also [41] **serves** other **purposes**, [42] **such as** [43] **aiding in** the reproductive, food-gathering, and communication processes. Anyway, does anybody [44] **want to** [45] **take a guess** at how bioluminescence might be used in [46] **protecting** the organism **against** predators' attacks?

S: You've [47] **taught us that** there are two strategies that animals employ when dealing with predators. I believe they are active defense strategy and passive defense strategy. My question is, does the same principle [48] **apply to** the marine life in the deep-layer zone?

P: Great question. Yes, the bioluminescent organisms utilize [49] **both** active **and** passive defense strategies. [50] **For** our **purpose**, let's look at… the crystal jellyfish. They are [51] **considered to be** the most influential bioluminescent organisms [52] **in the medical field**, because the chemical [53] **responsible for** their generation of light is used to locate cancerous tumors in the human body.

P: Anyway, when they initially detect a predator's threat, the jellyfish [54] **flashes light at** the predator. This flashing employs active defense strategies [55] **in two different senses**… [56] **What I mean** by two different senses is that there are two theories, [57] **as to** what [58] role **bioluminescence plays in** dealing with predators but no consensus exists as to which is correct. One theory explains that the jellyfish flash their light to seem daunting to the predator… You know, [59] **scare them off** [60] **in a sense**. To help illustrate this more clearly, um, think about thieves. [61] **Let's say** a thief is [62] **in the middle of** [63] **stealing jewelry from** your house and you flash a light in his face. What would his reaction be? Of course, he would [64] **try to** [65] **run away**, acknowledging that he has been caught…

P: The other theory posits that it [66] **exposes the predator to** its own predators. This theory was first hypothesized when scientists noticed that sometimes the jellyfish's predators were attacked while trying to [67] **feed on** them… and, um, there have been many experiments that showed this. One of these experiments artificially recreated the flashes that the jellyfish generated. Scientists then [68] **focused on** [69] **whether or not** squid, organisms that eat the jellyfish's predators but not the jellyfish, followed the flashes. And [70] **guess what**? They did. Squid actually swam to the signals, which proves that the flashes actually do play a role in attracting the predators' own predators.

P: Okay, that should be enough about active defense strategies. Now, let's move on to bioluminescence as a passive one! The use as a passive strategy is [71] **different than** the active one [72] **in that** bioluminescence is used to completely [73] **avoid encountering** predators. Um… do you guys remember our [74] **discussion on** the principle of camouflage?

S: Of course, it's used by animals to [75] **conceal** themselves **from** their predators. [76] **For instance**, some frogs and lizards deliberately change their skin color [77] **either to** [78] **make themselves more difficult** to see **or** to deceive their predators with colors that [79] **make them look** strong and dangerous. Oh, I get it now! Bioluminescence works similarly, doesn't it?

P: Excellent! That's exactly what it is. The organisms in the deep-zone, such as sea anemones, use the same mechanism, and use very conspicuous colors of bioluminescence to kind of… uh… [80] **deliver a warning message to** their predators. It's [81] **as if** they were saying, "I'm very toxic and dangerous, so you should not be [82] **considering me as** a meal today."

Bioluminescence

Listen to part of a lecture in a marine biology class

P: Last class we looked at the first two layers of the ocean and the marine life they contain. Well, today, we'll be moving on to the last, darkest layer of the ocean, named the deep-zone layer. Unlike the other two we've discussed so far, the deep-zone has some distinguishable characteristics. Yes, Isabella?

S: From what I've read, professor, the zone is quite a dangerous and challenging place for marine life to survive… it doesn't have as high of an oxygen level as the other two, the water pressure is high, and oh, it's also completely devoid of any light.

P: You're right. And, I would like to discuss the last condition: lack of light. Well, what first comes to mind when you hear that there is no light in the zone?

S: Well, I'm a little confused… I mean… I know that there are organisms living down there, but no light is kind of equivalent to no vision, right? So, how is it possible that there are organisms that thrive there without a problem?

P: Good question! Although the environment is seemingly uninhabitable, the marine life that lives there has adapted quite interesting ways to survive the harsh conditions. As you may have already guessed, the organisms that live in the zone have developed a trait that enables them to produce a type of chemical light, called "bioluminescence."

S: Um, correct me if I'm wrong, but isn't it the bacteria that are present in the water or within the organisms that glow, not the fish themselves?

P: Well, you're not completely wrong. There are fish like that, but that's a whole different category from bioluminescence. In fact, most fish with bioluminescence, which is, again, a chemical trait, not a type of bacteria, generate illumination within themselves to produce their own light. Okay now, we all know marine life down there has a chemical inherited from generation to generation that they use to produce light … In most cases, the light is blue… but other colors are also seen occasionally.

S: Professor, I understand that the color blue is the most functional color in the water in the sense that it travels the farthest in such an environment, but how is that of any help considering that… I mean… I thought the organisms in the deep-zone couldn't see anything because they had no visual senses at all. For bioluminescence to be functional, it needs to be seen, right?

P: Well, to some extent, you're right. But, it may come as a surprise to you that the fish in the zone actually do have the ability to see… but their visual senses are very limited. They only detect blue light, which is very fortunate since blue is the color of light that bioluminescence produces in most cases. It makes sense now, doesn't it? Although their vision is limited to one specific color, blue, they are capable of generating it themselves, thus enabling them to see in the darkness. Uh… there is one special type of fish, named the dragon fish, to which the blue light standard does not apply. They generate and see red light instead, and of course, this ability presents a tremendous advantage over others. Well… Dragon fish are not the topic of today's discussion, so let's move on.

P: We were talking about the benefits of bioluminescence. The main one we'll be looking into is the usefulness of bioluminescence when it comes to dealing with predators and their threats. Just for your information, though, it also serves other purposes, such as aiding in the reproductive, food-gathering, and communication processes. Anyway, does anybody want to take a guess at how bioluminescence might be used in protecting the organism against predators' attacks?

S: You've taught us that there are two strategies that animals employ when dealing with predators. I believe they are active defense strategy and passive defense strategy. My question is, does the same principle apply to the marine life in the deep-layer zone?

P: Great question. Yes, the bioluminescent organisms utilize both active and passive defense strategies. For our purpose, let's look at… the crystal jellyfish. They are considered to be the most influential bioluminescent organisms in the medical field, because the chemical responsible for their generation of light is used to locate cancerous tumors in the human body.

P: Anyway, when they initially detect a predator's threat, the jellyfish flashes light at the predator. This flashing employs active defense strategies in two different senses… What I mean by two different senses is that there are two theories, as to what role bioluminescence plays in dealing with predators but no consensus exists as to which is correct. One theory explains that the jellyfish flash their light to seem daunting to the predator… You know, scare them off in a sense. To help illustrate this more clearly, um, think about thieves. Let's say a thief is in the middle of stealing jewelry from your house and you flash a light in his face. What would his reaction be? Of course, he would try to run away, acknowledging that he has been caught…

P: The other theory posits that it exposes the predator to its own predators. This theory was first hypothesized when scientists noticed that sometimes the jellyfish's predators were attacked while trying to feed on them… and, um, there have been many experiments that showed this. One of these experiments artificially recreated the flashes that the jellyfish generated. Scientists then focused on whether or not squid, organisms that eat the jellyfish's predators but not the jellyfish, followed the flashes. And guess what? They did. Squid actually swam to the signals, which proves that the flashes actually do play a role in attracting the predators' own predators.

P: Okay, that should be enough about active defense strategies. Now, let's move on to bioluminescence as a passive one! The use as a passive strategy is different than the active one in that bioluminescence is used to completely avoid encountering predators. Um… do you guys remember our discussion on the principle of camouflage?

S: Of course, it's used by animals to conceal themselves from their predators. For instance, some frogs and lizards deliberately change their skin color either to make themselves more difficult to see or to deceive their predators with colors that make them look strong and dangerous. Oh, I get it now! Bioluminescence works similarly, doesn't it?

P: Excellent! That's exactly what it is. The organisms in the deep-zone, such as sea anemones, use the same mechanism, and use very conspicuous colors of bioluminescence to kind of… uh… deliver a warning message to their predators. It's as if they were saying, "I'm very toxic and dangerous, so you should not be considering me as a meal today."

Muon detector

Listen to part of a lecture in an archaeology class

P: I'm sure [01] **almost all** of you watched cartoons in your childhood that often portrayed archaeological elements. Watching these cartoons [02] **might have** [03] **given you** some **misconceptions** about the field of archaeology. I mean… Let me [04] **ask you this**: What is the image of archaeologists that you [05] **got from** those cartoons?

S: They dig here and there… [06] **hoping to discover** [07] **something significant** and valuable. I'm not [08] **trying to be** judgmental, but their job didn't [09] **seem to require** any sophisticated skill or anything.

P: I couldn't agree more. [10] **That's** exactly **how** they portray archaeology. It's funny [11] **in a sense**, but it's not how archaeologists actually [12] **carry out** their jobs… There certainly is some element of luck [13] **involved in** the discovery process, but overall, the job is a lot more professional, and it includes the use of high-tech tools. [14] **In contrast to** this common misconception, many archaeology-related institutions, [15] **such as** the Computerized Archaeology Laboratory, have [16] **devoted a tremendous amount of effort to developing** technology that could enrich the research environment. [17] **In fact,** they have invented [18] **one of the most effective tools**, the particle detector or, [19] **to be more specific**, the muon detector. I don't [20] **mean to say** that it's their only invention; they have developed other machines [21] **as well**, such as three-dimensional scanners that produce digital models of artifacts, but… I'[22] **d like to** primarily [23] **focus on** the muon detector today. We'll explore other machines [24] **in the next class**.

P: Okay. Umm… Let's [25] **get back to** our main topic. The muon detector uses subatomic particles [26] **called** muons, which [27] **result from** cosmic rays, you know, the high-energy protons that [28] **travel through** outer space [29] **at** [30] **close to the speed of** light. Those cosmic rays [31] **collide with** the Earth's atmosphere, and consequently, [32] **break down into** smaller, subatomic particles, which are [33] **known as** muons. Okay, you might be [34] **wondering about** how muons could [35] **be of any help** [36] **in the field of** archaeology; they're just particles, [37] **after all**. Well… Yes. They are particles but their properties can be exploited by archaeologists. Basically, since they are highly stimulated and energized particles, they [38] **are able to pass through**, or penetrate, solid matter. Archaeologists [39] **take advantage of** that property and [40] **use them to create** a visual image, [41] **similar to** a photograph. Let's say an archaeologist [42] **wanted to excavate** an ancient temple or an Egyptian pyramid and [43] **needed to** [44] **figure out** what types of artifacts were [45] **buried inside** without damaging the structure. Umm… It could [46] **be filled with** tombs or chambers. They could use the muon detector. The mechanism behind this is pretty straightforward and not too complicated. Muons lose energy as they [47] **go through** dense materials, such as a temple's posts, or a pyramid's walls [48] **in this case**. So [49] **the more** impediments they penetrate, **the more** energy they lose. Empty spaces, [50] **on the other hand**, don't [51] **pose any hindrance to** the muons, so less energy will be lost. Yes, Rebecca?

S: Okay, professor, I understand that [52] **the number of** energized muons varies [53] **depending on** the density of the spaces, but I'm still [54] **having a hard time** [55] **making sense** of how that principle could be deciphered or [56] **turned into** pictures.

P: Good question, Rebecca. [57] **As I mentioned previously**, more energized muons are present in empty spaces, whereas many are blocked or deflected by dense materials. To [58] **help you visualize** it more vividly, try to draw a circle and a square right [59] **in the middle of** it. Now, the square, in our case, is a chamber of a temple, and the surrounding space, the area [60] **between the circle and the square**, will represent the temple walls. As muons strike and eventually [61] **pass through** the temple, they kind of draw an image… like an X-ray image… for archaeologists to view. [62] **In other words**, when detected, the chamber, an empty area, will be much lighter than the temple walls, which reflect more muons than the open space.

P: [63] **In the past**, archaeologists were always [64] **at risk of** damaging important artifacts because they didn't have sophisticated tools like muon detectors to ensure their safety. With this technology, however, archaeologists have been able to [65] **avoid damaging** temples while excavating them.

P: Despite the advantages it presents today, the muon detector has only recently been fine-tuned [66] **enough to be** practical for this usage. Since its invention, it has gone through [67] **a lot of** modifications and many aspects of it have been enhanced. The earliest form of the muon detector was used by a physicist [68] **looking for** burial chambers in the Egyptian pyramids at Giza in 1967. Unfortunately, the one that he used [69] **at that time** had two major flaws… First, it was only functional if it was placed beneath the object to be scanned. It didn't work when [70] **placed on** the side of the object. This meant that if archaeologists wanted to scan the internal structures of a pyramid, they needed to bury the muon detector under it. Strenuous work, wasn't it? Also, the machine used in 1967 was very big and heavy, [71] **so it was quite difficult for archaeologists to carry it around with them**.

P: Today, however, modifications have solved the problems regarding the detector's burdensome size and technical limits. That doesn't necessarily mean that it's now a perfect form of technology, though. [72] **There are** still some issues that need to be [73] **worked out**, such as [74] **taking about half a year to produce** an image of the structure being scanned.

S: [75] **Half a year**? I can see that it improved [76] **in some ways**, but I would[77] **n't** call it much of an advance **at all**! I mean, if I were an archaeologist, I would never want to wait [78] **for six months** without being [79] **assured that** I would find something valuable.

P: Well, Rebecca, you have a point. But… Try to think about it [80] **this way**. Currently, there are Japanese scientists trying to [81] **map out** the interiors of volcanoes. If they didn't have the muon detector, what would their alternative be? [82] **Go inside** the volcanoes and explore? I think you get what I'm trying to say… Even though it does have some deficiencies that need to be overcome, it is the best tool we have for this type of scanning [83] **at the moment**.

Muon detector

Listen to part of a lecture in an archaeology class

P: I'm sure almost all of you watched cartoons in your childhood that often portrayed archaeological elements. Watching these cartoons might have given you some misconceptions about the field of archaeology. I mean… Let me ask you this: What is the image of archaeologists that you got from those cartoons?

S: They dig here and there… hoping to discover something significant and valuable. I'm not trying to be judgmental, but their job didn't seem to require any sophisticated skill or anything.

P: I couldn't agree more. That's exactly how they portray archaeology. It's funny in a sense, but it's not how archaeologists actually carry out their jobs… There certainly is some element of luck involved in the discovery process, but overall, the job is a lot more professional, and it includes the use of high-tech tools. In contrast to this common misconception, many archaeology-related institutions, such as the Computerized Archaeology Laboratory, have devoted a tremendous amount of effort to developing technology that could enrich the research environment. In fact, they have invented one of the most effective tools, the particle detector or, to be more specific, the muon detector. I don't mean to say that it's their only invention; they have developed other machines as well, such as three-dimensional scanners that produce digital models of artifacts, but… I'd like to primarily focus on the muon detector today. We'll explore other machines in the next class.

P: Okay. Umm… Let's get back to our main topic. The muon detector uses subatomic particles called muons, which result from cosmic rays, you know, the high-energy protons that travel through outer space at close to the speed of light. Those cosmic rays collide with the Earth's atmosphere, and consequently, break down into smaller, subatomic particles, which are known as muons. Okay, you might be wondering about how muons could be of any help in the field of archaeology; they're just particles, after all. Well… Yes. They are particles but their properties can be exploited by archaeologists. Basically, since they are highly stimulated and energized particles, they are able to pass through, or penetrate, solid matter. Archaeologists take advantage of that property and use them to create a visual image, similar to a photograph. Let's say an archaeologist wanted to excavate an ancient temple or an Egyptian pyramid and needed to figure out what types of artifacts were buried inside without damaging the structure. Umm… It could be filled with tombs or chambers. They could use the muon detector. The mechanism behind this is pretty straightforward and not too complicated. Muons lose energy as they go through dense materials, such as a temple's posts, or a pyramid's walls in this case. So the more impediments they penetrate, the more energy they lose. Empty spaces, on the other hand, don't pose any hindrance to the muons, so less energy will be lost. Yes, Rebecca?

S: Okay, professor, I understand that the number of energized muons varies depending on the density of the spaces, but I'm still having a hard time making sense of how that principle could be deciphered or turned into pictures.

P: Good question, Rebecca. As I mentioned previously, more energized muons are present in empty spaces, whereas many are blocked or deflected by dense materials. To help you visualize it more vividly, try to draw a circle and a square right in the middle of it. Now, the square, in our case, is a chamber of a temple, and the surrounding space, the area between the circle and the square, will represent the temple walls. As muons strike and eventually pass through the temple, they kind of draw an image… like an X-ray image… for archaeologists to view. In other words, when detected, the chamber, an empty area, will be much lighter than the temple walls, which reflect more muons than the open space.

P: In the past, archaeologists were always at risk of damaging important artifacts because they didn't have sophisticated tools like muon detectors to ensure their safety. With this technology, however, archaeologists have been able to avoid damaging temples while excavating them.

P: Despite the advantages it presents today, the muon detector has only recently been fine-tuned enough to be practical for this usage. Since its invention, it has gone through a lot of modifications and many aspects of it have been enhanced. The earliest form of the muon detector was used by a physicist looking for burial chambers in the Egyptian pyramids at Giza in 1967. Unfortunately, the one that he used at that time had two major flaws… First, it was only functional if it was placed beneath the object to be scanned. It didn't work when placed on the side of the object. This meant that if archaeologists wanted to scan the internal structures of a pyramid, they needed to bury the muon detector under it. Strenuous work, wasn't it? Also, the machine used in 1967 was very big and heavy, so it was quite difficult for archaeologists to carry it around with them.

P: Today, however, modifications have solved the problems regarding the detector's burdensome size and technical limits. That doesn't necessarily mean that it's now a perfect form of technology, though. There are still some issues that need to be worked out, such as taking about half a year to produce an image of the structure being scanned.

S: Half a year? I can see that it improved in some ways, but I wouldn't call it much of an advance at all! I mean, if I were an archaeologist, I would never want to wait for six months without being assured that I would find something valuable.

P: Well, Rebecca, you have a point. But… Try to think about it this way. Currently, there are Japanese scientists trying to map out the interiors of volcanoes. If they didn't have the muon detector, what would their alternative be? Go inside the volcanoes and explore? I think you get what I'm trying to say… Even though it does have some deficiencies that need to be overcome, it is the best tool we have for this type of scanning at the moment.

Math nights

Listen to part of a conversation between a student and his mathematics professor

S: Good afternoon, professor. I heard that you were 01) **looking for** me earlier this morning.

P: Hello, David. Yes, I was. I 02) **wanted to** 03) **offer you a job** 04) **related to** the new program our department is launching for the community. Have you 05) **heard of** math nights?

S: Math nights… Are you 06) **talking about** when schools host math-related games, and parents and kids 07) **participate in** them together? My parents and I 08) **loved going** to those when I was young.

P: Great! I was looking for someone who 09) **had experience** with them. Did you enjoy the activities, and did they 10) **help you** 11) **improve** your math **skills**?

S: Hmm… 12) **To be honest with you**, 13) **not only** was I horrible at math, **but** I really loathed it before I attended those programs. Seems ironic 14) **now that** I'm a math major, right? Those math nights really changed the way I 15) **looked at** math, and my parents were very 16) **supportive of** my 17) **decision to** 18) **choose to** 19) **major in** math in college, too.

P: That's exactly what our department 20) **is trying to** 21) **contribute to** our community: helping kids develop and 23) **figure out** their futures and 23) **teaching them** the profound and fundamental **concepts** of mathematics.

S: It sounds very 24) **intriguing to** me, but wouldn't I just be 25) **doing** kids' math **puzzles** with them? 26) **I'm not concerned with** the money being offered because 27) **I'd like to** 28) **focus on** gaining mathematics teaching experience, but doing puzzles won't help me learn that much about teaching math.

P: Well, you wouldn't 29) **have to** 30) **worry about** that at all because you'll be 31) **explaining** math concepts not only **to** the kids but **to** their parents 32) **as well**. 33) **You see**, the level of mathematics taught in schools has 34) **gotten** relatively **higher** 35) **over the past few decades**, so some parents are 36) **having a hard time helping** their kids with their homework.

S: Really? What level of math would I be teaching then?

P: Well, 37) **nothing higher than** 7th grade math will be required. But, uh… Try not to underestimate it, because the current level of 7th grade mathematics generally entails some high level stuff like graphing on the X-Y-Z plane and calculating probability.

S: Oh, wow, it surely 38) **sounds** a lot **harder** than when I was in 7th grade. I learned stuff like that in 9th grade.

P: Exactly! You can imagine how hard it must be 39) **for parents to teach** their kids subjects that they barely remember.

S: Yes, I can totally 40) **relate to** that. Well… 41) **the thing is** I still have to 42) **keep up with** 43) **a lot of** classes, and if I 44) **add work to** my schedule … I think it'll be too much.

P: Well, just 45) **give it a thought**. It involves about 15 hours of work 46) **per semester**, and it wouldn't be that 47) **difficult of** a job since you're a math major.

S: Sure, actually, 15 hours doesn't sound so bad. When do you need my answer?

P: Well, 48) **the sooner** you 49) **let us know, the better** it is for us because we 50) **need to have** a complete list of workers by next week for the administrator to sign and approve. Although we still have a few months until the actual launch, things like this are our priorities, and, also, a lot of people have inquired about the job. I hope you understand.

S: Of course, I won't 51) **take that long**. I'll 52) **give you a call** 53) **by the end of the week**.

P: That sounds great! Thanks, David.

S: No, 54) **thank you for the offer**, professor.

Math nights

Listen to part of a conversation between a student and his mathematics professor

S: Good afternoon, professor. I heard that you were looking for me earlier this morning.

P: Hello, David. Yes, I was. I wanted to offer you a job related to the new program our department is launching for the community. Have you heard of math nights?

S: Math nights… Are you talking about when schools host math-related games, and parents and kids participate in them together? My parents and I loved going to those when I was young.

P: Great! I was looking for someone who had experience with them. Did you enjoy the activities, and did they help you improve your math skills?

S: Hmm… To be honest with you, not only was I horrible at math, but I really loathed it before I attended those programs. Seems ironic now that I'm a math major, right? Those math nights really changed the way I looked at math, and my parents were very supportive of my decision to choose to major in math in college, too.

P: That's exactly what our department is trying to contribute to our community: helping kids develop and figure out their futures and teaching them the profound and fundamental concepts of mathematics.

S: It sounds very intriguing to me, but wouldn't I just be doing kids' math puzzles with them? I'm not concerned with the money being offered because I'd like to focus on gaining mathematics teaching experience, but doing puzzles won't help me learn that much about teaching math.

P: Well, you wouldn't have to worry about that at all because you'll be explaining math concepts not only to the kids but to their parents as well. You see, the level of mathematics taught in schools has gotten relatively higher over the past few decades, so some parents are having a hard time helping their kids with their homework.

S: Really? What level of math would I be teaching then?

P: Well, nothing higher than 7th grade math will be required. But, uh… Try not to underestimate it, because the current level of 7th grade mathematics generally entails some high level stuff like graphing on the X-Y-Z plane and calculating probability.

S: Oh, wow, it surely sounds a lot harder than when I was in 7th grade. I learned stuff like that in 9th grade.

P: Exactly! You can imagine how hard it must be for parents to teach their kids subjects that they barely remember.

S: Yes, I can totally relate to that. Well… the thing is I still have to keep up with a lot of classes, and if I add work to my schedule … I think it'll be too much.

P: Well, just give it a thought. It involves about 15 hours of work per semester, and it wouldn't be that difficult of a job since you're a math major.

S: Sure, actually, 15 hours doesn't sound so bad. When do you need my answer?

P: Well, the sooner you let us know, the better it is for us because we need to have a complete list of workers by next week for the administrator to sign and approve. Although we still have a few months until the actual launch, things like this are our priorities, and, also, a lot of people have inquired about the job. I hope you understand.

S: Of course, I won't take that long. I'll give you a call by the end of the week.

P: That sounds great! Thanks, David.

S: No, thank you for the offer, professor.

The accessibility of novels

Listen to part of a lecture in an English literature class

P: Last class I 01) **asked you to research** some of the popular English authors of the 19th century. As you may now know, 19th century England was marked by famous authors, 02) **such as** Charles Dickens. Before starting our discussion about the authors, however, I 03) **would first like to discuss** the accessibility of novels 04) **at the time**… like, you know, how readers 05) **used to** 06) **gain access to** novels.

Let's first 07) **talk about** what it was like to purchase novels during the 19th century. Novels of that time, which 08) **are now referred to as** classics, were extremely expensive. 09) **The amount of** money 10) **required to buy** a book was almost 11) **equal to** a laborer's average 12) **weekly wages**. I'm sure you guys are wondering how a single novel could be that costly, and trust me; I had the same exact question before 13) **doing more research**. What I found was that the high cost of novels was mainly 14) **due to** what they 15) **called** "triple deckers." What this means is that a single book was published 16) **in three volumes**. 17) **For instance**, to read a novel by, 18) **let's say**, Arthur Conan Doyle, the author of 19) **a series of** novels that we 20)'**re all well aware of**, Sherlock Holmes, you'd 21) **have to buy** 22) **not just** one book, **but** three separate books to finish it. This system highly 23) **discouraged** British readers **from purchasing** novels. It was 24) **so ingrained in England that** publishers argued that it was not a good place to launch a profitable business selling books. Quite 25) **unfortunate for** the publishers, wasn't it? One example of this was the famous American novel, Moby Dick, which 26) **was sold for** only $1.50 in America, but was $7.80 when it was published in England. Yet, as you well know, this novel was still read by millions of people at the time. Considering the burdensome expense required to purchase a novel, how do you think that was possible? Well, that's what we will be 27) **looking at** today!

One of the mediums that people invented was the 28) **so-called** lending library. Lending libraries were a little different from today's libraries in that people had to 29) **pay an annual fee** to borrow books. Some people found this ridiculous, but considering the amount of money they had to pay to purchase a book, this was still a good deal. Anyway, of the many lending libraries, Mudie's was the largest national company and had branches in most major English cities at the time. The way that C.E. Mudie, the owner of the libraries, 30) **ran his business** was that he would buy hundreds or even 31) **thousands of copies** of books 32) **at once to** 33) **satisfy the needs** of both his readers and the publishing companies. Since he purchased novels 34) **in such large quantities**, publishers did not have to 35) **worry about** their novels not 36) **being sold to** the public. Also, it was 37) **beneficial for** his customers at the same time, because it now 38) **became possible for them to read** the novels more cheaply. I think Mudie's idea was brilliant 39) **not only** because of the benefits his libraries presented, **but also** because he was smart 40) **enough to** 41) **take advantage of** the "triple deckers." 42) **Think about** it, since one novel was published in three volumes, Mudie 43) **made** 44) **three times as much profit**.

Because of the huge purchases required to 45) **fulfill** his business **plan**, he 46) **exerted a great influence over** the publishers' novel selections. Umm… He was a very conservative man and had the power to decide which books he would purchase and 47) **put into** his libraries. So, the publishers avoided novels with content that he might find offensive. Funny, right? This one library owner could basically say "yes" or "no" to the publication of a novel. His power of selection was so great that he could 48) **turn** an amateur writer **into** a best-selling author. Some people might think this is not fair, you know, having the choice of book selection for thousands of people in his hands, but neither the publishers nor the public could do anything about his decisions. That's how influential he was at the time.

Okay. That should be enough about Mudie's. Now, let's 49) **move on** to the second method that readers employed to gain access to novels. Has anyone here 50) **heard of** the "serial publication form"? Well, for those who don't know what it is, it means that the novels 51) **were divided into** chapters, and each of them was published weekly, or monthly, in a magazine or a newspaper, typically 52) **in chronological order**. Like I mentioned earlier, since buying several volumes of books at once 53) **came as** a great burden for the readers, the serial publication form became an efficient 54) **way to ameliorate** the financial concerns they had.

Hmm… Remember how I mentioned that books were lengthy and expensive because they were divided into three separate volumes? Well, this serial publication 55) **caused** the authors of the 19th century **to write** even longer novels. Anybody know why? No? Well, you see, the writers 56) **got paid** by the number of episodes their novels were published in, so they 57) **tried to** 58) **make up** extra lines and episodes just to 59) **make more profit**. Later, when all the chapters were bound for official publication, the book was much longer than the author had originally intended. Wait… I digressed a little, didn't I? Where was I… Oh, that's right. We were talking about how serialization made 19th century literature more accessible to the public, right? Okay. Charles Dickens and his publisher 60) **came up with** a new version of the serial publication form. 61) **Instead of** 62) **filling up** a magazine or a newspaper with a lot of content 63) **other than** the chapters of the books themselves, they simplified it. All their magazines and books had were a couple of illustrations and advertisements 64) **along with** the chapters.

Despite serial publications' 65) **contributions to** British readers, its proponents sometimes faced 66) **criticism from the public**. Since the authors were only releasing sections of their books periodically, they 67) **needed their readers to** 68) **rush out** and buy the next month's installment to ensure consistent profits. To do this, the authors would write episodes with cliffhangers or suspenseful endings, you know… so the readers would want to know what was going to happen and rush out to buy the next episode. A lot of readers at the time hated this system. Not all authors made their profit this way, however. Charles Dickens, for instance, avoided cliffhangers and used a different approach to 69) **keep his readers coming back**. Instead of writing suspenseful endings, his installments would 70) **end with** a man 71) **walking down the street**, kind of like the… uh… cinematic effects used in movies. You know… someone just 72) **walking off** 73) **into the distance**. Because of these more settled endings, Dickens 74) **was praised by** the public and attracted readers who 75) **were opposed to** the over-dramatization of other authors.

The accessibility of novels

Listen to part of a lecture in an English literature class

P: Last class I asked you to research some of the popular English authors of the 19th century. As you may now know, 19th century England was marked by famous authors, such as Charles Dickens. Before starting our discussion about the authors, however, I would first like to discuss the accessibility of novels at the time… like, you know, how readers used to gain access to novels.

Let's first talk about what it was like to purchase novels during the 19th century. Novels of that time, which are now referred to as classics, were extremely expensive. The amount of money required to buy a book was almost equal to a laborer's average weekly wages. I'm sure you guys are wondering how a single novel could be that costly, and trust me; I had the same exact question before doing more research. What I found was that the high cost of novels was mainly due to what they called "triple deckers." What this means is that a single book was published in three volumes. For instance, to read a novel by, let's say, Arthur Conan Doyle, the author of a series of novels that we're all well aware of, Sherlock Holmes, you'd have to buy not just one book, but three separate books to finish it. This system highly discouraged British readers from purchasing novels. It was so ingrained in England that publishers argued that it was not a good place to launch a profitable business selling books. Quite unfortunate for the publishers, wasn't it? One example of this was the famous American novel, Moby Dick, which was sold for only $1.50 in America, but was $7.80 when it was published in England. Yet, as you well know, this novel was still read by millions of people at the time. Considering the burdensome expense required to purchase a novel, how do you think that was possible? Well, that's what we will be looking at today!

One of the mediums that people invented was the so-called lending library. Lending libraries were a little different from today's libraries in that people had to pay an annual fee to borrow books. Some people found this ridiculous, but considering the amount of money they had to pay to purchase a book, this was still a good deal. Anyway, of the many lending libraries, Mudie's was the largest national company and had branches in most major English cities at the time. The way that C.E. Mudie, the owner of the libraries, ran his business was that he would buy hundreds or even thousands of copies of books at once to satisfy the needs of both his readers and the publishing companies. Since he purchased novels in such large quantities, publishers did not have to worry about their novels not being sold to the public. Also, it was beneficial for his customers at the same time, because it now became possible for them to read the novels more cheaply. I think Mudie's idea was brilliant not only because of the benefits his libraries presented, but also because he was smart enough to take advantage of the "triple deckers." Think about it, since one novel was published in three volumes, Mudie made three times as much profit.

Because of the huge purchases required to fulfill his business plan, he exerted a great influence over the publishers' novel selections. Umm… He was a very conservative man and had the power to decide which books he would purchase and put into his libraries. So, the publishers avoided novels with content that he might find offensive. Funny, right? This one library owner could basically say "yes" or "no" to the publication of a novel. His power of selection was so great that he could turn an amateur writer into a best-selling author. Some people might think this is not fair, you know, having the choice of book selection for thousands of people in his hands, but neither the publishers nor the public could do anything about his decisions. That's how influential he was at the time.

Okay. That should be enough about Mudie's. Now, let's move on to the second method that readers employed to gain access to novels. Has anyone here heard of the "serial publication form"? Well, for those who don't know what it is, it means that the novels were divided into chapters, and each of them was published weekly, or monthly, in a magazine or a newspaper, typically in chronological order. Like I mentioned earlier, since buying several volumes of books at once came as a great burden for the readers, the serial publication form became an efficient way to ameliorate the financial concerns they had.

Hmm… Remember how I mentioned that books were lengthy and expensive because they were divided into three separate volumes? Well, this serial publication caused the authors of the 19th century to write even longer novels. Anybody know why? No? Well, you see, the writers got paid by the number of episodes their novels were published in, so they tried to make up extra lines and episodes just to make more profit. Later, when all the chapters were bound for official publication, the book was much longer than the author had originally intended. Wait… I digressed a little, didn't I? Where was I… Oh, that's right. We were talking about how serialization made 19th century literature more accessible to the public, right? Okay. Charles Dickens and his publisher came up with a new version of the serial publication form. Instead of filling up a magazine or a newspaper with a lot of content other than the chapters of the books themselves, they simplified it. All their magazines and books had were a couple of illustrations and advertisements along with the chapters.

Despite serial publications' contributions to British readers, its proponents sometimes faced criticism from the public. Since the authors were only releasing sections of their books periodically, they needed their readers to rush out and buy the next month's installment to ensure consistent profits. To do this, the authors would write episodes with cliffhangers or suspenseful endings, you know… so the readers would want to know what was going to happen and rush out to buy the next episode. A lot of readers at the time hated this system. Not all authors made their profit this way, however. Charles Dickens, for instance, avoided cliffhangers and used a different approach to keep his readers coming back. Instead of writing suspenseful endings, his installments would end with a man walking down the street, kind of like the… uh… cinematic effects used in movies. You know… someone just walking off into the distance. Because of these more settled endings, Dickens was praised by the public and attracted readers who were opposed to the over-dramatization of other authors.

Predation risk effects

Listen to part of a lecture in an ecology class

P: Okay. Let's [01] **start from** where we [02] **left off** last time. We were [03] **talking about** the interactions of predators and prey and their relative [04] **effects on** [05] **each other**, right? You know…the survival methods that wild animals, um… prey specifically, [06] **employ to avoid** natural predators. Like I said last time, [07] **except for** [08] **apex predators**, [09] **such as** tigers and lions, most wild animals have natural predators. Since we didn't have [10] **enough** time **to go through** all of them, I briefly told you about the survival methods of gazelles and wolves. Today, we' [11] **re going to** [12] **bring** a third player **into** the game. The ecosystem! This term [13] **refers to** the areas in which wild organisms live and [14] **interact with** [15] **one another**. [16] **In a sense**, these ecosystems, which are [17] **analogous to** the communities in which we live, [18] **play a very significant role in** the study of ecology.

Okay… Now we're [19] **looking at** [20] **both predators and prey**, and their interactions with the ecosystems they occupy. With this integrative [21] **branch of** ecology, it's very important to discuss the effects of predation. [22] **As opposed to** what many of you are thinking, you know, that animals' predatory nature only affects them [23] **in terms of** their populations and such; it also plays a vital role in shaping biodiversity in the ecosystem. Okay, you guys [24] **are all aware of** the food chain, right? How an herbivore, or "vegan animal", eats plants, and a carnivore, or meat eating animal, then [25] **preys on** the herbivore. This chain [26] **is an** essential **key to sustaining** the healthy balance between populations of organisms in an ecosystem. When the principle is disturbed or changed, [27] **changes in** animal behavior [28] **commensurate with** the changes in the ecosystem. [29] **For instance**, when a species of animals [30] **lives in** an environment that does not have a population of natural predators, the most naturally occurring phenomenon is that they [31] **cease to employ** their survival mechanisms, such as [32] **looking around** to remain alert for the sudden appearance of predators. Yes, John?

S: Because they [33] **no longer** [34] **live with** the pressure from their predators' threats, right?

P: Exactly. Let's turn that around and [35] **try to imagine** what would happen if predators [36] **were** suddenly **introduced to** the environment. The carefree existence would be immediately terminated, right? Since the prey [37] **is not prepared to use**, or has not used their [38] **defense mechanisms** [39] **for a long time**, [40] **it is most likely that** they will be eaten by the predators [41] **as soon as** they are introduced. I mean, that is the impact of predation that we usually [42] **think of**. However, some animals will survive by [43] **forcing themselves to modify** their original behaviors or adapt new ones to lower their risk of predation. These changes in behavior occur [44] **due to** the increased risk of predation and are [45] **called** "predation risk effects." Umm… These risk effects also [46] **exert** major **influences on** the ecosystem.

S: Hmm.… Professor, I get the concept of predation risk effects but… I'm [47] **having** a **hard time visualizing** how these risk effects could affect the ecosystem… Is there a real world example that you could maybe tell us about?

P: [48] **Of course!** I [49] **m sure** many of you [50] **went on the school trip** to Yellowstone National Park last year. Well, for [51] **those of** you who didn't get a [52] **chance to visit**, umm… Yellowstone National Park was established by Congress in 1872. Its primary purpose was to protect [53] **not only the landscape, but also the wildlife** that inhabited the region. [54] **In the beginning**, however, the protection [55] **was only limited to** specific types of animals. [56] **For example**, carnivores were not protected [57] **at the time** and, [58] **with the exception of** bears, were continually hunted [59] **over the course of** the next few decades. [60] **As a result of** this peculiar regulation imposed by the government, wolves, coyotes, large cats, and other carnivores could be freely hunted. [61] **Not surprisingly**, by 1926, the wolves in the park had been [62] **wiped out** completely. So, what do you think happened in the park as a result of the disappearance?

S: Well, I guess, since the threat of wolves was no longer present, the animal that wolves [63] **preyed upon** thrived and their populations increased?

P: You're right! [64] **In this case**, elk, a type of large deer, were one of the animals that wolves preyed on most, so without the threat of the wolves, their range of activity increased dramatically. [65] **In addition to** that, something else increased in volume [66] **as well**… Anybody [67] **want to** [68] **take a guess**?

S: Well… Elk are herbivores, so they [69] **feed on** plants, right? As you mentioned previously, they most likely [70] **started living and roaming** [71] **without fear**. I'm guessing their range of food also expanded [72] **along with** their range of activity.

P: [73] **You got it!** Unfortunately, seedlings of aspens were the elk's main food source and they devoured them all around the park, including areas where elk had never been present before because of the presence of the wolves. This meant that the seedlings never got the chance to [74] **mature into** trees.

S: Trees… Correct me if I'm wrong, professor, but doesn't the [75] **decrease in** [76] **the number of** trees also mean that birds and other species that [77] **rely upon** them [78] **as a means of** survival were also negatively affected?

P: Great point! Yes, various species, such as birds, lost their habitats as a result of this phenomenon, and a large portion of the region's biodiversity decreased dramatically. Researchers realized that their mission to protect the wild life in the park [79] **was at risk of failing**. I mean, it didn't accomplish anything that it initially promised, right? To [80] **solve this problem**, they reintroduced wolves into the park in 1995. Their idea was not very complex; since the whole dilemma [81] **started with** the disappearance of wolves, they simply [82] **wished to reverse** the process.

S: And how exactly did that affect the elk's behavior?

P: Well, think about it. The main reason for the [83] **increase in** the elk population was the disappearance of the wolves, right? [84] **Now that** the wolves were no longer [85] **absent from** the park, the balance in the [86] **food chain** was re-established. Due to this, the elk [87] **needed to make** behavioral changes to minimize their risk of predation. For example, they became more nimble and attentive, and their activity range [88] **was once again restricted to** areas where they could easily spot wolves [89] **from a distance**. These forcibly [90] **imposed restrictions on** the elk's range of movement no longer [91] **allowed them to hinder** the maturation of the seedlings. Everything [92] **returned to** the way it was, and the once-lost biodiversity was restored.

Predation risk effects

Listen to part of a lecture in an ecology class

P: Okay. Let's start from where we left off last time. We were talking about the interactions of predators and prey and their relative effects on each other, right? You know…the survival methods that wild animals, um… prey specifically, employ to avoid natural predators. Like I said last time, except for apex predators, such as tigers and lions, most wild animals have natural predators. Since we didn't have enough time to go through all of them, I briefly told you about the survival methods of gazelles and wolves. Today, we're going to bring a third player into the game. The ecosystem! This term refers to the areas in which wild organisms live and interact with one another. In a sense, these ecosystems, which are analogous to the communities in which we live, play a very significant role in the study of ecology.

Okay… Now we're looking at both predators and prey, and their interactions with the ecosystems they occupy. With this integrative branch of ecology, it's very important to discuss the effects of predation. As opposed to what many of you are thinking, you know, that animals' predatory nature only affects them in terms of their populations and such; it also plays a vital role in shaping biodiversity in the ecosystem. Okay, you guys are all aware of the food chain, right? How an herbivore, or "vegan animal", eats plants, and a carnivore, or meat eating animal, then preys on the herbivore. This chain is an essential key to sustaining the healthy balance between populations of organisms in an ecosystem. When the principle is disturbed or changed, changes in animal behavior commensurate with the changes in the ecosystem. For instance, when a species of animals lives in an environment that does not have a population of natural predators, the most naturally occurring phenomenon is that they cease to employ their survival mechanisms, such as looking around to remain alert for the sudden appearance of predators. Yes, John?

S: Because they no longer live with the pressure from their predators' threats, right?

P: Exactly. Let's turn that around and try to imagine what would happen if predators were suddenly introduced to the environment. The carefree existence would be immediately terminated, right? Since the prey is not prepared to use, or has not used their defense mechanisms for a long time, it is most likely that they will be eaten by the predators as soon as they are introduced. I mean, that is the impact of predation that we usually think of. However, some animals will survive by forcing themselves to modify their original behaviors or adapt new ones to lower their risk of predation. These changes in behavior occur due to the increased risk of predation and are called "predation risk effects." Umm… These risk effects also exert major influences on the ecosystem.

S: Hmm…. Professor, I get the concept of predation risk effects but… I'm having a hard time visualizing how these risk effects could affect the ecosystem… Is there a real world example that you could maybe tell us about?

P: Of course! I'm sure many of you went on the school trip to Yellowstone National Park last year. Well, for those of you who didn't get a chance to visit, umm… Yellowstone National Park was established by Congress in 1872. Its primary purpose was to protect not only the landscape, but also the wildlife that inhabited the region. In the beginning, however, the protection was only limited to specific types of animals. For example, carnivores were not protected at the time and, with the exception of bears, were continually hunted over the course of the next few decades. As a result of this peculiar regulation imposed by the government, wolves, coyotes, large cats, and other carnivores could be freely hunted. Not surprisingly, by 1926, the wolves in the park had been wiped out completely. So, what do you think happened in the park as a result of the disappearance?

S: Well, I guess, since the threat of wolves was no longer present, the animal that wolves preyed upon thrived and their populations increased?

P: You're right! In this case, elk, a type of large deer, were one of the animals that wolves preyed on most, so without the threat of the wolves, their range of activity increased dramatically. In addition to that, something else increased in volume as well… Anybody want to take a guess?

S: Well… Elk are herbivores, so they feed on plants, right? As you mentioned previously, they most likely started living and roaming without fear. I'm guessing their range of food also expanded along with their range of activity?

P: You got it! Unfortunately, seedlings of aspens were the elk's main food source and they devoured them all around the park, including areas where elk had never been present before because of the presence of the wolves. This meant that the seedlings never got the chance to mature into trees.

S: Trees… Correct me if I'm wrong, professor, but doesn't the decrease in the number of trees also mean that birds and other species that rely upon them as a means of survival were also negatively affected?

P: Great point! Yes, various species, such as birds, lost their habitats as a result of this phenomenon, and a large portion of the region's biodiversity decreased dramatically. Researchers realized that their mission to protect the wild life in the park was at risk of failing. I mean, it didn't accomplish anything that it initially promised, right? To solve this problem, they reintroduced wolves into the park in 1995. Their idea was not very complex; since the whole dilemma started with the disappearance of wolves, they simply wished to reverse the process.

S: And how exactly did that affect the elk's behavior?

P: Well, think about it. The main reason for the increase in the elk population was the disappearance of the wolves, right? Now that the wolves were no longer absent from the park, the balance in the food chain was re-established. Due to this, the elk needed to make behavioral changes to minimize their risk of predation. For example, they became more nimble and attentive, and their activity range was once again restricted to areas where they could easily spot wolves from a distance. These forcibly imposed restrictions on the elk's range of movement no longer allowed them to hinder the maturation of the seedlings. Everything returned to the way it was, and the once-lost biodiversity was restored.

Housing department

Listen to a conversation between a student and an administrator in the housing department

A: Oh, hey, John! 01) **Long time no see**!

S: Hi, Ms. Brigida, I hope all has been well with you.

A: Thank you! So 02) **what brought you** all the way **here**? 03) **Aren't you supposed to** be 04) **spending time** at the beach?

S: Well, do you remember last semester when I 05) **talked** to you **about** donating the stuff that I couldn't 06) **take home with me**?

A: 07) **Of course** I remember, it was such a generous gesture.

S: Thanks. But I left **so** abruptly 08) **that** I had to just leave all my stuff in a box 09) **in front of** my dorm room door.

A: Ah, yes… If I remember correctly, the person who 10) **took summer courses** after you left used your things. Oh yes, and he wrote a 'thank you' letter 11) **for me to give** to you. 12) **Here it is**!

S: Oh, wow, I did not expect that. It sure 13) **makes me feel great**! I just thought that all my stuff 14) **had been** 15) **thrown out**. Anyway, I've come to formalize what I 16) **wanted to do** before the 17) **summer break**.

A: You're talking about your donation, right?

S: Yes, I'm sure 18) **a lot of** students experience the same problem that I had… 19) **leaving their stuff in** their dorms or simply throwing it out just because it's 20) **too** heavy **to** 21) **carry with** them on the plane. I'm sure a lot of it is still very useful, 22) **you know**, like clothes, books, and dishes.

A: I know exactly where you're 23) **coming from**. So, what can I do to help you?

S: Well, I've contacted several 24) **charity organizations**, and one of them 25) **is willing to schedule** pick-ups after 26) **every semester**. They have stores where they sell the donated stuff, and all of their profits 27) **are used to help** children in Africa.

A: Excellent! And… you 28) **need me to talk** to the administration about your idea, correct?

S: Yes! It would be great if you could help me with that…

A: Hmm…well, 29) **let's see**. I have a meeting this Saturday with some of the managers from university housing. I'm pretty sure they will 30) **agree with** you **on** this.

S: You 31) **think so**?

A: Yes, and I don't think there's any complicated procedure we need to 32) **follow** or any specific request process we 33) **have to** 34) **go through**.

S: Mhmm… I see. Now, what I need is to 35) **spread the word** about it before the semester ends. I was thinking maybe we could 36) **put** flyers and notices **on** the 37) **bulletin board** in the student center.

A: That 38) **sounds like** a great idea, but I think the fastest way would be to 39) **put** an advertisement **in** the university **newspaper**. You know, 40) **almost all** of the students read the paper, so word should spread quickly 41) **that way**.

S: That sure 42) **seems like** a great idea. I really hope this 43) **works out**!

A: I'm sure it will! Just leave your name and number here, and I'll contact you 44) **as soon as** I 45) **get the administration's permission**.

S: Thank you so much, Ms. Brigida!

Housing department

Listen to a conversation between a student and an administrator in the housing department

A: Oh, hey, John! Long time no see!

S: Hi, Ms. Brigida, I hope all has been well with you.

A: Thank you! So what brought you all the way here? Aren't you supposed to be spending time at the beach?

S: Well, do you remember last semester when I talked to you about donating the stuff that I couldn't take home with me?

A: Of course I remember, it was such a generous gesture.

S: Thanks. But I left so abruptly that I had to just leave all my stuff in a box in front of my dorm room door.

A: Ah, yes… If I remember correctly, the person who took summer courses after you left used your things. Oh yes, and he wrote a 'thank you' letter for me to give to you. Here it is!

S: Oh, wow, I did not expect that. It sure makes me feel great! I just thought that all my stuff had been thrown out. Anyway, I've come to formalize what I wanted to do before the summer break.

A: You're talking about your donation, right?

S: Yes, I'm sure a lot of students experience the same problem that I had… leaving their stuff in their dorms or simply throwing it out just because it's too heavy to carry with them on the plane. I'm sure a lot of it is still very useful, you know, like clothes, books, and dishes.

A: I know exactly where you're coming from. So, what can I do to help you?

S: Well, I've contacted several charity organizations, and one of them is willing to schedule pick-ups after every semester. They have stores where they sell the donated stuff, and all of their profits are used to help children in Africa.

A: Excellent! And… you need me to talk to the administration about your idea, correct?

S: Yes! It would be great if you could help me with that…

A: Hmm…well, let's see. I have a meeting this Saturday with some of the managers from university housing. I'm pretty sure they will agree with you on this.

S: You think so?

A: Yes, and I don't think there's any complicated procedure we need to follow or any specific request process we have to go through.

S: Mhmm… I see. Now, what I need is to spread the word about it before the semester ends. I was thinking maybe we could put flyers and notices on the bulletin board in the student center.

A: That sounds like a great idea, but I think the fastest way would be to put an advertisement in the university newspaper. You know, almost all of the students read the paper, so word should spread quickly that way.

S: That sure seems like a great idea. I really hope this works out!

A: I'm sure it will! Just leave your name and number here, and I'll contact you as soon as I get the administration's permission.

S: Thank you so much, Ms. Brigida!

Insight

Listen to part of a lecture in a psychology class

P: I can definitely see that 01) **almost all** of you are 02) **struggling with** the final 03) **term paper** that I assigned 04) **last week**… Well, when I was a college student, I 05) **confronted** similar adversities 06) **on a daily basis**, so I know how you must feel 07) **right now**. Frustrated, right? We all approach problems 08) **in a similar way**. After 09) **spending hours and hours tenaciously** 10) **trying to** 11) **come up with** a solution that just seems unreachable, what do you do? Well… One of the things you may do is 12) **step back** and 13) **take a break**, right? Maybe you go on your computer to 14) **socialize with** your friends or 15) **walk your dog** in the park… anything that 16) **keeps your mind off** of the problem. Then, a sudden 17) **light bulb goes on** and you finally grasp the solution that seemed 18) **out of reach** before. I'19) **m sure** all of you have experienced this phenomenon, which psychologists and researchers call "insight." Today, why don't we 20) **put aside** the assignments you're 21) **struggling with** and 22) **look at** how insight works instead?

Who 23) **pops up** into your head when 24) **thinking of** the world's most renowned physicist? Isaac Newton! Yes, he was a prestigious mathematician and physicist in the 1600's, and his work 25) **hundreds of years ago** has impacted and shaped many aspects of today's world. Uh… you guys 26) **are all aware of** the famous apple story, right? When Newton 27) **got stuck** trying to 28) **figure out** what 29) **keeps the moon in its orbit**, he 30) **reached a point** where he 31) **had to** 32) **withdraw from** the problem, and 33) **decided to** 34) **take a stroll** in a garden. While he was enjoying the view 35) **and such**, he saw an apple 36) **fall to the ground from a tree**. Seeing that, he 37) **was able to conclude** that the force that 38) **caused the apple to fall** to the ground, what we now call gravity, was the same force that 39) **kept the moon from** 40) **flying out of its orbit**. He didn't 41) **put any practical effort into solving the problem**. He simply looked at the apple 42) **falling to the ground**. Yet, his insight 43) **helped him establish** the fundamental governing rule of gravity and 44) **apply it to the moon**. So, you might be 45) **wondering about** exactly how insight works 46) **at this point**. Well, after 47) **a great deal of** scientific research by neuroscientists, they have successfully analyzed the phenomenon.

One of the **experiments** they 48) **carried out** analyzed brain activity that occurs when the insight phenomenon 49) **takes place**. All subjects, uh, the people who 50) **participated in** the experiment, 51) **were tasked with** solving 52) **a set of** word puzzles. While monitoring their brain activity, neuroscientists detected two unusual patterns.

The first unusual brain activity was detected in the frontal lobe area. Um… 53) **Try touching** your forehead. Yes, that's where the frontal lobe is located, the front part of your brain. It's the decision-making base, so when you plan things, decide which **actions** to 54) **take**, and initiate actions 55) **based on** logic and reason, your frontal lobe 56) **comes into play**. Anyway, when the subjects were doing the puzzles, this part of the brain was activated-which the scientists call the "preparatory phase"-and other sensory areas were 57) **shut down**. I mean, their brains were fully functional, but the senses that detect external stimuli, 58) **such as** the visual and auditory cortexes, were somehow slowed. As you may remember from our last class, the visual cortex is located in the occipital lobe, and the auditory cortex is in the temporal lobe. They, 59) **of course,** 60) **play vital roles** just like the frontal lobe, because they 61) **enable us to hear and see**, but when a person focuses, 62) **it seems that** the frontal lobe dominates the other two and 63) **switches them off** even though they are located in different parts of the brain. Well, I'd 64) **love to further explain** how that's possible, but since we don't have 65) **enough time to cover** that, let's 66) **stay on** topic. Anyway, it's quite logical that the two senses are shut down if you think about it… the sensory areas, the visual and auditory cortexes, were momentarily shut down or blocked because they could 67) **distract the brain from** 68) **focusing on** 69) **the task at hand**.

Okay. Now, the second unusual brain activity was found in the 70) **so-called** "search phase," which involves the part of the brain that controls the speech and language functions. Well, this also 71) **came as** no surprise to the scientists because if one was solving a word puzzle, then of course, the brain parts 72) **devoted to** "words" would be activated. What was significant and unusual about this phase happened about a few hundred milliseconds before the speech-language-production part of the brain was activated. The brain generated what we now 73) **know as**, "gamma rhythm" or "gamma waves." Although there is no consensus among neuroscientists on why gamma waves are generated, the most accepted theory states that the production of such waves is caused by the formation of new links between cells that are 74) **far from** 75) **one another**. So, imagine, uh… a telephone network. You know how all telephones 76) **are connected to** each other through a network line, so 77) **no matter where** you are you can contact people, 78) **as long as** you're within the network. Well, these so-called "gamma waves" 79) **sort of** 80) **work the same way**. What's intriguing about the waves is that they are only activated after someone experiences the same situation as yours. You know, try to 81) **solve a problem**, miserably 82) **fail at** it, and the brain just 83) **gives up** and goes into that dormant stage of "relaxing." Well, 84) **according to** the researchers, gamma waves 85) **are supposed to** 86) **help you obtain** that 'light bulb' moment because a relaxed brain, after 87) **failing to produce** a solution, produces gamma waves. These waves enable the building of networks between remote cells in a relaxed brain more successfully than in a frustrated brain like yours. Remember, 88) **the more** networks there are between the cells, **the faster** your brain can 89) **find a solution**.

Okay… As I mentioned earlier, I understand that the assignment is definitely not an easy one. Here's my advice for you. If you 90) **are stuck** 91) **at some point**, take a step back and just relax your frustrated brain. 92) **Go out**, take a stroll, and 93) **enjoy the views** of nature right 94) **in front of** you. Who knows? You might have one of those 'Isaac Newton' moments.

Insight

Listen to part of a lecture in a psychology class

P: I can definitely see that almost all of you are struggling with the final term paper that I assigned last week… Well, when I was a college student, I confronted similar adversities on a daily basis, so I know how you must feel right now. Frustrated, right? We all approach problems in a similar way. After spending hours and hours tenaciously trying to come up with a solution that just seems unreachable, what do you do? Well… One of the things you may do is step back and take a break, right? Maybe you go on your computer to socialize with your friends or walk your dog in the park… anything that keeps your mind off of the problem. Then, a sudden light bulb goes on and you finally grasp the solution that seemed out of reach before. I'm sure all of you have experienced this phenomenon, which psychologists and researchers call "insight." Today, why don't we put aside the assignments you're struggling with and look at how insight works instead?

Who pops up into your head when thinking of the world's most renowned physicist? Isaac Newton! Yes, he was a prestigious mathematician and physicist in the 1600's, and his work hundreds of years ago has impacted and shaped many aspects of today's world. Uh… you guys are all aware of the famous apple story, right? When Newton got stuck trying to figure out what keeps the moon in its orbit, he reached a point where he had to withdraw from the problem, and decided to take a stroll in a garden. While he was enjoying the view and such, he saw an apple fall to the ground from a tree. Seeing that, he was able to conclude that the force that caused the apple to fall to the ground, what we now call gravity, was the same force that kept the moon from flying out of its orbit. He didn't put any practical effort into solving the problem. He simply looked at the apple falling to the ground. Yet, his insight helped him establish the fundamental governing rule of gravity and apply it to the moon. So, you might be wondering about exactly how insight works at this point. Well, after a great deal of scientific research by neuroscientists, they have successfully analyzed the phenomenon.

One of the experiments they carried out analyzed brain activity that occurs when the insight phenomenon takes place. All subjects, uh, the people who participated in the experiment, were tasked with solving a set of word puzzles. While monitoring their brain activity, neuroscientists detected two unusual patterns.

The first unusual brain activity was detected in the frontal lobe area. Um… Try touching your forehead. Yes, that's where the frontal lobe is located, the front part of your brain. It's the decision-making base, so when you plan things, decide which actions to take, and initiate actions based on logic and reason, your frontal lobe comes into play. Anyway, when the subjects were doing the puzzles, this part of the brain was activated-which the scientists call the "preparatory phase"-and other sensory areas were shut down. I mean, their brains were fully functional, but the senses that detect external stimuli, such as the visual and auditory cortexes, were somehow slowed. As you may remember from our last class, the visual cortex is located in the occipital lobe, and the auditory cortex is in the temporal lobe. They, of course, play vital roles just like the frontal lobe, because they enable us to hear and see, but when a person focuses, it seems that the frontal lobe dominates the other two and switches them off even though they are located in different parts of the brain. Well, I'd love to further explain how that's possible, but since we don't have enough time to cover that, let's stay on topic. Anyway, it's quite logical that the two senses are shut down if you think about it… the sensory areas, the visual and auditory cortexes, were momentarily shut down or blocked because they could distract the brain from focusing on the task at hand.

Okay. Now, the second unusual brain activity was found in the so-called "search phase," which involves the part of the brain that controls the speech and language functions. Well, this also came as no surprise to the scientists because if one was solving a word puzzle, then of course, the brain parts devoted to "words" would be activated. What was significant and unusual about this phase happened about a few hundred milliseconds before the speech-language-production part of the brain was activated. The brain generated what we now know as, "gamma rhythm" or "gamma waves." Although there is no consensus among neuroscientists on why gamma waves are generated, the most accepted theory states that the production of such waves is caused by the formation of new links between cells that are far from one another. So, imagine, uh… a telephone network. You know how all telephones are connected to each other through a network line, so no matter where you are you can contact people, as long as you're within the network. Well, these so-called "gamma waves" sort of work the same way. What's intriguing about the waves is that they are only activated after someone experiences the same situation as yours. You know, try to solve a problem, miserably fail at it, and the brain just gives up and goes into that dormant stage of "relaxing." Well, according to the researchers, gamma waves are supposed to help you obtain that 'light bulb' moment because a relaxed brain, after failing to produce a solution, produces gamma waves. These waves enable the building of networks between remote cells in a relaxed brain more successfully than in a frustrated brain like yours. Remember, the more networks there are between the cells, the faster your brain can find a solution.

Okay… As I mentioned earlier, I understand that the assignment is definitely not an easy one. Here's my advice for you. If you are stuck at some point, take a step back and just relax your frustrated brain. Go out, take a stroll, and enjoy the views of nature right in front of you. Who knows? You might have one of those 'Isaac Newton' moments.

Shift from a nomadic lifestyle to sedentary settlements

Listen to part of a lecture in an Archaeology class

P: Last class we discussed the different types of social changes ancient people 01) **went through**. Well, today, we'll be narrowing that topic 02) **a bit** and 03) **looking at** one major social change that occurred centuries ago. Do you guys remember that one of the most significant changes 04) **in human history** was the 05) **shift from** a nomadic lifestyle **to** sedentary, year-round settlements?

S: Yes, and you also briefly mentioned some kind of cause that initiated the lifestyle change, right?

P: Good point! Researchers now believe that 06) **changes in** climate conditions ultimately triggered the lifestyle shift. When the glaciers from the last ice age 07) **receded to** the polar regions, a drastic climate change occurred 08) **across the globe** that 09) **enabled people to settle** in one region and 10) **cultivate crops** 11) **instead of** wandering 12) **from place to place**. 13) **There were** 14) **a number of** similar cases of lifestyle shifts around the world 15) **at about the same time**, but I think we should 16) **focus on** the most exemplary and studied case, which is the coastal plains of the eastern Mediterranean region, around present day Lebanon.

P: 17) **As you may know**, the eastern Mediterranean region is pretty much infertile and not 18) **suitable for** human habitation 19) **at this time**, but about 18,000 years ago, the region was open grasslands and woods. Such conditions 20) **were very likely to provide** 21) **a great deal of** convenience to hunter-gatherer groups whose survival heavily 22) **depended on** 23) **the amount of** food they hunted. Undoubtedly, the region was hugely 24) **attractive to** hunters. 25) **On top of** that, about 5,000 years after 26) **the advent of** their settlements in the region, another climate change occurred that 27) **resulted in** increased rainfall. What does that 28) **equal to**? Yes… An increased amount of precipitation equals richer and more fertile soil and ecosystems! Well, to verify everything I've just said, we need more than just statistical data concerning changes in precipitation and climate, right? Then… What kind of physical evidence should we 29) **be able to** find to 30) **support the claim** that sedentary settlements existed in the region?

S: That's pretty simple. If the hunters settled and lived there, they 31) **must have built** houses, right? So, evidence of houses 32) **must've been found**.

P: You got it! Architectural remains found in the region 33) **played a vital role in** 34) **helping researchers confirm** the existence of year-round settlements in the region. Most of the remains found in this area were from a people 35) **known as** the Natufians, who were the first group of people to inhabit and root their settlements in the eastern Mediterranean area.

P: 36) **Taking the Natufian housing structures into account**, we can observe that their houses were all uniform… Every house looked nearly 37) **identical to** every other one. They all had a rigid structure and were 38) **arranged in a semicircle**. The 39) **upper parts of** the houses 40) **were made of** brush and wood, while the lower parts 41) **were lined with** stones. The interesting thing is that these houses were partially dug into the ground. I mean, that is just brilliant! These people, thousands of years ago, were bright 42) **enough to** 43) **come up with** 44) **a way to construct** houses that could withstand occasional harsh weather 45) **and whatnot**… Also, um, the floors of the excavated houses had small circular holes in them, which indicates that they 46) **used posts and beams to support** the roofs. Why do you think this would be considered evidence of a sedentary lifestyle?

S: I'm a little confused… It can'47) **t** be evidence **at all**, can it? I mean, just because they had houses doesn't mean they couldn't 48) **move to** other places.

P: 49) **You have a point, but** you're missing 50) **something very important**. Anybody else 51) **want to** 52) **take a guess** before I 53) **give away** the answer?

S2: I was thinking that the houses 54) **seem to be** quite intricate 55) **in many ways**, and since the people 56) **put so much effort into** building them, they wouldn't just 57) **leave their houses behind** and build new ones 58) **on a seasonal basis**.

P: 59) **That's my point**! Why would they go through all the trouble of digging holes and such if they 60) **were just going to leave** the next season?

P: 61) **Along with** these architectural remains, researchers were able to find another type of valuable evidence – the tools they 62) **used to harvest** grains and 63) **large quantities of** stone mortars. 64) **As I previously stated**, the region that the Natufians inhabited had vast areas of rich soil, and wild cereal grains were abundant. What we can see from this is that the Natufians 65) **took advantage of** the environment and mainly harvested wheat and oats which they ground in their stone mortars.

S: Oh, I 66) **remember reading** something about that. They also used to plant grains, right?

P: That's exactly what I was thinking, because normally you'd expect 67) **that of** sedentary people. But, ironically enough, no evidence to support that assumption 68) **has yet to be found**. I mean, the tools used to harvest grains have been found, but no tools for planting grains have been discovered yet. Further, researchers think that the chances of them being found are pretty slim. They do, however, believe that the unintentional planting of seeds and grains 69) **might have taken place** 70) **during this time**, which, 71) **according to** them, is the only explanation for their continual 72) **reliance on** grains as a food source. This unintentional planting 73) **could have taken** place when seeds were spread by the wind and sprouted in other areas. So, you can say that the Natufians didn't actually do any planting work, but rather, nature did it for them.

P: 74) **Speaking of** their food sources, there is also evidence that indicates that they hunted animals. Bones of migratory birds and young gazelles found in the area indicate that the Natufians hunted those types of animals. Migratory birds often 75) **flew to** the area during the winter and young gazelles probably 76) **showed up** there around spring or summer. Now, do you see what I'm 77) **trying to say**? I mean, during the winter, migratory birds were hunted, and during spring or summer, young gazelles were hunted.

S2: Winter, summer, and spring… Mhmmm! This indicates that the hunting process 78) **took place** 79) **year around**, which means that the Natufians inhabited the region year around as well!

P: You've got it! That's exactly what happened. All of these great pieces of evidence 80) **point to** one logical conclusion: the Natufians built permanent settlements in the eastern Mediterranean region!

Shift from a nomadic lifestyle to sedentary settlements

Listen to part of a lecture in an Archaeology class

P: Last class we discussed the different types of social changes ancient people went through. Well, today, we'll be narrowing that topic a bit and looking at one major social change that occurred centuries ago. Do you guys remember that one of the most significant changes in human history was the shift from a nomadic lifestyle to sedentary, year-round settlements?

S: Yes, and you also briefly mentioned some kind of cause that initiated the lifestyle change, right?

P: Good point! Researchers now believe that changes in climate conditions ultimately triggered the lifestyle shift. When the glaciers from the last ice age receded to the polar regions, a drastic climate change occurred across the globe that enabled people to settle in one region and cultivate crops instead of wandering from place to place. There were a number of similar cases of lifestyle shifts around the world at about the same time, but I think we should focus on the most exemplary and studied case, which is the coastal plains of the eastern Mediterranean region, around present day Lebanon.

As you may know, the eastern Mediterranean region is pretty much infertile and not suitable for human habitation at this time, but about 18,000 years ago, the region was open grasslands and woods. Such conditions were very likely to provide a great deal of convenience to hunter-gatherer groups whose survival heavily depended on the amount of food they hunted. Undoubtedly, the region was hugely attractive to hunters. On top of that, about 5,000 years after the advent of their settlements in the region, another climate change occurred that resulted in increased rainfall. What does that equal to? Yes… An increased amount of precipitation equals richer and more fertile soil and ecosystems! Well, to verify everything I've just said, we need more than just statistical data concerning changes in precipitation and climate, right? Then… What kind of physical evidence should we be able to find to support the claim that sedentary settlements existed in the region?

S: That's pretty simple. If the hunters settled and lived there, they must have built houses, right? So, evidence of houses must've been found.

P: You got it! Architectural remains found in the region played a vital role in helping researchers confirm the existence of year-round settlements in the region. Most of the remains found in this area were from a people known as the Natufians, who were the first group of people to inhabit and root their settlements in the eastern Mediterranean area.

Taking the Natufian housing structures into account, we can observe that their houses were all uniform… Every house looked nearly identical to every other one. They all had a rigid structure and were arranged in a semicircle. The upper parts of the houses were made of brush and wood, while the lower parts were lined with stones. The interesting thing is that these houses were partially dug into the ground. I mean, that is just brilliant! These people, thousands of years ago, were bright enough to come up with a way to construct houses that could withstand occasional harsh weather and whatnot… Also, um, the floors of the excavated houses had small circular holes in them, which indicates that they used posts and beams to support the roofs. Why do you think this would be considered evidence of a sedentary lifestyle?

S: I'm a little confused… It can't be evidence at all, can it? I mean, just because they had houses doesn't mean they couldn't move to other places.

P: You have a point, but you're missing something very important. Anybody else want to take a guess before I give away the answer?

S2: I was thinking that the houses seem to be quite intricate in many ways, and since the people put so much effort into building them, they wouldn't just leave their houses behind and build new ones on a seasonal basis.

P: That's my point! Why would they go through all the trouble of digging holes and such if they were just going to leave the next season?

Along with these architectural remains, researchers were able to find another type of valuable evidence – the tools they used to harvest grains and large quantities of stone mortars. As I previously stated, the region that the Natufians inhabited had vast areas of rich soil, and wild cereal grains were abundant. What we can see from this is that the Natufians took advantage of the environment and mainly harvested wheat and oats which they ground in their stone mortars.

S: Oh, I remember reading something about that. They also used to plant grains, right?

P: That's exactly what I was thinking, because normally you'd expect that of sedentary people. But, ironically enough, no evidence to support that assumption has yet to be found. I mean, the tools used to harvest grains have been found, but no tools for planting grains have been discovered yet. Further, researchers think that the chances of them being found are pretty slim. They do, however, believe that the unintentional planting of seeds and grains might have taken place during this time, which, according to them, is the only explanation for their continual reliance on grains as a food source. This unintentional planting could have taken place when seeds were spread by the wind and sprouted in other areas. So, you can say that the Natufians didn't actually do any planting work, but rather, nature did it for them.

Speaking of their food sources, there is also evidence that indicates that they hunted animals. Bones of migratory birds and young gazelles found in the area indicate that the Natufians hunted those types of animals. Migratory birds often flew to the area during the winter and young gazelles probably showed up there around spring or summer. Now, do you see what I'm trying to say? I mean, during the winter, migratory birds were hunted, and during spring or summer, young gazelles were hunted.

S2: Winter, summer, and spring… Mhmmm! This indicates that the hunting process took place year around, which means that the Natufians inhabited the region year around as well!

P: You've got it! That's exactly what happened. All of these great pieces of evidence point to one logical conclusion: the Natufians built permanent settlements in the eastern Mediterranean region!

Brain's Left and Right Hemisphere

Listen to a conversation between a student and a psychology professor

S: Professor, do you have a minute?

P: Sure, Sarah, how can I help you?

S: Well… it's about the brain research you discussed yesterday.

P: Right.

S: You explained that the left and right hemispheres 01)**serve** different **functions** and… I 02)**kind of** started daydreaming.

P: No problem. Let's 03)**go back** a little and revisit some 04)**key points** first. Okay. Our brain 05)**consists of** left and right hemispheres connected by a bundle of commissural fibers 06)**called the corpus callosum**. The left and right sides of the brain communicate by sending signals.

S: I see… 07)**Is it possible to split** the hemispheres?

P: Well, actually that's possible. Let me 08)**give you an example** of the studies 09)**carried out** by Roger Walcott Sperry in the 1960s. He was a neuropsychologist who 10)**earned** the Noble **Prize** in Psychology or Medicine in 1981. While 11)**looking for** a cure for a patient with severe epilepsy, a neurological disorder 12)**characterized by** seizures, he 13)**came up with** the idea of splitting his patient's brain… literally 14)**cutting it in half**.

S: 15)**That sounds** radical and **dangerous to me**.

P: Indeed, many 16)**perceived it as an irrational decision**, but Sperry insisted that 17)**there were no** other **options** and conducted the surgery.

S: What happened? I wouldn't be surprised if it didn't 18)**go well**…

P: Well, the surgery was actually quite successful, 19)**except that** the patient experienced some unexpected 20)**side effects**, 21)**such as** insufficient speech production. The patient's seizures ceased, but the split-in-half brain, unsurprisingly, 22)**had some defects**.

S: Why? Was it because the communication between the hemispheres was 23)**cut off**?

P: Yes, neuroscientists believed that the left and right hemispheres uniformly 24)**performed** the same **functions**, but… ummm… if I 25)**put this pencil in your left visual field**, you can recognize it, right?

S: Of course, I'm not blind, professor.

P: 26)**What if** the patient's eye sight was perfectly normal, but he couldn't recognize an object presented in his left visual field but recognized it if it was in his right visual field? 27)**Regardless of** the type of object, the patient couldn't describe any stimulus in his left visual field.

S: Um… does that mean the left hemisphere was malfunctioning?

P: Actually, no. The left hemisphere 28)**corresponds to** the right visual field and the right hemisphere to the left visual field.

S: Right, I totally forgot about that.

P: Sperry additionally 29)**carried out** several other **tasks** to obtain 30)**in-depth** knowledge of the brain, and 31)**was able to** 32)**come to the conclusion** that each hemisphere 33)**specializes in** certain tasks. 34)**For instance**, the left hemisphere is 35)**associated with** analytical and verbal tasks, while the right hemisphere primarily controls spatial abilities, music, and creativity. So now you understand why the object in the left hemisphere wasn't recognized, right? It just wasn't the right hemisphere's job to recognize stuff 36)**in the first place**; it was the left hemisphere's job. The importance of the corpus callosum is quite noticeable to you now, isn't it? The communication between the two hemispheres is just… disabled once it's cut.

S: Yes, I understand that part. But, does that mean the patient 37)**had to** 38)**bear with** those symptoms 39)**for the rest of his life**? It 40)**must've been** really uncomfortable.

P: Not quite… because our brain, left or right, has the 41)**ability to learn**. So, 42)**over time**, the patient's left hemisphere "learned" the right hemisphere's jobs and 43)**vice versa**.

S: Ah, I get it now. The mystery of our brain… it's quite unbelievable. Well, thank you professor; that clarifies everything!

P: Yes it is, and no problem, Sarah!

Brain's Left and Right Hemisphere

Listen to a conversation between a student and a psychology professor

S: Professor, do you have a minute?

P: Sure, Sarah, how can I help you?

S: Well… it's about the brain research you discussed yesterday.

P: Right.

S: You explained that the left and right hemispheres serve different functions and… I kind of started daydreaming.

P: No problem. Let's go back a little and revisit some key points first. Okay. Our brain consists of left and right hemispheres connected by a bundle of commissural fibers called the corpus callosum. The left and right sides of the brain communicate by sending signals.

S: I see… Is it possible to split the hemispheres?

P: Well, actually that's possible. Let me give you an example of the studies carried out by Roger Walcott Sperry in the 1960s. He was a neuropsychologist who earned the Noble Prize in Psychology or Medicine in 1981. While looking for a cure for a patient with severe epilepsy, a neurological disorder characterized by seizures, he came up with the idea of splitting his patient's brain… literally cutting it in half.

S: That sounds radical and dangerous to me.

P: Indeed, many perceived it as an irrational decision, but Sperry insisted that there were no other options and conducted the surgery.

S: What happened? I wouldn't be surprised if it didn't go well…

P: Well, the surgery was actually quite successful, except that the patient experienced some unexpected side effects, such as insufficient speech production. The patient's seizures ceased, but the split-in-half brain, unsurprisingly, had some defects.

S: Why? Was it because the communication between the hemispheres was cut off?

P: Yes, neuroscientists believed that the left and right hemispheres uniformly performed the same functions, but… ummm… if I put this pencil in your left visual field, you can recognize it, right?

S: Of course, I'm not blind, professor.

P: What if the patient's eye sight was perfectly normal, but he couldn't recognize an object presented in his left visual field but recognized it if it was in his right visual field? Regardless of the type of object, the patient couldn't describe any stimulus in his left visual field.

S: Um… does that mean the left hemisphere was malfunctioning?

P: Actually, no. The left hemisphere corresponds to the right visual field and the right hemisphere to the left visual field.

S: Right, I totally forgot about that.

P: Sperry additionally carried out several other tasks to obtain in-depth knowledge of the brain, and was able to come to the conclusion that each hemisphere specializes in certain tasks. For instance, the left hemisphere is associated with analytical and verbal tasks, while the right hemisphere primarily controls spatial abilities, music, and creativity. So now you understand why the object in the left hemisphere wasn't recognized, right? It just wasn't the right hemisphere's job to recognize stuff in the first place; it was the left hemisphere's job. The importance of the corpus callosum is quite noticeable to you now, isn't it? The communication between the two hemispheres is just… disabled once it's cut.

S: Yes, I understand that part. But, does that mean the patient had to bear with those symptoms for the rest of his life? It must've been really uncomfortable.

P: Not quite… because our brain, left or right, has the ability to learn. So, over time, the patient's left hemisphere "learned" the right hemisphere's jobs and vice versa.

S: Ah, I get it now. The mystery of our brain… it's quite unbelievable. Well, thank you professor; that clarifies everything!

P: Yes it is, and no problem, Sarah!

Younger Dryas

Listen to part of a lecture in an Earth Science Class

P: Let's continue our discussion of historical global climate change. About 12,900 years ago, 01)**one of the** coldest **periods**, the "Younger Dryas," occurred. Previously, the Earth was gradually warming 02)**for about a thousand years**. Then, a sudden cooling happened.

S: Professor, 03)**correct me if I'm wrong**, but 04)**from what I've read**, didn't this affect North America?

P: Yes, Vicky. 05)**For those without this background knowledge**, 06)**let me explain** what happened in North America. As the main 07)**driving force** of the Younger Dryas, many scientists generally 08)**point to** a sudden 09)**influx of** freshwater into the Atlantic Ocean, 10)**the world's second largest** body of water, from a lake that covered much of Canada. The rush of the water disrupted oceanic currents and 11)**brought warmer temperatures to the region**. Another calamity occurred concurrently and caused the extinction of some mammalian species 12)**in the area**, 13)**such as** camels and mammoths, and the 14)**so-called** Clovis people 15)**disappeared without a trace**. While many have 16)**attempted to explain** these occurrences, archaeologist Dr. Douglas J. Kennett and his team 17)**came up with** a theory 18)**called the Younger Dryas impact**, or Clovis comet, hypothesis.

Kennett thought that a 19)**bundle of** comet fragments struck the North American continent and 20)**had** two major **effects**: they disrupted ocean currents and caused 35 21)**genera of** animals in the region to 22)**go extinct**. 23)**According to** him, they caused the sudden flow of lake water into the Atlantic Ocean, thereby altering the ocean's currents. He also 24)**suggested that** comets 25)**set** areas of North America **on fire**, causing the 26)**demise of** the animals and of the Clovis people who 27)**depended on** them for sustenance.

S: 28)**That sounds convincing**! What evidence did he have?

P: Well, he interpreted a layer of soil 29)**rich in** carbon found at about sixteen sites across North America and Europe. He 30)**was able to** extract microscopic diamonds called "nanodiamonds" from the very bottom sediment called the "black mat." How? Well… electron microscopes 31)**come in handy** when examining biological and inorganic specimens like cells, metals, and crystals. They comprise electrostatic and electromagnetic lenses too… well, that's not important now, let's revisit it later. So… black mat 32)**obtained its name from its distinctive color** and the 33)**discovery of** nanodiamonds there could be 34)**considered** critical evidence, because the force of asteroid impacts create them.

S: Oh, so that 35)**supports** his **claim** that comets struck the Earth, right?

P: Right! However, scientists 36)**point out** that Kennett's theory 37)**falls short** 38)**in some key ways**. His team said that "impact signs" are missing or cannot be found because the asteroid fragmented before it hit the ground. However, 39)**at least** one researcher says that 40)**it's impossible for a comet to vanish** 41)**without a trace**, such as a crater, and thus argues that Kennett's theory doesn't prove the occurrence of asteroids hitting the Earth. Another point of criticism arises because 42)**there is no evidence of** a population decline around that time… strange, huh? The 43)**disappearance of** the Clovis people, therefore, remains disputable and the demise or extinction of other species 44)**is also said to** be invalid because no evidence of continent-wide wildfires 45)**has been found**.

S: Um, what about the nanodiamonds? 46)**That seems** quite **convincing to me**.

P: Well, 47)**it's irrefutable that** nanodiamonds were found in the black mat at 16-impact sites around North America, but few researchers have 48)**looked for** them elsewhere. Maybe they're more common than we think. At least one researcher found nanodiamonds in non-impact sites in Europe from two 49)**thousand years ago**. 50)**Considering that** the Young Dryas happened 12,900 years ago, the origin of the nanodiamonds he discovered hardly proves the suggested 51)**occurrence of** asteroids.

S: Are you suggesting that his hypothesis is fundamentally wrong?

P: 52)**Not at all**. Theories are just theories. 53)**A lot of** them actually contain points that could be interpreted otherwise or 54)**proved** incorrect. 55)**That's the case here** 56)**as well**. Also, remember that the rebuttals are 57)**based on** the fact that valid "evidence" has not been found yet – "yet" being the key word. 58)**In the case of** the dinosaurs' extinction, criticism of the theory that the direct cause was 59)**a series of** impacts mounted, but evidence was eventually found in the Gulf of Mexico. Similarly, Kennett's theory just needs 60)**time to** be proven correct.

Younger Dryas

Listen to part of a lecture in an Earth Science Class

P: Let's continue our discussion of historical global climate change. About 12,900 years ago, one of the coldest periods, the "Younger Dryas," occurred. Previously, the Earth was gradually warming for about a thousand years. Then, a sudden cooling happened.

S: Professor, correct me if I'm wrong, but from what I've read, didn't this affect North America?

P: Yes, Vicky. For those without this background knowledge, let me explain what happened in North America. As the main driving force of the Younger Dryas, many scientists generally point to a sudden influx of freshwater into the Atlantic Ocean, the world's second largest body of water, from a lake that covered much of Canada. The rush of the water disrupted oceanic currents and brought warmer temperatures to the region. Another calamity occurred concurrently and caused the extinction of some mammalian species in the area, such as camels and mammoths, and the so-called Clovis people disappeared without a trace. While many have attempted to explain these occurrences, archaeologist Dr. Douglas J. Kennett and his team came up with a theory called the Younger Dryas impact, or Clovis comet, hypothesis.

Kennett thought that a bundle of comet fragments struck the North American continent and had two major effects: they disrupted ocean currents and caused 35 genera of animals in the region to go extinct. According to him, they caused the sudden flow of lake water into the Atlantic Ocean, thereby altering the ocean's currents. He also suggested that comets set areas of North America on fire, causing the demise of the animals and of the Clovis people who depended on them for sustenance.

S: That sounds convincing! What evidence did he have?

P: Well, he interpreted a layer of soil rich in carbon found at about sixteen sites across North America and Europe. He was able to extract microscopic diamonds called "nanodiamonds" from the very bottom sediment called the "black mat." How? Well… electron microscopes come in handy when examining biological and inorganic specimens like cells, metals, and crystals. They comprise electrostatic and electromagnetic lenses too… well, that's not important now, let's revisit it later. So… black mat obtained its name from its distinctive color and the discovery of nanodiamonds there could be considered critical evidence, because the force of asteroid impacts create them.

S: Oh, so that supports his claim that comets struck the Earth, right?

P: Right! However, scientists point out that Kennett's theory falls short in some key ways. His team said that "impact signs" are missing or cannot be found because the asteroid fragmented before it hit the ground. However, at least one researcher says that it's impossible for a comet to vanish without a trace, such as a crater, and thus argues that Kennett's theory doesn't prove the occurrence of asteroids hitting the Earth. Another point of criticism arises because there is no evidence of a population decline around that time… strange, huh? The disappearance of the Clovis people, therefore, remains disputable and the demise or extinction of other species is also said to be invalid because no evidence of continent-wide wildfires has been found.

S: Um, what about the nanodiamonds? That seems quite convincing to me.

P: Well, it's irrefutable that nanodiamonds were found in the black mat at 16-impact sites around North America, but few researchers have looked for them elsewhere. Maybe they're more common than we think. At least one researcher found nanodiamonds in non-impact sites in Europe from two thousand years ago. Considering that the Young Dryas happened 12,900 years ago, the origin of the nanodiamonds he discovered hardly proves the suggested occurrence of asteroids.

S: Are you suggesting that his hypothesis is fundamentally wrong?

P: Not at all. Theories are just theories. A lot of them actually contain points that could be interpreted otherwise or proved incorrect. That's the case here as well. Also, remember that the rebuttals are based on the fact that valid "evidence" has not been found yet – "yet" being the key word. In the case of the dinosaurs' extinction, criticism of the theory that the direct cause was a series of impacts mounted, but evidence was eventually found in the Gulf of Mexico. Similarly, Kennett's theory just needs time to be proven correct.

Leonardo's philosophical thinking

Listen to part of a lecture in an introductory computer science class

P: ⁰¹⁾**Let's review** last week's lecture. ⁰²⁾**When it comes to** designing computers, there are two major categories: exterior and interior design. The exterior is relatively simpler than the interior in ⁰³⁾**terms of** sophistication. Let's ⁰⁴⁾**think about** this. What does your computer ⁰⁵⁾**look like**? It could be black, beige, white, or another color, and it could ⁰⁶⁾**come in** different **shapes and sizes**. Since the introduction of personal computers, an… umm… evolution ⁰⁷⁾**has** ⁰⁸⁾**taken place** in the computer chassis, or case. Today, people employ ⁰⁹⁾**a number of** methods to ¹⁰⁾**distinguish their computers from others**, from lighting mods to body fillers ¹¹⁾**and so on**. It's a growing trend that's apparent in today's society. That's enough about the "look" of computers. Today, I ¹²⁾**want to** ¹³⁾**focus on** ¹⁴⁾**the other side** of computer design: technological design or how developers think and ¹⁵⁾**apply their thoughts to designing** and inventing computer systems and software, the "inside" of computers.

There is ¹⁶⁾**more** ¹⁷⁾**involved in** ¹⁸⁾**the process than** technological advances … I would say that philosophical aspects are just as important… Let me ¹⁹⁾**refer to** Leonardo da Vinci to illustrate my point.

²⁰⁾**As you know**, he was a great thinker and is arguably the most diversely inventive and talented person ever, ²¹⁾**not to mention** a profound artist from the Italian Renaissance. He was also a polymath who ²²⁾**made great contributions** in engineering, music, architecture, anatomy, and so on. In his work of anatomy, he demonstrated ²³⁾**a blend of** philosophical thinking in ²⁴⁾**both science and art**. But, I would say the ²⁵⁾**focal point** in his work is that, um, his understanding of human needs and problems were the primary ²⁶⁾**crux of** his thinking and of how he "designed." ²⁷⁾**In this sense**, developers ²⁸⁾**devoted to** technological design consider and apply both philosophical and technological aspects in their work.

Overall, there are two branches of technological design: old and new computing. Old computing refers to improving computing power and speed, the technical specifications of your computer. One may ²⁹⁾**cast doubt on** the philosophical aspects of memory capacity, but don't ³⁰⁾**get a wrong idea** here; these features are very important and ³¹⁾**play a** vital **role in** computer processing, which ultimately benefits society. We won't ³²⁾**go deep into** this because it's ³³⁾**irrelevant to** today's topic.

Um, Leonardo's ³⁴⁾**way of thinking** is ³⁵⁾**prevalent in** new computing. New computing, ³⁶⁾**in contrast to** old, elucidates an ³⁷⁾**approach to** technology design with the focus of ³⁸⁾**satisfying** people's **needs** and desires through computer usage. It ³⁹⁾**focuses on** what people can accomplish and do with their computers ⁴⁰⁾**instead of** what the computers can do, umm… like their capacity or abilities. What can you do with your computer? A myriad of tasks, correct? Things like researching, getting directions, communicating and socializing, ⁴¹⁾**disseminating information to others**, and so on. That's what developers of technology design do; they ⁴²⁾**try to think** ⁴³⁾**on behalf of** their users' goals and purposes for utilizing computers and create software programs that are easily usable by ⁴⁴⁾**the public**.

You can see how ⁴⁵⁾**important it is for developers to know** what users demand, right? The users' desires ultimately tell developers ⁴⁶⁾**what kinds of** programs to create. However, before they create new technology, they ⁴⁷⁾**need to** ⁴⁸⁾**make sure** that the technologies are ⁴⁹⁾**not only** efficient and useful **but also** easily manageable and executable… meaning they need to be ⁵⁰⁾**user-friendly**. These targeted users are not engineers with knowledge of processing and sophisticated technology, especially when it comes to computers. The focus here is usability ⁵¹⁾**along with** usefulness. So programmers try to avoid anything that may require substantial expertise, which ⁵²⁾**makes sense** right? But, we all know that's very ⁵³⁾**hard to** accomplish. Let's ⁵⁴⁾**put you in a** hypothetical **situation** where you are ⁵⁵⁾**working on** a ⁵⁶⁾**term paper**, and need to research and collect information. You would ⁵⁷⁾**go on websites** to find information, ⁵⁸⁾**of course**. ⁵⁹⁾**What if** the websites were organized ⁶⁰⁾**in a** confusing **way** that ⁶¹⁾**made you frustrated** before ⁶²⁾**looking for** the information? This commonly occurs in two ways: the information can be a million ⁶³⁾**clicks away** or it can be ⁶⁴⁾**jumbled with** ⁶⁵⁾**a bunch of** unnecessary information. We can conclude that this website has ⁶⁶⁾**failed to** ⁶⁷⁾**meet the** user's **demand**: usability.

This is where Leonardo's philosophical thinking ⁶⁸⁾**comes into play**. As I explained, the goal of these programs is to ⁶⁹⁾**solve problems**, not create more. Human-centered computing is perhaps the core of technology design as illustrated… ⁷⁰⁾**As a matter of fact**, professionals from fields ⁷¹⁾**such as** sociology and psychology ⁷²⁾**tend to** think similarly to enhance our daily lives, not complicate them. Anyway, this doesn't mean ⁷³⁾**that** old computing is unimportant… It is still an essential element of technological design as computer specifications, such as speed, are also important factors. Finding information or ⁷⁴⁾**communicating with** your friends wouldn't matter if it took you hours just to ⁷⁵⁾**get on** a website, right?

Leonardo's philosophical thinking

Listen to part of a lecture in an introductory computer science class

P: Let's review last week's lecture. When it comes to designing computers, there are two major categories: exterior and interior design. The exterior is relatively simpler than the interior in terms of sophistication. Let's think about this. What does your computer look like? It could be black, beige, white, or another color, and it could come in different shapes and sizes. Since the introduction of personal computers, an… umm… evolution has taken place in the computer chassis, or case. Today, people employ a number of methods to distinguish their computers from others, from lighting mods to body fillers and so on. It's a growing trend that's apparent in today's society. That's enough about the "look" of computers. Today, I want to focus on the other side of computer design: technological design or how developers think and apply their thoughts to designing and inventing computer systems and software, the "inside" of computers.

There is more involved in the process than technological advances … I would say that philosophical aspects are just as important… Let me refer to Leonardo da Vinci to illustrate my point.

As you know, he was a great thinker and is arguably the most diversely inventive and talented person ever, not to mention a profound artist from the Italian Renaissance. He was also a polymath who made great contributions in engineering, music, architecture, anatomy, and so on. In his work of anatomy, he demonstrated a blend of philosophical thinking in both science and art. But, I would say the focal point in his work is that, um, his understanding of human needs and problems were the primary crux of his thinking and of how he "designed." In this sense, developers devoted to technological design consider and apply both philosophical and technological aspects in their work.

Overall, there are two branches of technological design: old and new computing. Old computing refers to improving computing power and speed, the technical specifications of your computer. One may cast doubt on the philosophical aspects of memory capacity, but don't get a wrong idea here; these features are very important and play a vital role in computer processing, which ultimately benefits society. We won't go deep into this because it's irrelevant to today's topic.

Um, Leonardo's way of thinking is prevalent in new computing. New computing, in contrast to old, elucidates an approach to technology design with the focus of satisfying people's needs and desires through computer usage. It focuses on what people can accomplish and do with their computers instead of what the computers can do, umm… like their capacity or abilities. What can you do with your computer? A myriad of tasks, correct? Things like researching, getting directions, communicating and socializing, disseminating information to others, and so on. That's what developers of technology design do; they try to think on behalf of their users' goals and purposes for utilizing computers and create software programs that are easily usable by the public.

You can see how important it is for developers to know what users demand, right? The users' desires ultimately tell developers what kinds of programs to create. However, before they create new technology, they need to make sure that the technologies are not only efficient and useful but also easily manageable and executable… meaning they need to be user-friendly. These targeted users are not engineers with knowledge of processing and sophisticated technology, especially when it comes to computers. The focus here is usability along with usefulness. So programmers try to avoid anything that may require substantial expertise, which makes sense right? But, we all know that's very hard to accomplish. Let's put you in a hypothetical situation where you are working on a term paper, and need to research and collect information. You would go on websites to find information, of course. What if the websites were organized in a confusing way that made you frustrated before looking for the information? This commonly occurs in two ways: the information can be a million clicks away or it can be jumbled with a bunch of unnecessary information. We can conclude that this website has failed to meet the user's demand: usability.

This is where Leonardo's philosophical thinking comes into play. As I explained, the goal of these programs is to solve problems, not create more. Human-centered computing is perhaps the core of technology design as illustrated… As a matter of fact, professionals from fields such as sociology and psychology tend to think similarly to enhance our daily lives, not complicate them. Anyway, this doesn't mean that old computing is unimportant… It is still an essential element of technological design as computer specifications, such as speed, are also important factors. Finding information or communicating with your friends wouldn't matter if it took you hours just to get on a website, right?

The championship games

Listen to a conversation between a student and his soccer coach

C: ⁰¹⁾**Got a minute**, Mike?

S: ⁰²⁾**Of course**! Great game last night, right? Who ⁰³⁾**would've thought** that we would ⁰⁴⁾**make it to** the State Championships?

C: It's a huge improvement from last season. Since you became the team captain ⁰⁵⁾**at the beginning of** this season, team cooperation ⁰⁶⁾**has advanced** significantly.

S: That's quite flattering. Thanks, Coach! That means a lot. Oh, ⁰⁷⁾**by the way**, why did you ⁰⁸⁾**call me in**?

C: Oh, I ⁰⁹⁾**got** a little **sidetracked**, didn't I? I called you in because James told me that you might not ¹⁰⁾**be able to** ¹¹⁾**participate in** the championship games.

S: Oh, I'm sorry. I ¹²⁾**should've** ¹³⁾**consulted with** you ¹⁴⁾**in the first place**. Well… my internship interview is ¹⁵⁾**on the day** we leave for the game.

C: Oh wow, ¹⁶⁾**stepping up** your game, huh?

S: Yeah, it's for an internship with the university's advertising agency.

C: I see. Isn't there an ¹⁷⁾**alternative way** though? Like rescheduling the interview ¹⁸⁾**or something**?

S: I ¹⁹⁾**thought about** that, but I don't think it would ²⁰⁾**give them a good impression** of me as a candidate if I ²¹⁾**asked to reschedule**. It's a very popular and competitive position, you know?

C: I understand. ²²⁾**Let's see**. Well, we leave ²³⁾**on Wednesday** afternoon, but the games don't actually start until Thursday morning, so you could ²⁴⁾**consider taking** ²⁵⁾**public transportation** if it's not a problem for you. I'm sure the athletics department will ²⁶⁾**cover the cost**.

S: Well, actually, coach, I ²⁷⁾**looked into** the bus schedule, but the only ²⁸⁾**available time** for the bus that goes from here to the championship place is around 3 o'clock ²⁹⁾**in the morning**. And other transportation systems, like the subway, won't take me there unless I transfer like ³⁰⁾**a million times**.

C: I see… That won't be good since you wouldn't be able to play as hard without enough rest. But, you do know that the championship ³¹⁾**consists of** 3 games though, right? There's one game ³²⁾**each day**.

S: Really? Right, I totally forgot about that.

C: So, ³³⁾**even if** you missed the first game, you'd still be ³⁴⁾**a big help to** the team. If you ³⁵⁾**want to participate** in all of the games, ³⁶⁾**why not** ³⁷⁾**try to talk** to the agency and explain your situation?

S: Well, ³⁸⁾**like I said**, coach, I'd ³⁹⁾**hate to give** them a sense of inability or irresponsibility. I'm not implying that this internship position is any more important than the championship games. I've ⁴⁰⁾**devoted a lot of time and effort to practicing**, and we finally ⁴¹⁾**reached this point**, but this internship chance doesn't ⁴²⁾**come around** every day. I hope you can understand that.

C: Of course, Mike. As your coach, I've seen how passionate you are outside the field ⁴³⁾**as well**, and I will ⁴⁴⁾**support** whatever **decision** you ⁴⁵⁾**make**.

S: Thank you, coach. But like you suggested, I'll look into public transportation and try to be there for the second game! We, as one, worked very hard to get to the championship, and I don't want to ⁴⁶⁾**let my team down**.

C: Great, that sounds good, Mike! Well, I ⁴⁷⁾**wish you the best of luck** with the interview.

S: Thanks, coach, I'll see you later!

The championship games

Listen to a conversation between a student and his soccer coach

C: Got a minute, Mike?

S: Of course! Great game last night, right? Who would've thought that we would make it to the State Championships?

C: It's a huge improvement from last season. Since you became the team captain at the beginning of this season, team cooperation has advanced significantly.

S: That's quite flattering. Thanks, Coach! That means a lot. Oh, by the way, why did you call me in?

C: Oh, I got a little sidetracked, didn't I? I called you in because James told me that you might not be able to participate in the championship games.

S: Oh, I'm sorry. I should've consulted with you in the first place. Well… my internship interview is on the day we leave for the game.

C: Oh wow, stepping up your game, huh?

S: Yeah, it's for an internship with the university's advertising agency.

C: I see. Isn't there an alternative way though? Like rescheduling the interview or something?

S: I thought about that, but I don't think it would give them a good impression of me as a candidate if I asked to reschedule. It's a very popular and competitive position, you know?

C: I understand. Let's see. Well, we leave on Wednesday afternoon, but the games don't actually start until Thursday morning, so you could consider taking public transportation if it's not a problem for you. I'm sure the athletics department will cover the cost.

S: Well, actually, coach, I looked into the bus schedule, but the only available time for the bus that goes from here to the championship place is around 3 o'clock in the morning. And other transportation systems, like the subway, won't take me there unless I transfer like a million times.

C: I see… That won't be good since you wouldn't be able to play as hard without enough rest. But, you do know that the championship consists of 3 games though, right? There's one game each day.

S: Really? Right, I totally forgot about that.

C: So, even if you missed the first game, you'd still be a big help to the team. If you want to participate in all of the games, why not try to talk to the agency and explain your situation?

S: Well, like I said, coach, I'd hate to give them a sense of inability or irresponsibility. I'm not implying that this internship position is any more important than the championship games. I've devoted a lot of time and effort to practicing, and we finally reached this point, but this internship chance doesn't come around every day. I hope you can understand that.

C: Of course, Mike. As your coach, I've seen how passionate you are outside the field as well, and I will support whatever decision you make.

S: Thank you, coach. But like you suggested, I'll look into public transportation and try to be there for the second game! We, as one, worked very hard to get to the championship, and I don't want to let my team down.

C: Great, that sounds good, Mike! Well, I wish you the best of luck with the interview.

S: Thanks, coach, I'll see you later!

Earth's age

Listen to part of a lecture in a geology class

P: Geologists believe that Earth is about 4.54 billion years old. Using radiometric, or radioactive, dating, they calculated the ages of cosmic materials like meteorites, debris from asteroids and comets, and the oldest terrestrial samples. Ultimately they concluded that Earth's age is 01)**analogous to** the ages of these rocks. 02)**Prior to** this theory, there were major disputes regarding Earth's age, and today we'll explore some of those.

Okay, 03)**let's look at** Lord Kelvin's theory. 04)**I'm sure** you've 05)**heard of** the laws of thermodynamics, right? They are his biggest 06)**contributions to** the development of physics. He 07)**was able to** 08)**apply** his understanding of heat **to** his rudimentary understanding of Earth. He 09)**based** his theory **on** the assumption that Earth began 10)**in a** molten **state** and gradually became a solid body. 11)**It's said that** solid Earth's temperature was nearly the rock's 12)**melting point**, around 600 to 1200° C. As it cooled into a solid body, Earth 13)**radiated** heat **into** the relatively frigid outer space. Kelvin studied this phenomenon and posited that Earth's heat loss occurred through what he 14)**termed** "thermal diffusion."

S: You mean, heat diffusion?

P: 15)**More or less**. 16)**For those of you** who are **not familiar with** the concept, 17)**let me** 18)**give** you a simple example to illustrate it. 19)**Let's say** you're boiling water for coffee and realize that your craving 20)**went away**. Then, you 21)**put** the kettle **into** the freezer because you don't 22)**want to** waste the water. 23)**What** do you think would **happen**?

S: That's quite obvious; the temperature would drop.

P: Correct! But the cooling process is 24)**much more** complicated. Objects don't just go 25)**from** hot **to** cold instantaneously. It occurs gradually and the "layers" of the object have different temperatures, a temperature gradient. When the pot is put into the freezer, the outermost layer, the pot's exterior, would cool first, creating a temperature 26)**difference between** the surface layer and the layer 27)**just below** it. 28)**According to** the law of heat transfer, heat from a body 29)**at** a higher **temperature** 30)**flows to** a body at a lower temperature, meaning that heat would diffuse from deeper layers. Kelvin 31)**used** this property **to calculate** the length of earth's cooling 32)**by estimating** the difference between the original and current temperatures. He speculated that the original temperature was near the melting point of rocks and with some additional calculations, concluded that Earth was 33)**no more than** 100 million years old.

His theory initially 34)**received** great acknowledgment and **acclaim from** physicists, but it induced an uproar among geologists. Can anyone guess why?

S: Well… I'd assume 35)**it was because** geologists theorize that sedimentation and erosion take 36)**hundreds of millions of** years. So… it wouldn't 37)**make sense** for Earth to be 38)**less than** 100 million years old.

P: Exactly, Susan! 39)**As time passed** critics 40)**looked for** errors in Kelvin's calculations, but their arguments were 41)**just as** faulty and inadequate. By the early 1900's, radioactivity and heat 42)**release from** radioactive decay in Earth's interior were discovered. Scientists claimed that this additional heat source, which 43)**was absent from** Kelvin's calculations, would've made Earth much older than Kelvin's estimation. However, 44)**the amount of** radioactive heat is now 45)**considered** insignificant, so Kelvin's calculations wouldn't 46)**have been greatly affected** by it.

S: Then why was Kelvin's calculation wrong? I mean, his conclusion that Earth was only 100 million years old wasn't 47)**proven** incorrect…

P: Well, this is where it gets interesting. Kelvin had an assistant 48)**named** John Perry, who was a great patron of his employer. Um… how should I explain this? I would say 49)**it was** much **like** a coup d'état. Ironically, Perry disputed Kelvin's theory and discredited his calculations in 1895. He stated that Kelvin's assumption of a solid Earth was fundamentally wrong. 50)**In fact**, beneath Earth's crust was liquid, or semi-liquid. With further scrutiny, he discovered that thermal diffusion does not happen in liquid or semi-liquid bodies; 51)**instead**, convection, the circulation **of** hot material, occurs. Imagine heat following a circular pathway in the crust instead of the outward diffusion model. 52)**Not only** does the former keep 53)**large amounts of** heat spread through the whole, **but** it **also** suggests that cooling happens 54)**at** a much slower **rate**.

S: Were Perry's calculations 55)**close to** today's estimated age of the Earth?

P: It wasn't exactly 4.54 billion years, but considering the 56)**lack of** technology, his estimation of Earth's age, 3 billion years, was surprisingly accurate. Unfortunately, his work didn't 57)**receive** much **recognition from** his contemporaries because it was 58)**constructed on** a whole different framework. Later, when continental drift was proven, Perry's theory 59)**began receiving** the recognition it deserved.

Earth's age

Listen to part of a lecture in a geology class

P: Geologists believe that Earth is about 4.54 billion years old. Using radiometric, or radioactive, dating, they calculated the ages of cosmic materials like meteorites, debris from asteroids and comets, and the oldest terrestrial samples. Ultimately they concluded that Earth's age is analogous to the ages of these rocks. Prior to this theory, there were major disputes regarding Earth's age, and today we'll explore some of those.

Okay, let's look at Lord Kelvin's theory. I'm sure you've heard of the laws of thermodynamics, right? They are his biggest contributions to the development of physics. He was able to apply his understanding of heat to his rudimentary understanding of Earth. He based his theory on the assumption that Earth began in a molten state and gradually became a solid body. It's said that solid Earth's temperature was nearly the rock's melting point, around 600 to 1200° C. As it cooled into a solid body, Earth radiated heat into the relatively frigid outer space. Kelvin studied this phenomenon and posited that Earth's heat loss occurred through what he termed "thermal diffusion."

S: You mean, heat diffusion?

P: More or less. For those of you who are not familiar with the concept, let me give you a simple example to illustrate it. Let's say you're boiling water for coffee and realize that your craving went away. Then, you put the kettle into the freezer because you don't want to waste the water. What do you think would happen?

S: That's quite obvious; the temperature would drop.

P: Correct! But the cooling process is much more complicated. Objects don't just go from hot to cold instantaneously. It occurs gradually and the "layers" of the object have different temperatures, a temperature gradient. When the pot is put into the freezer, the outermost layer, the pot's exterior, would cool first, creating a temperature difference between the surface layer and the layer just below it. According to the law of heat transfer, heat from a body at a higher temperature flows to a body at a lower temperature, meaning that heat would diffuse from deeper layers. Kelvin used this property to calculate the length of earth's cooling by estimating the difference between the original and current temperatures. He speculated that the original temperature was near the melting point of rocks and with some additional calculations, concluded that Earth was no more than 100 million years old.

His theory initially received great acknowledgment and acclaim from physicists, but it induced an uproar among geologists. Can anyone guess why?

S: Well… I'd assume it was because geologists theorize that sedimentation and erosion take hundreds of millions of years. So… it wouldn't make sense for Earth to be less than 100 million years old.

P: Exactly, Susan! As time passed critics looked for errors in Kelvin's calculations, but their arguments were just as faulty and inadequate. By the early 1900's, radioactivity and heat release from radioactive decay in Earth's interior were discovered. Scientists claimed that this additional heat source, which was absent from Kelvin's calculations, would've made Earth much older than Kelvin's estimation. However, the amount of radioactive heat is now considered insignificant, so Kelvin's calculations wouldn't have been greatly affected by it.

S: Then why was Kelvin's calculation wrong? I mean, his conclusion that Earth was only 100 million years old wasn't proven incorrect…

P: Well, this is where it gets interesting. Kelvin had an assistant named John Perry, who was a great patron of his employer. Um… how should I explain this? I would say it was much like a coup d'état. Ironically, Perry disputed Kelvin's theory and discredited his calculations in 1895. He stated that Kelvin's assumption of a solid Earth was fundamentally wrong. In fact, beneath Earth's crust was liquid, or semi-liquid. With further scrutiny, he discovered that thermal diffusion does not happen in liquid or semi-liquid bodies; instead, convection, the circulation of hot material, occurs. Imagine heat following a circular pathway in the crust instead of the outward diffusion model. Not only does the former keep large amounts of heat spread through the whole, but it also suggests that cooling happens at a much slower rate.

S: Were Perry's calculations close to today's estimated age of the Earth?

P: It wasn't exactly 4.54 billion years, but considering the lack of technology, his estimation of Earth's age, 3 billion years, was surprisingly accurate. Unfortunately, his work didn't receive much recognition from his contemporaries because it was constructed on a whole different framework. Later, when continental drift was proven, Perry's theory began receiving the recognition it deserved.

Illegitimate theater

Listen to part of a lecture in a theater class

P: Before we begin today's lesson, let's review the main topics of our last class for those who were absent. Umm… legitimate theater was a form of theatrical art that 01)**relied on** spoken words without singing, dancing, or musical components. 02)**Due to** Great Britain's Licensing Act of 1737, strict 03)**restraints** were **put on** media and only certain theaters were 04)**permitted to** perform serious literary shows like Shakespeare's "Romeo and Juliet." Don't 05)**get** the wrong **idea** here; the censorship law didn't 06)**bar theaters from performing** less serious and more entertaining pieces, like comedies, but they were still 07)**under** governmental **control**. We 08)**refer to** this **as** illegitimate theater.

Let's 09)**look at** theatrical development in the United States. Significant cultural changes occurred as the 10)**conflict between the North and the South** gradually waned after the Civil War. More jobs 11)**became available to** 12)a greater **number of** people and rural residents 13)**flocked to** cities between 1870 through 1920. International immigration further increased the populations of the cities. 14)**As a consequence**, urban productivity and incomes skyrocketed 15)**as well**. As people had less strenuous jobs and more money, their 16)**attention turned to** leisure activities or travel. These two changes, demographic and economic, 17)**worked as** catalysts to begin a new era of the theatrical arts that we now refer to as popular theater. Popular theater was more like illegitimate theater 18)**in that** serious plays were rarely handled. Vaudeville was one of the main forms of popular theater that flourished 19)**at the time**.

For those of you who speak French, vaudeville may 21)**sound** quite **familiar**… Although the term's origin remains obscure, one of the suggested theories is that it described satirical songs that were once popular in France. Others theorize that it means "voice of the city" or "songs of the town." Anyway, let's not 22)**get hung up on** this, because the "vaudeville" we are discussing 23)**has nothing to do with** French songs.

Popular theater usually 24)**consisted of** 25)**a series of** ten unrelated acts or performances covering 26)**a wide spectrum of** theater-related options, 27)**such as** magic, acrobatics, comedies, 28)**and so on**. This property of popular theater may seem rather distracting and would 29)**fail to attract** people, but everyone 30)**had access to** every type of performance at the theater. To 31)**help you visualize**, think about a convenience store. You may not find "quality" products there, but the range of everyday commodities is a major benefit that convenience stores provide, right? 32)**In the same sense**, whatever your 33)**taste in** theater arts, whether it was comedies or musicals, it was there. Pretty convenient, huh?

Behind the exceptional success was the father of American vaudeville, Benjamin Franklin Keith. His entrepreneurial career 34)**began with** the establishment of the Gaiety Museum in Boston in 1883. His continuous endeavors and triumph 35)**allowed him to build** the Bijou Theater. Many theater historians note that his theater had two outstanding attractions: continuous performances and innovations.

First, continuous performances meant that the doors of his theater were open 36)**all day**, every day. He believed that the role of entertainment was to amuse people whenever they wanted. He would have his performers repeat their acts 37)**throughout the day** and the theater was 38)**designed to operate** twelve hours daily. Remember the increased urban income? It allowed workers to partake in 39)**leisure activities**, and vaudeville theaters were especially popular at the time. Keith 40)**intended to exploit** this through continuous performances 41)**in two ways**: always 42)**filling his theater with more people** and captivating the audience by 43)**decorating his theater with extravagant** and lavish details. Think about it… you 44)**walk into** a theater simply 45)**for** entertainment **purposes**, and you feel like you've 46)**come to** a luxurious hotel. Sounds tempting, right?

Let's shift our focus to elucidate his success as a vaudeville entrepreneur. His "fixed policy of cleanliness and order" represents his ideals as a stern businessman. He established rules by which everyone, his employees and the audience, had to 47)**abide**. These forbade acts that included profanity and 48)**prevented performers from using** 49)**offensive language**. This ensured that his theater would also 50)**appeal to** women and children. Similar restrictions were 51)**placed on** the audience, as well, in that they weren't allowed to interrupt the performances 52)**in any way**. Previously, Civil War-era audiences displayed low-brow behavior. They would stamp their feet or talk during the performances. Keith 53)**strove to change** this behavior by educating his audiences about appropriate theater behaviors.

We're actually 54)**running out of time**, so let's stop here until our next class. We'll 55)**continue** our **discussion on** entrepreneurs who followed the great work of Keith, so 56)**be sure to** 57)**do** some **research on** those people!

Illegitimate theater

Listen to part of a lecture in a theater class

P: Before we begin today's lesson, let's review the main topics of our last class for those who were absent. Umm… legitimate theater was a form of theatrical art that relied on spoken words without singing, dancing, or musical components. Due to Great Britain's Licensing Act of 1737, strict restraints were put on media and only certain theaters were permitted to perform serious literary shows like Shakespeare's "Romeo and Juliet." Don't get the wrong idea here; the censorship law didn't bar theaters from performing less serious and more entertaining pieces, like comedies, but they were still under governmental control. We refer to this as illegitimate theater.

Let's look at theatrical development in the United States. Significant cultural changes occurred as the conflict between the North and the South gradually waned after the Civil War. More jobs became available to a greater number of people and rural residents flocked to cities between 1870 through 1920. International immigration further increased the populations of the cities. As a consequence, urban productivity and incomes skyrocketed as well. As people had less strenuous jobs and more money, their attention turned to leisure activities or travel. These two changes, demographic and economic, worked as catalysts to begin a new era of the theatrical arts that we now refer to as popular theater. Popular theater was more like illegitimate theater in that serious plays were rarely handled. Vaudeville was one of the main forms of popular theater that flourished at the time.

For those of you who speak French, vaudeville may sound quite familiar… Although the term's origin remains obscure, one of the suggested theories is that it described satirical songs that were once popular in France. Others theorize that it means "voice of the city" or "songs of the town." Anyway, let's not get hung up on this, because the "vaudeville" we are discussing has nothing to do with French songs.

Popular theater usually consisted of a series of ten unrelated acts or performances covering a wide spectrum of theater-related options, such as magic, acrobatics, comedies, and so on. This property of popular theater may seem rather distracting and would fail to attract people, but everyone had access to every type of performance at the theater. To help you visualize, think about a convenience store. You may not find "quality" products there, but the range of everyday commodities is a major benefit that convenience stores provide, right? In the same sense, whatever your taste in theater arts, whether it was comedies or musicals, it was there. Pretty convenient, huh?

Behind the exceptional success was the father of American vaudeville, Benjamin Franklin Keith. His entrepreneurial career began with the establishment of the Gaiety Museum in Boston in 1883. His continuous endeavors and triumph allowed him to build the Bijou Theater. Many theater historians note that his theater had two outstanding attractions: continuous performances and innovations.

First, continuous performances meant that the doors of his theater were open all day, every day. He believed that the role of entertainment was to amuse people whenever they wanted. He would have his performers repeat their acts throughout the day and the theater was designed to operate twelve hours daily. Remember the increased urban income? It allowed workers to partake in leisure activities, and vaudeville theaters were especially popular at the time. Keith intended to exploit this through continuous performances in two ways: always filling his theater with more people and captivating the audience by decorating his theater with extravagant and lavish details. Think about it… you walk into a theater simply for entertainment purposes, and you feel like you've come to a luxurious hotel. Sounds tempting, right?

Let's shift our focus to elucidate his success as a vaudeville entrepreneur. His "fixed policy of cleanliness and order" represents his ideals as a stern businessman. He established rules by which everyone, his employees and the audience, had to abide. These forbade acts that included profanity and prevented performers from using offensive language. This ensured that his theater would also appeal to women and children. Similar restrictions were placed on the audience, as well, in that they weren't allowed to interrupt the performances in any way. Previously, Civil War-era audiences displayed low-brow behavior. They would stamp their feet or talk during the performances. Keith strove to change this behavior by educating his audiences about appropriate theater behaviors.

We're actually running out of time, so let's stop here until our next class. We'll continue our discussion on entrepreneurs who followed the great work of Keith, so be sure to do some research on those people!

TEST 4 SET 1-1

Final term papers

Listen to a conversation between a student and her biology professor

S: Hi professor, 01)**do you have a minute**?

P: Of course, Jenny, 02)**how have you been?** 03)**The semester's almost over**, so I'm guessing you 04)**must be** relaxing and enjoying your 05)**leisure time**.

S: Not exactly… It's that time of the semester. Final term papers 06)**are due**… I've 07)**been overwhelmed**. Thank you for 08)**extending the deadline** for the paper; that was very generous.

P: 09)**Of course**! That doesn't mean you didn't 10)**put** as much **effort into** 11)**the first draft** that I already received, does it?

S: Of course not! I 12)**started from scratch** and 13)**did** 14)**a ton of research**. 15)**I was wondering if** you 16)**had a chance to read** my paper 17)**over the weekend**.

P: I certainly did, and I have a few questions for you.

S: Sure, 18)**that's why** I 19)**came by**.

P: Okay, could you summarize the main theme of your paper?

S: Um, well the focus is honeybees – their 20)**way of** 21)**communicating with** 22)**one another** and how they utilize earth's magnetic field 23)**in the process**.

P: 24)**Use** the magnetic field **to facilitate communication**?

S: Umm… No, not quite. To 25)**help** them navigate by finding the right course.

P: Okay, now I'm 26)**starting to** understand your paper 27)**a bit** better. So, first, honeybees communicate with one another and second, they navigate using earth's 28)**magnetic field**, right?

S: Exactly!

P: Well, Jenny, your paper was quite vague 29)**in that sense**… I mean, it was 30)**difficult to** grasp those ideas separately in your thesis. Are you sure you understand the concepts?

S: I think so. I mean… what I learned through news articles and the internet was that honeybees 31)**employ** two different types of dances **to** 32)**deliver messages**. They 33)**perform** 34)**what's called** a round **dance** to 35)**tell others that** a food source is nearby and they perform a waggle dance, which is relatively more perplexing than the first, to tell them that the food source is 36)**far away** from their hive.

P: So their dances 37)**sort of** 38)**work as** food-location signals?

S: Right.

P: Um, okay, then where does the magnetic field part 39)**fit into** your paper?

S: 40)**Right after** that, I explain that honeybees have iron-rich granules in their cells, and they sense earth's magnetic field using them. It works almost like an internal compass – like the biological clock in plants. So 41)**even if** they 42)**lose their way** 43)**due to**… whatever the reason may be, they can 44)**get back** 45)**on course**.

P: Alright, good. Here's my advice; your paper 46)**seems to** 47)**lack** a clear **connection**, if there's any, between how honeybees communicate – their dances – and how they use earth's magnetic field to navigate. So I 48)**referred to** your citation list. The source you used…

S: 49)**Is there something wrong with** the source?

P: Yeah, it's not very academic. It contains 50)**a lot of** misused concepts, and it's a very subjective article that 51)**fails to** address the 52)**other side of** the matter. So 53)**I suggest you find** another source that has comprehensive knowledge of honeybees' communication methods and their 54)**relation to** earth's magnetic field. And see if you could, uh… clarify your paper a bit.

S: That 55)**sounds like** a great plan! 56)**Thank you** so much **for your help**, professor. I guess I 57)**need to hurry up** to 58)**meet the deadline**!

P: No problem. 59)**Stop by** anytime you need help, Jenny!

Final term papers

Listen to a conversation between a student and her biology professor

S: Hi professor, do you have a minute?

P: Of course, Jenny, how have you been? The semester's almost over, so I'm guessing you must be relaxing and enjoying your leisure time.

S: Not exactly… It's that time of the semester. Final term papers are due… I've been overwhelmed. Thank you for extending the deadline for the paper; that was very generous.

P: Of course! That doesn't mean you didn't put as much effort into the first draft that I already received, does it?

S: Of course not! I started from scratch and did a ton of research. I was wondering if you had a chance to read my paper over the weekend.

P: I certainly did, and I have a few questions for you.

S: Sure, that's why I came by.

P: Okay, could you summarize the main theme of your paper?

S: Um, well the focus is honeybees – their way of communicating with one another and how they utilize earth's magnetic field in the process.

P: Use the magnetic field to facilitate communication?

S: Umm… No, not quite. To help them navigate by finding the right course.

P: Okay, now I'm starting to understand your paper a bit better. So, first, honeybees communicate with one another and second, they navigate using earth's magnetic field, right?

S: Exactly!

P: Well, Jenny, your paper was quite vague in that sense… I mean, it was difficult to grasp those ideas separately in your thesis. Are you sure you understand the concepts?

S: I think so. I mean… what I learned through news articles and the internet was that honeybees employ two different types of dances to deliver messages. They perform what's called a round dance to tell others that a food source is nearby and they perform a waggle dance, which is relatively more perplexing than the first, to tell them that the food source is far away from their hive.

P: So their dances sort of work as food-location signals?

S: Right.

P: Um, okay, then where does the magnetic field part fit into your paper?

S: Right after that, I explain that honeybees have iron-rich granules in their cells, and they sense earth's magnetic field using them. It works almost like an internal compass – like the biological clock in plants. So even if they lose their way due to… whatever the reason may be, they can get back on course.

P: Alright, good. Here's my advice; your paper seems to lack a clear connection, if there's any, between how honeybees communicate – their dances – and how they use earth's magnetic field to navigate. So I referred to your citation list. The source you used…

S: Is there something wrong with the source?

P: Yeah, it's not very academic. It contains a lot of misused concepts, and it's a very subjective article that fails to address the other side of the matter. So I suggest you find another source that has comprehensive knowledge of honeybees' communication methods and their relation to earth's magnetic field. And see if you could, uh… clarify your paper a bit.

S: That sounds like a great plan! Thank you so much for your help, professor. I guess I need to hurry up to meet the deadline!

P: No problem. Stop by anytime you need help, Jenny!

Two galaxies

Listen to part of a lecture in an astronomy class

P: Yesterday we discussed our solar system and its contents. Today, we'll 01)**talk about** two galaxies, systems 02)**consisting of** billions of stars and other remnants, the Milky Way, which includes our solar system, and another 03)**named** Sagittarius.

Researchers 04)**have** recently **discovered** that larger galaxies 05)**tend to** 06)**absorb stars from smaller galaxies**. You may be wondering how this 07)**relates to** today's topic. 08)**You see**, the Milky Way 09)**is 10,000 times bigger** than Sagittarius and the research team found that Sagittarius' stars 10)**are being** 11)**pulled into**, or 12)**absorbed by**, the Milky Way. This is astonishing and interesting, because galaxies were commonly 13)**thought to** be gravitationally bound, and the idea of two galaxies 14)**fusing together**, or one 'stealing' stars from another, was seldom considered. Even when it was, researchers couldn't 15)**validate the point** 16)**due to** 17)**lack of** evidence, so the theories were 18)**viewed as** absurd and controversial. However, evidence arose that validated the theory. So, how did they prove what previous cosmologists couldn't?

19)**To begin**, let's 20)**go over** why previous researchers couldn't prove the phenomenon and what they were lacking. To 21)**help** you visualize it, 22)**let's say** you shredded two identical stacks of paper. If they were pure white with no distinguishing marks, would you 23)**be able to** sort them? Probably not unless you had some kind of 24)**supernatural power**, right? But 25)**what if** one stack was blue and the other red? Now, the scenario changes, and it becomes quite 26)**easy to distinguish** them.

That's exactly how the research team was able to determine the 27)**extent to** which the stars of the Sagittarius galaxy were being pulled into the Milky Way. They 28)**began by** studying galaxies... what they contain, what they're 29)**made of**, what properties they share, and things like that. Then, they realized that galaxies radiate thermal energy, or heat that 30)**gives off** infrared radiation or... infrared light. 31)**This might sound** a little more **familiar to you**... 32)**For those not familiar with** infrared radiation, 33)**think about** how 34)**detecting devices** are 35)**employed in** warzones or airports. I'm sure you've seen soldiers wearing bulky-looking goggles 36)**at night**. These night vision devices 37)**enable** soldiers **to**, uh... see objects by detecting the thermal radiation they give off, 38)**regardless of** the darkness – so the 'coldness' or 'hotness' of the objects determines the radiation's color, 39)**ranging from blue to red**. Also 40)**at the airport**, when you 41)**go through** the body-scanning process, you walk through a device that basically detects potentially dangerous items by measuring their temperature and 42)**distinguishing them from your body**, because the objects' temperature and the bodies' are usually different. We can 43)**apply** the same principle **to** the galaxies that the research team scrutinized.

Unfortunately, we don't have infrared-sensitive eyes or the 44)**ability to** just 45)**look at** the galaxies and 46)**discern one from another**, right? 47)**Infrared light**, which is 48)**a part of** the electromagnetic spectrum, is not within the visible spectrum, meaning that a special device is 49)**required to** detect the radiation that galaxies emit – 50)**a sort of** infrared-light detecting device like the body-scanning device or the night-vision goggles. Eventually, an appropriate device was developed: the infrared telescope. These telescopes don't 51)**differ** much **from** regular telescopes. The major difference is the location of the infrared telescope, because infrared radiation has lower energy than visible light, and... well, it would 52)**take** another period **to** explain the details, so 53)**let's get back** to that later; 54)**Be sure to remind** me though, because I might forget, and it's crucial that you understand it. So, as astronomers 55)**began looking** at the composition of stars in the Milky Way using infrared telescopes, they noticed that part of the galaxy, the peripheral space specifically, 56)**seemed to** be different, apparently containing unusual chemical patterns that didn't 57)**sync with** the Milky Way's chemical composition. After countless 58)**attempts to match** them, the astronomers finally found a secondary source of chemical compositions and 59)**identified** it **as** the Sagittarius Galaxy. As their research continued, they determined exactly how much of Sagittarius had been absorbed by the Milky Way. Furthermore, they found an 60)**attractive force** between the two, which they later identified as gravitational force. This force isn't 61)**dissimilar from** the one between Earth and the Moon, 62)**except that** the force exerted 63)**in the latter case** is much stronger.

This force has 64)**caused** the Milky Way **to** absorb or pull on Sagittarius 65)**for so long** that Sagittarius' shape has been 66)**stretched out** or 67)**transformed into** an elongated, elliptical shape. If this continues, as scientists predict it will, the galaxy will be destroyed and completely 68)**incorporated into** the Milky Way. Therefore, we now know that the belief that galaxies are bound is 69)**no longer** valid; rather, galaxies are ever evolving. 70)**Next time**, we'll discuss another 71)**contradictory point** about our solar system: that it actually 72)**belongs to** the Sagittarius Dwarf galaxy, not the Milky Way.

Two galaxies

Listen to part of a lecture in an astronomy class

P: Yesterday we discussed our solar system and its contents. Today, we'll talk about two galaxies, systems consisting of billions of stars and other remnants, the Milky Way, which includes our solar system, and another named Sagittarius.

Researchers have recently discovered that larger galaxies tend to absorb stars from smaller galaxies. You may be wondering how this relates to today's topic. You see, the Milky Way is 10,000 times bigger than Sagittarius and the research team found that Sagittarius' stars are being pulled into, or absorbed by, the Milky Way. This is astonishing and interesting, because galaxies were commonly thought to be gravitationally bound, and the idea of two galaxies fusing together, or one 'stealing' stars from another, was seldom considered. Even when it was, researchers couldn't validate the point due to lack of evidence, so the theories were viewed as absurd and controversial. However, evidence arose that validated the theory. So, how did they prove what previous cosmologists couldn't?

To begin, let's go over why previous researchers couldn't prove the phenomenon and what they were lacking. To help you visualize it, let's say you shredded two identical stacks of paper. If they were pure white with no distinguishing marks, would you be able to sort them? Probably not unless you had some kind of supernatural power, right? But what if one stack was blue and the other red? Now, the scenario changes, and it becomes quite easy to distinguish them.

That's exactly how the research team was able to determine the extent to which the stars of the Sagittarius galaxy were being pulled into the Milky Way. They began by studying galaxies… what they contain, what they're made of, what properties they share, and things like that. Then, they realized that galaxies radiate thermal energy, or heat that gives off infrared radiation or… infrared light. This might sound a little more familiar to you… For those not familiar with infrared radiation, think about how detecting devices are employed in warzones or airports. I'm sure you've seen soldiers wearing bulky-looking goggles at night. These night vision devices enable soldiers to, uh… see objects by detecting the thermal radiation they give off, regardless of the darkness – so the 'coldness' or 'hotness' of the objects determines the radiation's color, ranging from blue to red. Also at the airport, when you go through the body-scanning process, you walk through a device that basically detects potentially dangerous items by measuring their temperature and distinguishing them from your body, because the objects' temperature and the bodies' are usually different. We can apply the same principle to the galaxies that the research team scrutinized.

Unfortunately, we don't have infrared-sensitive eyes or the ability to just look at the galaxies and discern one from another, right? Infrared light, which is a part of the electromagnetic spectrum, is not within the visible spectrum, meaning that a special device is required to detect the radiation that galaxies emit – a sort of infrared-light detecting device like the body-scanning device or the night-vision goggles. Eventually, an appropriate device was developed: the infrared telescope. These telescopes don't differ much from regular telescopes. The major difference is the location of the infrared telescope, because infrared radiation has lower energy than visible light, and… well, it would take another period to explain the details, so let's get back to that later; Be sure to remind me though, because I might forget, and it's crucial that you understand it. So, as astronomers began looking at the composition of stars in the Milky Way using infrared telescopes, they noticed that part of the galaxy, the peripheral space specifically, seemed to be different, apparently containing unusual chemical patterns that didn't sync with the Milky Way's chemical composition. After countless attempts to match them, the astronomers finally found a secondary source of chemical compositions and identified it as the Sagittarius Galaxy. As their research continued, they determined exactly how much of Sagittarius had been absorbed by the Milky Way. Furthermore, they found an attractive force between the two, which they later identified as gravitational force. This force isn't dissimilar from the one between Earth and the Moon, except that the force exerted in the latter case is much stronger.

This force has caused the Milky Way to absorb or pull on Sagittarius for so long that Sagittarius' shape has been stretched out or transformed into an elongated, elliptical shape. If this continues, as scientists predict it will, the galaxy will be destroyed and completely incorporated into the Milky Way. Therefore, we now know that the belief that galaxies are bound is no longer valid; rather, galaxies are ever evolving. Next time, we'll discuss another contradictory point about our solar system: that it actually belongs to the Sagittarius Dwarf galaxy, not the Milky Way.

Biomimetics

Listen to part of a lecture in a biology class

P: Last lecture, I introduced a new field of biology 01)**called** biomimetics. It's basically imitating or borrowing natural systems and components 02)**for the purpose of** creating new commercial products. I'll 03)**give** you a few examples that'll 04)**make** it easier to understand.

You might be wondering how businesses can 05)**integrate** natural elements **into** their products, correct? Well… 06)**I'm** pretty **sure** you've noticed that birds, or insects like butterflies, have unique structures, 07)**such as** feathers or scales. 08)**For instance**, Morpho butterflies have mesmerizing green and blue scales on their wings. These colors are created 09)**in two ways**: pigmentation and structural coloration. 10)**The former** sounds more familiar than 11)**the latter**, doesn't it? For those not 12)**familiar with** pigments, let's 13)**look at** the colors of plants. Our common perception is that they're green. This color is 14)**due to** chlorophyll, a green pigment 15)**found in** the chloroplasts. The green wavelengths are reflected rather than 16)**absorbed by** the plants, and 17)**that's why** we see the color. Sunlight has 18)**a wide range of** colors, and green, specifically the green-light spectrum, 19)**fails to** be absorbed by the chlorophyll because… well, evidence proving why this happens remains unsubstantiated, but most scientists assume that green light is 20)**detrimental to** the process of photosynthesis, 21)**the process through** which plants 22)**produce** energy **from** sunlight. I think that's enough about pigmentation.

To understand structural coloration, which is also 23)**known as** schemochrome, we'll look at the Morpho butterfly. This type of coloration was first observed by Robert Hooke and Isaac Newton, and later elucidated by Thomas Young. Young explained that the creation of structural colors requires two elements: thin layers of films or scales and light. The morpho butterfly's wings are 24)**composed of** rows of tiny, tree-like scales, with gaps between them. As light hits these scales, they 25)**interact with** it, absorbing and reflecting certain wavelengths of colors, 26)**just as** pigments in the chloroplasts in plants. So, the blue wavelength is reflected multiple times and the coloration of the wings becomes visible.

27)**I don't know if** you've noticed it yet, but structural coloration is exactly what business people exploit when designing products. 28)**You see**, dyes and chemicals aren't necessary if structures can be used, right? So, fabric and fiber manufacturers can 29)**eliminate** the use of toxic elements **from** their formulas when coloring their products. Additionally, structural coloration is energy-efficient and not environmentally damaging because no additional energy consumption is 30)**required to** produce and 31)**apply** dyes to their products. Oh, I 32)**forgot to** mention that the wings are also 'water-proof,' didn't I?

The wings are structured 33)**so that** the gap between each layer is 34)**filled with** gas and 35)**works as** a 'water-barrier'. You see, if water droplets are 36)**dropped on** a flat surface, several adhesive forces govern them. One of these is the attraction between water droplets, which 37)**pull together** to form larger droplets. Another is the energy that 39)**causes water to** 40)**stick to** solids. This causes water droplets to 41)**flatten out** on smooth surfaces. However, the Morpho butterflies' wings are structured 42)**in such a way** that makes them bumpy and rough with air in the gaps. If you think of this 43)**in chemistry terms**, water doesn't stick to air as it does to solid, smooth surfaces. When water 44)**comes into contact with** a rough surface, it doesn't flatten out; it preserves its shape and slides right off. This also 45)**allows** dust particles on the wings **to** 47)**roll off** with the water droplets because, again, water has a strong affinity for solid matter, not rough surfaces.

You see where I'm going with this, right? These phenomena 48)**are prevalent in** nature, and are 49)**interesting to** manufacturers of commercial products. For instance, shirt manufacturers can incorporate the same principles. Let's imagine you are eating a greasy hamburger in a shirt with structural coloration. What do you think would happen if you accidently 50)**spilled** ketchup **on** your shirt? 51)**Of course**, the rough, layered material would bear the same results.

As I explained, the integration of biology and business gives us great promise for future generations and for technological advances. But, biomimicry can also 52)**have a** negative **impact on** creativity because… Well, 53)**let me** 54)**refer to** the three distinct steps or levels of biomimicry. First is the process of replicating aspects of the natural mechanisms of an organism, just like taking the tree-like structure of the butterflies' wings and duplicating it in their products. Next is the understanding of the phenomena – how these natural processes are created in nature. The third, and perhaps the most imperative, is that manufacturers 55)**need to** ensure that whatever they replicate and produce does not work as an 56)**impediment to** our thinking process. Original thinking is barely 57)**involved in** biomimicry, because it's simply observing natural phenomena and exploiting them. Don't misunderstand my point, though. Biomimicry presents noteworthy benefits to society, as I've explained.

Biomimetics

Listen to part of a lecture in a biology class

P: Last lecture, I introduced a new field of biology called biomimetics. It's basically imitating or borrowing natural systems and components for the purpose of creating new commercial products. I'll give you a few examples that'll make it easier to understand.

You might be wondering how businesses can integrate natural elements into their products, correct? Well… I'm pretty sure you've noticed that birds, or insects like butterflies, have unique structures, such as feathers or scales. For instance, Morpho butterflies have mesmerizing green and blue scales on their wings. These colors are created in two ways: pigmentation and structural coloration. The former sounds more familiar than the latter, doesn't it? For those not familiar with pigments, let's look at the colors of plants. Our common perception is that they're green. This color is due to chlorophyll, a green pigment found in the chloroplasts. The green wavelengths are reflected rather than absorbed by the plants, and that's why we see the color. Sunlight has a wide range of colors, and green, specifically the green-light spectrum, fails to be absorbed by the chlorophyll because… well, evidence proving why this happens remains unsubstantiated, but most scientists assume that green light is detrimental to the process of photosynthesis, the process through which plants produce energy from sunlight. I think that's enough about pigmentation.

To understand structural coloration, which is also known as schemochrome, we'll look at the Morpho butterfly. This type of coloration was first observed by Robert Hooke and Isaac Newton, and later elucidated by Thomas Young. Young explained that the creation of structural colors requires two elements: thin layers of films or scales and light. The morpho butterfly's wings are composed of rows of tiny, tree-like scales, with gaps between them. As light hits these scales, they interact with it, absorbing and reflecting certain wavelengths of colors, just as pigments in the chloroplasts in plants. So, the blue wavelength is reflected multiple times and the coloration of the wings becomes visible.

I don't know if you've noticed it yet, but structural coloration is exactly what business people exploit when designing products. You see, dyes and chemicals aren't necessary if structures can be used, right? So, fabric and fiber manufacturers can eliminate the use of toxic elements from their formulas when coloring their products. Additionally, structural coloration is energy-efficient and not environmentally damaging because no additional energy consumption is required to produce and apply dyes to their products. Oh, I forgot to mention that the wings are also 'water-proof,' didn't I?

The wings are structured so that the gap between each layer is filled with gas and works as a 'water-barrier'. You see, if water droplets are dropped on a flat surface, several adhesive forces govern them. One of these is the attraction between water droplets, which pull together to form larger droplets. Another is the energy that causes water to stick to solids. This causes water droplets to flatten out on smooth surfaces. However, the Morpho butterflies' wings are structured in such a way that makes them bumpy and rough with air in the gaps. If you think of this in chemistry terms, water doesn't stick to air as it does to solid, smooth surfaces. When water comes into contact with a rough surface, it doesn't flatten out; it preserves its shape and slides right off. This also allows dust particles on the wings to roll off with the water droplets because, again, water has a strong affinity for solid matter, not rough surfaces.

You see where I'm going with this, right? These phenomena are prevalent in nature, and are interesting to manufacturers of commercial products. For instance, shirt manufacturers can incorporate the same principles. Let's imagine you are eating a greasy hamburger in a shirt with structural coloration. What do you think would happen if you accidentally spilled ketchup on your shirt? Of course, the rough, layered material would bear the same results.

As I explained, the integration of biology and business gives us great promise for future generations and for technological advances. But, biomimicry can also have a negative impact on creativity because… Well, let me refer to the three distinct steps or levels of biomimicry. First is the process of replicating aspects of the natural mechanisms of an organism, just like taking the tree-like structure of the butterflies' wings and duplicating it in their products. Next is the understanding of the phenomena – how these natural processes are created in nature. The third, and perhaps the most imperative, is that manufacturers need to ensure that whatever they replicate and produce does not work as an impediment to our thinking process. Original thinking is barely involved in biomimicry, because it's simply observing natural phenomena and exploiting them. Don't misunderstand my point, though. Biomimicry presents noteworthy benefits to society, as I've explained.

19th century European art movements

Listen to a conversation between a student and her art history professor

S: Hi, professor, [01]**do you have a minute**?

P: Of course, [02]**what can I do for you**, Maria?

S: Well, it's about the group presentation on 19th century European art movements… I need help sorting my ideas.

P: Okay. Have you chosen a topic for the presentation?

S: Yes, [03]**I've done** some research, and the Barbizon school really [04]**caught** my **attention**, you know the French painters [05]**from** 1830 **to** 1880.

P: A very interesting topic. Ummm… [06]**Why don't you** [07]**tell** me what you've [08]**learned from** your research? [09]**Start with** the source of their name and the focus of their art.

S: Okay. [10]**From what I've read**, the name [11]**comes from** a village located just outside of Paris, because the painters' primary workplace was the nearby Fontainebleau Forest. I read that the forest attracted the artists because it preserved nature unaffected by modern civilization, so, it was a genuine representation of nature.

P: And their painting?

S: Oh right! They shared an understanding or recognition of landscape [12]**when it came to** painting and they were faithful painters. [13]**By that, I mean** they [14]**strove to** [15]**adhere to** capturing what they could see and avoided figurative elements or things that didn't exist in the natural scene.

P: I see… Okay. [16]**I'm not sure if** you've gotten this part yet, but did you know that their approach was quite [17]**different from** traditional French landscape painting, which included the use of imaginative elements inspired by classical poems?

S: Oh, I never knew that!

P: Great! Why don't you [18]**add** something **to** the presentation that will show the difference between the two? I'm sure it would be very informative.

S: I should definitely do that!

P: Okay, [19]**were** you **able to** find any other information?

S: Um, I read that the Barbizon painters often did basic, preliminary sketches for their paintings while out in the forest and then finished them in their studios. They also intentionally left some details of their work looking unfinished, but I [20]**need to do** more [21]**research on** those points.

P: Okay, that's great. [22]**Try to** [23]**make** your presentation concise and informative. Remember, It should be 5 minutes, not an hour.

S: Of course. Any suggestions on how I should proceed?

P: Well… [24]**let's see**. It seems that you've [25]**done** comprehensive **research**, but you're missing a central figure, like a paragon of the Barbizon school. I think Théodore Rousseau would be a good example, because… Well, you'll [26]**figure** it **out** through your research, but he was [27]**one of the** most prominent and noteworthy artists of the school. Try to do some research on his life and paintings and [28]**include** them **in** your presentation.

S: Perfect! Oh [29]**by the way**, I hear the art museum around the corner exhibits Barbizon paintings, so [30]**I'm going to** [31]**stop by** there also.

P: That's a great plan. I think [32]**you're all set** and good to go!

S: Thanks for your help, professor. I really appreciate it!

P: [33]**No problem at all**. Good luck with your presentation; I'll [34]**look forward to** it!

19th century European art movements

Listen to a conversation between a student and her art history professor

S: Hi, professor, do you have a minute?

P: Of course, what can I do for you, Maria?

S: Well, it's about the group presentation on 19th century European art movements… I need help sorting my ideas.

P: Okay. Have you chosen a topic for the presentation?

S: Yes, I've done some research, and the Barbizon school really caught my attention, you know the French painters from 1830 to 1880.

P: A very interesting topic. Ummm… Why don't you tell me what you've learned from your research? Start with the source of their name and the focus of their art.

S: Okay. From what I've read, the name comes from a village located just outside of Paris, because the painters' primary workplace was the nearby Fontainebleau Forest. I read that the forest attracted the artists because it preserved nature unaffected by modern civilization, so, it was a genuine representation of nature.

P: And their painting?

S: Oh right! They shared an understanding or recognition of landscape when it came to painting and they were faithful painters. By that, I mean they strove to adhere to capturing what they could see and avoided figurative elements or things that didn't exist in the natural scene.

P: I see… Okay. I'm not sure if you've gotten this part yet, but did you know that their approach was quite different from traditional French landscape painting, which included the use of imaginative elements inspired by classical poems?

S: Oh, I never knew that!

P: Great! Why don't you add something to the presentation that will show the difference between the two? I'm sure it would be very informative.

S: I should definitely do that!

P: Okay, were you able to find any other information?

S: Um, I read that the Barbizon painters often did basic, preliminary sketches for their paintings while out in the forest and then finished them in their studios. They also intentionally left some details of their work looking unfinished, but I need to do more research on those points.

P: Okay, that's great. Try to make your presentation concise and informative. Remember, It should be 5 minutes, not an hour.

S: Of course. Any suggestions on how I should proceed?

P: Well… let's see. It seems that you've done comprehensive research, but you're missing a central figure, like a paragon of the Barbizon school. I think Théodore Rousseau would be a good example, because… Well, you'll figure it out through your research, but he was one of the most prominent and noteworthy artists of the school. Try to do some research on his life and paintings and include them in your presentation.

S: Perfect! Oh by the way, I hear the art museum around the corner exhibits Barbizon paintings, so I'm going to stop by there also.

P: That's a great plan. I think you're all set and good to go!

S: Thanks for your help, professor. I really appreciate it!

P: No problem at all. Good luck with your presentation; I'll look forward to it!

The advent of literacy and cheap books

Listen to part of a lecture in a literature class

P: Okay, we ⁰¹⁾**looked at** the ⁰²⁾**access to** books by the 19th century English public last time, specifically how classics were ⁰³⁾**divided into** triple-deckers of three volumes. ⁰⁴⁾**Due to** this, book prices were extremely burdensome for ordinary people, so they ⁰⁵⁾**came up with** ⁰⁶⁾**ways to** ⁰⁷⁾**make** books more accessible and cheaper: lending libraries and, uh, the publication of books in magazines and newspapers. Well, interestingly, a similar phenomenon ⁰⁸⁾**existed from** the 15th century ⁰⁹⁾**all the way to** the 17th century, so we'll investigate some key points of the era today before we ¹⁰⁾**move on to** the modern era of literature.

Although the timing of this period is sometimes controversial, ¹¹⁾we**'re going to** ¹²⁾**refer to** it **as** the early ¹³⁾**modern period**, succeeding the Middle Ages of the post-classical era. This period was ¹⁴⁾**marked by** the advent of literacy and cheap books became readily ¹⁵⁾**available to** the general public, especially in France. These were small pamphlets, usually ¹⁶⁾**covering subjects** like chivalry – you know, medieval knights ¹⁷⁾**going on** adventures and exploring the world. Religious stories about the tension ¹⁸⁾**between** saints **and** demons were also covered in the books. However, ¹⁹⁾**don't get the wrong idea**; the stories were very light and entertaining. Philosophical components weren't involved, so everyday people ²⁰⁾**enjoyed reading** them. Those books were usually simple and cheaply-made, ²¹⁾**nothing like** the embellished manuscripts of the Middle ages, which covered ²²⁾**a range of** subjects ²³⁾**from** philosophy **to** art or science. These cheap books were ²⁴⁾**so** common **that** they were even sold by hawkers and peddlers.

S: Professor, you mentioned earlier, that some kind of stimulus or input always starts radical changes. What was it ²⁵⁾**in this case**?

P: Good question! You're asking what initiated this dramatic ²⁶⁾**change in** Western civilization, right? Well, Elizabeth Eisenstein, an American scholar and historian, explained the ²⁷⁾**transition from** the era of the manuscript **to** that of print culture.

In the late 1970's, she claimed that printing of cheap books and pamphlets was ²⁹⁾**responsible for** an unrecognized revolution that ³⁰⁾**resulted in** two significant ³¹⁾**long-term effects**. We'll discuss the 'unrecognized revolution' ³²⁾**in detail** later, so let's not ³³⁾**worry about** it yet, but the first change it ³⁴⁾**brought about** was printing technology, ³⁵⁾**a set of** new standards for books. I mean, popular stories ³⁶⁾**made way for** just one standard, the written version, because they were much more profitable and efficient ³⁷⁾**that way**. ³⁸⁾**Prior to the advent of** printing culture, however, stories were ³⁹⁾**passed down** orally. So, that was her first claim of a print revolution hypothesis, but this doesn't mean that the oral tradition was completely eradicated. She claimed ⁴⁰⁾**there would** always **be** a written version of stories, but people ⁴¹⁾**continued to** orally express them, because it was more convenient. Her second claim was that printing technology enabled the permanent preservation of materials, which were usefully employed by the critics of authority ⁴²⁾**at the time**. They were useful resources because the critics could ⁴³⁾**refer to** the books whenever evidence or differing perspectives were needed. To elucidate her point, she used the example of French writer, Michel de Montaigne.

Montaigne was ⁴⁴⁾**one of the** most prestigious and notable French Renaissance writers and his impact is still recognized today. His controversial essays were ⁴⁵⁾**considered** ⁴⁶⁾**detrimental to** tradition and authority rather than **as** innovations during his time. He's now considered the father of modern skepticism, but we needn't ⁴⁷⁾**go too deeply into** his biography now, so let's skip it. ⁴⁸⁾**Where were we**… right, okay. After scrutinizing his essays, Eisenstein found that he had access to information from many books and he borrowed ideas and concepts for his essays. ⁴⁹⁾**As I mentioned earlier**, his ⁵⁰⁾**points of view** were very well conveyed through his essays. ⁵¹⁾**For instance**, in his 1580 work ⁵²⁾**called** the Essais, which is considered his most noteworthy work, he expressed his ⁵³⁾**views on** subjects like politics, religion, and human nature.

I think that's ⁵⁴⁾**enough of** an explanation. Let me ask you, what do you think was the ⁵⁵⁾**driving force** of this revolution? Printing machines or people?

S: I would say printing machines actualized the revolution, because they ⁵⁶⁾**made it possible for people to develop** and use books more efficiently.

P: Some scholars argue that, but let's ⁵⁷⁾**take into consideration** ⁵⁸⁾**the accounts** of the French Revolution and the Industrial Revolution. The former lasted about 10 years, from 1789 to 1799, I believe, and the latter lasted much longer, fifty to seventy years. It's generally thought that fifty to seventy years is a long time for a 'revolution.' If you look at the printing revolution, it lasted about three hundred years. Do you think printing technology itself was ⁵⁹⁾**enough** of a driving force **to** ⁶⁰⁾**keep** the early modern period afloat for three centuries? Well, not quite. It's unfortunate that the people who brought about changes at the time aren't ⁶¹⁾**getting the credit** they deserve.

The advent of literacy and cheap books

Listen to part of a lecture in a literature class

P: Okay, we looked at the access to books by the 19th century English public last time, specifically how classics were divided into triple-deckers of three volumes. Due to this, book prices were extremely burdensome for ordinary people, so they came up with ways to make books more accessible and cheaper: lending libraries and, uh, the publication of books in magazines and newspapers. Well, interestingly, a similar phenomenon existed from the 15th century all the way to the 17th century, so we'll investigate some key points of the era today before we move on to the modern era of literature.

Although the timing of this period is sometimes controversial, we're going to refer to it as the early modern period, succeeding the Middle Ages of the post-classical era. This period was marked by the advent of literacy and cheap books became readily available to the general public, especially in France. These were small pamphlets, usually covering subjects like chivalry – you know, medieval knights going on adventures and exploring the world. Religious stories about the tension between saints and demons were also covered in the books. However, don't get the wrong idea; the stories were very light and entertaining. Philosophical components weren't involved, so everyday people enjoyed reading them. Those books were usually simple and cheaply-made, nothing like the embellished manuscripts of the Middle ages, which covered a range of subjects from philosophy to art or science. These cheap books were so common that they were even sold by hawkers and peddlers.

S: Professor, you mentioned earlier, that some kind of stimulus or input always starts radical changes. What was it in this case?

P: Good question! You're asking what initiated this dramatic change in Western civilization, right? Well, Elizabeth Eisenstein, an American scholar and historian, explained the transition from the era of the manuscript to that of print culture.

In the late 1970's, she claimed that printing of cheap books and pamphlets was responsible for an unrecognized revolution that resulted in two significant long-term effects. We'll discuss the 'unrecognized revolution' in detail later, so let's not worry about it yet, but the first change it brought about was printing technology, a set of new standards for books. I mean, popular stories made way for just one standard, the written version, because they were much more profitable and efficient that way. Prior to the advent of printing culture, however, stories were passed down orally. So, that was her first claim of a print revolution hypothesis, but this doesn't mean that the oral tradition was completely eradicated. She claimed there would always be a written version of stories, but people continued to orally express them, because it was more convenient. Her second claim was that printing technology enabled the permanent preservation of materials, which were usefully employed by the critics of authority at the time. They were useful resources because the critics could refer to the books whenever evidence or differing perspectives were needed. To elucidate her point, she used the example of French writer, Michel de Montaigne.

Montaigne was one of the most prestigious and notable French Renaissance writers and his impact is still recognized today. His controversial essays were considered detrimental to tradition and authority rather than as innovations during his time. He's now considered the father of modern skepticism, but we needn't go too deeply into his biography now, so let's skip it. Where were we… right, okay. After scrutinizing his essays, Eisenstein found that he had access to information from many books and he borrowed ideas and concepts for his essays. As I mentioned earlier, his points of view were very well conveyed through his essays. For instance, in his 1580 work called the Essais, which is considered his most noteworthy work, he expressed his views on subjects like politics, religion, and human nature.

I think that's enough of an explanation. Let me ask you, what do you think was the driving force of this revolution? Printing machines or people?

S: I would say printing machines actualized the revolution, because they made it possible for people to develop and use books more efficiently.

P: Some scholars argue that, but let's take into consideration the accounts of the French Revolution and the Industrial Revolution. The former lasted about 10 years, from 1789 to 1799, I believe, and the latter lasted much longer, fifty to seventy years. It's generally thought that fifty to seventy years is a long time for a 'revolution.' If you look at the printing revolution, it lasted about three hundred years. Do you think printing technology itself was enough of a driving force to keep the early modern period afloat for three centuries? Well, not quite. It's unfortunate that the people who brought about changes at the time aren't getting the credit they deserve.

The Industrial Revolution

Listen to part of a lecture in a history of technology class

P: Today, we'll continue our discussion of the Industrial Revolution that 01)**took place** from 1760 to around 1820 or 1840. 02)**As I mentioned** last time, it was the most prominent period in history, because of the developmental 03)**boom in** almost 04)**every aspect of** humanity 05)**due to** 06)**advances in** medication, transportation, food, 07)**and so on**. It started in England and 08)**spread across** Europe, eventually reaching the United States. Today, 09)**I'd like to** 10)**focus on** a specific technological advance made during the period: transportation. James?

S: If I remember correctly, the earliest steam-powered vehicles 11)**came about** during the mid-18th century. Right?

P: Yes, but these early steam vehicles had a major drawback. Although their engines powered their bodies, they were too heavy, averaging about 3,600kg. Due to this burdensome weight and manufacturing limitations, they weren't 12)**practical for** transportation unless they were on perfectly flat surfaces like iron tracks. Naturally, many companies 13)**turned to** developing locomotives, but the availability of new resources in the early 20th century, 14)**such as** petroleum and gasoline, 15)**led to** the introduction of the luxurious internal combustion powered vehicles that we use today and 16)**marked the end of** steam-powered vehicles.

Although the Industrial Revolution marked the introduction of mechanically produced products, human-powered transportation methods developed. Actually, they were more popular than steam engines because… Well, I think you should know 17)**by now**. What human-powered transportation methods 18)**are you aware of**?

S: Um, bicycles would be the most well-known, 19)**along with** skateboards, velomobiles, and cabin cycles.

P: Great! Today, there are many choices 20)**when it comes to** human-powered transportation, but in the 1800's, choices were more limited. Let's 21)**start with** the first human-powered vehicles 22)**called** horseless carriages, which had four wheels. First patented around 1800, a few different models were available and they accommodated 23)**up to** four riders. Despite their benefits, such as improved convenience on rough, rocky roads, the general public didn't 24)**accept** them **as** methods of transportation.

They were too heavy, so their operation was bothersome and since they were human-powered, human beings 25)**worked as** 'draft animals' to produce their mechanical energy. This was horrendous. Many owners were 26)**criticized** and debased **for** abusing their servants, so their use gradually waned.

After these four-wheeled carriages disappeared, a German carriage maker, Baron Karl Drais, 27)**came up with** the idea for the Dandy horse, or Laufmaschine, which somewhat resembled today's two-wheeled bicycles.

S: I'm sorry. Could you explain that term?

P: Of course. Drais 28)**referred to** it **as** 'Laufmaschine,' which 29)**translates to** 'running machine' in German. Others believe it 30)**comes from** the Latin words for 'fast' and 'foot' because of its shape. It was almost an extension of the human body – one would straddle it and push the ground 31)**as if** running. 32)**Think of** today's bicycle without pedals.

S: No pedals? I thought the earliest bicycle had a humongous front wheel and pedals.

P: You're 33)**referring to** the penny-farthing, which was invented in 1870. Oh wait… there was also another type of bicycle called the boneshaker that was 34)**introduced as** the first bicycle with pedals in the 1860's; you could also be referring to that. Well, whichever it is that you're implying, 35)**I'm on the same page** as you, but 36)**chronologically speaking**, the Laufmaschine was introduced in 1818, 37)**several decades earlier than** those two and was the 38)**starting point** in bicycle development.

S: How fast could it go without pedals… And did people like it?

P: Well, when Drais first demonstrated it in Germany it 39)**received** 40)**a fair amount of acclaim** and recognition, but when it was introduced to France it was largely ignored.

S: Professor, what was the difference?

P: I would say that geographical differences caused the different reactions. When he demonstrated it in Germany, Drais covered 14 kilometers 41)**in** 42)**less than an hour**, which was pretty good because walking would 43)**take** about **twice as long**, but we 44)**need to** 45)**look at** where he rode. The Laufmaschine worked best over smooth, level surfaces, such as where it was introduced in Germany. 46)**In contrast**, 47)**using** it **to** 48)**go up** a slope or through mud and forestland was very difficult. You could easily 49)**lose control** and cause injuries when going downhill. 50)**For these reasons**, the French 51)**were** never really **interested in** it, saying it provided hardly any benefits over walking.

However, Drais never 52)**succumbed to** this criticism and 53)**strove to** 54)**keep** the Laufmaschine alive. To do this, he changed his 55)**marketing strategy**, focusing on its 56)**use for** recreation 57)**rather than** transportation. He 58)**brought** his invention **to** parks and 59)**rented** them **out**. Pretty ingenious, huh?

Well… here's the point I 60)**want you to** understand: the significance of the Laufmaschine is not 61)**as weak as** it may seem. It 62)**inspired** other inventors **to** build better personal vehicles. As I mentioned, bicycles like the Penny-farthing and the boneshaker 63)**descended from** the Laufmaschine.

The Industrial Revolution

Listen to part of a lecture in a history of technology class

P: Today, we'll continue our discussion of the Industrial Revolution that took place from 1760 to around 1820 or 1840. As I mentioned last time, it was the most prominent period in history, because of the developmental boom in almost every aspect of humanity due to advances in medication, transportation, food, and so on. It started in England and spread across Europe, eventually reaching the United States. Today, I'd like to focus on a specific technological advance made during the period: transportation. James?

S: If I remember correctly, the earliest steam-powered vehicles came about during the mid-18th century. Right?

P: Yes, but these early steam vehicles had a major drawback. Although their engines powered their bodies, they were too heavy, averaging about 3,600kg. Due to this burdensome weight and manufacturing limitations, they weren't practical for transportation unless they were on perfectly flat surfaces like iron tracks. Naturally, many companies turned to developing locomotives, but the availability of new resources in the early 20th century, such as petroleum and gasoline, led to the introduction of the luxurious internal combustion powered vehicles that we use today and marked the end of steam-powered vehicles.

Although the Industrial Revolution marked the introduction of mechanically produced products, human-powered transportation methods developed. Actually, they were more popular than steam engines because… Well, I think you should know by now. What human-powered transportation methods are you aware of?

S: Um, bicycles would be the most well-known, along with skateboards, velomobiles, and cabin cycles.

P: Great! Today, there are many choices when it comes to human-powered transportation, but in the 1800's, choices were more limited. Let's start with the first human-powered vehicles called horseless carriages, which had four wheels. First patented around 1800, a few different models were available and they accommodated up to four riders. Despite their benefits, such as improved convenience on rough, rocky roads, the general public didn't accept them as methods of transportation.

They were too heavy, so their operation was bothersome and since they were human-powered, human beings worked as 'draft animals' to produce their mechanical energy. This was horrendous. Many owners were criticized and debased for abusing their servants, so their use gradually waned.

After these four-wheeled carriages disappeared, a German carriage maker, Baron Karl Drais, came up with the idea for the Dandy horse, or Laufmaschine, which somewhat resembled today's two-wheeled bicycles.

S: I'm sorry. Could you explain that term?

P: Of course. Drais referred to it as 'Laufmaschine,' which translates to 'running machine' in German. Others believe it comes from the Latin words for 'fast' and 'foot' because of its shape. It was almost an extension of the human body – one would straddle it and push the ground as if running. Think of today's bicycle without pedals.

S: No pedals? I thought the earliest bicycle had a humongous front wheel and pedals.

P: You're referring to the penny-farthing, which was invented in 1870. Oh wait… there was also another type of bicycle called the boneshaker that was introduced as the first bicycle with pedals in the 1860's; you could also be referring to that. Well, whichever it is that you're implying, I'm on the same page as you, but chronologically speaking, the Laufmaschine was introduced in 1818, several decades earlier than those two and was the starting point in bicycle development.

S: How fast could it go without pedals… And did people like it?

P: Well, when Drais first demonstrated it in Germany it received a fair amount of acclaim and recognition, but when it was introduced to France it was largely ignored.

S: Professor, what was the difference?

P: I would say that geographical differences caused the different reactions. When he demonstrated it in Germany, Drais covered 14 kilometers in less than an hour, which was pretty good because walking would take about twice as long, but we need to look at where he rode. The Laufmaschine worked best over smooth, level surfaces, such as where it was introduced in Germany. In contrast, using it to go up a slope or through mud and forestland was very difficult. You could easily lose control and cause injuries when going downhill. For these reasons, the French were never really interested in it, saying it provided hardly any benefits over walking.

However, Drais never succumbed to this criticism and strove to keep the Laufmaschine alive. To do this, he changed his marketing strategy, focusing on its use for recreation rather than transportation. He brought his invention to parks and rented them out. Pretty ingenious, huh?

Well… here's the point I want you to understand: the significance of the Laufmaschine is not as weak as it may seem. It inspired other inventors to build better personal vehicles. As I mentioned, bicycles like the Penny-farthing and the boneshaker descended from the Laufmaschine.

The reservation on a friday

Listen to a conversation between a student and an employee at the community center

S: Hello, 01)**I'm here for a meeting with** Ms. Magliozzi.

E: Oh, you 02)**must be**… Mr. James! I'm the one you're 03)**looking for**. I'm sorry… 04)**Were you waiting long**?

S: No, I was late myself because there was a 05)**traffic jam** on Main Street. There 06)**must've been** a 07)**car accident** on the 08)**leading road to** the highway.

E: 09)**What's happening** today? There was also a major accident 10)**on the other side of** town.

S: I hope no one was seriously injured. Anyway, about today's meeting…

E: Oh right. Let's see… I'm assuming you're 11)**familiar with** the community center.

S: I've 12)**spent** 13)**the majority** of my life here so I know pretty much everything about this town.

E: Great, 14)**come in** and 15)**take a seat**. I'll explain what you 16)**need to do** to 17)**make** your job a little easier and how to access the website you'll need.

S: Really? I'm just here to 18)**make a reservation** so my soccer club can have a practice session next Friday. I didn't 19)**expect it to** be so complicated.

E: Oh, wait. You're Mr. James, correct?

S: Yes, Mike James.

E: 20)**Give** me one second… I 21)**was supposed to** have a 22)**job interview** with Bryan James 20 minutes ago, but… Oh, my apologies. I must've 23)**mixed** you **up with** Bryan.

S: Well, that was out of the blue. I was confused 24)**for a second**. Okay, so about the reservation…

E: Right, when did you 25)**want to** make the reservation?

S: Next Friday. The manager 26)**asked** me **to** come and talk to you about it… I'm not sure why, though.

E: What's his name, may I ask?

S: Of course. It's Coach Stillman – Steven Stillman, just so 27)we're **on the same page** this time.

E: Oh, Steven is your coach? 28)**No wonder** he recommended that you see me.

S: I'm not sure 29)**I'm following**…

E: Steven and I 30)**go way back**. We met in high school, and we've 31)**had** a good **relationship** for almost 30 years now and… Whoops, I've deviated 32)**a little bit**, haven't I? Well, he asked you to see me because you would normally need to 33)**pay to** make any reservation on a Friday, unlike other days, and it's not so cheap since Fridays are extremely popular. But, for Steven, I…

S: Oh, I get it now. You must 34)**be willing to** give us a discount.

E: Well, for Steven's requests, I'm usually more generous than that. You won't need to pay anything.

S: Wow, 35)**I didn't see that coming**.

E: Here, just take these reservation forms and 36)**make sure** 37)**both** you **and** Steven sign them, okay? Once 38)you're **done**, you'll receive 39)**guest passes** for the number of people you're 40)**bringing in**. 41)**Are we clear**?

S: Yes, 42)**loud and clear**! Anything else?

E: Um, just one more thing. 43)**Tell** everyone on your team **to** bring the pass, because the security guards won't 44)**let** anyone **in** without them.

S: Perfect. I'll do that.

E: Okay, I think we're all set. 45)**Say hello to** your coach for me, will you?

S: 46)**Of course**! Thank you for your help.

E: My pleasure. Now, I guess I'll need to 47)**track down** the other Mr. James. Have a good day!

The reservation on a friday

Listen to a conversation between a student and an employee at the community center

S: Hello, I'm here for a meeting with Ms. Magliozzi.

E: Oh, you must be… Mr. James! I'm the one you're looking for. I'm sorry… Were you waiting long?

S: No, I was late myself because there was a traffic jam on Main Street. There must've been a car accident on the leading road to the highway.

E: What's happening today? There was also a major accident on the other side of town.

S: I hope no one was seriously injured. Anyway, about today's meeting…

E: Oh right. Let's see… I'm assuming you're familiar with the community center.

S: I've spent the majority of my life here so I know pretty much everything about this town.

E: Great, come in and take a seat. I'll explain what you need to do to make your job a little easier and how to access the website you'll need.

S: Really? I'm just here to make a reservation so my soccer club can have a practice session next Friday. I didn't expect it to be so complicated.

E: Oh, wait. You're Mr. James, correct?

S: Yes, Mike James.

E: Give me one second… I was supposed to have a job interview with Bryan James 20 minutes ago, but… Oh, my apologies. I must've mixed you up with Bryan.

S: Well, that was out of the blue. I was confused for a second. Okay, so about the reservation…

E: Right, when did you want to make the reservation?

S: Next Friday. The manager asked me to come and talk to you about it… I'm not sure why, though.

E: What's his name, may I ask?

S: Of course. It's Coach Stillman – Steven Stillman, just so we're on the same page this time.

E: Oh, Steven is your coach? No wonder he recommended that you see me.

S: I'm not sure I'm following…

E: Steven and I go way back. We met in high school, and we've had a good relationship for almost 30 years now and… Whoops, I've deviated a little bit, haven't I? Well, he asked you to see me because you would normally need to pay to make any reservation on a Friday, unlike other days, and it's not so cheap since Fridays are extremely popular. But, for Steven, I…

S: Oh, I get it now. You must be willing to give us a discount.

E: Well, for Steven's requests, I'm usually more generous than that. You won't need to pay anything.

S: Wow, I didn't see that coming.

E: Here, just take these reservation forms and make sure both you and Steven sign them, okay? Once you're done, you'll receive guest passes for the number of people you're bringing in. Are we clear?

S: Yes, loud and clear! Anything else?

E: Um, just one more thing. Tell everyone on your team to bring the pass, because the security guards won't let anyone in without them.

S: Perfect. I'll do that.

E: Okay, I think we're all set. Say hello to your coach for me, will you?

S: Of course! Thank you for your help.

E: My pleasure. Now, I guess I'll need to track down the other Mr. James. Have a good day!

Early European art movements

Listen to part of a lecture in an art history class

P: Let's continue our discussion of early European art movements by [01]**going over** some [02]**key points** from the 15th to 19th century, before [03]**moving on to** contemporary art.

You can see [04]**a myriad of** contemporary painting styles, philosophies, and perspectives [05]**embedded in** the paintings, but if you [06]**pay** close **attention to** the details, you'll find that they share one characteristic. How do you think they [07]**came up with** those sophisticated, rich, and delicate colors [08]**back then**? They all mixed and developed their own paints. Unlike today, they couldn't just [09]**pop into** an art store and [10]**ask for** tubes of paint. They [11]**needed to** [12]**go through** [13]**a lot of** experimentation to come up with [14]**not only** colorful, **but also** durable, paints that [15]**set** them **apart from** others. Further, they [16]**wanted to** preserve their paintings as long as they could… which [17]**makes sense**. Why would they [18]**want** their artwork **to** [19]**go to waste** after a short time?

That process lasted about 3 centuries, until a dramatic transition occurred in the art community [20]**between** the late 1700s **and** the early 1800s. Artists had [21]**had a** pretty good **understanding of** how to make rich, ornate paints [22]**on** their **own** [23]**by the end of** the 1700s, as the period's experimentation [24]**led to** stability. However, the need to make canvases – the fabrics on which they painted – [25]**became obsolete** [26]**due to** technological innovations. Unfortunately, the glue in these mechanically produced canvases [27]**made it** more **difficult for** the paint **to** stick to them. As the glue dried, it [28]**caused** the paint **to** crack and fade. Regrettably, the artists didn't know about this and quickly transitioned to mechanically produced canvases from making their own, which [29]**would've** required many hours of strenuous labor. Therefore, the European art movement from the early 1800s was… a total disaster [30]**in terms of** the longevity of their artwork.

Further "experimentation and innovation" changed the way artists learned. Previously, artists trained under master painters [31]**in a** studio or a similar **setting**. This method was interactive and intensive. However, in the early 1800s, art standards transformed as Napoleon III rebuilt Paris. Has anyone [32]**heard of** Académie des Beaux-Arts? I didn't think so. Well, they were [33]**a group of** art academies built around France that greatly impacted French art. Artists [34]**began to** [35]**adhere to** the rules and guidelines that they [36]**imposed on** their painters as many artists began to be educated at the academies. Thus, their preferences, [37]**such as** technique, color, and, um, subject selection, became the new standards for artists. [38]**For instance**, they valued religious and historical themes and caused their artists to paint [39]**in a way that** concealed their individual feelings and personalities. How? Well, again, they needed to follow certain rules, such as [40]**making** their paintings look as realistic as possible or using earnest and conservative colors, so individuality and creativity became more [41]**difficult to** discern. These "educated" artists were spared the responsibility of originality.

Later, another art movement arose [42]**in opposition to** the academies and their practice of art. Ummm… Does everyone remember the painting I [43]**showed** you last week? Impression, Sunrise by Claude Monet… He's now [44]**regarded as** [45]**one of the leading figures** of the Impressionist movement [46]**along with** Sisley, Pissarro, and Morisot. His work inspired the movement and [47]**contributed to** [48]**giving** "Impressionism" its name. Although their styles and techniques varied, the impressionists and their art were united by their pursuit of independence and rebellion. They [49]**abstained from** [50]**applying** the academies' regulations **to** their work, because they believed the paintings from the academies were unnatural. They [51]**held** their own impressionist **exhibitions** and, naturally, public awareness of the movement grew through their efforts.

You may be wondering how they [52]**differed from** the academies' artists. Or, should I say, how their paintings were [53]**distinguished from** those created by academy artists. Well, impressionists valued imagination and subjectivity and didn't [54]**attempt to** emulate the reality in their paintings. This development [55]**took off** as photography [56]**gained popularity** and cameras became portable. You see, they thought that there was no way they could create more accurate and realistic pictures than photographs. So, [57]**instead of** attempting to draw perfect representations, which seemed futile, they [58]**added** their views and imagination **to** their landscape paintings and such, to convey tidbits that photographs couldn't.

This became possible [59]**because of** another technological innovation. Pre-packaged paints, with both durability and rich colors, became readily available. [60]**In contrast to** the old masters, who needed to varnish their paintings to [61]**protect** them **from fading** and preserve them [62]**for long periods**, the impressionists didn't need to use artificial enhancements, because the new paints that came in tubes already had that ability. [63]**In addition to** this protection, varnish also gave colors depth, but, again, the impressionists didn't need it [64]**for the same reason**.

Next class we'll [65]**look at** five Impressionist works and discuss the individual artist's techniques and color usage.

Early European art movements

Listen to part of a lecture in an art history class

P: Let's continue our discussion of early European art movements by going over some key points from the 15th to 19th century, before moving on to contemporary art.

You can see a myriad of contemporary painting styles, philosophies, and perspectives embedded in the paintings, but if you pay close attention to the details, you'll find that they share one characteristic. How do you think they came up with those sophisticated, rich, and delicate colors back then? They all mixed and developed their own paints. Unlike today, they couldn't just pop into an art store and ask for tubes of paint. They needed to go through a lot of experimentation to come up with not only colorful, but also durable, paints that set them apart from others. Further, they wanted to preserve their paintings as long as they could… which makes sense. Why would they want their artwork to go to waste after a short time?

That process lasted about 3 centuries, until a dramatic transition occurred in the art community between the late 1700s and the early 1800s. Artists had had a pretty good understanding of how to make rich, ornate paints on their own by the end of the 1700s, as the period's experimentation led to stability. However, the need to make canvases – the fabrics on which they painted – became obsolete due to technological innovations. Unfortunately, the glue in these mechanically produced canvases made it more difficult for the paint to stick to them. As the glue dried, it caused the paint to crack and fade. Regrettably, the artists didn't know about this and quickly transitioned to mechanically produced canvases from making their own, which would've required many hours of strenuous labor. Therefore, the European art movement from the early 1800s was… a total disaster in terms of the longevity of their artwork.

Further "experimentation and innovation" changed the way artists learned. Previously, artists trained under master painters in a studio or a similar setting. This method was interactive and intensive. However, in the early 1800s, art standards transformed as Napoleon III rebuilt Paris. Has anyone heard of Académie des Beaux-Arts? I didn't think so. Well, they were a group of art academies built around France that greatly impacted French art. Artists began to adhere to the rules and guidelines that they imposed on their painters as many artists began to be educated at the academies. Thus, their preferences, such as technique, color, and, um, subject selection, became the new standards for artists. For instance, they valued religious and historical themes and caused their artists to paint in a way that concealed their individual feelings and personalities. How? Well, again, they needed to follow certain rules, such as making their paintings look as realistic as possible or using earnest and conservative colors, so individuality and creativity became more difficult to discern. These "educated" artists were spared the responsibility of originality.

Later, another art movement arose in opposition to the academies and their practice of art. Ummm… Does everyone remember the painting I showed you last week? Impression, Sunrise by Claude Monet… He's now regarded as one of the leading figures of the Impressionist movement along with Sisley, Pissarro, and Morisot. His work inspired the movement and contributed to giving "Impressionism" its name. Although their styles and techniques varied, the impressionists and their art were united by their pursuit of independence and rebellion. They abstained from applying the academies' regulations to their work, because they believed the paintings from the academies were unnatural. They held their own impressionist exhibitions and, naturally, public awareness of the movement grew through their efforts.

You may be wondering how they differed from the academies' artists. Or, should I say, how their paintings were distinguished from those created by academy artists. Well, impressionists valued imagination and subjectivity and didn't attempt to emulate the reality in their paintings. This development took off as photography gained popularity and cameras became portable. You see, they thought that there was no way they could create more accurate and realistic pictures than photographs. So, instead of attempting to draw perfect representations, which seemed futile, they added their views and imagination to their landscape paintings and such, to convey tidbits that photographs couldn't.

This became possible because of another technological innovation. Pre-packaged paints, with both durability and rich colors, became readily available. In contrast to the old masters, who needed to varnish their paintings to protect them from fading and preserve them for long periods, the impressionists didn't need to use artificial enhancements, because the new paints that came in tubes already had that ability. In addition to this protection, varnish also gave colors depth, but, again, the impressionists didn't need it for the same reason.

Next class we'll look at five Impressionist works and discuss the individual artist's techniques and color usage.

Antipredator adaptations

Listen to part of a lecture in a biology class

P: Okay, let's review some ⁰¹⁾**key points** before we begin today's lecture. Um, as you should know, prey animals ⁰²⁾**employ** various techniques **to** ⁰³⁾**avoid predation**, which we ⁰⁴⁾**call** "antipredator adaptations." These evolutionary traits and behaviors have been developed by animals ⁰⁵⁾**over** many **centuries** and include ⁰⁶⁾**a wide range of** camouflaging methods, ⁰⁷⁾**such as** crypsis and mimesis. This ⁰⁸⁾**allows** them **to** change their skin or scale colors and patterns. ⁰⁹⁾**For instance**, dark frogs can instantaneously ¹⁰⁾**change into** a vivid color, like red or yellow, as a signal of danger, toxicity, and ¹¹⁾**poison to** predators and ¹²⁾**warn** them **off**. ¹³⁾**In the same way**, animals can ¹⁴⁾**use** behavioral mechanisms **to** avoid predators. This will be off-topic today. Ummm… has anyone ¹⁵⁾**heard of** autotomy?

S: Isn't it when an animal detaches or releases a part of its body to momentarily distract a predator, thereby ¹⁶⁾**buying** it time to escape?

P: Exactly, Stephanie! This mechanism is usually ¹⁷⁾**found in** invertebrates like squids, spiders, and lobsters, but we'll ¹⁸⁾**look at** vertebrates such as salamanders, lizards, and geckos. These creatures can throw different body parts; salamanders drop their limbs – like their legs, geckos their skin, and lizards their tails. Today, we'll ¹⁹⁾**concentrate on** lizards and their ²⁰⁾**ability to** drop their tails.

Interestingly, there doesn't ²¹⁾**need to** be any physical contact between the lizards and their predators ²²⁾**for autotomy to occur**.

S: That's quite ²³⁾**different from** the geckos' release of their skin, isn't it? They only activate this mechanism when ²⁴⁾**in physical contact with** their predators, right?

P: Right, that certainly ²⁵⁾**draws a distinction** between the two species. However, in lizards ²⁶⁾**it seems that** the initial stage of autotomy is the result of a voluntary decision or ²⁷⁾**reflex to** threatening stimuli. Um, even though I said their tails could be lost voluntarily, ²⁸⁾**there are still questions** about the neural and physical ²⁹⁾**basis** of autotomy. More research is needed, but we know that there's ummm… an internal trigger that incites such a response. Looking at their anatomy, researchers have found that lizards have internal structures that facilitate the process, such as the "fracture plane."

Some lizards have multiple fracture planes, whereas others have only one within the vertebrae in their tails. Regardless, fracture planes ³⁰⁾**serve one purpose**: ³¹⁾**helping** lizards autotomize their tails. They drop them by contracting muscles ³²⁾**between** the vertebrae **and** severing the tail. Interestingly, the severed tails temporarily wiggle ³³⁾**as if** they were alive… Quite freaky, right?

S: How ³⁴⁾**is it possible that** the tail moves when there isn't a nervous system to stimulate the movement?

P: That's a great point, Stephanie. I was initially doubtful, too, but after seeing several studies about movement after tail detachment, I finally understand it. However, let's discuss that next time and ³⁵⁾**try to** stay ³⁶⁾**on track**. Anyway, when they successfully escape, the tail ³⁷⁾**healing process** begins almost immediately. I should also mention that, although the tails regenerate, the healed tails are not ³⁸⁾**identical to** the originals… The former comprise cartilage ³⁹⁾**rather than** vertebrae, but it ⁴⁰⁾**serves**, ⁴¹⁾**more or less**, the same purpose and **function**. Surprisingly, tail regeneration ⁴²⁾**takes only four to twelve weeks**, ⁴³⁾**depending on** the species.

Let's shift our focus here… we've discussed the primary purpose and benefit of tail autotomy, survival, but there are also costs involved. ⁴⁴⁾**You see**, lizards detach their tails as a survival mechanism, but then they become less effective predators themselves. Some believe that it's because they lose ⁴⁵⁾**a significant amount of** energy when their tails are dropped. However, others point out that their fat reserves, or their energy storage, are not lost since they are located ⁴⁷⁾**at the base of** the tails, which isn't detached. Confusing, huh? Anyway, let's think about how ⁴⁸⁾**the lack of** a tail would affect the lizard's ⁴⁹⁾**daily life**, which revolves around foraging and ⁵⁰⁾**feeding on** prey, and how their tails assist these activities. They are mainly ⁵¹⁾**used for** maintaining their body control and balance. Without tails, lizards can't move as freely, so they naturally ⁵²⁾**expend** more **energy negating** the impact of tail detachment. Another problem that arises after tail-drops is the ⁵³⁾**reduction in** ⁵⁴⁾**attractiveness to** the opposite-sex. ⁵⁵⁾**In addition**, female lizards ⁵⁶⁾**lay** fewer **eggs** that ⁵⁷⁾**result in** weaker offspring and male lizards ⁵⁸⁾**suffer from** lowered ⁵⁹⁾**social statuses**. There are several other costs, but we won't ⁶⁰⁾**go into** those, since they're quite redundant.

Remember that these disadvantages don't necessarily ⁶¹⁾**leave** the lizards completely vulnerable. They're ever-evolving creatures that consistently develop evolutionary traits ⁶²⁾**according to** their changing conditions and environments. For instance, they may ⁶³⁾**spend** less **time chasing** prey in open fields and more time ⁶⁴⁾**looking out for** predators. They may also change their activity time – from diurnal to nocturnal and ⁶⁵⁾**vice versa** – ⁶⁶⁾**depending on** the species.

Antipredator adaptations

Listen to part of a lecture in a biology class

P: Okay, let's review some key points before we begin today's lecture. Um, as you should know, prey animals employ various techniques to avoid predation, which we call "antipredator adaptations." These evolutionary traits and behaviors have been developed by animals over many centuries and include a wide range of camouflaging methods, such as crypsis and mimesis. This allows them to change their skin or scale colors and patterns. For instance, dark frogs can instantaneously change into a vivid color, like red or yellow, as a signal of danger, toxicity, and poison to predators and warn them off. In the same way, animals can use behavioral mechanisms to avoid predators. This will be off-topic today. Ummm… has anyone heard of autotomy?

S: Isn't it when an animal detaches or releases a part of its body to momentarily distract a predator, thereby buying it time to escape?

P: Exactly, Stephanie! This mechanism is usually found in invertebrates like squids, spiders, and lobsters, but we'll look at vertebrates such as salamanders, lizards, and geckos. These creatures can throw different body parts; salamanders drop their limbs – like their legs, geckos their skin, and lizards their tails. Today, we'll concentrate on lizards and their ability to drop their tails.

Interestingly, there doesn't need to be any physical contact between the lizards and their predators for autotomy to occur.

S: That's quite different from the geckos' release of their skin, isn't it? They only activate this mechanism when in physical contact with their predators, right?

P: Right, that certainly draws a distinction between the two species. However, in lizards it seems that the initial stage of autotomy is the result of a voluntary decision or reflex to threatening stimuli. Um, even though I said their tails could be lost voluntarily, there are still questions about the neural and physical basis of autotomy. More research is needed, but we know that there's ummm… an internal trigger that incites such a response. Looking at their anatomy, researchers have found that lizards have internal structures that facilitate the process, such as the "fracture plane."

Some lizards have multiple fracture planes, whereas others have only one within the vertebrae in their tails. Regardless, fracture planes serve one purpose: helping lizards autotomize their tails. They drop them by contracting muscles between the vertebrae and severing the tail. Interestingly, the severed tails temporarily wiggle as if they were alive… Quite freaky, right?

S: How is it possible that the tail moves when there isn't a nervous system to stimulate the movement?

P: That's a great point, Stephanie. I was initially doubtful, too, but after seeing several studies about movement after tail detachment, I finally understand it. However, let's discuss that next time and try to stay on track. Anyway, when they successfully escape, the tail healing process begins almost immediately. I should also mention that, although the tails regenerate, the healed tails are not identical to the originals… The former comprise cartilage rather than vertebrae, but it serves, more or less, the same purpose and function. Surprisingly, tail regeneration takes only four to twelve weeks, depending on the species.

Let's shift our focus here… we've discussed the primary purpose and benefit of tail autotomy, survival, but there are also costs involved. You see, lizards detach their tails as a survival mechanism, but then they become less effective predators themselves. Some believe that it's because they lose a significant amount of energy when their tails are dropped. However, others point out that their fat reserves, or their energy storage, are not lost since they are located at the base of the tails, which isn't detached. Confusing, huh? Anyway, let's think about how the lack of a tail would affect the lizard's daily life, which revolves around foraging and feeding on prey, and how their tails assist these activities. They are mainly used for maintaining their body control and balance. Without tails, lizards can't move as freely, so they naturally expend more energy negating the impact of tail detachment. Another problem that arises after tail-drops is the reduction in attractiveness to the opposite-sex. In addition, female lizards lay fewer eggs that result in weaker offspring and male lizards suffer from lowered social statuses. There are several other costs, but we won't go into those, since they're quite redundant.

Remember that these disadvantages don't necessarily leave the lizards completely vulnerable. They're ever-evolving creatures that consistently develop evolutionary traits according to their changing conditions and environments. For instance, they may spend less time chasing prey in open fields and more time looking out for predators. They may also change their activity time – from diurnal to nocturnal and vice versa – depending on the species.

TEST 5 SET 2-1

Poetry reading

Listen to part of a conversation between a student and a professor

S: Good morning, professor.

P: ⁰¹⁾**Come on in**, Claire. ⁰²⁾**I'm glad to see you** back ⁰³⁾**on your feet** again! What a horrible injury you suffered… Anyway, ⁰⁴⁾**what brings you here**?

S: Well, it's about the poetry reading I recently attended. I'm ⁰⁵⁾**trying to** ⁰⁶⁾**come up with** an idea for the final ⁰⁷⁾**term paper**, but even after hours of contemplation, I can't ⁰⁸⁾**seem to** broaden my perspective.

P: I see… I'm sorry I couldn't attend the reading, so could you ⁰⁹⁾**tell** me ¹⁰⁾**what kind of** reading it was? I ¹¹⁾**need to** know where you're ¹²⁾**coming from** to help you.

S: ¹³⁾**Of course**! Um, it seemed conventional. I mean, the overall mood was quiet and calm, and the audience sat quietly and ¹⁴⁾**listened to** the poets. ¹⁵⁾**You know what I mean**?

P: Yes, I think I understand. You're probably right, that ¹⁶⁾**sounds like** a pretty conventional poetry reading.

S: Well, I was ¹⁷⁾**wondering if** there was… some other way of sharing poetry, maybe something more performance-like.

P: Sure. You're thinking of the poetry slam that was created during the Beat Generation… It ¹⁸⁾**goes back** to 1948, when Jack Kerouac, one of the pioneers of the movement, coined the term to express his and his proponents' anti-conformist attitudes towards politics and a rejection of contemporary American values.

S: Oh, that sounds fascinating. I guess I didn't know much about the history of American poetry. How are poetry slams ¹⁹⁾**different from** conventional readings?

P: Well, poetry slams are competitive. ²⁰⁾**A number of** poets ²¹⁾**engage in** a competition and are judged by selected audience members, usually 3 to 5 of them.

S: ²²⁾**I'm not following**…

P: Okay, let's ²³⁾**look at** Allen Ginsberg and his philosophies **as** a poet to ²⁴⁾**clear** it **up**. He was ²⁵⁾**one of the** most prominent and noteworthy **leaders** of the Beat Generation, ²⁶⁾**known for** his powerful, engaging performances. Poetry slams were almost ²⁷⁾**at the** opposite **end of** the spectrum as conventional poetry reading, because they emphasized energetic, loud readings, and the role of the audience was significant.

S: Audience? How?

P: So, as you stated, the audience's primary function is listening to poems in conventional readings, right? Their involvement is highly discouraged and silence is expected so others can listen ²⁸⁾**as well**. In poetry slams, the audience actively ²⁹⁾**responds to** the poet ³⁰⁾**by yelling** or cheering.

S: Wow, I ³¹⁾**would've** never **thought** of that! And, I'm sorry, but could we go back to what their poems were usually about?

P: Certainly. Okay, since the poems needed to ³²⁾**arouse emotions** ³³⁾**in order to** build ³⁴⁾**a connection with** the audience, the topics were just as controversial. Well, ³⁵⁾**you're going to** need to ³⁶⁾**do** further **research** to ³⁷⁾**get the details** because you know… it's going to be your topic.

S: Oh right. I'm sorry about that. I have a much clearer vision ³⁸⁾**as to** how to organize my paper now. Two contrasting poetry sharing styles… quite a topic, isn't it?

P: Of course! I ³⁹⁾**look forward to reading** it.

S: Thank you so much for your time and help, professor!

P: My pleasure, Claire. ⁴⁰⁾**Good luck with** the assignment!

Poetry reading

Listen to part of a conversation between a student and a professor

S: Good morning, professor.

P: Come on in, Claire. I'm glad to see you back on your feet again! What a horrible injury you suffered… Anyway, what brings you here?

S: Well, it's about the poetry reading I recently attended. I'm trying to come up with an idea for the final term paper, but even after hours of contemplation, I can't seem to broaden my perspective.

P: I see… I'm sorry I couldn't attend the reading, so could you tell me what kind of reading it was? I need to know where you're coming from to help you.

S: Of course! Um, it seemed conventional. I mean, the overall mood was quiet and calm, and the audience sat quietly and listened to the poets. You know what I mean?

P: Yes, I think I understand. You're probably right, that sounds like a pretty conventional poetry reading.

S: Well, I was wondering if there was… some other way of sharing poetry, maybe something more performance-like.

P: Sure. You're thinking of the poetry slam that was created during the Beat Generation… It goes back to 1948, when Jack Kerouac, one of the pioneers of the movement, coined the term to express his and his proponents' anti-conformist attitudes towards politics and a rejection of contemporary American values.

S: Oh, that sounds fascinating. I guess I didn't know much about the history of American poetry. How are poetry slams different from conventional readings?

P: Well, poetry slams are competitive. A number of poets engage in a competition and are judged by selected audience members, usually 3 to 5 of them.

S: I'm not following…

P: Okay, let's look at Allen Ginsberg and his philosophies as a poet to clear it up. He was one of the most prominent and noteworthy leaders of the Beat Generation, known for his powerful, engaging performances. Poetry slams were almost at the opposite end of the spectrum as conventional poetry reading, because they emphasized energetic, loud readings, and the role of the audience was significant.

S: Audience? How?

P: So, as you stated, the audience's primary function is listening to poems in conventional readings, right? Their involvement is highly discouraged and silence is expected so others can listen as well. In poetry slams, the audience actively responds to the poet by yelling or cheering.

S: Wow, I would've never thought of that! And, I'm sorry, but could we go back to what their poems were usually about?

P: Certainly. Okay, since the poems needed to arouse emotions in order to build a connection with the audience, the topics were just as controversial. Well, you're going to need to do further research to get the details because you know… it's going to be your topic.

S: Oh right. I'm sorry about that. I have a much clearer vision as to how to organize my paper now. Two contrasting poetry sharing styles… quite a topic, isn't it?

P: Of course! I look forward to reading it.

S: Thank you so much for your time and help, professor!

P: My pleasure, Claire. Good luck with the assignment!

Ethanol

Listen to part of a lecture in an environmental science class

P: As we discussed, 01)**a lot of** 02)**effort** has **gone into** finding an 03)**alternative to** petroleum-based fuel 04)**such as** gasoline, the fuel 05)**used in** internal combustion engines like cars, locomotives, airplanes; 06)**you name it**... Most vehicles 07)**rely on** this fuel, because it was 08)**believed to be** the most suitable and efficient fuel for engines, despite its environmental impact. However, scientists have discovered a new source 09)**known as** ethanol. 10)**For those of you not** 11)**familiar with it**, let me explain what it is. Ethanol, or ethyl alcohol, is the alcohol 12)**found in** alcoholic beverages.

S: Alcoholic beverages? That doesn't 13)**sound like** an ideal 14)**fit for** combustion engines.

P: It 15)**makes** more **sense** if you understand how it's produced. Most people 16)**think of** alcohol **as** simply a pre-made adult product, but most ethanol 17)**used as** fuel 18)**in the United States** is actually a corn product. That's right, the edible yellow grain. However, its production can be quite interesting. It 19)**begins with** fermenting the corn to produce sugars, which 20)**go through** 21)**a series of** 22)**chemical reactions** and ultimately produces ethanol and carbon dioxide as by-products. Then, the ethanol is 23)**distilled into** its concentrated, purified form, which is usable as a fuel. It's not 24)**different from** gasoline 25)**in that** it 26)**supplies** energy **to** 27)**internal combustion engines**. It's been widely used as an additive or alternative to gasoline in 28)**a number of** countries, with Brazil and the United States being the largest markets. Between 2000 and 2007, ethanol production 29)**increased from** 17 billion **to** nearly 52 billion liters. That's quite an increase 30)**considering that** the idea of using ethanol as a fuel is fairly new.

S: So, it must provide some benefits over gasoline, right?

P: 31)**Of course!** 32)**First of all**, unlike gasoline, it's renewable. 33)**I'm sure** 34)**you're** all **aware that** gasoline is a non-renewable resource 35)**extracted from** the ground, so its supply is limited and will eventually 36)**run out**. 37)**In contrast**, ethanol is not a fossil fuel, so it will be available 38)**as long as** corn crops are available. 39)**Speaking of** crops, ethanol also 40)**has an** economic **impact**. 41)**You see**, growing and harvesting crops doesn't just happen; it requires labor. Therefore, it creates economic security for farmers. Furthermore, commerce, ummm… trade between countries, 42)**brings** prosperity **to** countries that 43)**depend on** agriculture for economic growth. It's also more 44)**environmentally friendly** than gasoline, because it emits less carbon dioxide.

S: I heard that ethanol also had 45)**negative aspects**. Is that true?

P: Yes. Some researchers have 46)**pointed out** negative aspects of ethanol production and use.

First, even though the type of energy doesn't differ, there's a big 47)**quality** 48)**difference between** the two. 49)**In other words**, ethanol contains less energy than gasoline, so more is 50)**required to** produce the same amount of usable energy. Basically, 1.5 gallons of ethanol is 51)**equivalent to** 1 gallon of gasoline 52)**in terms of** 53)**energy efficiency**. Also, growing and harvesting crops like corn requires a lot more than just sowing seeds. To grow them successfully, supplements, such as fertilizers, are needed. I'm not sure if you're 54)**familiar with** fertilizers, but they are 55)**detrimental to** the environment.

S: Because they harm animals and people who eat crops 56)**drenched in** them?

P: Not quite. 57)**You're** not totally **off the track**, but I meant that the current process of fertilizer production 58)**entails the use of** fossil fuels. Actually, ethanol fermentation and distillation have the same problem. So, just because ethanol fuel doesn't emit 59)**as much** carbon dioxide **as** gasoline, it doesn't mean that it's completely environmentally friendly. 60)**On top of** that, transporting and distributing ethanol demands tremendous energy input. You see, ethanol, unlike petroleum, can't be transported through pipelines because it is easily tainted and it's unusable if 61)**mixed with** water.

S: Wait, how are water and pipelines connected? 62)**Am I missing something**?

P: Oops, I skipped something. I 63)**forgot to** mention that 64)**it's** practically **impossible to** build a long pipeline that doesn't leak a little water. So, it 65)**takes** more energy **to** distribute ethanol than petroleum 66)**across the country**, because pipelines can't be used.

Another thing about ethanol is that it holds future harm. By that, I mean that the 67)**part of** corn used to make ethanol is the kernel – the part that we eat. It may not 68)**seem like** a problem now, but some scholars warn that there will be a time 69)**in the future** when producing ethanol will be our 70)**priority over** feeding people. Others argue that ethanol is just as dangerous as gasoline, because it's highly flammable, so it's not an ideal alternative. We'll cover that next time, so let's 71)**wrap up** for today.

Before we leave, I'll 72)**give** you an assignment. Research other sources, other crops like sugar cane, which could be an alternative to corn in ethanol production and analyze their benefits over corn.

Ethanol

Listen to part of a lecture in an environmental science class

P: As we discussed, a lot of effort has gone into finding an alternative to petroleum-based fuel such as gasoline, the fuel used in internal combustion engines like cars, locomotives, airplanes; you name it... Most vehicles rely on this fuel, because it was believed to be the most suitable and efficient fuel for engines, despite its environmental impact. However, scientists have discovered a new source known as ethanol. For those of you not familiar with it, let me explain what it is. Ethanol, or ethyl alcohol, is the alcohol found in alcoholic beverages.

S: Alcoholic beverages? That doesn't sound like an ideal fit for combustion engines.

P: It makes more sense if you understand how it's produced. Most people think of alcohol as simply a pre-made adult product, but most ethanol used as fuel in the United States is actually a corn product. That's right, the edible yellow grain. However, its production can be quite interesting. It begins with fermenting the corn to produce sugars, which go through a series of chemical reactions and ultimately produces ethanol and carbon dioxide as by-products. Then, the ethanol is distilled into its concentrated, purified form, which is usable as a fuel. It's not different from gasoline in that it supplies energy to internal combustion engines. It's been widely used as an additive or alternative to gasoline in a number of countries, with Brazil and the United States being the largest markets. Between 2000 and 2007, ethanol production increased from 17 billion to nearly 52 billion liters. That's quite an increase considering that the idea of using ethanol as a fuel is fairly new.

S: So, it must provide some benefits over gasoline, right?

P: Of course! First of all, unlike gasoline, it's renewable. I'm sure you're all aware that gasoline is a non-renewable resource extracted from the ground, so its supply is limited and will eventually run out. In contrast, ethanol is not a fossil fuel, so it will be available as long as corn crops are available. Speaking of crops, ethanol also has an economic impact. You see, growing and harvesting crops doesn't just happen; it requires labor. Therefore, it creates economic security for farmers. Furthermore, commerce, ummm... trade between countries, brings prosperity to countries that depend on agriculture for economic growth. It's also more environmentally friendly than gasoline, because it emits less carbon dioxide.

S: I heard that ethanol also had negative aspects. Is that true?

P: Yes. Some researchers have pointed out negative aspects of ethanol production and use.

First, even though the type of energy doesn't differ, there's a big quality difference between the two. In other words, ethanol contains less energy than gasoline, so more is required to produce the same amount of usable energy. Basically, 1.5 gallons of ethanol is equivalent to 1 gallon of gasoline in terms of energy efficiency. Also, growing and harvesting crops like corn requires a lot more than just sowing seeds. To grow them successfully, supplements, such as fertilizers, are needed. I'm not sure if you're familiar with fertilizers, but they are detrimental to the environment.

S: Because they harm animals and people who eat crops drenched in them?

P: Not quite. You're not totally off the track, but I meant that the current process of fertilizer production entails the use of fossil fuels. Actually, ethanol fermentation and distillation have the same problem. So, just because ethanol fuel doesn't emit as much carbon dioxide as gasoline, it doesn't mean that it's completely environmentally friendly. On top of that, transporting and distributing ethanol demands tremendous energy input. You see, ethanol, unlike petroleum, can't be transported through pipelines because it is easily tainted and it's unusable if mixed with water.

S: Wait, how are water and pipelines connected? Am I missing something?

P: Oops, I skipped something. I forgot to mention that it's practically impossible to build a long pipeline that doesn't leak a little water. So, it takes more energy to distribute ethanol than petroleum across the country, because pipelines can't be used.

Another thing about ethanol is that it holds future harm. By that, I mean that the part of corn used to make ethanol is the kernel – the part that we eat. It may not seem like a problem now, but some scholars warn that there will be a time in the future when producing ethanol will be our priority over feeding people. Others argue that ethanol is just as dangerous as gasoline, because it's highly flammable, so it's not an ideal alternative. We'll cover that next time, so let's wrap up for today.

Before we leave, I'll give you an assignment. Research other sources, other crops like sugar cane, which could be an alternative to corn in ethanol production and analyze their benefits over corn.

A solar nebula

Listen to part of a lecture in a geology class.

P: You may recall that the solar system [01]**started as** a cloud of dust and gas, [02]**known as** a solar nebula, [03]**according to** the core accretion model. Then, the collapse of a part of the cloud caused the mass concentration of cosmic material [04]**at its center**, ultimately creating the Sun. The advent of the terrestrial planets, including Earth, [05]**took place** [06]**shortly after**, as the remaining materials [07]**began to** [08]**build up**. During Earth's formation, dense elements sank [09]**to the bottom**, forming its core, and the lighter ones formed its crust. Let's [10]**look at** issues regarding Earth's life-sustaining ability. We [11]**tend to** wonder about how Earth [12]**is able to** support life, whereas other plants are uninhabitable.

Before we begin, let's [13]**try to** remember that liquid water [14]**is essential for** life. The presence of this water is the most distinguishing facet of our planet. On other planets, flowing water occurs only rarely or [15]**in small quantities**, because it [16]**either** freezes **or** vaporizes [17]**depending on** the temperature. Earth has abundant water because… ummm… let me [18]**go over** [19]**one of the** most widely accepted **theories** to elucidate water's origin on Earth. [20]**It is believed that** water remained on Earth [21]**due to** the accumulation of greenhouse gases produced by early [22]**volcanic activity** [23]**around the time of** Earth's formation. If [24]**you**'re not **familiar with** [25]**greenhouse gases**, they're gases that trap heat and [26]**prevent it from escaping** Earth's atmosphere. These greenhouse gases ultimately [27]**played a role in** maintaining Earth's temperature, and consequently, the water remained liquid.

Recently, however, geologists who analyzed fragments of ancient meteorites suggested that volcanic activity is probably not the only factor that [28]**caused** Earth **to** retain water. [29]**In fact**, they contend that meteorites [30]**may have** [31]**brought** water to Earth and [32]**contributed to** the accumulation of greenhouse gases. [33]**In order for** you **to** understand their findings, you first [34]**need to** have a good idea of what happens when meteorites enter Earth's atmosphere. First, they [35]**reach the edge of** the atmosphere and encounter massive [36]**frictional forces** very rapidly. They sometimes completely disintegrate mid-air, but other times their fragments [37]**manage to** reach Earth. Scientists [38]**used** a catalyst, intense electricity, **to** produce the same conditions, heating the fragments to temperatures of 1,000° C. When they [39]**burned up**, two by-products remained, carbon dioxide, a common greenhouse gas, and water vapor. These contribute to maintaining warmer temperatures and [40]**introducing** water **to** the environment. [41]**Of course**, one meteor won't affect Earth much, considering the inconsequential amount of [42]**by-products** they yield, but, [43]**as the old proverb states**, "[44]**little strokes fell great oaks**." We now believe this is what happened after Earth's formation, around 4 billion years ago, which is also when the analyzed samples [45]**dated from**. [46]**Have you heard of** the lunar cataclysm? It's a hypothetical theory, but I believe that we can [47]**take it into account** to further our discussion.

The theory states that millions of asteroids [48]**collided with** celestial bodies in our solar system, including Mercury, the Moon, Earth, and Mars about 3.8 to 4.1 billion years ago. Evidence for this [49]**comes from** the impact melt rocks collected during the Apollo missions – you know, NASA's manned spaceflight program. Anyway, the rocks collected during these missions to the Moon [50]**were dated to** 4 billion years ago, and that's how we originally learned that [51]**a large number of** asteroids struck the early planets, including Earth. From this and the experiments [52]**carried out** on the meteor samples, scientists now believe that the "theoretical" meteors burned up in Earth's atmosphere and ultimately produced the by-products I previously mentioned. Subsequently, this meteoric water accumulated in the oceans and the greenhouse gases trapped heat and provided the correct temperature to prevent the oceans from freezing or vaporizing.

The question that remains is, "Why don't planets like Mars resemble Earth [53]**in terms of** its oceans and greenhouse gases if they were [54]**subjected to** the same bombardment?" Well, to answer that, you need a better understanding of the [55]**differences between** Earth **and** Mars.

You see, the meteors most likely did [56]**result in** the same consequence, but you also need to remember that, Earth, unlike Mars, has a strong [57]**magnetic field** from its core, which [58]**protects it from** solar winds and charged particles, [59]**such as** electrons and protons, [60]**released from** the Sun's upper atmosphere. We won't [61]**go into** much **detail** about this, because it's too complex, so let's just [62]**stay on topic**. Mars, without a strong magnetic field, is subjected to the solar winds, which [63]**blow away** its greenhouse gases. [64]**You see where I'm going with this**? If greenhouse gases don't exist in the atmosphere, the temperature falls and water freezes, as it did on Mars.

A solar nebula

Listen to part of a lecture in a geology class.

P: You may recall that the solar system started as a cloud of dust and gas, known as a solar nebula, according to the core accretion model. Then, the collapse of a part of the cloud caused the mass concentration of cosmic material at its center, ultimately creating the Sun. The advent of the terrestrial planets, including Earth, took place shortly after, as the remaining materials began to build up. During Earth's formation, dense elements sank to the bottom, forming its core, and the lighter ones formed its crust. Let's look at issues regarding Earth's life-sustaining ability. We tend to wonder about how Earth is able to support life, whereas other plants are uninhabitable.

Before we begin, let's try to remember that liquid water is essential for life. The presence of this water is the most distinguishing facet of our planet. On other planets, flowing water occurs only rarely or in small quantities, because it either freezes or vaporizes depending on the temperature. Earth has abundant water because... ummm... let me go over one of the most widely accepted theories to elucidate water's origin on Earth. It is believed that water remained on Earth due to the accumulation of greenhouse gases produced by early volcanic activity around the time of Earth's formation. If you're not familiar with greenhouse gases, they're gases that trap heat and prevent it from escaping Earth's atmosphere. These greenhouse gases ultimately played a role in maintaining Earth's temperature, and consequently, the water remained liquid.

Recently, however, geologists who analyzed fragments of ancient meteorites suggested that volcanic activity is probably not the only factor that caused Earth to retain water. In fact, they contend that meteorites may have brought water to Earth and contributed to the accumulation of greenhouse gases. In order for you to understand their findings, you first need to have a good idea of what happens when meteorites enter Earth's atmosphere. First, they reach the edge of the atmosphere and encounter massive frictional forces very rapidly. They sometimes completely disintegrate mid-air, but other times their fragments manage to reach Earth. Scientists used a catalyst, intense electricity, to produce the same conditions, heating the fragments to temperatures of 1,000° C. When they burned up, two by-products remained, carbon dioxide, a common greenhouse gas, and water vapor. These contribute to maintaining warmer temperatures and introducing water to the environment. Of course, one meteor won't affect Earth much, considering the inconsequential amount of by-products they yield, but, as the old proverb states, "little strokes fell great oaks." We now believe this is what happened after Earth's formation, around 4 billion years ago, which is also when the analyzed samples dated from. Have you heard of the lunar cataclysm? It's a hypothetical theory, but I believe that we can take it into account to further our discussion.

The theory states that millions of asteroids collided with celestial bodies in our solar system, including Mercury, the Moon, Earth, and Mars about 3.8 to 4.1 billion years ago. Evidence for this comes from the impact melt rocks collected during the Apollo missions – you know, NASA's manned spaceflight program. Anyway, the rocks collected during these missions to the Moon were dated to 4 billion years ago, and that's how we originally learned that a large number of asteroids struck the early planets, including Earth. From this and the experiments carried out on the meteor samples, scientists now believe that the "theoretical" meteors burned up in Earth's atmosphere and ultimately produced the by-products I previously mentioned. Subsequently, this meteoric water accumulated in the oceans and the greenhouse gases trapped heat and provided the correct temperature to prevent the oceans from freezing or vaporizing.

The question that remains is, "Why don't planets like Mars resemble Earth in terms of its oceans and greenhouse gases if they were subjected to the same bombardment?" Well, to answer that, you need a better understanding of the differences between Earth and Mars.

You see, the meteors most likely did result in the same consequence, but you also need to remember that, Earth, unlike Mars, has a strong magnetic field from its core, which protects it from solar winds and charged particles, such as electrons and protons, released from the Sun's upper atmosphere. We won't go into much detail about this, because it's too complex, so let's just stay on topic. Mars, without a strong magnetic field, is subjected to the solar winds, which blow away its greenhouse gases. You see where I'm going with this? If greenhouse gases don't exist in the atmosphere, the temperature falls and water freezes, as it did on Mars.

www.usherin.usher.co.kr

USHER

iBT TOEFL
INTERMEDIATE LISTENING
TEST 1 해설

TEST 1 set 1-1

Conversation
Accounting department

문단주제	본문내용	해석
	Listen to a conversation between a student and a professor in a university accounting department	학생과 영어교수의 대화를 들으시오.
단락 1 학생의 전공 변경 관련 고민 토로	**P:** Hi, Sam. I saw your paper on the net profits of Google this year. Your work was phenomenal… I was very impressed. **S:** Oh, I'm very glad to hear that. Thank you so much. **P:** No problem! I hope you keep up the good work. So, what brought you here today? If it's about the paper, I've just assured you that you've done a great job on it. **S:** [Q1-A] Well…that's not what I'm here about… [Q1] I'm actually here to ask for your help with… umm… What's been concerning me recently is that I feel the strong need to switch majors. **P:** Okay… What are you looking into right now? **S:** Well, prior to entering college, I did some research to ensure that I would choose the right route for myself, and I thought that accounting would be a suitable major. Now that I'm here, however, I have been doubting my decision… I'm thinking about switching to Business Management.	**P:** 안녕 Sam, 네가 작성한 Google의 실수익에 대한 레포트를 살펴봤는데, 아주 인상적이었어. **S:** 오, 그 말을 들으니 기쁜데요. 감사합니다. **P:** 천만에! 지금처럼 계속 잘 해주길 바래. 그래서, 오늘은 무슨 일로 날 찾아온 거니? 만약 레포트 때문이라면, 내가 방금 아주 잘했다고 말했는데… **S:** [Q1-A] 음, 그것 때문에 온 게 아니에요… [Q1] 사실 제가 여기 온 건 교수님 도움이 필요해서인데… 음… 최근에 고민이 생겼는데 전공을 바꿔야 할 필요성이 강하게 느껴져요. **P:** 그래… 무엇에 대해서 생각하고 있는데? **S:** 음, 대학교에 들어오기 전에는, 제 자신이 옳은 길을 선택했는지 확인하기 위해서 조사를 조금 해봤는데, 회계가 저에게 맞는 전공이라고 생각을 했었어요. 하지만, 여기 들어와보니까, 제 결정에 대해 의심이 들어요… 경영으로 바꿀까 생각 중이에요.
단락 2 학생의 고민 이유 및 동기	**P:** [Q5] Let's see… Your grades… Your participation in class… It doesn't look like you're doing badly at this point. **S:** You're right. I've always tried my best, but [Q2-C] my academic performance isn't the reason I'm considering switching majors. [Q2, Q3-D] I guess it's the amount of math required to acquire a degree in the field. And, I think it takes a lot more time to earn a degree in accounting than it does in business management. **P:** That's true. It can be quite overwhelming at times. Have you looked at the job prospects of both? **S:** Oh yeah! I totally forgot to check that out.	**P:** [Q5] 어디 보자. 네 성적들과… 수업 참여도… 네가 지금 잘 못하고 있는 것 같진 않은데? **S:** 맞아요. 전 항상 최선을 다해왔어요, 근데 [Q2-C] 학업 성과가 제가 전공을 바꾸려는 이유는 아니거든요. [Q2, Q3-D] 제 생각에는 이 분야에서 요구하는 수학의 양 때문인 것 같아요. 그리고, 제 생각엔 경영 분야에서 학위를 얻는 것보다 회계 분야에서 학위를 얻는데 시간이 더 오래 걸리는 것 같아요. **P:** 사실이야, 가끔은 부담이 될 수도 있어. 두 전공 모두의 취업 전망을 살펴본 적 있니? **S:** 아, 맞아요! 확인하는 걸 완전 잊고 있었네요.
단락 3 회계학 전공자와 경영 전공자의 취업 전망	**P:** [Q2-D] You see, graduates who have degrees in the accounting field have a variety of options when choosing their career paths. When a company is seeking a person with experience in finance, global marketing, or other business-related fields, accounting graduates are very likely to get hired. For instance, you could be a financial analyst, an auditor, a financial manager, and so on.	**P:** [Q2-D] 있잖아, 회계학 학위를 가진 대학 졸업자들은 진로를 결정할 때 많은 선택권이 있어. 회사들이 회계사, 글로벌 마케팅, 또는 경영에 관련된 학위를 가지고 있는 사람을 찾을 때, 회계를 전공한 졸업생들은 고용될 기회가 더 많아. 예를 들면, 넌 재정분석가나, 회계 감사관이나, 금융 매니저 등이 될 수 있어.

문단주제	본문내용	해석
	S: Mmm… I see. What about business management?	S: 음… 그렇군요. 그럼 경영 전공은 어떻죠?
	P: Well, my belief is that [Q3] the problem with business management is that since the major itself is very broad and general, you won't really be a specialist in any field like an accounting major would be. Therefore, the demand for people with a degree in business management in the industry is relatively lower. So, as I mentioned before, accounting graduates have a relatively easy time securing jobs, but that's usually not the case with business management graduates.	P: 음, 내가 알기로는 [Q3] 경영 전공의 문제점은 전공 자체가 매우 광범위하고 일반적이기 때문에, 회계 전공자처럼 특별한 분야에서 전문가가 될 수 없어. 그래서, 경영 분야에서의 학위를 가지고 있는 사람들에 대한 수요가 상대적으로 적지. 그래서, 내가 앞서 말했듯이, 회계학 졸업자들은 직업을 안정적으로 구할 수 있는데, 하지만 경영을 전공한 사람들의 경우는 보통 그렇지 않지.
	S: Are you implying that it's hard to get a job with a degree in business management?	S: 교수님 말씀은 경영학 학위를 가지고 있으면 직업을 가지기 힘들다는 건가요?
	P: Umm… From what I've seen through my former graduate students, I would say so. I understand that you're having a hard time with your first choice and the burdensome amount of work involved, but, looking at the long term, I'm not so sure if business management would be a positive move for you.	P: 음… 내가 이전 졸업생들을 보니까 그렇다고 말할 수 있어. 네가 처음 선택한 것에 대해서 힘들어하고 있고 부담스러운 양의 공부가 포함된 거 이해해. 하지만, 장기적으로 봤을 때, 경영학이 너에게 긍정적인 전망이 될지는 모르겠구나.
	S: I get your point… I guess I shouldn't make a rash decision, huh?	S: 무슨 말씀인지 알겠어요… 성급한 결정을 하면 안 되겠네요, 그쵸?
단락 4 학생의 다짐	P: Exactly. Other than the job prospects, there are also many other aspects to consider, like the examinations you will need to deal with, how much money you can make, and so on.	P: 바로 그거야. 취업 전망 이외에도, 고려해야 할 측면들이 많아, 앞으로 봐야 할 시험들과, 돈을 얼마나 벌 수 있을 지와 같은 것들 말야.
	S: Right… Okay, I guess I shouldn't be swayed by my impetuous emotions…	S: 맞아요… 알겠어요, 제 성급한 감정에 휘둘리면 안되겠네요.
	P: Of course not… Switching majors is certainly not an easy step to take, you know?	P: 당연하지… 전공을 바꾸는 것은 분명히 쉬운 일이 아니야, 알지?
	S: [Q4] Yes… Well, I'll take my time and do some more research before I make a decision about whether or not to change my major. Thank you for your advice, professor. I really appreciate it.	S: [Q4] 네… 음, 시간을 더 두고 전공을 바꿀지 말지에 대한 결정하기 전에 조사를 좀더 많이 해 봐야겠네요. 조언해주셔서 감사해요, 교수님. 정말 감사드려요
	P: No problem, Sam. I'm available anytime you need me. Good luck!	P: 천만에 Sam, 필요한 게 있으면 언제든지 말하렴. 행운을 빌게!

01. [Detail - Reason/Cause] Why does the student visit the accounting department?

(A) He needs help with a ~~term paper~~ that he's having a difficult time with. *(wrong fact)*

(B) He would like to talk to the professor about ~~his major's job prospects~~. *(wrong fact)*★

(C) He needs the professor's advice as to which ~~career to pursue~~ after earning his degree. *(wrong fact)*

(D) He wants to discuss and explore options other than his current major.

01. 학생이 회계 부서로 찾아간 이유는 무엇인가?

(A) 그는 어려움을 겪고 있는 학기말 논문에 도움을 필요로 한다.

(B) 그는 자신의 ~~전공의 취업~~ 전망에 대해 교수와 얘기하고 싶어한다. ★

(C) 그의 학위를 취득한 후 ~~어떤 직업을 구할지~~에 대해 교수의 조언이 필요하다.

(D) 그는 현재의 전공 이외의 다른 선택권에 대해 의논하고 알아보고 싶어한다

해설 | (A) 지문에 term paper에 대한 언급이 없으므로 오답이다. 맨 처음에 교수가 언급하는 레포트는 학생이 찾아간 이유가 아니라고 직접적으로 얘기한다. (B) Accounting과 Business Management 사이의 갈등을 다루면서 job prospect가 언급이 되지만 그 이유가 학생이 교수를 찾아간 이유는 아니다. (C) 학위 취득 후 구직하는 것은 교수가 학생에게 전공을 바꾸지 말 것을 조언하면서 든 이유 중 하나로, 학생이 교수를 찾아간 직접적인 이유가 아니다.

02. [Detail - Reason] Why is the student considering switching his major?

(A) Because it's hard for him to keep up with the amount of mathematical work.

(B) Because his first choice has too many ~~mandatory examinations~~. *(not mentioned)*

(C) Because he is ~~struggling~~ in terms of his academic performance in his current major. *(wrong fact)* ★

(D) Because there are only a ~~limited number of job options~~ after graduation for his current major. *(opposite fact)*

02. 학생이 전공을 바꾸려고 고려하는 이유는 무엇인가?

(A) 그는 수학 공부의 양을 따라가는 것이 힘들기 때문이다.

(B) 그의 첫 번째 선택은 ~~의무적인 시험이~~ 너무 많이 포함되어 있다.

(C) 그는 현재 전공에서 학업 성취에 ~~어려움을 겪고 있다~~. ★

(D) 그의 현재 전공으로 졸업을 하게 되면 ~~직업 선택권이 제한되기~~ 때문이다.

해설 | (B) 현재 전공의 의무적인 시험에 대한 언급도, 바꾸고자 하는 동기라고도 주장하지 않았다. (C) 교수가 학생의 성적을 확인해 본바, 학생은 현재 전공에서 크게 뒤 떨어지지 않는다. 또한, 학생 본인도 학업 성취의 어려움을 이유로 전공을 바꾸고자 하는 것이 아님을 명시했다. (D)는 정반대 되는 내용이므로 각각 오답이다.

03. [Detail – Disadvantage] According to the professor, what is the biggest drawback of the new major the student is considering?

(A) The society is ~~leaning more towards generalists~~ as opposed to specialists. *(opposite fact)* ★

(B) It could encumber the student with too ~~many examinations~~. *(not mentioned)*

(C) It's relatively tougher to pursue a career after earning a degree in the field.

(D) It entails an abundant amount of ~~mathematical work~~. *(wrong fact)*

03. 교수의 말에 따르면, 학생이 고려하고 있는 새로운 전공의 가장 큰 단점은 무엇인가?

(A) 사회는 특정 분야의 전문가 보다 ~~다방면에 걸친 전문가를 선호한다~~. ★

(B) ~~많은 시험들이~~ 학생에게 부담을 줄 수도 있다.

(C) 그 분야에서 학위를 얻은 후에 직업을 얻는 것이 상대적으로 어렵다

(D) 많은 양의 수학 공부를 수반하고 있다

해설 | (A) 사회는 현재 specialist를 선호하는 추세라고 교수는 말한다. 정반대이므로 오답. Generalist를 선호한다 해도 이는 drawback이 아닌 advantage로 문제가 묻고있는 바가 아니다. (B)는 언급되지 않는 내용이므로 오답이다. (D)는 학생이 꼽는 자신의 current major인 accounting의 단점이다.

04. [Inference - Infer] What is the student most likely to do after his consultation with the professor?

(A) He will follow the school's procedures and ~~fill out the papers~~ needed to switch majors. *(wrong fact)*

(B) He will delay his decision and collect more information about his options.

(C) He will ~~take a break~~ this semester and narrow his interests and options. *(not mentioned)* ★

(D) He will ~~spend the rest of his time~~ at his college with his ~~current major~~. *(wrong fact)*

04. 교수와의 상담 후에, 학생이 가장 할 가능성이 있는 일은 무엇인가?

(A) 그는 전공을 바꾸기 위해 학교 절차를 밟아, 필요한 문서들을 작성할 것이다.

(B) 그는 자신의 결정을 연기하고 선택권에 대해 더 많은 정보를 모을 것이다.

(C) 그는 이번 학기를 쉬고 자신의 관심사들과 선택권들의 범위를 좁힐 것이다.

(D) ~~현재의~~ 전공을 가지고 ~~남은 대학 생활을~~ 보낼 것이다.

해설 | A) he will follow procedures and fill out the papers= 그는 교수님과 대화를 통해서 전공을 바꾸는 일이 확정되지 않았고, 조금더 정보를 찾아보기로 했다. 아직 fill out papers 문서들에 절차를 밟을때가 아니다. C) take a break= 잠시 쉰다는 얘기인데, 그가 아직 쉰다는 얘기는 아무것도 없었다. D) he will spend his time with current major = 현재 전공으로 그의 시간을 사용한다는 것인데 리스닝에 의하면 아직 확정된것이 아무것도 없고 정보를 더 찾아보기로 하였다.

Listen again to part of the conversation. Then answer the question.

"Let's see… Your grades… Your participation in class… It doesn't look like you're doing badly at this point"

05. [Inference-Imply] What does the professor imply when she says? 🎧

"It doesn't look like you're doing badly at this point."

(A) That the student is ~~one of the top students~~ in her class. *(not mentioned)* ★

(B) That she ~~doesn't feel the need to help~~ the student with his problem. *(wrong fact)*

(C) That she doesn't understand why the student is having a hard time with his ~~term paper~~. *(partial error)*

(D) That it's difficult to understand why the student feels uncertain about his major.

대화의 일부를 다시 듣고, 물음에 답하시오.

"어디 한번 너의 성적들과… 수업 참여도를 한번 보자… 네가 지금 잘 못하고 있는 것 같진 않은데?"

05. 교수가 이 말을 할 때 무엇을 암시하는가? 🎧

"네가 지금 잘 못하고 있는 것 같진 않은데?"

(A) 학생은 교수의 수업에서 ~~가장 잘하는 학생들 중 한명~~이다. ★

(B) 교수는 학생의 문제를 ~~도와줘야 할 필요성을 못 느끼고 있다~~.

(C) 그녀는 학생이 왜 ~~학기말 논문~~을 힘들어 하는지 이해를 못하고 있다.

(D) 학생이 왜 자신의 전공에 대해 확신을 가지지 못하는지 이해하기 힘들다.

해설 | 교수는 학생이 academic performance가 나빠서 major를 바꾸고 싶어한다고 생각했는데, 수업 참여도와 성적이 우수해 이해하기 힘들다는 표현을 한다. (A) 성적과 수업 참여도로 미루어 보았을 때 전공을 바꿀 정도의 어려움을 겪고 있지 않다는 표현이지, top student라고 하는 것은 아니다. (B) 도와줄 필요성을 못 느끼는 것이 아니라 학생의 고민을 이해하지 못하는 것이다.
(C) 학생은 term paper가 아니라 전공 때문에 어려움을 겪고 있다.

TEST 1 set 1-2

Lecture 1
Ice age

문단주제 | **본문내용** | **해석**

단락 1
빙하기와 그 이론의 소개

Listen to part of a lecture in a climatology class

As we discussed in our last class, there have been a number of ice ages over the past few million years, such as the Permian and Ordovician Glaciation Periods, when much of the planet was covered with glaciers… [Q10-D/Q11-B] Scientists believe that the ice age theory is certainly one of the most compelling theories to explain the end of the dinosaur era. Well, fortunately for human beings, we are currently living in an "interglacial period", or a period between ice ages, during which the glaciers retreat to the polar regions and the Earth experiences a relatively milder climate. All of the ice ages have been separated by long mild interglacial periods of this type. Even though the last ice age, the Quaternary Glaciation, ended around ten thousand years ago, [Q11-A] there is considerable evidence to suggest that another ice age is coming.

기후학에 관한 강의를 들으시오.

우리가 지난 시간에 논의했듯이, 지난 수백만년 동안 페름기와 오르도비스기 같은 수많은 빙하기가 있어왔는데요, 지구 행성의 많은 부분이 빙하로 뒤덮여 있을 때였죠. [Q10-D/Q11-B] 과학자들은 확실히 빙하기 이론이 공룡시대의 종말을 설명해줄 수 있는 가장 강력한 이론 중 하나라고 믿고 있죠. 음, 인류에게는 다행히도, 우리는 현재 "간빙기" 혹은 빙하기 사이에 살고 있는데요, 이 시기는 빙하가 극지방으로 후퇴해서 지구가 상대적으로 온화한 기후를 경험하고 있죠. 모든 빙하기는 이런 종류의 기나긴 간빙기에 의해 분리되었는데요. 비록 마지막 빙하기인 제4기가 약 만년 전에 끝났지만, [Q11-A] 또 다른 빙하기가 다가오고 있다는 상당한 증거가 있어요.

단락 2
빙하기 이론의 근거: 산호초와 빙하 사이의 관계

But, um… In today's world, an immense emission of greenhouse gases from the burning of fossil fuels has caused global warming and led to a drastic increase in global temperatures. [Q11] So, you may be doubtful about how scientists can be so sure that we're living in an interglacial period. Well… I've mentioned before that scientists have collected evidence and are predicting the advent of another ice age, right? It's because ice ages have occurred so regularly that they must abide by some kind of pattern. Quite interesting, huh? Let's look at some geological information that relates to the relationship between coral reefs and glaciers to help you understand. We now know, from geological research on the ancient coral reefs, that ice sheets have formed and receded about every one hundred thousand years. See, oceans turn into ice sheets during ice ages, resulting in a decrease in the water level and temperature. Consequently, coral reefs that normally grow in warm shallow waters would wind up on dry land or be killed by the low temperatures during ice ages and stop growing. [Q7-B] As the ice ages give way to interglacial periods with much milder climates, the coral reefs would start growing a new layer again as the glaciers withdrew and the water levels rose. This pattern allows the dating of coral reef growth, which has become a very crucial tool for scientists and geologists.

하지만 음… 요즘 세상에는 화석연료를 연소할 때 나오는 거대한 온실가스의 방출은 지구 온난화를 야기시켰고 세계 온도를 급격하게 증가시켰어요. [Q11] 그래서, 여러분은 어떻게 해서 과학자들이 우리가 간빙기에 살고 있다고 확신하는지에 대해 의심을 가질지도 몰라요. 음… 과학자들이 증거를 모았고 또 다른 빙하기가 도래할 것을 예측하고 있다고 제가 앞서 언급했었죠? 이것은 빙하기가 규칙적으로 발생해서 그것들이 일종의 패턴을 확실히 남긴 게 틀림없기 때문이죠. 상당히 흥미롭죠? 여러분의 이해를 돕기 위해, 산호초와 빙하 사이의 관계와 관련된 지질학적 정보를 살펴봅시다. 우리는 고대 산호초에 대한 지질학적 연구를 통해 이제 알고 있죠. 빙하가 형성되었고 약 십만년마다 형성과 후퇴했다는 것을요. 그러니까, 빙하기에 바다는 빙하로 변하고, 따라서 해수면과 기온이 줄어드는 결과를 가져오죠. 그 결과, 보통 얕은 물에서 성장하는 산호초는 빙하기에 마른 땅에서 죽음을 맞거나 낮은 기온 때문에 죽음을 당하고 성장이 멈추게 되죠. [Q7-B] 빙하기가 훨씬 온화한 기후로 구성된 간빙기에 길을 내어줌에 따라, 빙하가 물러가고 해수면이 다시 증가하며, 산호초는 새로운 층에서 다시 자라기 시작하죠. 이러한 패턴은 산호초의 성장에 대한 연대 측정을 가능하게 하는데요, 이것은 과학자와 지질학자들에게 매우 중요한 방법이 되어왔어요.

문단주제	본문내용	해석
단락 3 산호초 내 화학물질들의 분석	For those of you who are still confused, let me explain further. [Q7] To date coral reef growth, they try to determine how old each layer is and recently, they've been able to analyze chemicals found in the coral reefs, such as uranium isotopes, to figure out that coral growth has happened with regularity. Let's say… If the first layer of the coral reef was dated as 500 years old and the second 300 years old, then the interval of non-growth between the two layers would be 200 years, right? By compiling data showing the regularly formed gaps between the ages of layers of coral, scientists can determine how long ice ages lasted and approximately how often they occurred. That's exactly how the dating works, and it has clarified that ice ages have occurred in regular cycles as well. This theory of ice age regularity is, however, a very recent idea.	여러분들 중 여전히 혼란스러워하는 몇몇 학생을 위해 제가 더 설명을 드릴께요. [Q7] 산호초의 연대를 측정하기 위해서, 그들은 각 층이 얼마나 오래 되었는가를 확인하려고 시도했고 최근에는, 우라늄 동위원소와 같은 산호초에서 발견되는 화학물질들을 분석해서 산호의 성장은 규칙적으로 발생했다는 것을 발견했죠. 이렇게 말해보죠… 만약 산호초의 첫 번째 층이 500년이 되었고, 두번째가 300년인 것으로 측정되었다면, 두 층 사이에 자라지 않은 간격이 200년일 거에요, 맞죠? 산호초 층들의 나이 사이의 간격이 규칙적으로 형성됨을 보여주는 데이터를 수집함으로써, 과학자들은 빙하기가 얼마나 오래 지속 되었는지와 대략적으로 얼마나 자주 발생했는지를 결정할 수 있어요. 이게 바로 연대 측정이 작동하는 원리이고, 빙하기가 규칙적인 주기로 발생했다는 사실을 명확하게 해주었죠. 하지만 빙하기가 규칙적으로 발생했다는 이 이론은 아주 최근에 나온 개념이에요.
단락 4 판 구조론과 그 한 계정	Of course, there are several other theories proposed, like… uh… [Q9-B, Q9-C] plate tectonics, which describes the movement of giant plates under the Earth's surface that cause natural phenomena like earthquakes and volcanic eruptions. Those movements might have caused changes in ocean currents and wind patterns that could play a role in triggering ice ages. But, here's my question to you all, "Doesn't the theory suggest that ice ages would happen randomly because earthquakes and volcanic eruptions are random?"… Anyone? Okay, the answer would be, yes. Although it may explain the changes in the global climate to some extent, it's missing the critical point that we've been discussing: the regularity of ice ages, so, we need a theory that supports this regularity. The Milankovitch theory fits perfectly with this.	물론, 몇몇 다른 이론들도 제기되었는데요… 음, [Q9-B, Q9-C] 판 구조론처럼, 지진과 화산 분출과 같은 자연현상을 야기시키는 지구 표면 아래에 있는 거대한 판의 움직임을 설명하는 것이죠. 이러한 움직임들은 아마도 빙하기를 촉발시키는데 역할을 한 해류와 바람 패턴의 변화를 야기시켰을지도 몰라요. 그런데 여기서 제가 여러분 모두에게 하고 싶은 질문이 있어요, "지진과 화산 분출은 불규칙적이니까 이 이론은 빙하기가 무작위로 발생한다는 것을 암시하지 않을까요?"… 아무도 없나요? 좋아요. 대답은 "예" 인데요. 비록 이것은 세계의 기후 변화를 어느 정도까지는 설명해줄지는 모르지만 우리가 토론하는 내용의 중요한 부분을 놓치고 있어요. 바로 빙하기의 규칙성이요. 그래서 우리는 빙하기의 규칙성을 지지하는 이론이 필요해요. 그리고 Milankovitch이론이 여기에는 아주 딱 들어맞죠.
단락 5 Milankovitch 이론의 소개	Milutin Milankovitch, a Serbian astrophysicist, consistently studied and eventually developed a scientific theory that showed that subtle oscillations in the Earth's movement play a vital role in causing regular ice ages. In the 1920s, he theorized that the Earth's rotation and orbit were major factors regulating the "come and go" of ice ages by precisely calculating their fluctuations.	Milutin Milankovitch는 세르비아의 천체물리학자로써 지속적으로 연구를 해서 마침내 지구의 움직임의 미묘한 진동이 규칙적인 빙하기를 유발하는데 결정적인 역할을 한다는 이론을 발전시켰어요. 1920년에 그는 변동을 정확하게 계산함으로써 지구의 자전과 공전 궤도가 빙하기의 도래와 후퇴를 통제하는 중요한 요소라는 이론을 정립했죠.

TEST 1 set 1-2

USHER

문단주제	본문내용	해석
단락 6 Milankovitch 이론의 근거: 지구 축의 기울기 변화	First, by observing the changes in the angle of the Earth's tilt with respect to its axis, Milankovitch was able to conclude that the tilt changes about three degrees every forty-one thousand years. [Q8-C] Furthermore, he was able to conclude that more tilt leads to more extreme summers and winters, and less tilt results in the opposite, milder summers and winters. You might be wondering how small fluctuations in the Earth's tilt could lead to such tremendous effects on the climate. [Q8] Um… It's because the Earth is composed of such perplexing and intricate systems that even very minimal fluctuations can result in huge changes. Well… It's not important to discuss these systems in this lecture, so let's stay on topic.	첫째, 지구의 축에 대한 기울기의 변화를 관찰함으로써, Milankovitch는 기울기가 41000년마다 약 3도씩 변한다고 결론지을 수 있었어요. [Q8-C] 더 나아가, 그는 기울기가 더 크면 여름과 겨울이 더 극단적이며, 적은 기울기는 그 반대 즉 온화한 여름과 겨울을 불러온다고 결론지을 수 있었죠. 여러분은 아마 어떻게 해서 작은 지구 기울기 변화가 기후에 이렇게 엄청난 영향을 미칠 수 있는지 궁금해할 수도 있어요. [Q8] 음… 이건 왜냐하면 지구가 매우 혼란스럽고 복잡한 체계로 구성되어 있어서 아주 작은 변화도 엄청난 결과를 초래할 수 있기 때문이죠. 음… 이번 강의에서 이러한 체계를 논의하는 건 별로 중요하지 않아요, 그래서 우린 주제를 고수할게요.
단락 7 Milankovitch 이론의 근거: 지구의 타원형 궤도	Now, there was another contributing factor to the global climate change that Milankovitch proposed. He also claimed that the Earth's orbit around the sun is elliptical, rather than perfectly circular. As you may have already guessed from what I've just said, at times, the Earth is closer to the sun than it is at other times. At present, the Earth's closest approach to the sun occurs in January, resulting in milder summers in the northern hemisphere. On the contrary, however, eleven thousand years ago, the closest approach of the Earth to the sun happened in July, making summers and winters much more extreme. [Q9] Okay… So now we know the two contributing factors he proposed: the changes in the Earth's tilt and Earth's uneven orbital pattern around the sun. What can we conclude from this? Well… We know they cause climate changes, sometimes cooler summers or warmer summers. These two phenomena could also have a huge impact on the formation and ebbing of ice sheets. For instance, in the northern hemisphere where most of the Earth's landmass is found, consecutive cooler summers would allow snow to accumulate and persist throughout the year. What do you think that will lead to? Of course, an ice age! On the other hand, consecutive warmer summers would cause the shrinkage of ice sheets, which would bring about an interglacial period, like the one we're living in right now.	자, 세계 기후 변화에 기여하는 요소로 Milankovitch가 제시하는 게 하나 더 있는데요. 그는 또한 태양 주위를 도는 지구의 궤도가 완벽한 원이라기보다는 타원이라고 주장했어요. 제가 방금 말한 것을 듣고 여러분이 이미 짐작했겠지만, 때때로 지구는 다른 시기보다 태양에 더 가까이 있죠. 현재, 태양에 지구가 가장 가깝게 접근하는 것은 1월에 일어나서 이는 북반구에 온화한 여름을 발생시키는데요. 하지만 대조적으로, 11000년 전에는 지구가 태양에 가장 가깝게 접근하는 것이 7월에 일어났고, 이는 여름과 겨울을 더욱 극단적으로 만들었죠. [Q9] 좋아요, 이제 우리는 그가 제안했던 두 개의 기여하는 요소를 알고 있어요: 지구의 기울기 변화와 태양 주변을 도는 지구의 불규칙한 공전 패턴이죠. 우리는 이것으로부터 어떤 결론을 내릴 수 있을까요? 음… 우리는 이것들이 때로는 더 시원한 여름 또는 더 무더운 여름 같은 기후변화를 초래했다는 것을 알죠. 이 두 현상은 빙하의 형성이나 후퇴에 엄청난 영향을 미칠 수 있어요. 예를 들어, 지구의 땅덩어리 대부분을 갖고 있는 북반구에서는 연속적으로 계속되는 더 시원한 여름들이 몇 년 동안 눈이 쌓이고 지속되게 할 수 있어요. 그게 무엇을 야기시킬 것 같나요? 물론 빙하기이죠! 반면에 계속 지속되는 무더운 여름은 빙하의 수축을 야기시킬 것이고, 이는 우리가 현재 살고 있는 것과 같은 간빙기를 불러올 거에요.

문단주제	본문내용	해석
단락 8 Milankovitch 이론의 한계점	Although the Milankovitch theory has some convincing elements, it does overlook some essential factors, such as cloud cover and variations in solar energy. [Q10] When compared to the other theories proposed so far, it is, by far, the most accepted, but I believe we should keep our options open and avoid thinking that it's the ultimate and most comprehensive explanation possible.	비록 Milankovitch 이론이 몇몇 설득력 있는 요소를 갖고 있긴 하지만, 이것은 구름이 하늘을 덮는 것과 태양에너지의 변동과 같은 몇몇 중요한 요소를 간과하고 있어요. [Q10] 지금까지 제시되어온 다른 이론들과 비교해봤을 때 이것은 확실히 가장 인정되는 이론이죠. 하지만 우리의 선택 가능성을 열어두고 이 이론이 궁극적이고 가장 종합적인 설명이라고 생각하는 것을 피해야 해요.

---

06. [Main Idea] What is the main topic of the lecture?

(A) ~~Characteristics~~ of ice ages and interglacial periods *(too general)*

(B) ~~The Milankovitch theory~~ that explains the effects of the Earth's rotation and orbit on global climate change *(too specific)* ★

(C) Evidence and theories that point to the predictability of ice ages and interglacial periods

(D) ~~Chronological exploration~~ of ice ages that have happened over the last few million years *(too specific)*

06. 강의의 주제는 무엇인가?

(A) 빙하기와 간빙기의 ~~특징~~

(B) 지구의 자전과 공전이 세계 기후변화에 끼치는 영향을 설명하는 ~~Milankovitch의 이론~~ ★

(C) 빙하기와 간빙기에 대한 예측을 나타내는 증거와 이론들

(D) 지난 몇 백만년 동안 발생한 빙하기의 ~~연대순 설명~~

> **해설** | (A)는 너무 포괄적이다. 빙하기의 예측성을 얘기하는 데에 background information으로 들어간 내용. (B)전체 내용의 일부분임. 강의의 주제라 하기에는 무리가 있음. (D)는 초반에 교수가 잠깐 예를 들어 얘기한 것으로 오답.

---

07. [Detail – Methodology] How did the scientists determine the regularity of coral reef growth?

(A) By calculating the difference between each layer's ~~thickness and length~~ *(not mentioned)*

(B) By dating the layers of coral reef ~~responsible for the changes~~ in the water level *(opposite fact)* ★

(C) By comparing coral reefs in the Northern Hemisphere with the ones in the ~~Southern Hemisphere~~ *(not mentioned)*

(D) By examining specific chemicals from coral reefs and the difference in the ages of the layers

07. 과학자들은 어떻게 산호초 성장의 규칙성을 측정하였는가?

(A) 각 층의 ~~두께 및 길이 간의~~ 차이를 계산함으로써

(B) 해수면의 ~~변화의 원인이 되는~~ 산호초 층들을 연대 측정함으로써 ★

(C) 북반구에 있는 산호초들을 ~~남반구에~~ 있는 산호초와 비교함으로써

(D) 산호초에서 나오는 특정 화학물질과 각 층의 나이의 차이를 조사함으로써

> **해설** | 답은 uranium isotope을 사용해 각 층의 coral reef의 나이를 계산해 중간 휴식 시간을 찾는 것. (A)는 언급 되지 않은 내용.
> (B)는 순서가 뒤 바뀌었다 - water level이 높아졌다 낮아졌다 함으로서 coral reef가 성장을 하게 됨.
> (C)는 왜곡 된 내용 - northern hemisphere는 Milankovitch theory에 나오는 내용.

08. [Detail – Characteristic] Which of the following is true about the Earth's tilt?

(A) The sun's ~~gravity~~ exerts a ~~great influence~~ on the Earth's tilt. *(not mentioned)*

(B) It ~~does not have~~ any significant impact on the global climate. *(opposite fact)*

(C) More tilt results in extreme summers and ~~mild~~ winters. *(partial error)* ★

(D) Small changes in the Earth's tilt could lead to substantial changes in the global climate.

08. 다음 중 지구의 기울기에 대한 설명으로 맞는 것은?

(A) 태양의 ~~중력이~~ 지구의 기울기에 큰 ~~영향을~~ 미친다.

(B) 그것은 지구 기후에 어떤 중요한 영향도 ~~미치지 않는다~~.

(C) 더 큰 기울기는 극단적인 여름과 ~~온화한~~ 겨울을 야기시킨다. ★

(D) 지구 기울기의 작은 변화는 지구 기후에 상당한 변화를 초래할 수 있다.

> **해설** | (A)는 언급되지 않은 내용. (B)는 Milankovitch가 주장했던 내용과 정 반대되는 내용.
> (C)는 교수가 설명한 내용과 다르다 - more tilt - extreme summers and extreme winters가 맞는 답.

09. [Detail - Reason] What are the causes of ice ages according to Milutin Milankovitch?

Click on 2 answers

(A) The relative position of the Earth's axis

(B) Changes in ocean currents and wind patterns *(unrelated to the question)*

(C) Continental drift and volcanic eruptions *(unrelated to the question)*

(D) The elliptical orbit of the Earth

09. Milutin Milankovitch에 따르면 빙하기의 원인은 무엇인가?

2개의 정답을 고르시오

(A) 지구의 축에 대한 상대적인 위치

(B) 해류와 바람의 패턴 변화

(C) 판 이동과 화산 분출

(D) 지구의 타원형 궤도

> **해설** | (B)와 (C)는 모두 plate tectonics에 관한 내용이다 - (C)로 인해 (B)같은 현상이 일어난다고 주장하는 theory.

10. [Inference – Opinion/Attitude] What is the professor's attitude towards the Milankovitch theory?

(A) He takes a detached position and also opens up the possibility of other theories.
(B) He criticizes the theory and debases the validity of it.
(too extreme, wrong fact)
(C) He acknowledges the absolute creditability of the theory.
(too extreme, wrong fact)
(D) He believes the theory is the most historically accurate one.
(wrong fact) ★

10. Milankovitch의 이론에 대한 교수의 태도는 무엇인가?

(A) 그는 공정한 입장을 취하고 있으며 다른 이론들에 대한 가능성을 열어두고 있다.
(B) 그는 이론을 비판하고 그 타당성을 폄하하고 있다.
(C) 그는 이론에 대해 절대적인 신뢰성을 부여하고 있다.
(D) 그는 이론이 역사적으로 가장 정확한 이론이라고 믿고 있다. ★

해설 | (B)와 (C)는 극단적인 표현 - 교수는 어느 정도의 credit을 주지만, 비판을 하거나 완전한 신뢰는 주지 않는다.
(D)는 ice age theory를 나타내는 것.

11. [Inference-Imply] What does the professor imply when he says:

> "So, you may be doubtful about how scientists can be so sure we're living in an interglacial period?"

(A) That there is not enough evidence to support his claim of the advent of another ice age *(opposite fact)*
(B) That he is also doubtful of the hypothesis scientists have established *(opposite fact)*
(C) That it is very difficult to predict when another ice age will take place *(opposite fact)* ★
(D) That it's hard for students to believe that another ice age will come

11. 교수가 다음 말을 할 때 암시하는 것은 무엇인가?

> "그래서, 여러분은 과학자들이 어떻게 우리가 간빙기에 살고 있다고 확신하는지에 대해 의구심을 가질 수 있을 거 같아요?"

(A) 또 다른 빙하기가 도래한다는 그의 주장을 뒷받침하는 충분한 증거가 없다.
(B) 그는 또한 과학자들이 정립한 가설에 대해 의심하고 있다.
(C) 언제 또 다른 빙하기가 발생할지 예측하는 것은 아주 어렵다. ★
(D) 학생들이 또 다른 빙하기가 올 거라고 믿기는 힘들다.

해설 | 교수는 global warming이 일어나고 있는 이 시대에 ice age가 곧 다시 올 것이라는 주장이 믿기 힘들 거라 말한다. (A)는 "there is considerable evidence to suggest that another ice age is coming" 이라 주장하는 교수의 말을 반대로 써놓은 것이고, (B)는 ice age theory를 설명하는 교수의 입장의 반대되는 말. (C) 헤드셋 문제(다시 듣기 문제)는 노트테이킹 한 부분 중 어느 지점에서 나왔는지 파악해야 한다. 그래야 어느 문맥에서 그 말을 했는지 파악할 수 있다. 이 문제에서 교수는 우리가 간빙기에 살고 있다고 학자들이 예측했다는 사실을 얘기하는게 아니라 학자들의 판단근거를 학생들에게 강의를 통해 알려주기 위해 유도하는 질문을 한다. 그러므로, 언제 ice age가 일어날 것인지에 대한 얘기와 전혀 관계가 없다.

TEST 1 set 1-3
Lecture 2
Drama class

문단주제	본문내용	해석

단락 1
고대 극장에 대한 소개

Listen to part of a lecture in an introduction to drama class

P: Up to now we've been looking at how the structure of a play and the stage where the play is performed are related to each other. Let's look back to the very beginning of theater development. You guys are aware that the first theaters were built by the Greeks in the 5th century B.C.E. right? Well, although in our modern sense, theaters are supposed to be indoors, back then, they were built outdoors in nature, usually on the top of a hill. [Q16-D] By locating them in this way, the Greek architects ensured that the natural scenery was well incorporated into the theaters' settings. On the other hand, the basic elements of today's theater are essentially the same as in ancient times… [Q12] So, today we will be looking more deeply into their similarities and differences, and as we go along, you'll notice how certain things in the theater world remain unchanged and others were modified or abandoned.

단락 2
합창단의 역할 및 중요성 : 현대 vs 고대

Let's begin our discussion with the space where the choruses performed their roles in ancient times. [Q13-C] Just like today's theater, the performing area for the chorus was called the orchestra, which meant "the dancing place" in ancient Greek. As far as I'm concerned, the similarities they share end about there. In order to understand the discrepancy, you need to notice that the chorus in ancient times had an extra role on top of that of today's choruses. [Q13-A] Yes, they certainly did dance and sing on the stage like they do today, but they also provided commentary on a variety of aspects of the play, including its theme, what the characters were thinking, and what they were doing. [Q13] Their occasional direct involvement in the plays clearly showed that one of their primary roles was to interact with the audience and react to the drama with them. This is quite different from today's choruses, isn't it? One could argue that the importance of the chorus has diminished greatly over time. Anyway… Does anyone know any other differences between today's choruses and ancient ones?

S: Well, [Q13-B] I've heard that the choruses' involvement was so significant that they were considered to have a distinct personality like any other character on stage.

P: 지금까지 우리는 연극의 구조와 연극이 행해지는 무대가 서로 어떻게 관련되어 있는지 살펴보고 있는데요. 극장 발전의 맨 처음을 되돌아 봅시다. 여러분 모두 첫 번째 극장이 기원전 5세기에 그리스인들에 의해서 지어졌다는 건 알고 있죠? 현대의 감각으로 보면 극장은 안에 있어야 되지만, 그 당시에는 야외에 자연 속에, 보통 언덕 위에 지어졌어요. [Q16-D] 이런 식으로 위치해 놓으면, 그리스 건축물들은 자연의 경관이 무대의 장치에 잘 녹아들어가게 되었죠. 반면에, 오늘날 극장의 기본적인 요소들이 기본적으로 고대와 똑같아요… [Q12] 그럼, 오늘 우리는 그것들의 유사점과 차이점에 대해서 더 깊게 살펴볼 건데요, 우리가 그러는 도중에, 극장세계에서 어떤 특정한 것들이 바뀌지 않고 남아있고, 다른 것들은 변형되거나 버려졌는지 알게 될 거에요.

고대에 합창단이 역할을 하던 공간으로 토론을 시작해봅시다. [Q13-C] 오늘날의 극장과 똑같이, 합창단이 공연하는 장소는 오케스트라라고 불렸는데요, 이것은 고대 그리스어로 "춤추는 장소"를 뜻했어요. 제가 알기로는… 그들의 공통점은 거기쯤에서 끝이 나죠. 차이점을 이해하기 위해서는, 고대의 합창단은 현대의 합창단 위에 추가적인 역할을 가지고 있었어요. [Q13-A] 네, 물론 그들은 현대처럼 무대에서 춤도 추고 노래도 불렀어요, 하지만 그들은 연극의 다양한 측면에 대한 코멘트를 제공했죠, 주제라던지, 등장인물들이 무엇을 생각하는지, 그리고 그들이 무엇을 하는지를 포함해서요. [Q13] 그들이 가끔씩 연극에 관여하는 것은 그들의 주요 역할 중 하나가 관중들과 상호작용하며 그들과 함께 드라마에 반응하는 것을 분명히 보여주었죠. 지금 현대의 합창단과는 조금은 달라요, 그렇죠? 합창단의 중요성이 시간이 흐르면서 많이 사라졌다고 주장할 수도 있겠죠. 어쨌든… 현재와 과거 코러스의 다른 차이점을 알고 있는 사람 있나요?

S: 음, [Q13-B] 제가 듣기로는 합창단의 개입이 무척 중요해서 무대 위의 다른 등장 인물들처럼 뚜렷한 성격이 있었어요.

문단주제	본문내용	해석
	P: Yes. That's exactly what Aristotle, the Greek philosopher, explained about the choruses' role… That they also had an active role in the drama! Yes, John?	**P:** 맞아, 그게 바로 그리스 철학자인 아리스토텔레스가 합창단의 역할에 대해 설명했던 부분이야. 그들은 또한 드라마에서 활발한 역할을 갖기도 했다는 것을 말야. John?
	S: Um… I saw Politis last summer, you know, the reenactment of the ancient one, and I witnessed something very strange during the play… It seemed like some of the action scenes were abridged. You see, when Politis was sent off, a messenger appeared on stage and announced to the audience that while Politis was riding in his chariot, a giant monster, a bull, if I remember correctly, sprang forth from the ocean and killed Politis. Then, as the messenger walked off, Politis was carried back on stage, and he was officially pronounced dead in front of the audience. I mean, the intense fighting scene, which would have been great to watch, was put into words and relayed to us by a messenger. I don't understand… What happened to the scene? Is this how the theaters presented their scenes in ancient times?	**S:** 음… 제가 작년 여름에 Politis라고 고대 연극을 재연한 걸 봤는데요, 연극하는 동안 매우 이상한 점을 발견했어요… 몇 가지 액션 장면이 생략된 것 같더라고요. 그러니까, Politis가 떠났을 때, 전달자가 무대 위에 나타나 관객들에게 Politis가 전차를 타고 있는데, 큰 괴물-제가 기억하는 게 맞다면-황소가 바다에서 튀어나와서 Politis를 죽였다고 발표했어요. 그리고는, 전달자가 무대에서 나가고, Politis가 무대 위로 운반되어 왔죠, 그리고는 그는 죽었다는 걸 관객들 앞에서 공식적으로 발표되었어요. 제 말은, 만약에 볼 수 있었다면 정말 대단했을 치열한 싸움 장면은 몇 단어로 표현되어 전달자에 의해 우리에게 알려줬어요. 전 이해가 안돼요… 그 장면은 어떻게 된 거죠? 예전에는 이런 식으로 몇 가지의 장면들을 보여준 건가요?
	P: [Q17] Great point! I was just about to move on to a topic that will answer your question, so hang on a minute.	**P:** [Q17] 좋은 지적이에요! 학생이 물어보는 질문에 답변을 해줄 수 있는 주제로 이제 막 넘어가려고 했어요, 그러니까 잠시만 기다려봐요.
단락 3 공연 장소 : stage vs skēnē	Okay. Now that we've looked at the chorus, let's take a look at where the actors performed. The modern term for where the actors perform is called the stage, as you all know. The Greeks, however, referred to it as the skēnē. I'm sure it sounds unfamiliar to all of you, as even scholars have two totally different interpretations of the word. Some scholars use the term strictly to refer to the structure behind the stage, whereas others use it in reference to both the structure and the stage itself. In this class, we'll be using the term with the latter purpose. Anyway, the skēnē evolved throughout the centuries. Prior to the advent of theaters, it was merely a wooden platform with no significance, but it went through a lot of modifications and became much more ornate and decorative over time. [Q14] With the establishment of theaters, it acted as background scenery. For instance, the front wall of the building was decorated, sometimes as a temple or as a palace, according to the setting of the story. Well… The problem with this was that they didn't have the technology to change the background for every scene like we do today.. [Q14-B] Instead, they had only one decorated skēnē, and that had to last throughout the entire play.	오케이. 자 여러분은 합창단을 살펴봤으니, 이제 배우들이 어디에서 공연했는지 보도록 하죠. 여러분 모두 알다시피, 배우들이 공연하는 장소를 현대 용어로 무대라고 부르죠. 하지만, 그리스인들은, 이걸 skēnē 이라고 불렀어요. 여러분에게 익숙치 않을 거에요, 심지어 학자들도 그 단어에 대해서 두 가지의 다른 해석을 가지고 있거든요. 어떤 학자들은 이 용어를 무대 뒤의 구조를 나타내는 데 엄격하게 사용하고, 반면에 다른 학자들은 구조와 무대 둘 다 나타내는데 사용해요. 이 수업에서는, 우린 이 용어의 후자의 뜻으로 사용할 거에요. 어쨌든, skēnē은 수 세기 동안 진화했어요. 극장에 출연하기 전에는, 그것이 중요한 의미 없이 단지 나무 판자에 불과했는데요, 하지만 시간이 지남에 따라 수많은 변화를 겪고 더욱 화려해지고 다듬어졌죠. [Q14] 극장이 설립됨에 따라, 그것은 배경 장면으로서 중요한 역할을 하게 되었어요. 예를 들면, 빌딩의 앞에 있는 벽은 이야기의 장면에 따라 때때로 사원이나 궁으로 장식되었어요. 음… 이것이 가진 문제점은 그들은 지금 우리가 하는 것처럼 모든 장면을 바꿀 수 있는 기술을 가지고 있지 않았다는 점이죠. [Q14-B] 대신 오직 하나의 skēnē를 장식해서, 연극 내내 유지했죠.

TEST 1 set 1-3

문단주제	본문내용	해석
	Therefore, as you mentioned, John, it was impractical for them to portray every single scene of the play, and sometimes some of the events had to be condensed into words instead of visual images. That's why the entire fight scene in Politis had to be reported by the messenger… The setting in which the fight took place was not the same as the one in which the rest of the play happened. In fact, I'll show you some other great examples of plays like the one that John mentioned in the next lesson.	그래서, John 네가 말했던 것처럼, 그들은 연극의 매 장면을 묘사하는 것이 불가능해서, 때때로 몇 몇 장면들은 볼 수 있는 이미지대신 짧게 줄여서 말로 표현했던 거죠. 그래서 Politis의 액션 부분 전체를 전달자가 보고해야 했던 거예요. 싸움이 벌어졌던 배경은 연극의 나머지 부분이 발생했던 것과 같지 않았죠. 사실, 전 다음 강의에서 John이 말했던 것과 같은 다른 좋은 예를 보여줄게요.
단락 4 관객들의 좌석: theatron	Anyway, the last aspect of the Greek theaters we will be discussing today is the seating area for the audience, which they called the theatron. [Q15] Well, it's just an idea, but I think it's quite ironic that they called it the theatron, which meant the 'seeing place,' when some theaters had numerous rows and accommodated about 14,000 spectators per play… I'm sure some of the people in the upper part of the place couldn't even watch the show and had to hear it instead… (laughs) Anyway, the theatron was constructed in such a way that it resembled a bowl, with rows of seats spreading outwards and upwards… Sometimes, they were cut in half, resulting in a semi-circular shape. [Q16] The bowl shape was very effective because it enabled the capturing of the sound and efficiently delivered it upwards, so that everyone, regardless of his/her seat location, could hear the performers.	어쨌든, 오늘 우리가 토론할 그리스 극장의 마지막 부분은 관객들의 좌석인데요, 이걸 theatron이라고 불렸어요. [Q15] 음, 이건 그저 내 생각이지만, 그들이 이것을 theatron이라고 부르는 건 꽤 아이러니한 것 같아요, 이 단어의 뜻은 '보는 장소'이고, 어떤 극장들은 수많은 좌석열이 있어서 매회 연극 당 거의 14,000명 정도의 관객을 수용할 수 있었거든요… 분명히 위쪽에 앉은 일부 사람들은 쇼를 보지 못하고 거의 듣기만 했을 테니까요… (웃음) 어쨌든, theatron은 그릇을 닮은 모양으로 건축되었는데요, 좌석열은 밖으로 그리고 위로 퍼지듯이 되어 있었어요. 가끔씩은, 반으로 잘라져서 반원모양을 하고 있기도 했죠. [Q16] 그릇 모양은 정말 효과적이었는데 왜냐하면 그것은 소리를 잡아서 그것을 위쪽으로 효율적으로 전달할 수 있었거든요, 그래서 좌석 위치에 상관없이 모든 사람들이 연기자들이 말하는 소리를 들을 수 있었어요.
	Okay. That should cover today's discussion. Well, you see, I've devoted a long time to studying the fields of drama and theater, and I get a sense of great joy and pleasure whenever I introduce new students like you to my approach… Some people might put great emphasis on today's theaters and overlook the very first theaters used by the Greeks, but the way I look at it is that modern theater wouldn't exist without the basic elements of the ancient theaters, so try to keep that in mind.	좋아요… 이 정도면 오늘 수업을 다 한 것 같네요. 음, 그러니까, 전 오랜 기간 동안 드라마와 극장 분야에 대해 연구해 왔거든요. 그래서 전 여러분 같은 새로운 학생들에게 저의 접근법을 소개할 때마다 큰 기쁨과 즐거움을 얻고 있어요… 어떤 사람들은 오늘날의 극장에 대해서 엄청 강조하고 그리스인들에 의해 사용된 최초의 극장들을 간과하지만, 제가 바라보는 관점은 현대 극장은 고대 극장을 이루고 있는 기본적인 요소가 없었다면 지금 존재하지 않았을 거라는 것이죠. 그래서 이 점을 염두에 두세요.

12. [Main Idea] What is the lecture mainly about?

(A) The location and ~~organization~~ of theaters in ancient Greece
 (too specific)

(B) The establishment of the theater world in the ~~5th century B.C.E.~~
 (too specific)

(C) **Exploration of the aspects of Greek theaters in comparison to modern ones**

(D) Distinct ~~roles~~ that the Greeks' chorus and actors played in contrast to those of today *(too specific)* ★

12. 강의는 주로 무엇에 대한 것인가?

(A) 고대 그리스 극장의 위치와 ~~조직체계~~

(B) ~~기원전 5세기~~ 때 설립된 극장 세계

(C) **그리스 극장의 여러 면들을 현대 극장과 비교하여 조사**

(D) 오늘날과 대조되는 그리스 시대의 합창단의 뚜렷한 ~~역할들~~ ★

해설 | 교수는 introduction부터 오늘의 theaere과 Greece의 처음 만들어진 theatre를 비교해보겠다고 하며 시작을 한다. 따라서 (A), (B), (D) 모두 오늘의 theater란 내용을 포함하고 있지 않기 때문에 오답이다.

13. [Detail – Difference/Contrast] How does the professor distinguish the chorus of the Greeks from today's chorus?

(A) ~~The Greek chorus~~ sang and danced on stage *(partial error)*

(B) The Greek chorus' roles ~~weren't as significant~~ as today's
 (opposite fact)

(C) Today, theaters are built indoors, while ancient theaters were built outdoors in nature. *(unrelated to the question)* ★

(D) **The Greek choruses often took a more active role in the play.**

13. 교수는 어떻게 오늘날의 합창단과 그리스 시대의 합창단을 구별하는가?

(A) ~~그리스 시대의 합창단은~~ 무대에서 노래를 부르고 춤도 췄다.

(B) 그리스 시대의 합창단은 오늘날의 합창단만큼 ~~중요하지 않았다~~.

(C) 오늘날의 극장은 실내에 지어지지만 고대의 극장은 실외에 자연 속에 지어졌다. ★

(D) **그리스 시대의 합창단은 보통 연극에서 좀 더 활발한 역할을 했다**

해설 | 해설(A)는 공통점이므로 오답. (B)는 오히려 반대되는 말을 하고 있으므로 오답, (C)는 합창단과 관계 없으므로 오답.

14. [Detail] What was the purpose of the skēnē in early theaters?

(A) It helped the audience in the back rows hear the play more easily. *(wrong fact)* ★

(B) It served to portray every single scene of the play through multiple background images. *(wrong fact)*

(C) Although it was just a wooden platform, it played a considerable role. *(opposite fact)*

(D) **It was a background image that made the play look more elaborate.**

14. 초기 극장에서 skēnē의 목적은 무엇이었는가?

(A) 뒷줄에 앉아있는 관객들이 연극을 좀 더 쉽게 들을 수 있게 도움을 줬다. ★

(B) 여러 배경 이미지를 통해 모든 장면을 묘사해주는 역할을 한다.

(C) 그저 나무판자 틀에 불과 했으나 중요한 역할을 했다.

(D) 연극을 좀 더 정교하게 보이게 만들어 주는 배경 이미지였다.

해설 | (A)는 theatron에 관련된 내용이므로 질문과 관련이 없다. (B) 오직 하나의 skēnē를 장식해서 연극 내내 유지했다는 교수의 설명과 어긋나므로 오답. 기술의 한계로 인해 모든 장면에 맞게 배경을 바꾸는 것이 불가능했다. (C)는 정 반대되는 내용이므로 각각 오답이다.

---

15. [Inference – Imply] What does the professor imply when she interprets the meaning of the term, "theatron"?

(A) **That the literal interpretation of the Greek term doesn't match with its practical function.**

(B) That the interpretation of the term is controversial among scholars. *(unrelated to the question)*

(C) That it's ironic that the shape of theatron was a semi-circle instead of a square. *(not mentioned)* ★

(D) That it's very likely that everyone in the audience was able to watch the play. *(opposite fact)*

15. 교수는 "theatron"이라는 용어의 의미를 해석할 때 무엇을 암시하는가?

(A) 그리스 용어에 대한 해석은 그것의 실용적인 기능과 맞지 않다.

(B) 그 용어에 대한 해석은 학자들 사이에서 논란이 되고 있다.

(C) theatron의 모양이 사각형이 아니라 반원 모양이었다는 것은 아이러니하다. ★

(D) 모든 관객들이 연극을 볼 수 있었을 가능성이 높다.

해설 | (B)는 skene에 관한 내용으로 질문과 관련이 없다. (C) 교수는 theatron의 그릇 모양이 관객들에게 소리를 효과적으로 전달했다고 말한다. 즉, 사각형 모양이 아니어서 아이러니 하다는 주장은 용어의 의미 해석에 암시되어 있지 않다.
(D)는 (A)와 정 반대되는 말이므로 오답이다.

16. [Detail] Why was the bowl shape of the theatron so important?

(A) It widened the viewing range of the audience. *(wrong fact)*

(B) The shape enabled more viewers, thus making the play more profitable. *(not mentioned)*

(C) It effectively funneled the sound upward and delivered it to the audience.

(D) It was well incorporated with nature, and, thus, made the theater grand and prestigious. *(fact, but unrelated to the question)* ★

> 해설 | (A)는 오는 사람 수의 비해 theatron은 effective 하게 viewing range를 제공해주지 못했다고 주장하는 교수의 입장과 어긋나는 말이므로 오답이다. (B)는 언급된 내용이 아니므로 오답이다. (D)는 5세기 그리스인들이 언덕 위에 극장을 지어 자연의 경관이 무대와 잘 어우러지게끔 했다는 내용으로, theatron 의 그릇 모양과는 연관이 없다.

16. 왜 그릇 모양의 theatron이 중요한가?

(A) 관객들의 시야 범위를 넓혀준다.

(B) 그 모양은 더 많은 관객들을 유치할 수 있게 해서 연극이 더 많은 수익을 올릴 수 있게 한다.

(C) 소리를 효과적으로 위로 모아서 관객들에게 전달한다.

(D) 그것은 자연과 잘 결합되어 있어서 결국 극장을 웅장하고 유명하게 만들었다. ★

**Listen again to part of the lecture.
Then answer the question.**

"Great point! I was just about to move on to a topic that will answer your question, so hang on a minute."

17. [Inference–Imply] Why does the professor say this: 🎧

> "So hang on a minute."

(A) She doesn't want the student to interrupt her lesson. ★

(B) Her next discussion would automatically answer the student's question.

(C) She needs time to collect her thoughts before she answers the student's question.

(D) She is not certain about the credibility of her answer, so she thinks more research needs to be done.

강의의 일부를 다시 듣고, 질문에 답하시오.

"좋은 지적이에요! 학생이 물어보는 질문에 답변을 해줄 수 있는 주제로 이제 막 넘어가려고 했어요, 그러니까 잠시만 기다려봐요."

17. 교수는 왜 이렇게 말하는가?: 🎧

> "그러니까 잠시만 기다려봐요."

(A) 그녀는 학생들이 자신의 수업을 방해하는걸 원치 않는다. ★

(B) 그녀가 다룰 다음 주제가 학생의 질문에 자동적으로 답변 할 것이다.

(C) 그녀는 학생의 질문에 답하기 전에 자신의 생각을 정리할 시간이 필요하다.

(D) 그녀는 자신의 답이 확실하지 않아서, 그래서 더 많은 연구가 필요하다고 생각한다.

> 해설 | 해설 교수는 앞서서 "I was just about to move on to a topic that will elucidate your question" 이라 말한다.
> 이를 통해, 교수가 말하고자 하는 바는 교수가 다음으로 얘기할 내용이 그 학생의 질문을 대답해 줄 것이니 잠깐 기다리라는 것이다.
> (A) 대답하기 싫은 것도, (C) 생각할 시간이 필요한 것도, (D) 연구가 필요한 것도 아니다.

TEST 1 set 2-1

Conversation — Library employee

문단주제	본문내용	해석

단락 1
학생이 겪은 어려움 토로

Listen to a conversation between a student and a library employee.

S: Hi, could you help me with something? I really need your help.

L: Of course, how may I help you?

S: [Q1] Well, I am working on a paper on the Wall Street Crash of 1929, you know the Great Depression, and while I was looking for resources, I came across this book, "Time of Great Struggle." But, its reference pages are all damaged and wrinkled, and I can't really decipher anything. [Q5] What are the odds?

L: [Q2-B] Give me one second; let me check if we have another copy for you.

S: Sure.

L: Well… It seems like the book you're holding is the only copy we have in the library…

S: Oh no… I can't finish my assignment without the reference pages…

L: Have you tried ordering a copy of the book online? I'm sure you could try other sources

S: The thing is, I need to finish my research for the assignment by tomorrow, so ordering a new copy will take too long…

단락 2
도서관 사서의 대응책 제시

L: Hmm… let me try tracking the book and see if any other libraries have it.

S: Sure, as long as I can get the book.

L: I'm browsing for the book... and… actually, there's one university in New York! Do you want to try that?

S: Great! How long will it take for it to get here?

L: Well, I think it could get here by tomorrow if we ordered it right now, [Q2] but you never know what kind of delays can happen during shipment. We've experienced some of these issues before.

S: Oh no… Is there any other way to get the book from the university?

학생과 도서관 사서의 대화를 들으시오.

S: 안녕하세요, 도와주실 수 있나요? 당신 도움이 정말 필요해서요.

L: 물론이죠, 어떻게 도와드릴까요?

S: [Q1] 음, 제가 1929년에 일어난 금융계 몰락, 즉 대공황에 대한 레포트를 쓰고 있거든요. 그래서 제가 자료를 찾다가, "Time of Great Struggle"이라는 책을 봤어요. 그런데, 참고문헌 페이지가 모두 손상되거나 주름이 져서, 아무것도 읽을 수가 없네요. [Q5] 왜 이렇게 된 거죠?

L: [Q2-B] 잠시만요, 다른 책이 있는지 확인해 볼게요.

S: 네

L: 음… 지금 학생이 갖고 있는 책이 이 도서관이 소유한 유일한 책 같네요.

S: 오 안돼요… 이 참고문헌 페이지 없이는 과제를 못 끝내는데……

L: 혹시 온라인상에서 구매를 해보려고 시도해 봤나요? 다른 자료들을 쓸 수도 있을 텐데요.

S: 사실은요, 제가 이 과제를 위한 조사를 내일까지 끝내야 해서, 새로운 책을 주문하면 시간이 너무 많이 들 거에요.

L: 흠…… 다른 도서관에 이 책이 있는지 제가 한번 찾아볼게요.

S: 물론이죠, 이 책을 구할 수만 있다면요.

L: 제가 지금 책을 찾고 있는 중인데… 음… 뉴욕에 있는 대학교에 한 개가 있네요! 한번 확인해 볼래요?

S: 잘됐네요! 여기까지 오는데 얼마나 걸릴까요?

L: 음, 지금 바로 주문하면 내일까지는 올 것 같네요. [Q2] 하지만 배송 중에 어떤 일이 생겨서 지연이 될지는 모르겠어요. 예전에도 이와 비슷한 상황이 있었어요.

S: 오 안돼요… 혹시 그 대학교에서 책을 가져올 수 있는 다른 방법이 있나요?

문단주제	본문내용	해석
	L: Well, I usually do not do personal favors for patrons during working hours, but…a former colleague of mine works at that university. Maybe I can ask if he can help.	L: 음, 제가 보통은 근무시간에 학생들의 편의를 따로 봐주지 않는데요…하지만 제 예전 동료가 그 대학교에서 지금 일을 하고 있어요. 도와줄 수 있는지 한번 물어보도록 할게요.
	S: That'd be great. But how do you think he could be of any help in my current situation?	S: 그래 주시면 감사하죠. 하지만 이런 상황에 그가 어떤 도움을 줄 수 있죠?
	L: Well, he could fax over the pages that you need, and then I could give them to you.	L: 음, 그가 학생이 원하는 페이지들만 팩스로 보내고, 그러면 제가 그걸 학생에게 줄게요.
	S: Perfect! How soon do you think you'll be able to contact him?	S: 완벽해요! 얼마나 빨리 그에게 연락할 수 있죠?
	L: [Q4] Well, you're forgetting the time difference. They're on Eastern Time, so… it's very late there now	L: [Q4] 음, 학생이 지금 시차에 대해 잊은 것 같군요. 거기는 지금 동부 시간대니까… 지금쯤이면 시간이 매우 늦었겠네요.
	S: I hadn't thought about that. Okay, so…what time will you be able to get in touch with him?	S: 거기까지는 생각을 못했네요. 알겠어요, 그럼… 몇 시쯤 그와 연락이 될까요?
	L: Actually, I'm sure the library is not open right now, but I have his home number. [Q3-D] I'll ring him right now and see what he can do, [Q4-A, B] but… If the book is already checked out, I don't know what else I could do for you… [Q3] Perhaps you could stay here and try finding other books on the Great Depression. You never know.	L: 사실, 제가 알기론 그 도서관은 지금 문을 안 열었어요. 하지만, 제가 연락처를 알고 있는데… [Q3-D] 지금 당장 전화해서 알아볼게요. [Q4-A, B] 하지만, 이미 누군가 책을 빌려갔다면, 달리 어떻게 학생을 도울 수 있을지 모르겠네요… [Q3] 학생이 여기에 있으면서 대공황에 관한 다른 책들을 찾아보는 건 어떨까요?
	S: Okay, that sounds like all I can do for now. Could you leave me a message if that works out or not? I really want to make sure I'm not waiting for something that's not going to happen.	S: 알겠어요, 그게 지금 제가 할 수 있는 일인 것 같네요. 일이 성공했는지 아닌지 저에게 메시지로 알려주실 수 있나요? 가능하지 않은 상황을 기다리고 싶지는 않거든요.
	L: Sure, just leave your phone number here.	L: 물론이죠, 여기에 연락처를 남겨주세요.
	S: Thanks for your help.	S: 도와주셔서 감사해요.
	L: I will let you know as soon as possible.	L: 가능한 한 빨리 알려드릴게요.

01. [Main Idea – Main Purpose] Why does the student go to see the librarian?

(A) ~~To ask directions~~ to a different university that has the book that he needs *(wrong fact)*

(B) To ask ~~whether the library can fix~~ some damaged pages of a book *(wrong fact)*

(C) To get help finding a different book that contains ~~more~~ information that he needs *(wrong fact)* ★

(D) To get help finding information that he needs for his assignment

01. 학생은 도서관사서를 보러 간 이유는 무엇인가?

(A) 자신이 필요한 책을 가진 다른 대학교로 ~~가는 길을 물어보려고~~

(B) 도서관 측이 책의 손상된 부분을 ~~고칠 수 있나~~ 물어보려고

(C) 학생이 필요한 정보를 더 가지고 있는 다른 책을 찾는데 도움을 얻으려고 ★

(D) 학생의 과제에 필요한 정보를 찾는데 도움을 받기 위해서

> **해설 |** 학생은 자신이 쓰고 있는 과제에 필요한 내용을 담고 있는 책의 reference pages가 다 손상되어 다른 방법을 구색하기 위해 도서관원을 찾아간다. (A)는 해당 없는 내용이다. (B)는 학생의 부탁과는 거리가 멀고, (C)는 도서관원이 해결책으로 제시한 것 중 하나로, 학생이 도서관원을 찾아간 이유는 아니다.

02. [Inference – Infer] What can be inferred about the library?

(A) It ~~often~~ encounters cases similar to that of the student. *(partial error)* ★

(B) It only has a ~~single copy of each~~ book. *(too extreme)*

(C) It has had problems regarding the delivery of materials from other places.

(D) It ~~does not own many books~~ regarding the Great Depression. *(too extreme)*

02. 도서관에 대해서 무엇을 추론할수 있습니까?

(A) 종종 학생의 경우와 비슷한 상황들을 마주한다. ★

(B) 그곳은 모든 책들을 ~~한 권씩만~~ 가지고 있다.

(C) 다른 곳에서 자료가 배송되는 것과 관련하여 문제점들이 있었던 적이 있다.

(D) 대공황에 대한 책들을 ~~많이 소유하고 있지 않다~~.

> **해설 |** 도서관 사서는 학생의 문제를 해결해주기 위해 해결책으로 다른 도서관에서 책을 주문하자 한다. 하지만, 도서관원은 사전에도 주문하는 과정에서 문제가 있었다고 경고한다. (A) 학생의 경우를 자주 마주 하는 것이 아니라 주문과정에서 문제를 자주 겪는다는 내용이므로 틀렸다. (B) 학생이 처음 찾아가서 어려움을 토로했을 때 사서가 다른 한 부가 있는지 찾아보는 것으로 미루어 보아 모든 책들이 한 권씩만 있는 것이 아니다. (D) 학생은 specific 하게 Time of Great Struggle을 찾는 것이기 때문에 다른 책의 여분에 대해선 추측할 수 있는 바가 없다.

03. [Inference – Further Action] What will the student probably do next?

(A) ~~Try to decipher~~ what he can from the damaged pages. *(wrong fact)*

(B) Leave his contact information and ~~head out of the library~~. *(wrong fact)* ★

(C) Search for a book that may have the information that he needs.

(D) ~~Talk~~ to the librarian's colleague ~~over the phone~~. *(wrong fact)*

03. 학생이 다음에 할 일은 무엇일까?

(A) 손상된 부분을 ~~읽어보려고 할 것이다~~.

(B) 연락처를 준 후에 ~~도서관을 나갈 것이다~~. ★

(C) 학생이 필요한 정보를 가지고 있을 법한 책들을 찾아볼 것이다.

(D) 도서관 사서의 동료와 ~~전화 통화를~~ 할 것이다.

> **해설 |** A) 이미 손상되어 있고 찢어진 부분이기 때문에 try to decipher = 해석하는것은 불가능 하다. B)head out of the library = 도서관 밖으로 나가야하기에는 내일 책에 대한 내용을 받을수 있을지가 명확하지 않아서 다른책을 찾아보는게 어떻겠냐고 사서가 대안책을 제시 해 주었다. D) Talk to the librarian's colleague = 사서관의 동료와 전화는 사서가 할일은 아니다.

04. [Detail – Characteristic] Which of the following is true about the book in the other library?

(A) It ~~has not~~ been checked out yet. *(not mentioned)*
(B) It will ~~definitely~~ get to the student by tomorrow. *(wrong fact)*
(C) It belongs to a library in New York that is probably closed.
(D) It belongs to a library that the librarian's friend ~~owns~~. *(partial error)* ★

04. 다음 중 다른 도서관에 있는 책에 해당하는 내용은 무엇인가?

(A) 아직 누군가가 빌려가지 ~~않았다~~.
(B) 학생은 내일까지 ~~확실히~~ 책을 받게 될 것이다.
(C) 아마 문이 닫혔을 뉴욕에 있는 도서관에 있다.
(D) 도서관 사서의 친구가 ~~소유한~~ 도서관의 소유물이다. ★

해설 | (A) 누가 이미 빌려 갔는지 안 빌려 갔는지는 아직 확인된 바가 없다. (B) 또한 불확실한 내용이므로 틀리다. (D)는 도서관원의 예전 동료가 일하는 곳이라고 해서 그 사람이 그 도서관을 운영한다는 뜻이 아니다.

Listen again to part of the conversation. Then answer the question.

"But its reference pages are damaged and wrinkled, and I can't really decipher anything. What are the odds?"

05. [Inference – Purpose] Why does the student say this: 🎧

"What are the odds?"

(A) To suggest that he is ~~used to~~ the library's poor management of the books *(opposite fact)*
(B) To show that it's unbelievable to him that only the pages of use to him are damaged
(C) To show his ~~anger~~ towards the likely outcome of his assignment *(too extreme)*
(D) To ask the librarian ~~how he could decipher~~ the reference pages *(wrong fact)*

대화의 일부를 다시 듣고, 물음에 답하시오.

"그런데, 참고문헌 페이지가 모두 손상되거나 주름이 져서, 아무것도 읽을 수가 없네요. 왜 이렇게 된 거죠?"

05. 학생은 왜 이런 말을 하는가?: 🎧

"왜 이렇게 된 거죠?"

(A) 도서관의 미흡한 책 관리에 본인이 ~~익숙하다는 것을~~ 이야기하기 위해
(B) 학생이 사용하는 부분만 손상되었다는 사실이 믿기 어려워서
(C) 예측되는 과제의 결과에 대한 학생의 분노를 나타내기 위해
(D) 참고문헌 페이지를 ~~어떻게 해독해야 할지~~ 사서에게 물어보기 위해

해설 | 학생은 책 전체 중에 꼭 자기가 필요한 부분만 손상된 거에 믿지 못하겠다는 표현을 한다. (A) 하필 자신이 필요한 부분이 손상되었다며 의아해하는 부분으로, 이와 같은 상황에 익숙하다는 해석은 반대된 해석이다. (C) 학생의 말투에는 분노가 아닌 아쉬움과 어려움을 극복하고자 하는 의지가 담겨 있다. (D) 손상된 참고문헌을 해독하고자 하는 것이 아니라 대안 탐색 및 의아함의 표현이 이 부분에 담긴 학생의 주된 의도이다.

TEST 1 set 2-2
Lecture 1
Bioluminescence

문단 주제	본문내용	해석
단락 1 심층의 특징	**Listen to part of a lecture in a marine biology class** P: Last class we looked at the first two layers of the ocean and the marine life they contain. Well, today, we'll be moving on to the last, darkest layer of the ocean, named the deep-zone layer. Unlike the other two we've discussed so far, the deep-zone has some distinguishable characteristics. Yes, Isabella? S: From what I've read, professor, the zone is quite a dangerous and challenging place for marine life to survive… it doesn't have as high of an oxygen level as the other two, the water pressure is high, and oh, it's also completely devoid of any light.	해양 생물학 강의의 일부를 들으시오. P: 지난 수업에서 바다의 첫 2개의 층과 그들이 포함하고 있는 해양 생물을 살펴보았죠. 음, 오늘은, 심층이라고 불리는 바다의 가장 어두운 마지막 층을 배울 거예요. 지금까지 우리가 토론해 온 다른 2개의 층과 달리, 심층은 몇 가지 독특한 특징들을 가지고 있어요. 네, Isabella? S: 교수님, 제가 읽은 바로는, 이 지역은 해양 생물들이 생존하기에는 상당히 위험하고 도전을 많이 받고 있어요…. 산소 수준이 다른 2개의 층들만큼 높지 않고, 수압이 높아요. 그리고 또, 빛이 전혀 없구요.
단락 2 빛의 부족	P: You're right. And, I would like to discuss the last condition: lack of light. Well, what first comes to mind when you hear that there is no light in the zone? S: Well, I'm a little confused… I mean… I know that there are organisms living down there, but no light is kind of equivalent to no vision, right? So, how is it possible that there are organisms that thrive there without a problem?	P: 학생 말이 맞아요. 그래서, 전 마지막 상태에 대해서 토의하고 싶어요: 빛의 부족이요. 음, 이 지역에 빛이 없다는 말을 듣게 되면 여러분은 어떤 생각이 먼저 떠오르죠? S: 음, 약간 혼란스러운데요… 제 말은… 생물들이 아래에 존재한다는 것은 알겠는데, 빛이 없다는 건 못 보는 것과 마찬가지잖아요, 맞죠? 그럼, 그곳의 생물들이 아무 문제없이 번영하는 게 어떻게 가능한 거죠?
단락 3 생체 발광을 통한 빛 생산	P: Good question! Although the environment is seemingly uninhabitable, the marine life that lives there has adapted quite interesting ways to survive the harsh conditions. As you may have already guessed, the organisms that live in the zone have developed a trait that enables them to produce a type of chemical light, called "bioluminescence." S: Um, correct me if I'm wrong, but isn't it the bacteria that are present in the water or within the organisms that glow, not the fish themselves? P: Well, you're not completely wrong. There are fish like that, but that's a whole different category from bioluminescence. [Q7] In fact, most fish with bioluminescence, which is, again, a chemical trait, not a type of bacteria, [Q7-C] generate illumination within themselves to produce their own light. Okay now, we all know marine life down there has a chemical inherited from generation to generation that they use to produce light … [Q7-D] In most cases, the light is blue… but other colors are also seen occasionally.	P: 좋은 질문이에요! 비록 그곳 환경이 생물이 살기에 불가능해 보이지만, 거기에 살고 있는 해양 생물들은 상당히 흥미로운 방법들로 적응을 해서 척박한 환경에서 살아남았어요. 여러분이 이미 추측하고 있겠지만, 그 지역에 살고 있는 생물들은 "생체 발광"이라고 불리는 일종의 화학적 빛을 생산해낼 수 있게 하는 능력을 발달시켜 왔어요. S: 음, 제가 틀렸다면 지적해주세요, 하지만 빛을 내는 건 물 속이나 생물들 안에 존재하는 박테리아들 아닌가요, 물고기들이 아니라? P: 음, 학생 말이 완전히 틀리지는 않아요. 그런 물고기들도 있죠, 하지만 그것은 생체 발광과는 확연히 다른 범주에 속해요. [Q7] 사실, 생체 발광을 하는 대부분의 물고기들은, 다시 말하면, 박테리아가 아닌 화학적 물질들은, [Q7-C] 물고기들이 스스로 빛을 내게끔 만들어요. 그래요 지금은, 우린 심층에 있는 모든 해양 생물들이 빛을 생산하기 위해서 화학적 물질을 대대로 물려받은 사실을 알고 있죠. [Q7-D] 대개의 경우, 빛은 파란색이지만… 때론 다른 색깔들이 보이기도 해요.

문단주제	본문내용	해석
단락 4 심층 생물들의 시력	S: Professor, I understand that the color blue is the most functional color in the water in the sense that it travels the farthest in such an environment, but how is that of any help, considering that… I mean… I thought the organisms in the deep-zone couldn't see anything because they had no visual senses at all. For bioluminescence to be functional, it needs to be seen, right? P: Well, to some extent, you're right. But, it may come as a surprise to you that the fish in the zone actually do have the ability to see… but their visual senses are very limited. They only detect blue light, which is very fortunate since blue is the color of light that bioluminescence produces in most cases. It makes sense now, doesn't it? Although their vision is limited to one specific color, blue, they are capable of generating it themselves, thus enabling them to see in the darkness. Uh… there is one special type of fish, named the dragon fish, to which the blue light standard does not apply. They generate and see red light instead, and of course, this ability presents a tremendous advantage over others. Well… Dragon fish are not the topic of today's discussion, so let's move on.	S: 교수님, 파란색이 바다에서 가장 기능적인 색깔로 그런 환경에서 가장 멀리까지 멀리 이동할 수 있다는 건 이해해요. 하지만, 그게 어떤 도움이 되는 거죠… 제 말은… 심층에 있는 생물들은 눈이 안 보이기 때문에 아무것도 볼 수 없다고 생각했는데요? 생체 발광이 실용적이려면, 보여야 하잖아요, 맞죠? P: 음, 어느 정도까진, 학생 말이 맞아요. 하지만, 학생에게 놀랍게 들릴지도 모르겠지만, 심층에 살고 있는 물고기들은 사실상 볼 수 있는 능력이 있어요… 하지만 그들의 시각적임 감각은 아주 제한되어 있죠. 그들은 오직 파란색 색깔만 감지할 수 있는데, 이건 아주 운이 좋은 거에요, 왜냐하면 파란색이 생체 발광이 대개 보여주는 색깔이기 때문이에요. 이제 이해가 되나요? 비록 그들의 시력이 파란색이라는 하나의 특정한 색깔에 제한되어 있기는 해도, 그들은 스스로 그것을 만들어 낼 수 있고, 그래서 어둠 속에서도 볼 수 있는 거에요. 어… 홍룡어라고 불리는 특별한 물고기가 있는데, 이 물고기에는 파란색 기준이 적용되지 않아요. 대신 그들은 빨간색 빛을 내고 볼 수가 있는데, 그리고 당연히, 이런 특이한 능력이 다른 물고기들에 비해 엄청난 이점을 주죠. 음… 홍룡어들이 오늘 토론의 주제가 아니에요, 그러니까 넘어가도록 할게요.
단락 5 생체 발광의 장점 및 유용성	We were talking about the benefits of bioluminescence. [Q6] The main one we'll be looking into is the usefulness of bioluminescence when it comes to dealing with predators and their threats. Just for your information, though, it also serves other purposes, such as aiding in the reproductive, food-gathering, and communication processes. Anyway, does anybody want to take a guess at how bioluminescence might be used in protecting the organism against predators' attacks? S: You've taught us that there are two strategies that animals employ when dealing with predators. I believe they are active defense strategy and passive defense strategy. My question is, does the same principle apply to the marine life in the deep-layer zone?	우리는 생체 발광이 주는 이득에 대해서 말하고 있었죠. [Q6] 우리가 주로 살펴볼 것은 포식자들과 그들의 위협에 대처할 때 발생하는 생체 발광의 유용성이에요. 하지만, 그냥 참조라고 말해주는 건데, 생체 발광은 생식하는 과정, 음식을 모으는 과정, 그리고 의사 소통하는 과정에 도움을 주는 것처럼 다른 목적으로도 사용돼요. 어쨌든, 생체 발광이 어떻게 포식자들의 공격으로부터 보호하는 데 사용될 수 있는지 누구 추측해 볼 사람 있나요? S: 동물들이 포식자들을 대할 때 사용하는 2가지의 전략이 있다고 교수님이 가르쳐 주셨어요. 그것들은 능동적인 방어 전략과 수동적인 방어 전략이에요. 제가 궁금한 건, 심층에 사는 해양 생물들에게도 똑같은 원칙이 적용되나요?
단락 6 수정 해파리의 능동적인 방어 전략	P: Great question. Yes, the bioluminescent organisms utilize both active and passive defense strategies. For our purpose, let's look at… the crystal jellyfish. [Q8, Q7-B] They are considered to be the most influential bioluminescent organisms in the medical field, because the chemical responsible for their generation of light is used to locate cancerous tumors in the human body.	P: 좋은 질문이에요. 맞아요, 생체 발광하는 생물들은 능동적인 방어전략과 수동적인 방어 전략을 모두 사용해요. 우리가 다루는 목적을 위해서는, 수정 해파리에 대해서 살펴 봅시다. [Q8, Q7-B] 그것들은 의학 분야에서 가장 영향력 있는 생체 발광 생물들인데, 왜냐하면 이것은 빛을 생산을 담당하는 화학 물질이 인간의 몸 속에 있는 암 종양의 위치를 파악하는 데 사용되기 때문이에요.

TEST 1 set 2-2

문단주제	본문내용	해석
	Anyway, when they initially detect a predator's threat, the jellyfish flashes light at the predator. This flashing employs active defense strategies in two different senses… What I mean by two different senses is that there are two theories, as to what role bioluminescence plays in dealing with predators but no consensus exists as to which is correct. [Q10-D] One theory explains that the jellyfish flash their light to seem daunting to the predator… You know, scare them off in a sense. To help illustrate this more clearly, um, think about thieves. Let's say a thief is in the middle of stealing jewelry from your house and you flash a light in his face. What would his reaction be? Of course, he would try to run away, acknowledging that he has been caught… The other theory posits that it exposes the predator to its own predators. This theory was first hypothesized when scientists noticed that sometimes the jellyfish's predators were attacked while trying to feed on them… and, um, there have been many experiments that showed this. [Q9] One of these experiments artificially recreated the flashes that the jellyfish generated. Scientists then focused on whether or not squid, organisms that eat the jellyfish's predators but not the jellyfish, followed the flashes. And guess what? They did. [Q8-D] Squid actually swam to the signals, which proves that the flashes actually do play a role in attracting the predators' own predators.	어쨌든, 포식자의 위협을 처음 감지하면, 해파리는 포식자에게 빛을 비춰요. 이렇게 빛을 비추는 것이 2가지 의미에서 능동적인 방어 전략을 사용하는 것이죠… 제가 2가지라고 말하는 건 포식자들을 대할 때 생체 발광이 하는 역할에 관한 2가지의 이론들인데, 어떤 것이 맞는지는 과학자들 사이에서 의견 일치가 안되고 있어요. [Q10-D] 그 중 한 이론은 해파리들이 포식자들에게 겁을 주기 위해 빛을 비춘다는 것인데요… 그러니까, 어떤 면에서는 겁을 주어 쫓아버리겠다는 뜻이죠. 이 부분을 좀 더 명확히 설명하려면, 음, 도둑을 생각해 보세요. 한 도둑이 여러분의 집에서 보석을 훔치는 중이어서 여러분이 그 도둑의 얼굴에 빛을 비추었다고 합시다. 도둑의 반응은 어떨까요? 물론 도둑은 자신이 들켰다는 사실을 깨닫고는 도망가려 하겠죠. 다른 이론은 포식자들을 그들의 포식자에게 노출시키는 것을 말해요. 이 이론은 과학자들이 때때로 해파리의 포식자들이 먹이를 먹으려고 할 때 오히려 공격을 받았다는 것을 발견했을 때 처음 이론화되었어요… 그리고, 많은 실험들이 시행되어 이 사실을 보여주었죠. [Q9] 이 실험들 중 하나는 해파리들이 만들어내는 빛을 인위적으로 재창조하는 것이었어요. 그런 다음에 과학자들은 해파리가 아니라 해파리의 포식자들을 먹는 생물체인 오징어가 빛을 따라가는지에 주목했죠. 그리고 어떻게 되었을까요? 그것들은 빛을 따라갔어요. [Q8-D] 오징어는 신호가 있는 곳에 헤엄쳐 갔고, 이것은 빛이 포식자의 포식자를 끌어들이는 역할을 한다는 사실을 증명했죠.
단락 7 수동적인 방어전략으로서의 생체발광	Okay, that should be enough about active defense strategies. Now, let's move on to bioluminescence as a passive one! [Q10] The use as a passive strategy is different than the active one in that bioluminescence is used to completely avoid encountering predators. Um… do you guys remember our discussion on the principle of camouflage? S: Of course, it's used by animals to conceal themselves from their predators. [Q10-C] For instance, some frogs and lizards deliberately change their skin color either to make themselves more difficult to see or to deceive their predators with colors that make them look strong and dangerous. Oh, I get it now! [Q11] Bioluminescence works similarly, doesn't it?	그래요, 이 정도면 능동적인 방어 전략에 대한 얘기는 충분한 것 같군요. 자, 수동적인 방어 전략으로서의 생체발광으로 얘기를 옮겨보도록 하죠. [Q10] 소극적인 전략은 생체 발광이 포식자들과의 대면을 완전히 피하는 데 쓰인다는 점에서 능동적인 전략과 달라요. 음… 위장의 법칙에 대해 토론했던 것 기억나요? S: 물론이죠, 동물들이 포식자들로부터 숨으려고 할 때 사용되잖아요. [Q10-C] 예를 들어, 개구리나 도마뱀은 일부러 피부 색깔을 바꿔서 자신을 찾기 어렵게 만들거나 혹은 포식자들을 속이기 위해 강하고 위험하게 보이도록 색깔을 바꾸잖아요. 오, 이제야 알겠네요! [Q11] 생체 발광도 비슷한 원리로 작동되는구나, 아닌가요?

문단주제	본문내용	해석
	P: Excellent! That's exactly what it is. The organisms in the deep-zone, such as sea anemones, use the same mechanism, and use very conspicuous colors of bioluminescence to kind of… uh… deliver a warning message to their predators. It's as if they were saying, "I'm very toxic and dangerous, so you should not be considering me as a meal today."	**P:** 훌륭해요! 바로 그거에요. 심층에 사는 말미잘 같은 바다 생물들은, 똑같은 기제를 사용하는데, 아주 눈에 잘 띄는 색깔들을 가지고 생체 발광을 해서.. 음, 그들의 포식자들에게 경고 메시지를 전달하죠. 그건 마치 "나는 매우 독이 있고 위험하므로, 너는 오늘 음식으로 나를 목표로 삼으면 안돼"라고 말하고 있는 듯 해요.

06. [Main Idea] What is the lecture mainly about?

(A) The ~~characteristics~~ of the deep-zone layer of the ocean and its organisms *(too general)*

(B) Two strategies, active and passive defense, that organisms use ~~when attacking predators~~ *(too general)*

(C) The use of an evolutionary trait by organisms in the deepest layer of the ocean

(D) The defensive strategies of sea animals and a general exploration of each strategy *(too narrow)* ★

06. 이 강의의 주된 내용은 무엇인가?

(A) 바다의 심층과 그 안에 있는 생물들의 ~~특징들~~

(B) 생물들이 ~~포식자들을 공격할 때~~ 사용하는 2가지 전략인 능동적인 방어와 수동적인 방어 전략

(C) 바다의 가장 깊은 층에 사는 생물들의 진화적인 특징의 사용

(D) 바다 동물들의 방어 전략들과 각각의 전략에 대한 일반적인 탐구 ★

해설 | (A)는 bioluminescence가 왜 필요한지 부가적인 설명을 할 때 들어간 내용이므로 main idea가 될 수 없다.
(B)는 bioluminescence의 두 category를 'when dealing with predators'라고 too general 설명해서 오답이다.
(D) 목적뿐만 아니라 다른 aspect, such as how it works까지 다 포함 되어 있기 때문에 오답이다 (too narrow).

07. [Detail – Characteristic] Which of the following is NOT true about bioluminescence?

(A) Its primary source of power is generated by both bacteria and chemicals.

(B) Its application in the medical field is plausible.

(C) It enables fish to generate light within themselves, without any external help.

(D) In most cases, it's blue, but it can sometimes be other colors, such as red.

07. 생체 발광에 대해 옳지 않은 것은 무엇인가?

(A) 이 힘의 주원료는 박테리아와 화학적 물질들 둘 다에 의해 만들어진다.

(B) 그것을 의학 분야에서 적용하는 것은 실현 가능하다.

(C) 외부의 도움 없이 물고기들 스스로가 빛을 만들어낼 수 있게 한다.

(D) 대부분의 경우 파란색이지만, 가끔은 빨간색처럼 다른 색깔일 수도 있다.

해설 | (A)는 bacteria가 포함되지 않기 때문에 오답이다. (B), (C), (D) 모두 강의에 포함되어 있는 내용이므로 정답.

08. [Detail – Advantage] According to the professor, why are crystal jellyfish influential to our society?

(A) Because they generate blue light and blue light is a ~~great resource when exploring the deep-zone of the ocean~~. *(not mentioned)*

(B) Because their bioluminescent chemical is used in cancer detection.

(C) Because the chemical responsible for its bioluminescence ~~can be used as a light source~~. *(not mentioned)* ★

(D) Because its bioluminescence works as a ~~gathering signal~~ for squid, and it helps fishermen ~~catch squid more efficiently~~. *(not mentioned)*

08. 교수에 따르면, 수정해파리들이 사회에 영향력이 있는 이유는 무엇인가?

(A) 왜냐하면 그들은 파란색 빛을 만들어내는데, 파란색은 ~~심층을 탐험할 때 매우 훌륭한 자원이다~~.

(B) 그들의 생체 발광 화학 물질은 암을 감지하는 데에 사용되기 때문이다.

(C) 생체 발광을 하게하는 화학 물질은 ~~빛 에너지로 사용될 수 있기 때문이다~~. ★

(D) 생체 발광은 오징어를 모으기 위한 ~~신호로 이용되어, 어부들이 효율적으로 오징어를 잡게 해주기 때문이다~~.

> **해설** | (A) 파란색 빛을 만들어내는 것은 맞지만 이것이 심층을 탐험하는 데에 이용된다는 내용은 본문에 언급 되어 있지 않다.
> (C) 수정해파리들의 생체 발광 화학물질이 light source로 쓰일 수 있다고 언급된 내용이 없으므로 오답.
> (D) 수정해파리들의 빛을 재현해서 실험해봤을 때 오징어가 신호가 있는 곳으로 헤엄쳐 갔다.
> 따라서, 빛이 포식자의 포식자를 끌어들이는 역할을 한다는 사실이 입증됐다는 내용을 왜곡 시킨 것으로 오답.

09. [Detail – Methodology/Finding] How did scientists prove that bioluminescence attracts predators' predators?

(A) They observed that flashes of light mimicking a jellyfish's flashes attracted squid.

(B) They ~~put squid and jellyfish together~~ and witnessed that the jellyfish flashed more when squid were around. *(wrong fact)* ★

(C) They spotted the ~~heaviest~~ accumulations of squid around jellyfish habitats. *(not mentioned)*

(D) They noticed that while the jellyfish's predators tried to feed on their prey, they were attacked. *(unrelated to the question)*

09. 과학자들은 생체 발광이 포식자들의 포식자들을 끌어들인다는 것을 어떻게 증명하였는가?

(A) 그들은 해파리들의 빛을 흉내 낸 빛이 오징어를 끌어들이는 것을 관찰했다.

(B) 그들은 ~~오징어와 해파리를 같이 놓고~~, 오징어가 주변에 있을 때 해파리가 빛을 더 많이 비추는 것을 목격했다. ★

(C) 해파리들의 거주지에 ~~가장 많은~~ 오징어들이 있는 것을 발견했다.

(D) 그들은 때때로 해파리의 포식자들이 먹이를 먹으려고 할 때 오히려 공격을 받았다는 것을 발견했다.

> **해설** | (B) 과학자들은 jellyfish를 직접적으로 넣은 게 아니라 그들의 flash를 recreate 해서 넣은 것이므로 오답.
> (C) 언급된 바가 없으므로 오답.
> (D) 는 이론이 증명된 방법이 아닌 처음 가설이 세워지게 된 계기이므로 질문이 묻는 바가 아니다.

10. [Detail – Difference/Contrast] How is passive defense strategy different from active defense strategy?

(A) A passive defense strategy is the ~~direct use~~ of flashing lights at predators. *(opposite fact)*

(B) **A passive defense strategy is used prior to any engagement between predator and prey.**

(C) A passive defense strategy enables the ~~jellyfish~~ to change its skin color. *(partial error)*

(D) A ~~passive defense strategy~~ enables organisms to seem daunting to the predator. *(opposite fact)* ★

10. 수동적인 방어 전략은 능동적인 방어 전략과 어떻게 다른가?

(A) 수동적인 방어 전략은 포식자들에게 빛을 ~~직접적으로~~ 비춘다.

(B) **수동적인 방어 전략은 포식자와 피식자가 대면하기 전에 사용된다.**

(C) 수동적인 방어 전략은 ~~해파리가~~ 자신의 피부색을 바꾸게 한다.

(D) ~~수동적인 방어~~ 전략은 해파리들이 포식자들에게 겁을 주기 위해 빛을 비출 수 있도록 한다. ★

> **해설** | (A)는 active defense strategy를 설명하는 거라 오답. (C) 피부색을 바꾸는 생물의 예로 교수가 든 것은 개구리와 도마뱀이었다.
> (D) active defense strategy를 뒷받침하는 첫 번째 이론이라고 설명된다. Passive defense strategy에 해당 되는 내용이 아니므로 오답.

---

11. [Inference – Purpose/Intention] Why does the professor mention the principle of camouflage?

(A) To explain that bioluminescence and camouflage are two examples ~~of the same phenomenon~~

(B) To claim that bioluminescence is also ~~inherent in terrestrial animals~~, such as frogs. *(not mentioned)*

(C) To indicate that bioluminescent organisms are capable of changing their skin color as well as the color of their flashes. *(wrong fact)*

(D) **To imply that the use of bioluminescence is similar to that of camouflage**

11. 교수가 위장의 법칙을 언급한 이유는 무엇인가?

(A) 생체 발광과 위장이 ~~똑같은 현상의~~ 2가지 예라는 것을 설명하기 위해서.

(B) 생체 발광이 개구리들처럼 ~~육지 동물들에게도 유전된다는 것을~~ 주장하기 위해서.

(C) 생체 발광하는 생물들이 그들의 빛 색깔 뿐만 아니라 피부 색깔을 바꿀 수 있다는 것을 나타내기 위해서

(D) **생체 발광의 사용이 위장의 사용과 비슷하다는 것을 시사하기 위해서**

> **해설** | passive defense strategy가 camouflage와 비슷하다고 설명하는 것이다. (A)는 same phenomenon이 아니기에 때문에 오답. (B) 육지동물에겐 camouflage가 있기 때문에 오답. 또한, 육지 동물의 생체발광 소유 여부는 언급된 바 없다. (C)는 camouflage의 내용을 왜곡해서 써놓은 거라 오답.

TEST 1 set 2-3
Lecture 2
Muon detector

문단주제	본문내용	해석

단락 1
고고학에 대한 잘못된 인식의 소개

Listen to part of a lecture in an archaeology class

P: I'm sure almost all of you watched cartoons in your childhood that often portrayed archaeological elements. Watching these cartoons might have given you some misconceptions about the field of archaeology. I mean… Let me ask you this: What is the image of archaeologists that you got from those cartoons?

S: [Q13] They dig here and there… hoping to discover something significant and valuable. I'm not trying to be judgmental, but their job didn't seem to require any sophisticated skill or anything.

P: I couldn't agree more. That's exactly how they portray archaeology. It's funny in a sense, but it's not how archaeologists actually carry out their jobs… There certainly is some element of luck involved in the discovery process, but overall, the job is a lot more professional, and it includes the use of high-tech tools. In contrast to this common misconception, many archaeology-related institutions, such as the Computerized Archaeology Laboratory, have devoted a tremendous amount of effort to developing technology that could enrich the research environment. In fact, they have invented one of the most effective tools, the particle detector or, to be more specific, the muon detector. I don't mean to say that it's their only invention; they have developed other machines as well, such as three-dimensional scanners that produce digital models of artifacts, [Q12] but… I'd like to primarily focus on the muon detector today. We'll explore other machines in the next class.

단락 2
뮤온탐지기의 원리

Okay. Umm… Let's get back to our main topic. The muon detector uses subatomic particles called muons, which result from cosmic rays, you know, the high-energy protons that travel through outer space at close to the speed of light. Those cosmic rays collide with the Earth's atmosphere, and consequently, break down into smaller, subatomic particles, which are known as muons. Okay, you might be wondering about how muons could be of any help in the field of archaeology; they're just particles, after all. Well… Yes. They are particles but their properties can be exploited by archaeologists. Basically, since they are highly stimulated and energized particles, they are able to pass through, or penetrate, solid matter.

고고학 강의의 일부를 들으시오.

P: 여러분 모두 어린 시절에 종종 고고학적 요소들을 묘사하는 만화를 봤다고 전 확신해요. 이런 만화를 시청하는 것은 여러분에게 고고학 분야에 대해 몇 가지 잘못된 인식을 주었을 거에요… 제 말은, 이런 질문을 하나 할게요. 만화에서 얻게 된 고고학자들의 이미지는 무엇이었나요?

S: [Q13] 여기저기 파는 거요… 뭔가 중요하고 가치있는 것을 발견할거라고 희망하면서요. 제멋대로 판단하려는 건 아닌데요, 하지만 그들이 하는 일은 정교한 기술이나 그런 게 필요한 것 같진 않아 보였어요.

P: 나도 완전 같은 생각이에요. 그게 바로 만화에서 고고학을 묘사하는 것이죠. 한편으로는 웃기지만, 고고학자들은 사실상 그런 식으로 일을 하지는 않거든요… 확실히 발견하는 과정에서 운도 관여하긴 하지만, 전반적으로 그 일은 훨씬 더 전문적이고, 첨단기구의 사용을 포함하고 있어요. 이러한 일반적인 오해와는 달리, 컴퓨터 고고학 연구소 같은 많은 고고학 관련 기관들이 연구 환경을 풍부하게 만들 수 있는 기술을 개발하는데 엄청난 노력을 하고 있죠. 사실, 그들은 가장 효과적인 도구 중 하나인 소립자 탐지기, 좀더 구체적으로 말하면, 뮤온 탐지기를 발명했어요. 그것이 그들이 개발한 유일한 기계라고 말하려는 건 아니네요, 유물의 디지털 모형을 제공하는 3D 스캐너 같은 다른 기계들도 개발했거든요. [Q12] 하지만 오늘 전 주로 뮤온 탐지기에 집중하고 싶네요. 그리고 다른 기계들은 다음 수업에서 좀 더 알아보도록 하죠.

그래요. 음… 다시 우리의 주제로 돌아가죠. 뮤온 탐지기는 우주 광선, 그러니까 빛에 가까운 속도로 우주 공간을 통과하는 고에너지 양성자에서 비롯된 뮤온이라고 불리는 아원자 입자를 사용하는데요…. 그 우주 광선들은 지구의 대기권과 충돌하고, 결과적으로 뮤온이라고 알려진 더 작은 아원자 입자로 쪼개어지죠. 좋아요. 여러분은 뮤온이 어떻게 고고학 분야에서 도움이 될 수 있는지 궁금해 할 거에요. 그것들은 단지 입자일 뿐이니까요. 음… 그래요. 그것들은 입자이지만, 그들이 가지고 있는 속성은 고고학자들에 의해 활용될 수 있어요. 기본적으로, 그것들은 매우 자극 되어진 에너지 입자이기 때문에, 고체를 뚫고 통과할 수 있어요.

문단주제	본문내용	해석
	[Q14] Archaeologists take advantage of that property and use them to create a visual image, similar to a photograph. Let's say an archaeologist wanted to excavate an ancient temple or an Egyptian pyramid and needed to figure out what types of artifacts were buried inside without damaging the structure. Umm… It could be filled with tombs or chambers. They could use the muon detector. The mechanism behind this is pretty straightforward and not too complicated. Muons lose energy as they go through dense materials, such as a temple's posts, or a pyramid's walls in this case. So the more impediments they penetrate, the more energy they lose. Empty spaces, on the other hand, don't pose any hindrance to the muons, so less energy will be lost. Yes, Rebecca? S: Okay, professor, I understand that the number of energized muons varies depending on the density of the spaces, but I'm still having a hard time making sense of how that principle could be deciphered or turned into pictures. P: Good question, Rebecca. As I mentioned previously, more energized muons are present in empty spaces, whereas many are blocked or deflected by dense materials. To help you visualize it more vividly, try to draw a circle and a square right in the middle of it. Now, the square, in our case, is a chamber of a temple, and the surrounding space, the area between the circle and the square, will represent the temple walls. As muons strike and eventually pass through the temple, they kind of draw an image… like an X-ray image… for archaeologists to view. In other words, when detected, the chamber, an empty area, will be much lighter than the temple walls, which reflect more muons than the open space.	[Q14] 고고학자들은 이 특징을 이용해서, 사진에 가까운 시각적 이미지를 만들어내는데요. 한 고고학자가 고대 사원이나 이집트의 피라미드를 발굴해서, 구조물을 훼손하지 않고 어떤 종류의 유물이 묻혀있는지 알아낼 필요가 있다고 해보죠. 음… 그곳은 무덤이나 방으로 채워져 있을 수도 있어요. 뮤온 탐지기를 사용할 수 있겠죠. 음… 이 뒤에 감춰진 작동원리는 꽤 간단하고 복잡한 건 없어요. 뮤온은 밀도가 촘촘한 소재ㅡ이 경우엔 사원의 기둥이나 피라미드의 벽이 되겠죠ㅡ를 통과하면서 에너지를 잃게 되는데, 그래서 더 많은 장애물을 통과할 수록 더 많은 에너지를 잃게 되는 거죠. 반면에, 빈 공간은 뮤온에 어떤 장애도 부과하지 않기 때문에, 에너지를 덜 잃게 되요. 네, Rebecca? S: 네, 교수님, 에너지화된 뮤온의 개수는 공간의 밀도에 따라 다른 건 이해가 가요. 하지만 저는 아직도 어떻게 그 원리가 해독하거나 사진으로 변환되는지에 대해서는 이해하기가 힘든데요. P: 좋은 질문이에요, Rebecca. 내가 앞서 말했듯이, 빈 공간에 에너지화된 뮤온이 더 많이 존재하는데, 반면에 고밀도 물질에서는 많은 뮤온이 차단되거나 굴절되죠. 여러분이 좀더 생생하게 상상할 수 있도록 도와주자면, 동그라미를 그리고 그 안 중간에 정사각형을 그려봐요. 자, 정사각형은 우리가 설명하는 경우 사원의 방이에요, 그리고 주변에 있는 공간, 즉 원과 정사각형 사이에 지역은 사원의 벽을 나타내요. 뮤온이 부딪혀서 결국엔 사원을 통과할 때, 그것은 일종의 이미지… 엑스레이 같은 사진을 그려내어 고고학자들이 볼 수 있게 되죠. 다른 말로 하면, 탐지할 때, 빈 공간인 방은 사원의 벽보다 훨씬 밝게 되는데, 이곳은 열린 공간보다 훨씬 더 많은 뮤온을 반사하죠.
단락 3 뮤온탐지기의 장점	In the past, archaeologists were always at risk of damaging important artifacts because they didn't have sophisticated tools like muon detectors to ensure their safety. With this technology, however, archaeologists have been able to avoid damaging temples while excavating them.	과거에, 고고학자들은 뮤온탐지기와 같이 안전을 보장할 수 있는 정교한 도구들이 없었기 때문에 중요한 유물들을 손상시킬 수 있는 위험에 항상 노출되어 있었어요. 하지만, 이런 기술을 통해서 발굴하는 동안 사원을 훼손시키는 것을 피할 수 있었어요.
단락 4 뮤온탐지기의 발달과정 및 초기모형의 문제점	Despite the advantages it presents today, the muon detector has only recently been fine-tuned enough to be practical for this usage. Since its invention, it has gone through a lot of modifications and many aspects of it have been enhanced. The earliest form of the muon detector was used by a physicist looking for burial chambers in the Egyptian pyramids at Giza in 1967.	오늘날 존재하는 장점에도 불구하고, 뮤온 탐지기는 최근에야 이용에 실제적으로 쓰일 만큼 개선되었어요. 기계가 개발된 이후, 많은 수정을 거쳤고, 많은 부분이 향상되었어요. 가장 초기의 뮤온 탐지기는 1967년에 Giza에 있는 이집트 피라미드의 매장실을 찾는 한 물리학자에 의해 사용되었죠.

TEST 1 set 2-3

문단주제	본문내용	해석
단락 5 초기 모형의 문제점 극복 및 현대 모형의 한계점	[Q15] Unfortunately, the one that he used at that time had two major flaws… [Q16-B] First, it was only functional if it was placed beneath the object to be scanned. It didn't work when placed on the side of the object. [Q15] This meant that if archaeologists wanted to scan the internal structures of a pyramid, they needed to bury the muon detector under it. Strenuous work, wasn't it? Also, the machine used in 1967 was very big and heavy, so it was quite difficult for archaeologists to carry it around with them. Today, however, modifications have solved the problems regarding the detector's burdensome size and technical limits. That doesn't necessarily mean that it's now a perfect form of technology, though. [Q16] There are still some issues that need to be worked out, such as taking about half a year to produce an image of the structure being scanned. S: Half a year? I can see that it improved in some ways, but I wouldn't call it much of an advance at all! I mean, if I were an archaeologist, I would never want to wait for six months without being assured that I would find something valuable. P: Well, Rebecca, you have a point. But… Try to think about it this way. [Q17] Currently, there are Japanese scientists trying to map out the interiors of volcanoes. If they didn't have the muon detector, what would their alternative be? Go inside the volcanoes and explore? (laughs) I think you get what I'm trying to say… Even though it does have some deficiencies that need to be overcome, it is the best tool we have for this type of scanning at the moment.	[Q15] 불행히도, 그 당시에 사용했던 도구에는 2가지의 주요 결함이 있었어요… [Q16-B] 첫째, 스캔 하려는 물체 아래에 배치하는 경우에만 기능이 작동되었어요. 물체의 옆면에 놓으면 작용하지 않았죠. [Q15] 이것은 고고학자들이 피라미드의 내부 구조를 검사하길 원하면, 뮤온 탐지기를 피라미드 아래에 묻어야 한다는 걸 의미했죠. 엄청 힘든 작업이죠, 그렇지 않나요? 또한, 1967년에 사용된 기계는 엄청 크고 무거웠는데, 그래서 고고학자들은 그것을 지니고 다니기에 힘들었어요. 하지만 오늘날에는 개선을 통해서 탐지기의 부담스러운 크기와 기술적 제한과 관련된 문제점들이 해결되었는데요. 그렇지만, 그게 지금은 완벽한 형태의 기술이 되었다는 걸 의미하지는 않아요. [Q16] 아직도 해결해야 할 몇 가지 문제점들이 여전히 있는데요, 예를 들면 스캔을 뜬 구조의 이미지를 생산하는데 반년이라는 시간이 걸리는 거에요. S: 반년이라고요? 어떤 면에서는 향상되었다는 걸 알겠는데요, 하지만 엄청 크게 좋아졌다고는 말할 수는 없겠네요! 제 말은, 제가 고고학자라면, 정말 가치 있는 것을 발견했다는 보장도 없는데 6개월이라는 시간을 기다리진 않을 것 같아요. P: 음, Rebecca, 좋은 지적이에요. 하지만… 이런 식으로 한번 생각해보세요. [Q17] 현재, 일본 과학자들이 화산 내부에 대한 지도를 그려내려고 시도 중이에요. 만약 뮤온 탐지기가 없다면, 다른 대안은 뭘까요? 화산 안으로 들어가서 탐험하는 거요? (웃음)… 제가 무슨 말을 하고 싶은지 여러분이 이해했다고 전 믿어요… 물론 아직 극복해야 결점들은 있지만, 그래도 이러한 타입의 스캐닝을 위해서는 현재 우리가 가지고 있는 최고의 도구라고 생각되고 있어요.

12. [Main Idea] What is the purpose of the lecture?

(A) Explaining the advancements made in the development of the muon detector *(too specific)* ★

(B) Explaining the differences between the ancient muon detector and the modern muon detector. *(too specific)*

(C) **Explaining a type of technology that archaeologists have utilized when excavating historic sites**

(D) Explaining how excavation sites, such as the Egyptian pyramids, have been explored by archaeologists *(too specific)*

12. 강의의 목적은 무엇인가?

(A) 뮤온 탐지기의 개발 중에 만들어진 진보에 대해 설명하는 것 ★

(B) 예전의 뮤온 탐지기와 현대의 뮤온 탐지기와의 차이점을 설명하는 것

(C) **유적지를 발굴할 때 고고학자들이 이용하는 한 기술에 대해 설명하는 것**

(D) 이집트 피라미드 같은 발굴 현장이 고고학자들에 의해 어떻게 탐사되었는지를 설명하는 것

해설 | (A) 강의는 뮤온 탐지기의 개발과정뿐만 아니라, 뮤온 탐지기의 원리, 고고학에서의 의의 등을 포함하기 때문에 강의의 주제로 잡기에는 너무 구체적이다. (B) 뮤온 탐지기의 개발과정을 설명하면서 예전과 현대의 뮤온 탐지기의 차이점이 묘사되긴 했으나, 그 차이점을 설명하는 것을 강의의 주된 목적으로 정의하기에는 매우 한정적이다. (D)는 초기 뮤온 탐지기의 한계점을 설명할 때 언급된 내용으로 강의의 주된 내용으로 보기는 너무 구체적이다.

13. [Inference – Opinion/Attitude] What is the professor's opinion about the misconceptions that cartoons give students regarding archaeology?

(A) He ~~approves~~ of the idea that archaeology ~~doesn't entail any high-tech tools~~. *(wrong fact)*

(B) He ~~opposes the student's opinion~~ that archaeologists don't have any sophisticated skills. *(wrong fact)*

(C) **He believes that cartoons have led many people to believe that most archaeological exploration is accomplished through guessing and luck.**

(D) He is critical of the portrayal of archaeology in cartoons and thinks it is ~~only meant to demean~~ the profession. *(too extreme)* ★

13. 고고학과 관련하여 만화가 학생들에게 주는 잘못된 인식에 대한 교수님의 의견은 무엇인가?

(A) 그는 고고학이 ~~어떠한 첨단 기술도 수반하지 않는다~~는 아이디어를 인정하고 있다.

(B) 그는 고고학자들이 정교한 기술이 전혀 갖고 있지 않다는 ~~학생의 의견에 반대한다~~.

(C) **그는 만화가 대부분의 고고학 탐사가 추측과 운을 통해 이루어졌다고 사람들이 믿게 만들었다고 생각한다.**

(D) 그는 만화에서 고고학이 잘못 묘사되어 있다고 비판하며, 만화는 그저 그 직업에 대한 ~~품위를 떨어뜨리고자 의도되었을 뿐이라고 생각한다~~. ★

해설 | (A)와 (B)는 정 반대되는 내용이므로 오답. (D)는 too extreme 하기 때문에 오답이다 - 잘못된 인식이 많다고 얘기는 하지만 교수는 이 정도로 극도의 의견을 갖고 있는 것으로 보여지지 않는다.

14. [Detail – Methodology] How are archaeologists able to determine the structure of excavation sites?

(A) They use a particle detector to measure muons, thus allowing them to produce a visual image of the internal structure.

(B) They ~~extract isotopes~~ from the chemicals found in the excavation sites and use them to draw structures. *(not mentioned)*

(C) They ~~simplify the models~~ of the structures into circles and squares to detect empty spaces. *(unrelated to the question)* ★

(D) They use a form of technology that is a combination of the ~~x-ray machine~~ and the muon scanner. *(partial error)*

14. 고고학자들은 어떻게 발굴 유적지의 구조를 확인할 수 있는가?

(A) 그들은 뮤온을 측정하는 입자 탐지기를 사용하여, 내부 구조의 시각적인 이미지를 만들어내게 한다.

(B) 그들은 발굴 현장에서 발견된 화학 물질의 ~~동위원소를 추출해서~~ 구조물을 그리는데 사용한다.

(C) 그들은 구조물들의 모델을 원과 사각형으로 단순화시켜 빈 공간을 찾아낸다. ★

(D) 그들은 ~~엑스레이 기계와~~ 뮤온 탐지기를 혼합한 기술을 사용한다.

해설 | (B)는 아예 언급 되지 않은 내용이므로 오답. (C) 뮤온 탐지기의 원리에 대한 학생의 이해를 돕기 위해 교수가 한 보조설명을 왜곡 시켜 놓은 것으로 오답. (D) x-ray machine이 틀려 전체가 오답.

---

15. [Detail – Problem/Difficulty] Which of the following are the deficiencies of early muon detectors?

Click on 2 answers

(A) The direction from which the scanning process could be performed was very limited.

(B) It ~~took too much time~~ to produce a visual image of the structure. *(wrong fact)* ★

(C) It was very ~~unstable~~ in terms of ~~image quality~~. *(not mentioned)*

(D) It wasn't practically portable.

15. 보기 중 초기의 뮤온 탐지기가 가졌던 결함은 무엇인가?

2개의 정답을 고르시오

(A) 스캔 과정을 적용할 수 있는 방향이 매우 제한적이었다.

(B) 구조물의 시각적 이미지를 생산하는데 ~~너무 많은 시간이 걸렸다~~. ★

(C) ~~이미지의 품질~~ 면에서 굉장히 ~~불안정했다~~.

(D) 그것은 실제로 휴대할 수 없었다.

해설 | (B)는 현대 뮤온 탐지기의 문제점으로 언급된 내용이기 때문에 오답. (C)는 언급된 내용이 아니므로 오답.

16. [Detail – Problem/Difficulty] Why is the modern muon detector still considered to be imperfect?

(A) It takes a great deal of time to produce an image.
(B) It works only if it is placed beneath the object to be scanned. ★
(C) It does not function well under certain circumstances, such as on hot volcanic sites. *(not mentioned)*
(D) Although it's light and easily portable, it fails to include every small detail. *(not mentioned)*

16. 왜 현대의 뮤온 탐지기는 여전히 불완전하다고 여겨지는가?

(A) 이미지를 생산하는데 많은 시간이 걸린다.
(B) 스캔 하려는 물체 아래에 배치하는 경우에만 기능이 작동된다. ★
(C) 뜨거운 화산 지역 같은 특정 지역에서는 작동이 잘되지 않는다.
(D) 비록 가볍고 들고 다니기 편하나, 작은 세부 사항들을 모두 포함시키지는 못한다.

해설 | (B) 현대의 뮤온 탐지기가 아닌 초기의 뮤온 탐지기가 가졌던 결함으로 언급된 내용이므로 오답.
(C) 지역의 환경에 따라 기능이 달라진다는 내용은 언급되지 않으므로 오답. (D)는 뒷부분이 언급된 내용이 아니라 오답.

Listen again to part of the lecture. Then answer the question.

"Currently, there are Japanese scientists trying to map out the interiors of volcanoes. If they didn't have the muon detector, what would their alternative be? Go inside the volcanoes and explore? (laughs) I think you get what I'm trying to say…"

강의의 일부를 듣고, 질문에 답하시오.

"현재, 일본 과학자들이 화산 내부에 대한 지도를 그려내려고 시도 중이에요. 만약 뮤온 탐지기가 없다면, 다른 대안은 뭘까요? 화산 안으로 들어가서 탐험하는 거요? (웃음) 제가 무슨 말을 하고 싶어 하는지 여러분이 이해했다고 전 믿어요..."

17. [Inference – Imply] What does the professor imply when he says this? 🎧

"I think you get what I'm trying to say…"

(A) That the student understands the reason that muon detectors are the only practical solution in some cases
(B) That the muon detector is applicable to various fields. *(not mentioned)* ★
(C) That the muon detector is often used to map out the interiors of volcanoes. *(not mentioned)*
(D) That the muon detector is only practical when examining volcanoes. *(wrong fact)*

17. 교수는 이 말을 할 때 무엇을 암시하는가: 🎧

"제가 무슨 말을 하고 싶어 하는지 여러분이 이해했다고 전 믿어요…"

(A) 몇몇의 경우에 뮤온 탐지기가 유일한 실용적인 해결책이 될 수 있다라는 것을 학생들이 이해했다.
(B) 뮤온 탐지기는 다양한 분야에 적용될 수 있다. ★
(C) 뮤온 탐지기는 화산 내부의 지도를 그리기 위해 자주 사용된다.
(D) 뮤온 탐지기는 화산을 탐사할 때만 유용하다.

해설 | 현대의 뮤온 탐지기의 한계점을 언급하지만, 그래도 volcanic site 같은 곳에선 하나밖에 없는 solution이라 제시한다.
(B) 화산 탐사 역시 고고학의 일부이므로 다른 분야에도 적용된다는 뜻으로 말한 것이 아니다. (C) volcanic site 같은 곳에서는 하나밖에 없는 방법이라는 것을 보여주기 위해 든 극단적인 예로, 뮤온 탐지기가 화산 내부 탐사 시 자주 사용된다는 의미를 내포하고 있지는 않다. (D) 뮤온 탐지기는 화산 탐사 이외에도 다양한 용도로 쓰이는 것이 강의에서 명시 됐으므로 오답.

www.usherin.usher.co.kr

USHER

iBT TOEFL
INTERMEDIATE LISTENING
TEST 2 해설

TEST 2 set 1-1

Conversation: Math nights

문단주제	본문내용	해석
단락 1 수학의 밤 소개	**Listen to part of a conversation between a student and his mathematics professor** S: Good afternoon, professor. I heard that you were looking for me earlier this morning. P: Hello, David. Yes, I was. I wanted to offer you a job related to the new program our department is launching for the community. Have you heard of math nights? S: Math nights… Are you talking about when schools host math-related games, and parents and kids participate in them together? My parents and I loved going to those when I was young. P: [Q1] Great! I was looking for someone who had experience with them. Did you enjoy the activities, and did they help you improve your math skills?	학생과 수학교수의 대화를 들으시오. S: 안녕하세요, 교수님, 아침에 저를 찾으셨다고 들었어요. P: 안녕, David. 그래 맞아. 지역 사회를 위해 우리 학과에서 추진하는 새로운 프로그램과 관련된 일자리를 제안하려고 불렀어. 수학의 밤에 대해 들어 봤니? S: 수학의 밤이요… 학교들이 수학과 관련된 게임을 개최하고 부모님들과 아이들이 함께 참가하는 것 말씀하시는 건가요? 제가 어렸을 때 부모님과 함께 가는 것을 좋아했어요. P: [Q1] 좋아! 경험이 있는 사람을 찾고 있는 중이었거든. 그 행사들은 즐겁고 너의 수학실력에 도움이 되었니?
단락 2 수학의 밤의 의의 및 이점	S: Hmm… To be honest with you, not only was I horrible at math, but I really loathed it before I attended those programs. Seems ironic now that I'm a math major, right? Those math nights really changed the way I looked at math, and my parents were very supportive of my decision to choose to major in math in college, too. P: [Q2] That's exactly what our department is trying to contribute to our community: helping kids develop and figure out their futures and teaching them the profound and fundamental concepts of mathematics.	S: 흠…… 솔직하게 말씀드리면, 전 수학을 끔찍하게 못 했을뿐더러, 그 프로그램에 참가 하기 전에는 수학을 정말 싫어했어요. 지금은 수학 전공하다니 아이러니하죠? 음, 그런 수학의 밤들이 수학을 바라보는 제 시선을 정말 바꿔 놓았고, 제 부모님도 대학에서 수학 전공을 선택하는 것에 대해 많은 지지를 해주셨어요. P: [Q2] 그게 바로 우리 학과가 지역 사회에 기여하려는 거야: 아이들의 발전에 도움이 되고, 자신의 미래에 대해 깨닫고, 수학에 대한 심오하고 중요한 개념에 대해서 가르쳐주는 거 말이야.
단락 3 학생의 첫 번째 우려 및 업무 관련 세부사항	S: It sounds very intriguing to me, but wouldn't I just be doing kids' math puzzles with them? I'm not concerned with the money being offered because I'd like to focus on gaining mathematics teaching experience, [Q3] but doing puzzles won't help me learn that much about teaching math. P: Well, you wouldn't have to worry about that at all because you'll be explaining math concepts not only to the kids but to their parents as well. You see, the level of mathematics taught in schools has gotten relatively higher over the past few decades, so some parents are having a hard time helping their kids with their homework.	S: 정말 흥미롭게 들리네요. 하지만 그냥 아이들이랑 수학 퍼즐을 하는 게 아닌가요? 돈에 대해서는 별로 신경 쓰지 않아요, 왜냐하면 수학을 가르치는 경험을 얻는데 우선 집중하고 싶거든요. [Q3] 그런데 퍼즐을 푸는 건 수학을 가르치는 것에 그다지 큰 도움이 되지 않을 것 같아요. P: 음, 그점에 대해서 전혀 걱정하지 않아도 되는데, 왜냐하면 아이들뿐만 아니라 부모님들에게도 또한 수학 개념을 설명하게 될 거야. 그러니까, 학교에서 가르치는 수학 수준이 지난 몇 십년간에 걸쳐 비교적으로 높아졌거든. 그래서 부모님들이 아이들의 숙제를 도와주는 걸 힘들어하고 있어.

문단주제	본문내용	해석
단락 4 학생의 두 번째 우려	S: Really? What level of math would I be teaching then? P: Well, nothing higher than 7th grade math will be required. [Q5] But, uh… Try not to underestimate it, because the current level of 7th grade mathematics generally entails some high level stuff like graphing on the X-Y-Z plane and calculating probability. S: [Q3-C] Oh, wow, it surely sounds a lot harder than when I was in 7th grade. I learned stuff like that in 9th grade. P: [Q5-C] Exactly! You can imagine how hard it must be for parents to teach their kids subjects that they barely remember. S: [Q3-D] Yes, I can totally relate to that. Well… the thing is I still have to keep up with a lot of classes, and if I add work to my schedule … I think it'll be too much. P: Well, just give it a thought. It involves about 15 hours of work per semester, and it wouldn't be that difficult of a job since you're a math major. S: Sure, actually, 15 hours doesn't sound so bad. When do you need my answer? P: [Q4] Well, the sooner you let us know, the better it is for us because we need to have a complete list of workers by next week for the administrator to sign and approve. Although we still have a few months until the actual launch, things like this are our priorities, and, also, a lot of people have inquired about the job. I hope you understand. S: Of course, I won't take that long. I'll give you a call by the end of the week. P: That sounds great! Thanks, David. S: No, thank you for the offer, professor.	S: 진짜요? 제가 어떤 수준의 수학을 가르치게 되는데요? P: 음, 7학년 수준 이상은 필요하지 않을 거야. [Q5] 하지만 음… 과소평가 하지 말아야 되는 게, 현재 7학년의 수학 수준이 일반적으로 X-Y-Z 평면에 그래프를 그리거나, 확률을 계산하는 것 같은 높은 난이도를 수반하기 때문이야. S: [Q3-C] 오, 와우, 확실히 제가 7학년에서 배웠던 것보다 훨씬 더 어려운 것 같네요. 전 그런 것을 9학년 때 배웠거든요. P: [Q5-C] 맞아. 부모님들이 잘 기억나지 않는 과정들을 자신의 아이들에게 가르쳐야 한다니 얼마나 힘든지 상상이 갈 거야. S: [Q3-D] 네, 이해가 가요. 음… 사실은, 제가 아직도 따라가야 할 수업들이 많아서요, 제 스케줄에 일을 추가하면… 너무 많을 것 같네요. P: 음, 그냥 한번 생각해봐. 한 학기당 15시간 동안 일을 하는 게 포함되고, 네가 수학 전공이니까 그렇게 힘들지는 않을 거야. S: 물론이죠, 사실, 15시간이면 나쁘지 않네요. 제가 언제까지 확답을 드려야 되죠? P: [Q4] 음, 빨리 말해 줄수록, 더 좋아, 왜냐하면 행정 부서에서 싸인과 함께 허락을 얻으려면 확실히 일 하는 사람들의 명단이 다음주까지 필요하거든. 실제로 개최하기까지 아직 몇 달이 남아있기는 한데, 이런 것들이 우리의 우선순위이고, 그리고 또한, 많은 사람들이 일자리에 대해서 문의를 많이 하고 있어. 이해해주길 바라. S: 물론이죠, 오래 걸리지 않을 거에요. 이번 주 끝나기 전까지 전화를 드릴께요. P: 좋아! 고마워, David. S: 아뇨, 제안해 주셔서 감사해요, 교수님.

01. [Main Idea-Main Purpose] Why does the professor want to speak to the student?

(A) To ask him ~~to help plan~~ the math nights that the department is arranging *(wrong fact)*

(B) To suggest that he ~~teach a group of 7th graders~~ at the math nights *(wrong fact)*

(C) To ask him to ~~write the questions~~ for a math night with problems related to calculating probability *(wrong fact)*

(D) **To inquire about his interest in a job at the math nights that the university is hosting**

01. 교수님이 학생과 이야기를 하고 싶어하는 이유는 무엇인가?

(A) 학과가 준비하는 수학의 밤에 대해 학생이 ~~계획하는데 도움을 달라고~~ 요청하기 위해

(B) 수학의 밤에서 ~~7학년 학생 그룹들을 가르치는 것을~~ 제안하기 위해 ★

(C) 확률을 계산하는 것과 같은 문제들처럼 수학의 밤을 위한 ~~문제들을 만들어 달라고~~ 부탁하기 위해

(D) **대학교가 주최하는 수학의 밤의 일자리에 관심이 있는지 물어보기 위해**

> 해설 | (A)와 (C)는 교수가 도움을 요청하는게 아니고 일 할 생각이 있냐고 물어보는 것이기 때문에 오답이다. (B) 교수가 나중에 수학 나이트의 수준을 설명할 때 7학년의 수학 난이도를 예로 제시한다. 그걸 왜곡해 쓴 것이므로 오답.

02. [Detail-Cause/Reason] According to the professor, what is the university department trying to accomplish through the math nights?

Click on 2 answers

(A) **Guiding kids in considering their futures using mathematics**

(B) **Helping parents and their kids understand important math concepts**

(C) Building ~~intimate relationships~~ between parents and their kids *(not mentioned)*

(D) ~~Improving the level of mathematics in~~ 7th grade *(not mentioned)*

02. 교수에 의하면, 대학교 학과가 수학의 밤을 통해 이루고자 하는 것은 무엇인가?

2개의 정답을 고르시오

(A) **수학을 이용하여 아이들에게 미래에 관심을 가지도록 안내하는 것**

(B) **도전적인 수학 개념들을 부모님들과 아이들이 이해하도록 돕는 것**

(C) 부모님들과 아이들간의 친밀한 관계를 형성하는 것 ★

(D) 7학년의 ~~수학 수준을 향상시키는 것~~

> 해설 | (C)는 부가적으로 따라 올 수 있는 현상이겠지만, 교수가 성취하고자 하는 바는 아니다. (D)또한 왜곡되어 써져 있으므로 틀리다 - 언급된 내용도 아니다.

03. [Detail-Reason] Why is the student reluctant to take the offer that the professor suggests at first?

(A) Because he ~~already has a job~~, which is a burden for him *(not mentioned)*

(B) **Because he believes the job won't provide good teaching experience**

(C) Because he ~~doesn't think he's capable of~~ explaining 7th grade math concepts to kids and parents *(wrong fact)*

(D) Because the classes he is taking are already too much to handle *(partial error)* ★

03. 왜 학생은 처음에 교수님이 제안한 일자리를 주저하는가?

(A) 그는 ~~아마 일자리가 있어서~~, 이점이 부담이 되기 때문에

(B) **일자리가 좋은 가르치는 경험을 줄거라고 믿지 않기 때문에**

(C) 그는 7학년의 수학 개념들을 아이들과 부모님들에게 설명할 수 있는 ~~능력이 없다고 생각하기~~ 때문에

(D) 그가 지금 듣고 있는 수업들이 충분히 많이 힘들기 때문에 ★

> 해설 | 학생은 돈에 크게 연연하지 않고 단순히 teaching skill을 습득 하고자 일을 하고 싶다 한다. (A)는 언급된 바가 없으며, (C)는 학생이 생각하는 '많이 어려워진' 7th grade math를 왜곡 되어 써놓은 것이다. (D)는 학생의 첫 번째 우려가 아닌 두 번째 우려였다.

04. [Detail–Reason] Why does the professor need to get the student's answer as soon as possible?

(A) Because she ~~needs to get approval from the schools~~ at which the university is hosting the math nights. *(not mentioned)*

(B) Because she needs to let the administrator know ~~in 15 hours~~. *(wrong fact)* ★

(C) Because the administrator has to approve the employment of workers by next week.

(D) Because she is ~~going on a vacation~~ next week and won't be reachable. *(not mentioned)*

| 04. 왜 교수는 학생에게 가능한 빨리 답을 받을 필요가 있는가?

(A) 그녀는 대학교가 수학의 밤을 개최하는 ~~학교들로부터 승인을 받아야~~ 하기 때문이다.

(B) 그녀는 ~~15시간 내에~~ 관리자에게 알려야 하기 때문이다. ★

(C) 관리자가 다음주까지 일하는 사람들의 명단을 승인해야 되기 때문이다.

(D) 그녀는 다음주에 ~~휴가를 떠나서~~ 연락이 가능하지 않기 때문이다.

해설 | (A)와 (D)는 언급된 내용이 아니다. (B)의 15 hours는 job에 연관 되어있는 말이므로 틀렸다.

05. [Inference – Imply] Why does the professor imply when she says this?

> "But, uh…Try not to underestimate it, because the current level of 7ᵗʰ grade mathematics generally entails some high level stuff like graphing on the X-Y-Z plane and calculating probability."

(A) To distinguish the training course from other regular classes the student has taken

(B) To let the student know about ~~the potential non-monetary compensation~~ that the job provides

(C) To tell the student that ~~the training course is a way of giving back to the community~~

(D) To inform the student that she will ~~be receiving homework~~ assignments in the training course, just like any other class

05. 교수는 이 말을 할 때 무엇을 암시하는가?

"음, 7학년 수준 이상은 필요하지 않을 거야. 하지만 음… 과소평가 하지 말아야 되는게, 현재 7학년의 수학 수준이 일반적으로 X-Y-Z 평면에 그래프를 그리거나, 확률을 계산하는 것 같은 높은 난이도를 수반하기 때문이야."

(A) 학생들은 듣는 일반적인 수업과 훈련 과정을 구별하기 위해

(B) 학생에게 직업이 제공하는 ~~잠재적인 돈 외의 보상을~~ 알려주기 위해

(C) 훈련 과정은 ~~사회에게 들려주는 방법~~이라는것을 알려주기 위해

(D) 다른 수업과 같이 훈련 과정에서도 ~~숙제를 받을 것이란~~ 것을 알려주기 위해

해설 | (B) 잠재적인 보상이 있는것이 아니다. (C) 사회에 환원 하는것에 대해서 얘기하는 것이 아니다. (D) 학생이 따로 숙제를 받지 않는다.

TEST 2 set 1-2 — Lecture 1: The accessibility of novels

문단 주제	본문내용	해석

단락 1 — 19세기 소설의 소개

Listen to part of a lecture in an English literature class

Last class I asked you to research some of the popular English authors of the 19th century. As you may now know, 19th century England was marked by famous authors, such as Charles Dickens. Before starting our discussion about the authors, however, [Q6] I would first like to discuss the accessibility of novels at the time… like, you know, how readers used to gain access to novels.

단락 2 — 19세기 소설의 출판 방식 및 가격

Let's first talk about what it was like to purchase novels during the 19th century. Novels of that time, which are now referred to as classics, were extremely expensive. The amount of money required to buy a book was almost equal to a laborer's average weekly wages. I'm sure you guys are wondering how a single novel could be that costly, and trust me; I had the same exact question before doing more research. What I found was that the high cost of novels was mainly due to what they called "triple deckers." What this means is that a single book was published in three volumes. [Q7] For instance, to read a novel by, let's say, Arthur Conan Doyle, the author of a series of novels that we're all well aware of, Sherlock Holmes, you'd have to buy not just one book, but three separate books to finish it. This system highly discouraged British readers from purchasing novels. It was so ingrained in England that publishers argued that it was not a good place to launch a profitable business selling books. Quite unfortunate for the publishers, wasn't it? [Q6-B, Q7-C] One example of this was the famous American novel, Moby Dick, which was sold for only $1.50 in America, but was $7.80 when it was published in England. Yet, as you well know, this novel was still read by millions of people at the time. Considering the burdensome expense required to purchase a novel, how do you think that was possible? Well, that's what we will be looking at today!

단락 3 — 대여 도서관의 운영 방식

One of the mediums that people invented was the so-called lending library. [Q8] Lending libraries were a little different from today's libraries in that people had to pay an annual fee to borrow books. Some people found this ridiculous, but considering the amount of money they had to pay to purchase a book, this was still a good deal.

영문학에 강의의 일부를 들으시오.

지난 시간에 제가 여러분에게 인기 있는 19세기 영국 작가들을 찾아보라고 했었죠. 이제 여러분이 알지도 모르겠지만, 19세기 영국은 Charles Dickens와 같이 유명한 작가들로 기록되고 있죠. 하지만 작가들에 대해 토론을 시작하기 전에, [Q6] 먼저 그 당시의 소설에 대한 접근성에 대해 이야기하고 싶은데요… 그러니까, 독자들이 소설에 어떻게 접근했는지를 말이에요.

먼저 19세기에 소설을 구매하는 건 어땠는지에 대해 얘기해봅시다. 그 당시의 소설들은, 현재 고전으로 일컬어지는데요, 매우 값이 비쌌어요. 책 한 권을 사는 데 드는 돈의 양은 거의 노동자 한 명의 평균 일주일치 임금이었어요. 여러분은 아마 어떻게 소설 한 권이 그렇게 비쌀 수 있었는지 궁금해 할거라고 생각되는데요. 저도 더 많은 연구를 하기 전에는 똑같은 의문을 갖고 있었어요. 제가 발견한 사실은 소설의 값이 비싼 건 주로 사람들이 "triple deckers"라 부르는 것 때문이었어요. 이것이 의미하는 바는 책 한 권이 3권으로 출판되는 것이었죠. [Q7] 예를 들어, 우리가 모두 잘 알고 있는 셜록 홈즈의 시리즈의 작가인 Arthur Conan Doyle의 소설을 읽기 위해서는, 하나의 책만을 사는 것이 아니라, 전체 소설을 끝내기 위해 세 개의 분리된 책들을 구매해야 했어요. 이러한 체계는 영국 독자들이 소설을 구매하는 걸 주저하게 만들었죠. 이것은 영국에서 뿌리 깊이 박혀서 출판사들은 영국이 책 판매로 수익성 있는 사업을 하기에는 적합한 곳이 아니라고 주장했어요. 출판사들에게는 정말 불운한 일이었죠, 그렇지 않나요? [Q6-B, Q7-C] 이에 대한 한가지 예는 미국의 유명한 소설인 Moby Dick이 미국에서는 단 $1.50에 판매되었는데, 영국에서는 처음 출판되었을 때 $7.80이었죠. 하지만 여러분들이 잘 알듯이, 이 소설은 당시에 수백만 명의 사람들에게 읽혀졌지요. 소설 한 권을 구매하는데 드는 부담스러운 비용을 고려해보면, 어떻게 이게 가능했다고 생각하나요? 음, 바로 그 점이 오늘 우리가 살펴볼 부분이에요.

사람들이 발명해낸 방법 중 하나는 소위 대여 도서관으로 일컬어지는 것이었는데요. [Q8] 대여 도서관은 사람들이 책을 빌리기 위해서는 연간 비용을 지불했어야 했다는 점에서 오늘날의 도서관과 약간 달랐어요. 어떤 사람들은 이것이 터무니없다고 생각했지만, 책을 구매하기 위해 지불해야 하는 돈의 양을 생각한다면, 그래도 이게 더 나은 거래였죠.

문단주제	본문내용	해석
단락 4 Mudie의 영향력	Anyway, of the many lending libraries, Mudie's was the largest national company and had branches in most major English cities at the time. The way that C.E. Mudie, the owner of the libraries, ran his business was that he would buy hundreds or even thousands of copies of books at once to satisfy the needs of both his readers and the publishing companies. Since he purchased novels in such large quantities, publishers did not have to worry about their novels not being sold to the public. Also, it was beneficial for his customers at the same time, because it now became possible for them to read the novels more cheaply. I think Mudie's idea was brilliant not only because of the benefits his libraries presented, but also because he was smart enough to take advantage of the "triple deckers." Think about it, since one novel was published in three volumes, Mudie made three times as much profit. Because of the huge purchases required to fulfill his business plan, he exerted a great influence over the publishers' novel selections. Umm… He was a very conservative man and had the power to decide which books he would purchase and put into his libraries. So, the publishers avoided novels with content that he might find offensive. Funny, right? (laughs) [Q11] This one library owner could basically say "yes" or "no" to the publication of a novel. His power of selection was so great that he could turn an amateur writer into a best-selling author. Some people might think this is not fair, you know, having the choice of book selection for thousands of people in his hands, but neither the publishers nor the public could do anything about his decisions. That's how influential he was at the time.	어쨌든, 많은 대여 도서관 중에서, Mudies가 가장 큰 전국적인 기업이었는데 당시 영국의 주요 도시 대부분에 퍼져있었죠. 도서관들의 소유주인 C.E. Mudie가 자신의 사업을 운영했던 방식은, 수백 개 또는 심지어 수천 개의 책들을 한번에 구매해서 독자들과 출판사들의 요구를 모두 충족시켰어요. 그는 거대한 양의 소설을 구매했기 때문에, 출판업자들은 소설이 대중에게 팔리지 않을 까봐 걱정을 할 필요가 없었죠. 또한, 동시에 소비자들한테도 이득이었는데, 왜냐하면 이제 그들도 소설을 더 싸게 읽을 수 있게 되었기 때문이에요. 저는 Mudie의 아이디어가 뛰어났다고 생각하는데, 이는 그의 도서관이 제공했던 이득뿐만이 아니라 그가 "triple deckers"를 이용할 정도로 충분히 똑똑했기 때문이에요. 생각해보세요, 하나의 소설이 세 권으로 만들어졌기 때문에, Mudie는 세 배나 많은 이윤을 낼 수 있었지요. 그의 사업 계획을 충족시키기 위해서는 어마어마한 구매가 요구되었기 때문에, 그는 출판사의 소설 선택에 엄청난 영향력을 행사했어요. 음… 그는 아주 보수적인 사람이었고 어떤 책을 구매해서 자신의 도서관에 넣을지 결정하는 권한이 있었거든요. 그래서, 출판사들은 그를 기분 나쁘게 할 수 있는 내용을 갖고 있는 소설들을 기피했죠. 재미있지 않나요? (웃음) [Q11] 이 도서관 소유주는 기본적으로 소설이 출판되는 데 있어 "예" 또는 "아니오"라고 말할 수 있었죠. 그의 선택할 수 있는 권한은 너무 커서 아마추어 작가를 베스트셀러 작가로 만들 수 있을 정도였어요. 몇몇 사람들은 이것이 공평하지 않다고 생각할지도 모르겠네요, 그러니까 수 천명의 사람들을 위한 책을 선택하는 것이 그의 손안에 있다는 점이요, 하지만 출판사와 대중 모두 그의 결정에 대해 할 수 있는 건 아무것도 없었어요. 그것이 바로 그가 당시에 얼마나 영향력 있는 사람인지를 보여주고 있죠.
단락 5 정기간행물	Okay. That should be enough about Mudie's. Now, let's move on to the second method that readers employed to gain access to novels. Has anyone here heard of the "serial publication form"? [Q9] Well, for those who don't know what it is, it means that the novels were divided into chapters, and each of them was [Q9-B] published weekly, or monthly, in a magazine or a newspaper, typically in chronological order. Like I mentioned earlier, since buying several volumes of books at once came as a great burden for the readers, the serial publication form became an efficient way to ameliorate the financial concerns they had.	좋아요. Mudie's에 대한 건 그 정도로 충분할 것 같네요. 자, 독자들이 소설에 접하기 위해 이용했던 두 번째 방법으로 옮겨 보도록 하죠. 여러분 중 "정기 간행물 형태"에 대해 들어본 사람 있나요? [Q9] 음, 이게 뭔지 잘 모르는 사람들을 위해, 이것은 소설들이 여러 개의 장으로 나뉘어서, 이것들의 각각이 [Q9-B] 일주일 또는 한 달 단위로 잡지나 신문에 시간 순서에 따라 출판되는 걸 의미해요. 제가 앞서 언급했듯이, 한번에 여러 권씩 사는 것은 독자에게 큰 부담이었기 때문에, 정기 간행물 형태는 사람들이 갖는 금전적인 우려를 개선하는 효율적인 방법이 되었어요.

TEST 2 set 1-2

문단주제	본문내용	해석
단락 6 정기간행물의 개량	Hmm… Remember how I mentioned that books were lengthy and expensive because they were divided into three separate volumes? [Q10-B] **Well, this serial publication caused the authors of the 19th century to write even longer novels.** Anybody know why? No? Well, you see, the writers got paid by the number of episodes their novels were published in, so they tried to make up extra lines and episodes just to make more profit. Later, when all the chapters were bound for official publication, the book was much longer than the author had originally intended. Wait… I digressed a little, didn't I? Where was I… Oh, that's right. We were talking about how serialization made 19th century literature more accessible to the public, right? Okay. Charles Dickens and his publisher came up with a new version of the serial publication form. Instead of filling up a magazine or a newspaper with a lot of content other than the chapters of the books themselves, they simplified it. All their magazines and books had were a couple of illustrations and advertisements along with the chapters.	흠… 책들이 각각 세 권으로 분리되어있기 때문에 길이가 길고 비싸다고 언급했던 거 기억하나요? [Q10-B] 음, 이 정기 간행물 형태는 19세기 작가들이 더 긴 소설을 쓰도록 만들었어요. 왜 그런지 아는 사람 있나요? 없어요? 음, 그러니까, 작가들은 출판되는 자신의 소설에 들어있는 에피소드의 개수에 비례해서 돈을 지불 받았어요. 그래서 그들은 더 많은 이윤을 위해 대사와 이야기를 추가하려고 노력했죠. 나중에 모든 장들을 모아서 공식적으로 출판할 때, 작가가 처음에 의도했던 것보다 책이 훨씬 더 길어졌어요. 잠시만요...제가 주제를 좀 벗어났네요, 그렇죠? 어디까지 했었죠?... 아 맞아요. 우린 어떻게 해서 정기간행물이 19세기 문학을 대중에게 더 다가갈 수 있게 했는지에 대해 얘기하고 있었어요, 맞나요? 좋아요. Charles Dickens과 그의 출판사는 새로운 정기간행 형태를 생각해냈는데요. 잡지나 신문을 책 자체의 장들 이외의 많은 내용으로 채우는 대신에, 그것을 단순화시켰어요. 그들이 출판하는 모든 잡지와 책에는 각 장과 함께 두 가지 정도의 삽화와 광고들이 전부였죠.
단락 7 정기 간행물의 한계점 및 작가들의 이윤 창출을 위한 수법	Despite serial publications' contributions to British readers, its proponents sometimes faced criticism from the public. Since the authors were only releasing sections of their books periodically, they needed their readers to rush out and buy the next month's installment to ensure consistent profits. [Q10] To do this, the authors would write episodes with cliffhangers or suspenseful endings, you know… so the readers would want to know what was going to happen and rush out to buy the next episode. A lot of readers at the time hated this system. [Q9-D] **Not all authors made their profit this way, however**. Charles Dickens, for instance, avoided cliffhangers and used a different approach to keep his readers coming back. Instead of writing suspenseful endings, his installments would end with a man walking down the street, kind of like the… uh… cinematic effects used in movies. You know… someone just walking off into the distance. Because of these more settled endings, Dickens was praised by the public and attracted readers who were opposed to the over-dramatization of other authors.	정기 간행물이 영국 독자들에게 한 기여에도 불구하고, 이것에 대한 지지자들은 때때로 대중으로부터 비판을 받았어요. 작가들이 책의 일부분만을 정기적으로 배포했기 때문에, 지속적인 이윤을 확보하기 위해서는 독자들이 서둘러서 다음 달의 연재물을 구매하는 것이 필요했어요. [Q10] 이를 위해서, 작가들은 손에 땀을 쥐는 장면이나 미결상태의 결말을 가진 글을 쓰곤 했는데요, 그러니까… 독자들이 다음에 무슨 일이 일어날지 알고 싶어해서 다음 에피소드를 구매하려 서두르도록 말에요. 당시의 많은 독자들이 이것을 싫어했어요. [Q9-D] 하지만 모든 작가들이 이런 방식으로 이윤을 만든 건 아니에요. 예를 들어, Charles Dickens는 아슬아슬한 결말을 만드는 것을 피하고 그의 독자들이 자신의 소설을 다시 찾게 하는 다른 접근법을 사용했어요. 미해결 상태의 결말을 싣는 대신, 그의 연재물은 거리를 따라 걸어가는 남자로, 마치 음… 영화 속의 하나의 효과 같은 끝났어요. 그러니까… 누군가 그냥 걸어서 먼 거리로 사라지는 거죠. 더 안정된 결말 때문에, Dickens는 대중들로부터 칭송을 받았고 다른 작가들의 지나친 각색 경향에 반대하던 독자들을 끌어들였어요.

06. [Main Idea] What is the main topic of the lecture?

(A) The reasons that purchasing books was so difficult in the 19th century. *(too narrow)* ★

(B) The differences between the composition of American and British novels. *(too narrow)*

(C) The prestigious English authors of the 19th century and their works. *(too narrow)*

(D) The methods that English readers used to gain access to novels in the 19th century.

06. 강의의 주제는 무엇인가?

(A) 19세기에 책을 구매하는 것이 매우 어려웠던 이유들 ★

(B) 미국 소설과 영국 소설의 구성 간의 차이점

(C) 19세기 영국의 명망있는 작가와 이들의 작품들

(D) 19세기에 독자들이 소설에 접하기 위해 이용했던 방법들

해설 | (A) 책이 왜 비쌌는지 까지는 포함하고 있지만, 이 문제를 해결하기 위해 어떤 방안들이 제시됐는지 언급하지 않아 오답이다. (B) 책이 세 개로 분리되어 출판되었던 영국의 체계로 인해 출판사들이 겪은 어려움에 대한 예로 미국과 영국에서의 Moby Dick의 판매가격을 비교한 것으로, 강의의 극히 일부분이다. (C)는 강의에서 제시한 예를 든거지 이것이 main topic이 되기에는 무리가 있다.

07. [Detail – Purpose] Why does the professor mention Arthur Conan Doyle?

(A) To illustrate the type of novels that were praised and bought by C.E. Mudie. *(unrelated to the question)*

(B) To provide an example of a great novelist from 19th century Britain. *(unrelated to the question)*

(C) To support his claim that novels were more expensive in England than in America *(unrelated to the question)* ★

(D) To give an example of a hindrance that discouraged readers from buying books

07. 왜 교수는 Arthur Conan Doyle을 언급하는가?

(A) C.E.Mudie가 칭송하고 구입했던 소설의 종류를 설명하기 위해

(B) 19세기의 영국의 위대한 소설가에 대한 예를 제공하기 위해

(C) 소설이 미국보다 영국에서 더 비쌌다는 그의 주장을 뒷받침하기 위해 ★

(D) 독자들이 책을 구매하는 것을 꺼리게 만들었던 장애물에 대한 예시를 주기 위해

해설 | 교수는 Arthur Conan Doyle에 앞서 'triple deckers'를 제시하면서 책을 사는게 비싸다고 설명한다. (A)는 C.E. Mudie가 Conan Doyle의 책을 자신의 도서관에 들여왔을 지는 몰라도, 문제와 상관 없는 내용이므로 오답. (B) 또한 사실이지만 질문과는 관련 없는 내용이다. (C) 미국과 영국에서의 소설 판매가격 비교의 예로 교수가 든 것은 Conan Doyle이 아닌 Herman Melville의 Moby Dick이다.

08. [Detail – Difference/Contrast] According to the professor, how were lending libraries different from today's libraries?

(A) Lending libraries were ~~located in cities~~, but never in rural areas *(not mentioned)*

(B) **Lending libraries profited by requiring an annual fee from all borrowers.**

(C) At lending libraries, people needed to pay a certain amount ~~every time they borrowed books~~. *(partial error)* ★

(D) Lending libraries had large quantities of ~~newspapers and magazines~~. *(not mentioned)*

08. 교수에 따르면, 대여 도서관은 오늘날의 도서관과 어떻게 달랐는가?

(A) 대여 도서관은 ~~도시에 위치해~~ 있었으며 시골 지역에는 전혀 없었다.

(B) **대여 도서관은 모든 대여자에게 연간 비용을 요구함으로써 수익을 냈다.**

(C) 대여 도서관에서 사람들은 ~~책을 빌릴 때마다~~ 특정 요금을 지불해야 했다. ★

(D) 대여 도서관은 많은 양의 ~~신문과 잡지~~를 갖고 있었다.

> 해설 | (A) 언급 된 내용이 아니므로 오답이다. (C) 빌릴 때마다 돈을 내야 했던 것이 아니라는 annual fee, 즉, 연간 회비를 내야 했던 것이다.
> (D)는 신문과 잡지는 serial publication form에서 다루는 내용이므로 lending libraries 와는 관련 없는 내용이다.

09. [Detail - Characteristic] Which of these characteristics is true about the serial publication form?

(A) The serial publication form was more ~~preferred by readers~~ than lending libraries. *(not mentioned)*

(B) All of a novel's contents were updated and presented to people ~~on a daily basis~~. *(partial error)* ★

(C) **Contents were released in a newspaper or magazine rather than being published as a novel.**

(D) ~~All writers~~ who used the serial publication form ended each episode with a suspenseful ending to attract more readers. *(too extreme)*

09. 정기 간행물 형태에 대한 특징으로 사실인 것은 무엇인가?

(A) 정기 간행물 형태는 대여 도서관보다 ~~독자들에게 더 선호되었다~~.

(B) 소설의 모든 내용이 ~~매일매일~~ 새롭게 변경되어 사람들에게 제공되었다. ★

(C) **내용들은 소설로 출판되기 보다는 신문이나 잡지로 발간되었다.**

(D) 정기 간행물 형태를 이용했던 모든 ~~작가들~~은 더 많은 독자들을 끌어들이기 위해 각각의 에피소드를 미완결 상태로 끝맺었다.

> 해설 | (A)는 언급된 내용이 아니므로 답이 아니다. (B)는 daily가 아니라 weekly 또는 monthly 이므로 틀린 답이다.
> (D) 모든 작가들이 이와 같은 방법을 쓴 것은 아니라고 교수는 직접 말한다. 그 예로 Charles Dicken를 들기도 하므로 오답.

10. [Detail – Problem] Why were most of the authors who used the serial publication form criticized by the public?

(A) Because they would employ unwelcome methods at the end of their stories to attract more readers

(B) Because they unnecessarily prolonged their novels to earn more profits *(fact, but unrelated to the question)* ★

(C) Because they were ~~against the practice~~ of lending libraries
(not mentioned)

(D) Because the ~~pure purpose~~ of newspapers and magazines ~~was tainted~~
(not mentioned)

10. 정기간행물 형태를 사용하는 작가들 대부분은 왜 대중에게 비판을 받았는가?

(A) 그들은 더 많은 독자들을 끌어들이기 위해 이야기의 끝부분에 환영 받지 못한 방법을 사용했기 때문이다.

(B) 그들은 더 많은 이윤을 위해 불필요하게 소설을 연장시켰기 때문이다. ★

(C) 그들은 대여 도서관의 행위에 반대했기 때문이다.

(D) 신문과 잡지의 순수한 목적이 더럽혀졌기 때문이다.

해설 | (B)는 맞는 말이기는 하지만, 그들이 criticize 된 이유는 아니므로 오답이다. (C)와 (D)는 언급된 내용이 아니므로 오답이다. 질문에서 most of the authors이라 하기 때문에 (A)가 답이 될 수 있다 - Charles Dickens는 그렇지 않다 하여도.

Listen again to part of the lecture. Then answer the question.

"This one library owner could basically say "yes" or "no" to the publication of a novel. His power of selection was so great that he could turn an amateur writer into a best-selling author."

11. [Inference – Imply] What does the professor mean when he says this: 🎧

> "This one library owner could basically say "yes" or "no" to the publication of a novel."

(A) That C.E. Mudie was also the head of a book publishing company
(not mentioned) ★

(B) That library ~~owners~~ during the 19th century were more influential than present-day librarians *(not mentioned)*

(C) That the influence of C.E. Mudie's preferences greatly affected publishers' decisions.

(D) That C.E. Mudie's conceited attitude was ridiculed by the public.
(not mentioned)

강의의 일부를 듣고, 질문에 답하시오.

"이 도서관 소유주는 기본적으로 소설이 출판되는데 있어 "예" 또는 "아니오"라고 말할 수 있는 권한은 너무 커서 아마추어 작가를 베스트셀러 작가로 만들 수 있을 정도였어요."

11. 교수는 이 말을 할 때 의미하는 것은 무엇인가: 🎧

> "이 도서관 소유주는 기본적으로 소설이 출판되는데 있어 "예" 또는 "아니오"라고 말할 수 있었죠."

(A) C.E. Mudie는 또한 책 출판사의 사장이었다. ★

(B) 19세기동안 모든 도서관 소유주들이 현재의 도서관 사서보다 훨씬 더 영향력이 있었다.

(C) C.E. Mudie가 선호하는 바가 출판사의 결정에 큰 영향을 끼쳤다.

(D) C.E. Mudie의 자만하는 태도는 대중들에 조롱을 받았다.

해설 | 이 말을 통해서 교수가 하고자 하는 말은 C.E. Mudie의 영향력이 컸기 때문에 모든 작가들이 그의 preference에 맞추기 위해 노력했다고 하는 내용이므로 (C)가 정답일 수밖에 없다. (A), (B), (D)는 모두 언급되지 않은 내용으로 오답.

TEST 2 set 1-3

Lecture 2
Predation risk effects

문단주제	본문내용	해석

Listen to part of a lecture in an ecology class

생태학에 강의의 일부를 들으시오.

단락 1
생태계의 소개

P: Okay. Let's start from where we left off last time. We were talking about the interactions of predators and prey and their relative effects on each other, right? You know…the survival methods that wild animals, um… prey specifically, employ to avoid natural predators. Like I said last time, except for apex predators, such as tigers and lions, most wild animals have natural predators. Since we didn't have enough time to go through all of them, I briefly told you about the survival methods of gazelles and wolves. Today, we're going to bring a third player into the game. The ecosystem! This term refers to the areas in which wild organisms live and interact with one another. In a sense, these ecosystems, which are analogous to the communities in which we live, play a very significant role in the study of ecology.

P: 좋아요, 지난 번에 멈췄던 부분에서부터 다시 시작하죠. 우리는 포식자와 피식자의 상호작용과, 그들이 서로에게 끼치는 상대적인 영향에 대해 얘기했었죠, 맞나요? 그러니까, 들짐승들의 생존 방법은, 음… 구체적으로 피식자들이, 자연적인 포식자들을 피하기 위해 적용하는 것이죠. 제가 지난 번에 말했던 것처럼, 호랑이와 사자처럼 먹이사슬의 꼭대기에 있는 동물들을 제외하고는, 대부분의 들짐승들이 자연적인 포식자들을 가지고 있어요. 우리가 그것들 모두를 살펴볼 시간이 없었기 때문에, 제가 가젤과 늑대의 생존 방법에 대해 간단하게 설명했었죠. 오늘은, 이 게임에 제 3자를 들여올 건데요. 바로 생태계이죠! 이 용어는 야생의 생물들이 살면서 서로 상호작용하는 장소를 일컬어요. 어떤 면에서는 이러한 생태계는 우리가 살고 있는 사회에 비유될 수 있는데, 생태학을 연구하는데 매우 중요한 역할을 해요.

단락 2
포식행위의 영향

Okay… Now we're looking at both predators and prey, and their interactions with the ecosystems they occupy. With this integrative branch of ecology, it's very important to discuss the effects of predation. [Q13] As opposed to what many of you are thinking, you know, that animals' predatory nature only affects them in terms of their populations and such; it also plays a vital role in shaping biodiversity in the ecosystem. Okay, you guys are all aware of the food chain, right? How an herbivore, or "vegan animal", eats plants, and a carnivore, or meat eating animal, then preys on the herbivore. This chain is an essential key to sustaining the healthy balance between populations of organisms in an ecosystem. When the principle is disturbed or changed, changes in animal behavior commensurate with the changes in the ecosystem. For instance, when a species of animals lives in an environment that does not have a population of natural predators, the most naturally occurring phenomenon is that they cease to employ their survival mechanisms, such as looking around to remain alert for the sudden appearance of predators. Yes, John?

Because they no longer live with the pressure from their predators' threats, right?

그래요… 지금 우리는 포식자와 피식자 모두와 그들이 점령하고 있는 생태계와의 상호작용들을 살펴보고 있는데요. 이러한 통합적인 생태학의 분야와 함께 포식행위의 영향에 대해 논의하는 것이 매우 중요해요. [Q13] 여러분 대부분이 생각하고 있는 것, 그러니까, 동물들이 포식행위를 하는 천성은 오직 개체수 같은 것에만 영향을 끼친다는 생각과는 반대로, 생태계 내의 생물의 다양성에 있어서도 또한 주도적인 역할을 하고 있죠. 그래요, 모두 먹이 사슬에 대해서 알고 있죠, 맞나요? "채식주의" 동물인 초식동물이 식물들을 먹고, 고기를 먹는 육식동물이 초식동물을 사냥하는 것이요. 이런 먹이사슬은 생태계에서 생물체의 개체수 사이의 균형을 유지하는데 필수적인 열쇠이죠. 이 원칙이 방해를 받거나 바뀌면, 동물의 행동 변화가 생태계의 변화와 상응하게 되요. 예를 들면, 한 종류의 동물들이 자연적인 포식자들이 없는 환경에 살고 있을 때, 가장 자연적으로 발생하는 현상은 포식자들의 접근에 대한 경계를 늦추지 않기 위해 항상 주변을 둘러보는 것 같은 자신의 생존 방법을 더 이상 사용하지 않는 거에요. 네, John?

왜냐하면 포식자들의 위협에 대한 압박을 받지 않고 살아도 되니까요, 맞죠?

문단주제	본문내용	해석
단락 3 포식 위험 효과	**P:** Exactly. Let's turn that around and try to imagine [Q14] what would happen if predators were suddenly introduced to the environment. The carefree existence would be immediately terminated, right? Since the prey is not prepared to use, or has not used their defense mechanisms for a long time, it is most likely that they will be eaten by the predators as soon as they are introduced. I mean, that is the impact of predation that we usually think of. However, some animals will survive by forcing themselves to modify their original behaviors or adapt new ones to lower their risk of predation. [Q14] These changes in behavior occur due to the increased risk of predation and are called "predation risk effects." Umm… These risk effects also exert major influences on the ecosystem. **S:** Hmm…. Professor, I get the concept of predation risk effects but… I'm having a hard time visualizing how these risk effects could affect the ecosystem… Is there a real world example that you could maybe tell us about?	**P:** 정확해요. 반대로 생각해서, 만약 [Q14] 포식자들이 갑자기 그 환경에 도입되었다고 생각해보세요. 그들의 태평스러운 삶은 즉시 없어질 거예요, 그렇죠? 피식자들은 자신의 방어체계를 사용할 준비가 되지 않았거나, 오랫동안 사용하지 않았기 때문에, 아마도 포식자들에게 노출되자마자 먹힐 가능성이 커요. 제 말은, 그것이 우리가 보통 생각하는 포식행위의 영향이죠. 하지만, 몇몇 동물들은 포식의 위험을 줄이기 위해 기존 행동들을 수정하거나 새로운 행동에 적응하도록 자기자신을 강요하죠. [Q14] 이런 행동의 변화는 높아진 포식의 위험 때문에 발생하며, "포식 위험 효과"라고 불려요. 음… 이런 위험 효과들은 또한 생태계에 큰 영향을 끼치죠. **S:** 흠… 교수님, 포식 위험 효과에 대한 개념은 알겠는데요, 하지만… 이런 위험 효과들이 어떻게 생태계에 영향을 끼치는지는 상상이 가지 않는데요… 교수님께서 말씀해 주실 수 있는 실제 예가 있을까요?
단락 4 Yellowstone 국립공원의 예시	**P:** Of course! I'm sure many of you went on the school trip to Yellowstone National Park last year. Well, for those of you who didn't get a chance to visit, umm… Yellowstone National Park was established by Congress in 1872. Its primary purpose was to protect not only the landscape, but also the wildlife that inhabited the region. [Q15] In the beginning, however, the protection was only limited to specific types of animals. For example, carnivores were not protected at the time and, with the exception of bears, were continually hunted over the course of the next few decades. As a result of this peculiar regulation imposed by the government, wolves, coyotes, large cats, and other carnivores could be freely hunted. [Q15-C] Not surprisingly, by 1926, the wolves in the park had been wiped out completely. So, what do you think happened in the park as a result of the disappearance? **S:** Well, I guess, since the threat of wolves was no longer present, the animal that wolves preyed upon thrived and their populations increased? **P:** You're right! In this case, elk, a type of large deer, were one of the animals that wolves preyed on most, so without the threat of the wolves, their range of activity increased dramatically. In addition to that, something else increased in volume as well… Anybody want to take a guess?	**P:** 물론이죠! 여러분 중 많은 학생들이 작년에 Yellowstone 국립공원으로 수학여행을 갔을 거예요. 음, 아직 방문해 본 적이 없는 학생들을 위해서, 음… Yellowstone 국립공원은 1872년에 미국 국회에 의해 설립되었어요. 이 시설의 주된 목적은 자연경관을 보호하는 것뿐만 아니라, 그 지역에 살고 있는 야생 동물들도 보호하는 것이었어요. [Q15] 하지만 처음에는, 특정한 종류의 동물들에게만 보호가 제한되어 있었어요. 예를 들어, 육식동물들은 그 당시에 보호를 받지 못했고 이후 몇 십 년간 곰을 제외하고는 지속적으로 사냥을 당해 왔어요. 이러한 특이한 정부의 규정 때문에, 늑대와 사자, 코요테, 큰 고양이과 동물들, 그리고 다른 육식동물들을 자유롭게 사냥할 수 있었죠. [Q15-C] 당연히, 1926년이 되자, 공원 안에 있던 늑대들이 완전히 사라졌어요. 그럼, 그들이 사라짐으로써 공원에 무슨 일이 발생했을까요? **S:** 음, 제 생각에는, 늑대들의 위협이 더 이상 존재하지 않아서, 늑대들이 먹이로 삼던 동물들이 번성해서 개체수가 증가하지 않았나요? **P:** 맞아요! 이 경우에는, 큰 사슴의 한 종류인 말코손바닥사슴이, 늑대들이 가장 많이 잡아먹었던 동물들 중 하나였죠. 그래서 늑대들로부터의 위협이 없자, 그들의 활동 범위는 극적으로 확대됐어요. 그것과 더불어서, 다른 것의 양도 늘었죠… 짐작이 가는 학생이 있나요?

TEST 2 set 1-3

문단주제	본문내용	해석
단락 5 말코손바닥 사슴의 번식과 식량 범위의 확대	**S:** Well… Elk are herbivores, so they feed on plants, right? As you mentioned previously, they most likely started living and roaming without fear. I'm guessing their range of food also expanded along with their range of activity? **P:** You got it! Unfortunately, aspen seedlings were the elk's main food source and they devoured them all around the park, including areas where elk had never been present before because of the presence of the wolves. [Q16-A] This meant that the seedlings never got the chance to mature into trees.	**S:** 음… 말코손바닥사슴이 초식동물이니까, 식물을 먹잖아요, 맞죠? 교수님이 앞서 말씀하셨듯이, 그들은 두려움 없이 살면서 돌아다니기 시작했을 거에요. 제 생각엔 식량의 범위 또한 활동 범위와 함께 확대되었을 것 같은데요? **P:** 그렇죠! 불행히도, 사시나무 묘목들이 말코손바닥사슴들의 주식이어서 말코손바닥사슴들이 늑대들 때문에 한번도 나타나지 않은 곳들을 포함해서 공원 주변에 있는 모든 것들을 집어 삼켰어요. [Q16-A] 이것은 묘목들이 나무로 성장할 수 있는 기회가 전혀 없었다는 걸 의미하죠.
단락 6 문제의 해결	**S:** Trees… Correct me if I'm wrong, professor, but doesn't the decrease in the number of trees also mean that birds and other species that rely upon them as a means of survival were also negatively affected? **P:** Great point! [Q16] Yes, various species, such as birds, lost their habitats as a result of this phenomenon, and a large portion of the region's biodiversity decreased dramatically. Researchers realized that their mission to protect the wild life in the park was at risk of failing. I mean, it didn't accomplish anything that it initially promised, right? [Q17] To solve this problem, they reintroduced wolves into the park in 1995. Their idea was not very complex; since the whole dilemma started with the disappearance of wolves, they simply wished to reverse the process. **S:** And how exactly did that affect the elk's behavior? **P:** Well, think about it. The main reason for the increase in the elk population was the disappearance of the wolves, right? Now that the wolves were no longer absent from the park, the balance in the food chain was re-established. Due to this, the elk needed to make behavioral changes to minimize their risk of predation. For example, they became more nimble and attentive, and their activity range was once again restricted to areas where they could easily spot wolves from a distance. These forcibly imposed restrictions on the elk's range of movement no longer allowed them to hinder the maturation of the seedlings. Everything returned to the way it was, and the once-lost biodiversity was restored.	**S:** 나무들이라구요…제 말이 틀렸으면 고쳐주세요, 교수님. 그런데 나무의 수가 줄어들면 생존 수단으로써 나무에 의존했던 새와 다른 종들이 또한 부정적인 영향을 받지 않았을까요? **P:** 좋은 지적이에요! [Q16] 그래요, 새와 같은 다양한 종들은, 이 현상의 결과로 서식지를 잃게 되었고, 이 지역의 생물의 다양성의 큰 부분이 현저하게 감소되었어요. 연구자들은 공원 안에 있는 야생동물을 보호하려는 자신들의 목적이 실패할 위험에 처해 있다는 걸 깨달았어요. 제 말은, 처음에 약속된 목표들 중 어느 것도 성취하지 못했잖아요, 그렇죠? [Q17] 이 문제를 해결하기 위해, 그들은 1995년에 늑대를 다시 공원으로 들여왔어요. 그들의 생각은 그다지 복잡한게 아니었어요; 모든 딜레마는 늑대들이 사라져서 발생했기 때문에, 그들은 단순히 그 과정을 뒤바꾸고 싶어했던 거죠. **S:** 그럼 그것이 말코손바닥사슴들의 행동에 정확히 어떤 영향을 끼친 거죠? **P:** 음, 한번 생각해보세요. 말코손바닥사슴의 개체 수 증가의 주 요인은 늑대들의 소멸 때문이죠, 맞나요? 늑대들이 공원에 더 이상 없기 때문에, 먹이사슬의 균형은 새롭게 만들어졌어요. 이것 때문에, 말코손바닥사슴은 포식행위의 위험을 줄이기 위해 행동에 변화를 주는 게 필요했죠. 예를 들면, 그들은 더 날렵해지고 더 많은 주의를 기울이게 되었고, 활동범위가 먼 거리에서도 늑대들을 볼 수 있을 만큼의 지역들로 다시 제한되었어요. 이렇게 말코손바닥사슴이 움직이는 범위에 강제적으로 제한을 두게 되자, 더 이상 묘목들의 성장이 방해 받지 않게 되었죠. 모든 것들이 원래대로 돌아왔고, 한때 없어졌던 생물의 다양성도 복원되었어요.

12. **[Main Idea]** What is the lecture mainly about?

(A) The process of ~~restoring biodiversity~~ to an infertile region *(too narrow)* ★

(B) **The influence of the interactions between predators and prey on an environment**

(C) The ~~success of Yellowstone National Park~~ to protect the wildlife in it *(too narrow)*

(D) Interactions of predators and prey and their relative effects on each other *(unrelated to the question)*

해설 | (A)는 Yellowstone National Park에 대한 outcome이기 때문에 오답. (C)는 하나의 예에 불과하기 때문에 오답이다. (D) 지난 시간에 다룬 내용이므로 본 강의의 주제라 할 수 없다.

12. 강의는 무엇에 대한 것인가?

(A) ~~불모 지역에서 생물의 다양성을 회복하는 과정~~ ★

(B) **포식자와 피식자의 상호작용이 환경에 끼치는 영향**

(C) ~~Yellowstone 국립공원~~ 안에 있는 야생 동물들을 보호하는 것에 대한 ~~성공~~

(D) 포식자와 피식자의 상호작용과, 그들이 서로에게 끼치는 상대적인 영향

---

13. **[Detail – Characteristic]** According to the professor, what is true about animals' predatory nature?

Click on 2 answers

(A) It causes them to cease to employ their survival mechanisms in the ~~presence~~ of their predators. *(wrong fact)*

(B) **It maintains balance in the ecosystems' biodiversity.**

(C) **It works as a driving force for the growth or decline of a population.**

(D) It can ultimately cause a species' ~~extermination or extinction~~. *(too extreme)* ★

해설 | (A) 동물들은 포식자가 없는 환경에 살고 있을 때, 자신의 생존 방법을 더 이상 사용하지 않게 된다는 교수의 설명을 왜곡시켜 놓은 것으로 오답. (D)는 (C)에 대한 너무 한쪽으로만 치우친 extreme case이기 때문에 오답이다.

13. 교수에 따르면, 동물의 포식하는 본성에 대해 올바른 것은 무엇인가?

2개의 정답을 고르시오

(A) 포식자들이 ~~있을 때~~, 자신의 생존 방법을 더 이상 사용하지 않도록 만든다.

(B) **생태계에서 생물의 다양성의 균형을 유지한다.**

(C) **개체수의 증가 또는 감소에 대한 원동력으로 작동한다.**

(D) 궁극적으로 한 종의 전멸과 ~~멸종~~의 요인이 된다. ★

14. [Detail - Cause] Which of the following could cause an increase in the predation risk effects of a species?

(A) ~~Competition~~ for food sources between various species *(wrong fact)*

(B) An animal's ~~failure to fully exploit~~ its survival skills and methods *(wrong fact)*

(C) A rapid explosion in ~~a species' population~~ *(too general)* ★

(D) The appearance of a previously nonexistent population of predators

14. 다음 중 한 종의 포식 위험 효과를 증가시키는 요인은 무엇인가?

(A) 다양한 종들 간의 먹이를 위한 ~~경쟁~~

(B) 한 동물이 생존 능력과 방법들의 완전한 활용의 ~~실패~~

(C) ~~한 종의 개체수의 빠른 급증~~ ★

(D) 이전에 존재하지 않았던 포식자들의 등장

> **해설** | Predation risk effect은 갑작스러운 predator population의 등장에 의해 일어나는 현상이기 때문에 (A), (B), (C) 모두 답이 될 수 없다. (C)가 근접하긴 하지만 직접적으로 predator에 관한 내용이 다뤄지지 않으므로 오답이다.

15. [Detail - Cause/Reason] According to the professor, why did Yellowstone National Park fail to accomplish its mission to protect the wild life in the park?

(A) Because it ~~ignored the importance of imposing any rules~~ on free hunting. *(wrong fact)*

(B) Because carnivores, except bears, were not protected at the time *(wrong fact)* ★

(C) Because it failed to foresee the level of elk hunting and indirectly caused an ~~increase in the wolf population~~. *(opposite fact)*

(D) Because it provided regulatory protection only for the herbivores.

15. 교수에 따르면, 왜 Yellowstone 국립공원은 공원 내에 있는 야생 동물을 보호하는 임무를 달성하는 데 실패했는가?

(A) 자유로운 사냥에 대한 ~~규제를 부과하는 것의 중요성을 무시~~했기 때문이다.

(B) 곰을 제외한 육식동물들은 그 당시에 보호를 받지 못했기 때문이다. ★

(C) 말코손바닥사슴의 사냥 양을 예측하는 데 실패해서 늘대의 개체수를 증가시켰기 때문이다.

(D) 초식 동물들에게만 보호규정이 제공되었기 때문이다.

> **해설** | (A) 초식 동물의 사냥에 대한 규제를 부과하긴 했다; 사냥 규제의 중요성을 무시한 것은 육식 동물에만 해당되므로 오답이다. (B) 곰 역시 보호를 받았으므로 오답 - 곰을 제외한 육식동물들이 모두 사냥 당했다는 내용을 왜곡시킨 것이다. (C)는 정 반대되는 내용 - wolf의 population이 없어졌고, 오히려 elk가 증가했다.

16. [Detail – Effect/Influence] Which of the following was an effect or result of the disappearance of wolves from the park?

(A) An ~~increase~~ in the growth rate of aspen seedlings *(opposite fact)*
(B) ~~Increased hunting of carnivores~~ as their replacements *(not mentioned)* ★
(C) The loss of habitats for birds
(D) A decrease in the population of the ~~wolves' predators~~ *(not mentioned)*

16. 다음 중 공원에서 늑대들이 사라져서 발생한 효과나 결과는 무엇인가?

(A) 사시나무 묘목들의 성장률 증가
(B) 대체용으로 ~~육식동물들의 사냥 증가~~ ★
(C) 새들의 서식지 손실
(D) ~~늑대의 포식자~~ 개체수 감소

해설 | (A)는 정반대되는 내용이다. 사시나무 묘목들의 성장은 증가가 아닌 감소했다. (B), (D) 모두 언급된 내용이 아니므로 오답.

---

17. [Detail – Solution] How did the researchers solve the problem created by the disappearance of the wolves from the national park?

(A) They recreated an environment where predators and prey co-existed.
(B) They ~~artificially precluded~~ the elk from feeding on the seedlings of aspens. *(not mentioned)*
(C) They imposed restrictions on the ~~free-hunting of herbivores~~. *(unrelated to the question)* ★
(D) They ~~segregated~~ the prey's habitats from those of the predators. *(not mentioned)*

17. 연구자들은 국립공원에서 늑대들이 사라져 발생한 문제점을 어떻게 해결하였는가?

(A) 그들은 포식자와 피식자가 공존하는 환경을 재창조했다
(B) 그들은 말코손바닥사슴들이 사시나무 묘목들을 못 먹게끔 ~~인위적으로 막았다~~.
(C) ~~초식 동물들을 자유롭게 사냥~~하는 것에 대해 제한을 두었다. ★
(D) 그들은 피식자들의 서식지를 포식자들의 서식지와 ~~분리시켰다~~.

해설 | 해결책으로 wolf를 다시 들여왔다. 그래서 답은 (A). (B), (D) 모두 언급된 내용이 아니므로 오답. (C)는 문제의 해결책이 아닌 원인이었으므로 오답.

TEST 2 set 2-1

Conversation: Housing department

문단주제	본문내용	해석
단락 1 지난 학기 학생의 물건 기증 경험	**Listen to a conversation between a student and an administrator in the housing department** A: Oh, hey, John! Long time no see! S: Hi, Ms. Brigida, I hope all has been well with you. A: [Q5] Thank you! So what brought you all the way here? Aren't you supposed to be spending time at the beach? (laughs) S: (laughs) Well, do you remember last semester when I talked to you about donating the stuff that I couldn't take home with me? A: Of course I remember, it was such a generous gesture. S: Thanks. But I left so abruptly that I had to just leave all my stuff in a box in front of my dorm room door.	학생과 주택 담당 부서의 관리자의 대화를 들으시오. A: 오, 안녕 존! 오랜만이야! S: 안녕하세요 Brigida씨, 잘 지내셨기를 바라요. A: [Q5] 고마워! 무슨 일 때문에 여기 찾아 온 거야? 지금은 바다에서 시간을 보내야 할 때가 아니니? (웃음)' S: (웃음) 제가 저번 학기에 집에 가지고 갈 수 없는 것들을 기증한다고 했던 것 기억하시나요? A: 물론 기억하지. 정말 너그러운 행동이었어. S: 네… 그런데 제가 너무 갑작스럽게 떠나는 바람에 박스 안에 있는 모든 것들을 기숙사 문 앞에 놔두고 갔거든요.
단락 2 물건 기증의 형식화	A: Ah, yes… [Q2-A] If I remember correctly, the person who took summer courses after you left used your things. Oh yes, and he wrote a 'thank you' letter for me to give to you. Here it is! S: [Q2] Oh, wow, I did not expect that. It sure makes me feel great! I just thought that all my stuff had been thrown out. [Q1] Anyway, I've come to formalize what I wanted to do before the summer break. A: You're talking about your donation, right? S: Yes, I'm sure a lot of students experience the same problem that I had… leaving their stuff in their dorms or simply throwing it out just because it's too heavy to carry with them on the plane. I'm sure a lot of it is still very useful, you know, like clothes, books, and dishes. A: I know exactly where you're coming from. So, what can I do to help you? S: [Q3] Well, I've contacted several charity organizations, and one of them is willing to schedule pick-ups after every semester. [Q3-A] They have stores where they sell the donated stuff, and all of their profits are used to help children in Africa. A: Excellent! And… you need me to talk to the administration about your idea, correct? S: Yes! It would be great if you could help me with that…	A: 그렇구나… [Q2-A] 내 기억이 맞다면, 네가 떠난 후에 여름학기를 수강했던 학생이 네 물건을 쓴 것 같은데. 아 맞다, 너에게 주라고 감사 편지를 내게 주었어. 여기 있어! S: [Q2] 오, 와우, 전혀 기대하지 않았는데, 기분 정말 좋은데요! 전 모든 물건들이 버려졌을 거라고 생각했거든요. [Q1] 그건 그렇고, 제가 지난 여름 전에 하고 싶었던 일을 조직하기 위해서 왔어요. A: 기증에 대해서 말하는 거지, 맞지? S: 네, 제가 경험했던 문제들을 많은 학생들이 겪고 있는 것 같아서요… 비행기에 싣기가 무거워서 기숙사에 물건들을 놓거나, 단순히 버리는 것 말이에요. 옷, 책, 그리고 접시와 같이 쓸만한 것들 것 분명히 있을 텐데 말이죠. A: 정확히 무슨 뜻인지 알겠어. 그래서, 어떻게 도와줄까? S: [Q3] 음, 제가 몇 자선 단체들에게 연락을 해봤는데, 매 학기마다 픽업을 할 수 있게끔 일정을 맞추기로 한 자선 단체가 있었어요. [Q3-A] 기증된 물건들을 파는 가게들도 있고, 그들의 모든 이익은 아프리카에 있는 아이들에게 사용돼요. A: 훌륭해! 그리고… 너의 의견을 내가 행정부서에 말해줬으면 좋겠지, 맞지? S: 맞아요! 그렇게 해주시면 정말 감사하겠는데…

문단주제	본문내용	해석
단락 3 물건 기증 시스템의 홍보	A: Hmm…well, let's see. [Q3-C] I have a meeting this Saturday with some of the managers from university housing. I'm pretty sure they will agree with you on this. S: You think so? A: Yes, and I don't think there's any complicated procedure we need to follow or any specific request process we have to go through. S: Mhmm… I see. Now, what I need is to spread the word about it before the semester ends. [Q4-B, Q4-D] I was thinking maybe we could put flyers and notices on the bulletin board in the student center. A: [Q4] That sounds like a great idea, but I think the fastest way would be to put an advertisement in the university newspaper. You know, almost all of the students read the paper, so word should spread quickly that way. S: That sure seems like a great idea. I really hope this works out! A: I'm sure it will! Just leave your name and number here, and I'll contact you as soon as I get the administration's permission. S: Thank you so much, Ms. Brigida!	A: 흠… 어디 한번 보자, 음, [Q3-C] 요번 주 토요일에 대학 주택 담당 부서의 몇몇 매니저들과 회의가 있어. 그들도 이것에 대해 충분히 의견을 같이 할 거야. S: 그렇게 생각하세요? A: 그래, 그리고 우리가 거쳐야 할 복잡한 절차나, 특정하게 요구되는 절차가 있다고 생각 되지 않는데. S: 흠… 그렇군요. 지금, 학기가 끝나기 전까지 사람들에게 알리는게 필요해요. [Q4-B, Q4-D] 광고 전단과 공고문을 학생 회관에 있는 게시판에 올릴까 생각하고 있었어요. A: [Q4] 정말 좋은 아이디어처럼 들리는데, 하지만 난 가장 빠른 방법이 대학 신문에 광고를 싣는 거라고 생각해. 그러니까, 거의 모든 학생들이 신문을 읽기 때문에, 홍보가 빨리 될 거야. S: 정말 좋은 아이디어네요. 일이 잘 되었으면 좋겠네요 A: 그렇게 될 거야! 여기에 네 연락처와 이름을 남기면, 관부서의 허가를 받자마자 네게 연락할게. S: 정말 고마워요, Brigida씨!

01. [Main Idea – Main Purpose] Why did the man go to see the administrator in the housing department?

(A) ~~To donate~~ the stuff he left behind when he left last semester
(wrong fact) ★

(B) **To organize his plan to build a link between a charity organization and his university**

(C) To inquire about a ~~job advertisement~~ he saw in the school paper
(wrong fact)

(D) ~~To retrieve~~ the stuff that he couldn't take with him last semester
(wrong fact)

01. 학생이 주택 담당 부서 직원을 찾아간 이유는 무엇인가?

(A) 그가 지난 학기에 남기고 간 물건들을 ~~기증하기 위해~~ ★

(B) **자선 단체와 대학교를 잇는 자신의 계획을 추진하기 위해**

(C) 학교 신문에서 본 ~~취업광고~~에 대해 물어보기 위해

(D) 지난 학기에 가지고 가지 못했던 물건들을 ~~되찾기 위해~~

해설 | 학생은 저번 학기에 버리고 간 물건을 동기로 다른 사람들의 물건도 쓸데없이 버려지지 않게 하기 위해 자선 단체와 그의 대학교를 잇는 계획을 추진하기 위해 담당 부서를 찾아간다. (A), (D) 지난 학기에 남기고 간 물건들은 이미 당시 기증을 하고 갔다. - 물건을 기증 하거나 되찾기 위해 담당 부서를 찾아간 것이 아니다. (C)는 관련 없는 내용이다.

---

02. [Detail – Misunderstanding] What did the man think happened to the stuff he left behind?

(A) That someone who lived in his dorm after he left ~~took it and used it~~
(wrong fact) ★

(B) That it was donated ~~to a charity organization~~ for a good cause *(wrong fact)*

(C) **That it was simply thrown away**

(D) That the housing department took it and ~~held it for future inquiries~~ by its owner *(not mentioned)*

02. 남자는 자신이 남기고 간 물건들이 어떻게 되었다고 생각하였는가?

(A) 그가 떠난 뒤에 자신의 기숙사에 살았던 누군가가 ~~가져가서 사용했다.~~ ★

(B) ~~자선 단체에~~ 좋은 뜻으로 기증이 되었다.

(C) **단순히 버려졌다.**

(D) 주택 담당부서가 가져가서 나중에 주인이 문의를 할 때를 ~~대비해 보관했다.~~

해설 | 학생은 자신이 버리고 간 물건이 버려졌다고 생각했기 때문에 다른 학생이 유용하게 썼다는 사실에 놀랍다 표현한다. (A)는 학생이 예상했던 바가 아니라 실제로 일어난 것이므로 오답. (B)는 학생이 추진하는 계획이고, (D)는 언급된 적이 없는 내용이다.

---

03. [Inference – Infer] What can be inferred about the charity organization that the student contacted?

(A) That it ~~directly sends~~ the donated things, such as clothes and dishes, to children in Africa. *(partial error)* ★

(B) That the university needs to collect the donated things and ~~drop them off at the organization~~. *(wrong fact)*

(C) That it ~~wants to have a meeting~~ with the university's administration to discuss it first. *(wrong fact)*

(D) **That it will pick up the students' donated items every semester as long as the university administration permits them to.**

03. 학생이 접촉한 자선 단체에 대해 무엇을 추론할 수 있는가?

(A) 옷이나 접시 같은 기증 물건들을 아프리카에 있는 아이들에게 ~~직접 보낸다.~~ ★

(B) 대학교에서 기증된 물건들을 모은 후, ~~단체에 갖다 줄~~ 필요가 있다.

(C) 대학교의 관리부서와 의논을 먼저 하기 위해 ~~회의를 하고 싶어 한다.~~

(D) **대학교의 관리부서에서 허가를 하면 매 학기마다 학생들이 기증한 물건들을 가지러 온다.**

해설 | (A)는 Africa에 기부하는 건 맞지만, 기증된 물건을 직접 보내는 것이 아니라 먼저 팔아서 남은 이윤으로 도와주는 것이다. (B) 대학에서 단체에 가져다 주는 게 아니라 단체가 직접 pick up 해 간다. (C) 담당 부서가 할 일이지 단체가 할 일은 아니다.

04. [Detail – Suggestion] What does the administrator suggest is the fastest way to advertise the new donation program?

(A) Advertising it in the school's paper
(B) Putting advertisements on the ~~bulletin board~~ in the student center
    (wrong fact) ★
(C) Having the ~~school's TV station~~ announce it every morning
    (not mentioned)
(D) Putting flyers and notices on the walls of the ~~campus buildings~~.
    (wrong fact)

04. 무엇이 관리자가 제안하는 가장 빠른 새로운 기부 프로그램에 광고 방법입니까?

(A) 학교 신문에 광고하는 것
(B) 학생 회관에 있는 ~~게시판~~에 광고를 붙여 놓는 것 ★
(C) ~~학교 방송국~~에 매일 아침마다 방송을 하게 하는 것
(D) ~~캠퍼스 건물들~~ 벽에 광고 전단지와 공지문들을 붙이는 것

해설 | (B)는 관리자가 제안하는 것이 아니라 학생이 직접 권유한 방법이며 가장 빠른 방법은 아니라고 infer할 수 있다. (C)는 언급된 내용이 아니고, (D)는 campus buildings이란 부분이 틀렸다 - 이 부분이 고쳐진다 해도, (B)와 같은 이유로 가장 빠른 방법이 아니므로 맞는 답이 될 수 없다.

Listen again to part of the conversation. Then answer the question.

"Thank you! So what brought you all the way here?
Aren't you supposed to be spending time at the beach?"

05. [Inference - Imply] What does the administrator mean when she says this: 🎧

> "Aren't you supposed to be spending time at the beach?"

(A) All of the students went to the beach as a school trip. *(not mentioned)*
(B) The student is supposed to be in Africa helping kids in school. *(not mentioned)*
(C) The student had told the administrator about spending his summer break at the beach. *(not mentioned)* ★
(D) She wonders why he is on campus before students are required to be there.

대화의 일부를 다시 듣고, 질문에 답하시오.

"고마워! 무슨 일 때문에 찾아 온 거야?
지금은 바다에서 시간을 보내야 할 때 아니니?"

05. 관리자가 이 말을 하고자 한 이유는 무엇인가? 🎧

> "지금은 바다에서 시간을 보내야 할 때 아니니?"

(A) 학교의 모든 학생들은 바다로 체험학습을 갔다.
(B) 학생은 아프리카의 학교에서 아이들을 돕기로 되어있다.
(C) 이전에 학생이 관리자에게 여름방학을 바닷가에서 보낼 계획에 대해 얘기 한 바 있다. ★
(D) 그녀는 그가 왜 학생들이 캠퍼스에 와야 할 시간 이전에 학교에 있는지 궁금해한다.

해설 | 담당 부서는 아직 학교가 시작도 안 한 상태에서 학생이 찾아 온 것에 대해 아직 '방학'임을 뜻하기 위해 beach란 표현을 써서 궁금증을 표현한다. (A), (B), (C)는 언급된 내용이 아니므로 다 틀린 내용이다.

TEST 2 set 2-2 — Lecture 1: Insight

문단주제	본문내용	해석
	Listen to part of a lecture in a psychology class.	심리학에 관한 강의를 들으시오.
단락 1 통찰의 소개	I can definitely see that almost all of you are struggling with the final term paper that I assigned last week… Well, when I was a college student, I confronted similar adversities on a daily basis, so I know how you must feel right now. Frustrated, right? We all approach problems in a similar way. After spending hours and hours tenaciously trying to come up with a solution that just seems unreachable, what do you do? Well… One of the things you may do is step back and take a break, right? Maybe you go on your computer to socialize with your friends or walk your dog in the park… anything that keeps your mind off of the problem. Then, a sudden light bulb goes on and you finally grasp the solution that seemed out of reach before. I'm sure all of you have experienced this phenomenon, which psychologists and researchers call "insight." Today, why don't we put aside the assignments you're struggling with and look at how insight works instead?	제가 지난 주에 숙제로 냈던 학기말 리포트를 하느라 여러분이 애쓰고 있는데 분명히 보이네요. 음, 제가 대학생이었을 때, 저도 매일 비슷한 어려움을 겪었어요. 그래서 여러분들이 지금 어떤 기분일지 알죠. 정말 스럽지요? 우리 모두 하나의 비슷한 방식으로 문제점에 다가가죠. 도달할 수 없을 것 같은 해결책을 생각해내기 위해 수많은 시간을 끈기 있게 보내고 나면, 여러분은 무엇을 하나요? 음… 여러분이 할지도 모르는 일 중 하나는 잠깐 뒤로 물러서서 휴식을 갖는 거죠, 그렇죠? 아마도 여러분은 컴퓨터에서 친구들과 시간을 보내거나 개와 함께 공원을 거닐 수도 있구요… 그저 문제로부터 생각을 벗어나게 해주는 어떤 것이든 하게 되죠. 그러면 갑자기 여러분의 머리에 빛이 떠오르고, 전에는 닿을 수 없을 것처럼 보였던 해결책을 마침내 잡게 되요. 저는 여러분 모두 이 현상을 경험했으리라 확신하는데요, 이것을 심리학자들과 연구자들은 "통찰"이라고 부르지요. 오늘은 여러분이 씨름하고 있는 숙제를 잠시 내려놓고 대신 통찰이 어떻게 작용하는지 살펴보는 건 어떨까요?
단락 2 통찰력의 예시: Isaac Newton	Who pops up into your head when thinking of the world's most renowned physicist? Isaac Newton! Yes, he was a prestigious mathematician and physicist in the 1600's, and his work hundreds of years ago has impacted and shaped many aspects of today's world. Uh… you guys are all aware of the famous apple story, right? When Newton got stuck trying to figure out what keeps the moon in its orbit, he reached a point where he had to withdraw from the problem, and decided to take a stroll in a garden. While he was enjoying the view and such, he saw an apple fall to the ground from a tree. Seeing that, he was able to conclude that the force that caused the apple to fall to the ground, what we now call gravity, was the same force that kept the moon from flying out of its orbit. [Q11] **He didn't put any practical effort into solving the problem. He simply looked at the apple falling to the ground.** [Q7] **Yet, his insight helped him establish the fundamental governing rule of gravity and apply it to the moon.** So, you might be wondering about exactly how insight works at this point. Well, after a great deal of scientific research by neuroscientists, they have successfully analyzed the phenomenon.	세계에서 가장 잘 알려진 물리학자를 생각하면 누가 떠오르죠? Isaac Newton! 맞아요, 그는 1600년대의 명망 있는 수학자이자 물리학자였고, 수 백 년 전에 행한 그의 업적은 많은 측면에 영향을 주고 오늘날의 세상을 형성했어요. 어… 여러분 모두 유명한 사과 이야기를 알고 있어요, 그렇죠? 뉴턴이 달을 궤도에 머물게 하는 건 무엇인지에 관한 문제에 매달려 있을 때, 그는 문제로부터 벗어나야만 하는 시점에 이르게 되고, 정원을 거닐기로 결심하죠. 그가 경치 등을 즐기는 동안 나무에서 떨어지는 사과 하나를 보았어요. 이를 보고, 그는 사과를 땅에 떨어뜨리는 힘, 우리가 현재 중력이라고 부르는 힘이 달이 궤도를 벗어나는 걸 막는 힘과 같다고 결론지을 수 있었어요. [Q11] 그는 문제를 푸는데 어떤 실질적인 노력도 하지 않았죠. 단지 땅에 떨어지는 사과를 보았을 뿐이에요. [Q7] 하지만, 그의 통찰력이 중력의 근본적인 지배 법칙을 확립하고 그것을 달에 적용하는 것을 도왔어요. 그럼, 현 시점에서 여러분은 통찰력이 정확히 어떻게 작용하는지 궁금할 거예요. 음, 신경과학자들이 엄청난 양의 과학 연구들을 한 뒤에 그들은 이 현상을 성공적으로 분석해냈어요.

문단주제	본문내용	해석
단락 3 실시된 실험의 소개 및 첫 번째 결과: "준비 단계"	One of the experiments they carried out analyzed brain activity that occurs when the insight phenomenon takes place. All subjects, uh, the people who participated in the experiment, were tasked with solving a set of word puzzles. While monitoring their brain activity, neuroscientists detected two unusual patterns. The first unusual brain activity was detected in the frontal lobe area. Um… Try touching your forehead. Yes, that's where the frontal lobe is located, the front part of your brain. It's the decision-making base, so when you plan things, decide which actions to take, and initiate actions based on logic and reason, your frontal lobe comes into play. Anyway, when the subjects were doing the puzzles, this part of the brain was activated-which the scientists call the "preparatory phase"-and other sensory areas were shut down. I mean, their brains were fully functional, but the senses that detect external stimuli, such as the visual and auditory cortexes, were somehow slowed. As you may remember from our last class, the visual cortex is located in the occipital lobe, and the auditory cortex is in the temporal lobe. They, of course, play vital roles just like the frontal lobe, because they enable us to hear and see, [Q8-A] but when a person focuses, it seems that the frontal lobe dominates the other two and switches them off even though they are located in different parts of the brain. Well, I'd love to further explain how that's possible, but since we don't have enough time to cover that, let's stay on topic. Anyway, it's quite logical that the two senses are shut down if you think about it… [Q8] the sensory areas, the visual and auditory cortexes, were momentarily shut down or blocked because they could distract the brain from focusing on the task at hand.	이들이 실시한 실험들 중 하나는 통찰현상이 발생할 때 일어나는 뇌의 활동을 분석하는 것이에요. 모든 실험대상자들, 어, 이 실험에 참여한 사람들은 한 세트의 단어퍼즐들을 풀라는 과제를 받았어요. 그들의 뇌 활동을 살펴보는 동안 신경과학자들은 두 가지 독특한 패턴을 발견했어요. 첫 번째 독특한 뇌의 움직임은 전두엽 부근에서 발견되었어요. 음… 여러분의 이마를 만져보세요. 그래요, 그곳이 전두엽, 뇌의 앞부분이 위치해 있는 곳이에요. 이것은 의사 결정시 기반이 되는 곳이죠, 그래서 여러분이 계획을 세우고, 어떤 행동들을 취할지 결정하고, 논리와 이성에 근거하여 행동들을 개시할 때, 여러분의 전두엽이 활동하게 돼요. 어쨌든, 실험 대상자들이 퍼즐을 풀 때, 뇌의 이 부분은 활성화 되었는데-과학자들은 이것을 "준비 단계"라고 부르죠-그리고 다른 감각 기관들은 비활성화 되었죠. 제 말은, 그들의 뇌는 완전하게 기능하고 있지만, 시각과 청각 대뇌 피질 같은 외부 자극을 감지하는 감각들은 어쩐지 느려지게 되었어요. 여러분이 지난 시간에 배웠던 걸 기억해보면, 시각 대뇌피질은 후두엽에 위치해 있고, 청각 대뇌피질은 측두엽에 있어요. 이들은 물론 전두엽과 똑같이 중추적인 역할을 하죠. 왜냐하면 이것들은 우리가 듣고 보게 만들어주기 때문이에요. [Q8-A] 하지만 사람이 집중할 때, 전두엽이 다른 두 곳을 지배해서, 비록 뇌의 다른 부분에 위치해 있더라도 이들이 차단됩니다. 음. 그게 어떻게 가능한지 제가 더 설명을 드리고 싶어요, 하지만 우리는 그것을 다룰 시간이 충분치 않기 때문에, 그냥 주제에 머물기로 해요. 어쨌든, 생각해보면, 두 감각이 차단된다는 건 꽤 논리적이에요… [Q8] 감각 기관들, 즉 시각과 청각 대뇌피질이 순간적으로 차단되거나 막히는데, 왜냐하면 이것들은 뇌가 당면하고 있는 과제에 집중하는 것을 방해할 수 있기 때문이죠.
단락 4 실험의 두 번째 결과: "탐색 단계"와 감마파의 생성	Okay. Now, [Q8-C] the second unusual brain activity was found in the so-called "search phase", which involves the part of the brain that controls the speech and language functions. Well, this also came as no surprise to the scientists because if one was solving a word puzzle, then of course, the brain parts devoted to "words" would be activated. [Q9-C] What was significant and unusual about this phase happened about a few hundred milliseconds before the speech-language-production part of the brain was activated. The brain generated what we now know as, "gamma rhythm" or "gamma waves."	좋아요, 이제, [Q8-C] 두 번째 독특한 뇌의 활동은 "탐색 단계"라 불리는 곳에서 발견되는데, 이는 말과 언어 기능을 지배하는 뇌의 부분을 포함하죠. 음, 과학자들에게 이것은 놀랍지 않은데요, 왜냐하면 만약 누군가 단어 퍼즐을 풀고 있을 때, 당연히 단어에 몰두하고 있는 뇌 부분이 활성화 될 것이기 때문이에요. [Q9-C] 이 단계에 대해 중요하고 독특했던 점은, 뇌의 말-언어 생성 부분이 활성화되기 몇 0.000001초 전에 발생한 것이에요. 뇌는 우리가 현재 "감마 주기" 또는 "감마파"라고 알고 있는 것을 생성했습니다.

TEST 2 set 2-2

문단주제	본문내용	해석
	[Q9] Although there is no consensus among neuroscientists on why gamma waves are generated, the most accepted theory states that the production of such waves is caused by the formation of new links between cells that are far from one another. So, imagine, uh… a telephone network. You know how all telephones are connected to each other through a network line, so no matter where you are you can contact people, as long as you're within the network. Well, these so-called "gamma waves" sort of work the same way. What's intriguing about the waves is that they are only activated after someone experiences the same situation as yours. You know, try to solve a problem, miserably fail at it (laughs), and the brain just gives up and goes into that dormant stage of "relaxing." Well, according to the researchers, gamma waves are supposed to help you obtain that 'light bulb' moment [Q10-A] because a relaxed brain, after failing to produce a solution, produces gamma waves. [Q10] These waves enable the building of networks between remote cells in a relaxed brain more successfully than in a frustrated brain like yours. Remember, the more networks there are between the cells, the faster your brain can find a solution. Okay… As I mentioned earlier, I understand that the assignment is definitely not an easy one. Here's my advice for you. If you are stuck at some point, take a step back and just relax your frustrated brain. [Q7-C] Go out, take a stroll, and enjoy the views of nature right in front of you. Who knows? You might have one of those 'Isaac Newton' moments.	[Q9] 비록 왜 감마파가 생성되었는지에 대한 신경과학자들 사이의 완벽한 합의는 없지만, 가장 인정받는 이론은 이러한 파장의 생성이 서로 멀리 떨어진 세포 사이의 새로운 연결 형성에 의하여 야기된다고 말해요. 그럼 상상해보세요, 음…전화망 같은. 여러분은 모든 전화들이 네트워크 노선을 통하여 어떻게 서로 연결되었는지를 알고 있어요, 그래서 여러분이 어디에 있든지 여러분이 네트워크 지역 안에 있는 한, 다른 사람들과 연락할 수 있습니다. 음, 그래서 이 감마파는 일종의 같은 방식으로 작용하지요. 음… 파장에 관하여 흥미로운 점은 누군가 여러분과 같은 경험을 한 이후에만 이것들이 가담한다는 것이에요. 여러분은 알아요, 문제를 풀기 위해 노력하고, 초라하게 이것에 대해 실패하고, (웃음), 그리고 뇌는 그저 포기하며 "휴식"의 활동중단 단계에 들어가지요. 음, 연구자들에 따르면, 감마파는 여러분이 그 '백열전구' 기회를 얻도록 하는데 도움을 준다고 추정됩니다. [Q10-A] 왜냐하면, 답을 도출하는 데 실패한 후 이완된 뇌는 감마파를 생성하기 때문이죠. [Q10] 이 파장들은 여러분과 같이 낙담한 뇌보다 이완된 뇌의 떨어진 세포들 사이에 네트워크를 더 성공적으로 구성할 수 있도록 해요. 기억하세요, 세포 사이 더 많은 네트워크가 있을수록, 여러분 뇌가 해결책을 찾는 것도 빠르답니다. 좋아요… 제가 앞서 말했듯이, 과제가 분명 쉽지 않다는 것을 이해해요. 여러분들에게 제가 조언을 해 드릴께요. 만약 여러분이 어느 시점에 머물게 된다면, 한 걸음 물러서서 여러분의 화난 마음과 낙담한 뇌를 그저 쉬게 해줄 것을 권합니다. [Q7-C] 나가서 산책을 하고 여러분의 눈앞에 있는 경치와 자연을 만끽하세요. 누가 아나요? 여러분이 '아이작 뉴턴'의 기회들을 하나 갖게 될지.

06. [Main Idea] What is the lecture mainly about?

(A) Gamma waves and their role in facilitating brain activity and enhancing the brain's capacity *(too narrow)* ★

(B) Isaac Newton's work and his approach to problem solving *(too narrow)*

(C) The professor's advice on the final term paper that he has assigned to his students *(unrelated to the question)*

(D) General exploration and explanation of insight with supporting details

06. 강의는 무엇에 대한 것인가?

(A) 감마파와 뇌활동 및 뇌 능력을 강화하는 이들의 역할 ★

(B) 아이작 뉴턴의 업적과 문제해결에 대한 그의 접근법

(C) 교수가 학생들에게 준 학기말 리포트에 대한 조언

(D) 통찰의 일반적 탐구와 설명 및 뒷받침 세부내용

해설 | (A)는 실험을 통해 발견된 사실이지 강의의 메인 아이디어가 되기엔 부족하다. (B)는 Insight를 설명하기 위한 부가적인 소개 글에 불과하고, (C)는 purpose가 될 수도 있지만 main idea가 되기는 부족하기 때문에 오답이다.

07. [Inference – Purpose/Intention] Why does the professor mention Isaac Newton at the beginning?

(A) ~~To remind his students~~ of the famous apple story. *(wrong fact)* ★

(B) To present an account that illustrates the concept of insight

(C) To encourage his students ~~to take an "Isaac Newton"~~ approach to solving problems. *(unrelated to the question)*

(D) To open up a discussion about ~~well-known physicists~~ of the 1600's *(wrong fact)*

07. 교수가 앞 부분에 왜 아이작 뉴턴을 언급했는가?

(A) ~~그의 학생들에게~~ 유명한 사과 이야기를 ~~상기시키기 위해~~ ★

(B) 통찰의 개념을 예증하기 위한 설명을 주기 위해

(C) 그의 학생들에게 "~~아이작 뉴턴~~"의 문제 해결 접근법을 권하기 위해

(D) 1600년대의 잘 알려진 ~~물리학자~~에 대해 토론을 하기 위해

해설 | (A)의 apple story는 언급된 내용이지만 Isaac Newton를 언급한 목적은 아니기 때문에 오답이다. (C)는 맨 마지막에 학생들을 위해 교수가 잠깐 팁으로 준 내용이고, (D)는 Isaac Newton의 apple story 다음에 부가적으로 따라오는 내용이 없으므로 오답이다.

08. [Detail – Characteristic] Which of the following is a characteristic of the preparatory stage?

(A) The visual cortex is ~~enhanced,~~ thereby facilitating problem solving that requires the brain to visualize. *(opposite fact)*

(B) Sensory areas, ~~other than~~ the visual and auditory cortexes, shut down. *(wrong fact)*

(C) The parts of the brain devoted to ~~speech and language production~~ are activated. *(unrelated to the question)* ★

(D) The lobes that sense external stimuli temporarily stop functioning.

08. 다음 중 준비 단계의 특징인 것은?

(A) 시각 대뇌 피질은 뇌의 시각화를 필요로 하는 문제 풀이를 용이하게 하기 위해 ~~강화된다~~.

(B) 시각, 청각 대뇌 피질을 ~~제외한~~ 모든 ~~감각이~~ 정지된다.

(C) ~~말과 언어 생성에~~ 관여되는 뇌 부분이 활성화 된다. ★

(D) 외부의 자극을 감지하는 엽은 일시적으로 기능을 멈춘다.

해설 | (A) sensory system이 느려진다는 내용의 정 반대되는 말이므로 오답이다. (B) 정지되는 감각 중 가장 직접적으로 언급 된 시각과 청각을 제외하기 때문에 오답이며, (C)는 preparatory stage가 아니라 search phase를 설명하는 내용이므로 오답이다.

---

09. [Inference – Infer] What can be inferred about gamma waves from the passage?

(A) There needs to be more research on the cause of their production.

(B) They are the core of the sensory system, including the ~~visual and auditory cortexes~~. *(wrong fact)* ★

(C) They are formed ~~right after~~ the speech-language-production part of the brain becomes active. *(wrong fact)*

(D) They are ~~only helpful~~ in the communication between ~~nearby~~ cells. *(wrong fact)*

09. 이 글에서 감마파에 대해 암시될 수 있는 것은 무엇인가?

(A) 이것의 생성 원인에 대한 더 많은 연구가 필요하다.

(B) 이것은 ~~시각, 청각 대뇌 피질을~~ 포함한 감각 체계의 주요 핵심이다. ★

(C) 이것은 뇌의 말-언어-생성 부분이 활성화된 ~~이후에 바로~~ 발생한다.

(D) 이들은 ~~주변~~ 세포 사이의 소통~~에만~~ 매우 도움이 된다.

해설 | (B)는 speech and language가 맞는 말이므로 오답이며, (C)는 after가 아니라 before 이므로 오답이다. (D)는 nearby 뿐만 아니라 멀리 있는 cells들의 소통에 도움을 준다.

10. [Detail – Characteristic] What is the primary function of the gamma rhythms?

(A) They help in the transition from a tense, stressed brain to a relaxed brain. *(wrong fact)*

(B) They block signals from the sensory areas of the brain during the search phase. *(opposite fact)*

(C) They form the connecting networks between distant cells.

(D) They enable the activation of the speech-language-production part of the brain. *(wrong fact)* ★

10. 다음 중 공원에서 늑대들이 사라져서 발생한 효과나 결과는 무엇인가?

(A) 이것은 긴장되고 스트레스 받은 뇌에서 이완된 뇌로 전환하는데 도움이 된다.

(B) 이것은 탐색단계 때 감각기관에서 나오는 신호를 막는다.

(C) 이것은 멀리 떨어진 세포들 사이에 연결 네트워크를 구성한다.

(D) 말-언어-생성부분의 활성화를 가능하게 한다. ★

> 해설 | (A) 이미 relaxed된 뇌가 감마 주기를 produce하기 때문에 오답이다. (B)는 정반대 되는 말이므로 오답. (D)는 activation의 여부는 gamma rhythm과는 전혀 상관이 없기 때문에 오답이다.

**Listen again to part of the lecture.
Then answer the question.**

"He didn't put any practical effort into solving the problem. He simply looked at the apple falling to the ground."

11. [Inference – Imply] Why does the professor say this: 🎧

> He simply looked at the apple falling to the ground.

(A) To claim that most of Newton's discoveries were rather accidental *(partial error)* ★

(B) To make the point that Newton's leisure time actually helped him with his discovery

(C) To show admiration to the amount of work Newton put into his unexpected discovery *(wrong fact)*

(D) To help his students visualize the design of the experiment that Newton executed with an apple. *(wrong fact)*

강의의 일부분을 다시 듣고 질문에 답하시오.

"그는 문제를 푸는데 어떤 실질적인 노력도 하지 않았죠. 그는 단지 땅에 떨어지는 사과를 보았습니다."

11. 교수가 이 말을 하고자 한 이유는 무엇인가? 🎧

> 그는 단지 땅에 떨어지는 사과를 보았습니다.

(A) 그의 발견 대부분은 다소 우연이었다는 것을 주장하기 위해 ★

(B) 그의 여가 시간이 실제로 발견에 도움을 주었다는 것을 제시하기 위해

(C) 예기치 못한 발견에 그가 기여한 작업 양에 대한 존경심을 표하기 위해

(D) 그의 학생들이 뉴턴이 사과를 가지고 실행한 실험 설계를 시각화하는데 돕기 위해

> 해설 | (A) 중력을 발견한 과정에서 얘기를 하는 것이지 뉴턴의 대부분의 발견을 말하는 것이 아니다. (C) 뉴턴의 존경심에 대해서 언급한게 아니다.
> (D) 우연히 발생한 사건이지 실험을 설계하지 않았다.

TEST 2 set 2-3 — Lecture 2
Shift from a nomadic lifestyle to sedentary settlements

문단주제	본문내용

단락 1
인류의 생활방식의 변화 및 원인

Listen to part of a lecture in an Archaeology class.

P: Last class we discussed the different types of social changes ancient people went through. Well, today, we'll be narrowing that topic a bit and looking at one major social change that occurred centuries ago. Do you guys remember that one of the most significant changes in human history was the shift from a nomadic lifestyle to sedentary, year-round settlements?

S: Yes, and you also briefly mentioned some kind of cause that initiated the lifestyle change, right?

P: Good point! Researchers now believe that changes in climate conditions ultimately triggered the lifestyle shift. [Q13] When the glaciers from the last ice age receded to the polar regions, a drastic climate change occurred across the globe that enabled people to settle in one region and cultivate crops instead of wandering from place to place. There were a number of similar cases of lifestyle shifts around the world at about the same time, but I think we should focus on the most exemplary and studied case, which is the coastal plains of the eastern Mediterranean region, around present day Lebanon.

단락 2
지중해 동쪽 지역의 특징 및 변화

S: As you may know, the eastern Mediterranean region is pretty much infertile and not suitable for human habitation at this time, but [Q12-A] about 18,000 years ago, the region was open grasslands and woods. Such conditions were very likely to provide a great deal of convenience to hunter-gatherer groups whose survival heavily depended on the amount of food they hunted. Undoubtedly, the region was hugely attractive to hunters. On top of that, about 5,000 years after the advent of their settlements in the region, another climate change occurred that resulted in increased rainfall. What does that equal to? Yes… An increased amount of precipitation equals richer and more fertile soil and ecosystems! [Q17] Well, to verify everything I've just said, we need more than just statistical data concerning changes in precipitation and climate, right? Then… What kind of physical evidence should we be able to find to support the claim that sedentary settlements existed in the region?

문단주제	본문내용	해석
단락 3 정착생활의 근거: 집과 집 구조	S: That's pretty simple. If the hunters settled and lived there, they must have built houses, right? So, evidence of houses must've been found. P: You got it! Architectural remains found in the region played a vital role in helping researchers confirm the existence of year-round settlements in the region. Most of the remains found in this area were from a people known as the Natufians, who were the first group of people to inhabit and root their settlements in the eastern Mediterranean area. Taking the Natufian housing structures into account, we can observe that their houses were all uniform… Every house looked nearly identical to every other one. They all had a rigid structure and were arranged in a semicircle. [Q14] The upper parts of the houses were made of brush and wood, while the lower parts were lined with stones. [Q14-B] The interesting thing is that these houses were partially dug into the ground. I mean, that is just brilliant! These people, thousands of years ago, were bright enough to come up with a way to construct houses that could withstand occasional harsh weather and whatnot… Also, um, the floors of the excavated houses had small circular holes in them, which indicates that they used posts and beams to support the roofs. Why do you think this would be considered evidence of a sedentary lifestyle? S: I'm a little confused… It can't be evidence at all, can it? I mean, just because they had houses doesn't mean they couldn't move to other places. P: You have a point, but you're missing something very important. Anybody else want to take a guess before I give away the answer? S2: I was thinking that the houses seem to be quite intricate in many ways, and since the people put so much effort into building them, they wouldn't just leave their houses behind and build new ones on a seasonal basis.	S: 그건 꽤 간단해요. 만약 사냥꾼들이 거기서 정착하고 살았다면, 그들이 집을 지었겠죠, 그렇죠? 그럼, 집이 증거가 되는걸 찾을 수 있겠네요… P: 바로 그거에요! 그 지역에서 발견된 건축물 유적이 연구자들로 하여금 그 지역에 일년 내내 정착생활이 존재했다는 것을 확증해주는데 중추적인 역할을 했죠. 이 지역에서 발견된 유적지의 대부분은 Natufians으로 알려진 사람들이 만든 것으로, 이들은 지중해의 동쪽 지역에 정착해서 뿌리를 내린 최초의 집단이에요. Natufians 들의 집 구조를 살펴보면, 우리는 집들이 모두 동일하다는 걸 알 수 있어요… 모든 집이 다 똑같이 생겼다는 말이에요. 그것들은 다 단단한 구조를 가지고 있고 반원형으로 배열되어 있죠. [Q14]집의 윗부분은 풀과 목재로 만들어져 있고, 아래 부분은 돌로 정렬되어 있어요. [Q14-B] 흥미로운 점은 집의 일부분이 땅 속으로 파져 있었다는 거에요. 제 말은, 이건 정말 놀라운 거죠! 몇 천년 전에 사람들이 때때로 발생하는 험한 날씨 등에 집이 잘 견디게끔 만들 만큼 똑똑했다는 거니까요… 또한, 음, 발굴된 집의 바닥에는 작은 원형의 구멍들이 있는데, 이것은 그들이 지붕이 지탱할 수 있게 기둥과 대들보를 사용했다는 걸 시사해주죠. 왜 이것이 정착생활의 증거로 여겨지는 걸까요? S: 전 좀 헷갈리는데요… 이건 절대 증거가 될 수 없어요, 그렇지 않나요? 제 말은, 집을 가지고 있었다고 해서 그들이 다른 지역으로 이동할 수 없었다고는 말할 수 없잖아요? P: 학생 말도 일리가 있어요, 하지만 굉장히 중요한 걸 놓치고 있어요. 내가 답을 알려주기 전에 혹시 추측해 볼 사람 있나요? S2: 제 생각에는 집들이 여러 면에 있어서 꽤 복잡한 것 같아요, 그리고 사람들이 집을 짓는데 많은 노력을 쏟아 부었기 때문에, 그냥 집을 버리고 계절마다 새 집을 짓지는 않았을 것 같은데요?
단락 4 정착생활의 근거: 도구	P: That's my point! Why would they go through all the trouble of digging holes and such if they were just going to leave the next season?	P: 내가 말하고 싶은게 바로 그거에요! 만약 다음 계절에 버리고 떠날거면 왜 땅을 파는 것 같은 수고를 하겠어요?

문단주제	본문내용	해석
단락 5 음식 공급원: 우연한 곡물의 수확	Along with these architectural remains, researchers were able to find another type of valuable evidence – the tools they used to harvest grains and large quantities of stone mortars. As I previously stated, [Q15-D] the region that the Natufians inhabited had vast areas of rich soil, and wild cereal grains were abundant. What we can see from this is that the [Q15-B] Natufians took advantage of the environment and mainly harvested wheat and oats which they ground in their stone mortars. S: Oh, I remember reading something about that. They also used to plant grains, right? P: That's exactly what I was thinking, because normally you'd expect that of sedentary people. But, ironically enough, no evidence to support that assumption has yet to be found. [Q15-A] I mean, the tools used to harvest grains have been found, but no tools for planting grains have been discovered yet. Further, researchers think that the chances of them being found are pretty slim. They do, however, believe that the unintentional planting of seeds and grains might have taken place during this time, which, according to them, is the only explanation for their continual reliance on grains as a food source. This unintentional planting could have taken place when seeds were spread by the wind and sprouted in other areas. So, you can say that the Natufians didn't actually do any planting work, but rather, nature did it for them.	이런 건축 유적과 함께, 연구자들은 또 다른 종류의 가치 있는 증거를 찾을 수 있었는데요 -곡물을 수확하기 위해 사용했던 도구들과 많은 양의 돌절구들이에요. 제가 앞에서 말했듯이, [Q15-D] Natufians가 거주했던 지역은 광대한 크기의 땅이 기름져서 야생 곡물들이 풍부했어요. 우리가 이것으로부터 알 수 있는 건 [Q15-B] Natufians는 환경을 이용해서 밀과 귀리를 수확하고 그것들을 돌절구에 갈았다는 거에요. S: 아, 제가 그것에 대해 읽었던 게 기억나네요. 그들은 또한 곡물을 심기도 했어요, 맞죠? P: 저도 똑같이 그렇게 생각했어요 왜냐하면 보통은 그것이 정착해서 사는 사람들에게 기대하는 것이니까요. 하지만, 모순적이게도, 그런 추측을 뒷받침하는 증거는 아직 발견되지 않았어요. [Q15-A] 제 말은, 곡물을 수확하는 도구들은 발견됐지만, 심는 도구들은 아직까지 찾지 못했어요. 나아가, 연구자들은 그것들이 발견될 확률이 꽤 희박하다고 생각하고 있어요. 하지만, 그들은 의도치 않게 씨앗과 곡물이 이 시기에 심어졌을지도 모른다고 믿고 있는데요, 연구자들에 따르면 이것이 지속적으로 곡물을 음식 공급원으로 의지할 수 있었던 것에 대해 단 하나의 설명이 되는 거죠. 이렇게 우연히 심는 경우는 바람에 의해 퍼져나가 다른 지역에서 싹이 터서 발생할 수 있었을 거에요. 그래서 Natufians는 심는 행위는 전혀 하지 않았고, 오히려 자연이 그렇게 해줬다고 말할 수 있겠어요.
단락 6 음식 공급원: 사냥	[Q16] Speaking of their food sources, there is also evidence that indicates that they hunted animals. Bones of migratory birds and young gazelles found in the area indicate that the Natufians hunted those types of animals. Migratory birds often flew to the area during the winter and young gazelles probably showed up there around spring or summer. Now, do you see what I'm trying to say? I mean, during the winter, migratory birds were hunted, and during spring or summer, young gazelles were hunted. S2: Winter, summer, and spring… Mhmmm! This indicates that the hunting process took place year around, which means that the Natufians inhabited the region year around as well! P: You've got it! That's exactly what happened. All of these great pieces of evidence point to one logical conclusion: the Natufians built permanent settlements in the eastern Mediterranean region!	[Q16] 음식 공급원에 대한 얘기가 나왔으니 말인데, 그들이 동물을 사냥했다는 걸 나타내는 증거도 있어요. 이 지역에서 발견된 철새들과 어린 가젤의 뼈들이 Natufians가 그 동물들을 사냥 했다는 걸 시사하고 있죠. 철새들은 종종 겨울을 보내기 위해 그 지역으로 날라왔고 어린 가젤들은 아마 봄이나 여름 즈음에 나타났을 거에요. 자, 제가 무슨 말을 하려고 하는지 알겠나요? 그러니까, 겨울에는 철새들이, 봄이나 여름에는 어린 가젤들이 사냥을 당했어요. S2: 겨울, 여름 그리고 봄… 음! 이러한 증거들은 사냥이 일년 내내 진행 되어 Naufians이 일년 내내 그 지역에 남아 있었다는 사실을 나타내주네요! P: 맞았어요! 바로 그런 일이 생겼던 거죠. 이 모든 굉장한 증거들은 하나의 논리적인 결론을 가리키고 있어요: Naufians이 지중해의 동쪽 지역에 영구 정착지를 건설했다는 것을요!

12. [Main Idea] What is the main topic of the lecture?

(A) The means that Natufians employed to ~~survive in a harsh environment~~ *(wrong fact)*

(B) A part of the world where a lifestyle shift occurred centuries ago *(too general)*

(C) Distinct characteristics of the Natufians' lifestyle in the eastern Mediterranean region *(too general)* ★

(D) A change in lifestyles that happened thousands of years ago and its evidence

12. 강의 주제는 무엇인가?

(A) Natufians 사람들이 ~~가혹한 환경에서 살아남기~~ 위해 사용했던 수단들

(B) 몇 세기 전에 생활방식이 변화했던 세계의 일부분

(C) 지중해 동쪽 지역에 사는 Natufians 사람들의 삶의 뚜렷한 특징들 ★

(D) 몇 천년 전에 발생했던 생활 방식의 변화와 그것의 증거

해설 | (A) Natufians 사람들이 거주했던 지중해의 동쪽 지역은 18,000년 전과 5,000년 전을 기점으로 사람들의 생존과 생활이 용이한 기후로 바뀌었다고 교수는 설명한다. 가혹한 환경에서 살아남았다고 보기 어렵다. (B)는 구체적인 내용을 담고 있지 못하므로 오답이다. (C) Natufians 사람들의 생활에 대한 증거에 대한 언급이 빠지므로 too general.

13. [Detail – Cause] Which of the following initiated the shift to permanent settlements?

(A) The end of a cold era that resulted in a dramatic change in the world's climate

(B) The glaciers that ~~remained stable~~ in the Mediterranean region after the ice age *(opposite fact)*

(C) An increase in rainfall ~~as a result of~~ the end of the last ice age *(wrong fact)* ★

(D) ~~The advent of tools~~ that eased agricultural practices *(wrong fact)*

13. 다음 중 영구적인 정착생활로의 변화를 야기했던 것은 무엇인가?

(A) 전세계 기후에 급격한 변화를 가져온 추운 시대의 종결

(B) 빙하 시대 이후 지중해의 동쪽 지역에 ~~안정적으로 남아있는~~ 빙하들

(C) 마지막 빙하시대가 끝난 ~~결과로~~ 강수량이 증가 ★

(D) 농업 활동을 용이하게 한 ~~도구의 출현~~.

해설 | 질문은 첫 시작점이 어디냐고 물어본다. (B)는 교수가 주장하고 있는 "glaciers receded to the polar regions"에 반대되는 말이므로 틀렸다. (C) 잘못된 인과관계 - 전혀 관련 없는 두 내용(빙하시대와 5,000년 전 지중해의 동쪽 지역에 일어난 강수량의 변화)을 연관시켜 놓은 것으로 오답. (D) 도구의 개발은 정착생활의 특징에 대한 부가적인 설명으로 언급되며, 정착생활로의 변화를 야기한 요인은 아니므로 오답.

14. [Detail – Methodology] How did the Natufians make their houses strong and stable?

(A) The Natufians only used heavy stones to build the ~~walls~~ of their houses. *(partial error)* ★

(B) The Natufians built houses that dug ~~deep into the ground~~. *(unrelated to the question)*

(C) The Natufians ~~arranged~~ their houses in a ~~semicircular shape~~ that bound them to one another. *(not mentioned)*

(D) The Natufians built the lower parts of their houses with stones and dug them into the ground.

14. 어떻게 나투피안들은 집을 튼튼하고 안정적으로 만들었습니까?

(A) Natufians 사람들은 무거운 돌만을 이용해 집의 ~~벽~~을 지었다. ★

(B) Natufians 사람들은 ~~땅 속으로 깊이 파고 드는~~ 집을 지었다.

(C) Natufians 사람들은 자신의 집들이 서로 붙어 있게 ~~반원형으로~~ ~~배열했다~~.

(D) Natufians 사람들은 집의 아래 부분을 돌로 만들어서 그것들을 땅 속에 넣었다.

해설 | (A)는 the lower part of the house was lined with stones의 부분을 왜곡 하여 walls라 해서 틀리고, (B)Natufians의 집들이 땅 속으로 살짝 ("partially") 파고 든다는 교수의 말과는 어긋나는 내용으로 오답. (C)는 각각의 집 모양이 반원형이었다는 내용을 왜곡 시킨 것으로 오답. 집들의 배열과는 관련이 없다.

15. [Detail – Characteristic] Which of the following are NOT true about the Natufians' agriculture?

Click on 2 answers

(A) The Natufians ~~planted~~ and harvested grains on a seasonal basis. *(wrong fact)*

(B) Large quantities of mortars were used to grind seeds and grains.

(C) Grains such as wheat were ~~cherished~~, whereas grains such as oats were ~~ignored~~. *(not mentioned)*

(D) The Natufians took advantage of the vast areas of fertile soil and continually relied on the abundant wild plants as a food source.

15. 다음 중 Naufians에 대해 사실이 아닌 것은 무엇인가?

2개의 답을 고르시오

(A) Natufians는 계절마다 곡식을 ~~심고~~ 수확하곤 했다.

(B) 많은 양의 절구들이 씨앗과 곡식을 가는데 사용되었다.

(C) 밀같은 곡식들은 ~~소중히 여겨졌는데~~, 귀리 같은 곡식은 ~~무시되었다~~.

(D) Natufians는 넓은 지역의 비옥토를 이용했고 음식 공급원으로써 야생 식물에 꾸준히 의존하게 되었다.

해설 | (A) 수확을 했다는 증거는 있으나 곡물을 심었다는 증거는 없다고 교수는 주장하므로 오답이다.
(C) 곡식의 종류에 따른 가치에 대한 언급은 지문에 나오지 않는다.

16. [Inference – Purpose/Intention] Why did the professor mention migratory birds and young gazelles?

(A) To give examples of the Natufians' ~~domesticated animals~~ (not mentioned)

(B) To inform her students that migratory animals took up a large portion of the Natufians' diet (wrong fact)★

(C) To explain that the Natufians ~~used the animals' feathers and leather~~ to withstand the harsh conditions. (not mentioned)

(D) **To present another available food source to support the claim of permanent residence**

16. 왜 교수님은 철새들과 어린 가젤을 언급했습니까?

(A) Natufians의 ~~가축동물~~의 예를 보여주기 위해

(B) 이주하는 동물들이 natufians 사람들의 식생활에 큰 부분을 차지했음을 얘기하기 위해 ★

(C) Natufians가 힘든 환경을 견디기 위해 동물들의 ~~깃털과 가죽을 이용했다~~는 걸 설명하기 위해

(D) **영구적인 정착지에 대한 주장을 뒷받침하기 위해 또 다른 음식 공급원이 있었다는 걸 제시하기 위해**

> 해설 | 교수는 bones of migratory birds and young gazelles를 Natufians들이 뭘 먹고 살았는지 알려주기 위해 언급한 것이다. (A)와 (C)는 언급된 바가 없고, (B) 교수가 이주하는 동물들을 언급하는 근본적인 이유가 아니므로 오답.

Listen again to part of the lecture. Then answer the question.

"Well, to verify everything I've just said, we need more than just statistical data concerning changes in precipitation and climate, right? Then… What kind of physical evidence should we be able to find to support the claim that sedentary settlements existed in the region?"

강의의 일부를 다시 듣고, 질문에 답하시오

"음, 제가 방금 말했던 모든 것들을 증명하기 위해서는, 우리는 강수량과, 기후 변화와 관련된 통계자료 이상의 것이 필요해요, 맞죠? 그렇다면… 정착이 그 지역이 존재 했다는 주장을 지지하는 물적 증거는 어떤 것이 있을까요?"

17. [Inference - Imply] What does the professor imply when she says:

"Then… What kind of physical evidence should we be able to find to support the claim that sedentary settlements existed in the region?"

(A) Sedentary settlements have apparent differences from cultures with nomadic lifestyles (unrelated to the question)

(B) **What she stated as pre-conditions of the shift in lifestyle aren't enough to prove the Natufians' permanent settlement**

(C) Her students ~~must have learned~~ about the physical evidence found in the region previously (not mentioned)

(D) She wants to give the students a chance to answer because they've asked her a ~~similar question~~ before. (not mentioned)

17. 교수가 이 말을 할 때 암시하는 바는 무엇인가?

"그렇다면… 정착이 그 지역이 존재 했다는 주장을 지지하는 물적 증거는 어떤 것이 있을까요?"

(A) 정착은 유목민의 삶의 방식과는 확실하게 차이가 있다.

(B) **삶의 방식의 변화에 대한 전제 조건으로 그녀가 언급한 것은 Natufians 사람들의 정착생활을 증명하기에는 부족하다**

(C) 그녀의 학생이 그 지역에서 발견되었던 물적 증거에 대해 ~~배운 적이 있는~~ 게 ~~틀림없다~~.

(D) 그녀는 이전에 ~~비슷한 질문을~~ 했기 때문에 학생들에게 답할 수 있는 기회를 만들어 주고 싶어한다.

> 해설 | 교수는 open grasslands와 increase in precipitation을 'statistical data'라 부르며, 이것들은 Natufians 사람들의 정착생활을 증명하는데 충분하지 않다고 설명한다. (A)는 맞는 말이지만 문제와 관련되지 않아 오답이다. (C) 학생들이 이전에 관련 내용을 배웠다고 추측할 수 있을 만한 내용이 지문에 없으므로 오답. (D) 역시 학생들이 앞서 비슷한 질문을 했다고 추측할 수 있을 만한 내용이 지문에 없다.

www.usherin.usher.co.kr

USHER
iBT TOEFL
INTERMEDIATE LISTENING
TEST 3 해설

TEST 3 set 1-1

Conversation
Brain's Left and Right Hemisphere

문단주제	본문내용	해석

단락 1
지난 수업 핵심 복습

Listen to a conversation between a student and a psychology professor.

S: Professor, do you have a minute?

P: Sure, Sarah, how can I help you?

S: [Q1-A] Well… it's about the brain research you discussed yesterday.

P: Right.

S: [Q1] You explained that the left and right hemispheres serve different functions and… I kind of started daydreaming.

P: No problem. Let's go back a little and revisit some key points first. Okay. Our brain consists of left and right hemispheres connected by a bundle of commissural fibers called the corpus callosum. The left and right sides of the brain communicate by sending signals.

S: I see… Is it possible to split the hemispheres?

단락 2
좌뇌와 우뇌의 소통 및 관련 실험

P: Well, actually that's possible. Let me give you an example of the studies carried out by Roger Walcott Sperry in the 1960s. He was a neuropsychologist who earned the Noble Prize in Psychology or Medicine in 1981. [Q2] While looking for a cure for a patient with severe epilepsy, a neurological disorder characterized by seizures, he came up with the idea of splitting his patient's brain… literally cutting it in half.

S: That sounds radical and dangerous to me.

P: Indeed, many perceived it as an irrational decision, but Sperry insisted that there were no other options and conducted the surgery.

S: What happened? I wouldn't be surprised if it didn't go well…

P: Well, the surgery was actually quite successful, except that the patient experienced some unexpected side effects, such as insufficient speech production. The patient's seizures ceased, but the split-in-half brain, unsurprisingly, had some defects.

S: Why? Was it because the communication between the hemispheres was cut off?

학생과 심리학 교수의 대화를 들으시오.

S: 교수님, 혹시 시간 되세요?

P: 그래 무슨 일이니?

S: [Q1-A] 그게 말이죠… 어제 수업 때 이야기한 뇌 연구에 관해서 여쭤보고 싶어서요.

P: 그래.

S: [Q1] 교수님께서 좌뇌와 우뇌가 다른 기능을 한다고 설명하셨고… 제가 그 다음부터는 백일몽에 빠졌어요.

P: 괜찮아. 일단 전에 나갔던 진도에 나왔던 몇 가지의 핵심들을 다시 한 번 살펴보자. 그래. 우리의 뇌는 뇌량이라고 불리는 교련 섬유로 연결된 좌뇌와 우뇌로 구성되어 있어. 좌뇌와 우뇌는 신호를 보내 의사 소통을 한다.

S: 그렇군요… 혹시 반구들을 분열시키는 게 가능한가요?

P: 뭐, 가능하긴 하지. 1960년도에 Roger Walcott Sperry가 수행한 실험을 예로 들려줄게. 그는 1981년도에 심리학 혹은 의학 노벨상을 수상한 신경심리학자였다. [Q2] 극한 뇌전증 또는 발작으로 특징된 신경질환의 환자를 위한 치유법을 개발하는 도중에, 그는 환자의 뇌를 말 그대로 반으로 잘라서 분열을 시켰어.

S: 극단적이고 위험하게 들리는데요.

P: 물론, 많은 사람들이 비이성적인 결정으로 여겼지만, Sperry는 다른 선택권이 없다며 수술을 진행했어.

S: 그래서 어떻게 됐나요? 실패였다고 해도 별로 놀라지 않을 거 같네요.

P: 뭐, 수술은 꽤나 성공적이었으나 환자는 언어장애와 같은 몇몇의 부작용들을 앓고 말아버렸지. 환자의 발작들은 멈췄지만 반으로 갈라진 뇌는, 놀랍지 않게도, 결함이 좀 있었어.

S: 왜 그런 건가요? 두 반구의 교신이 단절돼서 그런 건가요?

문단주제	본문내용	해석
단락 3 좌뇌와 우뇌의 역할	**P:** Yes, neuroscientists believed that the left and right hemispheres uniformly performed the same functions, [Q5] but… ummm… if I put this pencil in your left visual field, you can recognize it, right? **S:** Of course, I'm not blind, professor (laughs) **P:** What if the patient's eye sight was perfectly normal, but he couldn't recognize an object presented in his left visual field but recognized it if it was in his right visual field? Regardless of the type of object, the patient couldn't describe any stimulus in his left visual field. **S:** Um… does that mean the left hemisphere was malfunctioning? **P:** [Q3] Actually, no. The left hemisphere corresponds to the right visual field and the right hemisphere to the left visual field. **S:** Right, I totally forgot about that.	**P:** 그래, 신경심리학자들은 좌뇌와 우뇌가 균일하게 같은 기능을 한다고 생각해왔었어, [Q5] 그렇지만… 음… 만약에 내가 이 연필을 너의 좌측 시야에 두면, 너는 그것을 인지하지? **S:** 당연하죠, 제가 눈이 먼 것도 아닌데 (웃음) **P:** 만약에 그 환자의 시야에 아무런 이상이 없었는데, 왼쪽에 나타나는 사물은 인지하지 못하면서 오른쪽 시야에 두면 인지한다면? 사물의 종류 따위에 상관없이, 그 환자는 왼쪽 시야에 어떤 자극도 묘사하지 못 했다는 거야. **S:** 음… 그렇다면 좌뇌에 오작동이 있었다는 건가요? **P:** [Q3] 사실은 그렇지는 않았어. 좌뇌는 오른쪽 시야와 부합되고 우뇌는 왼쪽 시야와 부합되는 거야. **S:** 그렇구나, 그 사실을 완전히 잊고 있었어요.
단락 4 우뇌와 좌뇌의 단절된 소통의 극복	**P:** [Q2-B] Sperry additionally carried out several other tasks to obtain in-depth knowledge of the brain, and was able to come to the conclusion that each hemisphere specializes in certain tasks. For instance, [Q4-B] the left hemisphere is associated with analytical and verbal tasks, while [Q3-D, Q4-A] the right hemisphere primarily controls spatial abilities, music, and creativity. So now you understand why the object in the left hemisphere wasn't recognized, right? It just wasn't the right hemisphere's job to recognize stuff in the first place; it was the left hemisphere's job. The importance of the corpus callosum is quite noticeable to you now, isn't it? The communication between the two hemispheres is just… disabled once it's cut. **S:** Yes, I understand that part. [Q3-B] But, does that mean the patient had to bear with those symptoms for the rest of his life? It must've been really uncomfortable. **P:** Not quite… because our brain, left or right, has the ability to learn. So, over time, the patient's left hemisphere "learned" the right hemisphere's jobs and vice versa. **S:** Ah, I get it now. The mystery of our brain… it's quite unbelievable. Well, thank you professor that clarifies everything! **P:** (laughs) Yes it is, and no problem, Sarah!	**P:** [Q2-B] Sperry는 뇌에 대한 더 깊은 지식을 얻기 위해 더 많은 실험들을 수행해서 결국에는 각각의 반구체는 특정한 기능을 맡는다는 것을 발견했어. 예를 들어, [Q4-B] 좌뇌는 분석적이고 언어적인 과업들을 특수화하는 반면에 [Q3-D, Q4-A] 우뇌는 주로 공간능력, 음악, 그리고 창의력을 통제해. 그래서 왜 좌시야에 있는 사물이 인식 안 되었는지 이제 알겠지? 애초에 사물을 인지하는 것 자체가 우뇌의 일이 아니었어. 그건 바로 좌뇌가 할 일이었어. 뇌량의 중요성이 이제 눈에 띄게 부각되고 있지? 두 반구 사이의 교신이 끊어지는 순간 아예 교신이 불가능하다는 거지. **S:** 네 그 부분은 이해하겠는데, [Q3-B] 그렇다면 그 환자가 평생 그 증상들을 앓고 살아야 했다는 건가요? 엄청 불편했을 거 같아요. **P:** 그렇지만은 않아… 왜냐하면 좌뇌던 우뇌던 우리의 뇌는 배울 수 있는 능력을 갖고 있어. 그래서 시간이 지날수록 그 환자의 좌뇌는 우뇌의 일을 배우고 반대로 우뇌가 좌뇌의 일을 배우게 된 거지. **S:** 아 이제 알겠어요. 뇌의 수수께끼라는 게 참… 믿기지 않네요. **P:** (웃음) 맞아, 천만해, 사라!

01. [Main Idea – Main Purpose] Why does the student visit the professor?

(A) To ask the professor for advice on ~~his brain research~~ *(wrong fact)*

(B) To ask for help with designing an experiment to study the brain

(C) To get a better understanding of a recent lecture

(D) To get an idea of ~~what neuropsychologists do~~ in their field *(wrong fact)* ★

01. 학생은 왜 교수를 찾아갔는가?

(A) 그~~의 뇌~~ 연구에 대한 조언을 구하기 위해

(B) 뇌 연구에 대한 ~~실험을 설계하는데~~ 도움을 요청하기 위해

(C) 최근에 들은 강의를 보다 잘 이해하기 위해

(D) 신경심리학자들이 자기 분야에서 ~~무엇을 하는~~ 지 알아보기 위해 ★

해설│ (A) 지난 수업에서 다룬 이야기인 뇌 연구에 관해서 질문하러 왔다는 학생의 말을 왜곡시켜 놓은 것으로 오답. (B) 1960년도에 Roger Walcott Sperry가 설계한 실험에 대한 교수의 설명을 왜곡 시켜놓은 것으로 오답. (D) 좌뇌와 우뇌의 분열 가능성에 대한 설명으로 교수가 신경심리학자 Roger Walcott Sperry의 예를 들지만, 학생이 교수를 찾아간 구체적인 이유는 아니다.

02. [Detail – Intention] According to the professor, why did Roger Walcott Sperry decide to split the patient's brain in half?

(A) To treat his patient for severe convulsions

(B) ~~To collect more data~~ about the two hemispheres of the brain *(unrelated to the question)*

(C) ~~To analyze the function~~ of the corpus callosum of the brain *(wrong fact)* ★

(D) ~~To make sure~~ his patient's mental abnormalities ~~do not relapse~~ *(not mentioned)*

02. 교수에 의하면, Roger Walcott Sperry는 왜 환자의 뇌를 반으로 분열시키기로 결정을 내렸는가?

(A) 그의 발작환자를 치료하기 위해

(B) 두 반구체에 대한 ~~더 많은 정보를 수집하기 위해~~

(C) 뇌량의 기능을 분석하기 위해 ★

(D) 그의 환자의 정신질환들의 ~~재발을 방지하기 위해~~

해설│ (B) 뇌전증 환자의 수술 이후 뇌에 대한 연구를 계속한 이유였으며, 수술과는 관련 없는 내용이다. (C) 수술 이후 뇌의 두 반구의 교신 및 그 단절에 관해 Sperry가 깨달은 것과 관련되어 있을 수는 있으나 그가 환자의 뇌를 반으로 분열시킨 직접적인 이유가 아니다. (D) 환자의 재발은 Sperry의 고민거리로 언급되지 않는다.

03. [Detail – Misconception] What was the student's misconception about the left and right hemispheres in relation to visual fields?

(A) That the right hemisphere dictates the perception of objects in the left visual field *(fact, but unrelated to the question)*

(B) That once the brain was split, the visual fields would never be balanced again. *(unrelated to the question)* ★

(C) That the left hemisphere is connected with the left visual field

(D) That the right hemisphere corresponds to spatial abilitiesas *(unrelated to the question)*

03. 시야에 관한 좌반구와 우반구에 대해 학생은 어떤 오해를 갖고 있었는가?

(A) 우반구는 좌안 시야에 있는 사물들의 자각을 통제한다는 것

(B) 뇌가 분열되는 순간, 시야는 절대로 균형을 잡지 못한다는 것 ★

(C) 좌반구는 좌안 시야와 연결되어 있다는 것

(D) 우반구는 공간능력과 부합한다는 것

해설│ (A) 학생의 오해를 교수가 정정해 줄 때 했던 설명이므로 오답. (B) 학생이 오해했던 부분이 아니라 궁금해서 질문했던 점으로 오답. (D) 교수가 실제로 한 설명으로 학생이 오해했던 점은 아니다.

04. [Detail – Difference] How is the left hemisphere different from the right hemisphere?

> Click on 2 answers

(A) The left hemisphere is specialized in ~~imagination and creative thinking~~ *(wrong fact)* ★

(B) **The left hemisphere primarily involves the task of analysis and logical reasoning**

(C) The left hemisphere specializes in ~~auditory tasks~~ *(not mentioned)*

(D) **The left hemisphere plays a role in processing rhetorical tasks**

04. 좌뇌는 우뇌와 어떻게 다른가?

> 2개의 정답을 고르시오

(A) 좌뇌는 ~~상상력과 창의력에~~ 특수화한다는 점 ★

(B) **좌뇌는 주로 분석과 논리적 추론과 관련된 일을 맡는다는 점**

(C) 좌뇌는 ~~청각과 관련된 작업을~~ 수행하는데 특수화 되어있다.

(D) **좌뇌는 수사학적인 일들을 처리하는 역할을 갖고 있다는 점**

해설 | (A)는 우뇌의 역할이므로 오답. (C) 청각과 관련된 작업의 수행은 언급되지 않는다.

---

05. [Inference - Purpose/Intention] Why does the professor say this:

> "but… ummm… if I put this pencil in your left visual field, you can recognize it, right?"

(A) **To elucidate one of the side effects that the patient suffered after the surgery**

(B) To see if the student recognizes the ~~elements used in the experiment~~ *(wrong fact)* ★

(C) To illustrate that the left and right hemispheres of the brain ~~aren't different~~ in terms of their functions and tasks *(wrong fact)*

(D) ~~To show his doubt~~ that the student is paying enough attention to him *(wrong fact)*

05. 교수는 왜 이런 말을 하는가?

> "그렇지만 음... 만약에 내가 이 연필을 너의 좌측 시야에 두면, 너는 그것을 인지하지?"

(A) **수술 후에 환자가 앓았던 한 부작용을 설명하기 위해**

(B) ~~실험에 쓰였던 다양한 요소들을~~ 학생이 인지하는지 보기 위해 ★

(C) 좌뇌와 우뇌가 기능과 과제 면에서는 ~~다르지 않~~ 다는 것을 보여주기 위해

(D) 학생이 자기 말에 집중하는 것에 대한 ~~의문을 표하기 위해~~

해설 | (B) 실험에 쓰였던 요소와는 무관하므로 오답. (C) 각각의 반구체는 특정한 기능을 맡는다는 교수의 설명과 모순 되는 말로 오답. (D) 두 반구 간의 교신이 단절되어 Sperry의 환자가 수술 후 부작용에 시달렸냐는 학생의 질문에 잇따라 하는 말로, 학생의 집중 여부에 대한 의문 표시가 아닌 그 질문에 대한 대답임을 추측할 수 있다.

TEST 3 set 1-2 — Lecture 1: Younger Dryas

문단주제

단락 1 — Younger Dryas의 원인과 특징

단락 2 — Younger Dryas의 영향

단락 3 — Younger Dryas Impact 가설의 근거

본문내용

Listen to part of a lecture in an Earth Science Class.

P: Let's continue our discussion of historical global climate change. [Q7-D] About 12,900 years ago, one of the coldest periods, the "Younger Dryas" occurred. Previously, the Earth was gradually warming for about a thousand years. Then, a sudden cooling happened.

S: Professor, correct me if I'm wrong, but from what I've read, didn't this affect North America?

P: Yes, Vicky. For those without this background knowledge, let me explain what happened in North America. [Q7] As the main driving force of the Younger Dryas, many scientists generally point to a sudden influx of freshwater into the Atlantic Ocean, the world's second largest body of water, from a lake that covered much of Canada. The rush of the water disrupted oceanic currents and brought warmer temperatures to the region. Another calamity occurred concurrently and [Q7-A] caused the extinction of some mammalian species in the area, such as camels and mammoths, and the so-called Clovis people disappeared without a trace. [Q6] While many have attempted to explain these occurrences, archaeologist Dr. Douglas J. Kennett and his team came up with a theory called the Younger Dryas impact, or Clovis comet, hypothesis.

Kennett thought that a bundle of comet fragments struck the North American continent and had two major effects: they disrupted ocean currents and caused 35 genera of animals in the region to go extinct. According to him, they caused the sudden flow of lake water into the Atlantic Ocean, thereby altering the ocean's currents. He also suggested that comets set areas of North America on fire, causing the demise of the animals and of the Clovis people who depended on them for sustenance.

S: That sounds convincing! What evidence did he have?

P: Well, he interpreted a layer of soil rich in carbon found at about sixteen sites across North America and Europe.

해석

지구 과학 수업 강의의 일부분을 들으시오.

P: 저번 시간에 역사적인 지구 기온 변화에 대한 이야기를 이어서 이야기해 볼게요. [Q7-D] 약 12,900년 전에 'Younger Dryas'라는 가장 추운 시대 중 하나가 일어났습니다. 이 전에는 지구가 천년 동안 서서히 온난화 되고 있었다가 갑작스럽게 냉각이 일어난 것입니다.

S: 교수님, 제가 틀렸다면 말씀해주세요, 그런데 제가 읽은 거에 의하면 이 현상이 북미에 영향을 주지 않았나요?

P: 네, 맞아요 Vicky. 이 배경지식이 없는 분들께 북미에 어떤 일이 일어났는지 제가 설명해 드리죠. [Q7] 많은 과학자들은 일반적으로 캐나다의 많은 지역을 덮고 있는 호수에서부터 세상에서 두 번째로 큰 수역인 대서양으로의 갑작스러운 민물 유입이 Younger Dryas의 주요 원동력이라고 지적하고 있습니다. 물의 쇄도는 해류를 방해했고 그 지역에 따뜻한 기후를 가지고 왔습니다. 동시에 또 다른 재앙이 발생하여 [Q7-A] 낙타와 맘모스와 같은 일부 포유류 종의 멸종을 초래했으며 소위 클로비스 사람들이라 부르는 이들은 아무런 흔적도 없이 사라졌습니다. [Q6] 많은 사람들이 이러한 현상들을 설명하려고 시도하는 동안, 고고학자 인 Dr. Douglas J. Kennett과 그의 팀은 Younger Dryas 충돌 또는 Clovis 혜성이라는 가설을 발견했습니다.

Kennett은 혜성 파편들이 북미 대륙을 강타했으며 두 가지 주요 효과를 미쳤다고 생각했습니다: 첫 번째는 해류의 혼란을 일으켰고. 두 번째는 이 지역의 35종의 동물을 멸종시켰다는 것입니다. 그에 따르면, 혜성 파편들에 의해 호숫물이 갑작스럽게 대서양으로 흘러 들어가 해류를 바꾸었습니다. 또한, 그는 혜성이 북아메리카의 일부 지역을 화재로 몰아 넣음으로써 동물들과 생계를 위해 그에 의지한 클로비스 사람들을 죽음으로 몰아 넣었답니다.

S: 설득력 있는 얘기네요! 그에게 어떤 증거가 있었죠?

P: 음, 그는 북아메리카와 유럽의 약 16 곳에서 발견된 탄소가 풍부한 토양 층을 해석하고

문단주제	본문내용	해석
단락 4 Younger Dryas Impact 가설의 한계점	[Q8] He was able to extract microscopic diamonds called "nanodiamonds" from the very bottom sediment called the "black mat." How? Well... electron microscopes come in handy when examining biological and inorganic specimens like cells, metals, and crystals. They comprise electrostatic and electromagnetic lenses too... well, that's not important now, let's revisit it later. So... black mat obtained its name from its distinctive color and the discovery of nanodiamonds there could be considered critical evidence, because the force of asteroid impacts create them. S: Oh, so that supports his claim that comets struck the Earth, right? P: Right! However, scientists point out that Kennett's theory falls short in some key ways. His team said that "impact signs" are missing or cannot be found because the asteroid fragmented before it hit the ground. [Q8-C] However, at least one researcher says that it's impossible for a comet to vanish without a trace, such as a crater, and thus argues that Kennett's theory doesn't prove the occurrence of asteroids hitting the Earth. [Q9] Another point of criticism arises because there is no evidence of a population decline around that time... strange, huh? The disappearance of the Clovis people, therefore, remains disputable and the demise or extinction of other species is also said to be invalid because no evidence of continent-wide wildfires has been found. S: Um, what about the nanodiamonds? That seems quite convincing to me. P: Well, it's irrefutable that nanodiamonds were found in the black mat at 16-impact sites around North America, but few researchers have looked for them elsewhere. [Q9] Maybe they're more common than we think. At least one researcher found nanodiamonds in non-impact sites in Europe from two thousand years ago. Considering that the Young Dryas happened 12,900 years ago, the origin of the nanodiamonds he discovered hardly proves the suggested occurrence of asteroids. S: Are you suggesting that his hypothesis is fundamentally wrong?	[Q8] "black mat"라고 불리는 맨 아래 침전물에서 "나노 다이아몬드"라고 불리는 미세 다이아몬드를 추출 할 수 있었습니다. 어떻게 했냐고요? 음... 전자 현미경은 세포, 금속 및 결정체와 같은 생물학적 및 무기적 표본을 검사 할 때 편리합니다. 이 전자 현미경은 정전기 렌즈와 전자기 렌즈로 구성되어 있고... 아무튼 지금은 이 내용이 중요하지 않습니다, 나중에 다시 살펴 보도록 할게요. 그래서... "블랙 매트"는 그 독특한 색깔에서 파생된 이름이고, 그 곳에서 나노 다이아몬드가 발견되었다는 것이 중요한 증거로 여겨 질 수 있습니다. 그 이유는 소행성의 영향으로 나노 다이아몬드를 생성하기 때문이죠. S: 오, 그래서 그것이 혜성이 지구를 강타했다는 그의 주장을 입증하네요, 맞죠? P: 그렇죠! 하지만, 과학자들은 Kennett의 이론은 몇 가지 핵심적인 면에서 부족하다고 지적했어요. 그의 팀은 충돌하기 전에 소행성이 파편화 되었기 때문에 "충격 신호"가 없거나 발견되지 못했다고 말했어요. [Q8-C] 그러나 적어도 한 연구원은 혜성이 분화구처럼 흔적 없이 사라지는 것은 불가능하다고 주장하고, 따라서 Kennett의 이론은 지구에 충돌하는 소행성의 발생을 증명하지 못한다고 주장합니다. [Q9] 그리고 그 시기에 인구 감소의 증거가 없기 때문에 또 다른 비판이 제기됩니다. 이상하죠? 따라서 클로비스 사람들의 실종은 논쟁의 여지가 있고 다른 종의 종말이나 멸종은 대륙 전체 산불의 증거가 발견되지 않아 근거가 없습니다. S: 그렇다면 나노 다이아몬드는요? 그거는 꽤 설득력 있는 것 같은데요. P: 음, 나노 다이아몬드가 북미 주변 16개 지점의 black mat에서 발견되었다는 것은 확실하지만, 다른 곳에서 찾아 봤던 연구자들은 거의 없었습니다. [Q9] 아마 나노 다이아몬드는 우리가 생각하는 거 보다 더 흔할 수도 있어요. 적어도 한 연구원은 2천년 전 영향을 받지 않은 유럽 지역 곳곳에서 나노 다이아몬드를 발견했습니다. Young Dryas가 12,900년 전에 일어났던 것을 고려해 볼 때, 그가 발견 한 나노 다이아몬드의 기원은 소행성의 발생은 증명을 하지 못합니다. S: 그렇다면 그의 가설이 근본적으로 틀렸다는 건가요?

06. [Main Idea] What is the lecture mainly about?

(A) ~~Exploration of the events that took place~~ during the Younger Dryas period with scientific research

(B) The last ice age that ~~caused the demise~~ of the Clovis civilization and extinction of species in North America

(C) ~~The characteristics of nanodiamonds~~ and ~~the black mat~~ in which they are found

(D) **In-depth theories of the Younger Dryas period with supporting details**

06. 강의의 주요 내용은 무엇입니까?

(A) Younger Dryas 시대에 ~~일어난 사건들에 대한~~ 과학적 연구에 ~~탐구~~

(B) 북아메리카에서 클로비스 문명의 종말과 종의 멸종을 ~~초래한~~ 마지막 빙하기

(C) ~~나노다이아몬드~~와 그들이 찾은 ~~black mat~~의 특징

(D) **Younger Dryas 시대의 심층 이론과 그 내용을 뒷받침하는 연구**

해설 | (A) 영거 드라이아스 시대에 있었던 사건이 아니다. (B) 클로비스 문명과 종말을 초래한 부분이 아니다. (C) 나노 다이아몬드와 black mat의 내용은 강의에 큰 주제가 아니라 디테일이다.

---

07. [Detail – reason] According to the professor, what gave rise to the initiation of the Younger Dryas?

(A) ~~The extinction of the species~~ including mammoths in North America

(B) The disrupted ocean currents and global wind patterns ~~caused by deglaciation~~

(C) **The change in ocean currents in the Atlantic Ocean caused by an influx of lake water**

(D) ~~The end of the ice age~~ that took place about 12,900 years ago

07. 교수에 의하면 무엇이 Younger Dryas의 시작을 야기시켰는가?

(A) 북아메리카에서 매머드를 포함한 종들의 ~~멸종~~

(B) ~~해빙으로 야기된~~ 방해된 해류와 방해된 지구풍의 패턴

(C) **호수의 유입으로 인한 대서양 해류의 변화**

(D) 약 12,900년 전에 일어난 ~~빙하기의 끝~~

해설 | (A) 영거 드라이아스의 시작을 종의 멸종이 불러올수 없다. (B) 빙하가 녹는거는 빙하시대가 끝나면서 나타나는 증상이다. (D) 질문이 빙하기 끝을 뭐가 시작했는지 인데 정답이 빙하시대의 끝일수가 없다.

08. [Detail – Evidence] How were Kennett and his team able to support their claim that comets struck the Earth?

(A) By using an electron microscope and finding minerals that are synchronous with the Younger Dryas

(B) ~~By dating mammals' bones~~ that have remained in the black mat throughout centuries *(not mentioned)* ★

(C) By ~~examining the crater~~ that's been assumed to be created by the asteroid 12,900 years ago *(wrong fact)*

(D) By ~~running computer simulations~~ and calculating the possibility of the occurrence of asteroids during the Younger Dryas *(not mentioned)*

08. Kennett과 그의 팀은 어떻게 혜성이 지구를 강타했다는 주장을 뒷받침 할 수 있었는가?

(A) 전자 현미경을 사용하여 Younger Dryas와 동기식인 미네랄을 찾음으로써

(B) 수세기 동안 검은 매트에 남아있는 포유동물들의 뼈의 연대를 측정함으로써 ★

(C) 12,900 년 전에 소행성에 의해 생성 된 것으로 추측 된 분화구를 조사함으로써

(D) 컴퓨터 시뮬레이션을 실행하고 Younger Dryas 기간 동안 소행성의 발생 가능성을 계산함으로써

해설 | (B) 포유류의 뼈의 연대 측정에 관한 내용은 언급되지 않는다. (C) 분화구에 대한 내용은 Kennett의 이론에 대한 비판 중 혜성이 아무 흔적도 없이 사라지는 것이 불가능하다는 지적에서 나온다. 이를 왜곡시켜 놓은 것으로 오답. (D) 컴퓨터 시뮬레이션에 대한 내용은 지문에 언급되지 않으므로 오답.

09. [Detail – Perspective] Which two of the following are true about the critics' perspective about Kennett and his team's finding of nanodiamonds?

Click on 2 answers

(A) That although the theory is not sufficient enough as of now, ~~there is hope that there will be additional evidence~~ in near future *(unrelated to the question)*

(B) That their work is incomplete in a sense that other places than the impact-sites haven't been examined

(C) That their hypothesis is purely based on ~~coincidental events rather than periodic~~ phenomena. *(not mentioned)*

(D) That their finding doesn't support their claim that asteroids struck the Earth

09. 다음 중 Kennett과 그의 팀이 나노 다이아몬드를 발견 한 것에 대한 비평가들의 관점에 대해 사실인 것은 무엇인가?

2개의 정답을 고르시오

(A) 이론이 현재로서는 충분하지 않지만, 가까운 미래에 추가적인 증거가 있을 것이라는 희망이 있다는 것

(B) 영향을 받은 지역 이외의 다른 곳은 조사해 보지 않은 점에서 그들의 연구가 불완전하다는 것

(C) 그들의 가설은 순전히 주기적인 현상보다는 우발적인 사건에 기초한다는 것

(D) 찾은 증거가 운석이 지구에 떨어졌다는 주장을 지지하지 못합니다.

해설 | (A) 비평가들의 관점이 아닌 교수의 입장으로 오답. (C) 가설의 기초가 우발적이라는 지적은 본문에 언급되지 않는다.

10. [Inference – Opinion/Attitude] What is the professor's overall attitude towards the "Clovis comet hypothesis"?

(A) He takes a ~~negative standpoint~~ of the theory by giving an argument in line with the critics *(wrong fact)*

(B) He seems to be emotionally detached and ~~doesn't disclose any subjective perspective~~ on the hypothesis ★

(C) He takes a fairly neutral stance by illustrating that it's quite possible that additional evidence will be found in the future

(D) He explains that the hypothesis is just another ~~ephemeral theory~~ like the one that involves the demise of dinosaurs

10. 교수가 '클로비스 혜성 가설'에 대해 보이는 전반적인 태도는 어떤가?

(A) 그는 비평가들의 의견에 따라 논쟁을 함으로써 그 이론에 대해 ~~부정적인 관점을~~ 갖는다.

(B) 그는 정서적으로 무심한 것으로 보이고 가설에 대한 ~~아무런 주관적인 관점도 밝히지 않는다~~ ★

(C) 그는 앞으로 추가 증거가 발견될 가능성이 높다는 것을 보여 줌으로써 상당히 중립적인 입장을 취하고 있다.

(D) 그는 그 가설이 공룡의 붕괴와 마찬가지로 또 다른 ~~임시 이론~~일 뿐이라고 설명한다.

> **해설 |** (A) 교수는 객관적인 입장에서 비평가들의 의견을 대변할 뿐, 그들의 비판을 옹호하지 않으므로 오답. (B) Kennett의 이론이 옳다고 증명될 때까지 시간이 더 필요할 뿐이라는 그의 주장에는 주관적인 관점이 어느 정도 담겨 있으므로 오답. (D) 교수는 이론들의 임시적 유효함이 아닌 해석의 다양성과 부정확하게 증명될 가능성을 강조한다.

11. [Inference – Purpose/Intention] Why does the professor mention the extinction of dinosaurs at the end?

(A) To deliver a message that evidence to support Kennett's theory ~~could also be used to prove~~ the dinosaur theory *(wrong fact)*

(B) To make a comparison with Kennett's theory in that it ~~fails to entail proven evidence~~ *(wrong fact)* ★

(C) To further support his claim that new discoveries that could validate Kennett's theory are just yet to be found

(D) To point out that the demise of dinosaurs ~~was also caused by impacts~~ *(unrelated to the question)*

11. 교수는 왜 결국 공룡의 멸종에 대해 언급합니까?

(A) Kennett의 이론을 뒷받침하는 ~~증거가 공룡의 이론을 증명하는 데도 사용될 수 있다는~~ 메시지를 전달하기 위해서

(B) ~~입증된 증거를 수반하지 않는다는~~ 점에서 Kennett의 이론과 비교하기 위하여 ★

(C) 케넷의 이론을 입증할 수 있는 새로운 발견들이 아직 발견되지 않았다는 그의 주장을 뒷받침하기 위해서

(D) 공룡의 멸종 ~~또한 충격에 의해 야기되었다는 것~~을 지적하기 위해

> **해설 |** (A) 교수는 Kennett의 이론의 추후 입증 가능성에 대한 설명을 위해 그 사례로 공룡 이론을 언급한 것이며, 공룡의 이론과 Kennett의 이론 사이에 직접적인 과학적 연관을 짓지 않는다. (B) 교수는 두 이론의 비교를 통해 입증된 증거의 결핍을 주장하는 것이 아니라 증거가 입증되기까지 시간이 필요하다는 점을 강조한다. (D) 공룡의 멸종의 직접적인 원인이 일련의 충격이었다는 이론을 그대로 서술하는 것으로, 질문이 묻는 바와 관련이 없다.

TEST 3 set 1-3

Lecture 2
Leonardo's philosophical thinking

Listen to part of a lecture in an introductory computer science class.

P: Let's review last week's lecture. When it comes to designing computers, there are two major categories: exterior and interior design. The exterior is relatively simpler than the interior in terms of sophistication. Let's think about this. What does your computer look like? It could be black, beige, white, or another color, and it could come in different shapes and sizes. Since the introduction of personal computers, an… umm… evolution has taken place in the computer chassis, or case. Today, people employ a number of methods to distinguish their computers from others, from lighting mods to body fillers and so on. It's a growing trend that's apparent in today's society. That's enough about the "look" of computers. [Q12] Today, I want to focus on the other side of computer design: technological design or how developers think and apply their thoughts to designing and inventing computer systems and software, the "inside" of computers.

There is more involved in the process than technological advances … I would say that philosophical aspects are just as important… Let me refer to Leonardo da Vinci to illustrate my point.

As you know, he was a great thinker and is arguably the most diversely inventive and talented person ever, not to mention a profound artist from the Italian Renaissance. He was also a polymath who made great contributions in engineering, music, architecture, anatomy, and so on. In his work of anatomy, he demonstrated a blend of philosophical thinking in both science and art. But, [Q13] I would say the focal point in his work is that, um, his understanding of human needs and problems were the primary crux of his thinking and of how he "designed." In this sense, [Q17] developers devoted to technological design consider and apply both philosophical and technological aspects in their work.

Overall, there are two branches of technological design: old and new computing. [Q16-B] Old computing refers to improving computing power and speed, the technical specifications of your computer.

TEST 3 set 1-3

문단 주제	본문내용	해석
단락 4 신형 컴퓨팅	[Q16-D] One may cast doubt on the philosophical aspects of memory capacity, but don't get a wrong idea here; [Q14-A] these features are very important and play a vital role in computer processing, which ultimately benefits society. [Q14] We won't go deep into this because it's irrelevant to today's topic. Um, Leonardo's way of thinking is prevalent in new computing. New computing, in contrast to old, elucidates an approach to technology design with the focus of satisfying people's needs and desires through computer usage. It focuses on what people can accomplish and do with their computers instead of what the computers can do, umm… like their capacity or abilities. What can you do with your computer? A myriad of tasks, correct? Things like researching, getting directions, communicating and socializing, disseminating information to others, and so on. That's what developers of technology design do; they try to think on behalf of their users' goals and purposes for utilizing computers and create software programs that are easily usable by the public.	[Q16-D] 메모리 용량의 철학적인 측면에 대해 의문을 제기할 수도 있지만, 오해하지 마세요; [Q14-A] 이러한 특징들은 매우 중요하고, 궁극적으로 사회에 이익을 주는 컴퓨터 처리에 중요한 역할을 합니다. [Q14] 이 주제는 오늘의 주제와 무관하기 때문에 우리는 여기에 깊이 파고들지 않을게요. 음, 레오나르도의 사고 방식은 새로운 컴퓨터 분야에서 널리 퍼져 있어요. 신형 컴퓨팅은, 이전의 것과는 대조적으로, 컴퓨터 사용을 통해 사람들의 필요와 욕구를 충족시키는 데 초점을 맞추어 기술 디자인에 대한 접근을 유도합니다. 이것은 컴퓨터가 할 수 있는 것 대신에 사람들이 컴퓨터로 무엇을 하고 수행할 수 있는 것에 초점을 맞추고 있어요. 여러분은 여러분의 컴퓨터로 무엇을 할 수 있습니까? 수많은 업무들이 있죠? 조사, 길 찾기, 의사소통 및 친목, 정보의 전파 등과 같은 것들이 있죠. 그것이 기술 설계자들이 하는 일입니다; 그들은 컴퓨터를 사용하는 사용자들의 목적과 목적을 대신하여 생각하고 대중이 쉽게 사용할 수 있는 소프트웨어 프로그램을 만들려고 합니다.
단락 5 프로그램 개발의 필요조건	You can see how important it is for developers to know what users demand, right? [Q15] The users' desires ultimately tell developers what kinds of programs to create. However, before they create new technology, they need to make sure that the technologies are not only efficient and useful but also easily manageable and executable… meaning they need to be user-friendly. These targeted users are not engineers with knowledge of processing and sophisticated technology, especially when it comes to computers. [Q16-A] The focus here is usability along with usefulness. So programmers try to avoid anything that may require substantial expertise, which makes sense right? But, we all know that's very hard to accomplish. Let's put you in a hypothetical situation where you are working on a term paper, and need to research and collect information. You would go on websites to find information, of course. What if the websites were organized in a confusing way that made you frustrated before looking for the information? This commonly occurs in two ways: the information can be a million clicks away or it can be jumbled with a bunch of unnecessary information. We can conclude that this website has failed to meet the user's demand: usability.	사용자들이 무엇을 요구하는지에 대해 개발자들이 아는 것이 얼마나 중요한지 아시겠죠? [Q15] 사용자들의 욕구는 궁극적으로 어떤 종류의 프로그램을 만들지 개발자들에게 알려줍니다. 하지만, 새로운 기술을 개발하기 전에, 그들은 그 기술들이 효율적이고 유용하다는 것 뿐만 아니라 다루기 쉽고 실행 가능하다는 것을 확실히 할 필요가 있습니다… 그 말인즉슨 사용하기 쉬워야 된다는 거죠. 이러한 사용자들은 특히 컴퓨터에 관해서는 프로세싱 및 정교한 기술 지식을 가진 공학자가 아닙니다. [Q16-A] 여기서 주목할 점은 편리성과 더불어 유용성입니다. 따라서 프로그래머들은 상당한 전문성이 필요한 것은 무엇이든 피하려고 노력하는 게 말이 되죠? 하지만 우리는 그것이 성취하기 매우 어렵다는 것을 압니다. 여러분들이 논문을 작성하고, 정보를 조사하고 수집해야 하는 상황에 처해 있다고 가정해볼게요. 물론 정보를 찾기 위해 웹사이트에 접속하겠죠. 만약 웹사이트가 혼란스러운 방식으로 구성되어 있어서 정보를 찾기 전에 답답함을 느낀다면 어떨 것 같아요? 이것은 일반적으로 두 가지 방식으로 발생합니다. 정보는 백만 번의 클릭을 해야 비로소 얻어질 수 있거나 불필요한 정보와 같이 뒤죽박죽 되어 있을 수 있습니다. 우리는 이 웹 사이트가 사용자의 요구, 즉 유용성을 충족시키지 못했다고 결론을 내릴 수 있습니다.

문단주제	본문내용	해석
	This is where Leonardo's philosophical thinking comes into play. As I explained, the goal of these programs is to solve problems, not create more. Human-centered computing is perhaps the core of technology design as illustrated… As a matter of fact, professionals from fields such as sociology and psychology tend to think similarly to enhance our daily lives, not complicate them. Anyway, this doesn't mean that old computing is unimportant… It is still an essential element of technological design as computer specifications, such as speed, are also important factors. Finding information or communicating with your friends wouldn't matter if it took you hours just to get on a website, right?	이것이 레오나르도의 철학적 사고가 작용됩니다. 제가 설명했듯이, 이러한 프로그램의 목표는 더 이상 만들지 않도록 문제를 해결하는 것입니다. 인간 중심의 컴퓨팅은 보이는 것과 같이 기술 설계의 핵심일 수 있습니다. 사실, 사회학과 심리학과 같은 분야의 전문가들은 우리의 일상 생활을 복잡하게 만들지 않고 향상시키려고 비슷한 생각을 갖고 있습니다. 어쨌든 이것은 구형 컴퓨팅이 중요하지 않다는 것을 의미하지는 않습니다… 속도와 같은 컴퓨터 사양이 중요한 요소이기 때문에 구형 컴퓨팅은 기술 설계의 여전히 필수 요소입니다. 웹 사이트에 접속하거나 친구들이랑 소통하는데 몇 시간이 걸리면 아무 의미가 없겠죠?

12. [Main Idea – Main Purpose] What is the purpose of the lecture?

(A) To discuss Leonardo da Vinci's philosophical thinking ~~embedded in his work~~ *(wrong fact)*

(B) **To explain the fundamental roots of creating computer programs**

(C) To illustrate the distinctive characteristics of technological design ~~developers~~ *(partial error)*

(D) To show that human needs and wants are considered in ~~various fields~~ in today's society *(partial error)* ★

12. 강의의 목적이 무엇인가?

(A) 레오나르도 다빈치의 ~~작품 속~~ 그의 철학적 사고에 대해 논하기 위해

(B) **컴퓨터 프로그램 제작의 근본을 설명하기 위해**

(C) 기술 설계 ~~개발자~~의 특성을 설명하기 위해

(D) 오늘날 사회의 ~~다양한 분야에서~~ 인간의 필요와 욕구가 고려되고 있음을 보여주기 위해 ★

해설 | (A) 강의에서 교수가 강조한 레오나르도 다빈치의 철학적 사고는 컴퓨터 프로그램 개발에서의 유용성이며, 그의 작품 속에서의 의의는 강의의 목적에서 벗어난다. (C) 강의의 중점은 개발자가 아닌 그들이 하는 일인 기술 설계 개발 그 자체이다. (D) 인간의 필요와 욕구가 프로그램 개발에 고려되고 있음을 보여주기는 하나 이것을 보여주는 것은 강의의 초점이 아니다. 또한, 다양한 분야라고 하기에는 강의의 주제가 국한되어 있다.

13. [Detail – Characteristic] What part of Leonardo da Vinci's work does the professor stress as a critical aspect of his work?

(A) His ~~inventive and spontaneous~~ thinking process *(not mentioned)*

(B) His well-rounded ~~insight~~ as a philosopher, an artist, and a polymath. *(wrong fact)* ★

(C) His ~~enlightened perspectives~~ in the various fields he studied *(not mentioned)*

(D) **His designs that were meant to satisfy people's problems**

13. 교수는 레오나르도 다빈치의 연구에서 어느 부분이 중요한 측면이라고 강조하는가?

(A) 그의 ~~독창적이고 자발적인~~ 사고 과정

(B) 철학자, 예술가, 박식가로서의 균형 잡힌 ~~통찰력~~ ★

(C) 그가 연구한 다양한 분야에서의 ~~계몽된 관점~~

(D) **사람들의 문제를 충족시키기 위한 그의 디자인**

해설 | (A) 레오나르도 다빈치의 독창성과 자발성에 대한 내용은 본문에 언급되지 않는다. (B) 교수가 강조하는 것은 다빈치의 통찰력이 아닌 인간의 필요와 문제 해소를 목표로 한 그의 디자인이다. 초점이 벗어나 있음으로 오답. (C) 다양한 분야에서 그가 한 기여가 언급되기는 하나 그 관점의 특징에 대한 설명은 강의에서 다뤄지지 않는다.

14. [Inference – Purpose/Intention] Why does the professor stop from further explaining old computing?

(A) Because he believes old computing is ~~relatively less significant~~ than new computing *(not mentioned)* ★

(B) Because he wishes ~~to discuss~~ old computing ~~next time~~ *(not mentioned)*

(C) Because he supposes that new computing is the main point of his lecture, not old computing

(D) Because he thinks old computing is ~~not related~~ to new computing in any way *(not mentioned)*

14. 교수가 왜 구형 컴퓨팅에 대해 더 이상 설명하지 않는가?

(A) 구형 컴퓨팅이 신형 컴퓨팅보다 ~~상대적으로 덜 중요하다~~고 믿기 때문에 ★

(B) 구형 컴퓨팅은 ~~다음에 이야기하~~고 싶기 때문에

(C) 그는 구형 컴퓨팅이 아니라 신형 컴퓨팅이 이 강의의 핵심이라고 생각하기 때문에

(D) 구형 컴퓨팅이 신형 컴퓨팅과 ~~전혀 관련이 없다~~고 생각하기 때문에

> **해설** | (A) 교수는 구형 컴퓨팅의 중요성과 그 의의를 강조한다. 또한, 신형과 구형 컴퓨팅의 상대적 중요성에 대해서는 언급하지 않는다. (B) 교수는 구형 컴퓨팅이 본 강의의 주제와 무관해 깊이 파고들지 않을 것이라고만 한다. 다음시간에 구형 컴퓨팅에 대해 이야기 할 지는 추측 할 수 없는 바다. (D) 구형 컴퓨팅과 신형 컴퓨팅의 관계 및 관련성에 대해서는 강의에서 언급되지 않는다.

15. [Detail – Methodology] According to the professor, how do developers in the field of technology design, new computing, get their ideas?

(A) They ~~study works~~ by Leonardo da Vinci and apply his rules to their work. *(wrong fact)* ★

(B) They get advice from increasingly ~~popular websites with a massive database~~. *(not mentioned)*

(C) They refer to the public's demands and its purposes of using computers.

(D) They develop their work based on ~~futuristic and revolutionary~~ thinking. *(wrong fact)*

15. 교수에 의하면, 기술 디자인, 신형 컴퓨팅 분야의 개발자들은 어떻게 아이디어를 얻는가?

(A) 레오나르도 다빈치의 ~~작품을 연구하고 그의 규칙을~~ 일에 적용한다. ★

(B) 그들은 ~~방대한 데이터베이스를 가진 점점 인기~~를 끌고 있는 웹사이트로부터 조언을 받는다.

(C) 대중의 요구와 컴퓨터 사용의 목적을 본다.

(D) 그들은 ~~미래적이고 혁명적인~~ 사고에 기초하여 그들의 일을 발전시킨다.

> **해설** | (A) 다빈치의 작품 연구는 언급되지 않는다. 또한, 개발자들은 그의 규칙이 아닌 사고방식을 적용시킨다고 교수가 설명한다. (B) 인기 있는 웹사이트의 데이터베이스 참고는 강의에서 언급되지 않는다. (D) 미래적이고 혁명적인 사고와 인간 중심적인 사고는 무관하므로 오답.

16. [Detail – Difference/Contrast] In the lecture, the professor explains two branches of technological design. Indicate whether each of the following is a feature of old computing, new computing, both, or neither.

	Old Computing	New Computing	Both	Neither
(A) Concerns the effectiveness and usability of computers		○		
(B) Develops technologies involved in improving computer speed	○			
(C) Contributes to simplifying computer components that could otherwise be perplexing				○
(D) Involves the application of philosophy for the ultimate benefit of the society			○	

해설 | (C) 컴퓨터 구성 요소의 단순화는 신형 컴퓨팅과 구형 컴퓨팅의 목적 및 역할 그 어느 것으로도 언급되지 않기 때문에 오답.

---

17. [Detail – Similarity/Comparison] What do Leonardo da Vinci's work and new computing have in common?

(A) They are both ~~conservative~~. they preserve and consist of the ~~old principles and ideas~~ *(wrong fact)*

(B) Both are easily exploitable and ~~accessible by the public~~ *(partial error)* ★

(C) Both comprise ~~profound scientific research~~ and experiments *(not mentioned)*

(D) **They contain advances in both philosophical and mechanical aspects**

해설 | (A) 보수성과 오래된 아이디어의 보존은 신형 컴퓨팅과 레오나르도 다빈치의 작품 그 어느 것에도 해당되는 내용이 아니므로 오답. (B) 인간 중심의 사고에 기반한다는 점에서 이용의 용이함은 공통되지만 대중의 접근성은 신형 컴퓨팅에만 적용되는 내용이다. (C) 신형 컴퓨팅에만 해당되는 부분; 과학 연구와 실험이 레오나르도 다빈치의 작품을 구성했음은 언급되지 않는다.

TEST 3 set 2-1

Conversation
The championship games

문단주제	본문내용	해석

Listen to a conversation between a student and his soccer coach.

학생과 축구 코치의 대화를 들으시오.

단락 1
학생의 챔피언십 경기 불참석 사유

C: Got a minute, Mike?

S: Of course! Great game last night, right? Who would've thought that we would make it to the State Championships?

C: (laughs) It's a huge improvement from last season. [Q1-B] Since you became the team captain at the beginning of this season, team cooperation has advanced significantly.

S: That's quite flattering. Thanks, Coach! That means a lot. Oh, by the way, why did you call me in?

C: Oh, I got a little sidetracked, didn't I? [Q1] I called you in because James told me that you might not be able to participate in the championship games.

S: Oh, I'm sorry. I should've consulted with you in the first place. Well… [Q2] my internship interview is on the day we leave for the game.

C: Oh wow, stepping up your game, huh?

S: Yeah, [Q1-A] it's for an internship with the university's advertising agency.

C: 시간 좀 있어, 마이크?

S: 물론이죠! 어젯밤에 멋진 경기였죠? 우리가 주 챔피언십에 진출할 거라고 누가 생각 했겠어요?

C: (웃음) 지난 시즌보다 많이 늘었지. [Q1-B] 시즌 초반에 네가 팀 주장으로 나섰을 때부터 팀 협동이 상당히 발전했어.

S: 정말 기쁜 소식이네요. 고마워요, 코치님! 아, 그런데 왜 저를 부르셨죠?

C: 오, 내가 주제에서 벗어났지? [Q1] 네가 챔피언십 경기에 참가할 수 없을지도 모른다고 제임스가 말하길래 널 부른 거야.

S: 아, 죄송해요. 처음부터 코치님께 상의했어야 했는데. 사실… [Q2] 저희 게임 하러 떠나는 날에 인턴 면접이 있어서요.

C: 오 그렇구나, 열심히 하려고 노력하나 보네?

S: 네, [Q1-A] 대학 광고 대행사와의 인턴쉽을 위한 거예요.

단락 2
대안 제의

C: I see. Isn't there an alternative way though? Like rescheduling the interview or something?

S: I thought about that, but I don't think it would give them a good impression of me as a candidate if I asked to reschedule. It's a very popular and competitive position, you know?

C: I understand. Let's see. [Q3-D] Well, we leave on Wednesday afternoon, but the games don't actually start until Thursday morning, so you could consider taking public transportation if it's not a problem for you. I'm sure the athletics department will cover the cost.

S: Well, actually, coach, I looked into the bus schedule, but the only available time for the bus that goes from here to the championship place is around 3 o'clock in the morning. And other transportation systems, like the subway, won't take me there unless I transfer like a million times.

C: 그렇구나. 그래도 다른 방법이 없을까? 인터뷰 일정을 변경한다던가?

S: 그 점에 대해 생각해봤지만, 일정을 변경 해달라고 요청하면 후보자로서 좋은 인상을 주진 않을 거 같아요. 아주 인기 있고 경쟁적인 자리거든요.

C: 그래 이해한다. 어디 보자. [Q3-D] 우린 수요일에 떠나지만 경기는 목요일 아침까지는 시작 안 해. 그러니 문제가 되지 않는다면 대중교통을 이용할 수도 있어. 교통비는 체육학과 부서에서 부담 해 줄 거야.

S: 사실, 코치님, 제가 버스 스케줄을 봤는데요, 여기서부터 챔피언십 장소까지 가는 버스를 탈 수 있는 유일한 시간은 새벽 3시 밖에 없습니다. 그리고 지하철 같은 다른 교통 수단을 이용 했을 때 백만 번을 환승하지 않는 이상 못 가요.

문단주제	본문내용	해석
단락 3 챔피언십 경기 체계	**C:** I see… That won't be good since you wouldn't be able to play as hard without enough rest. [Q3] But, you do know that the championship consists of 3 games though, right? There's one game each day. **S:** Really? Right, I totally forgot about that. **C:** So, even if you missed the first game, you'd still be a big help to the team. If you want to participate in all of the games, why not try to talk to the agency and explain your situation? **S:** [Q4-A] Well, like I said, coach, I'd hate to give them a sense of inability or irresponsibility. [Q2-A/Q5-A] I'm not implying that this internship position is any more important than the championship games. [Q5] I've devoted a lot of time and effort to practicing, and we finally reached this point, but this internship chance doesn't come around every day. I hope you can understand that. **C:** Of course, Mike. As your coach, I've seen how passionate you are outside the field as well, and I will support whatever decision you make. **S:** Thank you, coach. But like you suggested, [Q4-B, Q4] I'll look into public transportation and try to be there for the second game! [Q2-D] We, as one, worked very hard to get to the championship, and I don't want to let my team down. **C:** Great, that sounds good, Mike! Well, I wish you the best of luck with the interview. **S:** Thanks, coach, I'll see you later!	**C:** 알겠다… 충분한 휴식 없이 열심히 경기를 뛸 수 없기 때문에 좋지 않을 거야. [Q3] 하지만 챔피언십은 3경기로 이루어져 있고 매일 한 경기가 있다는 거 알고 있긴 하지? **S:** 진짜요? 아 맞다, 완전히 잊고 있었네요. **C:** 첫 번째 게임을 놓쳤다고 하더라도 팀에 큰 도움이 될 거야. 모든 게임에 참가하고 싶다면, 회사와 이야기하고 상황을 설명하는 것이 어떨까? **S:** [Q4-A] 음, 제가 말했듯이, 코치님, 저는 그들에게 제가 무능하거나 무책임한 모습을 보여주고 싶지 않습니다. [Q2-A/Q5-A] 이 인턴쉽이 챔피언십 경기보다 더 중요하다는 뜻은 아니에요. [Q5] 저는 연습에 많은 시간과 노력을 쏟아 붓고 여기까지 왔지만 이런 인턴 기회는 매일 오는 게 아니라서 코치님께서 이걸 이해해주셨으면 합니다. **C:** 당연하지, 마이크. 너의 코치로서 나는 네가 경기장 밖에서도 얼마나 열정적인지 보았고, 네가 내리는 결정은 무엇이든 응원할거야. **S:** 감사합니다, 코치님. 하지만 코치님께서 제안하신 대로 [Q4-B, Q4] 대중교통을 알아보고 두 번째 게임에 참가하도록 하겠습니다! [Q2-D] 우리는 한 팀으로서 챔피언십에 진출하기 위해 엄청나게 열심히 노력했고, 저의 팀을 실망시키고 싶지 않아요. **C:** 좋아, 마이크! 인터뷰 잘가길 바랄게. **S:** 고맙습니다, 코치님. 나중에 봬요!

01. **[Main Idea – Main Purpose]** What does the coach want to talk about with the student?

(A) An upcoming interview for an internship at ~~the university~~ that the coach is ~~promoting~~ *(wrong fact)*

(B) The ~~student's contributions~~ to the team as the new captain *(too specific)*

(C) **The reason the student is undecided about attending the championship**

(D) The transportation methods by which the team can get to the championship games *(too specific)* ★

01. 코치는 학생과 무슨 이야기를 하고 싶어 하는가?

(A) 코치가 ~~홍보하는 대학~~ 인턴십 인터뷰에 대해

(B) 새 주장으로서 팀에 대한 ~~학생의 공헌~~에 대해

(C) **챔피언십에 참여하는 것에 대한 결정을 내리지 못하고 있는 이유에 대해**

(D) 팀이 챔피언쉽 게임에 참가할 수 있는 운송수단에 대해★

해설 | (A) 코치가 홍보하는지는 지문의 내용으로 추측할 수 없다. 또한, 대학 인턴쉽이 아닌 대학 광고 대행사와의 인턴쉽이므로 오답. (B) 초반에 인사말을 나눌 때 간단히 언급되기는 하나 대화의 극히 일부분이며 코치가 학생을 부른 궁극적인 이유가 아니다. (D) 대화 중 코치가 학생에게 몇 가지 해결책을 제안하는 것은 맞으나 코치가 학생을 찾은 궁극적인 이유는 아니므로 오답.

02. **[Detail – Problem/Difficulty]** According to the student, why is the interview for the internship position a problem?

(A) He ~~prioritizes the internship position over~~ the soccer captain position *(wrong fact)*

(B) The transportation system doesn't take the student ~~to the interview place~~ directly *(not mentioned)*

(C) It's not practical for an applicant to reschedule an interview *(unrelated to the question)* ★

(D) **The interview time overlaps with the championship games**

02. 학생에 따르면, 인턴쉽 면접이 왜 문제가 되는가?

(A) 학생은 축구팀 캡틴 자리보다 ~~인턴쉽 포지션을 우선시 하기~~ 때문에

(B) 학생을 ~~인터뷰 장소로 데려가 줄 직행의 교통수단이 없기~~ 때문에

(C) 지원자가 인터뷰 일정을 변경하는 것은 실용적이지 않기 때문에 ★

(D) **인터뷰시간은 챔피언십 경기와 겹치기 때문에**

해설 | (A) 학생은 인턴쉽이 챔피언십 경기보다 중요하다는 뜻이 아님을 명확하게 말하므로 오답. (B) 인터뷰 장소로의 이동에 대한 어려움은 언급되지 않는다. 챔피언십 경기장까지 지하철을 타고 갈 경우 환승을 여러 번 해야 한다는 번거로움을 왜곡시켜 놓은 것으로 오답. (C) 맞는 말이지만 인턴쉽 면접이 학생에게 문제가 되는 이유는 아니다. 인터뷰 일정을 변경하는 것은 어떠냐는 코치의 제안에 대한 학생의 의견일 뿐이다.

03. **[Detail – Misconception]** What was the student's misconception about the championship game?

(A) **That the champion is decided through a single game**

(B) That it's very burdensome to get to the championship place using public transportation *(unrelated to the question)*

(C) That the championship comprises several games over few days *(fact, but unrelated to the question)* ★

(D) That it actually takes place one day after the arrival at the game venue *(fact, but unrelated to the question)*

03. 챔피언십 경기에 대한 학생의 오해는 무엇인가?

(A) **우승팀은 한 경기를 통해 결정된다는 것**

(B) 대중교통을 이용해 챔피언십 경기장에 가는 것은 매우 부담스럽다는 것

(C) 챔피언십은 며칠 동안 여러 경기로 구성되어 있다는 것 ★

(D) 실제 경기는 경기장 도착 하루 뒤에 열린다는 것

해설 | (B) 학생이 오해한 것이 아닌 교통편을 알아본 후 내린 결론이기 때문에 질문이 묻는 바와 관련이 없다. (C), (D) 학생이 오해했던 것이 아닌 코치가 알려주는 사실이다. (C), (D)는 (B)와 마찬가지로 질문이 묻는 바와 관련이 없다.

04. [Detail – Solution] What is the student most likely to do about the 'internship or championship' dilemma?

(A) He will try to explain his situation to the agency and ~~delay his interview~~ *(wrong fact)*

(B) He will have to ~~abandon the championship game~~ for the internship position *(partial error)* ★

(C) He will attempt to attend both of the events

(D) He is going to ~~give up on the interview~~ because he wishes to participate in all of the games. *(wrong fact)*

04. 학생이 '인턴쉽 또는 챔피언쉽' 딜레마에 어떻게 할지에 대해 가장 가능성이 높은 것은 무엇인가?

(A) 그는 자신의 상황을 기관에 설명하고 ~~인터뷰를 연기하려고~~ 노력할거다.

(B) 인턴쉽 포지션을 위해 ~~챔피언십 경기를 포기해~~ 야 할 거다 ★

(C) 그는 두 행사 모두에 참석하려고 시도할 거다.

(D) 모든 경기에 참여하고 싶어서 ~~인터뷰를 포기할~~ 예정이다.

> 해설 | (A) 인턴쉽 인터뷰를 연기하라는 코치의 제의에 학생은 재차 본인이 무능하거나 무책임한 모습을 보여주기 싫음을 강조한다. (B) 학생은 챔피언십 경기를 완전히 포기하는 것이 아니라 세 경기 중 인터뷰 날과 겹치지 않는 나머지 두 경기에 참여할 수 있도록 노력할 것이라고 한다. (D) 학생은 인턴쉽 기회가 흔치 않아 포기하고 싶지 않다고 말한다.

05. [Inference – Imply] What does the student imply when he says this: 🎧

> "I've devoted a lot of time and effort to practicing, and we finally reached this point, but this internship chance doesn't come around every day. I hope you can understand that."

(A) That the interview for the internship is ~~more important~~ than the championship *(wrong fact)*

(B) That he has taken both into contemplation, and it's difficult for him to give up on the internship interview

(C) That once he misses this internship interview, he will ~~never get another chance~~ *(too extreme)* ★

(D) That he doesn't want to let the championship game ~~hinder his path~~ *(not mentioned)*

05. 학생은 이렇게 말하며 무엇을 암시하는가? 🎧

> "저는 연습에 많은 시간과 노력을 쏟아 붓고 여기까지 왔지만 이런 인턴 기회는 매일 오는게 아니라서 코치님께서 이걸 이해해주셨으면 합니다.."

(A) 인턴쉽 인터뷰가 ~~챔피언십보다 중요하다는 것~~

(B) 두 가지를 모두 숙고해 봤고 인턴쉽 면접을 포기하기 어렵다는 것

(C) 이번 인턴쉽 인터뷰를 놓친다면 ~~다시는 기회가 없을 거라는 것~~ ★

(D) 챔피언십 경기가 자신의 ~~진로에 방해가 되지 않~~ 길 바란다는 것

> 해설 | (A) 학생은 인턴쉽이 챔피언십 경기보다 중요하다는 뜻이 아님을 명확하게 말하므로 오답. (C) 인턴쉽 기회가 흔치 않다고 말을 하긴 하지만 기회가 다시 오지 않을 것이라는 해석은 너무 과장된 표현이므로 오답. (D) 학생은 본 대화에서 챔피언십과 진로 사이에 아무런 관련도 짓지 않는다. 따라서, 챔피언십 경기가 학생의 진로에 방해가 되는지는 추측할 수 없다.

TEST 3 set 2-2
Lecture 1
Earth's age

문단주제	본문내용	해석

Listen to part of a lecture in a geology class.

단락 1
지구의 나이에 대한 논쟁 및 Lord Kelvin의 이론

P: Geologists believe that Earth is about 4.54 billion years old. [Q9-C] Using radiometric, or radioactive, dating, they calculated the ages of cosmic materials like meteorites, debris from asteroids and comets, and the oldest terrestrial samples. Ultimately they concluded that Earth's age is analogous to the ages of these rocks. [Q6] Prior to this theory, there were major disputes regarding Earth's age, and today we'll explore some of those.

Okay, let's look at Lord Kelvin's theory. I'm sure you've heard of the laws of thermodynamics, right? They are his biggest contributions to the development of physics. [Q7-C] He was able to apply his understanding of heat to his rudimentary understanding of Earth. [Q6-D] He based his theory on the assumption that Earth began in a molten state and gradually became a solid body. [Q8-D] It's said that solid Earth's temperature was nearly the rock's melting point, around 600 to 1200° C. [Q7-B] As it cooled into a solid body, Earth radiated heat into the relatively frigid outer space. Kelvin studied this phenomenon and posited that Earth's heat loss occurred through what he termed "thermal diffusion."

S: You mean, heat diffusion?

단락 2
열확산

P: More or less. [Q8] For those of you who are not familiar with the concept, let me give you a simple example to illustrate it. Let's say you're boiling water for coffee and realize that your craving went away. Then, you put the kettle into the freezer because you don't want to waste the water. What do you think would happen?

S: That's quite obvious; the temperature would drop.

P: Correct! But the cooling process is much more complicated. Objects don't just go from hot to cold instantaneously. It occurs gradually and the "layers" of the object have different temperatures, a temperature gradient. When the pot is put into the freezer, the outermost layer, the pot's exterior, would cool first, creating a temperature difference between the surface layer and the layer just below it.

지질학 강의의 일부분을 들으시오.

P: 지질학자들은 지구의 나이가 약 45억 4천만 년이라고 믿어요. [Q9-C] 그들은 방사성 측정법 또는 방사성 연대 측정법을 사용하여 운석, 소행성, 혜성의 파편, 그리고 가장 오래된 육상 샘플과 같은 우주 물질들의 나이를 계산했습니다. 궁극적으로 그들은 지구의 나이는 이 암석의 나이와 유사하다고 결론 지었는데요. [Q6] 이 이론 이전에는 지구의 나이에 관한 주요한 논쟁이 있었고, 오늘 우리는 그 중 일부를 살펴볼 겁니다.

좋아요, Lord Kelvin의 이론을 한번 살펴보죠. 열역학 법칙에 대해 들어본 적 있을 텐데, 그렇죠? 이 법칙들은 그가 물리학 발전에 한 가장 큰 기여입니다. [Q7-C] 그는 열에 대한 이해를 지구에 대한 그의 기초적인 이해에 적용시킬 수 있었습니다. [Q6-D] 그는 지구가 용융 상태에서 시작되어 점차적으로 고체가 되었다는 가정을 그의 이론의 기반으로 삼았습니다. [Q8-D] 지구의 고체 온도는 암석의 융점인 약 600-1200 °C에 가까웠다고 합니다. [Q7-B] 고체로 냉각되면서 지구는 상대적으로 추운 우주 공간으로 열을 방출했습니다. 켈빈은 이 현상을 연구하고 지구의 열 손실은 그가 "열 확산"이라고 불렀던 것을 통해 발생했다고 가정했죠.

S: 열 확산을 말씀하시는 건가요?

P: 어느 정도죠. [Q8] 이 개념에 익숙하지 않은 분들을 위해 간단한 예를 하나 들어보겠습니다. 커피를 마시려고 물을 끓이고 있다가 갈망이 사라졌다는 것을 깨닫는다고 가정해볼게요. 그리고, 물을 낭비하고 싶지 않기 때문에 주전자를 냉동실에 넣는다고 생각해봅시다. 무슨 일이 일어날 것 같나요?

S: 뻔하죠, 온도가 떨어질 겁니다.

P: 맞습니다! 하지만 냉각 과정은 훨씬 더 복잡합니다. 물체는 순간적으로 뜨겁다가 차갑게 되지 않아요. 냉각 과정은 점차적으로 발생하고 물체의 "층"은 다른 온도, 즉 온도 변화도가 있습니다. 냄비를 냉동고에 넣었을 때 가장 바깥 쪽 층인 냄비의 외부가 먼저 냉각되어 표면층과 그 바로 아래의 층 사이에 온도 차이가 생깁니다.

문단주제	본문내용	해석
단락 3 Lord Kelvin의 이론이 받은 비판	[Q7] According to the law of heat transfer, heat from a body at a higher temperature flows to a body at a lower temperature, meaning that heat would diffuse from deeper layers. Kelvin used this property to calculate the length of earth's cooling by estimating the difference between the original and current temperatures. He speculated that the original temperature was near the melting point of rocks and with some additional calculations, concluded that Earth was no more than 100 million years old. His theory initially received great acknowledgment and acclaim from physicists, but it induced an uproar among geologists. Can anyone guess why? S: Well… I'd assume it was because geologists theorize that sedimentation and erosion take hundreds of millions of years. So… it wouldn't make sense for Earth to be less than 100 million years old. P: Exactly, Susan! As time passed critics looked for errors in Kelvin's calculations, but their arguments were just as faulty and inadequate. (laughs) By the early 1900's, radioactivity and heat release from radioactive decay in Earth's interior were discovered. [Q9] Scientists claimed that this additional heat source, which was absent from Kelvin's calculations, would've made Earth much older than Kelvin's estimation. However, the amount of radioactive heat is now considered insignificant, so Kelvin's calculations wouldn't have been greatly affected by it.	[Q7] 열 전달의 법칙에 따르면, 열은 온도가 더 높은 물체에서부터 온도가 더 낮은 물체로 흐르고, 이는 더 깊은 층으로부터 열이 확산된다는 것을 의미하죠. 켈빈은 이 특성을 사용하여 지구의 원래 온도와 현재 온도의 차이를 추정하여 냉각 기간을 계산했습니다. 그는 지구의 원래 온도가 암석의 융점 근처에 있었다고 추측했으며, 몇 가지 추가 계산을 통해 지구의 나이가 1억 년이 넘지 않았다고 결론 지었다. 그의 이론은 처음에는 물리학자들로부터 큰 인정과 찬사를 받았지만 지질 학자들 사이에서는 소동을 불러 일으켰습니다. 왜 그런지 짐작할 수 있는 사람 있나요? S: 글쎄요… 아마도 지질학자들이 침전과 침식이 수억 년이 걸린다고 이론을 세웠기 때문일 거예요. 그러니까… 지구가 1억 년 미만이라는 건 말이 안 된다는 거죠. P: 바로 그겁니다, Susan! 시간이 흐르면서 비평가들은 켈빈의 계산에서 오류를 찾았지만, 그들의 주장 역시 잘못되고 부적절 했습니다. (웃음) 1900년대 초에는 방사능과 지구 내부의 방사성 붕괴로부터 열 방출이 발견된 상태였습니다. [Q9] 과학자들은 켈빈의 계산에 없었던 이 추가적인 열원이 지구가 켈빈의 추정치보다 훨씬 오래 되었을 거라고 주장했습니다. 하지만 방사능 열의 양은 이제 미미한 것으로 간주되어 켈빈의 계산은 그에 크게 영향을 받지 않았을 겁니다.
단락 4 John Perry의 이의제기 및 계산법	S: Then why was Kelvin's calculation wrong? I mean, his conclusion that Earth was only 100 million years old wasn't proven incorrect… P: Well, this is where it gets interesting. Kelvin had an assistant named John Perry, who was a great patron of his employer. [Q11] Um… how should I explain this? I would say it was much like a coup d'état. Ironically, Perry disputed Kelvin's theory and discredited his calculations in 1895. He stated that Kelvin's assumption of a solid Earth was fundamentally wrong. [Q10] In fact, beneath Earth's crust was liquid, or semi-liquid.	S: 그렇다면 왜 켈빈의 계산이 틀렸나요? 지구가 겨우 1억 년밖에 되지 않았다는 그의 결론은 틀렸다는 것이 증명 되지는 않았잖아요… P: 음, 여기서 재미있어집니다. 켈빈에게는 고용주의 훌륭한 후원자이기도 했던 John Perry라는 조수가 있었습니다. [Q11] 음.. 어떻게 설명해야 할까? 쿠데타 같은 거였죠. 아이러니하게도 페리는 켈빈의 이론에 대해 논쟁을 벌였으며 1895년에 그의 계산에 이의를 제기했습니다. 그는 켈빈이 고체 지구의 기본적인 추측이 잘못되었다고 말했습니다. [Q10] 사실 지구의 지각 밑은 액체나 반액체였습니다.

TEST 3 set 2-2

문단주제	본문내용	해석
	[Q7-A] With further scrutiny, he discovered that thermal diffusion does not happen in liquid or semi-liquid bodies; instead, convection, the circulation of hot material, occurs. Imagine heat following a circular pathway in the crust instead of the outward diffusion model. Not only does the former keep large amounts of heat spread through the whole, but it also suggests that cooling happens at a much slower rate. S: Were Perry's calculations close to today's estimated age of the Earth? P: It wasn't exactly 4.54 billion years, but considering the lack of technology, his estimation of Earth's age, 3 billion years, was surprisingly accurate. Unfortunately, his work didn't receive much recognition from his contemporaries because it was constructed on a whole different framework. Later, when continental drift was proven, Perry's theory began receiving the recognition it deserved.	[Q7-A] 추가적인 조사를 통해, 그는 열 확산이 액체 또는 반액체에서는 발생하지 않는다는 것을 발견했습니다. 대신, 대류, 즉 뜨거운 물질의 순환이 발생합니다. 외향 확산 모델 대신 지각의 원형 경로를 따라가는 열을 상상해보세요. 전자는 전체에 많은 양의 열을 퍼뜨릴 뿐만 아니라 냉각이 훨씬 느린 속도로 발생한다는 것을 보여줍니다. S: 페리의 계산은 오늘날 지구의 추정 연령에 가까웠나요? P: 정확히 45억 4천만 년은 아니었지만, 기술 부족을 고려할 때, 그가 추정한 지구의 나이인 30억만 년은 놀라울 정도로 정확했어요. 안타깝게도 그의 연구는 완전히 다른 틀 위에 세워졌기 때문에 동시대인들로부터 많은 인정을 받지 못했습니다. 나중에 대륙 표류가 입증되었을 때, 페리의 이론은 받아야 마땅했던 인정을 받기 시작했어요.

06. [Main Idea] What is main topic of the lecture?

(A) Contrasting theories and opinions regarding the age of the earth
(B) Scientific studies of heat diffusion *(too specific)*
(C) Lord Kelvin's successful research that has helped today's scientists determine the earth's age *(too specific)* ★
(D) Research of the mechanisms behind the early formation of the earth *(too specific)*

06. 강의의 주제는 무엇인가?

(A) 지구의 나이에 관한 대조되는 이론과 의견
(B) 열 확산에 관한 과학적 연구
(C) 오늘날의 과학자들이 지구의 나이를 결정하는 데 도움이 된 켈빈의 성공적인 연구 ★
(D) 지구의 초기 형성에 대한 메커니즘 연구

해설 | (B) 열 확산은 Lord Kelvin이 지구 나이에 대한 이론을 세울 때 기반으로 사용한 개념이다. 강의는 열 확산의 연구가 아닌 지구의 나이 계산에 대한 논쟁을 집중적으로 다룬다. (C) 지구의 실제 나이와 가장 근접한 값을 계산한 존 페리의 연구는 켈빈의 연구에 기반하지 않았다. 페리는 켈빈의 계산의 한계점을 지적하고 새로운 개념을 적용시켜 계산했다는 점에서 켈빈의 연구는 성공적이었다고도, 오늘날의 과학자들에게 도움이 되었다고도 할 수 없다. (D) 지구의 형성과정은 교수가 켈빈의 이론의 가정을 설명할 때 간략히 언급한 것으로, 강의의 극히 일부분에 불과하다.

07. [Detail – Methodology] How did Lord Kelvin establish the fundamentals of his theory?

(A) He theorized that earth's heat loss occurred through ~~heat convection~~ *(wrong fact)*
(B) ~~He established~~ that the layers beneath earth's crust became solid through a cooling process. *(partial error)*
(C) He posited the laws of thermodynamics ~~to explain earth's cooling process.~~ *(wrong fact)* ★
(D) He demonstrated the direction in which heat contained in a solid body flowed.

07. 켈빈은 그의 이론의 근본을 어떻게 세웠는가?

(A) 그는 지구의 열 손실이 ~~열 대류~~를 통해 발생한다고 이론을 세웠다.
(B) 그는 지구의 지각 아래 층이 냉각 과정을 통해 단단해졌다는 것을 ~~입증했다~~.
(C) 그는 ~~지구의 냉각 과정을 설명하기 위해~~ 열역학의 법칙을 세웠다. ★
(D) 그는 고체에 들어있는 열이 흐르는 방향을 보여 주었다.

해설 | (A) 열 대류는 존 페리의 이론에서 사용 된 개념으로, 켈빈과는 관련이 없다. (B) 켈빈은 지구의 지각과 그 내부를 구분 지어 이론을 세우지 않았다. 냉각과정에 대해서 그는 지각 아래 층으로 한정 짓지 않고 지구 전체가 냉각과정을 통해 단단해졌다고 입증했다. (C) 열역학 법칙은 Lord Kelvin을 소개할 때 교수가 언급한 그의 대표적인 발견일 뿐, 이를 지구 나이의 이론을 위해 세웠다고 말하지 않는다. 즉, 열역학 법칙과 본 강의에서 소개 된 Lord Kelvin의 지구 나이의 계산법 사이에는 아무런 관련이 없다.

08. [Detail – Purpose] Why does the professor mention the boiling kettle?

(A) To help his students understand ~~that the earth was very hot~~ when it formed *(wrong fact)*

(B) To illustrate that the liquid interior of the earth worked as a ~~heat source for the entire earth~~ *(not mentioned)* ★

(C) To explain the mechanism of heat diffusion to his students

(D) To explain how the ~~melting point of rocks~~ is calculated *(wrong fact)*

08. 교수가 왜 끓는 주전자를 언급하는가?

(A) 지구가 형성되었을 때 ~~매우 뜨거웠다는 것을~~ 학생들이 이해하도록 돕기 위해

(B) 지구의 액체 내부가 ~~지구 전체의 열원으로~~ 작용했다는 것을 설명하기 위해 ★

(C) 학생들에게 열 확산 과정을 설명하기 위해

(D) ~~암석의 융점~~이 어떻게 계산되는지 설명하기 위해

해설 | (A) 끓는 주전자는 지구의 온도와는 전혀 관련 없는 비유이다. 매우 뜨거웠음을 이야기하는 것이 교수의 목적이었다면 끓는 주전자를 다시 냉동실에 넣는 가정은 하지 않았을 거다. (B) 지구의 열원에 대한 내용은 강의에서 언급되지 않는다. (D) 암석의 융점은 고체 상태의 지구 온도 설명 시 언급된다. 열 확산의 과정을 비유한 끓는 주전자와는 무관하다. 또한, 암석의 융점의 계산은 지문의 그 어떤 내용과도 관련이 없다.

09. [Detail – Problem] According to the critics of Lord Kelvin's theory, which of the following was false about his calculations?

(A) He failed to take all variables of heat production into account.

(B) He ~~underestimated~~ the amount of heat produced by radioactivity. *(wrong fact)* ★

(C) He falsely assumed that ~~asteroids and comets~~ actually struck the earth. *(wrong fact)*

(D) His calculations included ~~no evidence of the earth's heat loss~~ *(wrong fact)*

09. Lord Kelvin의 이론을 비판하는 사람들에 따르면, 다음 중 그의 계산에 대한 설명으로 옳지 않은 것은?

(A) 그는 열 생산의 모든 변수를 고려하지 못했다.

(B) 그는 방사능에 의해 생성되는 열의 양을 ~~과소평가했다.~~ ★

(C) 그는 ~~소행성과 혜성이~~ 실제로 지구를 강타했다고 잘못 추정했다.

(D) 그의 계산에는 ~~지구의 열 손실에 대한 어떠한 증거도 포함되지 않았다.~~

해설 | (B) 비평가들은 켈빈이 그 열의 양을 과소평가 한 것이 아니라 전혀 고려를 하지 않았음을 지적한다. (C) 소행성과 혜성에 대한 언급은 초반에 오늘날의 지질학자들이 지구의 나이를 계산한 방법에 대한 설명에서 언급되며, 켈빈의 이론과는 관련이 없다. 이를 왜곡시켜 놓은 것으로 오답. (D) 켈빈의 계산은 근본적으로 열 전달의 법칙에 근거하여 지구의 냉각기간을 계산했기 때문에 지구의 열 손실에 대한 증거는 충분히 고려했다고 볼 수 있다.

10. [Detail – Difference/Contrast] What basic assumption was Perry's theory based upon that differed from Kelvin's?

(A) That the earth's heat loss followed a circular path rather than diffusion *(unrelated to the question)* ★

(B) That the interior of the earth was in a liquid, or semi-liquid, state

(C) That the cooling process took place while the earth was being solidified *(unrelated to the question)*

(D) That the trapped heat ~~diffused~~ inward not outward *(wrong fact)*

10. 페리의 이론은 켈빈의 이론과 어떤 다른 가정을 기반으로 한 건가?

(A) 지구의 열 손실은 확산이 아닌 원형 경로를 따른다는 것 ★

(B) 지구 내부가 액체, 또는 반액체 상태라는 것

(C) 지구가 응고되는 동안 냉각 과정이 일어났다는 것

(D) 덫에 걸린 열이 바깥쪽으로 확산되지 않고, 안쪽으로 확산된다는 것

해설 | (A) 맞는 말이지만, 지구 내부가 액체와 반액체라는 사실을 가정하고 진행한 추가적인 조사를 통해 발견한 것이므로 문제가 묻는 "가정"과는 관련이 없다. (C) 켈빈의 이론에서 사용된 개념으로, 페리와는 관련이 없다. (D) 확산의 방향과 관련 없이 페리는 대류를 기반으로 본인의 이론을 입증했다.

---

11. [Inference – Imply] What does the professor mean when he says this : 🎧

> Um… how should I explain this?
> I would say it was much like a coup d'état.

(A) Perry's challenge to Kelvin encouraged a major shift in the ~~social structure~~ in the contemporary society *(wrong fact)*

(B) Perry's argument resembles a society in which the less powerful citizens rebel against the authority

(C) ~~Kelvin abused~~ his assistants and employees including Perry *(wrong fact)*

(D) Perry's action was thought to be ~~impetuous and rebellious~~ by the society at the time *(too extreme)*

11. 교수가 이렇게 말할 때 무엇을 의미하는가? 🎧

> "음...... 어떻게 설명해야 하지?
> 쿠데타 같은 일이라고 할 수 있죠."

(A) 켈빈에 대한 페리의 도전은 현대 ~~사회의 구조에~~ 큰 변화를 불러 일으켰다.

(B) 페리의 주장은 덜 강력한 시민들이 권위에 반항하는 사회와 유사하다.

(C) 켈빈은 페리를 포함한 조수와 직원들을 학대했다.

(D) 페리의 행동은 당시 사회에서 ~~성급하고 반항적~~으로 여겨졌다.

해설 | (A) 페리의 반론은 사회구조 변화와는 무관하므로 오답. (C) 비유의 주어는 켈빈이 아닌 페리이다. 또한, 교수는 쿠데타와 페리의 반론 사이에서 학대라는 유사점을 집어내지 않는다. (D) 페리가 켈빈과는 전혀 다른 틀에서 이론을 세웠다는 점에서 당시 인정을 받지 못하기는 했으나 이것이 성급하거나 반항적으로 여겨졌다고는 볼 수 없다.

TEST 3 set 2-3

Lecture 2
Illegitimate theater

문단 주제	본문내용	해석

Listen to part of a lecture in a theater class.

단락 1 정극과 비정극

P: Before we begin today's lesson, let's review the main topics of our last class for those who were absent. Umm… legitimate theater was a form of theatrical art that relied on spoken words without singing, dancing, or musical components. [Q16-B] Due to Great Britain's Licensing Act of 1737, strict restraints were put on media and only certain theaters were permitted to perform serious literary shows like Shakespeare's "Romeo and Juliet." Don't get the wrong idea here; the censorship law didn't bar theaters from performing less serious and more entertaining pieces, like comedies, but they were still under governmental control. We refer to this as illegitimate theater.

단락 2 대중적인 연극의 유래

[Q12] Let's look at theatrical development in the United States. Significant cultural changes occurred as the conflict between the North and the South gradually waned after the Civil War. [Q13] More jobs became available to a greater number of people and rural residents flocked to cities between 1870 through 1920. International immigration further increased the populations of the cities. As a consequence, urban productivity and incomes skyrocketed as well. As people had less strenuous jobs and more money, their attention turned to leisure activities or travel. [Q13] These two changes, demographic and economic, worked as catalysts to begin a new era of the theatrical arts that we now refer to as popular theater. Popular theater was more like illegitimate theater in that serious plays were rarely handled. Vaudeville was one of the main forms of popular theater that flourished at the time.

단락 3 보드빌의 어원

For those of you who speak French, vaudeville may sound quite familiar… Although the term's origin remains obscure, one of the suggested theories is that it described satirical songs that were once popular in France. Others theorize that it means "voice of the city" or "songs of the town." Anyway, let's not get hung up on this, because the "vaudeville" we are discussing has nothing to do with French songs.

연극 수업의 일부를 들으시오.

P: 오늘 수업을 시작하기 전에, 안 왔던 사람들을 위해 지난 수업의 주제를 복습해봅시다. 음… 정극(legitimate theater)은 노래, 춤 그리고 음악적인 요소 없이 구어에 기반하는 연극 예술의 한 형태입니다. [Q16-B] 대영제국의 1737년 Licensing Act 때문에 매체에 엄격한 제한이 걸렸고 일부 특정한 극장만이 셰익스피어의 "로미오와 줄리엣"같은 진지한 문학 공연을 하도록 허락되었습니다. 여기서 오해하지 마세요; 검열 법은 덜 진지하고 더 재미있는 희극과 같은 작품을 공연하는 것도 막지는 않았습니다. 하지만 그들은 여전히 정부의 통제 하에 있었습니다. 우리는 이것을 비정극(illegitimate theater)이라고 부릅니다.

[Q12] 미국에서 연극의 발전을 봅시다. 남북전쟁 이후 남과 북의 갈등이 서서히 줄어들면서 중요한 문화적 변화가 일어났어요. [Q13] 더 많은 일자리가 많은 사람들에게 접근 가능해졌고 1870년에서 1920년 사이에 시골에 살던 사람들은 도시로 떼지어 옮겨갔습니다. 국제적인 이주는 도시의 인구를 더욱더 늘렸습니다. 결과적으로, 도시의 생산성과 수입 역시 하늘로 치솟았죠. 사람들이 덜 고된 일을 하고 더 많은 돈을 벌자, 그들의 주의는 여가 활동과 여행으로 옮겨갔습니다. [Q13] 이 두 가지, 인구통계학적이고 경제적인 변화는 우리가 지금 대중적인 연극(popular theater)이라고 부르는 연극 예술의 새로운 시대를 여는 촉매제로 작동했습니다. 대중적인 연극은 진지한 극이 거의 다뤄지지 않았다는 점에서 비정극과 더 비슷했어요. Vaudeville (보드빌)은 그 당시 번성했던 대중적인 연극의 주된 형식 중 하나였습니다.

여러분 중 불어를 하시는 분에게는, vaudeville은 꽤 익숙하게 들리겠죠… 이 용어의 기원은 분명하지 않지만, 제기된 이론들 중 하나는 이것이 프랑스에서 한 때 유행했던 풍자적인 노래들을 말한다는 겁니다. 다른 사람들은 이것이 "도시의 목소리" 혹은 "도시의 노래"라는 의미라는 가설을 세웁니다. 아무튼, 여기에 매달리지 맙시다, 왜냐하면 우리가 얘기하는 "vaudeville"은 프랑스 곡들과 아무 상관 없으니까요.

문단주제	본문내용	해석
단락 4 대중적인 연극의 특징	Popular theater usually consisted of a series of ten unrelated acts or performances covering a wide spectrum of theater-related options, such as magic, acrobatics, comedies, and so on. This property of popular theater may seem rather distracting and would fail to attract people, but everyone had access to every type of performance at the theater. To help you visualize, think about a convenience store. [Q14-C] You may not find "quality" products there, but the range of everyday commodities is a major benefit that convenience stores provide, right? [Q14] In the same sense, whatever your taste in theater arts, whether it was comedies or musicals, it was there. Pretty convenient, huh?	대중적인 연극은 보통 넓은 범위의 극과 관련된 마술, 곡예, 희곡 등의 선택지 중 10개의 관련 없는 연기나 공연의 연속으로 구성되어있었습니다. 대중적인 연극의 이 특성은 오히려 산만해 보이고 사람들을 끄는 데 실패했을 것 같지만, 모든 사람은 극장에서 모든 종류의 공연에 접근할 수 있었습니다. 여러분이 머릿속에 떠올리는 것을 돕기 위해, 편의점을 생각해보세요. [Q14-C] 거기서 "질 좋은" 제품을 찾진 못할 수 있지만, 넓은 범위의 일용품이 편의점이 제공하는 주된 이점이죠, 그쵸? [Q14] 같은 의미에서, 연극 예술에서 당신의 취향이 무엇이든, 그것이 희극이든 뮤지컬이든, 그건 거기에 있었어요. 꽤 편리하죠, 그쵸?
단락 5 Bijou 극장과 그 성공의 요소	Behind the exceptional success was the father of American vaudeville, Benjamin Franklin Keith. His entrepreneurial career began with the establishment of the Gaiety Museum in Boston in 1883. His continuous endeavors and triumph allowed him to build the Bijou Theater. Many theater historians note that his theater had two outstanding attractions: continuous performances and innovations. First, continuous performances meant that the doors of his theater were open all day, every day. He believed that the role of entertainment was to amuse people whenever they wanted. He would have his performers repeat their acts throughout the day and the theater was designed to operate twelve hours daily. Remember the increased urban income? It allowed workers to partake in leisure activities, and vaudeville theaters were especially popular at the time. Keith intended to exploit this through continuous performances in two ways: always filling his theater with more people and [Q15-C] captivating the audience by decorating his theater with extravagant and lavish details. Think about it… [Q15-B] you walk into a theater simply for entertainment purposes, and you feel like you've come to a luxurious hotel. Sounds tempting, right?	이 예외적인 성공 뒤에는 미국 vaudeville의 아버지, Benjamin Franklin Keith가 있었어요. 그의 사업가적인 진로는 1883년 보스턴에 Gaiety Museum이 설립되면서 시작되었습니다. 그의 끊임없는 노력과 큰 성공은 그가 Bijou 극장을 지을 수 있게 했어요. 많은 연극사학자들은 그의 극장이 두 가지 놀라운 매력, 계속되는 공연과 혁신을 가지고 있었다고 말합니다. 첫 째로, 계속되는 공연은 그의 극장 문이 하루 종일, 매일 열려있었다는 의미입니다. 그는 오락의 역할은 사람들이 원할 때 언제든 사람들을 기쁘게 하는 것이라고 믿었어요. 그는 그의 공연자들이 하루 종일 그들의 연기를 반복하게 했고 극장은 매일 12시간씩 운영되도록 설계되었습니다. 늘어난 도시의 수입을 기억하나요? 그것은 노동자들이 여가 활동에 참여하게 했고, vaudeville 극장은 그 당시 특히 인기 있었습니다. Keith는 계속되는 공연을 통해 이것을 두 가지 방식으로 이용하려고 했습니다: 더 많은 사람들로 항상 그의 극장을 채우는 것과 [Q15-C] 그의 극장을 화려하고 호화로운 세부 사항들로 장식해서 관중을 사로잡는 것. 생각해보세요… [Q15-B] 그냥 오락 목적으로 극장에 갔는데 호화로운 호텔에 간 것처럼 느껴지는 거에요. 솔깃하죠, 맞죠?
단락 6 보드빌 사업가로서의 이상	Let's shift our focus to elucidate his success as a vaudeville entrepreneur. His "fixed policy of cleanliness and order" represents his ideals as a stern businessman. He established rules by which everyone, his employees and the audience, had to abide.	Vaudeville 사업가로서의 그의 성공을 설명하는 것으로 우리의 초점을 옮겨봅시다. 그의 "깨끗함과 질서에 대한 변치 않는 정책"은 엄격한 사업가로서 그의 이상을 보여줍니다. 그는 모든 사람, 그의 고용자들과 관중들이 견뎌야 하는 규칙을 세웠습니다.

문단주제	본문내용	해석
USHER	[Q16] These forbade acts that included profanity and prevented performers from using offensive language. [Q15-D, Q17] This ensured that his theater would also appeal to women and children. Similar restrictions were placed on the audience, as well, in that they weren't allowed to interrupt the performances in any way. Previously, Civil War-era audiences displayed low-brow behavior. They would stamp their feet or talk during the performances. Keith strove to change this behavior by educating his audiences about appropriate theater behaviors. We're actually running out of time, so let's stop here until our next class. We'll continue our discussion on entrepreneurs who followed the great work of Keith, so be sure to do some research on those people!	[Q16] 이것은 불경스러운 것이 포함된 연기를 막았고 공연자들이 공격적인 말을 쓰지 못하게 했습니다. [Q15-D, Q17] 이것은 그의 극장이 여성과 아이들에게도 매력적이라는 것을 보장했습니다. 비슷한 제한이 관중들에게 또한 주어졌습니다. 그들이 어떤 방식으로든 공연을 방해해선 안됐다는 점에서요. 이전에, 남북 전쟁시대에 관중들은 교양 없는 행동을 보였습니다. 그들은 공연 중에 발을 구르거나 이야기 했어요. Keith는 그의 관중들에게 적절한 극장 예절을 가르침으로써 바꾸려고 애썼습니다. 우리는 사실 시간이 없네요, 그래서 다음 수업까지 여기서 멈춥시다. 우리는 Keith의 이 위대한 업적을 이은 사업가들에 대한 토론을 이어나갈 거에요, 그러니까 이 사람들에 대해 좀 조사해와야 해요!

12. [Main Idea] What is main topic of the lecture?

(A) One of the major cultural changes in American theater history with supporting details.

(B) General discussions of various aspects of vaudeville theaters ~~after the civil war.~~ *(too specific)*

(C) ~~Biography~~ of Benjamin Franklin Keith and details of his figure as a successful businessman *(partial error)*

(D) ~~Social changes~~ in lifestyle that directly affected the popularity of popular theater *(partial error)* ★

12. 이 강의의 주제는 무엇인가?

(A) 미국 연극사의 주된 문화적 변화 중 하나와 뒷받침하는 세부 정보

(B) ~~남북전쟁 이후~~ vaudeville 연극의 다양한 측면에 대한 일반적인 토론

(C) Benjamin Franklin Keith의 ~~전기~~와 성공적인 사업가로서 그에 대한 세부 정보

(D) 대중적인 연극의 유명세에 직접적으로 영향을 미친 생활방식의 ~~사회적 변화~~ ★

해설 | (B) Vaudeville 연극 이외에도 legitimate, illegitimate, popular 연극 등 다양한 종류들이 설명된다. 또한, 강의의 내용은 남북전쟁 이후의 연극에만 국한 되어있지 않다 – 그 전과 후의 비교, 그리고 변화의 원인까지 다뤄지기 때문에 강의의 주제로 잡기에는 매우 좁다. (C) 대중적인 연극의 성공의 예로 그의 성공과 그 요소들이 설명되기는 하나 그의 전기는 강의에서 다뤄지지 않는다. (D) 강의의 초점은 연극의 유명세에 영향을 미친 사회적 변화가 아닌 사회적 변화로 인해 영향을 받은 연극의 유명세이다.

13. [Detail – Cause] Which of the following were the primary forces that bolstered the establishment of a new form of theater art?

Click on 2 answers

(A) Increasing urban populations at the end of the 19th century.

(B) Adaptation of ~~foreign cultures~~ brought in by immense immigration movements *(not mentioned)* ★

(C) Growth in the employment and income rates

(D) ~~Economic depression~~ in rural areas caused by mass movements to the cities *(not mentioned)*

13. 다음 중 새로운 형태의 연극 예술의 설립을 강화한 주된 영향력은 무엇이었는가?

2개의 정답을 고르시오

(A) 19세기 말 도시 인구의 증가

(B) 거대한 이주 움직임이 초래한 ~~외국~~ 문화의 적응 ★

(C) 고용과 소득수입률의 증가

(D) 도시로의 큰 이동이 초래한 지방의 ~~경제 불황~~

해설 | (B) 국내적, 국제적 이주는 맞으나, 그로 인한 외국 문화의 유입은 지문에서 언급되지 않는다. (D) 지방의 경제 불황 역시 지문에서 언급되지 않는다.

14. [Inference – Purpose/Intention] Why does the professor compare vaudeville theaters to convenience stores?

(A) ~~To posit~~ that bigger-marketed industries ~~soon surpassed~~ vaudeville theaters

(B) To accentuate the thought that vaudeville theaters were ~~as common as~~ convenience stores *(not mentioned)*

(C) To elucidate that Vaudevillian performances were ~~low-quality~~ *(partial error)* ★

(D) **To explain that a myriad of entertainments was accessible in vaudeville theaters, collectively**

14. 왜 교수는 vaudeville 극장을 편의점에 비교하는가?

(A) 큰 시장에 산업들이 vaudeville ~~극장을 뛰어넘을 것을 주장하기~~ 위해

(B) Vaudeville 극장이 편의점만큼 ~~흔했다는~~ 생각을 강조하기 위해서

(C) Vaudeville의 공연은 ~~질이 낮았다는~~ 것을 분명히 설명하기 위해서 ★

(D) **Vaudeville 극장에서는 많은 오락이 집단적으로 접근 가능했다는 것을 설명하기 위해서**

> **해설 |** (A) 교수는 Vaudeville 극장과 편의점의 경영 전략의 차이점이 아닌 공통점을 이야기 하므로 오답. (B) 교수는 선택지의 다양성의 장점과 메리트를 설명하고자 편의점의 비유를 든다. 선택의 다양성과 극장의 흔한 정도와는 관련이 없으므로 오답. (C) 교수는 질의 한계를 언급하기는 하나 그 한계를 보완하는 다양성과 넓은 범위를 강조하고자 Vaudeville 연극을 편의점에 비유한다.

15. [Detail – Methodology] How did Benjamin Franklin Keith make his vaudeville theater exceptional?

(A) **He increased the operating hours of his theater and embellished them with ornaments.**

(B) He built his theater ~~inside a luxurious hotel~~ to make it seem more grandiose. *(wrong fact)* ★

(C) He decorated the ~~performers' costumes~~ with extravagant details. *(partial error)*

(D) He allowed the admission of women and children into his theater ~~when most theaters didn't~~. *(not mentioned)*

15. Benjamin Franklin Keith는 어떻게 그의 vaudeville 극장을 특별하게 만들었는가?

(A) **그는 그의 극장의 운영 시간을 늘렸고 극장을 장식품으로 장식했다.**

(B) 그는 더 거창해 보이게 하기 위해 그의 극장을 ~~호화로운 호텔 안에~~ 지었다. ★

(C) 그는 공연자들의 ~~의상을~~ 호화로운 세공으로 장식했다.

(D) 그는 ~~대부분의 극장이 그렇지 않을 때~~ 여성과 아이들이 그의 극장에 들어오는 것을 허락했다.

> **해설 |** (B) 그의 극장이 마치 호화로운 호텔처럼 거창하게 장식되었다는 교수의 설명을 왜곡시켜 놓은 것으로 오답. (C) 그가 호화롭게 꾸민 것은 공연자들의 의상이 아닌 극장 그 자체였다. (D) 당시 극장들이 여성과 아이들의 입장을 제한했는지는 지문에 나오지 않는다. 또한, Keith의 극장이 불경스러운 요소들을 연극에서 배제하면서 여성과 아이들도 즐길 수 있도록 했다는 설명을 왜곡시켜 놓은 것으로 오답.

16. [Detail – Difference/Contrast] What is the difference between the traditional theaters of the American Civil War era and the one established by Benjamin Franklin Keith?

(A) Freedom of speech was greatly suppressed in Keith's theater ~~under the government's control.~~ *(wrong fact)*

(B) Serious literary shows were ~~predominant during the civil war~~ due to the government's censorship law. *(wrong fact)* ★

(C) The use of vulgarity and inappropriate behavior were greatly discouraged in Keith's theater.

(D) The traditional theaters had a ~~strong theme of illegitimate theater.~~ *(not mentioned)*

16. 미국 남북전쟁시기에 전통적인 극장과 Benjamin Franklin Keith가 세운 것의 차이는 무엇인가?

(A) ~~정부의 통제 하에~~ 언론의 자유는 Keith의 극장에서 매우 억압되었다.

(B) 정부의 검열 법 때문에 ~~남북전쟁 동안~~ 진지한 문학적 공연은 ~~지배적~~이었다. ★

(C) 음란물의 사용과 부적절한 행동은 Keith의 극장에서 매우 금지되었다.

(D) 전통적인 연극은 ~~비정극의 강력한 주제~~를 가졌다.

해설 | (A) Keith의 극장에서 음란물과 불경스러운 요소들이 금지된 것은 맞으나 그것은 Keith의 재량 하에 이루어진 것이며, 정부의 통제에 인한 것은 아니었다. (B) 진지한 문학적 공연은 1737년 Licensing Act에 의해 엄격한 제한이 걸렸다. 또한, 이것은 남북전쟁 시기 (1861~1865) 이전부터 제한되었던 것이었으므로 오답. (D) 언급되지 않았으므로 오답.

---

17. [Inference – Imply] What does the professor imply when he says this: 🎧

> "This ensured that his theater would also appeal to women and children."

(A) That Keith's theater mainly consisted of ~~romantic and humorous~~ elements. *(not mentioned)*

(B) That the women and children's influence was ~~greater than~~ that of men during the time. *(not mentioned)*

(C) That Keith advocated the equality of his audience and was able to make more profits than the discriminatory theaters

(D) That Keith's theaters consisted of elements that ~~attracted more~~ female and young customers than male customers. *(wrong fact)*

17. 교수가 이 말을 했을 때 어떤 것을 암시했나? 🎧

> "이것은 그의 극장이 여성과 아이들에게도 매력적이라는 것을 보장했습니다."

(A) Keith의 극은 주로 ~~낭만적이고 재미있는~~ 요소로 구성되었다는 것

(B) 여성과 아이들의 영향이 그 당시 남성들의 ~~영향보다 컸다는~~ 것

(C) Keith는 그의 관중의 평등을 지지했고 차별적인 극장보다 더 많은 이윤을 낼 수 있었다는 것

(D) Keith의 극은 남성 고객보다 여성 고객과 어린 고객을 ~~더 사로잡는~~ 요소로 구성되었다는 것

해설 | (A) 불경스러운 요소들을 배제한 것은 맞으나 이것을 낭만적이고 재미있었다는 뜻으로 해석하기에는 매우 제한적이다. (B) 여성과 아이들의 영향과 남성들의 영향을 비교하는 내용은 지문에 언급되지 않는다. (D) 여성과 아이들을 더 사로잡은 것이 아니라 그들 또한 사로잡았다는 뜻이다.

www.usherin.usher.co.kr

# USHER

iBT TOEFL
INTERMEDIATE LISTENING
TEST 4 해설

TEST 4 set 1-1

Conversation — Final term papers

문단주제	본문내용	해석
단락 1 학생의 근황	**Listen to a conversation between a student and her biology professor.** S: Hi professor, do you have a minute? P: Of course, Jenny, how have you been? The semester's almost over, so I'm guessing you must be relaxing and enjoying your leisure time. S: Not exactly… It's that time of the semester. [Q1] Final term papers are due… I've been overwhelmed. Thank you for extending the deadline for the paper; that was very generous. P: Of course! That doesn't mean you didn't put as much effort into the first draft that I already received, does it? (laughs) S: Of course not! I started from scratch and did a ton of research. I was wondering if you had a chance to read my paper over the weekend. P: I certainly did, and I have a few questions for you. S: Sure, that's why I came by.	학생과 생물학 교수의 대화를 들으시오. S: 안녕하세요, 교수님. 잠시 시간 괜찮으세요? P: 물론이지, Jenny. 잘 지냈니? 학기가 거의 끝나니까 아마 지금 좀 편하게 여가 시간을 즐기고 있겠구나. S: 별로 그렇지도 않아요… 이번 학기의 그 시기에요. [Q1] 기말 보고서들도 제출 해야 하고… 저는 어쩔 줄 모르겠어요. 보고서 제출 기한을 연장해주셔서 감사해요. 정말 관대하셨어요. P: 물론이지! 그게 내가 이미 받은 초안에 네가 충분히 노력을 투입하지 않았단 뜻은 아니지, 그치? (웃음) S: 물론 아니죠! 저는 아무 것도 없는 상태에서 시작해서 아주 많이 조사를 했어요. 주말 동안 제 보고서를 읽어보실 기회가 있었는지 궁금하네요. P: 물론 있었지, 그리고 너에게 몇 가지 질문이 있단다. S: 그럼요, 그게 제가 여기 온 이유인걸요.
단락 2 학생의 보고서의 주제	P: Okay, could you summarize the main theme of your paper? S: Um, well [Q2] the focus is honeybees – their way of communicating with one another and how they utilize earth's magnetic field in the process. P: Use the magnetic field to facilitate communication? S: Umm… No, not quite. To help them navigate by finding the right course. P: Okay, now I'm starting to understand your paper a bit better. So, first, honeybees communicate with one another and second, they navigate using earth's magnetic field, right? S: Exactly!	P: 그래, 네 보고서의 주된 주제를 요약해줄 수 있니? S: 음, 글쎄요, [Q2] 꿀벌에게 초점을 맞췄어요 - 그들이 서로 의사 소통하는 방식이랑 어떻게 꿀벌들이 지구의 자기장을 그 과정에 활용하는지요. P: 의사소통을 하기 위해 자기장을 이용한다고? S: 음… 아뇨, 그렇다기 보다는. 그들이 맞는 길을 찾게 해서 그들이 방향을 알게 돕는 것이요. P: 그래, 이제 너의 보고서를 좀 더 이해하겠구나. 그래서 첫째로, 꿀벌들이 서로 의사소통하고, 두 번째로 지구의 자기장을 이용해서 길을 찾는다는 거지, 그치? S: 바로 그거에요!
단락 3 꿀벌들의 메시지 전달의 종류	P: Well, Jenny, your paper was quite vague in that sense… I mean, it was difficult to grasp those ideas separately in your thesis. Are you sure you understand the concepts?	P: 음, Jenny, 그런 의미에서 네 보고서는 좀 모호해… 내 말은, 네 글에서 그 아이디어들을 구별해서 파악하기가 어려워. 이 개념들을 이해한 것이 확실하니?

문단주제	본문내용	해석
	S: I think so. I mean… what I learned through news articles and the internet was that honeybees employ two different types of dances to deliver messages. [Q3] They perform what's called a round dance to tell others that a food source is nearby and they perform a waggle dance, which is relatively more perplexing than the first, to tell them that the food source is far away from their hive. P: So their dances sort of work as food-location signals? S: Right. P: Um, okay, then where does the magnetic field part fit into your paper?	S: 그런 것 같아요. 제 말은… 제가 신문 기사와 인터넷을 통해 배운 것은 꿀벌들은 메시지를 전달하기 위해 두 가지 다른 종류의 춤을 사용한다는 거에요. [Q3] 그들은 근처의 먹이 있는 곳을 다른 꿀벌들에게 말하기 위해 원형 춤이라고 불리는 것을 춰요. 그리고 그들의 벌집에서 멀리 떨어진 먹이가 있는 곳을 말해줄 때는 첫 번째 것보다 상대적으로 더 복잡한 8자 춤을 춰요. P: 그래서 그들의 춤이 먹이의 위치를 알리는 신호 같은 것으로 작동한단 거지? S: 맞아요. P: 음, 그래, 그러면 너의 보고서에서 자기장은 어디에 들어가는 거니?
단락 4 꿀벌들의 자기장 활용	S: Right after that, [Q4] I explain that honeybees have iron-rich granules in their cells, and they sense earth's magnetic field using them. It works almost like an internal compass – like the biological clock in plants. So even if they lose their way due to… whatever the reason may be, they can get back on course.	S: 네 그 다음에, [Q4] 저는 꿀벌들이 그들의 세포에 철이 풍부한 과립을 가지고 있고 이걸 사용해서 지구의 자기장을 지각할 수 있다고 설명했어요. 이건 거의 몸 안의 나침반처럼 작동해요 - 식물의 생체 시계처럼요. 그래서 어떤 이유로든 그들이 길을 잃는다고 해도, 그들은 다시 길로 돌아올 수 있는 거죠.
단락 5 학생 보고서의 문제점 및 보완방법	P: Alright, good. Here's my advice; your paper seems to lack a clear connection, if there's any, between how honeybees communicate – their dances – and how they use earth's magnetic field to navigate. So I referred to your citation list. The source you used… S: Is there something wrong with the source? P: Yeah, [Q5-B] it's not very academic. It contains a lot of misused concepts, and it's a very subjective article that fails to address the other side of the matter. [Q5] So I suggest you find another source that has comprehensive knowledge of honeybees' communication methods and their relation to earth's magnetic field. And see if you could, uh… clarify your paper a bit. S: That sounds like a great plan! Thank you so much for your help, professor. [Q5-A] I guess I need to hurry up to meet the deadline! P: No problem. Stop by anytime you need help, Jenny!	P: 그래, 좋아. 이게 내 조언이야; 네 보고서는 어떻게 꿀벌이 의사소통 하는지- 그들의 춤- 그리고 어떻게 그들이 지구의 자기장을 길을 찾는 데 이용하는지 사이에 명확한 연결이 부족해 보여, 연결이 있긴 하다면 말이야. 그래서 난 네 참고문헌을 봤어. 네가 사용한 자료의 출처 말이야… S: 자료 출처와 관련해서 잘못된 것이 있나요? P: 그래, [Q5-B] 그게 별로 학문적이지 않아. 거기에는 많은 잘못 사용된 개념들이 포함되어 있고 문제의 반대 쪽을 다루지 못한 매우 주관적인 기사야. [Q5] 그래서 나는 네가 꿀벌의 의사소통 방법이랑 이것과 지구의 자기장의 관계에 대해 더 포괄적인 지식이 있는 다른 출처를 찾아보면 좋겠어. 그리고 네가 음… 네 보고서를 좀 더 명확하게 할 수 있는지 보자. S: 아주 좋은 계획처럼 들리네요! 도와주셔서 정말 감사해요, 교수님. [Q5-A] 제출기한에 맞추려면 서둘러야 할 것 같네요! P: 문제 없어. 도움이 필요하면 언제든 들르렴, Jenny!

01. [Main Idea] What is the conversation mainly about?

(A) The student's last term paper for the semester in her Biology class

(B) Honeybees' usage of their dances and the magnetic field as their survival mechanism *(too specific)* ★

(C) Student's request that the professor ~~extends the deadline~~ for the Biology paper that is due soon *(not mentioned)*

(D) The professor's advice on the student's difficulty of grasping the concept of honeybees' navigation methods *(wrong fact)*

01. 이 대화는 주로 어떤 것에 관한 것인가?

(A) 학생의 생물학 수업 학기 마지막 보고서

(B) 꿀벌들의 생존 방법으로써의 춤과 자기장의 사용 ★

(C) 곧 제출해야 하는 생물학 보고서의 ~~제출기한을 연장해달라는~~ 학생의 요청

(D) 꿀벌들의 길 찾기 방법을 이해하는 것에 대한 학생의 어려움을 위한 교수의 조언

> **해설** | (B) 대화의 주제가 아닌 학생의 보고서의 내용으로 너무 좁다. (C) 대화 초반에 학생은 교수에게 보고서 제출기한을 연장시켜준 것에 대해 고마움을 표한다. 이를 학생의 요청사항으로 왜곡시켜 놓은 것으로 오답. (D) 학생의 보고서 중, 꿀벌들의 의사소통 방법과 자기장의 이용에 대한 명확하지 못한 연결에 대한 교수의 지적을 왜곡시켜 놓은 것으로 오답. 꿀벌들의 길 찾기 방법을 이해하는 것은 본 대화에서 학생이 겪는 어려움으로 보여지지 않는다.

02. [Main Idea] What is the main idea addressed in the student's paper?

(A) How honeybees accomplish communication using earth's magnetic field *(too specific)* ★

(B) Comparison between ~~plants' biological clocks~~ and honeybees' internal clocks *(wrong fact)*

(C) ~~Insects~~' survival and foraging methods *(too general)*

(D) Communication and navigation methods utilized by honeybees

02. 학생의 보고서에서 다룬 주된 주제는 무엇인가?

(A) 꿀벌이 지구의 자기장을 이용해 의사소통을 하는 방법 ★

(B) ~~식물의 생체 시계와~~ 꿀벌의 내부 시계의 대조

(C) 곤충의 생존과 먹이 찾는 방법

(D) 꿀벌이 사용하는 의사소통과 길 찾기 방법

> **해설** | (A) 꿀벌이 지구의 자기장을 이용하는 내용이 나오기는 하지만 일정 부분에서만 나올뿐 글 전체의 내용이 아니다. (B) 식물의 생체 시계와 꿀벌의 내부 시계를 비교 하지 않는다. (C) 곤충의 생존이 아닌 꿀벌의 생존이다.

03. [Detail – Cause and Effect] According to the student, what affects honeybees' decision to use either the round dance or the waggle dance?

(A) ~~Their position~~ in the highly complex social structure *(not mentioned)*

(B) The strength of the ~~earth's magnetic field~~ they sense *(wrong fact)* ★

(C) The location of their food sources with respect to that of their hives

(D) Their individual and distinctive ~~duties~~ *(not mentioned)*

03. 학생의 말에 따르면, 어떤 것이 꿀벌이 원형 춤과 8자 춤 중 무엇을 사용할 지 결정하는 데 영향을 미치는가?

(A) 매우 복잡한 ~~사회 구조 속~~ 그들의 위치

(B) 그들이 감지하는 ~~지구의 자기장의~~ 세기 ★

(C) 그들의 먹이가 있는 곳부터 그들의 벌집의 위치

(D) 그들의 개별적이고 특별한 ~~의무~~

> **해설** | (B) 꿀벌들은 지구의 자기장을 이용해 길을 찾고 방향을 잡는다 - 자기장의 세기와 그들의 춤과는 아무런 관련이 없으므로 오답. 학생은 꿀벌들의 (A) 사회적 위치와 (D) 개별 의무를 춤의 종류 결정과 연관 짓지 않는다.

04. [Detail – Ethodology] How are honeybees able to navigate?

(A) By sensing earth's magnetic field with iron in their bodies

(B) By responding to and orienting themselves to ~~external stimuli, such as wind~~ *(not mentioned)*

(C) By using their internal, biological clock to ~~detect the amount of sunlight~~ *(not mentioned)*

(D) By detecting traces of ~~iron in earth's magnetic field~~ *(wrong fact)* ★

04. 꿀벌들은 어떻게 길을 찾을 수 있는가?

(A) 그들 몸의 철로 지구의 자기장을 지각함으로써

(B) ~~바람과 같은 외부 자극들~~에 반응하고 자기 자신을 그 쪽으로 향하게 함으로써

(C) ~~햇빛의 양을 탐지하는데~~ 그들의 내부 생체 시계를 사용함으로써

(D) ~~지구의 자기장~~ 속 철의 흔적들을 탐지함으로써 ★

해설 | (B) 외부자극의 사용은 언급되지 않는다. (C) 햇빛 양의 탐지는 언급되지 않는다. (D) 꿀벌들이 그들의 세포 속 철이 풍부한 과립을 이용해 지구의 자기장을 지각한다는 설명을 왜곡시켜 놓은 것으로 오답.

---

05. [Inference – Future Action] What is the student most likely to do after the conversation with the professor?

(A) She will ~~finish~~ her other assignments ~~before~~ revising her Biology paper *(wrong fact)*

(B) She will revise her paper using her ~~original sources~~ *(wrong fact)*

(C) She ~~will come back~~ to the professor for help again *(partial error)* ★

(D) She will find another suitable source of information

05. 학생은 교수와의 대화 후에 할 것으로 가능성이 가장 높은 것은?

(A) 그녀는 다른 과제들을 ~~먼저 마치고~~ 생물학 기말 과제를 수정할 것이다.

(B) 그녀는 자신이 ~~원래 썼던 자료 출처~~를 써서 자신의 보고서를 수정할 것이다.

(C) 그녀는 도움을 받으러 ~~다시 교수님께 올 것이다~~. ★

(D) 그녀는 다른 적절한 정보의 출처를 찾을 것이다

해설 | (A) 학생은 제출기한에 맞추려면 서둘러야 할 것 같다고 마지막에 이야기한다. 때문에, 다른 과제를 먼저 마치고 생물학 과제를 수정할 가능성은 낮다. (B) 교수는 학생이 쓴 자료의 출처에 대해서 학문적이지 않으며 잘못된 개념들이 포함되어 있다며 지적을 한다. 따라서, 학생이 원래 썼던 자료를 다시 활용할 가능성은 매우 낮다. (C) 교수를 다시 찾아오는 것에 대한 언급은 마지막에 도움이 필요하면 언제든 찾아오라는 교수의 인사말 정도 밖에 없기 때문에 학생이 확실히 교수를 다시 찾아올 것을 예측할 수 있는 근거가 충분치 않다.

Lecture 1
Two galaxies

Listen to part of a lecture in an astronomy class.

P: Yesterday we discussed our solar system and its contents. [Q6] Today, we'll talk about two galaxies, systems consisting of billions of stars and other remnants, the Milky Way, which includes our solar system, and another named Sagittarius.

Researchers have recently discovered that larger galaxies tend to absorb stars from smaller galaxies. You may be wondering how this relates to today's topic. You see, the Milky Way is 10,000 times bigger than Sagittarius and the research team found that Sagittarius' stars are being pulled into, or absorbed by, the Milky Way. [Q11] This is astonishing and interesting, because galaxies were commonly thought to be gravitationally bound, and the idea of two galaxies fusing together, or one 'stealing' stars from another, was seldom considered. Even when it was, researchers couldn't validate the point due to lack of evidence, so the theories were viewed as absurd and controversial. However, evidence arose that validated the theory. So, how did they prove what previous cosmologists couldn't?

To begin, let's go over why previous researchers couldn't prove the phenomenon and what they were lacking. To help you visualize it, let's say you shredded two identical stacks of paper. If they were pure white with no distinguishing marks, would you be able to sort them? Probably not unless you had some kind of supernatural power, right? But what if one stack was blue and the other red? Now, the scenario changes, and it becomes quite easy to distinguish them.

[Q7] That's exactly how the research team was able to determine the extent to which the stars of the Sagittarius galaxy were being pulled into the Milky Way. They began by studying galaxies… what they contain, what they're made of, what properties they share, and things like that. [Q8] Then, they realized that galaxies radiate thermal energy, or heat that gives off infrared radiation or… infrared light. This might sound a little more familiar to you…

문단주제	본문내용	해석
단락 3 적외선 망원경을 이용한 은하들의 복사 탐지	For those not familiar with infrared radiation, think about how detecting devices are employed in warzones or airports. I'm sure you've seen soldiers wearing bulky-looking goggles at night. [Q7-D] These night vision devices enable soldiers to, uh… see objects by detecting the thermal radiation they give off, regardless of the darkness – so the 'coldness' or 'hotness' of the objects determines the radiation's color, ranging from blue to red. Also at the airport, when you go through the body-scanning process, you walk through a device that basically detects potentially dangerous items by measuring their temperature and distinguishing them from your body, because the objects' temperature and the bodies' are usually different. We can apply the same principle to the galaxies that the research team scrutinized. Unfortunately, we don't have infrared-sensitive eyes or the ability to just look at the galaxies and discern one from another, right? [Q9] Infrared light, which is a part of the electromagnetic spectrum, is not within the visible spectrum, meaning that a special device is required to detect the radiation that galaxies emit – a sort of infrared-light detecting device like the body-scanning device or the night-vision goggles. Eventually, an appropriate device was developed: the infrared telescope. [Q9-B, Q9-C] These telescopes don't differ much from regular telescopes. The major difference is the location of the infrared telescope, because infrared radiation has lower energy than visible light, and… well, it would take another period to explain the details, so let's get back to that later; Be sure to remind me though, because I might forget, and it's crucial that you understand it. So, as astronomers began looking at the composition of stars in the Milky Way using infrared telescopes, they noticed that part of the galaxy, [Q8-D] the peripheral space specifically, seemed to be different, apparently containing unusual chemical patterns that didn't sync with the Milky Way's chemical composition. After countless attempts to match them, the astronomers finally found a secondary source of chemical compositions and identified it as the Sagittarius Galaxy. As their research continued, they determined exactly how much of Sagittarius had been absorbed by the Milky Way.	적외선을 잘 모르는 사람들은 교전지역이나 공항에서 탐지기가 어떻게 쓰이는지 생각해보세요. 여러분은 밤에 병사들이 커다란 고글을 쓰고 있는 것을 본 적 있을 거라 생각하는데요. [Q7-D] 이 밤에 보게 해주는 장치는 병사들이 음, 사물을 어둠과 상관없이 보게 해줍니다. 그것들이 방출하는 열 복사를 탐지함으로써요. 그러니까 그 물체들의 '차가움'이나 '뜨거움'이 파랑에서 빨강에 이르기까지 그 복사의 색깔을 결정해요. 공항에서도, 여러분이 몸수색 절차를 지날 때, 그 장치는 기본적으로 그 온도를 측정하고 여러분의 몸과 그것을 구별해서 위험할 수도 있는 물건을 찾는 거에요. 왜냐면 사물의 온도와 몸의 온도는 보통 다르니까요. 우리는 연구팀이 정밀 조사한 은하들에도 똑같은 원리를 적용할 수 있습니다. 불운하게도, 우리는 적외선에 민감한 눈이나 은하를 그냥 보고 이 은하와 다른 걸 구별할 능력은 갖고 있지 않아요, 그죠? [Q9] 전자기 스펙트럼의 일부인 적외선은 가시광선 스펙트럼에 있지 않아요. 이는 은하들이 방출하는 복사를 탐지하기 위해서는 특별한 장치-몸수색장치나 밤에 보게 해주는 고글처럼 적외선 빛을 감지하는 어떤 장치-가 필요하다는 의미이죠. 마침내, 적절한 장치가 개발되었습니다: 적외선 망원경. [Q9-B, Q9-C] 이 망원경은 일반 망원경과 크게 다르지 않습니다. 주된 차이는 적외선 망원경의 위치입니다. 왜냐하면 적외선은 가시광선보다 에너지가 낮고 그래서 음, 자세히 설명하려면 또 다른 시간이 필요하겠네요, 그래서 이건 다음에 다시 할게요. 그런데 제가 까먹을 수 있고 이걸 이해하는 게 아주 중요하니까 꼭 다시 알려주시고요. 그래서, 천문학자들이 적외선 망원경을 써서 Milky Way의 별 구성을 보기 시작하자, 그들은 은하의 일부, [Q8-D] 특히 주변적인 부분이 달라 보인다는 것을 알아차렸어요. 분명히 Milky Way의 화학적 구성이랑 맞지 않는 흔하지 않은 화학 패턴을 가지고 있었어요. 그들을 맞춰보려는 셀 수 없는 시도 끝에, 천문학자들은 마침내 화학 구성요소의 두 번째 출처를 찾아냈고 그게 Sagittarius 은하에서 온 것을 밝혀냈어요. 연구를 계속하면서, 그들은 Sagittarius에서 정확히 얼마나 Milky Way로 흡수되었는지 밝혔어요.

문단주제	본문내용	해석
단락 4 은하들의 끊임없는 진화	Furthermore, they found an attractive force between the two, which they later identified as gravitational force. [Q10-C] This force isn't dissimilar from the one between Earth and the Moon, except that the force exerted in the latter case is much stronger. This force has caused the Milky Way to absorb or pull on Sagittarius for so long that Sagittarius' shape has been stretched out or transformed into an elongated, elliptical shape. [Q10] If this continues, as scientists predict it will, the galaxy will be destroyed and completely incorporated into the Milky Way. Therefore, we now know that the belief that galaxies are bound is no longer valid; rather, galaxies are ever evolving. Next time, we'll discuss another contradictory point about our solar system: that it actually belongs to the Sagittarius Dwarf galaxy, not the Milky Way.	게다가, 그들은 중력의 힘이라고 나중에 밝혀진, 둘 사이의 인력을 찾았어요. [Q10-C] 이 힘은 지구와 달 사이의 힘과 다르지 않았어요. 후자에서 가해지는 힘이 훨씬 더 세다는 것만 빼면요. 이 힘은 너무 오랫동안 Milky Way가 Sagittarius를 당기거나 흡수하게 해서 Sagittarius의 모양은 늘어났고, 비정상적으로 가늘고 긴 타원 모양으로 바뀌었어요. [Q10] 이게 계속된다면, 과학자들이 예상한 것처럼 계속된다면, 그 은하는 파괴되고 완전히 Milky Way로 합쳐질 거예요. 그래서, 우리는 이제 은하들이 묶여있다는 믿음이 더 이상 타당하지 않다는 걸 알겠죠. 오히려, 은하들은 계속 진화하죠. 다음 시간에, 우리는 우리 태양계의 또 다른 모순되는 점을 얘기해볼게요: 사실 그건 Milky Way가 아니라 Sagittarius 왜소은하에 속해있다는 걸요.

06. [Main Idea] What is the lecture mainly about?

(A) ~~Comparison~~ between the distinct properties and characteristics of two galaxies *(too specific)* ★

(B) Discoveries regarding the relationship between two galaxies that differ in size

(C) The effect of gravitational forces on ~~the formation~~ and coordination of galaxies *(too specific)*

(D) The ~~origin~~ of our solar system, which has been misunderstood for a long time *(not mentioned)*

06. 강의의 주요 내용이 무엇인가?

(A) 두 은하의 구별된 속성과 특징의 ~~비교~~ ★

(B) 크기가 다른 두 은하의 관계에 대한 발견

(C) 은하의 ~~형성~~과 조직에 대한 중력의 영향

(D) 오랫동안 잘못 이해되어온 우리 태양계의 ~~기원~~

해설 | (A) 두 은하의 크기가 비교되는 것은 사실이지만, 강의의 극히 일부이며 이외의 특징들은 비교되지 않으므로 강의의 주제로 보기에는 너무 좁다. (C) 중력은 Milky Way가 Sagittarius에게 미치는 영향의 근거를 설명하기 위해 간단히 언급되었을 뿐이기 때문에 주제로 보기에는 너무 좁으며, 본 강의는 그로 인한 은하의 형성이 아닌 소멸을 중점적으로 다룬다. (D) 태양계의 기원은 언급되지 않는다.

---

07. [Detail – Purpose] Why does the professor mention 'two identical stacks of paper'?

(A) To give his students a better understanding of how galaxies are ~~initially formed~~ *(not mentioned)*

(B) To help his students grasp the idea that stars of several galaxies are ~~always jumbled up~~ *(wrong fact)*

(C) To help his students understand the universally accepted method of distinguishing galaxies ~~using the colors blue and red~~ *(wrong fact)* ★

(D) To simplify the concept of the technology that was developed to distinguish galaxies from one another

07. 교수는 왜 '똑같은 두 무더기의 종이'를 언급했는가?

(A) ~~처음에 은하가 어떻게 만들어졌는지~~에 대해 학생들이 더 잘 이해하게 해주려고

(B) 몇 은하의 별들은 ~~항상 뒤섞여있다는~~ 아이디어에 대한 학생들의 이해를 도우려고

(C) 학생들이 ~~파란색과 빨간색을 써서~~ 은하를 구분하는 널리 받아들여지는 방법을 이해하게 도와주려고 ★

(D) 은하들을 서로 구별하기 위해 개발된 기술의 개념을 간단하게 설명하려고

해설 | (A) 은하기의 초기 생성은 "똑같은 두 무더기 종이" 비유를 통해 교수가 전하고자 했던 은하들의 구별 방법과 아무런 관련이 없을 뿐만 아니라 강의를 통해서도 관련이 전혀 없는 내용이다. (B) 항상 뒤섞여 있다는 사실을 전달하려는 것이 아닌 그 뒤섞여 있던 별들을 두 분류로 구분하는 방법을 이야기한다. (C) Night vision devices의 열 복사 탐지와 그 온도를 파랑과 빨강의 색 범위 안에서 나타내는 것은 은하를 구분하는데 쓰인 기술이 아니다. 화학적 구성의 차이를 이용해 두 은하를 구별하는 원리를 비유적으로 설명한 것이지 두 경우의 기술적 일치를 뜻하는 것은 아니다.

08. [Detail – Characteristic] What property of galaxies helped the research team make a distinction between two different chemical compositions?

(A) The ~~gravitational pull~~ that exists between galaxies
    (unrelated to the question)

(B) The galaxies' emission of light photons created by their heat energy

(C) Bigger galaxies' ~~tendency~~ to fuse with relatively smaller galaxies
    (unrelated to the question) ★

(D) The unique chemical patterns found ~~at the center of~~ each galaxy
    (wrong fact)

08. 은하의 어떤 특징이 연구팀이 두 가지 다른 화학 구성을 구별할 수 있게 도와주었는가?

(A) 은하 간에 존재하는 ~~중력의 당김~~

(B) 은하가 그들의 열 에너지로 만드는 광자의 방출

(C) 상대적으로 더 작은 은하들과 합치는 더 큰 은하들의 ~~경향성~~ ★

(D) 각 은하의 ~~중심에서~~ 발견되는 독특한 화학 패턴

해설 | (A)와 (C)는 연구팀이 발견한 은하들의 특징일 뿐, 두 가지 다른 화학 구성을 구별 할 수 있게 도와준 것은 아니다. 문제가 묻는 바가 아니므로 오답. (D) 독특한 화학 패턴은 중심이 아닌 주변부에서 주로 발견되었다고 교수는 설명한다.

---

09. [Detail – Cause/Reason] According to the professor, why is a special type of device needed to measure chemical patterns of galaxies?

(A) Because the light that galaxies radiate is not within the visible-light spectrum

(B) Because galaxies ~~become so dark~~ that they are not visible through a ~~regular telescope~~ *(not mentioned)*

(C) Because galaxies ~~release light composed of blinding chemicals~~
    (opposite fact) ★

(D) Because the ~~distance~~ between galaxies and Earth makes it impossible for ordinary telescopes to detect them *(not mentioned)*

09. 교수에 따르면, 왜 은하의 화학적 패턴을 측정하기 위해 특별한 종류의 장치가 필요한가?

(A) 은하가 내뿜는 빛이 가시광선 스펙트럼에 있지 않기 때문에

(B) 은하들이 일반 망원경으로 보이지 않을 만큼 ~~어두워지기~~ 때문에

(C) 은하수가 눈을 멀게하는 화학 요소로 구성된 빛을 내뿜기 때문에★

(D) 은하들과 지구의 ~~거리가~~ 일반 망원경이 탐지하지 못하게 만들기 때문에

해설 | (B) 적외선 망원경과 일반 망원경의 비교를 왜곡시켜 놓은 것으로 오답. 또한, 은하들이 어두워지는 것에 대한 이야기는 언급되지 않는다. (C) 적외선은 가시광선보다 에너지가 낮기 때문에 오답. (D) 은하들과 지구 사이의 거리, 또는 일반 망원경의 한계점은 언급되지 않는다.

10. [Inference - Imply] What do scientists imply about the future of the Milky Way and Sagittarius galaxies?

(A) That the entirety of the Milky Way will be ~~absorbed by Sagittarius~~ *(wrong fact)* ★

(B) That fusion of the galaxies will eventually cause ~~both~~ to be completely destroyed *(wrong fact)*

(C) That the gravitational force between the Moon and Earth ~~will eventually interrupt~~ the one between two galaxies *(wrong fact)*

(D) That the incessant attractive force will ultimately lead to total disappearance of the Sagittarius

10. 과학자들은 Milky Way와 Sagittarius 은하의 미래에 대해 어떤 것을 암시하는가?

(A) Milky Way의 전체가 ~~Sagittarius에 의해 흡수될~~ 것이라는 것 ★

(B) 은하들의 융합은 결국 ~~양 쪽 다~~ 완전히 없어지게 할 것이라는 것

(C) 달과 지구 사이의 중력이 두 은하 사이의 중력을 ~~결국 방해할~~ 것이라는 것

(D) 끊임없는 인력이 결국 Sagittarius가 완전히 없어지게 할 것이라는 것

해설 | (A) 두 은하의 관계가 잘못 설립되어 있다. Sagittarius에 의해 Milky Way가 흡수되는 것이 아니라 Milky Way에 의해 Sagittarius가 흡수되는 것이다. (B) 완전히 없어지는 것은 Sagittarius 은하에만 해당하는 내용이므로 오답. (C) Sagittarius와 Milky Way 사이의 인력인 중력이 지구와 달 사이의 힘과 비슷하다는 교수의 설명을 왜곡시켜 놓은 것으로 오답.

Listen again to part of the lecture. Then answer the question.

"This is astonishing and interesting, because galaxies were commonly thought to be gravitationally bound"

11. [Inference - Imply] What does the professor imply when he says this: 🎧

"galaxies were commonly thought to be gravitationally bound"

(A) That the gravitational pull from the Earth ~~inhibited physical contact~~ between galaxies *(not mentioned)*

(B) That the astronomers from the past didn't believe that it was possible for galaxies to affect each other

(C) That the gravitational force that once existed ~~no longer exists~~ *(wrong fact)*

(D) That the previous generations were conservative and ~~never made attempts to override existing theories~~ *(too extreme)*

강의의 일부분을 다시 듣고 질문에 답하시오.

"이거는 놀랍고 흥미로운데요, 왜냐면 일반적으로 은하들은 중력으로 묶여있다고 생각되었거든요."

11. 교수는 이 말을 할 때 어떤 것을 암시하는가? 🎧

"일반적으로 은하들은 중력으로 묶여있다고 생각되었거든요."

(A) 지구가 중력으로 당기는 것이 은하들의 ~~물리적인 접촉을 막는다는~~ 것

(B) 과거의 천문학자들은 은하들이 서로에게 영향을 미칠 수 있다고 생각하지 않았다는 것

(C) 이전에 존재하던 중력이 ~~더 이상 존재하지 않는다는~~ 것

(D) 이전 세대는 보수적이었고 ~~존재하는 이론들을 기각하는 시도를 하지 않았다는~~ 것

해설 | (A) 강의에서 언급되지 않은 내용이므로 오답. (C) 중력으로 묶여있음이 부정된 것과 중력의 존재 자체가 부정된 것은 별개이므로 오답. (D) 과거의 천문학자들의 착오를 객관적인 입장에서 전달하는 교수가 암시하는 것이라고 보기에는 너무 편중되어있다. 또한, 존재하는 이론의 기각 시도에 대한 내용은 언급되지 않는다.

TEST 4 set 1-3

Lecture 2
Biomimetics

문단 주제	본문 내용	해석

Listen to part of a lecture in a biology class.

단락 1
생체 모방 기술의 소개와 예시

P: Last lecture, I introduced a new field of biology called biomimetics. [Q12] It's basically imitating or borrowing natural systems and components for the purpose of creating new commercial products. I'll give you a few examples that'll make it easier to understand.

You might be wondering how businesses can integrate natural elements into their products, correct? Well… I'm pretty sure you've noticed that birds, or insects like butterflies, have unique structures, such as feathers or scales. For instance, Morpho butterflies have mesmerizing green and blue scales on their wings. These colors are created in two ways: pigmentation and structural coloration. The former sounds more familiar than the latter, doesn't it? For those not familiar with pigments, let's look at the colors of plants. Our common perception is that they're green. [Q13] This color is due to chlorophyll, a green pigment found in the chloroplasts. The green wavelengths are reflected rather than absorbed by the plants, and that's why we see the color. Sunlight has a wide range of colors, and green, specifically the green-light spectrum, fails to be absorbed by the chlorophyll because… well, evidence proving why this happens remains unsubstantiated, but [Q13-A] most scientists assume that green light is detrimental to the process of photosynthesis, the process through which plants produce energy from sunlight. I think that's enough about pigmentation.

단락 2
Morpho 나비의 구조적 천연색

[Q16-C] To understand structural coloration, which is also known as schemochrome, we'll look at the Morpho butterfly. This type of coloration was first observed by Robert Hooke and Isaac Newton, and later elucidated by Thomas Young. [Q16-A] Young explained that the creation of structural colors requires two elements: thin layers of films or scales and light. The morpho butterfly's wings are composed of rows of tiny, tree-like scales, with gaps between them. [Q14] As light hits these scales, they interact with it, absorbing and reflecting certain wavelengths of colors, just as pigments in the chloroplasts in plants. So, the blue wavelength is reflected multiple times and the coloration of the wings becomes visible.

생물학 수업의 일부를 들으시오.

P: 지난 시간, 생물학의 새로운 분야인 생체 모방 기술에 대해 배웠었죠. [Q12] 생체 모방 기술은 기본적으로 새로운 상업용 제품을 만들 목적으로 자연의 체계나 구성요소들을 모방 혹은 차용하는 것입니다. 이해하기 쉽도록 몇 가지 예시를 들어볼게요.

아마도 여러분들은 어떻게 비즈니스에 자연의 요소를 자신들의 제품에 연결시킬 수 있는 지 궁금할 겁니다, 맞나요? 음.. 여러분은 나비와 같은 새나 곤충이 날개나 비늘처럼 특이한 구조를 가지고 있다는 걸 알고 있을 거예요. 예를 들어, Morpho 나비는 아름다운 날개에 푸른 비늘을 가지고 있죠. 이러한 색은 두 가지 방식으로 만들어집니다. 색소 형성과 구조적인 천연색이죠. 전자가 후자보다 우리에겐 더 친숙하게 들리죠, 그렇지 않나요? 색소에 친숙하지 않은 분들을 위해서, 식물의 색상을 먼저 살펴봅시다. 우리의 일반적인 인식은 이것들이 초록빛이라는 거죠. [Q13] 이 색은 엽록소 때문인데, 엽록체에서 발견되는 녹색 색소죠. 녹색 파장은 식물이 흡수시키기보다는 반사하죠. 그렇기 때문에 우리가 그 색을 볼 수 있는 이유랍니다. 햇빛에는 광범위한 색이 있으며, 녹색, 특히 녹색 빛의 스펙트럼은 엽록소가 흡수하지 못하죠. 왜냐하면, 왜 이런 일이 일어나는 지에 대한 증거는 입증되지 않았어요. 하지만 [Q13-A] 대부분의 과학자들은 녹색 빛이 식물이 햇빛에서 에너지를 생산하는 과정인 광합성 과정에서 해롭다고 추정합니다. 저는 그것이 색소 형성에 대해 충분하다고 생각해요.

[Q16-C] Schemochrome이라고 알려진 구조적 천연색을 이해하기 위해서는 Morpho 나비를 살펴봐야 합니다. 이러한 천연색의 형태는 Robert Hooke와 Isaac Newton이 처음 발견했죠. 이후에 Thomas Young이 설명했죠. [Q16-A] Young은 구조적 천연색을 형성하는 데 두 가지의 요소가 필요하다고 설명했습니다. 얇은 층의 껍질이나 비늘과 빛이죠. Morpho 나비의 날개는 작고 나무 같은 비늘의 열로 이루어져 있고 그 사이에는 틈이 있습니다. [Q14] 빛이 이 비늘을 관통하면, 날개가 빛에 반응하여 특정한 색상의 파장들을 흡수하고 반사시킵니다. 식물의 엽록체에 있는 색소들처럼 말이에요. 그래서, 푸른 파장은 여러 번 반사되면서 날개의 천연색이 뚜렷해지는 것이죠.

문단 주제	본문내용	해석
단락 3 구조적 천연색의 사업적 활용	I don't know if you've noticed it yet, but [Q16-D] **structural coloration is exactly what business people exploit when designing products.** You see, dyes and chemicals aren't necessary if structures can be used, right? So, fabric and fiber manufacturers can eliminate the use of toxic elements from their formulas when coloring their products. Additionally, structural coloration is energy-efficient and not environmentally damaging because no additional energy consumption is required to produce and apply dyes to their products. Oh, I forgot to mention that the wings are also 'water-proof,' didn't I?	알고 있을 지는 모르겠지만, [Q16-D] 구조적 천연색이 바로 사업가들이 제품을 디자인 할 때 이용하는 것입니다. 알다시피, 구조를 이용하면 물감이나 화학제품을 사용할 필요가 없겠죠? 그래서 천과 섬유 생산업자들은 자신들의 제품을 염색할 때의 방식에서 독성 물질을 제거할 수 있습니다. 추가적으로 구조적 천연색은 에너지 효율적이며 친환경적입니다. 왜냐하면 제품을 생산하고 염색약을 넣는 데에 추가적인 에너지 낭비를 하지 않아도 되기 때문입니다. 오, 날개가 방수도 된다고 말하는 걸 깜빡 했네요, 아닌가요?
단락 4 Morpho 나비의 날개의 방수성	[Q15] **The wings are structured so that the gap between each layer is filled with gas and works as a 'water-barrier'.** You see, [Q15-B] if water droplets are dropped on a flat surface, several adhesive forces govern them. One of these is the attraction between water droplets, which pull together to form larger droplets. Another is the energy that causes water to stick to solids. This causes water droplets to flatten out on smooth surfaces. However, the Morpho butterflies' wings are structured in such a way that makes them bumpy and rough with air in the gaps. If you think of this in chemistry terms, water doesn't stick to air as it does to solid, smooth surfaces. When water comes into contact with a rough surface, it doesn't flatten out; it preserves its shape and slides right off. This also allows dust particles on the wings to roll off with the water droplets because, again, water has a strong affinity for solid matter, not rough surfaces. You see where I'm going with this, right? These phenomena are prevalent in nature, and are interesting to manufacturers of commercial products. For instance, shirt manufacturers can incorporate the same principles. Let's imagine you are eating a greasy hamburger in a shirt with structural coloration. [Q17] What do you think would happen if you accidently spilled ketchup on your shirt? Of course, the rough, layered material would bear the same results.	[Q15] 날개는 구조적이기 때문에 각 층의 틈은 가스로 채워져 있으며 이것은 '물의 장벽'으로서 기능합니다. 여러분도 알다시피, [Q15-B] 평평한 표면에 작은 물방울이 떨어지면, 약간의 접착력이 물방울을 통제하게 됩니다. 이들 중 하나는 물방울 사이의 인력이며, 더 큰 물방울을 형성하기 위해 끌어당깁니다. 또 다른 힘은 물이 고체에 달라붙도록 하는 힘입니다. 이 힘은 물방울이 부드러운 표면에 평평하게 펴지도록 합니다. 그러나 Morpho 나비의 날개는 그 틈이 울퉁불퉁하고 공기로써 거칠게 만들어졌습니다. 이것을 화학적인 용어로 생각하자면, 물은 고체나 부드러운 표면에서처럼 공기에 달라붙지 않습니다. 물이 거친 표면과 닿으면, 평평해지지 않습니다. 그것의 모양을 보존하면서 미끄러져 내려갑니다. 이는 또한 날개의 먼지 입자가 물방울과 함께 굴러 떨어지는데, 왜냐하면, 즉, 물이 거친 표면이 아니라 고체 물질에 강한 친화성을 가지기 때문입니다. 제가 무엇을 설명하는 지는 알겠죠? 이러한 현상은 자연에서 널리 퍼져있으며, 상업용 제품을 생산하는 사람들에게는 흥미로운 것이었습니다. 예를 들어, 셔츠 제조업자들은 동일한 원칙을 수용할 수 있습니다. 구조적 천연색이 있는 셔츠를 입고 기름진 햄버거를 먹는다고 상상해보십시오. [Q17] 만약 여러분이 우연히 셔츠에 케첩을 흘렸다면, 무슨 일이 생길까요? 물론, 거칠고 겹겹이 쌓인 물질이 같은 결과를 만들 것입니다.
단락 5 생물 모방 기술의 부정적 영향	As I explained, the integration of biology and business gives us great promise for future generations and for technological advances.	제가 설명했듯이, 생물학과 경영학의 통합은 기술 진보와 미래 세대를 위한 위대한 장래의 촉망입니다.

TEST 4 set 1-3

USHER

문단주제	본문내용	해석
	But, biomimicry can also have a negative impact on creativity because… Well, let me refer to the three distinct steps or levels of biomimicry. First is the process of replicating aspects of the natural mechanisms of an organism, just like taking the tree-like structure of the butterflies' wings and duplicating it in their products. Next is the understanding of the phenomena – how these natural processes are created in nature. The third, and perhaps the most imperative, is that manufacturers need to ensure that whatever they replicate and produce does not work as an impediment to our thinking process. [Q16-B] Original thinking is barely involved in biomimicry, because it's simply observing natural phenomena and exploiting them. Don't misunderstand my point, though. Biomimicry presents noteworthy benefits to society, as I've explained.	하지만 생물 모방 기술은 또한 창의력에 부정적인 영향력을 미치고 있습니다. 왜냐하면… 생물 모방 기술의 세 가지 단계에 대해 이야기해봅시다. 첫째는 유기체의 자연적인 기제를 복제하는 측면의 과정입니다. 나비의 날개의 나무 같은 구조를 차용해 자신들의 상품에 복제하는 것 같은 것이죠. 다음은 현상에 대한 이해입니다. 어떻게 이러한 자연적인 과정들이 자연적으로 형상되는 지 말입니다. 다음으로는, 아마도 가장 중요한 것으로서, 제조업자들이 차용하여 생산하는 것이 무엇이든 간에 우리의 사고 단계의 장애물이 아니라는 것을 확실시 해야 합니다. [Q16-B] 독창적인 생각은 생물 모방 기술에 거의 포함되지 않는데, 왜냐하면 그것은 단지 자연 현상을 관찰해서 이용하는 것이기 때문입니다. 하지만 제 얘기를 오해하지는 마세요. 제가 설명했듯이 생물 모방 기술은 우리 사회에 현저한 이익을 가져다 주기 때문입니다.

12. [Main Idea] What is the lecture mainly about?

(A) Methods of color production employed by diverse species with feathers and scales *(too specific)*

(B) ~~Pros and cons~~ of biomimicry used in many industries and ~~potential threats~~ *(too specific)* ★

(C) The application of natural processes in modern commercial endeavors

(D) Contributing factor to the ~~development of structural coloration~~ in the modern society *(not mentioned)*

해설 | (A) 자연에서 찾아 볼 수 있는 색상 생산 방법이 상업분야에서 어떻게 활용되는지가 강의의 주된 내용이다. 이 중 일부만 포함하고 있으므로 주제로 보기에는 너무 한정적이다. (B) 산업에서 이용되는 생물 모방 기술의 장단점이 언급되는 하지만 강의의 극히 일부이므로 주제로 보기에는 너무 한정적이다. (D) 구주적 천연색을 활용한 산업의 발전은 언급되지만 구조적 천연색 그 자체의 발전은 강의에서 다뤄지지 않으므로 오답.

13. [Detail – Cause/Reason] According to the professor, why aren't plants able to absorb the green wavelength?

(A) Because the green wavelengths are ~~used during photosynthesis~~ so the chloroplasts absorb them *(opposite fact)*

(B) Because the chlorophyll in the leaves reflects the green wavelengths of light from the sun's rays

(C) Because the leaves of plants have strong ~~affinity~~ for all colors but green *(not mentioned)* ★

(D) Because the wavelength of green the sun disseminates is ~~not substantial enough for plants to detect~~ *(not mentioned)*

해설 | (A) 식물이 녹색 파장을 흡수하지 못하는지에 대한 증거는 아직 입증 되지 않았지만 대부분의 과학자들은 녹색 빛이 광합성 과정에 해롭다고 추정한다고 교수는 설명한다. 이에 반대되므로 오답. (C) 교수는 식물의 녹색 파장의 흡수와 그 파장과의 친화성을 연관 짓지 않기 때문에 오답. (D) 녹색 파장이 식물이 감지하기에 불충분하다는 내용은 언급되지 않는다.

14. [Detail – Cause] How do Morpho butterflies appear blue when no pigment is existent in their bodies?

(A) Their scales are ~~too pale to absorb~~ the blue wavelengths in ultraviolet light *(not mentioned)*

(B) The unique chemical called schemochromes ~~makes them reflect the blue wavelength~~ *(wrong fact)* ★

(C) The multiple surfaces of their scales reflect the blue light from the ultraviolet spectrum

(D) Their ~~wing movements~~ and the ~~angle at which the sunlight hits them~~ makes them appear to be blue *(not mentioned)*

14. 어떻게 Morpho 나비의 몸에 색소가 없는데도 푸른 색을 띄는가?

(A) 날개가 자외선의 파란 파장을 ~~흡수하기에 너무 창백하다.~~

(B) Schemochromes라고 불리는 독특한 화학물질이 파란 파장을 반사하도록 만든다. ★

(C) 나비의 비늘의 다양한 표면이 자외광선 스펙트럼의 빛을 반사한다.

(D) 나비의 ~~날갯짓과 햇빛을 통과하는~~ 각도가 날개를 파란색으로 보이도록 한다.

> **해설** | (A)와 (D)는 언급되지 않은 내용이므로 오답. (B) 색소가 없음에도 불구하고 푸른 색을 띄는 나비의 날개는 schemochrome의 예일 뿐, 그로 인한 결과가 아니다. 둘의 관계가 잘못 설립 되어있으므로 오답. 또한, schemochrome은 화학물질이 아닌 구조적 천연색이다.

15. [Detail – Characteristic] What property of the scales of Morpho butterflies makes the wings water-resistant?

(A) The air-filled gaps in between their scales

(B) The adhesive forces ~~between each layer~~ of their scale *(wrong fact)*

(C) The rough, multi-layered structure of their scale ~~caused by the chemical called schemochromes~~ *(wrong fact)* ★

(D) Their individual cells' ~~hemophilic membrane~~ that prevents the entrance of water *(not mentioned)*

15. Morpho 나비 비늘의 어떠한 속성이 날개를 방수로 만드는가?

(A) 날개 사이에 있는 공기로 찬 틈

(B) 비늘의 ~~각 층 사이의~~ 접착력

(C) ~~schemochromes라고 불리는 화학물질에 의~~한 거칠고 다양한 층을 가진 비늘 ★

(D) 물의 입구를 막는 나비 비늘 각 세포의 ~~혈우병에 걸린~~ 막

> **해설** | (B) 평평한 표면에 물방울이 떨어질 경우 물방울들 사이에서, 그리고 물방울과 고체 사이에서 작용하는 접착력에 대한 교수의 설명을 왜곡시켜 놓은 것으로 오답. 비늘 사이의 접착력은 언급되지 않는다. (C) 거친 표면에 의해 물이 바로 미끄러져 내려가는 것은 맞으나 schemochromes에 의한 것은 아니다. 인과관계가 잘못 설립되어 있으므로 오답. (D) 언급되지 않은 내용이므로 오답.

16. [Detail – Difference/Contrast] In the lecture, the professor explains two different ways in which colors are created in nature. Indicate whether each of the following is a feature of pigmentation, structural coloration, or none.

	Pigmentation	Structural Coloration	None
(A) Requires thin layers of films or scales and light		○	
(B) Heavily involves original thinking			○
(C) Also known as schemochrome		○	
(D) Less exploited by business people when designing products	○		

해설 | 본문에 표시된 각 선택지의 근거 참고

Listen again to part of the lecture. Then answer the question.

"What do you think would happen if you accidentally spilled some ketchup on your shirt? Of course, the rough, layered material would bear the same results"

17. [Inference – Imply] **What does the professor mean when she says this:** 🎧

"Of course, the rough, layered material would bear the same results"

(A) That the ketchup would slide off the shirt without staining it

(B) That all everyday commodities like the shirt could be modified the same way *(unrelated to the question)*

(C) That using pigments on the shirt isn't necessary anymore because the shirts are already structurally colored *(unrelated to the question)*

(D) That applying the discipline of structural coloration to shirts is as effective as the layers of the butterflies' wings *(unrelated to the question)* ★

해설 | (B) 교수는 일상 제품들의 개선 방법을 제시하는 것이 아니라 생체모방기술을 적용시킨 셔츠 역시 이에 영감을 준 Morpho 나비들의 날개와 같은 원리가 적용할 것임을 이야기한다. (C) 이전에 설명 된 나비의 날개의 푸른 비늘이 색을 띄는 방법인 색소 형성과 구조적 천연색을 왜곡시켜 놓은 것으로 오답. 본 문제에서 다시 재생된 부분의 요점인 물질의 질감과는 관련 없는 내용이다. (D) 구조적 천연색은 본 문제의 요점인 물질의 질감과 그로 인한 방수성과 관련이 없으므로 오답.

TEST 4 set 2-1

Conversation: 19th century European art movements

문단주제	본문내용	해석
단락 1 발표 주제 소개	Listen to a conversation between a student and her art history professor. S: Hi, professor, do you have a minute? P: Of course, what can I do for you, Maria? S: [Q1] Well, it's about the group presentation on 19th century European art movements… I need help sorting my ideas. P: Okay. Have you chosen a topic for the presentation? S: Yes, I've done some research, and the Barbizon school really caught my attention, you know the French painters from 1830 to 1880.	학생과 예술사 교수님의 대화를 들어보시오. S: 교수님 안녕하세요, 시간 있으세요? P: 물론이지, 무슨 일이니, 마리아? S: [Q1] 음, 19세기 유럽의 미술 운동에 대한 그룹 발표 때문인데요. 생각을 정리하는 데 도움이 필요해요. P: 좋아. 발표 주제는 정했니? S: 네, 조사를 좀 해봤어요. 바르비종 학파가 정말로 제 관심을 끌더라구요. 1830년부터 1880년대까지의 프랑스 화가들 말이에요.
단락 2 조사 내용: 이름의 유래와 작품의 초점	P: A very interesting topic. Ummm… Why don't you tell me what you've learned from your research? Start with the source of their name and the focus of their art. S: Okay. [Q2-D] From what I've read, the name comes from a village located just outside of Paris, because the painters' primary workplace was the nearby Fontainebleau Forest. [Q2] I read that the forest attracted the artists because it preserved nature unaffected by modern civilization, so, it was a genuine representation of nature. P: And their painting? S: Oh right! They shared an understanding or recognition of landscape when it came to painting and they were faithful painters. By that, I mean they strove to adhere to capturing what they could see and avoided figurative elements or things that didn't exist in the natural scene.	P: 매우 흥미로운 주제지. 음… 조사를 해본 내용을 나에게 말해주는 건 어때? 이름의 시초와 그들 작품의 중점부터 시작해봐. S: 네. [Q2-D] 제가 읽은 바로는, 그 이름은 파리 외곽에 위치한 한 마을에서 유래되었어요. 왜냐하면 화가들의 주요 작업 장소가 Fontainebleau 숲 근처였기 때문이었어요. [Q2] 제가 읽기로는 그 숲이 예술가들의 흥미를 끌었대요, 왜냐하면 현대 문명의 영향을 받지 않은 자연을 보존하고 있었기 때문이에요. 그래서 그 숲은 정말 자연의 묘사였죠. P: 그리고 그들의 그림은 어땠지? S: 아 맞아요! 그들은 그림에 대한 풍경의 이해나 인식을 공유했어요. 그들은 신뢰 깊은 화가들이었죠. 그때까지, 제 말은 그들은 자기가 볼 수 있었던 것을 포착하는 데 충실히 노력했고, 자연에서 존재하지 않는 비유적인 요소나 사물은 피했어요.
단락 3 전통적인 프랑스 풍경화와의 차이점	P: I see… Okay. I'm not sure if you've gotten this part yet, [Q3] but did you know that their approach was quite different from traditional French landscape painting, which included the use of imaginative elements inspired by classical poems? S: Oh, I never knew that! P: Great! Why don't you add something to the presentation that will show the difference between the two? I'm sure it would be very informative. S: I should definitely do that! P: Okay, were you able to find any other information?	P: 알겠어. 좋아. 이 부분을 알고 있는지는 아직 모르겠지만, [Q3] 이러한 접근이 고전 시의 영향을 받아 상상적인 요소를 사용했던 전통적인 프랑스 풍경화와 꽤 다르다는 것을 알고 있니? S: 오, 전혀 몰랐어요! P: 좋아! 두 가지의 차이를 보여주는 것을 발표에 추가하는 게 어때? 굉장히 유익하리라고 확신해. S: 당연히 그래야죠! P: 좋아. 또 다른 정보를 찾을 수 있었니?

문단주제	본문내용	해석
단락 4 교수의 조언: Theodore Rousseau	**S:** Um, I read that the Barbizon painters often did basic, preliminary sketches for their paintings while out in the forest and then finished them in their studios. They also intentionally left some details of their work looking unfinished, but I need to do more research on those points. **P:** Okay, that's great. [Q5-D] Try to make your presentation concise and informative. [Q5] Remember, It should be 5 minutes, not an hour. **S:** Of course. Any suggestions on how I should proceed? **P:** Well… let's see. [Q4-C] It seems that you've done comprehensive research, but you're missing a central figure, like a paragon of the Barbizon school. [Q4] I think Théodore Rousseau would be a good example, because… Well, you'll figure it out through your research, but he was one of the most prominent and noteworthy artists of the school. Try to do some research on his life and paintings and include them in your presentation. **S:** Perfect! Oh by the way, I hear the art museum around the corner exhibits Barbizon paintings, so I'm going to stop by there also. **P:** That's a great plan. I think you're all set and good to go! **S:** Thanks for your help, professor. I really appreciate it! **P:** No problem at all. Good luck with your presentation; I'll look forward to it!	**S:** 음, 제가 읽은 바로는 바르비종 화가들은 종종 그림을 위해 기본적이고 임시적인 스케치를 숲에 나갔을 때 그리고 자신들의 스튜디오에서 마무리했다고 해요. 그들은 또한 의도적으로 자신의 작업의 디테일을 미완성처럼 보이게 했는데, 이 부분에 대해서는 더 조사가 필요해요. **P:** 좋아, 훌륭해. [Q5-D] 발표를 간결하고 유익하게 만들도록 노력해봐. [Q5] 기억해야 할 것은 발표가 1시간이 아니라 5분이라는 거야. **S:** 물론이죠. 제가 어떻게 해야 할 지 조언 좀 해주시겠어요? **P:** 음, 글쎄요. [Q4-C] 학생은 꽤 포괄적인 조사를 한 것 같아. 하지만 핵심을 놓치고 있어. 예를 들면 바르비종 학파의 핵심 인물이라든지. [Q4] 내 생각에는 Theodore Rousseau가 좋은 예가 될 것 같아. 왜냐하면… 음, 조사를 통해서 알게 되겠지만 그는 그 학파에서 가장 뛰어나고 주목할 만한 사람 중 하나야. 그의 삶과 작품에 대해서 조사를 해보고 발표에 포함시키도록 해봐. **S:** 완벽해요! 오, 그런데, 코너에 있는 미술관에서 바르비종 전시회를 한다고 들었어요. 거기 또한 들려 보려고요. **P:** 좋은 계획이야. 모든 게 다 정리되었으니 가도 될 거 같아. **S:** 도와주셔서 감사해요, 교수님. 정말로 감사해요! **P:** 천만해. 발표 잘 할거야. 기대할게.

01. [Main Purpose] Why does the student visit the professor?

(A) To organize her thoughts and get advice on an upcoming assignment

(B) To discuss the ~~Barbizon paintings that she will observe~~ in the art museum around the corner *(wrong fact)*

(C) To consult with the professor on the problems she's having ~~with her group members~~ *(not mentioned)*

(D) To inquire about the ~~lifestyle~~ of French painters in the in the mid-19th century *(not mentioned)* ★

01. 학생은 교수를 왜 찾아가는가?

(A) 자신의 생각을 정리하고 임박한 과제에 대해 조언을 얻으려고

(B) 코너에 있는 미술관에서 ~~관찰할~~ 바르비종 작품들에 대해 이야기하려고

(C) ~~조원들과의~~ 문제에 대해 교수와 상의하려고

(D) 19세기 중반 프랑스 화가들의 ~~생활양식~~에 대해 물어보려고 ★

해설 | (B) 19세기 유럽의 미술 운동은 그룹 발표과제의 주제이다. 이에 대한 토론은 대화에서 언급되지 않는다. (C) 조원들과의 문제 역시 언급되지 않으므로 오답. (D) 대화 마지막에 학생이 코너에 있는 미술관에서 하는 바르비종 전시회에 가볼 것이라는 내용으로 대화의 극히 일부이며, 학생이 교수를 찾아간 이유는 아니다.

---

02. [Detail – Characteristic] According to the student, what property of the Fontainebleau Forest did the painters of the Barbizon school cherish?

(A) Its distinct landscape features ~~that other forests did not have~~ *(not mentioned)*

(B) The existence of its untouched nature

(C) The fusion of ~~modern civilization~~ and preserved ~~relics from ancient times~~ *(wrong fact)*

(D) Its location just outside of the ~~village in Paris where the painters lived~~ *(wrong fact)* ★

02. 학생에 따르면 바르비종 학파의 화가들이 Fontainebleau 숲의 어떤 속성을 아꼈는가?

(A) ~~다른 숲에서는 볼 수 없는~~ 뚜렷한 풍경의 특성

(B) 때묻지 않은 자연의 존재

(C) 현대 문명과 보존된 ~~고대 문명의 유물~~의 혼합

(D) ~~화가들이 살았던 파리의 마을~~ 바로 밖의 위치 ★

해설 | (A) 학생은 Fontainebleau 숲과 다른 숲을 비교하지 않으므로 오답. (C) 학생 말에 의하면, Fontainebleau 숲이 화가들의 이목을 끈 것은 현대 문명의 영향을 받지 않은 풍경을 볼 수 있어서였다. 또한, 고대유물은 아예 언급되지 않으므로 오답. (D) 숲의 위치는 파리 외곽의 한 마을 근처이다. 바르비종 학파의 이름의 유래에 대한 내용을 왜곡시켜 놓은 것으로 오답. 또한, 화가들의 거주지에 대한 내용은 언급되지 않는다.

---

03. [Detail – Difference/Contrast] How did the Barbizon way of landscape painting differ from that of an earlier period?

(A) ~~The former's artists~~ used imagination as a key component *(wrong fact)*

(B) ~~The latter~~ presented an honest, truthful depiction of nature *(wrong fact)*

(C) The former didn't require any part of paintings to be fabricated

(D) The former's artists mostly worked in forests undisturbed by modern civilization *(unrelated to the question)* ★

03. 바르비종의 풍경화 기법은 초기의 풍경화 기법과 어떻게 다른가?

(A) ~~바르비종의 예술가들은~~ 상상력을 핵심 요소로 사용했다.

(B) ~~초기의 풍경화 기법은~~ 자연을 정직하고 진실되게 묘사했다.

(C) 바르비종의 풍경화는 그림의 어떠한 부분도 조작을 필요로 하지 않았다.

(D) 바르비종의 예술가들은 대부분 현대 문명의 방해를 받지 않는 숲에서 작업했다. ★

해설 | (A) 바르비종의 풍경화 기법이 아닌 전통적인 프랑스 풍경화 기법에 대한 설명이므로 오답. (B) 전통적인 프랑스 풍경화 기법이 아닌 바르비종의 풍경화 기법에 대한 설명이므로 오답. (D) 맞는 말이지만, 전통적인 프랑스 예술가들의 작업 공간이 어떠했는지 알 수 없기 때문에 대조가 불가하다.

04. [Inference – Purpose/Intention] Why does the professor mention Théodore Rousseau?

(A) To explain that he was one of the most prestigious artists of the time *(unrelated to the question)* ★

(B) To give the student an exemplary person whom she could possibly use for her assignment

(C) To support his claim that the student's paper is well-organized and comprehensive *(wrong fact)*

(D) To claim that Théodore Rousseau was responsible for founding the Barbizon school *(not mentioned)*

04. 교수는 왜 Theodore Rousseau를 언급하는가?

(A) 그가 그 당시에 가장 유명한 예술가 중 하나였다고 설명하기 위해서 ★

(B) 그녀의 과제에 사용할 수 있는 아마도 좋은 예가 되는 사람을 학생에게 알려주기 위해서

(C) 학생의 과제가 잘 정리되었고 포괄적이라는 그의 주장을 뒷받침하기 위해서

(D) Theodore Rousseau가 바르비종 학파의 설립을 담당하였다고 주장하기 위해서

해설 | (A) 맞는 말이기는 하나 교수의 의도와는 무관하므로 오답. (C) 교수는 학생의 조사가 포괄적이기는 하나 핵심을 놓치고 있다고 말한다. 이를 보완하기 위해 조사하기를 권한 주제가 바로 Theodore Rousseau이기 때문에 마냥 칭찬만 하기 위해서 Rousseau가 언급된 것은 아니다. (D) 교수는 Theodore Rousseau와 바르비종 학파의 설립을 연관 짓지 않는다.

05. [Inference – Imply] What does the professor imply when he says this: 🎧

> "Remember, It should be 5 minutes, not an hour."

(A) That the student didn't pay enough attention to the presentation guidelines *(not mentioned)*

(B) That the student may be trying to present too much information

(C) That he made a change in the requirements of the assignment and shortened the presentation's duration *(not mentioned)*

(D) That in his opinion, all presentations should be concise and informative within 5 minutes *(wrong fact)* ★

05. 교수가 이 말을 할 때 암시하는 것은 무엇인가? 🎧

> "기억해야 할 것은 발표가 1시간이 아니라 5분이라는 거야."

(A) 학생이 발표 지침을 주의 깊게 숙지 하지 않았다는 것

(B) 학생이 너무 많은 정보를 발표하려고 하는 것 같다는 것

(C) 그가 과제에 대한 요구 조건을 바꾸었고 발표 시간을 줄였다는 것

(D) 모든 발표가 5분안에 간결하고 유익 해야 한다고 그가 생각한다는 것 ★

해설 | (A) 학생이 발표 지침을 주의 깊게 숙지 하지 않음을 보여주는 부분은 대화에 나오지 않는다. 따라서, 교수가 의심할 이유가 없는 부분이다. (C) 발표의 요구 사항 및 조건의 변화에 대한 내용은 대화에서 언급되지 않는다. (D) 주어진 5분의 발표시간은 본 발표에서 학생들이 따라야 할 조건일뿐, 교수의 의견과는 무관하다. 또한, 이러한 조건은 모든 발표 (all presentations)가 아닌 이번 발표에만 해당하는 것이므로 오답.

TEST 4 set 2-2

Lecture 1
The advent of literacy and cheap books

문단주제	본문내용	해석

단락 1
지난 시간 복습 및 초기현재 시기의 소개

Listen to part of a lecture in a literature class.

P: Okay, we looked at the access to books by the 19th century English public last time, specifically how classics were divided into triple-deckers of three volumes. Due to this, book prices were extremely burdensome for ordinary people, so they came up with ways to make books more accessible and cheaper: lending libraries and, uh, the publication of books in magazines and newspapers. [Q7] Well, interestingly, a similar phenomenon existed from the 15th century all the way to the 17th century, [Q6] so we'll investigate some key points of the era today before we move on to the modern era of literature.

영문학 강의의 일부를 들으시오.

P: 자, 우리 저번 시간에 19세기 영국 대중이 책에 접근한 것에 대해, 특히 어떻게 고전이 세 권의 3부작으로 나눠졌는지 봤죠. 이 때문에 책값은 평범한 사람들한테 너무 많이 비쌌고, 그래서 그들은 책을 더 접근 가능하고 싸게 만드는 방법을 생각해냈어요: 도서관에서 빌리고, 음, 잡지나 신문으로 책을 출판해냈어요. [Q7] 음, 흥미롭게도, 비슷한 현상은 15세기에서 17세기까지 계속 되었습니다. [Q6] 오늘 우리는 현대 문학으로 넘어가기 전에 이 시기의 몇 중요한 포인트에 대해 살펴볼 거에요.

단락 2
초기현대 시기와 당시 책의 특징

Although the timing of this period is sometimes controversial, we're going to refer to it as the early modern period, succeeding the Middle Ages of the post-classical era. This period was marked by the advent of literacy and cheap books became readily available to the general public, especially in France. [Q8-B] These were small pamphlets, usually covering subjects like chivalry – you know, medieval knights going on adventures and exploring the world. Religious stories about the tension between saints and demons were also covered in the books. However, don't get the wrong idea; [Q8] the stories were very light and entertaining. Philosophical components weren't involved, so everyday people enjoyed reading them. Those books were usually simple and cheaply-made, nothing like the embellished manuscripts of the Middle ages, which covered a range of subjects from philosophy to art or science. [Q8] These cheap books were so common that they were even sold by hawkers and peddlers.

이 시기가 정확히 언제였는지는 가끔 논쟁거리가 되지만, 우리는 이 시기를 초기 현대라고 부를 거에요. 중세의 후기 고전 시기의 뒤에 오는. 이 시기는 특히 프랑스에서, 문해가 도래했고 일반 대중들한테 싼 책이 쉽게 접근 가능해졌다는 특징이 있습니다. [Q8-B] 이것들은 보통 기사도, 알죠? 그 중세의 기사들이 모험을 떠나고 세계를 탐험하는 그 기사도와 같은 주제를 다뤘던 작은 팜플렛입니다. 성인들과 악마 사이의 긴장에 관한 종교적인 이야기 또한 책에서 다뤄졌죠. 하지만, 오해하지는 마세요, [Q8] 이 이야기들은 매우 가볍고 재미있었어요. 철학적인 부분들은 포함되지 않았고, 그래서 평범한 사람들은 이런 책을 읽는 것을 즐겼습니다. 이 책들은 보통 단순했고 저렴하게 만들어졌으며 철학부터 예술이나 과학에 달하는 주제를 다루던 장식된 중세의 필사본들과는 전혀 달랐어요. [Q8] 이 싼 책들은 너무 흔해서 심지어 행상인과 보따리 장수들이 팔았을 정도였습니다.

단락 3
값싼 책의 인쇄의 영향

S: Professor, you mentioned earlier, that some kind of stimulus or input always starts radical changes. What was it in this case?

P: Good question! You're asking what initiated this dramatic change in Western civilization, right? Well, Elizabeth Eisenstein, an American scholar and historian, explained the transition from the era of the manuscript to that of print culture.

S: 교수님, 저번에 교수님께서 어떤 종류의 자극이나 투입이 늘 근본적인 변화를 이끈다고 하셨잖아요. 이 경우엔 어떤 것이 있었나요?

P: 좋은 질문이에요! 어떤 것이 서구 문명의 이 극적인 변화를 시작했는지 묻는 거죠, 맞죠? 음, 미국의 학자이자 역사학자인 Elizabeth Eisenstein은 필사본의 시대에서 인쇄 문화의 시대로의 전환을 설명합니다.

문단주제	본문내용	해석
	In the late 1970's, she claimed that printing of cheap books and pamphlets was responsible for an unrecognized revolution that resulted in two significant long-term effects. We'll discuss the 'unrecognized revolution' in detail later, so let's not worry about it yet, but the first change it brought about was printing technology, a set of new standards for books. I mean, popular stories made way for just one standard, the written version, because they were much more profitable and efficient that way. Prior to the advent of printing culture, however, stories were passed down orally. So, that was her first claim of a print revolution hypothesis, but this doesn't mean that the oral tradition was completely eradicated. [Q9] She claimed there would always be a written version of stories, but people continued to orally express them, because it was more convenient. Her second claim was that printing technology enabled the permanent preservation of materials, which were usefully employed by the critics of authority at the time. They were useful resources because the critics could refer to the books whenever evidence or differing perspectives were needed. [Q6-B] To elucidate her point, she used the example of French writer, Michel de Montaigne.	1970년대 후반, 그녀는 싼 책과 팜플렛의 인쇄는 두 가지 중요한 장기 효과를 가져온 인정받지 못했던 혁명을 가져왔다고 주장했습니다. 우리는 이 "인정받지 못한 혁명"을 다음에 자세히 알아볼 것이니까 아직 이것에 대해 걱정하지는 말고요, 하지만 이 것이 가져온 첫 번째 변화는 인쇄 기술, 즉 책에 대한 새로운 기준들이었습니다. 제 말은, 인기 있는 이야기들은 쓰여진 버전, 그 단 하나의 표준에 길을 내줬어요. 그렇게 하는 게 훨씬 이윤이 남고 효율적이었으니까요. 인쇄 문화가 도래하기 전에는 하지만 이야기들은 구전되어 전해졌어요. 그래서 이게 인쇄 혁명 가설에 대한 그녀의 첫 번째 주장이었지만 이것은 구전의 전통이 아예 없어졌다는 뜻은 아니었어요. [Q9] 그녀는 이야기의 쓰여진 버전은 늘 있었겠지만 사람들은 그게 더 편하기 때문에 계속 말로 그 이야기를 표현해왔을 거라고 주장했어요. 그녀의 두 번째 주장은 인쇄 기술이 당시의 권위 있는 비평가들이 유용하게 사용한 자료의 영구 보존을 가능하게 했을 것이라는 것이었습니다. 그것들은 비평가들이 증거나 다른 관점이 필요할 때 언제나 책을 인용할 수 있었다는 점에서 유용한 자원이었어요. [Q6-B] 그녀의 요점을 명료하게 하기 위해, 그녀는 프랑스 작가, Michel de Montaigne의 예시를 들었습니다.
단락 4 Montaigne의 작품 및 특징	Montaigne was one of the most prestigious and notable French Renaissance writers and his impact is still recognized today. [Q10] His controversial essays were considered detrimental to tradition and authority rather than as innovations during his time. He's now considered the father of modern skepticism, but we needn't go too deeply into his biography now, so let's skip it. Where were we… right, okay. After scrutinizing his essays, Eisenstein found that he had access to information from many books and he borrowed ideas and concepts for his essays. As I mentioned earlier, his points of view were very well conveyed through his essays. For instance, in his 1580 work called the Essais, which is considered his most noteworthy work, he expressed his views on subjects like politics, religion, and human nature.	Montaigne는 프랑스 르네상스시기의 가장 명망 있고 주목할만한 작가 중 한 명이었고 그의 영향은 오늘날까지 아직도 인정받고 있습니다. [Q10] 그의 논쟁적인 에세이는 그의 시대에는 혁신이라기 보다는 전통과 권위를 해하는 것으로 여겨졌어요. 그는 지금은 현대 회의론의 아버지로 여겨지지만, 우리는 오늘 그의 전기를 깊이 들어갈 필요는 없으니 넘어갑시다. 우리가 어디까지 얘기했었죠.. 아, 네. 그의 에세이를 자세히 살펴본 후, Eisenstein은 그가 여러 책들에서 나온 정보에 접근할 수 있었고 그는 그의 에세이를 위해 아이디어와 개념들을 빌려왔다는 사실을 발견했습니다. 앞서 이야기했듯, 그의 관점은 그의 에세이를 통해 매우 잘 전달되어요. 예를 들어, 가장 주목할 가치가 있는 그의 작품이라고 여겨지는, Essais라고 불리는 그의 1580 작품에서 그는 정치학, 종교, 그리고 인간의 본성과 같은 주제에 대한 그의 견해를 드러냅니다.
단락 5 혁명의 원동력	I think that's enough of an explanation. Let me ask you, what do you think was the driving force of this revolution? Printing machines or people?	설명은 이만하면 충분한 것 같네요. 질문 하나 할게요. 여러분들은 이 혁명을 이끈 힘이 무엇이었다고 생각하나요? 인쇄기인가요 아니면 사람들인가요?

문단주제	본문내용	해석
	S: I would say printing machines actualized the revolution, because they made it possible for people to develop and use books more efficiently. **P:** Some scholars argue that, but let's take into consideration the accounts of the French Revolution and the Industrial Revolution. The former lasted about 10 years, from 1789 to 1799, I believe, and the latter lasted much longer, fifty to seventy years. [Q11] It's generally thought that fifty to seventy years is a long time for a 'revolution.' If you look at the printing revolution, it lasted about three hundred years. Do you think printing technology itself was enough of a driving force to keep the early modern period afloat for three centuries? Well, not quite. It's unfortunate that the people who brought about changes at the time aren't getting the credit they deserve.	**S:** 저는 인쇄기가 혁명을 실현했다고 봐요, 왜냐하면 인쇄기가 사람들이 책을 발전시키고 더 효율적으로 사용할 수 있게 만들어줬으니까요. **P:** 몇 학자들은 그걸 주장하죠, 하지만 프랑스 혁명과 산업혁명의 이야기를 생각해 봅시다. 전자는 10년이 걸렸어요, 1789년부터 1799년까지, 그리고 후자는 훨씬 더 걸렸죠, 50년에서 70년. [Q11] 일반적으로 50년에서 70년이 "혁명"에 필요한 긴 기간이라고 여겨져요. 인쇄 혁명을 보시면, 이건 약 300년이 걸렸어요. 인쇄 기술 그 자체가 초기 현대시기가 3세기 동안 떠있도록 할 만큼 충분한 원동력이라고 생각하나요? 글쎄요, 별로요. 그 당시 변화를 가져온 사람들이 그들이 마땅히 받을만한 인정을 받고 있지 못한 것은 불운한 일이지요.

06. [Main Purpose] What is the main purpose of the lecture?

(A) To discuss the causes and effects of the development of accessible literature in the early modern period

(B) To explain remarkable works by French scholars, such as Michel de Montaigne *(too specific)*

(C) To compare and contrast the revolution that took hold in the 19th century with the early modern period *(wrong fact)* ★

(D) To address the transition from the manuscript culture to print culture *(not mentioned)*

06. 이 강의의 주된 목적은 무엇인가?

(A) 초기 현대시기에 접근 가능한 문학이 발전한 것의 인과관계를 논의하기 위해서

(B) Michel de Montaigne와 같은 프랑스 학자들의 훌륭한 작품을 설명하기 위해서

(C) 19세기에 일어난 혁명과 초기 현대시기에 일어난 것을 비교대조하기 위해서 ★

(D) 필사본 문화에서 인쇄 문화로의 전환을 이야기하기 위해서

해설 | (B) Michel de Montaigne은 인쇄 기술이 당시의 비평가들의 자료 인용 및 참고를 용이하게 했다는 Elizabeth Eisenstein의 주장의 예로 언급되었다. 강의의 극히 일부이므로 문제가 묻는 강의의 주된 목적으로 정의하기에는 너무 좁다. (C) 19세기의 영국은 강의 초반에 지난 시간 수업을 복습하기 위한 목적으로 언급된 것이며, 초기 현대시기와 근본적인 공통점이 있음을 시사하는 것 이외에는 본 강의와 크게 관련성이 없다. (D) 강의에서 주로 다뤄지는 변화는 책 값의 하락으로 인한 대중의 접근성의 변화이다. 필사본 문화는 언급되지 않는다.

07. [Inference – Purpose/Intention] Why does the professor mention what happened in England in the 19th century at the beginning of the lecture?

(A) To explain that the printing revolution continued all the way through the 19th century *(wrong fact)*

(B) To explain how classics were divided into triple-deckers of three volumes *(fact, but unrelated to the question)* ★

(C) To imply that the last class' discussion shares a similarity with today's lecture

(D) To introduce the idea that revolutions have taken place throughout Europe since the printing era began *(not mentioned)*

07. 교수는 왜 강의를 시작할 때 19세기 영국에서 일어난 일을 언급했는가?

(A) 인쇄 혁명이 19세기까지 계속 이어졌음을 설명하기 위해서

(B) 고전이 세 권의 3부작으로 나눠졌음을 설명하기 위해서 ★

(C) 지난 시간의 논의가 오늘의 강의와 비슷한 점이 있음을 시사하기 위해서

(D) 인쇄 시기가 시작된 이후로 유럽 전역에서 혁명이 일어났다는 아이디어를 소개하기 위해서

해설 | (A) 인쇄 혁명에 대한 내용은 강의 마지막에 "인정 받지 못한 혁명"의 원동력에 대해 이야기 할 때 언급된다. 이를 왜곡시켜 놓은 것으로 오답. (B) 사실이지만, 이로 인해 비쌌던 책값에 대한 사람들의 대응책과 15세기에서 17세기 사이의 현상의 유사점을 이끌어내려고 한 말로, 본 강의와 직접적인 연관이 없다. (D) 교수는 혁명의 시초를 정의하지 않으므로 오답.

08. [Detail – Characteristic] Which of the following are the characteristics of cheap books made during the early modern period?

Click on 2 answers

(A) They contained light stories that most people enjoyed reading

(B) Unlike ~~those of the medieval period~~, they ~~avoided~~ philosophical topics like medieval knights and religious stories *(wrong fact)* ★

(C) They required ~~sophisticated logical reasoning skills~~ *(wrong fact)*

(D) They were easily accessible and sometimes sold by street vendors

08. 초기 현대 시기에 만들어진 싼 책의 특징은 무엇인가?

2개의 정답을 고르시오

(A) 대부분의 사람들이 읽기 좋아할 가벼운 이야기를 담고 있었다.

(B) ~~중세시대의 책들과~~는 달리, 중세의 기사들과 종교적인 이야기 같은 철학적인 주제를 ~~다루지 않았다.~~ ★

(C) 복잡한 논리적 추론 기술을 요구했다.

(D) 그것들은 쉽게 접근 가능했고 가끔 행상인이 팔았다.

해설 | (B) 중세시대 책들의 특징은 강의에서 언급되지 않으며, 초기현대 시기의 책들과 비교되지 않는다. 또한, 중세의 시가들과 종교적인 이야기가 가볍게 다뤄졌다는 교수의 설명과 어긋나므로 오답. (C) 책의 내용은 일반적으로 매우 가볍고 재미있었으며, 철학적인 요소가 포함되어 있지 않았다는 교수의 설명과 어긋나므로 오답.

09. [Inference – Imply] What does the professor imply about the oral tradition?

(A) That it was a ~~reliable source~~ of preserving ideas and stories for future generations *(not mentioned)*

(B) That its role didn't vanish or succumb to printing machines

(C) That it ~~died out~~ when the printing era began taking over *(wrong fact)* ★

(D) That its importance ~~surpassed~~ that of the printing machines *(not mentioned)*

09. 교수가 구전 전통에 대해 암시한 것은 무엇인가?

(A) 그것은 미래 세대를 위해 아이디어와 이야기를 보존하기에 ~~믿을만한 원천~~이라는 것

(B) 그것의 역할은 사라지거나 인쇄기술에 굴복한 것이 아니라는 것

(C) 그것이 인쇄 시기가 중요해지기 시작할 때 ~~멸종되었다는 것~~ ★

(D) 그것의 중요성은 인쇄기의 중요성을 ~~넘었다는 것~~

해설 | (A) 교수는 구전 전통의 신뢰도를 평가하지 않으므로 오답. (C) 구전 전통의 편리성 때문에 계속 말로 이야기가 전달됐을 거라는 Elizabeth Eisenstein의 주장과 어긋나므로 오답. (D) 교수는 구전 전통과 인쇄기의 중요성을 비교하지 않으므로 오답.

10. [Detail – Opinion/Attitude] According to the professor, what was the contemporary public's opinion of Montaigne's essays?

(A) They were thought of as ~~innovative and experimental~~ *(wrong fact)*

(B) **They were viewed adversely because of their argumentative tendency**

(C) They were most ~~popular and sensational~~ with politicians of his time *(opposite fact)*

(D) The authorities ironically ~~favored them~~, for they identified their shortcomings *(not mentioned)* ★

10. 교수에 따르면, Montaigne의 에세이에 대한 당대 대중의 의견은 어떠했는가?

(A) 그것들은 혁신적이고 실험적이라고 여겨진다.

(B) **그것들은 시비를 거는 경향 때문에 부정적으로 여겨진다.**

(C) 그것들은 당시 정치인들 사이에서 ~~가장 유명했고 돌풍을 일으켰다.~~

(D) 권위자들은 그들의 단점을 밝혔기 때문에, 역설적으로 그것들을 좋아했다. ★

해설 | (A) 그의 에세이가 "혁신이라기 보다는 전통과 권위를 해하는 것으로 여겨졌다"는 교수의 설명과 정반대 되므로 오답. (C) 전통과 권위를 위협한다고 여겨졌기에 정치인들 사이에서는 더욱 더 부정적인 시각을 받았음을 유추할 수 있으므로 오답. (D) 언급되지 않은 내용이므로 오답.

**Listen again to part of the lecture.
Then answer the question.**

"It's generally thought that fifty to seventy years is a long time for a 'revolution.' If you look at the printing revolution, it lasted about three hundred years. Do you think printing technology itself was enough of a driving force to keep the early modern period afloat for three centuries?"

강의의 일부분을 다시 듣고 질문에 답하시오.

"일반적으로 50년에서 70년이 "혁명"에 필요한 긴 기간이라고 여겨져요. 인쇄 혁명을 보시면, 이건 약 300년이 걸렸어요. 인쇄 기술 그 자체가 초기 현대시기가 3세기 동안 떠있도록 할 만큼 충분한 원동력이라고 생각하나요?"

11. [Inference - Imply] What does the professor imply when she asks this: 🎧

> "Do you think printing technology itself was enough of a driving force to keep the early modern period afloat for three centuries?"

(A) **That the focus of attention should be on the people of the period not the technology**

(B) That she believes ~~other technologies~~ facilitated the revolution's longevity *(wrong fact)*

(C) That the biggest contribution ~~to the early modern period~~ was the scholars' work *(unrelated to the question)* ★

(D) That she's in line with those who argue that the printing technology was the ~~essence of the revolution~~ *(wrong fact)*

11. 교수가 이렇게 물을 때 무엇을 암시하는가? 🎧

"인쇄 기술 그 자체가 초기 현대시기가 3세기 동안 떠있도록 할 만큼 충분한 원동력이라고 생각하나요?"

(A) **기술이 아니라 그 시기 사람들에게 주의가 집중되어야 한다는 것**

(B) 그녀는 ~~다른 기술들이~~ 혁명이 오래 지속되도록 했다고 믿는다는 것

(C) 초기 현대 시기에 가장 큰 기여를 한 것은 학자들의 작품이라는 것 ★

(D) 그녀는 인쇄 기술이 ~~혁명의 가장 중요한 부분~~이라고 주장하는 사람들과 같은 의견이라는 것

해설 | (B) 교수는 다른 기술들이 아닌 당대 사람들의 영향이라고 주장하므로 오답. (C) 초기 현대 시기의 기여가 아닌 혁명의 원동력을 논하고 있으므로 오답. (D) 교수는 너무 오랜 시간 지속된 인쇄 혁명은 그 영향력에 한계가 있었다고 지적하며 인쇄 기술이 아닌 당시 사람들이 더 큰 원동력이라고 주장한다. 이에 어긋나므로 오답

TEST 4 set 2-3
Lecture 2
The Industrial Revolution

문단주제	본문내용	해석
	Listen to part of a lecture in a history of technology class.	기술사 수업의 일부를 들으시오.
단락 1 산업혁명과 그로 인한 개발 돌풍	P: Today, we'll continue our discussion of the Industrial Revolution that took place from 1760 to around 1820 or 1840. As I mentioned last time, it was the most prominent period in history, because of the developmental boom in almost every aspect of humanity due to advances in medication, transportation, food, and so on. It started in England and spread across Europe, eventually reaching the United States. [Q12] Today, I'd like to focus on a specific technological advance made during the period: transportation. James? S: If I remember correctly, the earliest steam-powered vehicles came about during the mid-18th century. Right?	P: 오늘 우리는 1760년부터 1820년 혹은 1840까지 지속되었던 산업혁명에 대하여 계속해서 논할 것입니다. 지난 시간에 얘기했듯이, 산업혁명은 역사에서 가장 중요한 시기였습니다. 왜냐하면 의약, 교통, 식품의 진보 등 인류의 거의 모든 분야에서 개발 돌풍이 일어났기 때문입니다. 산업혁명은 영국에서 시작되어 유럽 전역으로 확대되었으며 심지어 미국까지 도달하였습니다. [Q12] 오늘 우리는 이 기간 동안에 발생한 특정 기술 진보에 대하여 집중하고자 합니다: 교통이죠. 제임스? S: 제가 정확히 기억하는 게 맞다면, 초기 증기를 동력으로 하는 운송수단들이 18세기 중반에 등장했죠. 맞나요?
단락 2 초기 증기 운송수단의 단점	P: Yes, but these early steam vehicles had a major drawback. [Q13-A] Although their engines powered their bodies, they were too heavy, averaging about 3,600kg. [Q13] Due to this burdensome weight and manufacturing limitations, they weren't practical for transportation unless they were on perfectly flat surfaces like iron tracks. Naturally, many companies turned to developing locomotives, but the availability of new resources in the early 20th century, such as petroleum and gasoline, led to the introduction of the luxurious internal combustion powered vehicles that we use today and marked the end of steam-powered vehicles. Although the Industrial Revolution marked the introduction of mechanically produced products, human-powered transportation methods developed. [Q17] Actually, they were more popular than steam engines because… Well, I think you should know by now. What human-powered transportation methods are you aware of? S: Um, bicycles would be the most well-known, along with skateboards, velomobiles, and cabin cycles.	P: 맞습니다. 그러나 초기 증기 운송수단들은 심각한 결점이 있었습니다. [Q13-A] 엔진이 몸체에 동력을 공급했음에도 불구하고, 평균적으로 3,600kg정도로 매우 무거웠습니다. [Q13] 이러한 성가신 무게와 생산의 한계 때문에, 초기 운송수단은 철제 도로처럼 완벽히 평평한 표면에 있는 것이 아니고서는 실용적이지 않았습니다. 당연히 많은 회사들은 기관차를 개발하는 데 집중했고, 20세기 초의 석유나 가솔린 같은 새로운 자원의 가능성이 화려한 내부 연소로 동력을 공급하는 운송수단을 도입하지 않을 수 없었습니다. 이는 오늘날의 우리가 사용하고 있는 것이며, 증기 운송수단의 종말을 고하는 것이었죠. 산업혁명이 제품의 기계 생산의 시작을 알렸지만, 인간이 동력을 공급하는 운송 수단들도 개발되었습니다. [Q17] 실제로 이것들은 증기 엔진보다 더 대중적이었습니다. 왜냐하면… 그런데, 지금쯤은 이미 여러분들이 알아야 할 것 같은데요. 우리가 아는 것 중 인간이 동력을 공급하는 운송수단이 뭐가 있습니까? S: 음, 자전거가 가장 유명하죠. 스케이트보드, 벨로모빌, 그리고 캐빈 오토바이가 있죠.
단락 3 인간 동력의 운송수단: "말 없는 마차"	P: Great! Today, there are many choices when it comes to human-powered transportation, but in the 1800's, choices were more limited.	P: 훌륭합니다! 오늘날 인간이 동력하는 운송 수단들이 많이 있지만, 1800년대에는 훨씬 선택권이 적었죠.

문단주제	본문내용	해석
단락 4 Drais의 Laufmaschine	Let's start with the first human-powered vehicles called horseless carriages, which had four wheels. First patented around 1800, a few different models were available and they accommodated up to four riders. Despite their benefits, [Q14-C] such as improved convenience on rough, rocky roads, the general public didn't accept them as methods of transportation. [Q14] They were too heavy, so their operation was bothersome and since they were human-powered, human beings worked as 'draft animals' to produce their mechanical energy. This was horrendous. Many owners were criticized and debased for abusing their servants, so their use gradually waned. After these four-wheeled carriages disappeared, a German carriage maker, Baron Karl Drais, came up with the idea for the Dandy horse, or Laufmaschine, which somewhat resembled today's two-wheeled bicycles. S: I'm sorry. Could you explain that term? P: Of course. Drais referred to it as 'Laufmaschine,' which translates to 'running machine' in German. Others believe it comes from the Latin words for 'fast' and 'foot' because of its shape. It was almost an extension of the human body – one would straddle it and push the ground as if running. Think of today's bicycle without pedals. S: No pedals? I thought the earliest bicycle had a humongous front wheel and pedals. P: You're referring to the penny-farthing, which was invented in 1870. Oh wait… there was also another type of bicycle called the boneshaker that was introduced as the first bicycle with pedals in the 1860's; you could also be referring to that. [Q15] Well, whichever it is that you're implying, I'm on the same page as you, but chronologically speaking, the Laufmaschine was introduced in 1818, several decades earlier than those two and was the starting point in bicycle development. S: How fast could it go without pedals… And did people like it?	그럼 4개의 바퀴를 가지고 있고, '말 없는 마차'라고 불리는 최초의 인간 동력 운송수단부터 시작해 봅시다. 1800년경에 먼저 출원되어, 몇 개의 다른 모델이 출시되었으며, 4명의 사람들을 태울 수 있었습니다. [Q14-C] 거칠고 돌이 많은 길에서 훨씬 더 편리하다는 이점에도 불구하고, 일반 대중들은 이것을 운송 수단으로 받아들이지 않았습니다. [Q14] '말 없는 마차'는 너무 무거웠기 때문에 운전하는 것도 까다로웠습니다. 뿐만 아니라 인간이 동력을 공급해야 했으므로, 인간이 기계 에너지를 창출하기 위해 인간 스스로 '짐수레 끄는 동물'의 역할을 해야 했습니다. 무서운 일이죠. (이 마차를 소유한) 많은 주인들이 그들의 하인을 학대해서 비판과 질타를 받았습니다. 그래서 이 마차의 사용은 점차 줄어들었습니다. 이러한 4개의 바퀴를 가진 마차가 사라지고 난 이후, 독일인 마차 제작자 Baron Karl Drais는 Dandy Horse 혹은 Laufmaschine에 대한 아이디어를 생각해냈습니다. 이것은 오늘날의 두발 자전거와 다소 유사했습니다. S: 죄송한데, 그 용어 좀 설명해주시겠어요? P: 물론이죠. Drais는 'Laufmaschine'이라고 그것을 언급했습니다. 독일어로 번역하자면 '달리는 기계'이지요. 다른 사람들은 그것의 모양 때문에 '빠른' 혹은 '발'이라는 라틴어에서 이름이 유래했다고 믿었습니다. 그것은 거의 인간 신체의 확장판과도 같았습니다. 마치 달리기처럼 사람이 다리를 벌리고 그 위에 걸터앉아 땅을 밀어내는 것이지요. 페달이 없는 오늘날의 자전거를 생각해보십시오. S: 페달이 없었다고요? 저는 초기 자전거에 엄청나게 큰 앞 바퀴와 페달이 있었을 거라고 생각했는데요. P: Penny-Farthing을 말하는 거군요. 1870년에 발명되었죠. Boneshaker라고 불리는 또 다른 자전거 유형 중 하나는 1860년대에 발명된 페달이 있는 최초의 자전거였습니다. 이 자전거를 말하는 것일 수도 있겠죠. [Q15] 아무튼, 학생과 제가 이해하는 내용이 같습니다. 하지만 시간적으로 말하자면 Laufmaschine은 1818년에 발명되었습니다. 나머지 두 개가 발명된 시기보다 몇십 년 전이며, 자전거 개발의 시발점이었죠. S: 페달이 없이도 얼마나 빨리 달릴 수 있었나요? 사람들이 그걸 좋아했나요?

TEST 4 set 2-3

문단주제	본문내용	해석
단락 5 Laufmaschine에 대한 각지 사람들의 반응	**P:** Well, when Drais first demonstrated it in Germany it received a fair amount of acclaim and recognition, but when it was introduced to France it was largely ignored. **S:** Professor, what was the difference? **P:** [Q16] I would say that geographical differences caused the different reactions. When he demonstrated it in Germany, Drais covered 14 kilometers in less than an hour, which was pretty good because walking would take about twice as long, but we need to look at where he rode. The Laufmaschine worked best over smooth, level surfaces, such as where it was introduced in Germany. In contrast, using it to go up a slope or through mud and forestland was very difficult. You could easily lose control and cause injuries when going downhill. For these reasons, the French were never really interested in it, saying it provided hardly any benefits over walking. However, Drais never succumbed to this criticism and strove to keep the Laufmaschine alive. To do this, he changed his marketing strategy, focusing on its use for recreation rather than transportation. He brought his invention to parks and rented them out. Pretty ingenious, huh? Well… here's the point I want you to understand: the significance of the Laufmaschine is not as weak as it may seem. It inspired other inventors to build better personal vehicles. As I mentioned, bicycles like the Penny-farthing and the boneshaker descended from the Laufmaschine.	**P:** 글쎄요, Drais가 처음 독일에서 그 자전거를 선보였을 때 많은 환호와 인정을 받았습니다. 그러나 프랑스에 소개되었을 때는 처참히 무시당했죠. **S:** 교수님, 무슨 차이였는데요? **P:** [Q16] 지리적인 차이가 다른 반응을 만들어 냈습니다. 그가 독일에서 선보였을 때는 1시간도 안 되어서 14킬로미터를 갔었죠. 꽤 괜찮았어요, 왜냐하면 걸어서 가면 두 배는 걸리니까요. 하지만 우리는 그가 어디에서 탔는가를 살펴보아야 합니다. Laufmaschine은 소개된 독일처럼 부드럽고 평탄한 표면에서 가장 잘 작동했습니다. 그러나 경사진 곳을 오르고 진흙이나 삼림을 지나가기에는 매우 어려웠습니다. 내리막길을 내려갈 때에는 쉽게 통제력을 잃고 부상을 당하기 쉬웠죠. 이러한 이유 때문에, 걷는 것 보다 이득이 거의 없다며 프랑스 사람들은 Laufmaschine에 전혀 관심을 갖지 않았습니다. 그러나 Drais는 이러한 비판에 전혀 동요되지 않았고 Laufmaschine을 활성화하기 위해 노력했습니다. 이를 위해서 마케팅 전략을 바꿔 사용 목적을 운송 수단보다는 여가 생활을 위한 것으로 집중했습니다. 그는 자신의 발명품을 공원으로 가져가 사람들에게 빌려주었습니다. 꽤 기발하지 않나요? 아무튼, 제가 여러분들이 알았으면 하는 점: Laufmaschine의 중요성은 보이는 것보다 약하지 않다는 것입니다. Laufmaschine는 더 나은 개인 운송수단을 만들 수 있도록 다른 발명가들에게 영감을 주었습니다. 제가 말했듯 Penny-farthing이나 Boneshaker과 같은 자전거들은 Laufmaschine의 영향을 받은 것입니다.

12. [Main Purpose] What is the lecture mainly about?

(A) The continuing history and development of bicycles *(too specific)*
(B) ~~Comparison~~ between advances in automobile technology ~~before and after~~ the Industrial Revolution *(wrong fact)* ★
(C) The causes and effects of the ~~Industrial Revolution~~ in the 18th century *(unrelated to the question)*
(D) **Technological development in transportation over several decades**

12. 강의의 주요 내용이 무엇인가?

(A) 자전거에 대한 지속적인 역사와 발전
(B) 산업혁명 전후 시기의 자동차 기술의 발전 ~~비교~~ ★
(C) 18세기 ~~산업혁명의~~ 원인과 결과
(D) **수십 년간의 운송수단의 기술적 발전**

해설 | (A) 본 강의는 자전거 이외에도 '말 없는 마차' 등 이외의 운송수단에 대해서도 논한다. 자전거를 주제로 잡기에는 매우 제한적이다.
(B) 산업혁명의 전과 후가 아닌 그 당시에 있었던 운송수단 기술의 발전이다. 때문에, 비교 역시 강의의 내용에 포함되지 않는다.
(C) 강의의 주제는 산업혁명 자체가 아닌 그 시기에 있었던 기술적 발전이다.

13. [Detail – Problem] What does the professor identify as the earliest steam-powered vehicles' problem?

(A) They were ~~so heavy that~~ their engines could not power their bodies *(wrong fact)* ★
(B) **They could not be utilized on rough roads because of their massive density**
(C) They were ~~slower~~ than other transportation methods *(not mentioned)*
(D) They were prone to sudden ~~breakdowns and stalling~~ *(not mentioned)*

13. 최초의 증기 동력 운송수단의 문제점에 대하여 교수가 말한 것이 무엇인가?

(A) ~~매우 무거워서 엔진이 몸체에 동력을 공급하지 못했다.~~ ★
(B) **엄청난 부피 때문에 거친 도로에서 이용될 수 없었다.**
(C) 다른 교통 수단보다 ~~느렸다~~.
(D) 갑자기 ~~고장 나거나 멈추기~~ 쉬웠다.

해설 | (A) 엔진이 몸체에 동력을 공급했으며, 평균무게가 매우 무거웠다는 교수의 설명을 잘못된 인과관계로 왜곡시켜 놓은 것으로 오답.
(C) 최초의 증기 동력 운송수단의 비교적 속도 역시 강의에서 언급되지 않으므로 오답. (D) 잦은 고장 또한 언급되지 않으므로 오답.

14. [Detail – Cause/Reason] Why were Baron Karl Drais' horseless carriages criticized by the public?

(A) Because the ~~draft animals~~ used were abused by their owners *(wrong fact)* ★

(B) Because they ~~failed to accommodate more people~~ than previous inventions *(not mentioned)*

(C) Because their use was ~~limited to certain landscapes~~ *(wrong fact)*

(D) **Because they employed 'draft people', which was viewed as immoral**

14. Baron Karl Drais의 '말 없는 마차'가 왜 대중으로부터 비판을 받았는가?

(A) 마차의 주인들이 수레를 끄는 동물을 학대했기 때문에 ★

(B) 이전의 발명품보다 더 많은 인원을 수용할 수 없었기 때문에

(C) 사용이 특정한 지형으로만 한정되었기 때문에

(D) 비도덕적으로 보이는 '수레를 끄는 사람'을 썼기 때문에

해설 | (A) 동물들이 학대가 된 것이 아니라 수레를 끄는 동물의 역할을 했던 사람들이 학대 되었다고 비판을 받았다.
(B) 언급되지 않는 내용이므로 오답. (C) 교수는 '말 없는 마차'의 이점으로 거칠고 돌 많은 길에서의 편리성을 꼽는다. 이와 어긋나므로 오답.

---

15. [Detail – Reaction/Response] How does the professor react to the student's doubt that the Laufamaschine was the first bicycle?

(A) She takes the ~~same stance~~ and ~~does not understand~~ why researchers call it the first bicycle *(wrong fact)*

(B) **She opposes the student's point and explains why it was the first bicycle**

(C) She ~~partially shares~~ the opinion of the student ★

(D) She believes that the Laufmaschine deserves credit as the first bicycle ~~along with other two types, the Penny-farthing and the boneshaker~~ *(wrong fact)*

15. 학생이 어떻게 Laufmaschine이 최초의 자전거였냐고 의문을 가졌을 때 교수는 어떻게 반응하는가?

(A) 같은 입장을 취하며 왜 연구자들이 Laufmaschine을 최초의 자전거라고 부르는 지 이해하지 못한다.

(B) 학생의 주장에 대해 반대하면서 왜 최초의 자전거였는지 설명한다.

(C) 학생의 의견에 부분적으로 동의한다. ★

(D) 다른 두 종류의 자전거인 Penny-farthing과 boneshaker와 같이 Laufmaschine도 최초의 자전거라고 평가 받을 자격이 있다고 믿는다.

해설 | (A) 교수는 1818년에 Laufmaschine이 발명되고 이후 1860년대와 1870에 각각 Penny-farthing과 boneshaker가 나왔다고 지적한다. 따라서 학생과 완전히 같은 입장이라고 볼 수 없다. (C) 교수는 Laufmaschine (1818)이 Penny-farthing (1870) 과 boneshaker (1860년대)보다 빨리 발명된 것이 명확하다고 밝히므로 아무런 동의도 하지 않는다. (D) 언급되지 않는 내용이므로 오답.

16. [Detail – Cause/Reason] Why did the public's opinions about the Laufmaschine vary in France and Germany?

(A) Because the French had ~~different taste in bicycles~~ than the German people *(not mentioned)*

(B) Because the idea of utilizing human-powered transportation ~~wasn't popular~~ in France at the time *(not mentioned)*

(C) Because it received a fair amount of acclaim and recognition when it was demonstrated in Germany *(unrelated to the question)* ★

(D) **Because geographical conditions in the regions where the machine was introduced were very different**

16. 왜 Laufmaschine에 대한 대중의 의견이 프랑스와 독일에서 달랐는가?

(A) 프랑스 사람들이 독일 사람들과 ~~다른 자전거 취향을~~ 가졌기 때문에

(B) 인간이 동력을 만드는 운송수단을 이용한다는 생각이 그 당시 프랑스에서는 ~~대중적이지 못했기~~ 때문에

(C) 독일에서 선보였을 때 많은 환호와 인정을 받았기 때문에 ★

(D) **기계가 도입된 지역의 지리적 조건이 매우 달랐기 때문에**

해설 | (A), (B) 각지 사람들의 취향은 언급되지 않으므로 오답. (C) 맞는 말이지만 대중의 의견이 프랑스와 독일에서 달랐던 이유는 아니므로 문제가 묻는 바가 아니다.

Listen again to part of the lecture. Then answer the question.

"Actually, they were more popular than steam engines because… Well, I think you should know by now."

강의의 일부분을 다시 듣고 질문에 답하시오.

"실제로, 이것들은 증기 엔진보다 더 대중적이었습니다. 왜냐하면… 그런데, 지금쯤은 이미 여러분들이 알아야 할 것 같은데요."

17. [Inference – Imply] What does the professor imply when she asks this: 🎧

"Well, I think you should know by now"

(A) That she believes everyone in her class has done ~~research before the lecture~~ *(wrong fact)*

(B) That the students can figure out the problem ~~using common sense~~ *(wrong fact)* ★

(C) That she has as ~~little knowledge~~ of the concept as the students *(wrong fact)*

(D) **That she has previously explained the concept to the class**

17. 교수가 이 말을 할 때 암시하는 것은 무엇인가? 🎧

"그런데 지금쯤은 이미 여러분이 알아야 할 것 같은데요"

(A) ~~수업 전에 학생들 전원이 아마 연구했다고~~ 믿기 때문에

(B) 학생들이 ~~기본상식을 이용해서~~ 문제를 이해할 수 있기 때문에 ★

(C) 학생들만큼 해당 개념에 대한 ~~지식이 거의 없기~~ 때문에

(D) **강의에서 해당 개념을 이미 설명한 바 있기 때문에**

해설 | 교수는 이 말을 하기 직전 최초 증기 운송수단의 결점 (성가신 무게, 제한된 지형에서의 원활한 작동 등) 에 대해 설명한다. 때문에, 인간이 동력을 공급하는 운송 수단이 증기 엔진보다 대중적이었던 이유는 학생들이 쉽게 유추할 수 있을 것이라는 뜻에서 교수는 이와 같은 말을 하므로 (A), (B), (C) 모두 오답.

www.usherin.usher.co.kr

USHER

iBT TOEFL
INTERMEDIATE LISTENING
TEST 5 해설

TEST 5 set 1-1

Conversation: The reservation on a friday

문단주제	본문내용	해석
단락 1 인사	**Listen to a conversation between a student and an employee at the community center.** S: Hello, I'm here for a meeting with Ms. Magliozzi. E: Oh, you must be… Mr. James! I'm the one you're looking for. I'm sorry… Were you waiting long? S: No, I was late myself because there was a traffic jam on Main Street. [Q2-D] There must've been a car accident on the leading road to the highway. E: What's happening today? There was also a major accident on the other side of town. S: I hope no one was seriously injured. Anyway, about today's meeting…	시민 문화 회간에서의 학생과 종업원의 대화를 들으시오. S: 안녕하세요, 저는 Ms. Magliozzi를 만나러 왔는데요. E: 오, Mr. James시겠군요! 제가 당신이 찾는 사람이랍니다. 죄송해요… 오래 기다리셨나요? S: 아니에요, Main Street에 차가 막혀서 저도 늦었어요. [Q2-D] 고속도로로 가는 길에 차 사고가 있었나 봐요. E: 오늘 무슨 일일까요? 동네 반대 쪽에도 큰 사고가 있었거든요. S: 심하게 다친 사람이 없으면 좋겠네요. 아무튼, 오늘 만난 거에 대해서는….
단락 2 주민센터 소개	E: Oh right (laughs). Let's see… I'm assuming you're familiar with the community center. S: [Q2] I've spent the majority of my life here so I know pretty much everything about this town. E: Great, come in and take a seat. I'll explain what you need to do to make your job a little easier and how to access the website you'll need.	E: 오 맞아요(웃음). 어디 봅시다… 주민센터에 익숙하신 것 같네요. S: [Q2] 제 인생의 대부분을 여기서 보냈죠. 그래서 이 동네의 모든 것에 대해 꽤 잘 알아요. E: 좋아요, 들어와서 앉으세요. 당신의 일을 조금 쉽게 만들기 위해 해야 하는 일들을 설명해드리고 필요하실 웹사이트에 어떻게 접속하는지 설명할게요.
단락 3 이름 혼동	S: Really? [Q1] I'm just here to make a reservation so my soccer club can have a practice session next Friday. I didn't expect it to be so complicated. E: Oh, wait. You're Mr. James, correct? S: Yes, Mike James. E: [Q5] Give me one second… I was supposed to have a job interview with Bryan James 20 minutes ago, but… Oh, my apologies. I must've mixed you up with Bryan. S: Well, that was out of the blue. I was confused for a second. Okay, so about the reservation… E: Right, when did you want to make the reservation? S: Next Friday. The manager asked me to come and talk to you about it… I'm not sure why, though. E: What's his name, may I ask?	S: 정말요? [Q1] 전 그냥 다음주 금요일에 제 축구 동아리가 연습을 할 수 있게 예약하러 온 건데요. 이렇게 복잡할 지는 몰랐네요. E: 오, 잠시만요. 당신 Mr. James씨죠, 맞죠? S: 네, Mike James요. E: [Q5] 잠시만요… 제가 Bryan James랑 20분 전에 취직 면접을 하기로 되어 있었거든요… 그런데… 오, 죄송해요. 제가 Bryan이랑 당신을 헷갈렸나봐요. S: 네, 난데없었어요. 잠깐 헷갈렸네요. 네, 그래서 그 예약 말인데요… E: 맞아요, 언제 예약하시고 싶다고요? S: 다음주 금요일이요. 매니저가 와서 이것에 대해 당신이랑 얘기하라고 했어요… 왜인지는 모르지만요. E: 그의 이름이…. 물어봐도 될까요?

문단주제	본문내용	해석
단락 4 코치와 종업원의 우정	**S:** Of course. It's Coach Stillman – Steven Stillman, just so we're on the same page this time (laughs). **E:** Oh, Steven is your coach? No wonder he recommended that you see me. **S:** I'm not sure I'm following… **E:** Steven and I go way back. We met in high school, and we've had a good relationship for almost 30 years now and… Whoops, I've deviated a little bit, haven't I? Well, he asked you to see me because you would normally need to pay to make any reservation on a Friday, unlike other days, and it's not so cheap since Fridays are extremely popular. But, for Steven, I… **S:** Oh, I get it now. You must be willing to give us a discount. **E:** [Q3] Well, for Steven's requests, I'm usually more generous than that (laughs). You won't need to pay anything.	**S:** 물론이죠. 코치 Stillman - Steven Stillman이요. 이번에는 저희가 똑같이 이해하기 위해서 (웃음). **E:** 오, Steven이 당신의 코치인가요? 그가 당신한테 저를 보러 오라고 추천한 것이 놀랍지 않네요. **S:** 제가 잘 알아듣고 있는지 모르겠네요…. **E:** Steven과 저는 한참 예전으로 거슬러가죠. 우리는 고등학교에서 만났고 지금 거의 30년 째 좋은 관계를 유지하고 있죠… 아이고, 좀 딴 길로 샜네요, 그쵸? 음, 다른 날과 다르게 금요일에는 보통 어떤 예약을 하든 돈을 내야 해서, 그리고 금요일이 엄청나게 인기 있기 때문에 싸지가 않아서 그가 절 보러 가라고 했을 거예요. 하지만, Steven에게라면, 저는…. **S:** 오, 이제 알겠어요. 저희에게 할인해주려 하시는 거군요. **E:** [Q3] 글쎄, Steven의 요청이라면, 저는 보통 그것보다 더 관대하죠 (웃음). 돈 내지 않아도 돼요.
단락 5 축구 연습 예약 진행	**S:** Wow, I didn't see that coming. **E:** [Q4] Here, just take these reservation forms and make sure both you and Steven sign them, okay? [Q4-A] Once you're done, you'll receive guest passes for the number of people you're bringing in. Are we clear? **S:** Yes, loud and clear! Anything else? **E:** Um, just one more thing. Tell everyone on your team to bring the pass, because the security guards won't let anyone in without them. **S:** Perfect. I'll do that. **E:** Okay, I think we're all set. Say hello to your coach for me, will you? **S:** Of course! Thank you for your help. **E:** My pleasure. Now, I guess I'll need to track down the other Mr. James. Have a good day!	**S:** 와, 그렇게 될 줄은 몰랐네요. **E:** [Q4] 자, 이 예약서를 가져가서 당신과 Steven 둘 다 여기 꼭 사인을 하세요, 알았죠? [Q4-A] 다 하면, 당신이 데려 올 인원수만큼 손님 출입증을 받게 될 거예요. 이해됐나요? **S:** 네, 아주 분명하게 이해했어요. 또 다른 게 있나요? **E:** 음, 하나만 더요. 팀 모두 다에게 출입증을 가져오라고 하세요, 왜냐면 그게 없으면 안전요원이 아무도 들여보내지 않거든요. **S:** 좋아요. 그렇게 할게요. **E:** 네, 다 된 것 같군요. 코치에게 제 안부를 전해주세요, 네? **S:** 물론이죠! 도와주셔서 감사합니다. **E:** 천만에요. 그럼 저는 이제 다른 Mr. James를 찾아내야겠네요. 좋은 하루 되세요!

01. **[Main Purpose]** Why does the student visit the employee at the community center?

(A) Because his soccer coach has asked him ~~to hand in a reservation form~~ *(wrong fact)* ★

(B) Because he is supposed to have a ~~job interview~~ *(wrong fact)*

(C) Because he needs to book a space for an upcoming club activity

(D) Because he needs to meet the deadline for the ~~club registration date~~ *(not mentioned)*

01. 왜 학생은 주민센터의 직원을 찾아왔는가?

(A) 그의 축구 코치가 그에게 ~~예약서를 내라고 해서~~ ★

(B) 그가 ~~취직 인터뷰~~를 하기로 해서

(C) 그는 다가오는 동아리 활동을 위해 장소를 예약해야 해서

(D) 그는 ~~동아리 등록 날짜~~ 기한을 맞춰야 해서

해설 | (A) Ms. Magliozzi를 찾아가 장소 예약에 관해 이야기 해보라는 코치의 이야기를 왜곡시켜 놓은 것으로 오답. 코치는 구체적으로 예약서를 내라고 하지는 않았다. (B)취직 인터뷰는 학생 (Mike James)이 아닌 Bryan James가 하기로 한 것이었으므로 오답. (D) 동아리 등록에 관해서는 대화에서 언급되지 않는다.

02. **[Inference – Infer]** What can be inferred about the student from the conversation?

(A) That it's natural for him to know almost everything about his town

(B) That he is late because traffic jams ~~occur frequently~~ on Main Street *(too extreme)* ★

(C) That he is ~~not familiar~~ with the town because he has ~~just moved there~~ *(wrong fact)*

(D) That he ~~knows for certain~~ that the traffic jam was caused by a vehicle accident *(wrong fact)*

02. 대화 속 학생에 대해 어떤 것을 추론할 수 있는가?

(A) 그가 그의 동네의 거의 모든 것을 아는 것은 자연스럽다는 것

(B) 그가 늦은 것은 Main Street에 차가 ~~자주 막히~~기 때문이라는 것 ★

(C) 그가 ~~막 이사 와서~~ 동네를 ~~잘 모른다는~~ 것

(D) 그가 교통체증이 차 사고 때문이라는 것을 ~~확실히 안다는~~ 것

해설 | (B) 이 날 Main Street에 차가 막혀서 늦은 것은 맞으나 단지 이것을 통해 Main Street에 차가 자주 막힌다는 것을 추론하는 것은 무리이다. (C) 막 이사 왔다는 것은 틀리므로 오답. (D) Main Street에 차가 막혀 늦었다며 학생은 고속도로로 가는 길에 차 사고가 있었을 것이라고 추측한다. 추측이기 때문에 확실히 안다고 하는 것은 틀리므로 오답.

03. **[Detail – Cause/Reason]** Why has the student's coach asked him to make an arrangement specifically with the employee?

(A) Because he wants to exploit the special treatment she gives him in regard to the reservation fee

(B) Because he knows pretty much everything about the town *(unrelated to the question)* ★

(C) Because his team ~~has not received funds~~ from the sports department *(not mentioned)*

(D) Because he wants to ~~invite the employee~~ to the soccer practice next Friday *(not mentioned)*

03. 학생의 코치는 왜 특별히 그 직원과 약속을 잡도록 했는가?

(A) 그는 그녀가 예약비용과 관련해서 그에게 제공하는 특별한 대우를 누리고 싶었기 때문에

(B) 그는 그 동네의 모든 것에 대해 꽤 잘 알기 때문에 ★

(C) 그의 팀은 운동부에서 ~~지원을 못 받았기~~ 때문에

(D) 그는 직원을 다음 주 금요일 축구 연습에 ~~초대~~하고 싶었기 때문에

해설 | (B) 코치가 아닌 학생에 대한 설명으로 오답. 또한, 특별히 그 직원을 찾도록 한 이유와는 무관하므로 오답. (C) 운동부의 지원은 언급되지 않으므로 오답. (D) 학생은 직원에게 축구 연습에 올 것을 권유하지 않으므로 초대의 목적은 없다는 것을 알 수 있다.

04. [Inference – Future Action] What is the student most likely to do right after the conversation?

(A) He will ~~give out the guest passes~~ to his team members *(wrong fact)*

(B) **He and his coach will sign the registration forms and return them**

(C) He will ~~ask for guest passes~~ for the number of people in his team *(wrong fact)* ★

(D) He will visit the team members individually ~~to get their signatures~~ on the registration form *(wrong fact)*

> **해설 |** 손님 출입증은 예약서에 코치와 학생이 사인을 한 후 받게 될 것이라고 직원은 설명하기 때문에, 대화 후에 바로 (A) 출입증을 팀원들에게 나누어 주는 것이나 (C) 출입증을 달라고 요구하는 것은 불가능하다. 직원은 마지막에 다른 Mr. James를 찾는다고 말한다. 학생은 이에 대해 아무런 말도 하지 않는 것으로 보아 직원을 도와줄 것이라고 예측할 수 없다. (D) 직원은 학생에게 예약서를 주면서 학생과 코치가 사인할 것을 요구한다. 따라서 학생은 팀원들의 사인을 받을 이유가 없다.

Listen again to part of the conversation. Then answer the question.

"**E:** Give me one second… I was supposed to have a job interview with Bryan James 20 minutes ago, but… Oh, my apologies. I must've mixed you up with Bryan.

S: Well, that was out of the blue."

05. [Inference - Imply] What does the student mean when he says this: 🎧

> "Well, that was out of the blue."

(A) That he's surprised that the job interview ~~finished~~ 20 minutes ago *(wrong fact)* ★

(B) **That he had not expected the misunderstanding that occurred**

(C) That he's having a hard time trying to understand how the employee could make ~~such a silly mistake~~ *(too extreme)*

(D) That he ~~happens to know the other guy~~ with whom the employee has mixed him up *(not mentioned)*

> **해설 |** (A) 면접이 아예 이뤄지지 않았으므로 20분 전에 끝났다는 것에 놀랄 이유가 없으므로 오답. (C) 직원의 실수로 인해 학생이 헷갈린 것은 맞으나 '멍청한 실수'라고 여길 만큼의 극한 감정을 갖는 것으로 보이지 않으므로 오답. (D) 학생은 Bryan James를 아는 기색을 전혀 보이지 않으므로 오답.

TEST 5 set 1-2

Lecture 1
Early European art movements

문단주제	본문내용	해석

USHER

단락 1
15세기부터 19세기의 중요한 유럽예술 운동

Listen to part of a lecture in an art history class.

P: [Q6] Let's continue our discussion of early European art movements by going over some key points from the 15th to 19th century, before moving on to contemporary art.

You can see a myriad of contemporary painting styles, philosophies, and perspectives embedded in the paintings, but if you pay close attention to the details, you'll find that they share one characteristic. How do you think they came up with those sophisticated, rich, and delicate colors back then? They all mixed and developed their own paints. [Q7-C] Unlike today, they couldn't just pop into an art store and ask for tubes of paint. [Q7] They needed to go through a lot of experimentation to come up with not only colorful, but also durable, paints that set them apart from others. Further, they wanted to preserve their paintings as long as they could… which makes sense. Why would they want their artwork to go to waste after a short time?

단락 2
1700년대의 물감

That process lasted about 3 centuries, until a dramatic transition occurred in the art community between the late 1700s and the early 1800s. Artists had had a pretty good understanding of how to make rich, ornate paints on their own by the end of the 1700s, as the period's experimentation led to stability. However, the need to make canvases – the fabrics on which they painted – became obsolete due to technological innovations. Unfortunately, the glue in these mechanically produced canvases made it more difficult for the paint to stick to them. As the glue dried, it caused the paint to crack and fade. Regrettably, the artists didn't know about this and quickly transitioned to mechanically produced canvases from making their own, which would've required many hours of strenuous labor. [Q8] Therefore, the European art movement from the early 1800s was… a total disaster in terms of the longevity of their artwork.

Further "experimentation and innovation" changed the way artists learned. Previously, artists trained under master painters in a studio or a similar setting. This method was interactive and intensive.

예술사 강의의 일부를 들으시오.

P: [Q6] 현대 예술로 넘어가기 전에 15세기에서 19세기의 중요한 포인트 몇 개를 복습하면서 초기 유럽 예술 운동에 대한 우리의 토론을 이어가 봅시다.

여러분은 그림에 들어가있는 수많은 당시 회화양식, 철학 그리고 관점들을 보실 수 있을 거에요. 하지만 세부사항에 잘 집중해본다면, 그들이 한 가지 특징을 공유한다는 것을 알 수 있습니다. 그 옛날에 어떻게 이렇게 정교하고, 풍부하며, 섬세한 색깔을 낼 수 있었을까요? 그들은 다 그들의 물감을 섞고 개발했어요. [Q7-C] 오늘날과 달리 그들은 그냥 화방에 들어가서 물감을 달라고 할 수 없었어요. [Q7] 그들은 다채로울 뿐 아니라 오래 가는, 다른 것과 구별되는 물감을 만들어내기 위해서 수많은 실험을 거쳐야만 했어요. 게다가, 그들은 그들의 그림이 가능한 오래가길 원했어요, 그럴 만하죠. 그들이 왜 그들의 예술작품이 곧 망가지길 바랐겠어요?

이 과정은 1700년대 후기와 1800년대 초기 사이에 예술계에 일어난 극적인 전환이 있을 때까지 3세기 정도 계속되었습니다. 예술가들은 1700년대 말쯤 스스로 풍부하고 현란한 물감을 어떻게 만드는지에 대해 잘 이해하고 있었어요. 그 시대의 실험이 오래가게 만들면서요. 하지만, 캔버스-그들이 그림 그리는 천-를 만들 필요는 기술의 혁신과 함께 사라졌습니다. 불운하게도, 이 기계로 만들어진 캔버스의 풀은 물감이 거기 붙어있기 더 어렵게 했어요. 그 풀이 마르면서, 그것은 물감이 갈라지고 희미해지게 했어요. 애석하게도, 예술가들은 이것을 몰랐고 오랜 시간의 몹시 힘든 노동을 필요로 하는 스스로 캔버스 만들기에서 빠르게 기계로 만든 캔버스로 넘어갔어요. [Q8] 그래서, 1800년대 초기의 유럽 예술 운동은 음… 예술 작품이 오래갔는지의 측면에서는 완전 재앙이었죠.

계속된 "실험과 혁신"이 예술가들이 학습하는 방법을 바꾸었습니다. 이전에는, 예술가들은 스튜디오나 비슷한 환경에서 대가의 밑에서 훈련 받았어요. 이 방법은 서로 소통하는 것이었고 집중적이었죠.

문단주제	본문내용	해석
단락 3 1800년대 예술원	However, in the early 1800s, art standards transformed as Napoleon III rebuilt Paris. Has anyone heard of Académie des Beaux-Arts? (pause) I didn't think so. Well, they were a group of art academies built around France that greatly impacted French art. Artists began to adhere to the rules and guidelines that they imposed on their painters as many artists began to be educated at the academies. Thus, their preferences, such as technique, color, and, um, subject selection, became the new standards for artists. For instance, they valued religious and historical themes and caused their artists to paint in a way that concealed their individual feelings and personalities. How? Well, again, they needed to follow certain rules, such as making their paintings look as realistic as possible or using earnest and conservative colors, so individuality and creativity became more difficult to discern. [Q11] **These "educated" artists were spared the responsibility of originality.**	하지만, 초기 1800년대에, 예술의 기준은 나폴레옹 3세가 파리를 재건하면서 바뀌었습니다. Académie des Beaux-Arts에 대해 들어본 사람 있나요? (일시정지) 없는 것 같군요. 음, 그들은 프랑스 예술에 크게 영향을 준 프랑스 근처에 지어졌던 예술원들이에요. 많은 예술가들이 이 예술원들에서 교육받으면서 그들은 그들이 화가에게 부과한 규칙과 지침들을 고수하기 시작했어요. 그래서, 그들의 기술, 색깔, 그리고, 음, 주제 선택에 대한 그들의 선호는 예술가들에 대한 새로운 기준이 되었어요. 예를 들어, 그들은 종교적이고 역사적인 주제에 가치를 부여했고 그들의 예술가가 자신의 감정과 성격을 숨기는 방식으로 그리게 되었습니다. 어떻게냐구요? 음, 다시, 그들은 그들의 그림을 가능한 최대한 현실적으로 보이게 하거나 진중하고 보수적인 색깔을 쓰는 등의 특정한 기준에 따라야 했고, 그래서 성격과 창의성은 알아차리기 더 어려워졌어요. [Q11] 이 "교육받은" 예술가들은 독창성의 책임으로부터 자유로웠죠.
단락 4 예술행위의 반하는 예술 운동	Later, another art movement arose in opposition to the academies and their practice of art. Ummm… Does everyone remember the painting I showed you last week? Impression, Sunrise by Claude Monet… He's now regarded as one of the leading figures of the Impressionist movement along with Sisley, Pissarro, and Morisot. His work inspired the movement and contributed to giving "Impressionism" its name. Although their styles and techniques varied, the impressionists and their art were united by their pursuit of independence and rebellion. They abstained from applying the academies' regulations to their work, because they believed the paintings from the academies were unnatural. [Q9-A] They held their own impressionist exhibitions and, naturally, public awareness of the movement grew through their efforts. You may be wondering how they differed from the academies' artists. Or, should I say, how their paintings were distinguished from those created by academy artists. Well, impressionists valued imagination and subjectivity and didn't attempt to emulate the reality in their paintings. This development took off as photography gained popularity and cameras became portable.	후에, 이 예술원과 그들의 예술 행위에 반하는 또 다른 예술 운동이 일어났어요. 음.. 제가 저번 주에 보여준 그림 기억하는 사람 있나요? Claude Monet의 인상, 해돋이요. 그는 지금은 Sisley, Pissarro, Morisot과 함께 인상주의 운동을 이끈 인물 중 하나로 여겨지죠. 그의 작품은 그 운동에 영감을 주었고 "인상주의"의 이름을 붙이는 데 기여했습니다. 그들의 스타일과 기술은 달랐지만, 인상주의자들과 그들의 작품은 그들이 독립과 반항을 추구했다는 점에서 같습니다. 그들은 그들의 작품에 예술원의 규칙을 적용하는 것을 피했어요. 그들은 예술원의 그림은 자연스럽지 않다고 생각했기 때문입니다. [Q9-A] 그들은 그들만의 인상주의 전시를 열었고, 자연스럽게 그들의 노력을 통해 대중들이 그들의 운동을 더 알게 되었습니다. 여러분은 아마 그들이 어떻게 예술원의 예술가들과 달랐는지 궁금할텐데요. 아니면 제가 말하죠, 그들의 그림이 예술원 예술가들이 만든 것과 어떻게 구별되었는지요. 음, 인상주의자들은 상상과 주관성에 가치를 두었고 그들의 그림에 현실을 모방하려고 시도하지 않았습니다. 이 발전은 사진술이 인기를 얻고 카메라가 휴대 가능해지면서 시작되었어요.

TEST 5 set 1-2

문단주제	본문내용	해석
단락 5 기술적 혁신이 예술에 미친 영향	[Q9] You see, they thought that there was no way they could create more accurate and realistic pictures than photographs. So, instead of attempting to draw perfect representations, which seemed futile, they added their views and imagination to their landscape paintings and such, to convey tidbits that photographs couldn't. This became possible because of another technological innovation. [Q10-A/Q10-D] Pre-packaged paints, with both durability and rich colors, became readily available. [Q7-B/Q10-C] In contrast to the old masters, who needed to varnish their paintings to protect them from fading and preserve them for long periods, [Q10-B] the impressionists didn't need to use artificial enhancements, because the new paints that came in tubes already had that ability. In addition to this protection, varnish also gave colors depth, but, again, the impressionists didn't need it for the same reason. Next class we'll look at five Impressionist works and discuss the individual artist's techniques and color usage.	[Q9] 보시면, 그들은 사진보다 더 정확하고 현실적인 그림을 만들어낼 방법은 없다고 생각했어요. 그래서 완벽한 표상을 그리려고 시도하는 것, 무의미해 보이는 그것 대신 그들은 그들의 풍경화 등등에 그들의 관점과 상상을 더했어요, 사진이 줄 수 없는 맛을 더하기 위해서요. 이건 또 다른 기술적 혁신 때문에 가능했습니다. [Q10-A/Q10-D] 오래 가고 색깔이 풍부한 포장된 물감이 쉽게 접근 가능해졌거든요. [Q7-B/Q10-C] 희미해지는 걸 막고 오래 보존하기 위해 그들의 그림에 광을 내야 했던 예전의 대가들과 대조적으로, [Q10-B] 인상주의자들은 인공적인 효과를 쓸 필요가 없었어요. 왜냐면 튜브에 들어있는 새 물감은 이미 그 능력을 가지고 있었으니까요. 이런 보호뿐 아니라 광택제는 색깔에 깊이를 주었는데, 하지만, 역시, 인상주의자들은 같은 이유로 그럴 필요가 없었습니다. 다음 시간에 우리는 다섯 명의 인상주의자의 작품을 보고 각각 예술가의 기술과 색깔 사용에 대해 이야기해볼 것입니다.

06. [Main Idea] What is the lecture mainly about?

(A) ~~Conflicts~~ between the old standards of art and the rules imposed by the Académie des Beaux-Arts *(partial error)*

(B) ~~Impressionists'~~ philosophies and beliefs expressed through their paintings *(too specific)*

(C) Art transitions that took hold over a few centuries ~~in Paris~~ *(too specific)* ★

(D) Contrasting features of European art movements that occurred over several centuries

06. 이 강의의 주제는 무엇인가?

(A) 오래된 예술의 규준과 Académie des Beaux-Arts가 부과한 규칙 사이의 갈등

(B) 그들의 그림에 드러난 인상주의자들의 철학과 신념

(C) 파리에서 몇 세기 동안 강력했던 예술의 전환 ★

(D) 몇 세기 동안 일어난 유럽 예술 운동의 대조적인 특성

해설 | (A) 교수는 예술의 규준의 갈등이 아닌 변화 또는 전환에 초점을 맞춘다. 또한, 오래된 예술의 규준과 Académie des Beaux-Arts 이외에도 인상주의, 기술의 발전 등을 다루므로 오답. (B) 강의는 인상주의 이외에도 다양한 기술의 발전, 예술가들의 학습 방법 등 다양한 주제를 다룬다. 이상주의에만 국한되지 않으므로 오답. (C) 강의의 중점은 파리만이 아닌 유럽 전체의 예술의 전환이다. 너무 구체적이므로 오답.

07. [Detail – Characteristic] Which of the following are true about the paints used by painters before the 19th century?

Click on 2 answers

(A) They were durable and colorful

(B) They had rich colors even ~~without the use of varnish~~ *(wrong fact)* ★

(C) They were easily portable and convenient because they were ~~sold in tubes~~ *(wrong fact)*

(D) They could be used to identify the artist

07. 다음 중 19세기 전에 화가들이 사용한 물감에 대해 옳은 것은 무엇인가?

2개의 정답을 고르시오

(A) 그것들은 오래가고 다채로웠다.

(B) 그것들은 광택제를 쓰지 않아도 색깔이 풍부했다. ★

(C) 그것들은 튜브로 판매되었기 때문에 휴대가 쉽고 편리했다.

(D) 그것들은 예술가를 알아보는 데에 쓰였다.

해설 | (B) 교수는 19세기 전에 화가들은 작품이 희미해지는 것을 막고 오래 보존하기 위해 그들의 그림에 광을 내야 했다고 설명한다. 이와 어긋나므로 오답. (C) 튜브로 판매되는 물감은 인상주의 시대부터 사용되었으므로 오답.

08. [Inference – Infer] According to the professor, what can be inferred about the European paintings from the early 1800s before the Impressionism movement?

(A) They were ~~heavily affected by~~ the paintings of old art masters, such as ~~Claude Monet~~ *(wrong fact)* ★

(B) Those that still exist are most likely in bad quality

(C) ~~Landscape and life~~ are the common themes found in them *(not mentioned)*

(D) The painters found ~~spontaneity~~ to be the main source of ideas for their work *(not mentioned)*

08. 교수에 따르면, 1800년대 초기부터 인상주의 운동 전까지 유럽의 그림에 대해 추론할 수 있는 것은 무엇인가?

(A) 그것들은 ~~Claude Monet~~같은 오래된 예술 대가들에게서 ~~큰 영향을 받았다~~. ★

(B) 지금까지 남아있는 것들은 안 좋은 상태일 가능성이 높다.

(C) ~~풍경이나 정물~~은 그 그림들에게서 발견되는 흔한 주제이다.

(D) 화가들은 즉흥성이 그들의 작품에 대한 아이디어의 주된 원천이라고 보았다.

> **해설 |** (A) 인상주의 화가였던 Claude Monet가 그 이전 시대에 영향을 미쳤다는 것은 시기적으로 어긋나는 말이므로 오답. (C)와 (D)는 언급되지 않으며, 이를 암시하는 내용도 전혀 없으므로 오답.

09. [Detail – Cause/Reason] Why did impressionists not admire emulating reality in their paintings?

(A) Because the exhibitions where they displayed their paintings ~~didn't allow reality-based art~~ *(not mentioned)*

(B) Because they loathed the academies' principles of art *(unrelated to the question)* ★

(C) Because the ~~public's attention~~ shifted to favoring work of abstract imagination *(wrong fact)*

(D) Because a technological produced better quality results

09. 왜 인상주의자들은 그들의 그림에 현실을 복제하는 것을 중요시하지 않았는가?

(A) 그들이 그들의 그림을 전시한 전시들이 ~~현실 기반의 예술을 허용하지 않았기~~ 때문에

(B) 그들이 예술원의 예술에 대한 원칙들을 싫어했기 때문에 ★

(C) ~~대중의 관심이~~ 추상적인 상상을 표현한 작품을 좋아하게 바뀌었기 때문에

(D) 기술적인 것이 더 높은 질의 결과물을 낼 수 있었기 때문에

> **해설 |** (A) 언급되지 않는 내용이다. 또한, 인상주의 화가들이 그들만의 전시를 열어 그들의 운동을 알렸다는 내용을 왜곡시킨 것으로 오답. (B) 예술원이 지정하는 원칙을 따르는 것을 싫어한 것은 맞으나, 그 이유 때문에 그들의 그림에 현실을 복제하는 것을 중요시하지 않은 것은 아니다. 문제가 묻는 바가 아니므로 오답. (C) 강의에서 대중의 관심에 대한 얘기는 언급되지 않으므로 오답.

10. [Detail – Difference/Contrast]
In the lecture, the professor explains two different types of paints. Indicate whether each of the following is a feature of paints used by impressionists, ones used by old masters, or both.

	Impressionists' paints	Old masters' paints	Both
(A) had durability and rich colors	○		
(B) required the use of artificial enhancements		○	
(C) aroused preservation issues like fading		○	
(D) were prepackaged products	○		
(E) were able to produce colors according to painters' desires and intentions			○

해설 | (A) 기술적 혁신으로 접근하기 쉬워졌던 포장된 물감에 대해 교수는 오래 가고 색깔이 풍부했다고 말하므로 인상주의자들의 물감에 해당하는 특징. (B), (C) 예전의 대가들은 자신의 작품이 희미해지는 걸 막고 오래 보존하기 위해 varnish를 써야 했다고 설명하므로 옛 거장들의 물감에 해당하는 내용. (D) 기술적 혁신으로 인해 물감들이 포장되어 판매되기 시작했다고 설명되므로 인상주의자들의 물감에 해당하는 내용. (E) 교수는 포장된 물감이 풍부한 색감을 표현했다고 말한다. 또한, 강의 초반에 옛 화가들은 물감을 섞고 개발하는 등의 수 많은 실험을 통해 정교하고, 풍부하며, 섬세한 색깔을 낼 수 있었다고 설명된다. 따라서, 인상주의자들의 물감과 옛 거장들의 물감의 공통된 특징.

11. [Inference – Imply]
What does the professor mean when he says this:

> "These 'educated' artists were spared the responsibility of originality."

(A) The artists of the academies began to ~~copy each other's work~~
(not mentioned)

(B) Their ~~spontaneity~~ enabled them to expand the theme of their work
(not mentioned) ★

(C) The followers of the academies only adhered to the established formulas when creating art

(D) The academies contributed to making the process of drawing a ~~relatively easier task~~ *(not mentioned)*

해설 | (A), (B), (D) 모두 언급되지 않으므로 오답.

TEST 5 set 1-3

Lecture 2
Antipredator adaptations

문단주제	본문내용	해석

Listen to part of a lecture in a biology class.

생물학 수업의 강의 중 일부를 들으시오.

단락 1
반포식자 적응의 소개

P: Okay, let's review some key points before we begin today's lecture. Um, as you should know, prey animals employ various techniques to avoid predation, which we call "antipredator adaptations." [Q17-A] These evolutionary traits and behaviors have been developed by animals over many centuries and include a wide range of camouflaging methods, such as crypsis and mimesis. This allows them to change their skin or scale colors and patterns. For instance, dark frogs can instantaneously change into a vivid color, like red or yellow, as a signal of danger, toxicity, and poison to predators and warn them off. In the same way, animals can use behavioral mechanisms to avoid predators. This will be off-topic today. Ummm… has anyone heard of autotomy?

P: 자, 오늘의 강의를 시작하기 전에 주요 사항 몇 개 복습합시다. 음, 아시겠지만, 먹이가 되는 동물들은 먹히는 것을 피하기 위해 우리가 "반포식자 적응"이라고 부르는 다양한 기술을 씁니다. [Q17-A] 이 진화적인 특성과 행동은 여러 세기에 걸쳐 동물들에 의해 발달되었고 은폐와 모방 같은 넓은 범위의 위장 기술을 포함합니다. 이것은 그들이 피부나 비늘 색깔과 모양을 바꾸게 합니다. 예를 들어, 참개구리는 포식자에게 위험, 유독성, 독극물의 신호로 빨강이나 노랑 같은 선명한 색깔로 순간적으로 바뀔 수 있고 그래서 포식자들을 경고해서 쫓아버릴 수 있습니다. 같은 방법으로, 동물들은 포식자를 피하기 위해 행동적인 방법을 쓸 수도 있습니다. 이건 오늘은 주제에서 벗어난 거겠네요. 음…. 자기절단에 대해 들어본 사람 있나요?

단락 2
척추동물의 자기절단

S: Isn't it when an animal detaches or releases a part of its body to momentarily distract a predator, thereby buying it time to escape?

S: 동물들이 잠시 포식자의 주의를 돌리고 그래서 도망갈 시간을 벌 수 있게 자기 몸의 일부를 떼어내거나 내버리는 것 아닌가요?

P: Exactly, Stephanie! This mechanism is usually found in invertebrates like squids, spiders, and lobsters, but we'll look at vertebrates such as salamanders, lizards, and geckos. These creatures can throw different body parts; salamanders drop their limbs – like their legs, geckos their skin, and lizards their tails. [Q12] Today, we'll concentrate on lizards and their ability to drop their tails.

P: 정확해요, Stephanie! 이 메커니즘은 보통 오징어, 거미, 랍스터와 같은 무척추동물에서 주로 발견되지만, 우리는 도롱뇽, 도마뱀, 도마뱀붙이와 같은 척추동물을 살펴볼 겁니다. 이 생물들은 신체의 다른 부분을 버릴 수 있어요. 도롱뇽은 그들의 사지를 떨어뜨리고 - 그들의 다리 같은 거요. 도마뱀붙이는 그들의 피부, 도마뱀은 그들의 꼬리죠. [Q12] 오늘, 우리는 도마뱀과 그들의 꼬리를 떨어뜨리는 능력에 집중할 겁니다.

단락 3
도마뱀의 자기절단

[Q12-B] Interestingly, there doesn't need to be any physical contact between the lizards and their predators for autotomy to occur.

[Q12-B] 흥미롭게도, 자기절단이 일어나기 위해 도마뱀과 그들의 포식자들 사이에는 물리적인 접촉이 일어날 필요가 없습니다.

S: [Q13] That's quite different from the geckos' release of their skin, isn't it? They only activate this mechanism when in physical contact with their predators, right?

S: [Q13] 그건 도마뱀붙이가 피부를 내버리는 거랑 꽤 다르네요, 그죠? 그들은 포식자와 물리적으로 닿았을 때만 그 메커니즘을 실행하잖아요, 맞죠?

P: Right, that certainly draws a distinction between the two species. However, in lizards it seems that the initial stage of autotomy is the result of a voluntary decision or reflex to threatening stimuli. [Q14] Um, even though I said their tails could be lost voluntarily, there are still questions about the neural and physical basis of autotomy.

P: 맞아요, 그게 분명 그 두 종간의 차이를 만들죠. 하지만, 도마뱀에서 자기절단의 시작 단계는 자발적인 선택이나 위협적인 자극에 대한 반사의 결과로 보여요. [Q14] 음, 그들의 꼬리가 자발적으로 잃어질 수 있다고 제가 말했지만, 자기절단의 신경, 물리적 기초에는 여전히 의문점이 있습니다.

문단주제	본문내용	해석
	More research is needed, but we know that there's ummm… an internal trigger that incites such a response. Looking at their anatomy, researchers have found that lizards have internal structures that facilitate the process, such as the "fracture plane." [Q13-D] Some lizards have multiple fracture planes, whereas others have only one within the vertebrae in their tails. Regardless, fracture planes serve one purpose: helping lizards autotomize their tails. They drop them by contracting muscles between the vertebrae and severing the tail. Interestingly, the severed tails temporarily wiggle as if they were alive… Quite freaky, right?	더 많은 연구가 되어야 하지만, 우리는 음… 그런 반응을 일으키는 내부 촉발요인이 있다는 걸 알아요. 그들의 자기절단을 보면, 연구자들은 도마뱀이 "파단면"과 같은 그 과정을 일으키는 내부 구조를 갖고 있음을 밝혔습니다. [Q13-D] 어떤 도마뱀은 여러 파단면을 갖고 있지만 어떤 도마뱀은 그들의 꼬리 속 척추골에 단 하나만 가지고 있습니다. 이와 상관없이, 파단면은 하나의 역할을 하죠: 도마뱀이 자기 꼬리를 자르게 돕는 거요. 그들은 척추뼈 사이의 근육을 수축시키고 꼬리를 자름으로써 그걸 떨어뜨립니다. 흥미롭게도, 떨어진 꼬리는 살아있는 것처럼 잠시 씰룩거립니다.… 좀 이상하죠, 그죠?
	S: [Q14-B] How is it possible that the tail moves when there isn't a nervous system to stimulate the movement?	S: [Q14-B] 움직임을 자극할 신경계가 없는데 어떻게 꼬리가 움직일 수 있죠?
단락 4 꼬리의 재생	P: That's a great point, Stephanie. I was initially doubtful, too, but after seeing several studies about movement after tail detachment, I finally understand it. However, let's discuss that next time and try to stay on track. Anyway, when they successfully escape, the tail healing process begins almost immediately. I should also mention that, [Q4] although the tails regenerate, the healed tails are not identical to the originals… The former comprise cartilage rather than vertebrae, but it serves, more or less, the same purpose and function. Surprisingly, [Q15-A] tail regeneration takes only four to twelve weeks, depending on the species.	P: 좋은 지적이에요, Stephanie. 저도 처음에는 미심쩍었어요, 하지만 꼬리가 떨어지고 난 후 움직임에 관한 몇몇 연구를 보고 나자, 마침내 이해하게 되었답니다. 하지만, 이건 다음에 얘기하고 하던 얘기를 계속 합시다. 아무튼, 그들이 성공적으로 탈출했을 때, 꼬리 치유 과정이 거의 바로 시작됩니다. [Q4] 꼬리가 다시 생겨나도, 치료된 꼬리는 원래 것과 같진 않다는 것도 말해야겠네요. 전자는 척추뼈가 아니라 연골뼈로 구성되었지만, 거의 같은 목적과 기능을 수행합니다. 놀랍게도, [Q15-A] 꼬리 재생은 종에 따라 4주에서 12주 밖에 안 걸립니다.
단락 5 꼬리 절단으로 인한 손실	Let's shift our focus here… we've discussed the primary purpose and benefit of tail autotomy, survival, but there are also costs involved. You see, lizards detach their tails as a survival mechanism, but then they become less effective predators themselves. Some believe that it's because they lose a significant amount of energy when their tails are dropped. However, [Q16-A] others point out that their fat reserves, or their energy storage, are not lost since they are located at the base of the tails, which isn't detached. Confusing, huh? Anyway, let's think about how the lack of a tail would affect the lizard's daily life, which revolves around foraging and feeding on prey, and how their tails assist these activities. They are mainly used for maintaining their body control and balance.	여기서 우리의 주의를 전환해봅시다… 우리는 꼬리 자기절단의 주된 목적과 이득, 즉 생존을 이야기했었죠, 하지만 거기는 관련된 손실도 있습니다. 보면, 도마뱀은 생존 메커니즘으로 그들의 꼬리를 떼어내지만, 그러면 그들 자신은 덜 효율적인 포식자가 됩니다. 어떤 사람들은 이것이 그들의 꼬리가 떨어질 때 상당한 양의 에너지를 잃기 때문이라고 생각합니다. 하지만, [Q16-A] 다른 사람들은, 그들의 비축된 지방, 혹은 저장된 에너지는 떨어지지 않은 꼬리의 기반 부분에 있기 때문에 없어지지 않는다고 주장합니다. 헷갈리죠, 그죠? 아무튼, 꼬리가 없는 것이 먹이를 찾고 먹이를 먹는 것 중심으로 돌아가는 도마뱀의 일상에 어떤 영향을 줄지 생각해봅시다. 그리고 어떻게 그들의 꼬리가 이 활동을 도왔는지요. 그 꼬리들은 주로 몸의 통제와 균형을 유지하는 데에 쓰입니다.

TEST 5 set 1-3

문단주제	본문내용	해석
단락 6 도마뱀의 진화 가능성	[Q16] Without tails, lizards can't move as freely, so they naturally expend more energy negating the impact of tail detachment. Another problem that arises after tail-drops is the reduction in attractiveness to the opposite-sex. In addition, female lizards lay fewer eggs that result in weaker offspring and male lizards suffer from lowered social statuses. There are several other costs, but we won't go into those, since they're quite redundant. Remember that these disadvantages don't necessarily leave the lizards completely vulnerable. They're ever-evolving creatures that consistently develop evolutionary traits according to their changing conditions and environments. [Q17] For instance, they may spend less time chasing prey in open fields and more time looking out for predators. They may also change their activity time – from diurnal to nocturnal and vice versa – depending on the species.	[Q16] 꼬리 없이, 도마뱀은 그만큼 자유롭게 움직일 수 없고, 그래서 그들은 꼬리를 떼어낸 것의 영향을 없애기 위해 자연스럽게 더 많은 에너지를 씁니다. 꼬리를 떨어뜨린 후 생기는 또 다른 문제는 이성에 대한 매력이 줄어드는 것입니다. 게다가, 암컷 도마뱀은 알을 덜 낳는데 이는 더 약한 자손을 초래하고, 수컷 도마뱀은 낮아진 사회적 지위로 고통 받습니다. 또 다른 몇 개의 비용이 있지만, 그것은 하지 않을게요, 그것들이 좀 불필요해서요. 이 불리한 점들이 꼭 도마뱀을 완전히 무력하게 만드는 것은 아니라는 걸 기억하세요. 그들은 변화하는 조건과 환경에 맞춰 진화적인 특성을 끊임없이 개발해가는 계속 진화하는 생물입니다. [Q17] 예를 들어, 그들은 탁 트인 들판에서 먹이를 쫓는데 시간을 덜 쓰고 포식자를 찾는데 더 시간을 쓸 거예요. 그들은 또 활동 시간을 - 낮 시간에서 밤 시간으로, 혹은 반대로 - 바꾸기도 합니다, 종에 따라서요.

12. [Main Idea] What is the main topic of the lecture?

(A) The ~~interaction~~ between predators and prey and its effects on both *(wrong fact)*

(B) The definition of autotomy as an animal's reaction to threat *(too specific)* ★

(C) An antipredator adaptation of a reptile species and its effects

(D) A variety of evolutionary traits that predators have developed to increase their chances of capturing prey *(too specific)*

12. 이 강의의 주제는 무엇인가?

(A) 포식자와 먹이의 ~~상호작용~~과 그것이 양쪽에 미치는 영향

(B) 위협에 대한 동물들의 반응으로서의 자기절단의 정의 ★

(C) 파충류 종들의 반포식자 적응과 그 영향

(D) 먹이를 잡을 확률을 높이기 위해 포식자들이 개발해 온 다양한 진화적 특성

해설 | (A) 강의의 주는 포식자가 아닌 먹이와 그 생존방식이다. 때문에, 상호작용과는 관계가 없다. (B) 자기절단의 정의 및 근본적인 설명은 강의의 극히 일부이다. 강의의 중점은 자기절단의 정의 자체가 아닌 자기절단과 이후의 재생과정과 그 영향이다. (D) 변화하는 환경에 따라 도마뱀들도 진화한다는 예로 교수는 탁 트인 들판에서 먹이를 쫓는 시간을 줄이고 포식자를 찾는 시간을 늘린다고 설명한다. 강의의 극히 일부로, 주제라고 볼 수 없다.

13. [Detail – Difference/Contrast] How is autotomy in geckos different from that in lizards?

(A) Geckos drop their tails when under threat, but ~~only at night~~ *(not mentioned)*

(B) Lizards ~~release their fragile skin~~ to slip away from predatory attacks *(wrong fact)*

(C) The former employ autotomy when they're in direct contact with their predators

(D) ~~The former~~ have multiple fracture planes, whereas the latter have only one *(not mentioned)* ★

13. 도마뱀붙이의 자기절단은 도마뱀의 것과 어떻게 다른가?

(A) 도마뱀붙이는 위협이 있을 때, 하지만 ~~밤에만~~ 꼬리를 떨어뜨린다.

(B) 도마뱀은 포식자의 공격에서 빠져나가기 위해 ~~그들의 약한 피부를 내버린다~~.

(C) 전자는 그들의 포식자와 직접적인 접촉이 있을 때 자기절단을 사용한다.

(D) ~~전자~~는 여러 파단면을 가지고 있고, 반면 후자는 하나만 가지고 있다. ★

해설 | (A) 언급되지 않는 내용이므로 오답. (B) 피부를 내버리는 것은 도마뱀붙이의 특징이므로 오답. (D) 어떤 도마뱀은 여러 파단면을 갖고 있는 반면 어떤 도마뱀은 단 하나만 가지고 있다는 교수의 설명을 왜곡시켜 놓은 것으로 오답. 도마뱀붙이의 파단면 소유 여부는 언급되지 않는다.

14. [Inference – Imply] What does the professor imply about the studies that explain the voluntary detachment of tails?

(A) That they fall short of proving ~~that tails have their own nervous systems~~ *(wrong fact)* ★

(B) That they've yet to effectively validate the phenomenon with sufficient evidence

(C) That improvements need to be made regarding the understanding of ~~differences between geckos and lizards~~ *(unrelated to the question)*

(D) That they're ~~complete~~ and the discovery of body structures like fracture planes is the evidence viewed as immoral *(wrong fact)*

14. 자발적인 꼬리 자르기를 설명하는 연구에 대해 교수는 어떤 것을 암시하는가?

(A) 그것들은 꼬리가 ~~그만의 신경계를 가지고 있다~~는 것을 증명하지 못했다는 것 ★

(B) 그것들은 아직 그 현상을 충분한 증거로 효과적으로 타당화하지는 못했다는 것

(C) ~~도마뱀붙이와 도마뱀의 차이~~에 대한 이해를 바탕으로 발전이 이뤄져야 한다는 것

(D) 그것들은 ~~완성되었고~~ 파단면과 같은 몸의 구조는 부도덕하게 관찰된다는 증거이다.

| 해설 | (A) 도마뱀의 꼬리에는 신경계가 없음은 확실하므로 이를 증명하는 연구는 의미가 없으므로 오답. (C) 교수는 도마뱀과 도마뱀붙이의 차이점에 의미를 두지 않으므로 오답. (D) 교수는 직접적으로 연구가 더 필요하다고 말하므로 연구의 완전함은 어떤 식으로든 암시하지 않음을 알 수 있다. |

---

15. [Detail – Characteristic] Which of the following is true about the regenerated tails of lizards?

(A) Regeneration ~~begins~~ about four to twelve weeks ~~after the detachment~~ *(wrong fact)* ★

(B) They are different from the original tails in terms of their physical compositions

(C) They are ~~smaller and weaker~~ than the original tails *(not mentioned)*

(D) Lizards ~~aren't able to~~ autotomize regenerated tails again *(not mentioned)*

15. 다음 중 도마뱀의 재생된 꼬리에 대해 맞는 것은 무엇인가?

(A) 분리 후 약 4주에서 12주 후에 재생이 ~~시작된다~~. ★

(B) 물리적 구성 측면에서 원래 꼬리와는 다르다.

(C) 그것들은 원래 꼬리보다 ~~작고 약하다~~.

(D) 도마뱀은 다시 재생된 꼬리를 자기 절단~~하지 못한다~~.

| 해설 | (A) 꼬리 재생은 종에 따라 4주에서 12주 정도 걸린다는 교수의 설명을 왜곡시켜 놓은 것으로 오답. (C) 교수는 원래 꼬리와 재생된 꼬리의 구성의 차이점은 설명하지만 그 특징의 비교는 하지 않으므로 오답. (D) 재생된 꼬리의 절단 가능성에 대한 내용 역시 언급되지 않으므로 오답. |

16. [Detail – Cause/Reason] Why do lizards lose a great amount of energy after tail autotomization?

(A) Because lizards' energy storage mechanisms are located in the section of the tail that isn't detached *(unrelated to the question)*

(B) Because regenerating tails requires a massive amount of energy *(not mentioned)* ★

(C) **Because lizards need to compensate for their restricted movement**

(D) Because lizards suffer from degradation of their social status and ~~expend extra energy earning it back~~ *(partial error)*

16. 꼬리 자기절단 후에 도마뱀은 왜 많은 양의 에너지를 잃는가?

(A) 도마뱀의 에너지 저장 메커니즘은 꼬리의 떼어지지 않는 부분에 있기 때문에

(B) 꼬리를 다시 만드는 것은 많은 양의 에너지를 필요로 하기 때문에 ★

(C) **도마뱀은 제한된 움직임을 보충해야 하기 때문에**

(D) 도마뱀은 그들의 사회적 지위가 낮아진 것으로 고통 받고 ~~다시 그것을 얻기 위해 추가적인 에너지를 쓰기~~ 때문에

> **해설 |** (A) 맞는 말이지만 저장된 에너지가 떼어지지 않기 때문에 에너지를 잃지 않는다는 주장이 설명된다. 문제가 묻는 에너지의 손실과는 무관하므로 오답. (B) 꼬리 재생 시 필요한 에너지에 대해서는 언급되지 않으므로 오답. (D) 꼬리 절단 후 사회적 지위가 낮아지는 것은 맞으나 이를 회복하기 위해 추가적인 에너지는 쓴다는 내용은 언급되지 않는다.

17. [Detail – Solution] How do lizards adapt to living without their tails and overcome the disadvantages it causes?

(A) They develop additional traits, such as ~~crypsis and mimesis~~ *(wrong fact)* ★

(B) **They change their behavior patterns and the time of their activity**

(C) They exert more energy ~~to speed their tail regeneration~~ *(not mentioned)*

(D) They forage ~~in social groups~~ rather than hunting individually *(not mentioned)*

17. 도마뱀은 어떻게 꼬리 없이 사는 것에 적응하고 그것이 일으키는 불리한 점을 극복하는가?

(A) 그들은 ~~은폐와 모방~~ 같은 추가적인 특성을 개발한다. ★

(B) **그들은 그들의 행동 패턴과 활동 시간을 바꾼다.**

(C) 그들은 그들의 ~~꼬리 재생성을 더 빠르게 하기 위해~~ 더 많은 에너지를 가한다.

(D) 그들은 개별적으로 사냥하지 않고 ~~사회적 무리~~로 먹이를 찾는다.

> **해설 |** (A) 은폐와 모방은 강의 초반부에 교수가 동물들의 진화적 특성을 설명할 때 든 위장 기술의 예로, 도마뱀의 꼬리 자기절단 후 적응 방법과는 연관이 없으므로 오답. (C)와 (D)는 언급되지 않으므로 오답.

TEST 5 set 2-1

Conversation: Poetry reading

Listen to part of a conversation between a student and a professor.

S: Good morning, professor.

P: Come on in, Claire. [Q2] I'm glad to see you back on your feet again! What a horrible injury you suffered… Anyway, what brings you here?

S: [Q1] Well, it's about the poetry reading I recently attended. I'm trying to come up with an idea for the final term paper, but even after hours of contemplation, I can't seem to broaden my perspective.

P: I see… [Q2-B] I'm sorry I couldn't attend the reading, so could you tell me what kind of reading it was? I need to know where you're coming from to help you.

S: Of course! [Q2-D] Um, it seemed conventional. I mean, the overall mood was quiet and calm, and the audience sat quietly and listened to the poets. You know what I mean?

P: Yes, I think I understand. You're probably right, that sounds like a pretty conventional poetry reading.

S: Well, I was wondering if there was… some other way of sharing poetry, maybe something more performance-like.

P: Sure. You're thinking of the poetry slam that was created during the Beat Generation… It goes back to 1948, when Jack Kerouac, one of the pioneers of the movement, [Q3] coined the term to express his and his proponents' anti-conformist attitudes towards politics and a rejection of contemporary American values.

S: Oh, that sounds fascinating. I guess I didn't know much about the history of American poetry. How are poetry slams different from conventional readings?

P: Well, poetry slams are competitive. A number of poets engage in a competition and are judged by selected audience members, usually 3 to 5 of them.

S: I'm not following…

문단주제	본문내용	해석
단락 5 관중의 역할 및 대조	P: [Q4] Okay, let's look at Allen Ginsberg and his philosophies as a poet to clear it up. He was one of the most prominent and noteworthy leaders of the Beat Generation, known for his powerful, engaging performances. Poetry slams were almost at the opposite end of the spectrum as conventional poetry reading, because they emphasized energetic, loud readings, and the role of the audience was significant. S: Audience? How? P: So, as you stated, the audience's primary function is listening to poems in conventional readings, right? Their involvement is highly discouraged and silence is expected so others can listen as well. In poetry slams, the audience actively responds to the poet by yelling or cheering. S: Wow, I would've never thought of that! And, I'm sorry, but could we go back to what their poems were usually about?	P: [Q4] 좋아, 명확하게 설명하기 위해서 Allen Ginsberg과 시인으로서의 그의 철학에 대해서 살펴보죠. 그는 Beat 세대에서 가장 유명하고 눈에 띄는 리더 중 하나였죠. 강력하고 매력적인 연기로 유명했어요. Poetry slam은 상투적인 시 낭독과 거의 가장 대척점에 있었어요. 왜냐하면 그들은 활동적이고 시끄럽게 낭독하는 것을 강조했고, 관중의 역할도 중요했죠. S: 관중들이요? 어떻게요? P: 네가 말했듯, 관중의 주요 기능은 상투적인 낭독을 듣는 거지, 맞지? 관객들의 개입은 꽤 배제되고, 침묵해야 하지, 다른 사람들이 잘 들을 수 있도록. Poetry Slam에서 청중은 소리를 지르거나 응원을 해서 시인들에게 적극적으로 반응하지. S: 와, 그런 건 생각도 못해봤어요. 근데 죄송한데, 그 사람들의 시가 주로 무엇에 관한 것인지에 대해 돌아가도 될까요?
단락 6 Beat Generation 의 시의 주제	P: Certainly. Okay, since the poems needed to arouse emotions in order to build a connection with the audience, the topics were just as controversial. [Q5] Well, you're going to need to do further research to get the details because you know… it's going to be your topic (laughs). S: Oh right. I'm sorry about that (laughs). I have a much clearer vision as to how to organize my paper now. Two contrasting poetry sharing styles… quite a topic, isn't it? P: Of course! I look forward to reading it. S: Thank you so much for your time and help, professor! P: My pleasure, Claire. Good luck with the assignment!	P: 물론이지. 자, 관중과 소통하기 위해서 시는 감정을 불러 일으켜야만 했어. 주제는 꼭 논쟁적이었어. [Q5] 음, 세부적인 내용을 알기 위해서는 네가 추가적인 조사를 직접 해야 해, 너도 알겠지만.. 이게 곧 너의 주제가 될 거니까. (웃음) S: 맞아요. 그 점은 죄송해요. (웃음) 이제 제 페이퍼를 어떻게 정리해야 할지 훨씬 명확한 그림을 그렸어요. 시를 이야기하는 두 가지의 대조적인 양식.. 꽤 그럴싸 하죠, 아닌가요? P: 물론이지! 기대할게. S: 시간 내주셔서 도와주셔서 감사합니다, 교수님! P: 천만해, Claire. 과제 잘 하렴!

01. [Main Purpose] Why does the student visit the professor?

(A) To get help with ~~distinguishing~~ conventional poetry readings from ~~poetry slams~~ *(wrong fact)* ★

(B) To discuss the poetry reading event that recently took place ~~on campus~~ *(not mentioned)*

(C) **To organize her thoughts on her paper**

(D) To examine the significance of Allen Ginsberg as a prominent leader of the Beat Generation *(unrelated to the question)*

01. 학생은 교수를 왜 방문하는가?

(A) 상투적인 시 낭독과 Poetry Slam을 ~~구분하는 데~~ 도움을 얻으려고 ★

(B) 최근 ~~캠퍼스에서~~ 개최된 시 낭독 행사에 관해 논의하려고

(C) **학생의 페이퍼에 대해 학생의 생각을 정리하려고**

(D) Beat 세대의 유명한 리더로써의 Allen Ginsberg의 중요성을 살펴보기 위해서

> **해설** | (A) Poetry Slam은 교수가 학생에게 소개시켜 준 시 공유 방식으로 상투적인 시 낭독과 구분하는 것은 학생이 교수를 방문하는 이유가 될 수 없다. (B) 시 낭독 행사가 캠퍼스에서 개최되었는지는 언급되지 않으므로 알 수 없다. (D) Allen Ginsberg는 교수가 poetry slam에 대해 부가적으로 설명할 때 언급되는 인물로, 학생이 교수를 방문하는 이유가 아니다.

---

02. [Inference – Infer] What can be inferred about the student?

(A) **That she was momentarily handicapped due to an injury**

(B) That she is distressed about the poetry reading ~~she missed recently~~ *(wrong fact)* ★

(C) That she ~~did not spend much time~~ planning her paper *(wrong fact)*

(D) That she ~~dislikes~~ conventional poetry reading *(not mentioned)*

02. 학생에 대해 무엇이 암시 가능한가?

(A) **그녀는 부상 때문에 잠시 불편했었다.**

(B) 그녀는 ~~최근에 참석하지 못했던~~ 시 낭송회에 대해 당황하고 있다. ★

(C) 그녀의 페이퍼를 계획하는 데 ~~많은 시간을 쓰지 않았다.~~

(D) 그녀는 상투적인 시 낭송회를 ~~좋아하지 않는다.~~

> **해설** | (B) 낭송회에 참석하지 못한 것은 학생이 아닌 교수이므로 오답. (C) 학생은 기말 페이퍼를 위해 아이디어를 생각하는 데 오랜 시간을 보냈다고 직접 말하기 때문에 오답. (D) 학생은 최근에 참석한 시 낭송회의 상투적인 분위기를 묘사할 때 매우 객관적으로 이야기하므로 이에 대한 그녀의 의견은 짐작 할 수 없다.

---

03. [Detail – Characteristic] According to the professor, what was the focal point of the Beat Generation?

(A) Connecting with the audience and involving them in the ~~creation process~~ *(partial error)* ★

(B) **A contentious attitude toward traditional beliefs and values**

(C) Implicit acceptance by ~~main-stream society~~ *(not mentioned)*

(D) ~~Violent riots and rebellion~~ against the government *(too extreme)*

03. 교수의 말에 다르면, Beat 세대의 중점은 무엇인가?

(A) ~~창작 과정에~~ 관객과 소통하여 그들을 참여시키는 것 ★

(B) **전통적인 믿음과 가치에 대한 논쟁적인 태도**

(C) ~~주류 사회의~~ 맹목적인 수용

(D) 정부에 대한 폭력적인 폭동과 반란

> **해설** | (A) Beat Generation의 Poetry Slam에서 관객과의 소통이 중요시 된 것은 맞으나 교수는 그것이 창작 과정이 아닌 낭독 과정에서의 특징이었다고 설명하므로 오답. (C) 언급되지 않으므로 오답. (D) 정부 체제에 대한 반항을 표현한 것은 맞으나 이것이 폭력적이었다고 설명되지는 않으므로 오답.

04. [Detail – Purpose] Why does the professor mention Allen Ginsberg?

(A) To explain that his practice of reading poetry in poetry slams ~~inspired lots of young writers~~ *(not mentioned)*

(B) To illustrate his philosophies as a poet ~~to introduce the Beat Generation~~ *(wrong fact)*

(C) **To show the difference between the styles of conventional poetry readings and poetry slams**

(D) To demonstrate that conventional poetry reading and poetry slams can be ~~classified into a spectrum~~ *(partial error)* ★

04. 왜 교수는 Allen Ginsberg를 언급하는가?

(A) Poetry Slam에서 그가 시를 읽는 습관이 ~~많은 젊은 시인들에게 영감을 주었다는 것을~~ 설명하기 위해서

(B) 시인으로서의 그의 철학을 묘사해 ~~Beat 세대를 소개하기~~ 위해서

(C) **상투적인 시 낭독과 Poetry Slam의 방식의 차이를 보여주기 위해서**

(D) 상투적인 시 낭송회와 poetry slam이 ~~spectrum으로 분류될~~ 수 있다는 것을 보여주기 위해서 ★

> 해설 | (A) 교수는 Allen Ginsberg가 Beat 세대의 유명한 리더 중 하나로 강력하고 매력적인 연기로 유명했다고 설명하긴 하지만 젊은 시인들에게 영감을 주었다고 말하지는 않으므로 오답. (B) 교수는 Allen Ginsberg를 언급하기 이전에 이미 Beat 세대를 소개하기 때문에 오답. (D) 교수의 설명의 목적 및 중점은 분류 방식이 아닌 차이점이므로 오답.

Listen again to part of the conversation. Then answer the question.

"Well, you're going to need to do further research to get the details because you know… it's going to be your topic (laughs)."

05. [inference-imply] What does the professor imply when he says this: 🎧

"Well, you're going to need to do further research to get the details because you know… it's going to be your topic."

(A) **That he wishes to avoid giving away too much information to the student**

(B) That he is ~~not familiar~~ with the details of the topic

(C) That the details are ~~too complicated for~~ him to explain on the spot

(D) That he thinks that the student ~~is apathetic~~ about her research topic

대화의 일부를 다시 듣고, 문제에 답하시오.

"음, 세부적인 내용을 알기 위해서는 네가 추가적인 조사를 직접 해야 해, 너도 알겠지만.. 이게 곧 너의 주제가 될 거니까. (웃음)"

05. 교수가 이 말을 할 때 암시하는 것은 무엇인가? 🎧

"음, 세부적인 내용을 알기 위해서는 네가 추가적인 조사를 직접 해야 해, 너도 알겠지만.. 이게 곧 너의 주제가 될 거니까."

(A) **그는 너무 많은 정보를 학생들에게 주는것을 피하고 싶어한다.**

(B) 그가 주제에 ~~세부사항을 잘 모른다~~.

(C) 지금 그 자리에서는 설명하기에는 세부사항이 ~~너무 복잡하다~~.

(D) 그는 학생들이 그에 주제에 대해서 너무 ~~무관심~~ 하다고 생각한다.

> 해설 | It's going to be your topic= 너네 주제가 될것이기 때문이다. 학생들이 앞으로 글을써야하는 주제이기 때문에 교수님이 알려주지 않는것이다. B) 주제와 익숙하지 않은것이 아니다. C) 너무 복잡한것이 아니다 D) 학생들이 무관심 하기에 말하는것이 아니다.

TEST 5 set 2-2 — Lecture 1: Ethanol

Listen to part of a lecture in an environmental science class.

P: As we discussed, a lot of effort has gone into finding an alternative to petroleum-based fuel such as gasoline, the fuel used in internal combustion engines like cars, locomotives, airplanes; you name it... Most vehicles rely on this fuel, because it was believed to be the most suitable and efficient fuel for engines, despite its environmental impact. However, scientists have discovered a new source known as ethanol. For those of you not familiar with it, let me explain what it is. Ethanol, or ethyl alcohol, is the alcohol found in alcoholic beverages.

S: Alcoholic beverages? That doesn't sound like an ideal fit for combustion engines.

P: [Q11] It makes more sense if you understand how it's produced. Most people think of alcohol as simply a pre-made adult product, but most ethanol used as fuel in the United States is actually a corn product. That's right, the edible yellow grain. However, its production can be quite interesting. It begins with fermenting the corn to produce sugars, which go through a series of chemical reactions and ultimately produces ethanol and carbon dioxide as by-products. Then, the ethanol is distilled into its concentrated, purified form, which is usable as a fuel. It's not different from gasoline in that it supplies energy to internal combustion engines. [Q7-D] It's been widely used as an additive or alternative to gasoline in a number of countries, with Brazil and the United States being the largest markets. Between 2000 and 2007, ethanol production increased from 17 billion to nearly 52 billion liters. [Q7] That's quite an increase considering that the idea of using ethanol as a fuel is fairly new.

S: So, it must provide some benefits over gasoline, right?

P: Of course! First of all, unlike gasoline, it's renewable. I'm sure you're all aware that gasoline is a non-renewable resource extracted from the ground, so its supply is limited and will eventually run out. In contrast, ethanol is not a fossil fuel, so it will be available as long as corn crops are available.

문단주제	본문내용	해석
단락 4 에탄올의 단점	Speaking of crops, ethanol also has an economic impact. You see, growing and harvesting crops doesn't just happen; it requires labor. Therefore, it creates economic security for farmers. [Q8] Furthermore, commerce, ummm… trade between countries, brings prosperity to countries that depend on agriculture for economic growth. It's also more environmentally friendly than gasoline, because it emits less carbon dioxide. P: I heard that ethanol also had negative aspects. Is that true? S: Yes. Some researchers have pointed out negative aspects of ethanol production and use. P: [Q7-C] First, even though the type of energy doesn't differ, there's a big quality difference between the two. In other words, ethanol contains less energy than gasoline, so more is required to produce the same amount of usable energy. [Q9-A] Basically, 1.5 gallons of ethanol is equivalent to 1 gallon of gasoline in terms of energy efficiency. Also, growing and harvesting crops like corn requires a lot more than just sowing seeds. [Q9] To grow them successfully, supplements, such as fertilizers, are needed. I'm not sure if you're familiar with fertilizers, but they are detrimental to the environment. S: Because they harm animals and people who eat crops drenched in them? P: Not quite. You're not totally off the track, but [Q9] I meant that the current process of fertilizer production entails the use of fossil fuels. Actually, ethanol fermentation and distillation have the same problem. [Q9-C] So, just because ethanol fuel doesn't emit as much carbon dioxide as gasoline, it doesn't mean that it's completely environmentally friendly. On top of that, transporting and distributing ethanol demands tremendous energy input. [Q10] You see, ethanol, unlike petroleum, can't be transported through pipelines because it is easily tainted and it's unusable if mixed with water. S: Wait, how are water and pipelines connected? Am I missing something?	옥수수에 대해서 얘기하자면, 에탄올은 경제적 효과도 있죠. 여러분도 알겠지만, 작물을 심고 거둬들이는 것은 그냥 있는 일이 아니죠. 노동이 필요합니다. 그러므로 농부들에게 경제적 안전을 보장할 수 있는 것이죠. [Q8] 게다가 상업… 그러니까… 나라간 무역에서도 (국가) 경제 성장에서 농업에 의존하고 있는 국가들에게 번영을 가져다 줍니다. 에탄올은 또한 가솔린보다 더 친환경적이므로, 이산화탄소를 덜 배출합니다. P: 에탄올도 문제점이 있다고 들었는데요. 맞나요? S: 맞습니다. 어떤 연구자들은 에탄올 생산과 사용의 부정적인 측면을 지적해왔습니다. P: [Q7-C] 먼저, 심지어 에너지의 유형이 다르지 않지만, 에탄올과 가솔린 차이에는 큰 질적 차이가 존재합니다. 다시 말해, 에탄올은 가솔린 보다 더 적은 양의 에너지를 포함합니다. 그래서 유효한 에너지의 같은 양을 생산하기 위해서 더 많은 양이 필요합니다. [Q9-A] 기본적으로 에탄올 1.5 갤런은 가솔린 1 갤런과 에너지 효율이 같습니다. 뿐만 아니라, 옥수수 같은 작물을 기르고 거둬들이는 것은 씨앗을 파종하는 것 보다 더 많은 (자원이) 필요합니다. [Q9] 옥수수를 잘 기르기 위해서, 비료와 같은 보조제가 필요합니다. 비료를 잘 모르는 학생들이 있을 지 모르겠지만, 비료는 환경에 해롭죠. S: 비료가 뿌려진 작물을 동물과 사람이 먹으면 해롭기 때문이죠? P: 꼭 그렇지만은 않아요. 학생이 주제에서 완전히 벗어난 것은 아니지만, [Q9] 오늘날 비료 생산을 하는 과정에서 화석 연료를 사용하기 때문이었어요. 실제로, 에탄올 발효와 증류도 같은 문제가 있죠. [Q9-C] 그래서 에탄올 연료가 가솔린만큼 많은 이산화탄소를 배출하는 것이 아니라고 해서 완전히 친환경적이라는 것도 아니에요. 무엇보다, 에탄올을 운반하고 배분하는 데에 많은 에너지 투입이 필요합니다. [Q10] 알다시피, 석유와는 다르게 에탄올은 수송관을 통해서 운반될 수 없어요. 왜냐하면 물과 섞일 경우 쉽게 썩으며 사용할 수 없게 되기 때문이에요. S: 잠시만요, 어떻게 수송관과 물이 무슨 상관이죠? 제가 뭔가 놓치고 있나요?

문단 주제	본문내용	해석
	P: Oops, I skipped something. [Q10-D] I forgot to mention that it's practically impossible to build a long pipeline that doesn't leak a little water. [Q8-A] So, it takes more energy to distribute ethanol than petroleum across the country, because pipelines can't be used. Another thing about ethanol is that it holds future harm. By that, I mean that the part of corn used to make ethanol is the kernel – the part that we eat. It may not seem like a problem now, but some scholars warn that there will be a time in the future when producing ethanol will be our priority over feeding people. [Q10-A] Others argue that ethanol is just as dangerous as gasoline, because it's highly flammable, so it's not an ideal alternative. We'll cover that next time, so let's wrap up for today.	P: 오, 제가 그냥 지나쳤네요. [Q10-D] 적은 양의 물이라도 들어가지 않는 긴 수송관을 만드는 것 자체가 실질적으로 불가능 하다고 말할 것을 까먹었네요. [Q8-A] 그래서, 국토를 가로질러 석유보다 에탄올을 배분하는 게 더 많은 에너지가 필요하다는 것입니다. 왜냐하면 수송관을 사용할 수 없기 때문이에요. 에탄올에 대한 또 다른 점은 잠재적인 위험이 있다는 것입니다. 때문에, 에탄올을 만들기 위해 사용되는 옥수수의 일부분은 열매입니다, 우리가 먹는 부분이죠. 지금은 문제가 아닌 것처럼 보일지 몰라도, 몇몇 학자들은 나중에 사람들을 먹이는 것 보다 에탄올을 생산하는 것이 더 우위에 설 순간이 올지도 모른다고 경고합니다. [Q10-A] 다른 학자들은 에탄올은 가솔린만큼 위험하다고 주장합니다. 왜냐하면 에탄올은 매우 불타기 쉬워서 이상적인 대체재가 아닌 것이죠. 다음 시간에 다시 얘기해보고, 오늘 배운 내용을 정리해봅시다.
단락 5 다음 수업 과제	Before we leave, I'll give you an assignment. Research other sources, other crops like sugar cane, which could be an alternative to corn in ethanol production and analyze their benefits over corn.	끝내기 전에, 과제를 하나 내 줄게요. 사탕 수수 같은 다른 자원들을 조사해보세요. 에탄올 생산에서 옥수수를 대체할 수 있고, 옥수수보다 많은 이점을 조사해보세요.

06. [Main Idea] What is the main topic of the lecture?

(A) ~~Social responsibilities~~ and the production of ethanol as a fuel source
(not mentioned)

(B) The efficiency of ethanol in contrast to that of gasoline *(too specific)* ★

(C) **The pros and cons of an alternative to gasoline as a fuel**

(D) The ~~deficiency of gasoline alternatives~~ with supporting details
(partial error)

06. 강의의 주제가 무엇인가?

(A) ~~사회적 책임과~~ 연료 자원으로서의 에탄올 생산

(B) 가솔린과 비교하였을 때의 에탄올의 효율성 ★

(C) **연료로서의 가솔린의 대체재의 장단점**

(D) 상세한 뒷받침 내용을 통한 ~~가솔린 대체재의 결핍~~

해설 | (A) 사회적 책임은 언급되지 않으므로 오답. (B) 언급되기는 하지만 강의의 일부이므로 주제로 잡기에는 너무 좁다. (D) 가솔린 대체재를 찾기 위해 많은 노력이 있었음은 언급되지만 교수는 그 결과 개발된 에탄올에 중점을 둔다. 즉, 강의의 중점은 결핍이 아니라 가솔린 대체재 중 하나이다.

07. [Inference – Infer] What can be inferred about ethanol fuel from the lecture?

(A) ~~Most countries~~ are using it, contributing to a dramatic increase in its production *(partial error)*

(B) **Its use has been accepted by many despite its relatively short history**

(C) The quality of ~~the energy it produces~~ is substandard and inferior to gasoline *(partial error)* ★

(D) It's ~~too costly~~ for countries without ethanol fermentation technology to produce *(not mentioned)*

07. 강의를 통해 에탄올 연료에 대해서 알 수 있는 내용이 무엇인가?

(A) ~~대부분의 국가가~~ 에탄올을 사용하고 있으며 생산량을 극적으로 증가시키고 있다.

(B) **짧은 역사에도 불구하고 다수가 사용하고 있다.**

(C) ~~에탄올이 생산하는 에너지의 품질은~~ 가솔린보다 품질이 좋지 않다. ★

(D) 에탄올 발효 기술이 없는 나라가 생산하기에는 ~~너무 비싸다~~.

해설 | (A) 교수는 에탄올이 대부분의 국가가 아닌 "몇몇 국가"에서 사용되고 있다고 말하므로 오답.
(C) 교수는 에탄올이 생산하는 에너지가 아닌 에탄올 그 자체의 질적 한계를 지적하므로 오답.
(D) 언급되지 않는 내용이므로 오답.

08. [Detail – Effect/Influence] According to the professor, how does the use of ethanol fuel contribute to the welfare of society?

(A) Since it requires extra transportation, it ~~creates jobs~~ for distributors *(wrong fact)* ★

(B) Because growing and harvesting crops ~~just happens~~, it ~~doesn't require~~ much labor *(opposite fact)*

(C) It ~~inhibits the use of~~ environmentally harmful chemicals, such as fertilizers and oil *(not mentioned)*

(D) It works as a catalyst for businesses in countries with abundant amount of agricultural resources

08. 교수의 말에 따르면, 에탄올 사용이 어떻게 사회 복지에 기여하는가?

(A) 운송수단이 더 필요하기 때문에 유통업자를 위한 ~~직업을 생산한다~~. ★

(B) 작물을 심고 거둬들이는 것은 ~~그냥 일어나는 일~~이므로, 많은 노동력을 ~~필요로 하지 않는다~~.

(C) 비료나 기름 같은 환경적으로 해로운 화학 물질의 ~~사용을 근절한다~~.

(D) 농업 자원이 풍부한 국가의 무역 촉매제로 기능한다.

해설 | (A) 교수는 에탄올이 수송관을 통해 운송 될 수 없기 때문에 에너지가 더 필요하다고 말한다. 교수가 설명하는 직업의 생산은 작물 재배의 결과이다. 잘못된 인과관계이므로 오답. (B) 작물을 심고 거둬들이는 것은 그냥 일어나는 일이 아니기 때문에 노동력이 필요하다는 교수의 설명과 정반대되는 말이므로 오답. (C) 언급되지 않는 내용이므로 오답.

09. [Detail – Effect/Influence] Which of the following are environmental impacts of ethanol fuel?

Click on 2 answers

(A) It takes about 1.5 gallons of ethanol ~~to produce the same amount of CO2~~ as 1 gallon of gasoline *(not mentioned)* ★

(B) Creating ethanol from corn is energy-intensive in that it requires the production of toxic chemicals

(C) It ~~completely eradicates~~ the emission of carbon dioxide *(wrong fact)*

(D) Fermenting corn kernels and purifying ethanol entails the use of fossil fuels

09. 에탄올 연료의 환경적 영향이 무엇인가?

2개의 정답을 고르시오

(A) 가솔린 1 갤런당 ~~생산되는 이산화탄소와 같은 양~~을 위해 에탄올 1.5 갤런이 필요하다. ★

(B) 독성 화학 물질을 생산해내므로 옥수수에서 에탄올을 생산하는 데에는 많은 에너지가 필요하다.

(C) 이산화탄소의 방출을 ~~완전히 근절한다~~.

(D) 옥수수 열매를 발효시키고 에탄올의 불순물을 제거하는 데에 화석 연료가 필요하다.

해설 | (A) 에탄올 1.5 갤런이 가솔린 1 갤런과 에너지 효율이 같다는 교수의 설명을 왜곡시켜 놓은 것으로 오답. (C) 교수는 비료 생산 과정에서 화석 연료가 사용되며 에탄올 발효와 증류도 같은 문제가 있다며 이산화탄소 배출이 어느 정도 있다고 설명한다. 때문에, 이산화탄소 방출을 완전히 근절한다고 할 수 없다.

10. [Detail – Cause/Reason] Why can't ethanol be transported via pipelines like oil?

(A) Because its high flammability ~~makes it unsuitable for~~ such a transportation method *(wrong fact)*

(B) Because it starts a chemical reaction and ~~causes rusting~~ in response to its contact with steel *(not mentioned)*

(C) Because it loses its usefulness as a fuel when tainted by water

(D) Because it's ~~economically impossible~~ to build a pipeline network just for ethanol *(partial error)* ★

해설 | (A) 교수는 에탄올의 인화성을 언급하기는 하지만 이를 운송수단과 연결 짓지 않으므로 오답. (B) 언급되지 않는 내용이므로 오답. (D) 교수는 적은 양의 물이라도 들어가지 않는 긴 수송관을 만드는 것이 실질적으로 불가능 하다고 말하며 기술적 한계를 지적한다. 경제적 한계를 탓하지 않기 때문에 오답.

Listen again to part of the lecture. Then answer the question.

"It makes more sense if you understand how it's produced. Most people think of alcohol as simply a pre-made adult product, but most ethanol used as fuel in the United States is actually a corn product."

11. [Inference - Imply] What does the professor imply when he says this: 🎧

> "Most people think of alcohol as simply a pre-made adult product, but most ethanol used as fuel in the United States is actually a corn product."

(A) That most people don't realize that the alcohol they drink is a corn product that can be used as a fuel

(B) That corn, ~~unlike all other crops~~, is used in the production of alcohol *(not mentioned)*

(C) That not all corn products are edible *(partial error)*

(D) That it makes more sense if the students understand how ~~alcoholic beverages~~ are produced *(partial error)* ★

해설 | (B) 다른 작물 및 그 비교는 전혀 언급되지 않으므로 오답. (C) 맞는 말이지만 교수의 의도와는 무관하므로 오답. (D) "It makes more sense if you understand how it's produced."의 "it"은 알코올성 음료가 아닌 에탄올을 가리키는 대명사이므로 오답.

TEST 5 set 2-3 — Lecture 2: A solar nebula

Listen to part of a lecture in a geology class.

P: You may recall that the solar system started as a cloud of dust and gas, known as a solar nebula, according to the core accretion model. Then, the collapse of a part of the cloud caused the mass concentration of cosmic material at its center, ultimately creating the Sun. The advent of the terrestrial planets, including Earth, took place shortly after, as the remaining materials began to build up. During Earth's formation, dense elements sank to the bottom, forming its core, and the lighter ones formed its crust. [Q12] Let's look at issues regarding Earth's life-sustaining ability. We tend to wonder about how Earth is able to support life, whereas other plants are uninhabitable.

Before we begin, let's try to remember that liquid water is essential for life. The presence of this water is the most distinguishing facet of our planet. On other planets, flowing water occurs only rarely or in small quantities, because it either freezes or vaporizes depending on the temperature. Earth has abundant water because… ummm… let me go over one of the most widely accepted theories to elucidate water's origin on Earth. [Q14-D] It is believed that water remained on Earth due to the accumulation of greenhouse gases produced by early volcanic activity around the time of Earth's formation. [Q13] If you're not familiar with greenhouse gases, they're gases that trap heat and prevent it from escaping Earth's atmosphere. These greenhouse gases ultimately played a role in maintaining Earth's temperature, and consequently, the water remained liquid.

[Q14] Recently, however, geologists who analyzed fragments of ancient meteorites suggested that volcanic activity is probably not the only factor that caused Earth to retain water. In fact, they contend that meteorites may have brought water to Earth and contributed to the accumulation of greenhouse gases. In order for you to understand their findings, you first need to have a good idea of what happens when meteorites enter Earth's atmosphere. First, they reach the edge of the atmosphere and encounter massive frictional forces very rapidly.

문단주제	본문내용	해석
	[Q15-D] They sometimes completely disintegrate mid-air, but other times their fragments manage to reach Earth. Scientists used a catalyst, intense electricity, to produce the same conditions, heating the fragments to temperatures of 1,000° C. When they burned up, two by-products remained, carbon dioxide, a common greenhouse gas, and water vapor. These contribute to maintaining warmer temperatures and introducing water to the environment. [Q17] Of course, one meteor won't affect Earth much, considering the inconsequential amount of by-products they yield, but, as the old proverb states, "little strokes fell great oaks." We now believe this is what happened after Earth's formation, around 4 billion years ago, which is also when the analyzed samples dated from. Have you heard of the lunar cataclysm? It's a hypothetical theory, but I believe that we can take it into account to further our discussion.	[Q15-D] 운석은 가끔 완전히 공중에서 분해되지만, 어쩔 때는 그 조각이 지구에 도달하기도 합니다. 과학자들은 조각을 1,000도로 가열시키는 동일한 조건을 만들기 위해 강한 전기를 촉매제로 이용했습니다. 조각이 탈 때, 두 가지 부산물이 산출되는데 일반적인 온실 가스인 이산화탄소와 수증기입니다. 이 부산물들은 더 따뜻한 온도를 유지해서 해당 환경에 물을 만들어낸 것입니다. [Q17] 물론, 어떤 유성은 유성이 만들어내는 미미한 양의 부산물 탓에 지구에 많은 영향을 미치지는 않습니다. 하지만 "작은 때림이 나무를 쓰러뜨린다 (열 번 찍어 안 넘어가는 나무 없다)"라는 오랜 속담이 있습니다. 우리는 이제 분석된 샘플의 나이이기도 한 40억 년 전 지구가 형성 되었을 때 이러한 일들이 있었다고 믿습니다. 달의 지각 변동을 들어봤나요? 가설적인 이론이지만, 우리는 이에 대해 더 토론해 볼 수 있습니다.
단락 4 Lunar Cataclysm 이론	The theory states that millions of asteroids collided with celestial bodies in our solar system, including Mercury, the Moon, Earth, and Mars about 3.8 to 4.1 billion years ago. Evidence for this comes from the impact melt rocks collected during the Apollo missions – you know, NASA's manned spaceflight program. [Q15] Anyway, the rocks collected during these missions to the Moon were dated to 4 billion years ago, and that's how we originally learned that a large number of asteroids struck the early planets, including Earth. From this and the experiments carried out on the meteor samples, scientists now believe that the "theoretical" meteors burned up in Earth's atmosphere and ultimately produced the by-products I previously mentioned. Subsequently, this meteoric water accumulated in the oceans and the greenhouse gases trapped heat and provided the correct temperature to prevent the oceans from freezing or vaporizing.	이론은 약 38억에서 41억 년 전에 수성, 달, 지구, 목성을 포함한 태양계의 행성이 수백만 소행성과 충돌했다고 주장합니다. 이에 대한 근거는 아폴로 작전 동안 수집된 "impact melt rock"을 통해 알 수 있습니다. 여러분도 알다시피 (아폴로 작전은) NASA의 유인 우주비행 프로그램이죠. [Q15] 어쨌든 달에서 이루어진 이 작전 동안 수집된 암석은 40억 년 전의 것으로 추정되며, 이것이 우리가 처음에 어떻게 지구를 포함한 초기 행성과 많은 소행성이 충돌하였는지를 알 수 있는 점입니다. 이뿐만 아니라 유성 샘플로 이루어진 실험을 통해, 과학자들은 '이론적인' 유성이 지구의 대기에서 타 버렸으며, 마침내 제가 이미 언급했던 부산물들을 만들어낸 것입니다. 결과적으로, 이러한 유성의 물은 바다에 축적되어왔으며, 온실가스는 따뜻하게 유지되어 바다가 얼어붙거나 증발하지 않도록 적절한 온도를 유지한 것입니다.
단락 5 지구와 화성의 차이	The question that remains is, [Q16-C] "Why don't planets like Mars resemble Earth in terms of its oceans and greenhouse gases if they were subjected to the same bombardment?" Well, to answer that, you need a better understanding of the differences between Earth and Mars.	(여전히) 남는 의문점은 [Q16-C] "화성 같은 행성들도 똑같은 충격에 가해졌으면 왜 지구의 바다와 온실 가스를 닮지 않았을까"입니다. 음, 답변하자면, 지구와 화성의 차이에 대해 더 이해해야 한다는 것입니다.

문단주제	본문내용	해석
단락 6 도마뱀의 진화 가능성	You see, the meteors most likely did result in the same consequence, but you also need to remember that, [Q16] Earth, unlike Mars, has a strong magnetic field from its core, which protects it from solar winds and charged particles, such as electrons and protons, released from the Sun's upper atmosphere. We won't go into much detail about this, because it's too complex, so let's just stay on topic. Mars, without a strong magnetic field, is subjected to the solar winds, which blow away its greenhouse gases. You see where I'm going with this? [Q16-B] If greenhouse gases don't exist in the atmosphere, the temperature falls and water freezes, as it did on Mars.	여러분도 알다시피, 유성은 대부분 같은 결과를 만들어내는 경향이 있습니다. 하지만 여러분들이 기억해야 할 것은, [Q16] 화성과 달리 지구는 그 핵에 엄청난 자기장이 있어 태양의 상부 대기에서 방출되는 전자와 양성자 같은 태양풍과 하전 입자를 막아줍니다. 이런 내용에 대해 자세히 얘기하지는 않겠습니다. 왜냐하면 너무 복잡하니까요. 주제로 다시 돌아가봅시다. 강력한 자기장이 없는 화성은 온실가스를 날려버리는 태양풍을 맞습니다. 무슨 말인지 아시겠죠? [Q16-B] 만약 온실가스가 대기에 존재하지 않으면, 온도가 떨어져 물은 얼어붙습니다. 화성에서 그랬던 것처럼 말이죠.

12. [Main Idea] What is the lecture mainly about?

(A) ~~Proven theories~~ regarding the formation of ~~Earth~~ and its ability to maintain liquid water *(too specific)* ★

(B) ~~Geological differences~~ between planets such as Earth, Mars, and the Moon *(too specific)*

(C) The climate conditions of planets in regard to their ability to maintain liquid water

(D) The ~~influence of water~~ and greenhouse gases on the planets of our solar system *(partial error)*

12. 강의의 주제가 무엇인가?

(A) ~~지구~~의 형성과 액체 상태의 물을 유지하기 위한 지구의 능력에 관한 ~~증명된 이론~~ ★

(B) 지구, 화성, 달과 같은 행성들 사이의 ~~지질학적 차이~~

(C) 액체상태인 물을 보존할 수 있는 행성의 능력에 관한 행성의 기후 환경

(D) 우리 태양계에 있는 행성의 물과 온실가스~~의 영향~~

해설 | (A) 교수는 증명된 이론이 아닌 "널리 받아들여지는" 이론과 "가설적인" 이론을 소개하므로 오답. 또한, 강의는 지구 이외의 태양계 행성들도 다루기 때문에 주제를 지구에만 국한 시킬 수 없다. (B) 행성 간의 지질학적 비교는 지구와 화성에 대해서만 이루어지며, 강의의 극히 일부이므로 주제로 잡기에는 너무 좁다. (D) 강의에서 온실가스의 영향이 다뤄지는 것은 맞지만 물에 대해서는 그 영향이 아닌 그 존재와 초기 생성의 이론이 다뤄진다.

13. [Detail – Effect/Influence] According to the professor, what role did greenhouse gases play in the early formation of Earth?

(A) They prevented water from vaporizing into space

(B) They produced heat and maintained constant warmer temperatures *(partial error)* ★

(C) They worked as a barrier and minimized the impact of meteors on Earth *(unrelated to the question)*

(D) They kept heat from escaping the atmosphere

13. 교수의 말에 따르면, 초기 지구 형성에서 온실가스가 어떠한 역할을 하는가?

(A) 물이 우주로 증발하는 것을 막았다.

(B) 열을 내어 따뜻한 온도를 유지했다. ★

(C) 온실가스는 장벽으로서 지구에 미치는 유성의 영향력을 최소화했다.

(D) 대기를 벗어나는 열을 보존했다.

해설 | (A) 온실가스가 따뜻한 온도를 유지하여 증발하는 것을 막은 것이 아니라 어는 것을 막은 것이므로 오답. (B) 열을 직접 생산한 것이 아니라 열기를 가두어 지구의 대기에서 이탈하는 것을 막는 보다 간접적인 역할을 했으므로 오답. (C) 대기의 역할이므로 문제가 묻는 바가 아니다.

14. [Inference – Infer] What can be inferred about the volcanic activity theory suggested in the lecture?

(A) It is outdated and its proponents have now ~~shifted to~~ the lunar cataclysm theory *(wrong fact)*

(B) It doesn't ~~take into account the greenhouse gases~~ that prevented heat from escaping into space *(wrong fact)*

(C) **It falls short of validating all origins of liquid water on Earth**

(D) It fails to take the ~~transformation of liquid water~~ into account and explain it thoroughly *(not mentioned)* ★

14. 강의에서 제시된 화산 활동 이론에 대해 무엇을 추론할 수 있는가?

(A) 구식의 이론이며 지지자들은 달의 지각변동 ~~이론으로 갈아탔다.~~

(B) 열이 우주로 빠져나가는 것을 막는 온실가스를 ~~고려하지 않았다.~~

(C) **지구에서 물의 존재에 대한 모든 근원을 규명하는 데 실패하였다.**

(D) ~~액체 상태의 물의 변화~~를 고려하여 완전히 설명하는 데에 실패했다. ★

> 해설 | (A) Lunar cataclysm 이론은 교수가 소개하는 또 하나의 가설적인 이론일 뿐, 화산 활동 이론과의 경쟁에 대해 언급하지 않으므로 오답. (B) 화산 활동 이론은 초기 화산 활동에 의해 온실가스가 축적되었음을 주장한다고 설명된다. 이를 통해 화산활동 이론은 온실가스를 분명히 고려한 것을 알 수 있다. (D) 액체 상태의 물의 변화는 화산 활동 이론에서 전혀 언급되지 않으므로 오답.

15. [Detail – Purpose/Intention] Why does the professor mention the Apollo missions?

(A) ~~To praise~~ NASA's accomplishments, which brought significant changes to the history of mankind *(wrong fact)*

(B) **To support his claim that the tests on meteorites proved that asteroids struck Earth around 4 billion years ago**

(C) To argue that ~~meteors hit Earth~~ around the time they struck other planets when Earth was forming *(partial error)* ★

(D) To prove his point that asteroids are usually incinerated in Earth's atmosphere before they reach the surface *(unrelated to the question)*

15. 왜 교수는 아폴로 작전을 언급했는가?

(A) 인류 역사의 중요한 변화를 가져온 NASA의 공로를 ~~치하하기 위해서~~

(B) **유성에 대한 실험을 통해 약 40억년 전에 소행성이 지구에 부딪혔다는 그의 주장을 뒷받침하기 위해서**

(C) ~~유성~~은 지구가 형성 될 때 다른 행성을 때릴 즈음에 ~~지구에 충돌했다는~~ 것을 주장하기 위해 ★

(D) 소행성은 주로 지구의 표면에 닿기 전에 지구의 대기에서 소각되었다는 것을 증명하기 위해

> 해설 | (A) 교수는 객관적인 입장에서 아폴로 작전과 그 사실에 대해서만 언급하므로 치하하기 위한 목적은 전혀 찾아볼 수 없다. (C) 유성 자체가 아닌 소행성이 행성들에 충돌한 것이므로 오답. (D) 맞는 말이지만 교수는 이 사실을 아폴로 작전과 연관 짓지 않으므로 질문과 관련이 없다.

16. [Detail – Characteristic] Which of the following is true about Mars?

(A) It lacks a key feature of Earth that shields it from solar winds

(B) Its water was ~~vaporized~~ due to the lack of a strong magnetic field *(partial error)* ★

(C) It was ~~not~~ subjected to the same bombardment as Earth, hence the different resemblance of oceans and greenhouse gases *(wrong fact)*

(D) It doesn't sustain water because of low its ~~gravitational force~~ *(not mentioned)*

16. 화성에 대해 사실인 것은 무엇인가?

(A) 태양풍을 막아주는 지구의 핵심적인 기능이 부족하다.

(B) 강한 자기장이 없기 때문에 물이 ~~증발~~해버렸다. ★

(C) 화성은 지구에 가해졌던 충격과 똑같은 영향을 받지 ~~않았기~~ 때문에 지구의 바다와 온실가스를 닮지 않은 것이다.

(D) 화성의 낮은 ~~중력 탓~~에 물을 지속하지 않는다.

해설 | (B) 증발이 아닌 냉각이므로 오답. (C) 화성과 지구는 같은 충격에 가해졌으므로 오답. 또한, 태양풍과 하전 입자를 막아주는 자기장의 부재로 인해 화성에는 액체 상태의 물이 없는 것이다. 따라서, 잘못된 인과관계로 오답. (D) 교수는 화성의 중력에 대해서 언급하지 않으므로 오답.

Listen again to part of the lecture. Then answer the question.

"Of course, one meteor won't affect Earth much, considering the inconsequential amount of by-products they yield, but, as the old proverb states, 'little strokes fell great oaks'."

17. [Inference - Imply] What does the professor mean when she says this: 🎧

> "but, as the old proverb states, 'little strokes fell great oaks'."

(A) When meteors continuously struck Earth, it began to be ~~negatively affected~~ by them *(partial error)*

(B) The effect of the meteors' hitting Earth was ~~quite insubstantial~~ *(partial error)*

(C) Little strokes of meteor yield inconsequential amounts of by-products *(partial error)* ★

(D) When accumulated in large quantities, the small impact of the meteors caused a great change

강의의 일부분을 다시 듣고 질문에 답하시오.

"물론, 어떤 유성은 유성이 만들어내는 미미한 양의 부산물 탓에 지구에 많은 영향을 미치지는 않습니다. 하지만 '작은 때림이 나무를 쓰러뜨린다 (열 번 찍어 안 넘어가는 나무 없다)' 라는 오랜 속담이 있습니다."

17. 이에 대해 교수가 말하고자 하는 바가 무엇인가? 🎧

> "하지만 '작은 때림이 나무를 쓰러뜨린다 (열 번 찍어 안 넘어가는 나무 없다)' 라는 오랜 속담이 있습니다."

(A) 유성이 지속적으로 지구에 부딪혔을 때, 지구는 유성의 ~~부정적인 영향을 받기~~ 시작했다.

(B) 지구를 강타하는 유성의 효과는 ~~꽤 미미하다~~.

(C) 적은 양의 유성들은 미미한 양의 부산물을 생산한다. ★

(D) 많은 양이 쌓이면 유성의 작은 영향력도 큰 변화를 일으킨다.

해설 | (A) 유성에 의해 지구에 물이 생성된 것이기 때문에 그 영향이 부정적이라고 할 수 없으므로 오답. (B) 교수의 말은 유성 하나의 효과는 미미하지만 개수가 늘면 그 영향력도 커진다는 의미를 내포하므로 오답. (C) 맞는 말이지만, 교수는 이러한 미미한 영향이 축적됐을 때 미치는 큰 영향을 강조하고자 위와 같은 속담을 언급하므로 오답

첨삭권 소개

01 스피킹/라이팅 첨삭이 필요한 이유?

대체로 독학을 할 수 있다고 생각하는 리딩, 리스닝과는 달리 스피킹 라이팅은 독학이 힘듭니다.

이유는? "내가 뭘 틀렸는지 모르니까!!!"
대안은?? 독학이라고 했으니, 과외나, 학원은 빼고, 남는 건 첨삭이나, 그냥 혼자 틀린 걸 계속 보거나….

그런데, 첨삭을 받으러 검색을 해보면 가격이 라이팅 한편당 23000…원…?
한편만 첨삭 받으면 끝날 것 같진 않은 내 실력을 봐서는…
비용 감당 안됨. 어쩌지?

02 학원까지 다니고 싶진 않은데 스피킹/라이팅 첨삭만 받을 순 없나요?

라이팅 첨삭
10회권은 어셔수강생에게만 제공됩니다
(2025.07. 현재)

1회권	어셔	1회 첨삭권 25,000원	최저가 1회당 25,000원
	해**	1회권 없음 2회 첨삭권 54,000원	1회당 27,000원
	영**	1회 첨삭(1일 소요)권 28,000원	1회당(1일 소요)권 28,000원
5회권	어셔	5회 첨삭권 100,000원	최저가 1회당 20,000원
	해**	5회권 없음	5회권 없음
	영**	5회 첨삭(1일 소요)권 119,000원	1회당(1일 소요)권 23,800원
10회권 *어셔 수강생 한정	어셔	10회 첨삭권 150,000원	최저가 1회당 15,000원
	해**	10회권 없음	10회권 없음
	영**	10회권 없음	10회권 없음

스피킹 첨삭
(2025.07. 현재)

1회권	어셔	1회 첨삭권 15,000원	최저가 1회당 15,000원
	해**	1회권 없음 2회 첨삭권 54,000원	1회당 27,000원
	영**	1회 첨삭(1일 소요)권 16,000원	1회당(1일 소요)권 16,000원
5회권	어셔	5회 첨삭권 60,000원	최저가 1회당 12,000원
	해**	5회권 없음	5회권 없음
	영**	5회 첨삭(1일 소요)권 68,000원	1회당(1일소요)권 13,600원
10회권 *어셔 수강생 한정	어셔	10회 첨삭권 110,000원	최저가 1회당 11,000원
	해**	10회권 없음	10회권 없음
	영**	10회권 없음	10회권 없음

03 첨삭 구성은 어떻게 되나요?

스피킹 첨삭

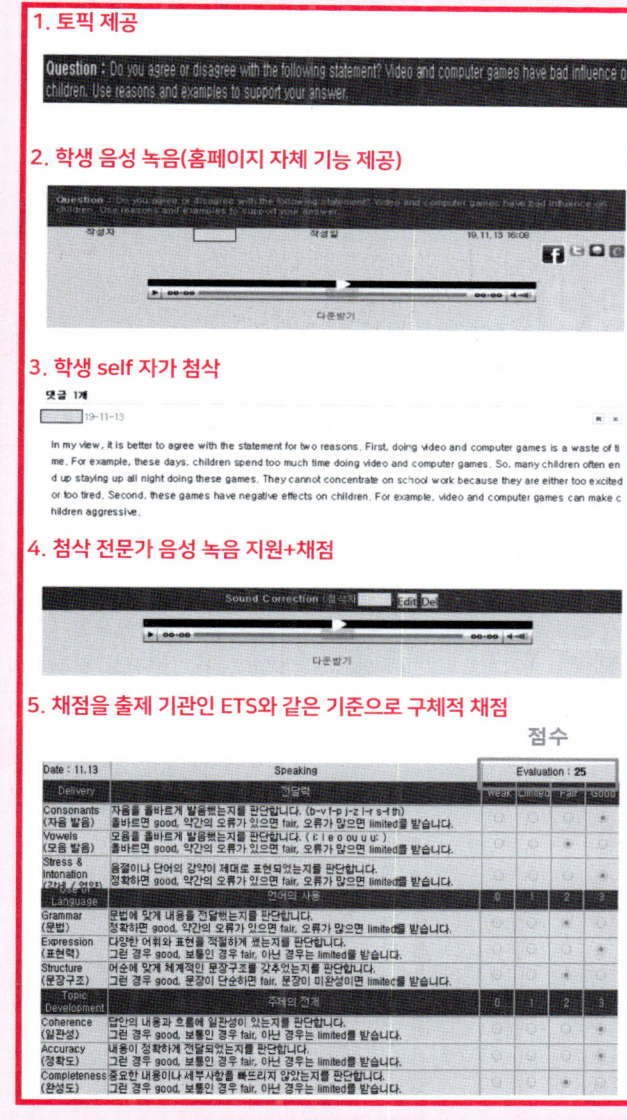

라이팅 첨삭

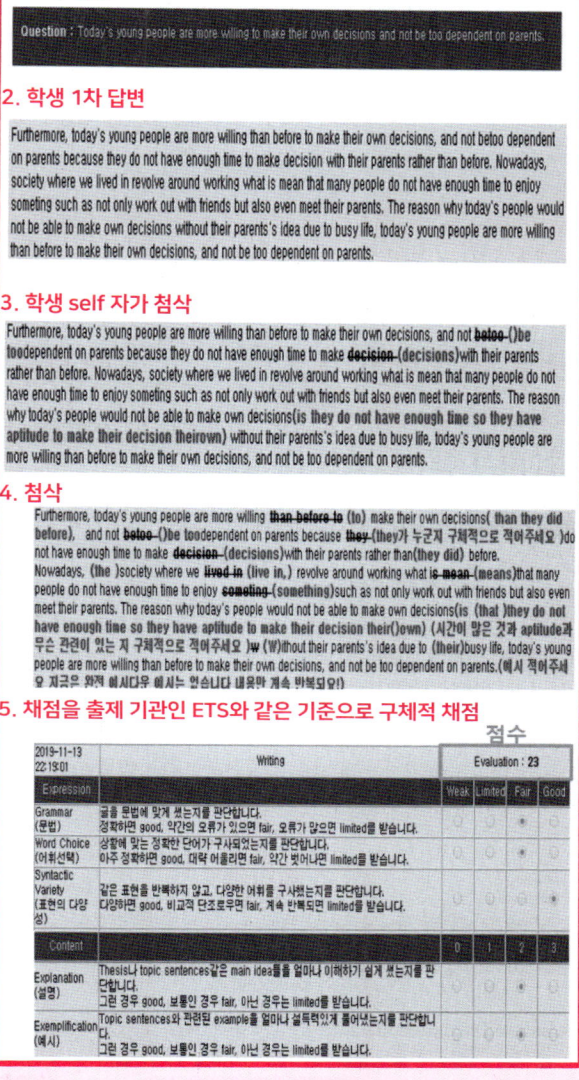

04 첨삭 신청하기

라이팅 첨삭권

1회 첨삭권	5회 첨삭권	10회 첨삭권
사용기간 15일	사용기간 30일	사용기간 60일
25,000원	~~125,000원~~ → 100,000원	~~250,000원~~ → 150,000원

10회권은 어셔수강생에게만 제공됩니다

스피킹 첨삭권

1회 첨삭권	5회 첨삭권	10회 첨삭권
사용기간 15일	사용기간 30일	사용기간 60일
15,000원	~~75,000원~~ → 60,000원	~~150,000원~~ → 110,000원

10회권은 어셔수강생에게만 제공됩니다

첨삭은 근무일 기준(평일)으로 진행되며, 주말 또는 휴일은 익일 평일에 진행됩니다.

강의대상

1. 책으로 토플을 공부해왔지만 컴퓨터로 실전 대비가 필요한 학생
2. 단기간 실전과 같은 형식의 문제풀이를 통한 실전감각이 필요한 학생
3. 토플 공부를 제대로 해본 적은 없지만 급하게 제출할 점수가 필요한 학생
4. 영어 실력이 어느정도 있고 실전 연습을 통해 빠르게 점수를 만들고 싶은 학생

강의목표

종이로 공부하고 시험보는 것이 아닌,
컴퓨터로 보는 실제 시험 환경에서,
시험당일 시험보는 스케줄대로 시험을 보고
시험 당일엔 확인할 수 없는 답안들을 확인하는
Reading과 Listening 수업을 듣고,
점수만 주는 Speaking & Writing 시험이 아닌,
점수와, 점수의 근거와, 점수를 올리기 위한 첨삭까지
모든 걸 포함하는 풀 케어 서비스

별도 구매 가능

모의토플
시장 최저가로 준비된 시험가격

~~50,000원~~
50% 추가 할인가
25,000원

가격소개
*시중에 나와있는 3사를 비교한 표입니다.

시장구성	USHER	D사	H사
구성	Half and Full (new 토플 반영)	Half and Full (new 토플 반영)	자체시험 (4가지 영역중 하나선택)
가격	27,000원/50,000원	33,000원/62,000원	66,000원
응시날짜	언제든지 응시가능	언제든지 응시가능	매주 토요일
첨삭	있음	없음	있음

등록하기

25% off
3일 등록
~~600,000원~~
450,000원
하루 15만원

50% off
5일 등록
~~1,000,000원~~
500,000원
하루 10만원

50% off
7일 등록
~~1,400,000원~~
700,000원
하루 10만원

가격구성

모의토플 + 첨삭 + 수업

05 모의토플
시장 최저가로 준비된 시험가격

~~50,000원~~
50% 추가 할인가
25,000원

가격소개
*시중에 나와있는 3사를 비교한 표입니다.

시장구성	USHER	D사	H사
구성	Half and Full (new 토플 반영)	Half and Full (new 토플 반영)	자체시험 (4가지 영역중 하나선택)
가격	27,000원/50,000원	33,000원/62,000	66,000원
응시날짜	언제든지 응시가능	언제든지 응시가능	매주 토요일
첨삭	있음	없음	있음

06 스피킹 첨삭

시장 최저가 첨삭 가격!!!

스피킹 1일 4문제
~~60,000원~~

50% 추가 할인가
30,000원

+

01 스피킹 첨삭
2025. 07. 기준

1회권	어셔	1회 첨삭권 15,000원	**최저가** 1회당 15,000원
	해**	1회권 없음 2회 첨삭권 54,000원	1회당 27,000원
	영**	1회 첨삭(1일소요)권 16,000원	1회당(1일소요)권 16,000원
5회권	어셔	5회 첨삭권 60,000원	**최저가** 1회당 12,000원
	해**	5회권 없음	5회권 없음
	영**	5회 첨삭(1일소요)권 68,000원	1회당(1일소요)권 13,600원
10회권 *어셔 수강생 한정	어셔	10회 첨삭권 110,000원	**최저가** 1회당 11,000원
	해**	10회권 없음	10회권 없음
	영**	10회권 없음	10회권 없음

07 라이팅 첨삭

시장 최저가 첨삭 가격!!!

라이팅 1일 2문제
~~50,000원~~

50% 추가 할인가
25,000원

+

02 라이팅 첨삭
2025. 07. 기준

1회권	어셔	1회 첨삭권 25,000원	**최저가** 1회당 25,000원
	해**	1회권 없음 2회 첨삭권 54,000원	1회당 27,000원
	영**	1회 첨삭(1일소요)권 28,000원	1회당(1일소요)권 28,000원
5회권	어셔	5회 첨삭권 100,000원	**최저가** 1회당 20,000원
	해**	5회권 없음	5회권 없음
	영**	5회 첨삭(1일소요)권 119,000원	1회당(1일소요)권 23,800원
10회권 *어셔 수강생 한정	어셔	10회 첨삭권 150,000원	**최저가** 1회당 15,000원
	해**	10회권 없음	10회권 없음
	영**	10회권 없음	10회권 없음

08 수업
국내 유일 수업!

수업 1일 4시간
~~40,000원~~

50% 추가 할인가
20,000원

**국내유일
비교대상이 없음**

기초 영단어 / 토플 단어

01 계획표 짤 준비

밑빠진 독에 물붓기 + 일정량 무조건 나가기

다수의 학생들이 단어를 공부 할 때는 대부분 초반에 하루, 잘하면 이틀 정도만 제대로 하고는
곧 포기하곤 합니다. 이런 일들을 가능케 하는 것은 대충하겠다는 생각으로 시작했다기 보다는,
너무 잘하겠다는, 즉 확실하게 암기하겠다는 생각으로 하루하루는 정말 잘하지만,
그런 자세가 오히려 지나친 부담으로 다가와 결국 다음날 스스로 공부하는데
큰 방해가 되게 된다는 점입니다.

그러므로, 너무 부담 갖지 마십시오. 할 수 있는 이게 팔굽혀펴기 다섯 개라면
그냥 다섯 개를 쭉 하다 보면, 어느날 문득 열 개를 해도 될 것 같다는 생각이 들 때가 있고,
이런 일이 반복되면, 어느 순간 50개 60개씩 늘어나는 것입니다.

하지만, 대부분의 경우에는 그저 옆 사람이 60개씩 한번에 하는 것이 부럽기만 할 뿐
그 사람이 그렇게 되는데까지 걸린 과정은 무시하고 지나가는 경우가 결정적인 실패의 요인이 됩니다.
그러므로 너무 무리하지 말고, 그냥 편하게 하십시오. 하지만, 절대 정한 양은 지키는 철저함은 필요합니다.

02 계획 잡는 방법

하루 200개씩 intensive하게 공부할 수 있는 사람이라면, 책의 편집대로 따르면 13일에 마쳐지게 되고, 한 달에 두 번을 보게 됩니다.
하지만, 다른 공부나 일을 병행하기 때문에 200개씩이 부담스러운 경우에도 임의의 숫자대로 30개 또는 50개 등으로 목표를 잡되,
절대 다음 B와 같이 하지 마십시오.

	A	B	C
	단어 공부시간 확보된 경우	하루 30개 목표 잘못된 경우	하루 30개 목표 추천 계획
1일차	1-200	1-30	1-30
2일차	201-400	31-60	201-230
3일차	401-600	61-90	401-430
4일차	601-800	91-120	601-630
⋮	⋮	⋮	⋮
13일차	1회독 완성	부분 1회독 완성	부분 1회독 완성
14일차	201	391-420	(1-30 간단 복습 후) 31-60
15일차	401	421-450	(201-230 간단 복습 후) 231-260
16일차	601	451-480	(401-430 간단 복습 후) 431-460
17일차	801	481-510	(601-630 간단 복습 후) 631-660
⋮	⋮	⋮	⋮
26일차	2회독 완성	책 앞부분 1/5도 못보고 포기 가능성 높고, 앞부분 기억도 잘 안남	같은 1/5봤지만, 포기확률 적고, 기억할 가능성 높음.

처음에 절대 양을 많이 잡지 말 것
너무 적게 잡았다면 중간에 늘려도 됩니다.

■ 토플 Listening 공부방법

리딩 점수에 따라서

- 20점 미만이라면, 리스닝에는 너무 많은 힘을 쓰지 말고, 단어와 리딩에 집중 바랍니다.
  둘 다 하려다 하나도 못 할 수 있습니다.

- 20점 이상이라면, **1.** 단어 **2.** 구문 **3.** 딕테이션 **4.** 열번읽기 까지 꼼꼼히 처리 바랍니다.

- 25점 이상이면, 단어, 구문은 거의 알 겁니다.
  대략 틀린 것 정도 간단히 마무리 하고 **딕테이션 및 오답 패턴 확인**에 집중하면 됩니다.

각각의 과정을 적으면 다음과 같습니다.

Step 1. 문제풀이

Step 2. TAGGING

Step 3. 단어 / 구문시험

Step 4. 딕테이션

Step 5. 열번읽기 (내 발음 체크 = 말 할 수 있으면 들린다)

과정 순서대로 공부를 해야하는 구체적인 이유와 방법을 적어보겠습니다.

Step 1. 문제풀이 (Note Taking)

- 문제 풀이는 실전 화면처럼 컴퓨터로 직접 풀면서 익숙해지는게 좋습니다.

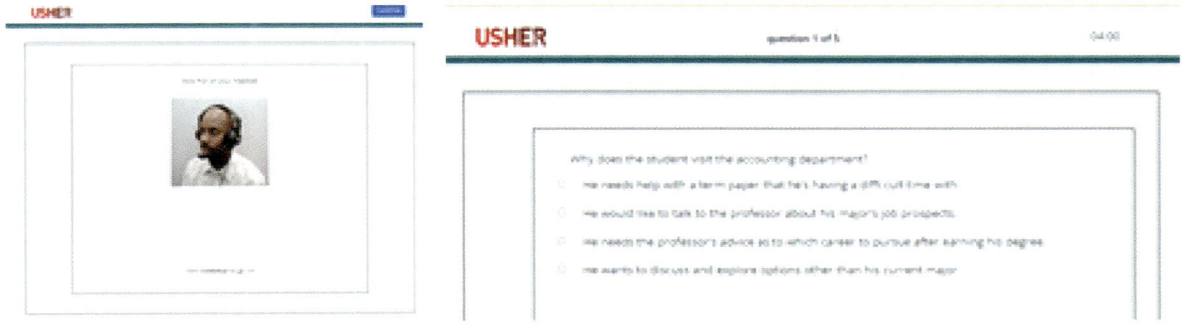

Step 2. TAGGING

- 문제 풀이 **직후, 잊기 전에,** 문제 풀면서 가장 짜증 났던 부분 = 즉, 이해하기 힘들었던 부분을 체크해둬야 합니다.

Step 3. 단어 / 구문시험

- **귀찮은 거 압니다.** 그래도 해두시기 바랍니다. 리딩 20점 미만은 실력 없어서 하기 싫어도 해야 하고, 리딩 25점 넘는 분들은 별로 할 것도 없겠지만, 그래도 다 챙겨 두시기 바랍니다.

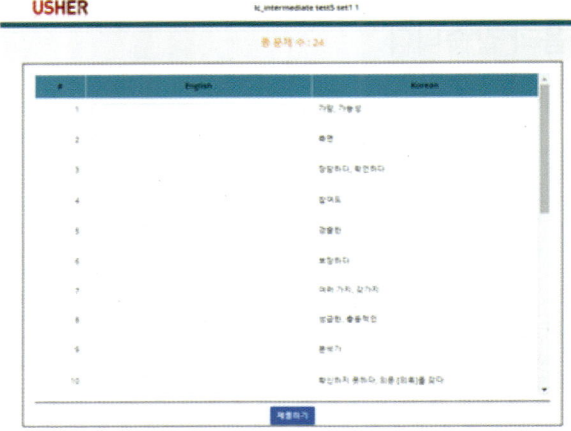

Step 4. 딕테이션

- 리딩 20점 미만은 실력이 없으니, 파악+ 실력 자체를 늘리기 위해 필요합니다.
- 리딩 25점 이상은 만점 받기 위해서, 본인이 어느 부분이 약한지 "샅샅이 훑어야 할 때", 가장 강력한 툴입니다.
  "30점의 절박함과 귀찮음 중", 더 강한 것이 여러분의 행동을 바꿀겁니다.

Step 5. 열번읽기 (내 발음 체크 = 말 할 수 있으면 들린다)

- 리딩 20점 미만의 학생들에게 가장 중요한 점은 "말 할 수 없으면, 들을 수 없다!!!" 입니다.

- 본인만 아는 이상한 발음으로 기억하면, 절대 못듣습니다.
  이그제그래이션? Exaggeration을 이렇게 읽는 학생. 답 없습니다.

- 말 할 수 있는지는, 학원 프로그램이 모두 파악해 줍니다. 채점까지.
  여러분은 성실함만 있으면 됩니다.

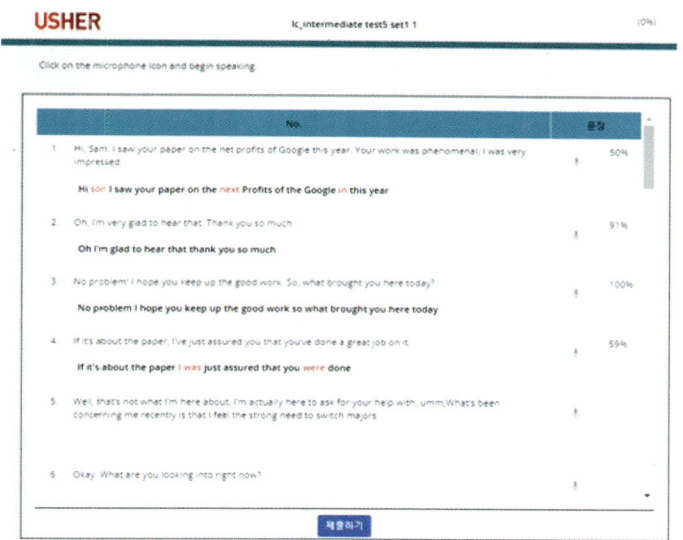

어셔어학원을 다니면,

어셔어학원을 다니면, 이 과정을 모두 스터디 시간에 합니다.

하지만, 인강을 듣거나 프로그램만 구매하시는 분들은,

반드시, 위 내용들을 기억하고, 실향하면, 실력 향상에 도움 되실겁니다.

USHER 단어암기 프로그램 소개

1. 듣고 - 아직도 눈으로만 외우나요?
 어셔단어 프로그램에서는 듣고, 쓰고, 품사외우고, 동의어까지 한번에 진행합니다.

2. 말하고 - 아직도 발음을 못하나요?
 발음 연습을 정확하게 프로그램이 읽어, 단어 외우면서 발음까지 한번에 준비할 수 있습니다.

3. 집중 암기하고 - 천천히 성장 VS 고성장
 90일 동안 외울 단어를 13일 안에 끝내므로 반복효과 및 고성장을 이루어 낼수있습니다.

4. internet based test - 즉시채점+틀린것만 계속 테스트
 틀린 단어들만 다시 시험보기가 가능합니다.

5. 기분좋은 성취 확인 - 향상 기록 personal trainer
 본인이 본 시험 기록 내용이 누적 확인되어 본인에 성취를 확인 할수있습니다.

1. 어셔 책으로 공부하는 법

1. 타사 책으로 공부하는 법

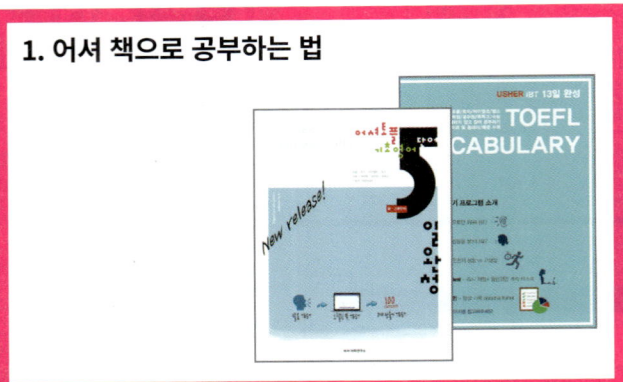
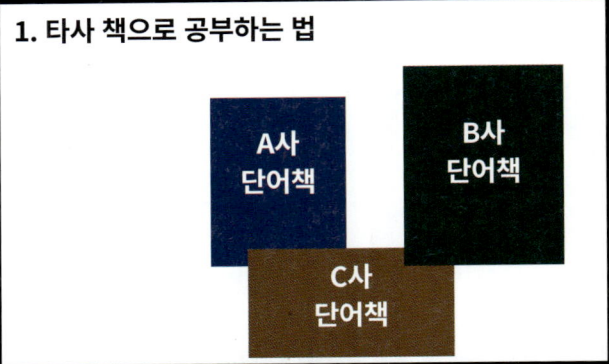

2. 발음을 먼저 듣고

2. 읽지도 못하는 발음기호 주고

3. 들어본 발음 시켜보고

3. 내가 읽은 발음이 맞는지 모르고

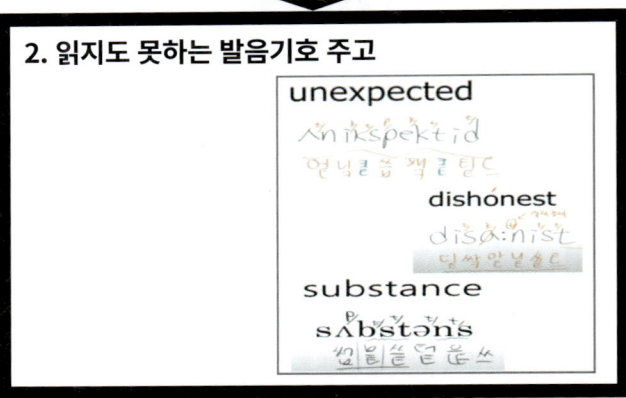
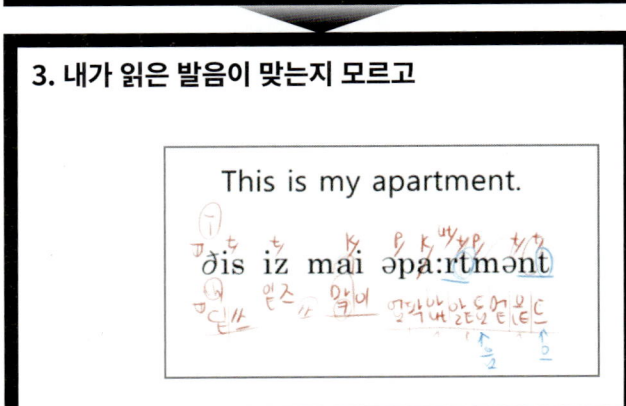

4. 분량을 나눠서 모의시험

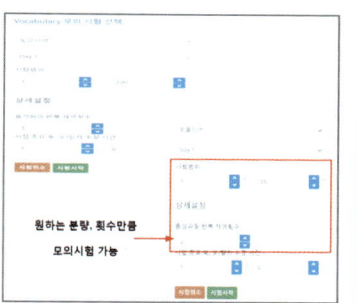
원하는 분량, 횟수만큼
모의시험 가능

4. 빽빽이 써가면서 단어 외워야하는데

5. 준비되면 실전시험!
듣고 → 스펠링 → 품사 → 뜻 순으로 적기

5. 학교 or 학원가서 종이에
한글 또는 스펠링 중 하나만 시험

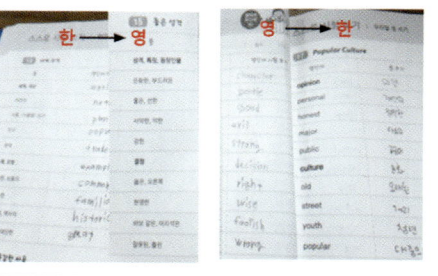

6. 하나라도 틀리면 오답처리
시험결과 자동체크

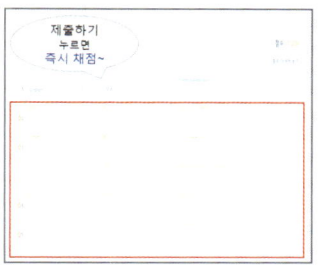

6. 채점을 내가 하면 잘못 외운 스펠링체크 못해주고
친구가 해주면 우정으로 틀린 것도 맞다고 해주고

7. 틀린 단어 묶음으로 즉시 **오답노트** 만들어줌

7. 내가 뭘 틀렸는지 일일히 추려내야 하지만...
보통은 보지도 않고 그냥 버리게 됨

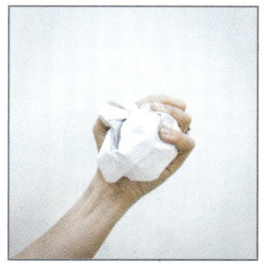

8. 틀린 개수 0으로 만들기 틀린 단어만 재시험

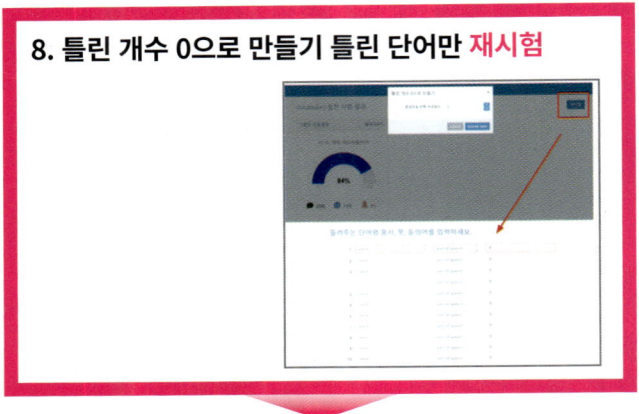

8. 틀린 단어가 뭔지 보지도 않고

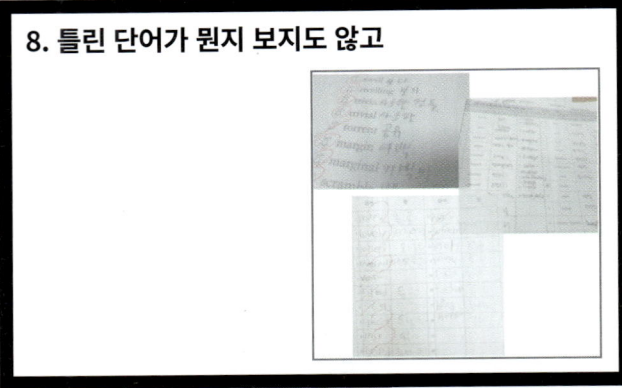

9. 한달 동안 시험 본 모든 기록 체크해주며 자극주는 시스템

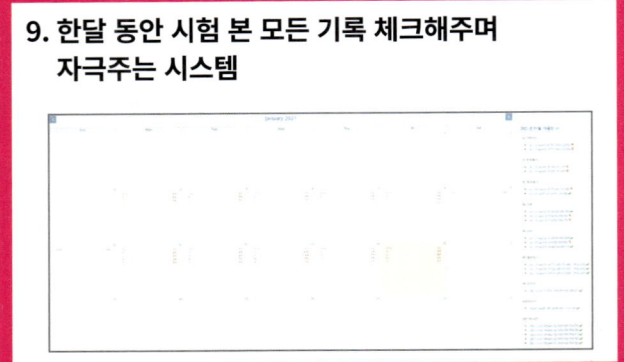

9. 종이가 너덜너덜해지면 그냥 버림

단어 프로그램 가격 소개

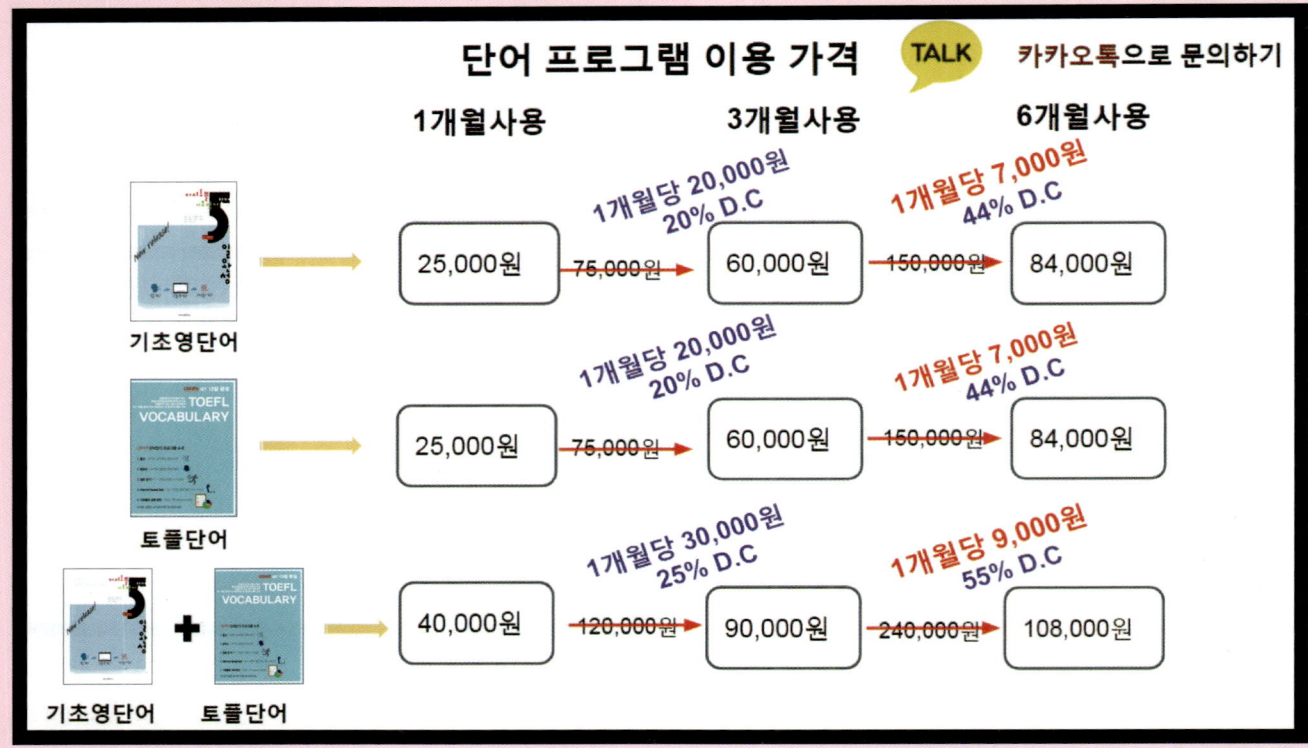

usherin.usher.co.kr

usherin.usher.co.kr